FRAME BY FRAME—
A BLACK FILMOGRAPHY

FRAME BY FRAME–
A BLACK FILMOGRAPHY

Phyllis Rauch Klotman

Indiana University Press
Bloomington   London

for my husband

Manufactured in the United States of America

Library of Congress Cataloging in Publication Data

Klotman, Phyllis Rauch.
  Frame by frame.

  1. Afro-Americans in the motion picture industry—
Dictionaries.   2. Afro-American actors and actresses—
Dictionaries.   3. Moving-pictures—United States—
Catalogs.   I. Title.
PN1995.9.N4K57   791.43'0909'352   78-20403
ISBN 0–253–16423–0   2 3 4 5 83 82 81 80

Contents

Foreword

All the older intellectual disciplines rely on standard bibliographies, a few of which, after many years of faithful use, are referred to by shortened, slightly reverential names. The historian reaches for his "Seignobos," the political scientist his "Schmeckebier," the literary critic his "Leary," and so on. Cinema bibliographies, filmographies, and other compendia have elicited no such endearing response from their users. Indeed most of them are referred to with a slight sneer because none is complete enough or free enough of error to have earned a respectful nickname.

When I first heard of Phyllis Klotman's black filmography, I was seized with no great wave of enthusiasm. Not that I had reason to expect a less than professional accomplishment. Rather, the dismal chronicle of cinematic research tools simply did not allow the expectation that a compiler could assemble funds, staff, and time enough to accomplish the goal.

This is not to say that we have lacked for useable books. The American Film Institute's decade-by-decade feature film catalogue project occasionally groaned and brought forth a new volume. But so *slowly!* Documentary film could be found in several well-known university audio-visual catalogues—Berkeley, Syracuse, Indiana, and NYU. Then there are the specialized catalogues, such as that of the National Audio-Visual Center. Or the careful student-culled titles and sources of films from the footnotes of the cinema histories written in traditional scholarly style. And for feature film rentals there is the bible of film societies, James L. Limbacher's periodically revised *Feature Films on 8 MM and 16 MM,* much admired because it included sources and addresses.

The user of films, either in the classroom or on the Steenbeck viewing table, knows that every filmography left a void because of its specialization, so that no single volume served the needs of the student of black film. Limbacher and the AFI catalogue indexed only feature films; institutional catalogues included only their own holdings; and so on. Therefore, dozens of anthropological, avant-garde, experimental, and documentary films were lost from view.

Over a period of many months, I have observed the growth of *Frame by Frame —A Black Filmography* as it gradually closed many of the gaps that had baffled seekers after black film. More than a filmography, union list, or rental catalogue, the book answers the need for a compendium of titles, credits, synopses, and sources for worldwide black film.

Take one film as an example of the uses of this volume. One of the most informative and yet elusive films of the 1940s is *The Negro Soldier,* an Army training film later released to civilian audiences by the Office of War Information. A rich document from the World War II era, when liberalism meant good "race relations" in the spirit of FDR's "Four Freedoms" speech, it has remained in-accessible to all but a few film scholars.

Only a specialist would know of a print in the National Archives, a shorter version warehoused by the Army, another in a university collection, a "bootleg" print, and finally a fresh print for sale at the National AV Center. Now, *Frame by Frame* will allow such fugitive films to come to light, complete with credits and location, thereby opening them to broader usage.

This wider access to films is also served by viewing "black" in its broadest compass as African as well as "Third World," Latin, Afro-American, documentary, anthropological, "independent," Hollywood feature, "race movies" made for ghetto audiences from the 1920s to the 1950s, and early "primitive" film—the entire black world on film. To gain access to this world, merely turn the pages of your "Klotman," which should take its place on the shelf between your "Cyr" and your "Limbacher."

Morgan State University   THOMAS CRIPPS
Baltimore, Maryland

Acknowledgments

A number of people labored long and hard to help assemble *Frame by Frame —A Black Filmography:* Charles Meyers, who designed the computer program, and Lynn Zonakis who spoke its (the computer's) language; Joseph Russell and Thomas Schwen, who actually believed in and supported the entire project; Al Lowe, for whom the book is "sub-titled" the Albert Lowe Memorial Project; as well as the following graduate and undergraduate students: Bob Sloan, Carolyn Denard, Michael Henderson, Adrienne Seward, Lee Foster, Alix Martin, Adriane Livingstone; and secretaries: Lois Smith, Ruthetta Lee, Frances Palmer, Dawn Jimeson, Anne DeCurtis.

I am indebted as well to Charles Silver of the Museum of Modern Art and to Patrick Sheehan and Barbara Humphreys at the Library of Congress for their patience and help during my frequent trips to New York and Washington.

Finally, my special thanks to Thomas Cripps, who not only spent hours going over computer printouts, helping me check for gross errors and glaring omissions, but also dredged up arcane facts from his vast fund of knowledge.

There are others whose indirect help I would like to acknowledge: Leonard Maltin and Richard H. Bann, whose book, *Our Gang: The Life and Times of the Little Rascals,* was published in time for me to verify numerous facts or fill in missing information; Helen Cyr, whose *Filmography of the Third World,* and Stephen Ohrn and Rebecca Riley, whose *Africa from Real to Reel,* provided necessary information especially in the areas of Black African, Afro-Caribbean, and Black Latin American features and documentaries; Henry Sampson, whose *Blacks in Black and White* helped with the "ghetto cinema"; David Meeker, whose *Jazz in the Movies* helped verify information on black musicians in films; and Edward Mapp, whose very recent *Directory of Blacks in the Performing Arts* includes not only musicians but all performing artists, e.g., film, stage, television, opera, etc. Judy Peiser allowed me to cite a number of revelant folklore documentaries from the *Index of Folklore Films,* which are acknowledged in the annotations as being "Provided by the Center for Southern Folklore."

Permission to use annotations of films distributed by the Indiana University Audio-Visual Department was granted by the Indiana University Audio-Visual Center, William Cuttill, Director of Media Resources.

Introduction

For many years it was assumed that Afro-Americans and other black peoples of the world had little or nothing to do with the art of filmmaking. Their presence in films often went uncredited, and even as late as the thirties, type names were often given in cast lists, such as Snowflake instead of Fred Toones, Sleep 'n' Eat instead of Willie Best, Sambo instead of Joffre Pershing Johnson. Until a few years ago, when scholars began publishing in this area, black film companies were scarcely known to have existed; yet the Johnson brothers incorporated the Lincoln Motion Picture Company as early as 1916, and Bill Foster had made some films earlier than that. Serious scholars are now giving their attention to black participation in a medium that has profoundly influenced attitudes over the years, from before *The Birth of a Nation* to the present time.

Because of such efforts to acknowledge the contribution of Blacks to film—whether in bit roles in primarily white vehicles, or as major stars, directors, writers, or producers in black films—it is important to have a research tool to facilitate serious study. Indeed *Frame by Frame—A Black Filmography* is the result of research undertaken in order to teach a course at Indiana University-Bloomington, "Images of Blacks in Film," in the Afro-American Studies Department, under the direction of Joseph J. Russell, Chairperson, in the spring of 1975. The course was supported by special funds authorized by K. Gene Faris, Dean of Learning Resources, and was ably assisted by Professor Thomas Schwen and his office of Instructional Systems Technology/Audio-Visual Services. Professor Schwen's assistant, Albert Lowe, first suggested the idea of producing a research tool from the hundreds of film cards I had amassed. Those card entries have become a computerized filmography that will be systematically updated as more information is gathered: additions to entries (of missing information) when and if "lost" films are found; corrections to those and other entries if necessary; additional entries of completely new items. This volume represents the total information available at the time of publication and is designed for use not only by students and scholars, as a tool for designing courses and research projects, but also as a guide to community groups concerned with disseminating more and better information to the general public about the cultural contributions of black peoples. Although there are other resources that can assist in this process, *Frame by Frame* is uniquely designed to bring together as much information as possible under one cover.

How to Use This Volume

Frame by Frame—A Black Filmography is a compendium of over 3,000 film items. Films listed are those with black themes or subject matter—even before Blacks acted in them; films that have substantial participation by Blacks as writers, actors, producers, directors, musicians, animators, or consultants; and films in which Blacks appeared in ancillary or walk-on roles. "Black" here encompasses the following:

Afro-American/Black American (U.S.)

Third World: Black Latin American (Mexico, Central America, South America)

Black African (mainly sub-Saharan)

Afro-Caribbean

The letter *b* is capitalized when "Black" refers to or is synonymous with Afro-American or Negro and is used as a noun, singular or plural, even when it is used without a hyphen, as in Black American. It is *not* capitalized when used as an adjective, e.g., black middle class. The foregoing racial designations are used interchangeably throughout the text, although more references will be found to Black American and Afro-American than to Negro. All are used as denotations of respect.

Although the filmography as well as the film course(s) began as Afro-American, it became increasingly clear that the black experience in film as well as in history went far beyond the boundaries of the United States or the North American continent. Whether it was our own films with the domestically patronizing "natives" of *Tarzan* or the African films of Ousmane Sembene, with complex characters and situations; the European films of Paul Robeson or the "whiteman's burden" documentaries of Africa; the Ethiopian docu-drama of Haile Gerima or the recent compelling Jamaican features—all of these constitute an important body of knowledge. Hence, a larger, world view is reflected in such entries. The time period covered is 1900 through 1977.

The following information was sought, although not with equal success for each entry:

Film Title/Series Title
Narrator/Cast
Writer: screenplay/adaptation
Producer
Director
Studio/Company
Technical information: film size/color/sound
(silent)/no. of reels/time

Date/Country of origin
Type
Distributor/Archive
Annotation

1. *Film Title/Series Title*
Entries are listed alphabetically according to the first word of the title, exclusive of the article. Series titles follow, e.g.:

Film Title: *Pigskin Palooka*   *Meeting at Midnight*
Series Title: *Our Gang*   *Charlie Chan*

Alternate or translated titles are crosslisted, with the information given under one title only, the original, if that could be determined, e.g.:

Title: *Sweet Love, Bitter*
Alt: *It Won't Rub Off, Baby*

Foreign films are listed in the original language and crosslisted by English translation if that title had or has some official currency in the English-speaking world, e.g.:

Title: *Orfeu Negro*
Alt: *Black Orpheus*

2. *Narrator/Cast*
Blacks are identified by an asterisk following the name; an asterisk is used for identification not only of black narrators and actors, but also for directors, writers, musicians, producers, consultants, animators, and interviewees, as is sometimes the case in documentaries.

No distinction has been made in this entry between narrator and actor. It should be clear that for documentaries, the term "narrator" is appropriate; that fact is usually stated in the annotation.

3. *Writer: Screenplay/Story*
The writer of the screenplay is listed first, followed by the term "story," which refers to the writer of an original story or of an adaptation from another work: a novel, a play, a short story.

4. *Producer*
For feature films of most recent vintage, the producer listed is an individual(s). For earlier films, particularly those for which no prints have yet been found, e.g., *The Trooper of Troop K,* a production company may be listed.

5. *Director*
A designation that applies mainly to fictional films, of all varieties, rarely to documentaries—unless they are dramatized (i.e., docu-dramas or cinema vérité).

6. *Studio/Company*
Hollywood films are identified by the studio that produced them, e.g., MGM, United Artists, etc., but many black films were made wherever the filmmaker could shoot them. "Studio" for independents is a somewhat pretentious term. "Company" is appropriate for the Lincoln Motion Picture organization of the

Johnson brothers and for the Colored Players of Philadelphia. Neither "studio" nor "company" is quite the appropriate term for documentaries.

7. *Technical Information*

Includes film size (8mm, 16mm, 35mm); whether the film is in color or black and white; whether it is silent or sound; the number of reels and the running time. Silent film is projected at a different rate of speed from sound film: 24 frames per minute versus 16. When the running time of a silent film was not available, the length of footage was substituted.

This kind of information is important for planning, as is such information as "dubbing" or English subtitles with foreign films, and cinemascope with later films, because a special lens is required for projection.

8. *Date/Country of Origin*

Documenting film history is a nearly impossible task. Because there are so many possible dates—year of production, release, copyright, etc.—the date that could best be authenticated is the one that appears. The date that appears on the film is the one that was considered the most reliable. In the absence of that information, release date is used, a date that could be confirmed from reviews in the *New York Times Film Reviews,* the *American Film Institute Catalogs,* the *Motion Picture Daily Yearbook,* the *Film Daily Yearbook,* trade papers, scholarly publications, and distributor catalogues.

Country of origin is used for fictional films and for most documentaries, although for documentaries on Africa, the country in which or about which the film was made is often listed as well; e.g., Britain/Kenya. A key to the viewpoint (political and social) can often be ascertained from the "country of origin" and the "producer," for example, in films made in South Africa by the Ministry of Information.

9. *Type*

Fiction films are categorized as *Feature* or *Dramatic Short,* or if made for television, *TV Feature;* non-fiction films are categorized as *Documentary, TV Documentary,* or *Dramatized Documentary* (the terms "cinema vérité" or "docudrama" are not used to classify, although those terms may be referred to in the annotations). Short films (usually less than an hour) come under the headings *Comedy Short, Musical Short, Sports Short, Animated Short* (cartoons), or, as above, *Dramatic Short* (the way most Biograph films before the twenties are classified), and *Newsreels,* although there are very few of the last.

Documentary, for a variety of reasons, is the most complicated category. It also includes, for example, Army training films, which fact is made clear in the annotation, and folklore and anthropological films, also referred to in the annotation. Like fiction films, documentaries can be almost any length, but no subset by length appears in the text. In fact, a number of short documentaries had to be omitted because of space constraints. Since the need for a black filmography arose out of an Afro-American context, the emphasis in *Frame by Frame* is on Blacks in the Americas. Therefore, documentaries depicting the "Old" World experience (Africa, Europe), which take less than 20 minutes running time, were deleted if not located through either a distributor or an archive (U.S./abroad), unless they were of particular historic or aesthetic relevance. For more complete information on the shorter documentary, see *Filmography of the Third World* by Helen Cyr and *Africa from Real to Reel,* compiled by Steven Ohrn and Rebecca Riley.

Soundies must also be mentioned in the sin-of-omission category. Soundies are three-minute films that were made between the twenties and the forties for a machine-like variant of the juke box. For a dime, it produced a sound film on a glass screen. Many of the performers were black, some of them the best musicians of the day. When the soundies fad faded in the United States, many of the prints were sold to television and to film collectors; a number are now available on 16mm from film distributors. An excellent source for those made here and abroad (called Scopitone in Europe) is David Meeker's *Jazz in the Movies.*

10.   *Distributor/Archive*

Film distributors and archives in the United States and abroad are listed if the film is extant and has been located, even if it does not circulate. No distinction has been made between distributor and archive except by key, e.g.:

Distributor/Archive: KPF and MOMA or MMA

The key to the above entry is Kit Parker Films/Museum of Modern Art. Distributors and archives appear immediately after the "Alphabetical Listing of Films" section, listed by key and containing the most recent address it was possible to locate.

Distributor catalogues are available, usually upon request, but many community and university libraries collect them.

No distinction is made in the distributor entry between rental and purchase options. Many distributors offer prints for both rental and purchase, and have prices listed accordingly. Prices change from time to time; therefore, it is always best to get the most recent information available on prices and terms. Also, be careful to note that distribution rights change not infrequently.

Archives. Some films are located in archives or private collections and are only available for viewing by scholars; e.g., *Native Son* at the Library of Congress, *Borderline* at the International Museum of Photography. They do not circulate, or at least, at this time they do not. Information about archives and their restricted use is given in the Archives listing. Be sure to refer to this section before requesting permission to screen archived films.

11. *Annotation*

Because general information about many of the films is easily available elsewhere, the emphasis in *Frame by Frame* is on the presence and participation of Blacks; each is identified and full cast lists have been assembled wherever possible. Likewise, the annotations address the black theme in the film, even if it is a minor one, and identify the roles played by black actors, if that information was available. Every effort has been made *not* to editorialize or to be judgmental, not to express repugnance at obvious racist attitudes and tones, themes, and stereotypes, but to describe as objectively as possible the content of the film. A monumental effort was made to eschew aesthetic judgments and personal biases as well.

No matter how assiduous the researcher, some errors are bound to appear. For the human errors I am solely responsible. Peculiarities of the computer ("glitches"), however, are somewhat out of my control. Technology does at times seem to take on a life of its own, even in this small realm of academic computing.

FRAME BY FRAME–
A BLACK FILMOGRAPHY

Alphabetical Listing of Films

"BABY MARIE" OSBORNE SERIES
Nar/Cast: Joffre Pershing Johnson*
Date/Country: 192- + USA   Type: Comedy Short
Annotation: Joffre Johnson, child actor, usually listed in
    the credits as "Sambo," played Ebenezer Eczema, Abraham
    White (and other such types) in this series of comedy
    shorts directed to the young audience.

"BIG" BILL BLUES   Director: Jean Delire
Tech Info: 18 min.
Date/Country: 1956 + Belgium   Type: Documentary
Annotation: Documentary film record of a club performance by
    "Big" Bill Broonzy* singing and playing several numbers.

"BIG" BILL BROONZY
Tech Info: 9 min.
Date/Country: USA   Type: Documentary
Annotation: A film record of "Big" Bill Broonzy* sitting on
    a front porch and playing "Twelve bar blues."

"BLIND" GARY DAVIS   Director: Harold Becker
Tech Info: 11 min.
Date/Country: 1964 + USA   Type: Documentary
Annotation: Documentary about the Blues guitarist Gary
    Davis, includes two numbers.

"BUCK AND BUBBLES" SERIES
Nar/Cast: Ford Lee Washington* + John Sublette*   Story:
    Hugh Wiley
Producer: Bill Foster*
Studio/Company: Pathe
Tech Info: bw/sound/2 reels
Date/Country: 1929-1930   Type: Comedy Shorts

Annotation: Washington and Sublette appear as "Buck and Bubbles," a dance and comedy duo in these 2-reelers which Pathe hired black filmmaker Bill Foster to produce as competition for the Christie Comedies: <u>Black Narcissus</u>, <u>Darktown Blues</u>, <u>Darktown Follies</u>, <u>Foul Play</u>, <u>High Toned</u>, <u>Honest Crooks</u>, <u>In and Out</u>.

"I HAVE A DREAM..." THE LIFE OF MARTIN LUTHER KING
Series: Of Black America
Producer: CBS
Tech Info: 16 mm/sound/bw/33 min./1 reel
Date/Country: 1968 + USA   Type: Dramatized Documentary
Distr/Arch: tribu + kpf + iu + bfa
Annotation: Study of King's life through news footage tracing his development from Baptist minister to Civil Rights leader.

"KING" COLE AND HIS TRIO
Nar/Cast: Nat "King" Cole* + Irving Ashby* + Joe Comfort* + Jack Costanzo* + Benny Carter and His Orchestra* + Dolores Parker* + "Scat Man" Crothers*   Director: Will Cowan
Studio/Company: UniversalInternational
Tech Info: 15 min.
Date/Country: 1950 + USA   Type: Musical Short
Annotation: Above musicians are featured performing such numbers as "Route 66" and "Ooh Kick Arooney."

"LIGHTNIN'" SAM HOPKINS
Producer: University of Washington Archives of Ethnic Music and Dance
Tech Info: 16 mm/sound/bw/8 min.
Date/Country: 1967 + USA
Annotation: Short program of a "Lighnin'" Hopkins blues performance on guitar, includes "Mojo Hand."

"WITH ALL DELIBERATE SPEED"
Nar/Cast: Lloyd Hollar* + Hank Ross* + Gus Fleming*   Type: Dramatized Documentary
Distr/Arch: bfa
Annotation: Historical re-enactment of Brown vs. the Board of Education and some of the results. Lloyd Hollar plays Thurgood Marshall; Gus Fleming is Dr. Kenneth Clark.

$10,000 TRAIL, THE
Nar/Cast: Sidney P. Dones* + Nina Rowland* + Dorothy Dumont* + Frances Henderson* + Clinton Ross* + "Kid" Herman* + Joel Teal* + Master Henry Feltenburg* + E. Patrick* + Henry Smith* + J. Crockett* + E. M. Dennis*
Producer: Sidney P. Dones*
Studio/Company: Bookertee Investment Company
Date/Country: 1921 + USA
Annotation: Dones plays ranchman "Smiling Bob" Woodson whose rugged ways no longer appeal to Kate, his fiancee who returns from the East with her head turned by her education. Her visiting cousin Rosemary is however attracted to Bob and they get together after her hair-raising kidnapping by bandits and Bob's heroic rescue of her.

$100,000.00 MISUNDERSTANDING, THE
Producer: NET
Tech Info: 16 mm/sound/bw/1 reel/19 min.
Date/Country: 1971 + USA   Type: Documentary
Distr/Arch: iu
Annotation: Focuses on the Inner City Business Improvement
    Forum (ICBIF) of Detroit, a non-profit, black-controlled
    economic development group which has aided over 100 medium
    and large manufacturing businesses. Indicates the UCBIF
    requires the businesses it helps to re-invest their
    profits in black and poor communities. Established on a
    '$100,000.00 misunderstanding' following the Detroit civil
    disorders of 1967.

A FIL DI SPADA
Nar/Cast: John Kitzmiller*
Date/Country: 1953 + Italy   Type: Feature

A LUTA CONTINUA
Alt Title(s): Struggle Continues, The
Nar/Cast: Robert Van Lierop*
Screenplay: Robert Van Lierop*
Producer: Robert Van Lierop*   Director: Robert Van Lierop*
Studio/Company: Independent
Tech Info: 16 mm/sound/color/1 reel/32 min./English narra-
    tion
Date/Country: 1971 + Mozambique   Type: Documentary
Distr/Arch: tri
Annotation: A Luta Continua focuses on the national libera-
    tion movement in Mozambique, a strategically located
    country in Southern Africa. Historical background is
    presented on Portugese colonialism in Africa and analyses
    are made of the various economic interests that have a
    stake in the status quo in Southern Africa. Filmed in
    Niassa Province, September and October, 1971.

A NOUS DEUX, LA FRANCE   Director: Desire Ecare
Tech Info: 60 min.
Date/Country: 1970 + France + Ivory Coast   Type: Feature
Annotation: A serio-comic treatment of French racism and
    African social problems, second part of a trilogy. Music
    by Memphis Slim*.

A ROPIN' RIDIN' FOOL
Nar/Cast: Martin Turner* + Pete Morrison
Screenplay: Jay Inman Kane + Bob Williamson
Studio/Company: William Steiner Productions
Tech Info: 35 mm/silent/bw/5 reels
Date/Country: 1925 + USA   Type: Feature
Annotation: Martin Turner plays Major "a gentleman of many
    parts," to Pete Morrison's Jim Warren, the Texas ranger
    hero who solves all the problems in this "western
    melodrama."

A THOUSAND AND ONE NIGHTS
Nar/Cast: Cornel Wilde + Evelyn Keyes + Phil Silvers + Rex
    Ingram*
Screenplay: Wilfred Pettitt + Jack Henley

Producer: Samuel Bischoff   Director: Alfred Green
Studio/Company: Columbia
Tech Info: 16mm/ sound/ bw/ 93 min.
Date/Country: 1948 + USA   Type: Feature
Distr/Arch: bud + new
Annotation: The story of Alladin and his magic lamp, except
    that the genie who comes out to help Alladin is female and
    jealous (Keyes).   Rex Ingram plays the giant in this
    version.

A VENT 'ANNI E SEMPRE FESTA
Nar/Cast: John Kitzmiller*
Date/Country: 1957 + Italy   Type: Feature

A. PHILIP RANDOLPH
Series: Portrait in Black
Producer: Rediscovery Productions
Tech Info: 16 mm/sound/color/10 min.
Date/Country: 1972 + USA   Type: Documentary
Distr/Arch: nacc + sef
Annotation: Randolph meets with Roosevelt and Kennedy about
    the continuing struggle of black Americans.

A.K.A. CASSIUS CLAY
Nar/Cast: Richard Kiley + Muhammad Ali* + Gus D'Amato
Producer: William Cayton   Director: Jim Jacobs
Studio/Company: United Artists
Tech Info: 16mm/ sound/ color/ 3 reels/ 87 min.
Date/Country: 1970 + USA   Type: Documentary
Distr/Arch: uas
Annotation: The film traces Ali's career from the early days
    to his return to the ring against Jerry Quarry in Atlanta.
    Included in the film is fight footage, e.g. the first
    Ali-Liston fight. Music score by Teo Macero. Narrated by
    Richard Kelly.

AARON LOVES ANGELA
Nar/Cast: Moses Gunn* + Kevin Hooks* + Ernestine Jackson*
    Director: Gordon Parks, Jr.*
Studio/Company: Columbia
Tech Info: 16 mm/sound/color/3 reels/99 min.
Date/Country: 1975 + USA   Type: Feature
Distr/Arch: swa
Annotation: Story of a black youth and a Puerto Rican girl
    romantically involved in the slums of New York City.

ABBY
Nar/Cast: William Marshall* + Carol Speed* + Terry Carter*
    Director: William Girdler
Studio/Company: American International
Tech Info: 16 mm/sound/color/91 min.
Date/Country: 1974 + USA   Type: Feature
Distr/Arch: swa
Annotation: An unknown demon is unleashed during an archae-
    ological expedition and inhabits the body of an attractive
    minister's wife. Abby touches upon some aspects of Afri-
    can lore and folkways.

ABOUT MRS. LESLIE
Nar/Cast: Shirley Booth + Robert Ryan + Maidie Norman*
Screenplay: Ketti Frings + Hal Kanter
Producer: Hal B. Wallis   Director: Daniel Mann
Studio/Company: Paramount
Date/Country: 1954 + USA   Type: Feature
Annotation: Maidie Norman has a small role as Camilla in
    this story of a middle-aged landlady (Booth) whose
    poignant reminiscences in flashback include a love affair
    on a once a year basis with Mr. Leslie (Ryan).   He turns
    out to be an unhappily married airplane tycoon who comes
    to an untimely end.

ABRAHAM LINCOLN
Nar/Cast: Walter Huston + Una Merkel + Henry B. Walthall +
    Kay Hammond + Lucille LaVerne
Screenplay: D.W. Griffith   Story: Stephen Vincent Benet
Producer: Joseph Schenck   Director: D.W. Griffith
Studio/Company: Feature Productions + United Artists
Tech Info: 16 mm/sound/bw/90 min.
Date/Country: 1930 + USA   Type: Feature
Distr/Arch: aim + alb + emg + fce + ima + kil + kpf + mma +
    mog + tfc + cfm + cie + csv + ima + ncs + nil + moma
Annotation: The highlights of Abraham Lincoln's life are
    covered in this, D.W. Griffith's first sound movie.
    Blacks are present as atmosphere. Scenes showing Lincoln
    taking direct action against slavery (e.g. stopping a
    master from beating a slave) were deleted. In the
    original version, the first shot showed blacks being
    brought over in slave ships, whipped and tossed into the
    sea.

ABSENT
Nar/Cast: Clarence Brooks* + George Reed* + Virgil Owens* +
    Rosa Lee Lincoln* + Floyd Shackeford*
Producer: Rosebud Film Corporation
Date/Country: 1928 + USA   Type: Feature
Annotation: Suffering from loss of memory after his world
    war experience, a young black veteran goes West to a
    mining camp. He regains his memory during a fight in the
    camp and is able to begin his life again.

ACES HIGH
Nar/Cast: Brock Peters* + Eli Wallach + Terence Hill + Bud
    Spencer
Screenplay: Giusippe Colizzi
Producer: Crono Cinematografica   Director: Giuseppe Colizzi
Studio/Company: Paramount
Tech Info: sound/color/122 min.
Date/Country: 1969 + Italy   Type: Feature
Annotation: A revenge western with Terrence Hill in the
    Clint Eastwood role. Colizzi presents a western featuring
    intellectually attuned hombres, including Brock Peters as
    Thomas. Released in Italy in 1968 as I Quattro dell' Ave
    Maria.

ACQUE AMARE
Nar/Cast: John Kitzmiller*

Date/Country: 1955 + Italy   Type: Feature

ACROSS 110TH STREET
Nar/Cast: Anthony Quinn + Yaphet Kotto* + Paul Benjamin + Ed
    Bernard + Richard Ward*
Screenplay: Luther Davis   Story: Wally Ferris   Director:
    Barry Shear
Studio/Company: United Artists
Tech Info: 16 mm/sound/color/3 reels/102 min.
Date/Country: 1972 + USA   Type: Feature
Distr/Arch: uas
Annotation: Struggling to survive in the Harlem ghetto, a
    few men mastermind the robbery of a Mafia "bank" and be-
    come tragically caught between the police and gangsters.
    Music by J.J. Johnson* and Bobby Womack*.

ACT OF MURDER, AN
Nar/Cast: Clarence Muse* + Florence Eldredge + Fredric March
    Director: Michael Gordon
Studio/Company: Universal
Tech Info: 16 mm/sound/bw/90 min.
Date/Country: 1948 + USA   Type: Feature
Distr/Arch: uas
Annotation: One of Muse's bit parts, this one with the hus-
    band-wife team of Eldredge and March.

ADELAIDE VILLAGE   Director: Pierre L'Amare
Studio/Company: National Film Board of Canada
Tech Info: color/15 min.
Date/Country: 1974   Type: Animated Short
Distr/Arch: pho
Annotation: Describes the Caribbean people and their
    changing lifestyle.

ADIEU ONCLE TOM
Alt Title(s): Farewell Uncle Tom + Goodbye Uncle Tom
Nar/Cast: John Kitzmiller*
Screenplay: Gualtierro Jacopetti + Franco Prosperi
Producer: Euro International Films   Director: Gualtiero
    Jacopetti + Franco Prosperi
Studio/Company: Cannon + Solter, Sabinson and Roshin, Inc
Date/Country: 1971 + Italy   Type: Feature
Annotation: An attempt at "docudrama" to show the inhumanity
    of slavery.

ADVENTURES OF ROBINSON CRUSOE, THE
Nar/Cast: James Fernandez* + Dan O'Herlihy
Screenplay: Phillip Roll + Luis Bunuel
Producer: Oscar Dancigers + Henry Ehrlich   Director: Luis
    Bunuel
Tech Info: sound/color
Date/Country: 1953 + France   Type: Feature
Annotation: James Fernandez is Friday in this faithful
    adaptation of DeFoe's novel shot in Mexico with O'Herlihy
    as Crusoe.

AFFAIR OF THE SKIN, AN
Nar/Cast: Diana Sands* + Viveca Lindfors + Kevin McCarthy +

Osceolo Archer* + Lee Grant
Screenplay: Ben Maddow
Producer: Helen Levitt + Ben Maddow   Director: Ben Maddow
Studio/Company: Zenith International
Tech Info: sound/bw/3-4 reels/102 min
Date/Country: 1963 + USA   Type: Feature
Distr/Arch: mac
Annotation: Diana Sands plays a talented young photographer
   in the midst of several interlocking, disintegrating rela-
   tionships in this drama set in New York's Greenich Vil-
   lage. She acts as friend and confidante to the leads.

AFFECTIONATELY YOURS
Nar/Cast: Merle Oberon + Dennis Morgan + Rita Hayworth +
   Hattie McDaniel* + Butterfly McQueen*
Screenplay: Edward Kaufman   Story: Fanya Foss + Aleen
   Leslie   Director: Lloyd Bacon
Studio/Company: Warners
Tech Info: 16 mm/sound/bw/3 reels/88 min.
Date/Country: 1941   Type: Feature
Distr/Arch: uas
Annotation: In this comedy a newspaper reporter tries to
   remarry his ex-wife. Humor is provided by McQueen, a maid
   who cries at the slightest provocation.

AFRICA ASTIR
Producer: Hector Acebes
Tech Info: 16 mm/sound/color/1 reel/24 min.
Date/Country: 1961   Type: Documentary
Distr/Arch: iu
Annotation: Studies some of the little-known peoples of
   western Africa, emphasizing the effects of European influence on fast-disappearing cultures. Includes con-
   siderable history of the area and shows parts of the
   cities of Dakar, Mopti, Bondiagara, Djiune, Timbuktu, Gao,
   and Fianga.

AFRICA AWAKENS: MODERN NIGERIA
Producer: Atlantis Production, Inc.
Tech Info: 16 mm/sound/color/1 reel/23 min.
Date/Country: 1961   Type: Documentary
Distr/Arch: iu
Annotation: Depicts various peoples of Nigeria and their
   accomplishments and reviews African history from the
   Islamic conquerors of the seventh century to the modern
   period.

AFRICA IS MY HOME
Producer: Atlantis Productions, Inc.
Tech Info: 16 mm/sound/color/1 reel/22 min.
Date/Country: 1960   Type: Documentary
Distr/Arch: iu
Annotation: Presents the life story of Malobi, a young
   Nigerian woman, as it is interwoven with the progress of
   her people toward independence.

AFRICA JOINS THE WORLD
Series: National Archives Gift Collection

Tech Info: 16 mm/3 reels/partly edited
Annotation: Part of Record Group 200 HF series, Harmon
    Foundation Collection.

AFRICA_REBORN
Producer: Ghana Information Service
Tech Info: 16 mm/sound/bw/20 min.
Date/Country: 1963 + Ethiopia   Type: Documentary
Distr/Arch: gis
Annotation: The founding of the Organization of African Un-
    ity.

AFRICA:_EAST_AFRICAN_ARISTOCRATS_-_MASAI
Producer: Wayne State University
Tech Info: 16 mm/sound/color/1 reel/29 min.
Date/Country: 1961 + East Africa   Type: Documentary
Distr/Arch: wsu
Annotation: The film presents various facets of Masai life
    and culture, land, house types, dress, economy, etc. Al-
    so, the film discusses change and its effect on the Masai.

AFRICA:_EAST_AND_WEST
Producer: Tribune Films + Pan Am World Airlines
Tech Info: 16 mm/sound/color/1 reel/28 min.
Date/Country: 1967 + East Africa + West Africa   Type: Docu-
    mentary
Distr/Arch: tribu + panwa + aim
Annotation: The European influences on East Africa--
    supermarkets, modern cities and industrialization--are
    contrasted to the mosques and other influences of West
    Africa.

AFRICA:_THE_HIDDEN_FRONTIER
Producer: NET
Tech Info: 16 mm/sound/bw/59 min.
Date/Country: 1963-64 + Kenya   Type: TV Documentary
Distr/Arch: iu
Annotation: Depicts Kenya's attempts to unify its numerous
    ethnic groups into a coherent nation.

AFRICA'S_FUTURE
Studio/Company: WCBS-TV + NET
Tech Info: 16 mm/sound/bw/29 min.
Date/Country: 1959 + Ethiopia + Ghana + South Africa   Type:
    Documentary
Distr/Arch: iu
Annotation: The views of African teenagers on African in-
    dependence.

AFRICA'S_GIFT
Series: Black African Heritage
Nar/Cast: Gordon Parks*
Producer: Eliot Elisofon
Tech Info: 16 mm/sound/color/35 min.
Date/Country: 1973 + Ivory Coast + Sennfo   Type: Docu-
    mentary
Distr/Arch: webc
Annotation: The film examines the influence of Africa--

music, art, etc.--on American culture.   Gordon   Parks   is
the narrator.

AFRICAN ADVENTURE
Producer: Marty Stouffer
Studio/Company: Crown International
Tech Info: 16 mm/sound/color/3 reels/93 min.
Date/Country: 1964 + Botswana   Type: Documentary
Distr/Arch: mac + unf
Annotation: Various scenes of Bushman life including a hunt.
  Film also shows area wildlife.

AFRICAN MANHUNT
Nar/Cast: Myron Healey + Karen Booth + James Edwards*
Screenplay: Arthur Hoerl   Story: Arthur Hoerl
Producer: Jerry Thomas   Director: Seymour Friedman
Studio/Company: Republic
Date/Country: 1957 + USA   Type: Feature
Annotation: A melodrama of two men and a woman   escorting   a
  criminal "to the coast."

AFRICAN QUEEN, THE
Nar/Cast: Humphrey Bogart + Katherine Hepburn
Screenplay: James Agee + John Huston   Story: C.S. Forrester
Producer: S.P. Eagle   Director: John Huston
Studio/Company: United Artist
Tech Info: 16 mm/sound/color/4 reels/104 min.
Date/Country: 1952 + East Africa   Type: Feature
Distr/Arch: mab + aim + aca + roa + as
Annotation: In German East   Africa   during   WWI   gin   soaked
  Charlie Allnut (Bogart) and a prissy lady missionary (Hep-
  burn) battle each other along with   malaria,   rapids   and
  German gunboats.   Filmed on location in what is now Zaire.
  Blacks play very minor background roles.

AFRIQUE DUR SEINE
Nar/Cast: Paulin Soumanou Vieyra* + Mamamou Sarr*
Screenplay: Mamamou Sarr*
Producer: Groupe   Africain   Director: Paulin   Soumanou
  Vieyra* + Mamamou Sarr*
Studio/Company: Ethnographic Film Committee of the Museum of
  Man, Paris
Tech Info: bw/22 min./French commentary
Date/Country: 1955 + France   Type: Dramatic Short
Annotation: Depicts living and coping as a young African   in
  Paris.   It   deals   with   alienation and the bitterness of
  emigration. (Made by the first African film   group   under
  the   auspices   of   the   Ethnographic Film Committee of the
  Museum of Man, Paris.

AFRO-AMERICAN DANCE: ESTABLISHING A CULTURAL HERITAGE
Producer: Raymond Fischer + Stanley Woodward
Tech Info: 16 mm/sound/color/20 min.
Date/Country: 1971 + USA   Type: Documentary
Distr/Arch: tl
Annotation: A group of black students try   to   preserve   and
  understand   aspects   of African culture by establishing an
  African dance organization.

AFRO-AMERICAN WORKSONGS IN A TEXAS PRISON
Nar/Cast: Bruce Jackson + W.D. Alexander
Producer: Peter Seeger + Daniel Seeger + Toshi Seeger +
  Bruce Jackson + W.E. Alexander + Folklore Research Films
Tech Info: 16 mm/sound/bw/1 reel/29 min.
Date/Country: 1966 + USA   Type: Documentary
Distr/Arch: rad
Annotation: This film records seven Afro-American worksongs
  at the Ellis Unit of the Texas Department of Corrections,
  near Huntsville.   Black prisoners are seen being tran-
  sported by truck to woods and fields early in the morning,
  then   at   work   singing tree-chopping songs, e.g. "John, O
  John", "Early in the Morning."

AFRODITE LEA DELL' AMORE
Nar/Cast: John Kitzmiller*
Date/Country: 1958 + Italy   Type: Feature

AFTER HOUSE
Tech Info: 27 min.
Date/Country: 1961 + USA
Annotation: A program of music by Coleman Hawkins* in a
  night club setting. Originally produced for TV.

AH QUELLE EQUIPE   Director: Roland Quignon
Tech Info: 96 min./color
Date/Country: 1956 + France
Annotation: Comedy with popular French variety stars, in-
  cluding Sidney Bechet* and the orchestra of Andre
  Reweliotty.

AIN'T GONNA EAT MY MIND
Producer: Tony Batten
Studio/Company: WNET-TV
Tech Info: 16 mm/sound/color/1 reel/34 min.
Date/Country: 1972 + USA   Type: TV Documentary
Distr/Arch: carouf + imp
Annotation: Gang wars and street life in U.S. ghettos are
  shown in this Emmy Award winning film. Attempts made by
  gang members to explore differences and end violence.

AIN'T MISBEHAVIN'
Nar/Cast: Fats Waller* + Meade Lux Lewis* + Nat King Cole
  Trio*   Director: Peter Neal + Anthony Stern
Tech Info: 85 min.
Date/Country: 1974 + British   Type: Dramatized Documentary
Annotation: The film uses clips from features, shorts and
  newsreels.

AKKI: A BLACK POET
Producer: WKYC
Tech Info: 16 mm/sound/color/25 min.
Date/Country: 1972   Type: TV Documentary
Distr/Arch: fi
Annotation: The background, inner thoughts and writings of
  Akki Onyango, a young black poet.

AL STACEY HAYES
Producer: Canaiel
Tech Info: 16 mm/sound/color/28 min.
Date/Country: 1970 + USA   Type: Documentary
Distr/Arch: jas
Annotation: The pre-election canvassing of a black Missis-
    sippi town by a black teenager.

ALADDIN'S LANTERN
Series: Our Gang
Nar/Cast: Our Gang + Billie Thomas*
Screenplay: Hal Law + Robert A. McGowan
Producer: Jack Chertok   Director: Gordon Douglas
Studio/Company: MGM
Tech Info: bw/sound/1 reel
Date/Country: 1938 + USA   Type: Comedy Short
Annotation: The gang stages a show about Aladdin and his
    lamp.   Porky and Buckwheat keep interrupting the show to
    do a soft shoe rendition of 'Strolling Through the Park
    One Day'. Billie Thomas plays Buckwheat.

ALFALFA'S AUNT
Series: Our Gang
Nar/Cast: Our Gang + Billie Thomas*
Screenplay: Hal Law + Robert A. McGowan
Producer: Jack Chertok   Director: George Sidney
Studio/Company: MGM
Tech Info: bw/sound/1 reel
Date/Country: 1939 + USA   Type: Comedy Short
Annotation: Alfalfa mistakenly thinks his aunt is plotting
    to kill him. During one scary murder mystery sequence
    Buckwheat is frightened by a scream which makes his hair
    stand on end. Billy Thomas stars as Buckwheat.

ALFALFA'S DOUBLE
Series: Our Gang
Nar/Cast: Our Gang + Billie Thomas*
Screenplay: Hal Law + Robert A. McGowan
Producer: Jack Chertok   Director: Edward Cahn
Studio/Company: MGM
Tech Info: bw/sound/1 reel
Date/Country: 1940 + USA   Type: Comedy Short
Annotation: A prince and the pauper story involving Alfalfa
    and his twin brother Cornelius. Billie Thomas plays Buck-
    wheat.

ALI BABA GOES TO TOWN
Nar/Cast: Eddie Cantor + Cab Calloway*   Director: David
    Butler
Tech Info: 81 min.
Date/Country: 1937 + USA   Type: Feature
Annotation: An Eddie Cantor comedy featuring Cab Calloway.

ALI-FRAZIER FIGHT
Date/Country: 1971 + USA   Type: Documentary

ALIAS MARY DOW
Nar/Cast: Ray Milland + Clarence Muse* + Lola Lane

Screenplay: Gladys Unger   Director: Kurt Neumann
Studio/Company: Universal
Tech Info: sound/bw
Date/Country: 1935 + USA   Type: Feature
Annotation: To save his seriously ill wife, Mr. Dow hires a
    waitress to play his daughter, who was kidnapped 18 years
    earlier. All goes well until those involved begin having
    difficulty distinguishing fact from fiction. A bit role
    for Clarence Muse.

ALIBI, THE
Alt Title(s): see L'Alibi

ALICE ADAMS
Nar/Cast: Hattie McDaniel* + Katharine Hepburn + Fred McMur-
    ray
Screenplay: Dorothy Yost + Mortimer Offner   Story: Booth
    Tarkington
Producer: Pandro S. Berman   Director: George Stevens
Studio/Company: RKO Radio Pictures
Tech Info: 16 mm/sound/bw/99 min.
Date/Country: 1935 + USA   Type: Feature
Distr/Arch: fnc
Annotation: A tragi-comedy about a family's pretensions to
    gentility. Hattie McDaniel portrays a hired maid who can
    see through the family's make-believe world.

ALICE'S RESTAURANT
Alt Title(s): The Alice's Restaurant Massacre
Nar/Cast: Arlo Guthrie + Pat Quinn + James Broderick +
    Michael McClanathan + Geoff Outlaw + Pete Seeger + Vinette
    Carroll*
Screenplay: Venable Herndon + Arthur Penn   Story: Arlo
    Guthrie
Producer: Hillard Elkins + Joe Manduke   Director: Arthur
    Penn
Studio/Company: United Artists
Tech Info: 16 mm/sound/color/111 min.
Date/Country: 1969 + USA   Type: Feature
Distr/Arch: uas
Annotation: Film is woven around the song of the same name,
    about how a conviction for littering keeps Arlo Guthrie
    out of the army. Mirrors life in the late sixties, but is
    biographical. Vinette Carroll plays a lady clerk.

ALL ABOUT HASH
Series: Our Gang
Nar/Cast: Our Gang + Billie Thomas*
Screenplay: Hal Law + Robert A. McGowan
Producer: Jack Chertok + Richard Goldstone   Director:
    Edward Cahn
Studio/Company: MGM
Tech Info: bw/sound/1 reel
Date/Country: 1940 + USA   Type: Comedy Short
Annotation: The gang writes a radio skit to help solve a
    marital problem at Mickey's house that results from
    mother's Monday night hash. Billie Thomas plays Buck-
    wheat.

ALL AMERICAN NEWS
Nar/Cast: Frankie "Sugar Chile" Robinson*
Tech Info: 8 min.
Annotation: Seven-year old "Sugar Chile" Robinson performs
   at the piano.

ALL GOD'S STEPCHILDREN
Alt Title(s): see God's Stepchildren

ALL MY BABIES
Producer: George Stoney + Center for Mass Communications,
   Columbia University
Tech Info: 16 mm/sound/bw/55 min.
Date/Country: 1952 + USA   Type: Documentary
Distr/Arch: uca
Annotation: A licensed midwife demonstrates the method by
   which black babies in Georgia were being delivered.

ALL NIGHT LONG
Nar/Cast: Charles Mingus* + Geoffrey Holder* + Patrick Mc-
   Goohan + Marti Stevens + Paul Harris*
Screenplay: Mel King* + Peter Achilles
Producer: Relph Michael   Director: Basil Dearden
Studio/Company: Rank Organization
Tech Info: sound/bw/95 min.
Date/Country: 1962 + Britain   Type: Feature
Annotation: Johnny Cousin (McGoohan), Aurelius Rex (Har-
   .ris)'s jealous drummer, tries to break up Rex's marriage
   to his devoted (white) wife, played by Marti Stevens.
   Much drama revolves around the jealousy but Johnny is not
   successful. The film is as much music as drama.

ALL THE FINE YOUNG CANNIBALS
Nar/Cast: Pearl Bailey* + Robert Wagner + Natalie Wood +
   Louise Beavers* + George Hamilton
Screenplay: Robert Thom   Story: Rosamond Marshall
Producer: Pandero S. Berman   Director: Michael Anderson
Studio/Company: MGM
Tech Info: 16 mm/sound/color/4 reels/122 min.
Date/Country: 1960 + USA   Type: Feature
Distr/Arch: fnc
Annotation: Pearl Bailey plays a Bessie Smith type in this
   film about a young white musician's (Robert Wagner) rise
   in the jazz world.

ALL THE PEOPLE AGAINST SOME OF THE PEOPLE
Series: The Turning Points: America in the 20th Century
Producer: Koplin and Grinker
Tech Info: 16 mm/sound/color/15 min.
Date/Country: 1970 + USA   Type: Documentary
Distr/Arch: pic
Annotation: In 1963 Governor Wallace of Alabama tried to
   prevent black students from registering at the Universty
   of Alabama.

ALL THE WAY HOME
Producer: Dynamic Films, Inc.

Tech Info: 16 mm/sound/bw/1 reel/30 min.
Date/Country: 1963 + USA   Type: Dramatized Documentary
Distr/Arch: iu + dync
Annotation: Presents the conflicts that arise when an
   elderly couple shows a Negro family their house which is
   for sale. Dramatizes the crisis of community pressure as
   neighbors face the possiblility of change to an interracial neighborhood.

ALL_THE_YOUNG_MEN
Nar/Cast: Sidney Poitier* + Alan Ladd + James Darren + In-
   gemar Johansson + Mort Sahl
Screenplay: Hall Barlett
Producer: Hall Barlett   Director: Hall Barlett
Studio/Company: Columbia
Tech Info: 16 mm/sound/bw/3 reels/87 min.
Date/Country: 1960 + USA   Type: Feature
Distr/Arch: arg + bud + cin + cha + mac + mod + mot + roa +
   tfc + twy
Annotation: Poitier plays a sergeant during the Korean con-
   flict who is unexpectedly thrown into a position of com-
   manding white soldiers during the heat of battle. Tempers
   and prejudice flare while the men take refuge in a
   deserted farmhouse in the dead of Korean winter. When
   Kincaid (Alan Ladd) requires a blood transfusion it is
   Towler (Poitier) who acts as donor.

ALL_THIS_AND_RABBIT_STEW
Series: Merrie Melodies
Producer: Leon Schlesinger
Studio/Company: Warner Brothers Cartoons
Tech Info: 16 mm/technicolor/sound/10 min.
Date/Country: 1941 + USA   Type: Animated Short
Distr/Arch: kpf
Annotation: Stepin-Fetchit-like character is out rabbit
   hunting, but is outwitted by Bugs Bunny. Bugs even out-
   shoots him at craps, ending up with gun, clothes, etc.

ALL_THROUGH_THE_NIGHT
Nar/Cast: Humphrey Bogart + Sam McDaniel* + Conrad Veidt +
   Peter Lorre
Screenplay: Leonard Spigelgass + Edwin Gilbert   Director:
   Vincent Sherman
Studio/Company: Warner Brothers
Tech Info: 16 mm/sound/bw/107 min.
Date/Country: 1942 + USA   Type: Feature
Distr/Arch: uas
Annotation: Humphrey Bogart stars as a Broadway tough guy
   who gets involved in trying to break a Nazi spy ring be-
   fore they can do any major damage. Sam McDaniel has a bit
   role.

ALL-AMERICAN_SWEETHEART
Nar/Cast: Frank Wilson*   Director: Lambert Hillyer
Date/Country: 1938 + USA   Type: Feature

ALL-COLORED_VAUDEVILLE_SHOW
Nar/Cast: Adelaide Hall* + The Nicholas Brothers* + The Five

Racketeers* + Eunice Wilson*   Director: Roy Mack
Studio/Company: Warner Brothers + Vitaphone
Tech Info: 35 mm/sound/bw/1 reel/9 min.
Date/Country: 1935 + USA   Type: Musical Short
Distr/Arch: lc
Annotation: This musical short features Adelaide Hall and
    the Nicholas Brothers. Music includes "Minnie the
    Moocher", "Sweet Sue", and "Stars and Stripes."

ALMOS'_A_MAN
Series: American Short Story
Nar/Cast: LeVar Burton* + Madge Sinclair* + Robert DoQui*
Screenplay: Leslie Lee*   Story: Richard Wright*
Producer: Robert Geller + PBS   Director: Stan Laleman
Studio/Company: PBS
Tech Info: 16 mm/sound/color
Date/Country: 1977 + USA   Type: TV Feature
Annotation: Richard Wright's short story about a young black
    Southerner who is trapped by the sharecropping system in
    the South. Music by Taj Majal*.

ALOMA_OF_THE_SOUTH_SEAS
Nar/Cast: Noble Johnson* + Gilda Gray + Percy Marmont +
    Warner Baxter + William Powell   Director: Maurice
    Tourneur
Tech Info: 35 mm/bw/9 reels
Date/Country: 1925 + USA   Type: Feature
Annotation: Noble Johnson has a small role in this melodrama
    about Aloma (Gray), her South Seas paradise island, and
    some interlopers.

AM_I_GUILTY?
Alt Title(s): Racket Doctor
Nar/Cast: Ralph Cooper* + Sybil Lewis* + Dewey "Pigmeat"
    Mackham* + Sam "Deacon" McDaniel* + Lawrence Criner* +
    Monte Hawley* + Reginald Fenderson* + Clarence Brooks* +
    Marcella Moreland* + Arthur T. Ray* + Cleo Desmond* + Jes-
    se Brooks* + Napolean Simpson* + Ida Coffin* + Lillian
    Randolph* + Vernon McCalla* + Eddie Thompson* + Mae
    Turner* + Alfred Grant* + Guernsey Morrow*
Producer: A.W. Hackel
Studio/Company: Supreme Pictures
Date/Country: 1940 + USA
Annotation: Dr Dunbar (Ralph Cooper) gets involved unwit-
    tingly with the Bennett gang led by "Trigger" Bennett
    (Lawrence Criner) when his clinic is partially funded by
    Bennett. Although forced to accompany the gang, he
    remains unsullied throughout the action and excitement
    including the demise of Bennett. Clarence Brooks plays
    the police lieutenant.

AMATEUR_DETECTIVE
Nar/Cast: Mantan Moreland* + Frankie Darro   Director:
    Howard Bretherton
Date/Country: 1940 + USA   Type: Feature
Annotation: One of the series in which Darro and Moreland
    team up to solve crimes/bring criminals to justice.   See
    Chasing Trouble, for example.

AMAZING GRACE
Nar/Cast: Moms Mabley* + Stepin Fetchit* + Butterfly Mc-
  Queen* + Moses Gunn* + Slappy White* + Rosalind Cash*
Screenplay: Matt Robinson*
Producer: Matt Robinson*   Director: Stan Lathan*
Studio/Company: United Artists
Tech Info: 16 mm/sound/color/3 reels/99 min.
Date/Country: 1974 + USA   Type: Feature
Distr/Arch: uas
Annotation: Campaign of a black candidate for Mayor of
  Baltimore is led by an old woman (Mabley) who defies con-
  vention and traditional politics with comedy and the
  strength of her convictions.

AMERICAN MUSIC - FROM FOLK TO JAZZ AND POP   Director:
  Stephen Fleishman
Tech Info: 49 min.
Date/Country: 1969 + USA
Annotation: An illustrated history of American popular music
  with a section devoted to the story of jazz; includes ap-
  pearances by Duke Ellington*. Billy Taylor*, the Preserva-
  tion Hall Band*, others.

AMERICAN MUSIC: FROM FOLK TO JAZZ TO POP
Producer: ABC
Tech Info: 16 mm/sound/bw/2 reels/46 min.
Date/Country: 1967 + USA   Type: Documentary
Distr/Arch: iu + mghf
Annotation: Introduces development of jazz and pop music
  from folk music origins and features original performances
  of prominent musicians. Features commentary and analysis
  by Duke Ellington*, Richard Rodgers, and Billy Taylor*.

AMERICAN NEGRO SINGS, THE
Producer: Futura
Tech Info: 16 mm/sound/color/24 min.
Date/Country: 1968 + USA   Type: Documentary
Distr/Arch: mla
Annotation: Black roots and aspirations are explored with
  music and song.

AMERICAN SHOESHINE
Nar/Cast: Sparky Greene*
Date/Country: 1975 + USA
Annotation: The expression of black filmmaking made entirely
  by Blacks.

AMERICAN TALL TALE HEROES
Producer: Coronet Instructional Media
Tech Info: 16 mm/sound/color/1 reel/15 min.
Date/Country: 1974 + USA   Type: Animated Short
Distr/Arch: iu + corf
Annotation: Portrays through animation the adventures of
  four American folk heroes: John Henry, Stormalong, Paul
  Bunyan, Pecos Bill. Describes John Henry's steel-driving
  abilities, Stormalong's adventures as a great sailor,
  Bunyan's accomplishments as a lumber-jack, and why Pecos

Bill was considered king of the cowboys.

AMOS AND ANDY TV SHOWS
Tech Info: 16 mm/sound
Date/Country: USA   Type: TV Feature
Distr/Arch: emg
Annotation: Different segments of the Amos and Andy TV show
with black actors in the roles.

AN ADVENTURER RETURNS
Producer: Moustapha Allassane*
Tech Info: sound/color/39 min./French with English subtitles
Date/Country: 1965 + Niger   Type: Dramatic Short
Annotation: An African parody of American Westerns and a
comment on cultural and social change in the context of
the story of Jimi who returns home from America with cowboy clothes for himself and his friends and shoots up the
village.

AN AFRICAN IN LONDON
Nar/Cast: Robert Adams*
Producer: Colonial Film Unit   Director: George Pearson
Date/Country: 1943 + Britain   Type: Feature
Annotation: Adams has a featured role.

AN AFRO-AMERICAN THING
Producer: Royce Vaughn   Director: Oscar Williams*
Studio/Company: Royce Vaughn and Associates
Tech Info: 16 mm/sound/bw/1 reel/28 min.
Date/Country: 1969 + USA   Type: Documentary
Distr/Arch: kpf
Annotation: Music and dance provide the principal background
for a film which expresses the similarities and contrasts
of African and Afro-American cultures. Film sponsored by
Neighborhood Arts Alliance, San Francisco Arts Commission.

ANACOSTIA: MUSEUM IN THE GHETTO
Producer: NET
Tech Info: 16 mm/sound/bw/1 reel/18 min.
Date/Country: 1968 + USA   Type: Documentary
Distr/Arch: iu
Annotation: Describes how a branch museum of the Smithsonian
Institution enlarges the lives of children in a Washington
D. C., ghetto. Depicts the museum's policy to involve the
children in its activities.

ANATOMY OF A MURDERER
Nar/Cast: James Stewart + Lee Remick + Ben Gazzara + George
C. Scott + Duke Ellington*
Screenplay: Wendell Mayes   Story: Robert Traver
Producer: Otto Preminger   Director: Otto Preminger
Studio/Company: Columbia
Tech Info: 16 mm/sound/bw/160 min.
Date/Country: 1959 + USA   Type: Feature
Distr/Arch: arg + bud + cwf + ics + mac + mod + mot + nat +
roa + swa + tfc + wcf + wel + who
Annotation: Jimmy Stewart and George C. Scott clash in this
courtroom drama in which Stewart is defending an Army

lieutenant accused of murder, after the man allegedly
raped the lieutenant't wife. Duke Ellington is Pie Eye.

ANATOMY_OF_A_PERFORMANCE   Director: George Wein + Sidney J.
   Stiber
Date/Country: 1970 + USA   Type: Documentary
Annotation: A documentary of Louis Amstrong's final per-
   formance at Newport.

ANCIENT_AFRICANS,_THE
Tech Info: 16 mm/sound/color/1 reel/28 min.
Date/Country: 1970   Type: Documentary
Distr/Arch: iu + iff
Annotation: Uses animation and color photography to explain
   the early history of African civilizations from the Stone
   Age to the 16th century. Studies the ancient kingdoms of
   Kush, Axum, Mali, Sonhay and the stone ruins of Zimbabwe.

ANDERSON_PLATOON,_THE
Nar/Cast: Joseph Anderson + Pierre Schoendorffer
Producer: Pierre   Schoendorffer   Director: Pierre
   Schoendorffer
Studio/Company: Office de Radiodiffusion-Television Fran-
   caise
Tech Info: 16 mm/sound/bw/65 min./2 reels/English Narration
Date/Country: 1967 + France   Type: TV Documentary
Distr/Arch: con + cal
Annotation: Lieutenant Joseph B. Anderson, a black graduate
   of West Point, and his men were filmed in Vietnam as they
   ate, slept, fought and died. Schoendorffer narrates.
   Presented in U.S. by CBS TV.

ANDROCLES_AND_THE_LION
Nar/Cast: Jean Simmons + Alan Young + Victor Mature + Woody
   Strode*
Screenplay: Chester Erskine + Ken Englund   Story: G.
   Bernard Shaw
Producer: Gabriel Pascal   Director: Chester Erskine
Studio/Company: RKO Radio
Tech Info: 16 mm/sound/bw/93 min.
Date/Country: 1952 + USA   Type: Feature
Distr/Arch: jan
Annotation: Film adaptation of Shaw's story of Christian
   martyrs thrown to the lions only to be saved by a meek
   tailor who once pulled a thorn from a lion's paw. Woody
   Strode plays the lion.

ANDROMEDA_STRAIN,_THE
Nar/Cast: Arthur Hill + David Wayne + James Olson + Kate
   Reid + Paula Kelly*
Screenplay: Nelson Gidding   Story: Michael Crichton
Producer: Robert Wise   Director: Robert Wise
Studio/Company: Universal
Tech Info: 16 mm/soundcolor/130 min.
Date/Country: 1971 + USA   Type: Feature
Distr/Arch: uni + swa + cwf + twy
Annotation: Science-fiction film about the earth's first
   biological crisis. Paula Kelly plays a nurse in a small

role.

ANGEL LEVINE, THE
Nar/Cast: Harry Belafonte* + Zero Mostel + Ida Kaminska + Gloria Foster* + Barbara Ann Teer*
Screenplay: William Gunn* + Ronald Ribman   Story: Bernard Malamud
Producer: Chiz Shultz   Director: Jan Kadar
Studio/Company: United Artists
Tech Info: 16 mm/sound/color/114 min.
Date/Country: 1970 + USA   Type: Feature
Distr/Arch: mac + uas
Annotation: Reality and fantasy are interwoven in this story of a black Jewish "angel" sent to earth to save the wife and fortunes of a New York tailor played by Zero Mostel. Belafonte is the angel opposite Mostel whom he seeks to convince that he is real.

ANGEL ON MY SHOULDER
Nar/Cast: Paul Muni + Anne Baxter + Claude Rains
Screenplay: Harry Segall + Roland Kibbee
Producer: Charles R. Rogers   Director: Archie Mayo
Studio/Company: United Artists
Tech Info: 16 mm/sound/bw/99 min.
Date/Country: 1946 + USA   Type: Feature
Distr/Arch: ivy + kpf + cie
Annotation: In a reworking of Here Comes Mr. Jordan, a recently deceased mobster makes a deal with the devil to do his bidding if returned to the living. One of the first Hollywood films to show well dressed blacks in crowd scenes.

ANGELA DAVIS: PORTRAIT OF A REVOLUTIONARY
Producer: Yolande du Luart   Director: Yolande du Luart
Studio/Company: New Yorker
Tech Info: 16 mm/sound/bw/2 reels/64 min./also available in 35 min. version
Date/Country: 1971 + USA   Type: Documentary
Distr/Arch: nyf
Annotation: A documentary profile of Angela Davis, filmed by UCLA students over an eight-month period during which she was dismissed from her post as a philosophy instructor on the grounds of her membership in the Communist party.

ANGELA: LIKE IT IS
Producer: WABC-TV
Tech Info: 16 mm/sound/bw/60 min.
Date/Country: 1970 + USA   Type: Documentary
Distr/Arch: imp
Annotation: A TV documentary-interview, etc. with Angela Davis.

ANGELITOS NEGROES
Alt Title(s): Little Dark Angels
Nar/Cast: Pedro Infante + Emilia Guiu + Rita Montaner + Titina Romay + Chela Castro + Nicholas Rodriguez
Producer: Manuel R. Ojeda   Director: Joselito Rodriguez
Studio/Company: Rodriguez Brothers

Tech Info: 16 mm/sound/bw/3 reels/95 min./with English subtitles
Date/Country: 1948 + Mexico   Type: Feature
Distr/Arch: twf
Annotation: Popular singer Jose Carlos (Pedro Infante) falls
   in love with blonde, beautiful but sheltered, Ana Luisa
   and convinces her that they should marry. Unknown to Ana
   Luisa, however, her mother is black Nana, her maid.   When
   Ana Luisa's own black child is born she blames her husband
   and neglects the child. The tragic death of Nana finally
   brings about a change in Ana Luisa. No black actors appear.

ANGELO
Nar/Cast: Renato Baldini + Umberto Spadaro + Angelo* + M.
   Hussein*
Screenplay: Francesco De Robertis   Director: Francesco de
   Robertis
Tech Info: 16 mm/bw/sound/95 min./Italian with subtitles or
   dubbed
Date/Country: 1951 + Italy
Distr/Arch: ics
Annotation: Five-year old Angelo is the mulatto child of an
   Italian woman, a victim of war. The husband, in prison,
   when the child was born, learns to love little Angelo who
   has problems being accepted by the village children. Hus-
   sein plays the boy's uncle from America who comes to take
   Angelo to the U.S.

ANGOLA: THE PEOPLE HAVE CHOSEN
Alt Title(s): Second War of Liberation   Director: Herbert
   Risz
Tech Info: 16 mm/sound/color/50 min.
Date/Country: 1975 + Congo   Type: Documentary

ANGRY NEGRO, THE
Series: Radical Americans
Producer: NET
Tech Info: 16 mm/sound/bw/1 reel/30 min.
Date/Country: 1966 + USA   Type: Documentary
Distr/Arch: iu
Annotation: The Angry Negro includes interviews with Elijah
   Muhammed*, Daniel Watts*, Jimmy Garrett*, Fannie Lou
   Hamer*, John Lewis*, Julian Bond*, Andrew Young*, and Bill
   Epton* examining their opinions about the best methods to
   use to achieve equality for black people in the United
   States.

ANGRY PROPHET: FREDRICK DOUGLASS, THE
Nar/Cast: Jaye Williams*
Producer: NBC
Tech Info: 16 mm/sound/color/1 reel/23 min.
Date/Country: 1970 + USA   Type: Documentary
Distr/Arch: fnc + iu + roa
Annotation: The social views of Fredrick Douglass are
   presented through the dramatic interpretation of actor
   Jaye Williams. Outlined are Douglass' predictions
   regarding the continued mistreatment of oppressed groups.

ANGRY VOICES OF WATTS, THE
Series: Civil Rights Movement
Producer: NBC
Tech Info: 16 mm/sound/bw/50 min.
Date/Country: 1966 + USA   Type: TV Documentary
Distr/Arch: cal + fnc
Annotation: Expressions of black writers in Budd Schulberg's
    writers workshop regarding the 1965 riot in Watts, Cali-
    fornia. Shows streets and faces of people in the Watts
    area.

ANIMAL CRACKERS
Nar/Cast: Four Marx Brothers + Lillian Roth + Margaret
    Dumont
Screenplay: Morris Ruskind   Director: Victor Heerman
Studio/Company: Paramount
Tech Info: 16 mm/sound/sepia tone/97 min.
Date/Country: 1930 + USA   Type: Feature
Distr/Arch: cwf + swa + twy + uas
Annotation: Marx Brothers madness includes Groucho's en-
    trance on a stretcher borne by 4 African natives who are
    simply background to a one liner.

ANNA LUCASTA
Nar/Cast: Rex Ingram* + Eartha Kitt* + Sammy Davis, Jr.* +
    Frederick O'Neal* + James Edwards* + Henry Scott* + Ge-
    orgia Burke* + Isabelle Cooley* + Rosetta LeNoire* + Alvin
    Childress*
Screenplay: Phillip Yordan   Story: Phillip Yordan
Producer: Sidney Harmon + Longridge Enterprises   Director:
    Arnold Laven
Studio/Company: United Artists
Tech Info: sound/color/97 min.
Date/Country: 1958 + USA   Type: Feature
Annotation: Problems of a young woman (played by Eartha
    Kitt) who is thrown out of the house by a tyrannical
    father and then takes to the streets.

ANNABELLE'S AFFAIRS
Nar/Cast: Victor McLaglen + Jeanette McDonald + Louise
    Beavers*   Director: Alfred Werker
Studio/Company: Fox Film Corp.
Date/Country: 1931 + USA   Type: Feature
Annotation: A farce about the rich set with Louise Beavers
    playing a maid.

ANNAPOLIS FAREWELL
Nar/Cast: Sir Guy Standing + Tom Brown + Louise Beavers* +
    John Howard
Screenplay: Dale Van Every + Frank Craven   Director:
    Alexander Hall
Studio/Company: Paramount
Tech Info: sound/bw
Date/Country: 1935 + USA   Type: Feature
Annotation: Story of a retired commander in the Navy who
    tries to instill a love of country and service in the mid-
    dies of the Naval Academy. Louise Beavers plays Miranda.

ANNIVERSARY TROUBLE
Series: Our Gang
Nar/Cast: Our Gang + Hattie McDaniel* + Matthew Beard* +
    Billie Thomas*
Producer: Hal Roach   Director: Gus Meins
Studio/Company: MGM
Tech Info: super 8 mm/bw/sound/1 reel/20 min.
Date/Country: 1935 + USA   Type: Comedy Short
Distr/Arch: kpf + roa + bla
Annotation: Stymie (Matthew Beard) is the president of the
    Woodchucks, Spanky is the treasurer. Spanky misappropri-
    ates the club's money and gets in trouble when his mother
    thinks it is her anniversary present from her husband.
    Spanky disguises himself as Buckwheat in an unsuccessful
    attempt to escape the wrath of the club members. Buck-
    wheat is female here, the 'daughter' of Mandy the maid,
    played by Hattie McDaniel.

ANOTHER PART OF THE FOREST
Nar/Cast: Fredric March + Dan Duryea + Ann Blyth + Libby
    Taylor* + Robert "Smokey" Whitfield*
Screenplay: Vladimir Pozner   Story: Lillian Hellman
Producer: Jerry Bresler   Director: Michael Gordon
Studio/Company: Universal International
Tech Info: 16 mm/sound/bw/108 min.
Date/Country: 1948 + USA   Type: Feature
Distr/Arch: uni
Annotation: How the evil in "The Little Foxes" took root in
    the Hubbard family is the subject of Lillian Hellman's
    play set just before and during the Civil War. Libby
    Taylor, in the usual domestic role, came to Hollywood as
    Mae West's maid.

ANTONIO DAS MORTES
Nar/Cast: Mauricio Do Valli + Odete Laru + Othon Bastor +
    Hugo Carvana + Jofre Soares + Lorival Pary + Rosa Maria
    Penna + Mario Gasmas*
Screenplay: Glauber Rocha
Producer: Claude-Antoini Mapa   Director: Glauber Rocha
Tech Info: 16 mm/sound/color/100 min./3 reels
Date/Country: 1969 + Brazil   Type: Feature
Distr/Arch: fnc + gro
Annotation: Glauber Rocha (leader of Cinema Nova) links
    Latin and African cultures together in this film about the
    struggle of Brazilian peasants against the landowners.
    Rosa Maria Penna as the "saint" and a black disciple are
    the only survivors of a bloody battle by hired killers
    against the beatos. A prologue describes the importance
    of the legend of St. George and the dragon and the
    similarities between Christian and African religious
    heritage of Brazil.

ANY NUMBER CAN PLAY
Nar/Cast: Clark Gable + Alexis Smith + Leo Ames + Caleb
    Peterson*
Screenplay: Richard Brooks
Producer: Arthur Freed   Director: Mervyn Leroy

Studio/Company: MGM
Tech Info: 16 mm/sound/bw/112 min.
Date/Country: 1949 + USA   Type: Feature
Annotation: Caleb Peterson plays Sleigh in this story of a
    gambling king (Gable) who eventually opts for a more
    peaceful life, giving up his successful gambling
    establishment.

ANYBODY'S WAR
Nar/Cast: Moran and Mack + Joan Peers + Neil Hamilton
Studio/Company: Paramount
Tech Info: sound/bw
Date/Country: 1930 + USA   Type: Feature
Annotation: The vaudeville team of Moran and Mack, the "two
    Black Crows" go to war (WWI) and attempt to ruin it in
    their own way. Romance furnished by Joan Peers and Neil
    Hamilton. Moran (played in this film by Bert Swor) and
    Mack wear their usual blackface make-up.

APEMEN OF AFRICA
Producer: MGM
Studio/Company: MGM
Tech Info: 16 mm/sound/color/1 reel/20 min.
Date/Country: 1972 + East Africa   Type: Documentary
Distr/Arch: fi + umnav
Annotation: In 1924, a South African gold miner found a fos-
    sil and sent it to Professor of Anatomy Raymond Dart and
    with it Professor Dart theorized that man may have
    originated in Africa, not Asia, contrary to popular
    belief. His work was ignored until later corroborated by
    others.

APPALOOSA, THE
Nar/Cast: Frank Silvera* + Marlon Brando + Anjanette Comer
Screenplay: James Bridges + Roland Kibbee
Producer: Alan Miller   Director: Sidney J. Furie
Studio/Company: Universal
Tech Info: 16mm/ sound/ color/ 98 min.
Date/Country: 1966 + USA
Distr/Arch: twy + uas
Annotation: Frank Silvera plays Ramos, a Mexican goatherd,
    who protects Brando by allowing him and Trini (Comer) to
    hide in his hut. Ramos is then murdered by one of the
    villains because he refuses to inform on Brando, a buffalo
    hunter, who eventually escapes with his woman and his
    horse, an Appaloosa stallion, across the border.

ARBOR DAY
Series: Our Gang
Nar/Cast: Our Gang + Billie Thomas* + Hattie McDaniel*
Producer: Hal Roach   Director: Fred Newmeyer
Studio/Company: MGM + Roach
Tech Info: 16 mm/super 8 mm/bw/sound/2 reels/15-20 min.
Date/Country: 1936 + USA   Type: Comedy Short
Distr/Arch: roa + bla
Annotation: Two runaway midgets disguised as children are
    caught by a truant officer and forced to sit through the
    gang's arbor day pageant. Asked to participate, the two

are discovered by their circus employer. Billie Thomas
stars as Buckwheat.

ARE WORKING GIRLS SAFE?
Nar/Cast: Ebony Players*
Producer: Ebony Film Corporation
Date/Country: 1918 + USA

ARENA, THE
Nar/Cast: Pam Grier* + Margaret Markov + Lucretia Lone
   Director: Steve Carver
Studio/Company: New World
Tech Info: 16 mm/sound/color/90 min.
Date/Country: 1975 + USA   Type: Feature
Distr/Arch: fnc
Annotation: Among girls kidnapped by a slave merchant for
   sale in the market at Brundisiom are a Druid priestess and
   an African dancer (Pam Grier). They soon find themselves
   fighting for survival in the arena, billed as female
   gladiators.

ARETHA FRANKLIN, SOUL SINGER
Nar/Cast: Aretha Franklin*
Producer: ABC
Tech Info: 16 mm/sound/color/1 reel/25 min.
Date/Country: 1969 + USA   Type: Documentary
Distr/Arch: con
Annotation: Behind the scenes profile of Aretha Franklin, in
   rehearsals, with friends, on stage, and at home. She dis-
   cusses how she began her career in the choir of her
   father's church and sings such songs as "Respect", and
   "Natural Woman."

ARGUMENT ABOUT A MARRIAGE
Series: Kung and /Gwi Bushmen
Producer: John Marshall
Tech Info: 16 mm/sound
Date/Country: 1966 + Botswana   Type: Documentary
Distr/Arch: der + psu
Annotation: Conflict between two !Kung bands over a child
   born out of wedlock and legitimacy of a marriage. Made in
   1955, the film gives background information, as well as
   dealing with questions of bride-service and leadership.

ARIZONIAN, THE
Nar/Cast: Willie Best* + Richard Dix + Margot Grahame
Screenplay: Dudley Nichols   Story: Dudley Nichols
Producer: Cliff Reid   Director: Charles Vidor
Studio/Company: RKO
Date/Country: 1935 + USA   Type: Feature
Annotation: Willie Best is Pompey in this thirties western.

ARROWSMITH
Nar/Cast: Ronald Colman + Helen Hayes + Myrna Loy + Clarence
   Brooks*   Story: Sinclair Lewis   Director: John Ford
Studio/Company: Sam Goldwyn + Paramount
Tech Info: 16 mm/bw/sound
Date/Country: 1931 + USA   Type: Feature

Annotation: Film adaptaton of Sinclair Lewis' novel about   a
   young doctor's zealous medical research, which at times
   mars his home life. Clarence Brooks plays Dr. Marchand, a
   Howard Medical graduate who offers people of his island
   for medical experiment.

ART IN THE NEGRO SCHOOLS
Series: National Archives Gift Collection
Tech Info: 16 mm/silent/2 reels/bw
Annotation: Art education in Negro Colleges, particularly
   from the point of view of its contribution to a well
   rounded life. (Part of Record Group 200 HF series, Harmon
   Foundation Collection).

ARTHUR CRUDUP: BORN IN THE BLUES
Producer: Dave Deutsch + Jeffrey Abramson + WETA-TV
Tech Info: 16 mm/sound/color/28 min.
Date/Country: 1973 + USA   Type: Documentary
Distr/Arch: weta
Annotation: Crudup*, a native of Mississippi, makes comments
   about his life and sings some of his songs.   Provided by
   Center for Southern Folklore.

ARTISTS AND MODELS
Nar/Cast: Jack Benny + Ida Lupino + Louis Armstrong*
Screenplay: Walter LeLeon + Francis Martin
Producer: Lewis E. Gensler   Director: Raoul Walsh
Studio/Company: Paramount
Tech Info: 16 mm/sound/bw/97 min.
Date/Country: 1937 + USA   Type: Feature
Distr/Arch: uni
Annotation: In this musical comedy Jack Benny heads a strug-
   gling ad firm trying to land a big account. This picture
   was a cause celebre because of the integrated musical
   number between Martha Raye and Louis Armstrong (Satchmo).

AS THE WORLD ROLLS ON
Nar/Cast: Jack Johnson* + Blanche Thompson*
Producer: Andlauer Production Company
Tech Info: 35 mm/silent/bw/7 reels/5.600 ft.
Date/Country: 1921 + USA   Type: Feature
Annotation: Jack Johnson plays himself in this film about
   Joe Walker, a physically weak young man who learns physi-
   cal fitness and the art of self-defense from the great
   ex-heavy weight champion. The young man (Joe) also wins
   the affection of Polly (Blanche Thompson).

ASK GRANDMA
Series: Our Gang
Nar/Cast: Our Gang + Allen Hoskins*
Screenplay: Hal Roach
Producer: Hal Roach   Director: Robert McGowan
Studio/Company: Pathe
Tech Info: silent/bw/2 reels
Date/Country: 1925 + USA   Type: Comedy Short
Annotation: With his grandmother's help Mickey escapes his
   mom's 'sissfying' ways--by getting in a fight with the
   local bully. Allen Hoskins stars as Farina.

ASSAULT_ON_A_QUEEN
Nar/Cast: Errol John* + Frank Sinatra + Virni Lisi   Story:
   Jack Finney
Producer: William Goetz   Director: Jack Donohue
Studio/Company: Seven Arts Productions + Sinatra Enterprises
   + Paramount
Tech Info: sound/color/106 min.
Date/Country: 1966 + USA   Type: Feature
Annotation: A group of adventurers dream up the idea of hi-
   jacking the Queen Mary, among them Errol John as Linc
   Langley, a partner of Frank Sinatra (Mark Brittain) in an
   unsuccessful charter boat business in Florida.   After a
   wild and abortive attempt, three of the adventurers
   (Langley, Brittain and Rosa Lucchesi-Virni Lisi) survive
   and at the end of the film are drifting toward South
   America.

AT_THE_CIRCUS
Nar/Cast: Marx Brothers + Eve Arden   Director: Edward Buz-
   zell
Studio/Company: MGM
Tech Info: 16 mm/sound/bw/87 min.
Date/Country: 1939 + USA
Annotation: Black musical sequence with Harpo includes
   boogie, blues, and parodies of Rudy Vallee and Guy
   Lombardo. Ends with Harpo playing a medley of "Blue
   Moon", "Swing Low, Sweet Chariot" and applause from the
   black singers.

ATLANTIC_CITY
Nar/Cast: Constance Moore* + Brad Taylor + Louis Armstrong*
   and his Orchestra + Buck and Bubbles*   Director: Ray Mc-
   Carey
Studio/Company: Republic Pictures
Date/Country: 1945 + USA   Type: Feature
Annotation: A musical about how Atlantic City came to be a
   resort spot-- leaning more toward fiction than fact.
   Louis Armstrong and his band perform in night club scene.

ATTICA   Director: Cinda Firestone
Studio/Company: Tri-Continental
Tech Info: 16 mm/color and bw/90 min.
Date/Country: 1973 + USA   Type: Documentary
Distr/Arch: cal + tri
Annotation: The film explores the events and conditions that
   led to the rebellion as well as its aftermath, examining
   prisoner's grievances and the degrading conditions of the
   correctional system.

ATTORNEY_FOR_THE_DEFENSE
Nar/Cast: Edmund Lowe + Evelyn Brent + Clarence Muse*
   Story: J.K. McGuinness   Director: Irving Cummings
Studio/Company: Columbia
Tech Info: sound/bw
Date/Country: 1932 + USA   Type: Feature
Annotation: A brilliant prosecuting attorney becomes a
   defender of the accused after he sends someone to the

electric chair who may have been innocent. He goes on to
defend himself when he is falsely accused of murder by a
racketeer. Clarence Muse plays Jeff.

ATUMPAN: THE TALKING DRUMS OF GHANA
Producer: UCLA
Tech Info: 16 mm/sound/color/42 min.
Date/Country: 1964 + Ghana   Type: Documentary
Distr/Arch: ieucla
Annotation: Describes the part drums play in the social and
    political life of the Ashanti.

AUF WIEDERSEHN
Nar/Cast: Louis Armstrong*   Director: Harold Philipp
Tech Info: 98 min.
Date/Country: 1961 + West Germany   Type: Feature
Annotation: Comedy about three German-Americans who are sent
    to the United States as spies during World War II.   Louis
    Armstrong makes a cameo appearance.

AUTO ANTICS
Series: Our Gang
Nar/Cast: Our Gang + Billie Thomas*
Screenplay: Hal Law + Robert A. McGowan
Producer: Jack Chertok   Director: Edward Cahn
Studio/Company: MGM
Tech Info: bw/sound/1 reel
Date/Country: 1939 + USA   Type: Comedy Short
Annotation: Butch fails to sabotage Spanky and Alfalfa's
    rocket propelled soap box car.   Billie Thomas stars as
    Buckwheat.

AUTOBIOGRAPHY OF MISS JANE PITTMAN, THE
Nar/Cast: Cicely Tyson* + Thalmus Rasulala* + Roy Poole +
    Josephine Premice* + Richard A. Dysart + Katherine Helmond
    + Michael Murphy + Collin Wilcox-Horne + Beatrice Winde +
    Odetta*
Screenplay: Tracy Keenan Wynn   Story: Earnest Gaines*
    (novel)
Producer: Robert Christiansen + Rick Rosenberg   Director:
    John Korty
Studio/Company: CBS-TV + Learning Corp.
Tech Info: 16 mm/sound/color/109 min.
Date/Country: 1974 + USA   Type: TV Feature
Distr/Arch: con + roa + ics + arg + bud + cal + cwf + mmm +
    mod + mct + new + tfc + twy + wcf
Annotation: The fictional life of a 110 year old black woman
    is traced from her birth as a slave to the Civil Rights
    movement of the sixties. Cicely Tyson stars as Miss Jane.
    Winner of nine Emmies.

AWFUL TOOTH, THE
Series: Our Gang
Nar/Cast: Our Gang + Billie Thomas*
Producer: Hal Roach   Director: Nate Watt
Studio/Company: MGM + Roach
Tech Info: super 8 mm/16 mm/bw/sound/1 reel/10 min.
Date/Country: 1938 + USA   Type: Comedy Short

Distr/Arch: roa
Annotation: The gang needs money. Buckwheat tells them he
    got a dime by putting a tooth under his pillow. Alfalfa
    decides they can get a lot of money having all their teeth
    pulled. The dentist scares them, then rewards them with
    two baseballs, a glove and catcher's mitt. Buckwheat,
    scared, begins to pray. Billie Thomas stars as Buckwheat.

BABY BLUES
Series: Our Gang
Nar/Cast: Our Gang + Billie Thomas*
Screenplay: Hal Law + Robert A. McGowan
Producer: MGM   Director: Edward Cahn
Studio/Company: MGM
Tech Info: bw/sound/1 reel
Date/Country: 1941 + USA   Type: Comedy Short
Annotation: Mickey's fear that his mother will give birth to
    a Chinese baby (since he's learned every fourth child born
    is Chinese) leads to an instructive meeting with a
    Chinese/American family. Billie Thomas stars as Buck-
    wheat.

BABY BROTHER
Series: Our Gang
Nar/Cast: Our Gang + Allen Hoskins* + Jannie Hoskins*
Screenplay: Hal Roach
Producer: Hal Roach   Director: Anthony Mack + Charles Oelze
Studio/Company: Pathe
Tech Info: silent/bw/2 reels
Date/Country: 1927 + USA   Type: Comedy Short
Annotation: Lonely Joe is taken to the other side of the
    tracks where he makes friends and buys a baby that Farina
    has painted white. Also shown is an automated assembly
    line for the care and feeding of infants. Allen Hoskins
    stars as Farina and Jannie Hoskins stars as Mango.

BABY CLOTHES
Series: Our Gang
Nar/Cast: Our Gang + Allen Hoskins*
Screenplay: Hal Roach
Producer: Hal Roach   Director: Robert McGowan
Studio/Company: Pathe
Tech Info: silent/bw/2 reels
Date/Country: 1926 + USA   Type: Comedy Short
Annotation: A conniving couple who have been collecting
    $50.00 a week from a rich uncle end up in more trouble
    when they hire Joe and Mickey to impersonate young
    children. Allen Hoskins stars as Farina.

BABY THE RAIN MUST FALL
Nar/Cast: Estelle Hemsley* + Steve McQueen + Lee Remick
Screenplay: Horton Foote
Producer: Alan Pakula   Director: Robert Mulligan
Studio/Company: Columbia
Tech Info: 16 mm/sound/bw/100 min.
Date/Country: 1965 + USA   Type: Feature
Distr/Arch: arg + ccc + cwf + mod + mot + roa + swa + twy +
    unf + who

Annotation: Estelle Hemmsley is Catherine, a small role in a
    drama about a woman who comes to a small Texan town to
    rejoin her husband who has just been released after
    serving a prison term.

BACK STAGE
Series: Our Gang
Nar/Cast: Our Gang + Allen Hoskins* + Ernie Morrison*
Screenplay: Hal Roach
Producer: Hal Roach   Director: Robert McGowan
Studio/Company: Pathe
Tech Info: silent/bw/2 reels
Date/Country: 1923 + USA   Type: Comedy Short
Annotation: The opening scene features one of the more in-
    genious devices devised by the gang members, a double-
    decker tour bus powered from the inside by a mule. The
    rest of the film has the gang helping a tacky vaudevilli-
    an, totally ruining his performance. Allen Hoskins stars
    as Farina and Ernie Morrison stars as Sunshine Sammy.

BAD BOY
Nar/Cast: Johnny Downs* + Rosaline Keith* + Helen MacKellar*
    + James Robbins* + Holmes Herbert* + Matt Moore* + Bobby
    Clark* + Spencer Williams* + Clarence Brooks*
Studio/Company: Gateway Productions
Date/Country: 1937 + USA   Type: Feature

BAD MEN OF MISSOURI
Nar/Cast: Dennis Morgan + Jane Wyman + Wayne Morris + Sam
    McDaniel*
Screenplay: Charles Grayson   Director: Ray Enright
Studio/Company: Warners
Tech Info: 16 mm/sound/bw/71 min.
Date/Country: 1941 + USA   Type: Feature
Distr/Arch: uas
Annotation: Sam McDaniel has a few sparkling bit lines in
    this romanticized history of the Younger brothers.

BADDEST DADDY IN THE WHOLE WORLD, THE
Nar/Cast: Muhammad Ali*   Director: Fred Haines
Tech Info: 16 mm/sound/color/2 reels/52 min.
Date/Country: 1972 + USA   Type: Documentary
Distr/Arch: nyf
Annotation: Muhammad Ali prepares for the Juergen-Blin fight
    in Switzerland. The film shows Ali briefly with his fam-
    ily and entertaining his fans in and out of the ring.

BADOU BAY   Director: Djibril Diop-Mambety*
Tech Info: 160 min.
Date/Country: 1970 + Dakar + Senegal
Annotation: Made originally in 1967 as a comic short, Badou
    Bay was remade in a longer version with more "bite" be-
    cause the director was not satisfied with it.   Not
    released in longer version until 1972 because the censor
    asked Diop to cut the playing of the national anthem over
    the shanty town shots, one of the many scenes which shows
    the ways of the city as a dull-witted policeman chases a
    young boy through Dakar.

BAHAMA PASSAGE
Nar/Cast: Madeline Carroll + Sterling Hayden + Flora Robson
   + Leo G. Carroll + Leigh Whipper* + Dorothy Dandridge*
   Story: Nelson Hayes
Producer: Edward H. Griffith   Director: Edward H. Griffith
Studio/Company: Paramount
Date/Country: 1942 + USA   Type: Feature
Annotation: In this love story of a woman with a "tainted"
   past and a gentleman planter in the Bahamas, Leigh Whipper
   (Morales) and Dorothy Dandridge (Thalia) make brief ap-
   pearances as locals of the island.

BAIT, THE
Nar/Cast: Donna Mills + Michael Constantine + Thalmus
   Rasulala*
Screenplay: Don M. Mankiewicz + Gordon Cotler
Producer: Peter Nelson   Director: Leonard Horn
Studio/Company: Spelling-Goldberg + ABC
Date/Country: 1975 + USA   Type: TV Feature
Annotation: An attractive undercover policewoman risks her
   life to lure a woman killer into a trap.

BAKS
Alt Title(s): Yamba + Joint
Nar/Cast: Mago Ne N'Diaye* + Papa Fall* + Mareme Niang*
Screenplay: Momar Thiam*
Producer: Societe Nationale de Cinemathographie + Les Films
   Momar   Director: Momar Thiam*
Tech Info: sound/color/110 min./in Wolf with French sub-tit-
   les
Date/Country: 1974 + Senegal   Type: Feature
Annotation: Idrissa, the 12-year old son of Souleye and
   Patou, often left to his own devices, begins to be a
   truant from school and becomes an "apprentice" to "Brother
   Thie" who traffics in drugs. When "Brother Thie" and his
   gang are captured and sent to prison, Idrissa is sent to
   reform school to learn a trade. Film concentrates on the
   evils of Yamba, the "weed."

BALCONY, THE
Nar/Cast: Shelley Winters + Peter Falk + Lee Grant + Ruby
   Dee* + Leonard Nimoy
Screenplay: Ben Maddoev   Story: Jean Genet
Producer: Walter Reude, Jr.,   Director: Joseph Strick
Studio/Company: Sterling Films + Allen Hodgden Production
Tech Info: 16 mm/sound/bw/3 reels/84 min.
Date/Country: 1963 + USA   Type: Feature
Distr/Arch: bud + cal + wrs + kpf
Annotation: In this film adaptation of Genet's play about
   role playing and man's illusions of his own self-im-
   portance, Ruby Dee recreates the role of the thief.

BALLAD IN BLUE
Alt Title(s): see Blues for Lovers

BALLAD OF FRANKIE AND JOHNNY
Producer: Learning Corporation of America

Tech Info: 16 mm/sound/color/8 min.
Date/Country: 1969 + USA   Type: Animated Short
Distr/Arch: lcoa
Annotation: An animated film about the legend of Frankie and
  Johnny set in the context of a courtroom melodrama.
  Provided by Center for Southern Folklore.

BALLETS (LES) DU NIGER   Director: Jean Rouch
Date/Country: 1961 + France
Distr/Arch: saf
Annotation: Archived only.

BAND OF ANGELS
Nar/Cast: Clark Gable + Yvonne DeCarlo + Sidney Poitier*
Screenplay: John Twist + Ivan Goff + Ben Roberts   Story:
  Robert Penn Warren
Producer: Warner Brothers   Director: Raoul Walsh
Studio/Company: Warner Brothers
Date/Country: 1957 + USA   Type: Feature
Annotation: An antebellum belle (DeCarlo) learns that she
  has Negro blood. Sold into slavery and made the mistress
  of a millionaire Louisiana planter, she comes to learn the
  meaning of freedom. Sidney Poitier plays Rau-Ru, a
  favored slave.

BAND PARADE   Director: Josef Berne
Tech Info: 10 min.
Date/Country: 1943 + USA   Type: Documentary
Annotation: A couple of numbers performed by Count Basie*
  and His Band with solos.

BANJO ON MY KNEE
Nar/Cast: Barbara Stanwyck + Joel McCrea + Buddy Ebsen +
  Hall Johnson Choir* + Water Catlett
Screenplay: Nunnally Johnson   Director: John Cromwell
Studio/Company: 20th Century Fox
Tech Info: 16 mm/bw/sound/105 min.
Date/Country: 1936 + USA   Type: Feature
Distr/Arch: fnc
Annotation: Story of the life of shanty boaters on the Mis-
  sissippi with the Hall Johnson Choir providing the music
  of "The St. Louis Blues," Buddy Ebsen the dancing, Walter
  Catlett the comedy.

BAOBOB PLAY
Producer: John Marshall
Tech Info: 16 mm/sound/color/1 reel/8 min.
Date/Country: 1972 + Botswana   Type: Documentary
Distr/Arch: der
Annotation: Film depicts a pastime of children and teenagers
  in Botswana which includes using the baobob tree.

BAR SINISTER, THE
Producer: Edgar Lewis Photodrama
Studio/Company: Frank Hall Productions
Date/Country: 1917 + USA   Type: Dramatic Short
Annotation: An early "tragic mulatto" melodrama which turns
  out white, and happily.

BARBARY COAST GENT
Nar/Cast: Louise Beavers* + Wallace Beery + Binnie Barnes
Screenplay: William Lipman + Grant Garrett + Harry Ruskin
Producer: Orville Dull   Director: Roy del Ruth
Studio/Company: MGM
Date/Country: 1946 + USA   Type: Feature
Annotation: Beavers is Bedelia, a small role, in this Wal-
  lace Beery western of the 1880's.

BARBER OF DARKTOWN
Studio/Company: Keystone
Date/Country: 1915 + USA   Type: Comedy Short
Annotation: Whites in blackface play the razor carrying bar-
  ber and his "dusky" girlfriend.

BARBERSHOP BLUES
Nar/Cast: Nicholas Brothers* + Claude Hopkins band*
Screenplay: Joseph Henabery   Director: Joseph Henabery
Date/Country: 1932 + USA   Type: Musical Short
Annotation: The Nicholas Brothers are dancing bootblacks in
  a black barbershop setting. The plot involves the winning
  of a new barbershop on a bet while the band plays, among
  other numbers, "Loveless Love" and "St. Louis Blues."

BARGAIN DAY
Series: Our Gang
Nar/Cast: Our Gang + Matthew Beard* + Allen Hoskins*
Screenplay: H. M. Walker
Producer: Hal Roach   Director: Robert F. McGowan
Studio/Company: MGM + Roach
Tech Info: super 8 mm/16 mm/bw/sound/2 reels/20 min.
Date/Country: 1931 + USA   Type: Comedy Short
Distr/Arch: roa + bla
Annotation: The gang gets into mischief in a large mansion.
  Stymie is mistaken by the young lady of the house for the
  son of the family chauffeur. His response to her question
  is: "Un-un, my daddy ain't no chauffeur. My daddy's just
  a crap shootin' fool." This and other of Stymie's crap
  shooting sequences may be deleted from extant prints.
  Matthew Beard stars as Stymie and Allen Hoskins stars as
  Farina.

BARGAIN WITH BULLETS
Alt Title(s): Gangsters on the Loose
Nar/Cast: Ralph Cooper* + Lawrence Criner* + Edward Thomp-
  son* + Reginald Fenderson* + Clarence Brooks* + Al Duvall*
  + Theresa Harris* + Halley Harding* + John Lester Johnson*
  + Sam McDaniel* + Art Murray* + Ray Martin* + Francis
  Turnham* + Billy McClain* + Milton Shockley*
Screenplay: Ralph Cooper* + Phil Dunham   Story: Ralph
  Cooper* + Phil Dunham
Producer: Million Dollar Productions
Date/Country: 1937 + USA
Annotation: An underworld melodrama with Ralph Cooper as
  "Mugsy" a man who deals in stolen furs and who is also
  attractive to women - Kay and Grace (Frances Turnham and
  Theresa Harris).

BARNUM AND RINGLING, INC.
Series: Our Gang
Nar/Cast: Our Gang + Allen Hoskins*
Producer: Hal Roach   Director: Robert McGowan
Studio/Company: MGM + Roach
Tech Info: super 8 mm/bw/silent/2 reels/20 min.
Date/Country: 1928 + USA   Type: Comedy Short
Distr/Arch: kpf + roa + bla
Annotation: Farina, as a hotel bellboy, lets the gang into
   the hotel lobby where they decide to put on a circus,
   animals and all. The circus is broken up by the hotel
   detective and a chaotic chase ensues. Stars Alan Hoskins
   as Farina.

BARNUM WAS RIGHT
Nar/Cast: Glenn Tryon + Merna Kennedy + Otis Harlan + Louise
   Beavers*
Screenplay: Hutchinson Boyd   Director: Del Lord
Studio/Company: Universal
Date/Country: 1929 + USA   Type: Feature
Annotation: Mr. Loche promises his daughter in marriage to a
   young man if he makes some run down swampland, where the
   family estate is located, into valuable property. A
   legend of buried treasure almost ruins the hotel which the
   fiance has put up on the property, but in the end the
   treasure is found and the property is even more valuable.
   Louise Beavers has a bit part.

BARRAVENTO
Alt Title(s): Turning Wind, The   Director: Glauber Rocha
Tech Info: 16 mm/sound/bw/2 reels/76 min./Portugese with
   English subtitles
Date/Country: 1962 + Brazil   Type: Feature
Distr/Arch: nyf
Annotation: Barravento is set on the Bahian seacoast in a
   small fishing village where the people live in a state of
   blissful ignorance of the modern world. The town's peace
   is shattered by the arrival of Firmino, a native who has
   returned to his home from the big city. How he goes about
   bringing the town from its superstitious past into a via-
   ble present is the story of Barravento.

BASIN STREET REVUE
Nar/Cast: Lionel Hampton* + Sarah Vaughan* + Martha Davis +
   Mantan Moreland* + Nipsy Russell* + The Larks* + Little
   Buck + Nat "King" Cole* + Count Basie* + Helen Humes +
   Amos Wilburn* + The Three Businessmen of Rhythm* + Dinah
   Washington* + Freddy and Flo* + The Clovers* + Paul Willi-
   ams* + Jimmy Brown*   Director: Joseph Kohn
Studio/Company: Studio Films, Inc.
Tech Info: 35 mm/sound/tinted/8 reels
Date/Country: 1955 + USA   Type: Feature
Distr/Arch: lc
Annotation: Acts from the Harlem Variety Revue at the Apollo
   Theater.

BATAAN

Nar/Cast: Robert Taylor + George Murphy + Thomas Mitchell +
   Lloyd Nolan + Desi Arnaz + Kenneth Spencer*
Screenplay: Robert Andrews   Story: George White
Producer: Irving Starr   Director: Tay Garnett
Studio/Company: MGM
Tech Info: 16 mm/bw/sound/3 reels/93 min.
Date/Country: 1943 + USA   Type: Feature
Distr/Arch: fnc
Annotation: Wesley Epps (Spencer) is an American soldier
   during WWII fighting in the Pacific. His regiment, com-
   posed of the many ethnic groups that represent the
   pluralistic population of America valiantly attempts to
   hold the island to the last man.

BATTLE_BENEATH_THE_EARTH
Nar/Cast: Earl Cameron* + Kerewin Mathews
Screenplay: Lance Hargreaves
Producer: Charles Reynolds + Charles Vetter   Director:
   Montgomery Tully
Studio/Company: MGM
Tech Info: 16 mm/sound/color/92 min.
Date/Country: 1968 + USA + Britain   Type: Feature
Distr/Arch: fnc
Annotation: Cameron plays Sgt. Seth Hawkins in this science
   fictin melodrama about nuclear weapons, bombs and the
   Chinese communists.

BATTLE_HYMN_OF_THE_REPUBLIC.__THE
Studio/Company: Vitagraph
Date/Country: 1911 + USA
Annotation: Literal dramatization of Julia Ward Howe's song
   (which evades the phrase "to make men free") has newly
   emancipated slaves genuflecting to a savior-like Lincoln.

BATTLE_HYMN
Nar/Cast: Rock Hudson + Anna Kashfi + Dan Duryea + Don De-
   fore + Alan Hale + James Edwards*
Screenplay: Charles Grayson + Vincent Evans
Producer: Ross Hunter   Director: Douglas Sirk
Studio/Company: Universal-International
Tech Info: 16 mm/sound/color/111 min.
Date/Country: 1956 + USA   Type: Feature
Distr/Arch: uni
Annotation: The true life story of "the flying parson"
   (colonel Dean Hess) features James Edwards in a minor role
   as a Lieutenant (Maples) in the Air Force aiding Hess
   (Hudson) in his efforts to care for Korean orphans.   In
   one scene, Edwards sings an old spiritual as a lullaby.

BATTLE_OF_BROADWAY
Nar/Cast: Victor McLaglen + Brian Donlevy + Hattie McDaniel*
   + Louis Hovick
Screenplay: Lou Breslow + John Patrick   Story: Norman
   Houston
Producer: Sol M.Kurtzell   Director: George Marshall
Studio/Company: 20th Century Fox
Tech Info: sound/bw
Date/Country: 1938 + USA   Type: Feature

Annotation: McDaniel in the usual role, here as Agatha, in
an American Legion romp in New York.

BATTLE OF EAST SAINT LOUIS, THE
Studio/Company: CBS-TV
Tech Info: 16 mm/sound/bw/40 min.
Date/Country: 1970 + USA   Type: Documentary
Distr/Arch: adl + carouf
Annotation: The film focuses on selected participants in a
3-day sensitivity training program involving the local
police and members of a black ghetto community. The four
featured participants, 2 white policemen, a young black
militant and a middle-aged black woman, exchange ideas on
attitudes and issues.

BATTLE, THE
Nar/Cast: Blanche Sweet + Charles West
Producer: D.W. Griffith   Director: D.W. Griffith
Studio/Company: Biograph
Tech Info: 35 mm/silent/bw/1,135 ft./1 reel/10-15 min.
Date/Country: 1911 + USA   Type: Dramatic Short
Distr/Arch: moma
Annotation: One of the first films on the American Civil War
to romanticize the old South. The Battle contained
several elements that would later make famous Griffith's
The Birth of a Nation. Blacks as background.

BEALE STREET MAMA
Nar/Cast: July Jones* + Spencer Williams* + Rosalie Lar-
rimore* + Allen and Allen* + Joyce McElrath*
Producer: Bert Goldberg   Director: Spencer Williams*
Studio/Company: Sack Amusement
Date/Country: 1946 + USA   Type: Feature
Distr/Arch: lc
Annotation: A streetcleaner (Jones) and Bad News Johnson
(Williams) find some stolen money which they use to try to
establish themselves in the good life. They are found out
and end up losing everything.

BEAR FACTS
Series: Our Gang
Nar/Cast: Our Gang + Billie Thomas*
Producer: Hal Roach   Director: Gordon Douglas
Studio/Company: MGM + Roach
Tech Info: super 8 mm/16 mm/bw/sound/1 reel/11 min.
Date/Country: 1938 + USA   Type: Comedy Short
Distr/Arch: roa + bla
Annotation: Alfalfa fabricates a story that he can hypnotize
wild bears into submission for Darla whose father owns a
circus the gang hopes to work for. Dad overhears Al-
falfa's tale, dresses up as a bear, and scares the gang
back to their clubhouse. Billie Thomas stars as Buck-
wheat.

BEAR SHOOTERS
Series: Our Gang
Nar/Cast: Our Gang + Allen Hoskins*
Producer: Robert F. McGowan + Hal Roach   Director: Robert

f. McGowan
Studio/Company: MGM
Tech Info: bw/sound/2 reels
Date/Country: 1930 + USA   Type: Comedy Short
Annotation: The gang goes on a camping trip in search of
    bears, but instead finds a man dressed in a gorilla suit
    to frighten the kids away from a bootleg operation and a
    swarm of unfriendly bees. Farina contributes a bathtub to
    their equipment from which he fishes. Allen Hoskins stars
    as Farina.

BEAST_MUST_DIE,_THE
Nar/Cast: Calvin Lockhart*   Director: Paul Annett
Date/Country: 1974 + USA   Type: Feature

BEAST_OF_BORNEO
Tech Info: 78 min.
Annotation: The film includes voodoo and zombie mysteries
    and the search for a method of rejuvenation.

BEAT_GENERATION,_THE
Nar/Cast: Steve Cochran + Fay Spain + Mamie Van Doren +
    Louis Armstrong* + Billy Daniels*
Screenplay: Richard Matheson + Lewis Meltzer
Producer: Albert Zugsmith   Director: Charles Haas
Tech Info: 93 min.
Date/Country: 1959 + USA   Type: Feature
Annotation: Louis Armstrong is featured in this convoluted
    melodrama about beatnicks in the fifties.   Billy Daniels
    plays Dr. Elcott.

BEAU_SABREUR
Nar/Cast: Oscar Smith* + Gary Cooper + Evelyn Brent + Noah
    Beery
Producer: Adolph Zukor + Jesse L. Lasky   Director: John
    Waters
Studio/Company: Paramount
Date/Country: 1927 + USA   Type: Feature
Annotation: Oscar Smith plays Djikhi, a Sengalese soldier,
    in this tale of a French legionnaire who fulfills his duty
    to France by securing a treaty with a sheik, falls in love
    with an American journalist, and at the same time avenges
    a grudge with a traitor.

BEDFORD_INCIDENT,_THE
Nar/Cast: Richard Widmark + Sidney Poitier* + Martin Balsam
    + Wally Cox + Eric Portman + James MacArthur
Screenplay: James Poe   Story: Mark Rascovich
Producer: James B. Harris +   Richard Widmark Production
    Director: James B. Harris
Studio/Company: Columbia Pictures
Tech Info: 16 mm/bw/sound/102 min.
Date/Country: 1966 + USA   Type: Feature
Distr/Arch: mac + arg + bud + ccc + cwf + mot + new + roa +
    tfc + wcf + wel + who
Annotation: Ben Munceford (Sidney Poitier), a cool and ar-
    rogant newspaperman, is one of several thorns in the side
    of a U.S. naval captain (Richard Widmark) obsessed with

stalking a Soviet vessel during the cold war period.

BEDTIME WORRIES
Series: Our Gang
Nar/Cast: Our Gang + Matthew Beard*
Producer: Robert F. McGowan + Hal Roach   Director: Robert
    F. McGowan
Studio/Company: MGM + Roach
Tech Info: 16 mm/bw/sound/1 reel/20 min.
Date/Country: 1933 + USA   Type: Comedy Short
Distr/Arch: kpf + bla
Annotation: Spanky matches wits with a burglar who gets into
    the house through his bedroom. Although Spanky manages to
    knock out his father during the ensuing fight, the crook
    is caught in the end. Matthew Beard stars as Stymie.

BEGGARS OF LIFE
Nar/Cast: Louise Brooks + Richard Arlen + Wallace Beery +
    Edgar "Blue" Washington*   Story: Jim Tully   Director:
    William Wellman
Date/Country: 1928 + USA   Type: Feature
Annotation: Washington plays Mose, a black hobo, who, along
    with a white hobo (Richard Arlen) helps a young girl who
    has accidentally killed her father, escape to Canada.

BEGINNER'S LUCK
Series: Our Gang
Nar/Cast: Our Gang + Matthew Beard* + Billie Thomas* + The
    Five Cabin Kids*
Producer: Hal Roach   Director: Gus Meins
Studio/Company: MGM + Roach
Tech Info: 16 mm/bw/sound/1 reel/15-20 min.
Date/Country: 1935 + USA   Type: Comedy Short
Distr/Arch: roa
Annotation: There's a local amateur contest and Spanky's
    mother has big plans for him. Spanky wins in spite of all
    the gang's shenanigans. The Cabin Kids also perform.
    Billie thomas is Buckwheat.

BEGINNINGS...THE STORY OF BAGGS ACADEMY
Producer: Rediscovery
Tech Info: 16 mm/sound/color/12 min.
Date/Country: USA   Type: Documentary
Distr/Arch: nacc
Annotation: Baggs Academy is the only predominantly black
    prep school that is accredited and Oscar McCloud* of the
    Presbyterian church began his education there.

BELLE OF THE NINETIES
Nar/Cast: Libby Taylor* + Mae West + Johnny Mack Brown +
    Katherine DeMille + Duke Ellington and orchestra*
Screenplay: Mae West   Director: Leo McCarey
Studio/Company: Paramount
Tech Info: 16 mm/sound/bw/76 min.
Date/Country: 1934 + USA   Type: Feature
Distr/Arch: uni
Annotation: Libby Taylor plays Mae West's maid, Jasmine, in
    this saga of old New Orleans and its sporting world over-

seen by Miss West as Ruby Carter.   actress   Libby   Taylor
was   also   Mae   West's   maid   offscreen.   Duke   Ellington
orchestra on screen and off.

BELLE STARR
Nar/Cast: Randolph Scott + Gene Tierney + Louise Beavers*
Screenplay: Lamar Trotti   Director: Irving Cummings
Studio/Company: Fox
Tech Info: sound/color
Date/Country: 1941 + USA   Type: Feature
Annotation: Beavers is Mammy Lou who tells the story of Bel-
    le   (Tierney),   a   southern   woman who takes to the hills,
    guerilla like, to drive out the Carpetbaggers, bad Yankees
    and upstart Blacks.

BEN HUR
Nar/Cast: Noble Johnson* + Ramon Novarro + Francis X. Bush-
    man + May McAvory
Producer: Louis B. Mayer + Samuel Goldwyn + Irving Thalberg
    Director: Fred Niblo
Studio/Company: MGM
Tech Info: bw/silent
Date/Country: 1925 + USA   Type: Feature
Annotation: Ben-Hur,   a   wealthy Jew is betrayed by a Roman
    friend and is sentenced to be a galley slave.   When he
    later   becomes   a wealthy charioteer. Ben Hur avenges the
    Roman who betrayed him, finds his lost mother and sister
    and   they become Christian followers after the crucifixion
    in Jerusalem. Noble Johnson plays a charioteer.

BEND OF THE RIVER
Nar/Cast: Stepin Fetchit* + James Stewart + Julie Adams
Screenplay: Borden Chase   Story: Bill Gulick
Producer: Aaron Rosenberg   Director: Anthony Mann
Studio/Company: UniversalInternational
Tech Info: 16 mm/sound/color/3 rels/91 min.
Date/Country: 1952 + USA   Type: Feature
Distr/Arch: uni
Annotation: Indian fighting and   a   wagon   train   to   Oregon
    round   cut   this   western in which Stepin Fetchit provides
    his brand of comic relief.

BENEATH THE PLANET OF THE APES
Nar/Cast: James Franciscus + Kim Hunter + Don Pedro Colley*
    + Charlton Heston
Screenplay: Paul Dehn
Producer: Arthur P. Jacobs   Director: Ted Post
Studio/Company: 20th Century Fox
Tech Info: 16 mm/sound/color/3 reels/93 min.
Date/Country: 1970 + USA   Type: Feature
Distr/Arch: fnc
Annotation: In this sequel to Planet of the Apes James
    Franciscus, as an astronaut sent to find out what happened
    to Charlton Heston, crash lands on the planet and together
    with Heston escape the apes only to fall   prey   to   people
    who   worship   a   live   atom bomb. Don Pedro Colley is the
    "Negro."

BENITO CERENO
Nar/Cast: Roscoe Lee Brown* + Lester Rawlins
Studio/Company: NET
Tech Info: 16mm/ sound/ bw/ 105 min.
Date/Country: 1965 + USA   Type: Feature
Distr/Arch: mmm
Annotation: Adaptation of Melville's story with Roscoe Lee
   Brown in the role of Babo who leads the mutiny.

BENJAMIN BANNEKER: MAN OF SCIENCE
Series: Afro-American History
Producer: Steve Krantz Films
Tech Info: 16 mm/sound/color/1 reel/9 min.
Date/Country: 1971 + USA   Type: Documentary
Distr/Arch: iu + ebec
Annotation: Portrays   the   life   and   accomplishments   of
   Benjamin Banneker, a free black in 18th century America
   who was the grandson of a former slave. Shows how Ban-
   neker excelled in science, math, and astronomy and records
   his appointment to the commission planning the new capital
   city of Washington, D.C.

BENJAMIN FRANKLIN, JR.
Series: Our Gang
Nar/Cast: Our Gang + Billie Thomas*
Screenplay: Hal Law + Robert F. McGowan
Producer: MGM   Director: Herbert Glazer
Studio/Company: MGM
Tech Info: bw/sound/1 reel
Date/Country: 1943 + USA   Type: Comedy Short
Annotation: The gang produces a skit to teach disgruntled
   neighborhood kids the meaning of patriotism in time of
   war. Billie Thomas stars as Buckwheat.

BENNY GOODMAN STORY, THE
Nar/Cast: Sammy Davis, Jr.* + Lionel Hampton* + Teddy
   Wilson* + Steve Allen + Donna Reed
Screenplay: Valentine Davies
Producer: Aaron Rosenberg   Director: Valentine Davies
Studio/Company: Universal-International
Tech Info: 16 mm/sound/color/117 min.
Date/Country: 1956 + USA   Type: Feature
Distr/Arch: uni
Annotation: Steve Allen stars in the title role in this film
   story of the career of jazzman Benny Goodman. Featured
   are   Sammy   Davis,   Jr.   as   musician-composer   Fletcher
   Henderson; vibraphonist Lionel Hampton plays himself.

BERIMBAU
Nar/Cast: Emile de Antonio   Director: Toby Talbot
Tech Info: 16 mm/sound/color/1 reel/12 min.
Date/Country: Brazil   Type: Short
Distr/Arch: nyf
Annotation: The berimbau, a one-stringed musical bow derived
   from the hunting bow, was brought from Angola to Brazil in
   the 16t century. It was used as an accompaniment for the
   capoeria, a dance in which the dancers simulate a fight.
   Brazilian slaves danced it to practice fighting techniques

and perpetuate African culture. The well-known black
Brazilian musician, Nana, demonstrates the berimbau's complete versatility.

BERNIE CASEY: BLACK ARTIST
Producer: Multi-Cul
Tech Info: 16 mm/sound/color/21 min.
Date/Country: 1971 + USA   Type: Documentary
Distr/Arch: aci
Annotation: A former football player is now a successful
    painter.

BESSIE SMITH   Director: Charles I. Levine
Tech Info: 16 mm/sound/bw/13 min.
Date/Country: 1969 + USA   Type: Dramatic Short
Distr/Arch: can
Annotation: Footage from Bessie Smith's only extant film
    (1929) combined with newsreels of a Mississippi civil
    rights demonstration.

BET ONE I CAN MAKE IT
Producer: Peter Askin
Tech Info: 16 mm/sound/bw/22 min.
Date/Country: 1969 + USA   Type: Dramatized Documentary
Distr/Arch: dir
Annotation: Several boys from Southeast Bronx tell about
    their lives in a series of improvisations. Provided by
    Center for Southern Folklore.

BETRAYAL, THE
Alt Title(s): Wind From Nowhere (book)
Nar/Cast: Leroy Collins* + Lou Vernon* + Verlie Cowan* +
    Harris Gaines* + Jessie Johnson* + Myra Stanton* + Frances
    DeYoung* + Arthur McCoo* + Barbara Lee* + Verlie Cowan* +
    Alice B. Russell* + Edward Fraction*
Screenplay: Oscar Micheaux*   Story: Oscar Micheaux*
Producer: Oscar Micheaux*   Director: Oscar Micheaux*
Studio/Company: Astor Pictures release
Tech Info: 180 min.
Date/Country: 1948 + USA   Type: Feature
Annotation: A young black farmer in South Dakota refuses the
    love of a woman he believes is white--only to marry her
    after discovering she is a Mulatto. The film also ex-
    plores black and white community relationships.

BETTER MOVIES
Series: Our Gang
Nar/Cast: Our Gang + Allen Hoskins*
Screenplay: Hal Roach
Producer: Hal Roach   Director: Robert F. McGowan
Studio/Company: Pathe
Tech Info: silent/bw/2 reels
Date/Country: 1925 + USA   Type: Comedy Short
Annotation: The gang organizes an entire motion picture con-
    cern, complete with elaborate sets and even a fake al-
    ligator. Allen Hoskins stars as Farina.

BEWARE OF CHILDREN

Nar/Cast: Earl Cameron* + Leslie Philips + Gerald McGiven   +
    Pearl Prescod*
Screenplay: Norman Hudis + Robin Estridge
Producer: Peter Rogers   Director: Gerald Thomas
Studio/Company: G.H. Productions + American International
Tech Info: 16 mm/sound/bw/87 min.
Date/Country: 1961 + Britain   Type: Feature
Distr/Arch: mac + mod + tfc
Annotation: Cameron and Prescod are the "colored" father and
    mother in this comedy drama about a vacation resort for
    privileged children.

BEWARE
Nar/Cast: Louis Jordan* + Frank Wilson* + Valerie Black* +
    Ernest Calloway* + Milton Woods*   +   Emory Richardson*   +
    Jordan's Tympanny Five + Dimpler Daniels*
Producer: Bud Pollard   Director: Bud Pollard
Studio/Company: Astor Pictures Corporation
Tech Info: 16 mm/sound/bw/60 min.
Date/Country: 1946 + USA   Type: Feature
Distr/Arch: ncs + lc
Annotation: Musical romance with Lucius (Louis) Jordan
    coming to the rescue of his alma mater, Ware College, by
    exposing the unscrupulous tactics of Benjamin Ware III
    (Milton Woods). He also woos and wins his former love,
    athletics instructor Annabella Brown (Valerie Black).
    "Beware" is the title of the song which Jordan writes in
    honor of the college.

BEYOND MOMBASA
Nar/Cast: Cornel Wilde + Donna Reed + Leo Genn
Screenplay: Richard English + Gene Levitt   Story: James
    Eastwood
Producer: Tony Owen   Director: George Marshall
Studio/Company: Columbia
Tech Info: 16 mm/sound/color/3 reels/90 min.
Date/Country: 1957 + USA   Type: Feature
Distr/Arch: roa
Annotation: An American adventurer arrives in Africa to help
    his brother work a uranium mine in the jungles only to
    find his brother murdered supposedly by a native religious
    cult known as the Leopard Men. Usual African flora, fauna
    and witchcraft.

BEYOND THE VALLEY OF THE DOLLS
Nar/Cast: Harrison Page* + Jim Inglehart* + Marcia McBroom*
    + Dolly Reed + Cynthia Meyers + Pamela Grier* + Lavelle
    Roby*
Screenplay: Roger Ebert   Story: Ebert and Meyer
Producer: Russ Meyer   Director: Russ Meyer
Studio/Company: Fox
Tech Info: 16mm/ sound/ color/ 109 min.
Date/Country: 1970 + USA   Type: Feature
Distr/Arch: fnc
Annotation: Meyer's x-rated film about Hollywood: sin, sex,
    and show business. The most important characters are
    singers in an all-girl rock trio which includes black and
    beautiful Petronella, played by Marcia McBroom. Harrison

Page is Emerson Thorne who becomes her lover, then husband; Lavelle Roby is Vanessa; Pam Grier has a bit part as "4th Woman."

BIENVENUE a ... DUKE ELLINGTON   Director: Guy Job
Tech Info: 75 min.
Date/Country: 1973 + France   Type: Documentary
Annotation: Documentary focuses on Duke Ellington* during one of his last European tours. Includes, an excerpt from his ballet.

BIG BEN   Director: Johann van der Keuken
Tech Info: 31 min.
Date/Country: 1967 + Netherlands   Type: Documentary
Annotation: Ben Webster is studied and interviewed in Europe, with guest Don Byas.

BIG BIRD CAGE, THE
Nar/Cast: Pam, Grier*   Director: Jack Hill
Date/Country: 1974 + USA   Type: Feature

BIG BOY
Nar/Cast: Al Jolson + Claudia Dice
Screenplay: William Wills + Perry Vekroff   Story: Harold Attridge   Director: Alan Crosland
Studio/Company: Warners
Tech Info: 16 mm/sound/bw/69 min.
Date/Country: 1930 + USA   Type: Feature
Annotation: Al Jolson as Gus is blackface throughout, except for a brief postlogue in this musical comedy billed as an evening of "rollicking levity."

BIG BROADCAST OF 1936
Nar/Cast: Jack Oakie + George Burns + Gracie Allen + Harold Nicholas* + Fayard Nicholas*
Screenplay: Walter DeLeon + Francis Martin + Ralph Spence
Producer: Benjamin Glazer   Director: Norman Taurog
Studio/Company: Paramount
Tech Info: 16 mm/sound/bw/97 min.
Date/Country: 1935 + USA   Type: Feature
Distr/Arch: uni
Annotation: A variety show of entertainment with a farcical plot features performances by the Nicholas Brothers as Dot (Harold) and Dash (Fayard) and a scene with radio's Amos n' Andy characters as managers of a grocery store.

BIG BROADCAST, THE
Nar/Cast: Stuart Erwin + Bing Crosby + Burns and Allen + Kate Smith + The Mills Brothers* + Cab Calloway and his band* + Benny Carter
Screenplay: George Marion, Jr.   Story: William Ford Manley   Director: Frank Tuttle
Studio/Company: Paramount
Tech Info: 16 mm/sound/bw/197 min.
Date/Country: 1932 + USA   Type: Feature
Distr/Arch: uni
Annotation: The ups and downs of a radio broadcast studio provide musical entertainment and comedy. Cab Calloway

does his "Minnie the Moocher."

BIG BUSINESS
Series: Our Gang
Nar/Cast: Our Gang + Ernie Morrison* + Allen Hoskins* + Jan-
   nie Hoskins*
Screenplay: Hal Roach
Producer: Hal Roach   Director: Robert F. McGowan
Studio/Company: Pathe
Tech Info: super 8 mm/16 mm/bw/silent
Date/Country: 1924 + USA   Type: Comedy Short
Distr/Arch: bla
Annotation: The gang sets up a barber shop which tends to
   revolutionize the hair styles of the other kids in the
   nighborhood, much to their mother's dismay. They do have
   a notable sucess in transforming Mickey into a normal
   looking boy. Ernie Morrison stars as Sunshine Sammy, Al-
   len Hoskins stars as Farina and Jannie Hoskins stars as
   Mango.

BIG CITY
Alt Title(s): see Reouh-Takh

BIG EARS
Series: Our Gang
Nar/Cast: Our Gang + Matthew Beard*
Screenplay: H. M. Walker
Producer: Robert F. McGowan + Hal Roach   Director: Robert
   F. McGowan
Studio/Company: MGM
Tech Info: bw/sound/2 reels
Date/Country: 1931 + USA   Type: Comedy Short
Annotation: With Stymie's advice and help, Wheezer makes
   himself sick as a way to reconcile his squabbling parents.
   Matthew Beard stars as Stymie.

BIG FELLA
Nar/Cast: Paul Robeson* + Elizabeth Welch* + Roy Emerton +
   James Hayter + Lawrence Brown + Eslanda Robeson*   Story:
   Claude McKay*   Director: J. Elder Wills
Studio/Company: British Lion-Hammer
Tech Info: sound/bw
Date/Country: 1938 + Britain   Type: Feature
Annotation: Paul Robeson is featured in this film story of
   the Marseilles waterfront. Loosely based on McKay's Banjo
   the film also provides a small role for Eslanda Robeson;
   he plays the title role and sings "Lazin'" "Roll Up
   Sailorman," and "You Didn't Orta Do Such Things."

BIG MO
Nar/Cast: Bernie Casey* + Bo Svenson + Janet MacLachlan* +
   Stephanie Edwards + Maidie Norman* + Bill Walker*
Screenplay: Douglas Morrow
Producer: Frank Ross + Douglas Morrow Production   Director:
   Daniel Mann
Studio/Company: High Key Limited
Tech Info: 16 mm/sound/color/110 min.
Date/Country: 1973 + USA   Type: Feature

Distr/Arch: swa
Annotation: The courageous story of Maurice Stokes, professional basketball star who is struck down by a fatal disease and helped back to a temporary recovery by a white
teammate. Received the NAACP Image Award for best
picture. Janet MacLachlan plays Dorothy Parsons, the girl
he loves; Maidie Norman is his mother.

BIG PARADE, THE
Nar/Cast: Rex Ingram* + John Gilbert + Renee Adore
Screenplay: Laurence Stallings   Director: King Vidor
Studio/Company: MGM
Tech Info: 16 mm/3 reels/bw with color sequences/silent
(music and sound effects)/130 min.
Date/Country: 1925 + USA   Type: Feature
Annotation: Rex Ingram plays the old, faithful servant who,
in the opening scene is seen waking and then shaving the
pampered, lazy Southern rich boy. He appears at the end
when the boy returns a man after the dreadful experience
of war.

BIG PREMIERE, THE
Series: Our Gang
Nar/Cast: Our Gang + Billie Thomas*
Screenplay: Hal Law + Robert F. McGowan
Producer: Jack Chertok + Richard Goldstone   Director:
Edward Cahn
Studio/Company: MGM
Tech Info: bw/sound/1 reel
Date/Country: 1940 + USA   Type: Comedy Short
Annotation: After being chased away from a big Hollywood
premiere, the gang stages one of its own. Much is made of
Buckwheat's getting stuck in a box of cement as he tries
to leave his footprints. Billie Thomas stars as Buck-
wheat.

BIG SHOW, THE
Series: Our Gang
Nar/Cast: Our Gang + Allen Hoskins* + Ernie Morrison*
Screenplay: Hal Roach
Producer: Hal Roach   Director: Robert F. McGowan
Studio/Company: Pathe
Tech Info: silent/bw/2 reels
Date/Country: 1923 + USA   Type: Comedy Short
Annotation: Influenced by the opening of the county fair,
the gang decides to put on its own show, with various
makeshift rides, acts and exhibits. They also manage to
chase away the real fair's mean animal trainer. Allen
Hoskins stars as Farina and Ernie Morrison stars as Sun-
shine Sammy.

BIG STREET, THE
Nar/Cast: Louise Beavers* + Henry Fonda + Lucille Ball
Screenplay: Leonard Spigelgass   Story: Damon Runyan
Producer: Damon Runyan   Director: Irving Reis
Studio/Company: RKO
Date/Country: 1943 + USA   Type: Feature
Annotation: Louise Beavers plays Ruby in this comedy-drama

about "Little Pinks" (Fonda), a Broadway bus boy, and his
devotion to a self-centered nightclub singer (Ball).

BIG T-N-T SHOW, THE
Alt Title(s): T.N.T. Show, The
Nar/Cast: Joan Baez + Ike Turner* + Tina Turner* + The Byrds
  + Roger Miller + Ray Charles** and his orchestra + Donovan
  + Petula Clark + The Ronettes + Bo Diddley*
Producer: Phil Spector   Director: Larry Peerce
Studio/Company: American International Productions + 16 + 16
  mm/sound/color/3 reels/93 min. + 17 + 1965 + USA
Distr/Arch: kpf + bud + sel + wil
Annotation: Filmed before a live audience of more than
  30,000 in Hollywood, this musical revue is hosted by David
  McCallum.

BIG TIME
Nar/Cast: Stepin   Fetchit*   +   Lee   Tracy   +   Mae   Clark
  Director: Kenneth Hawks
Studio/Company: Fox
Tech Info: sound/bw
Date/Country: 1929 + USA   Type: Feature
Annotation: Fetchit does his slow talking, selective memory
  routine in this early talking picture which stars Lee
  Tracy as a joke-and-dance man (with Mae Clark as his part-
  ner/wife Lily) who wants to make the "big time."

BIG TIMERS
Nar/Cast: Moms Mabley* + Stepin Fetchit* + Francine Everett*
  + Duke Williams* + Lou Swarz* + Milton Woods* + Dots John-
  son* + Walter Earl* + Lucky Brown*   Director: Bud Pollard
Studio/Company: All American News + Astor Pictures
Tech Info: 35 mm/bw/sound/4 reels
Date/Country: 194- + USA   Type: Feature
Distr/Arch: lc

BIG TOWN, THE
Series: Our Gang
Nar/Cast: Our Gang + Allen Hoskins* + Eugene Jackson*
Screenplay: Hal Roach
Producer: Hal Roach   Director: Robert F. McGowan
Studio/Company: Pathe
Tech Info: silent/bw/2 reels
Date/Country: 1925 + USA   Type: Comedy Short
Annotation: The gang gets locked into an empty boxcar and
  ends up in New York City. Here they commandeer a double-
  decker bus to sight see until the police finally run them
  down. On the return train trip, they let loose a hoard of
  insects which totally disrupt the train. Allen Hoskins
  stars as Farina.

BIGGEST BUNDLE OF THEM ALL, THE
Nar/Cast: Godfrey Cambridge* + Robert Wagner + Raquel Welch
  + Vittorio De Sica
Screenplay: Sy Salkowitz   Story: Joseph Shaftel
Producer: Joseph Shaftel + Sy Stewart Production   Director:
  Ken Annakin
Studio/Company: MGM

Tech Info: 16 mm/sound/color/3-4 reels/106 min.
Date/Country: 1968 + USA   Type: Feature
Distr/Arch: fnc
Annotation: Crooks (Godfrey Cambridge among them) as "Benny"
  kidnap an ex-Mafioso who cannot afford the ransom in this
  crime comedy set in Italy.

BILL COSBY ON PREJUDICE
Nar/Cast: Bill Cosby*
Tech Info: 16 mm/sound/color/1 reel/24 min.
Date/Country: 1971 + USA   Type: Dramatic Short
Distr/Arch: iu + pyr + roa
Annotation: Presents Bill Cosby in a satiric monologue in
  which a super bigot, who sees himself as the common man on
  the street, characterizes different minority types. Emphasizes, by implication, the contradictions and paradoxes
  inherent in attributing characteristics to different
  minority groups.

BILL CRACKS DOWN
Nar/Cast: Grant Withers + Beatrice Roberts + Eddie Anderson*
    Director: William Nigh
Studio/Company: Republic
Tech Info: 16 mm/sound/bw/54 min.
Date/Country: 1937 + USA   Type: Feature
Distr/Arch: ivy

BILL OF RIGHTS IN ACTION, THE: DEFACTO SEGREGATION
Series: The Bill of Rights in Action
Producer: BFA
Tech Info: 16 mm/sound/color/1 reel/25 min.
Date/Country: 1972 + USA   Type: Documentary
Distr/Arch: iu + bfa
Annotation: Dramatizes the problems involved in using busing
  as a means to desegregate the schools in a segregated
  city. Features four speakers giving their reasons for and
  against busing.

BILL OF RIGHTS IN ACTION, THE: EQUAL OPPORTUNITY
Series: The Bill of Rights in Action
Producer: BFA
Tech Info: 16 mm/sound/color/1 reel/22 min.
Date/Country: 1969 + USA   Type: Documentary
Distr/Arch: iu + bfa + roa
Annotation: Presents the case of two factory workers - one
  black, one white - who are competing for the same promo-
  tion, to review the constitutional issues involved in
  establishing policies of equal opportunities. Suggests
  that there are many ways to interpret 'discrimination' and
  concludes open-endedly.

BILLIE
Nar/Cast: Rafer Johnson* + Patty Duke + Warren Berlinger
Screenplay: Ronald Alexander
Producer: Don Weis   Director: Don Weis
Studio/Company: United Artists
Tech Info: 16 mm/sound/color/87 min.
Date/Country: 1965 + USA   Type: Feature

Distr/Arch: uas
Annotation: Rafer Johnson* is athletic technical advisor in
    this domestic comedy about a 16-year old female athlete.

BINGO LONG TRAVELING ALL-STARS AND MOTOR KINGS, THE
Nar/Cast: Billy Dee Williams* + Richard Pryor* + James Earl
    Jones* + Marcia McBroom* + Emmett Ashford* + Rico Dawson*
    + Sam Brison* + Leon Wagner* + Ted Ross* + DeWayne Jessie*
    + John McCurry* + Tony Burton + Melvin Franklin + Alvin
    Childress* + Bertha DeWitt* + Carl Gordon + Ken Force +
    Henry Dunbar
Screenplay: Hal Barwod + Matthew Robbins   Story: William
    Brashler
Producer: Robert Cohen + Motown Pictures   Director: John
    Badham
Studio/Company: Universal
Tech Info: 16 mm/sound/color/111 min.
Date/Country: 1976 + USA   Type: Feature
Distr/Arch: swa + uni
Annotation: Set against the depression-ridden midwest in
    1939, a group of players from baseball's Negro National
    League become dissatisfied with exploitation by their
    management and deide to form a club of their own.

BIOGRAPHY OF A ROOKIE
Nar/Cast: Mike Wallace
Producer: David Wolpek
Studio/Company: Wolper-Sterling Production
Tech Info: 16 mm/sound/bw/50 min.
Date/Country: 1961 + USA   Type: Documentary
Distr/Arch: fnc + ste
Annotation: The rise of Dodger baseball player Willie Davis*
    to the major leagues is retold in this documentary.

BIP BAM BOOGIE
Nar/Cast: Lena Horne* + Ebony Trio* + Alex Brown*
Date/Country: 194-

BIRTH MARK
Producer: Bill Foster*
Studio/Company: Foster Photoplay Company
Date/Country: 191- + USA

BIRTH OF A NATION, THE
Nar/Cast: Mae Marsh + Lillian Gish + Henry B. Walthall +
    Wallace Reid + George Seigmann + Walter Long + George
    Reed* + Elmo Lincoln + Madame Sul-te-Wan* + Raoul Walsh +
    Eugene Pallette + Bessie Love + Jennie Lee + Tom Wilson +
    Erich von Stroheim + Mary Alden
Screenplay: D.W. Griffith + Frank Woods   Story: Thomas
    Dixon
Producer: D.W. Griffith   Director: D.W. Griffith
Studio/Company: Epoch
Tech Info: 16 mm/bw/silent/3 reels/195 min./8 mm (super and
    standard)/ bw/silent/also one with musical sound track/6
    reels
Date/Country: 1915 + USA   Type: Feature
Distr/Arch: bud + cha + rad + jan + kpf + mac + pyr + thu +

bla
Annotation: Made   from Dixon's The Clansman (original title
   of film) and The Leopard's Spots, The Birth of a Nation
   was the southerner's version of the Civil War, Reconstruction, and the rise of the Ku Klux Klan. Griffith's extraordinary skill made his controversial film one of the most
   widely disseminated,   in spite of   protests   by   the
   N.A.A.C.P.   and other anti-racist groups.   A few black
   actors, like George Reed and Madame Sul-te-Wan (who spits
   on the old colonel) appear, along with whites in blackface, like Jennie Lee as Mammy, Walter Long as Gus, Mary
   Alden as Lydia Brown, etc.

BIRTH OF A RACE
Alt Title(s): Lincoln's Dream
Screenplay: Emmett J. Scott
Producer: Emmett J. Scott
Tech Info: silent/bw/12 reels/3 hours
Date/Country: 1918 + USA   Type: Feature
Annotation: The film intended to counteract the effects and
   respond to the racial allegations in Birth of Nation.
   Ended up as a kind of patchwork extravaganza beginning in
   the Garden of Eden. It took over two years to make at a
   cost of over $1,000,000.

BIRTH OF THE BLUES
Nar/Cast: Bing Crosby + Mary Martin + Brian Donlevy + Eddie
   Anderson* + J. Carroll Naish + Ruby Elzy*   Story: Harry
   Tugend   Director: Victor Schertzinger
Studio/Company: Paramount
Tech Info: 16 mm/sound/bw/3 reels/85 min.
Date/Country: 1941 + USA   Type: Feature
Distr/Arch: uni
Annotation: An essentially plotless musical, Birth of the
   Blues follows the wanderings of clarinetist Jeff Lambert
   (Crosby) from jam session to jam session. Eddie Anderson
   is featured as Lovey, a member of Jack Teagarden's
   orchestra.

BIRTH
Series: The Family of Man
Producer: BBC-TV
Studio/Company: BBC-TV
Tech Info: 16 mm/sound/color/2 reels/45 min.
Date/Country: 1971 + Botswana   Type: Documentary
Distr/Arch: tim
Annotation: Film of how women in different cultures react to
   pregnancy and birth - why do women in more "primitive"
   cultures seem to have easier births than their more
   "civilized" couterparts, are cravings common to women of
   all cultures, do they all get tired as term draws to an
   end? Film focuses on these and other points.

BIRTHDAY BLUES
Series: Our Gang
Nar/Cast: Our Gang + Matthew Beard* + Bobbie Beard* +
   Carolina Beard*
Producer: Robert F. McGowan + Hal Roach   Director: Robert

F. McGowan
Studio/Company: MGM + Roach
Tech Info: super 8 mm/16 mm/bw/sound/2 reels/20 min.
Date/Country: 1932 + USA   Type: Comedy Short
Distr/Arch: bla
Annotation: Stymie helps Dickie and Spanky raise money for a
    dress for their mother by having a bake sale. They bake a
    cake, put prizes inside it, and sell slices by advertising
    surprise gifts in every piece. The inevitable disaster
    ensues, but all works out in the end.

BIRTHRIGHT, ≤1
Nar/Cast: J. Homer Tutt* + Evelyn Preer* + Salem Tutt Whit-
    ney* + Lawrence Chenault* + W.B.F. Crowell* + Callie
    Mines* + E.G. Tatum* + Edward Elkas + Alma Sewall*
Studio/Company: Micheaux Film Corporation
Tech Info: 35 mm/bw/silent/10 reels/9,500 ft
Date/Country: 1924 + USA   Type: Feature
Annotation: Young idealistic Harvard graduate settles in a
    small southern town where he hopes to be a service to his
    people and encounters brutality and prejudice from both
    races.

BIRTHRIGHT, ≤2
Nar/Cast: Ethel Moses* + Alec Lovejoy* + Carmen Newsome* +
    Laura Bowman* + George Vessey
Producer: Micheaux Film Corporation*
Tech Info: bw/sound
Date/Country: 1939 + USA   Type: Feature
Annotation: Remake of 1924 film, with some changes, but
    basic issue of the young Harvard graduate struggling
    against prejudice and bigotry remains.   Intra-racial
    prejudice still is a factor.

BISCUIT EATER, THE
Nar/Cast: Billy Lee + Fred Toones* + Cordell Hickman*
Screenplay: Stuart Anthony + Lillie Hayward   Story: James
    Street
Producer: Stuart Heisler   Director: Jack Moss
Studio/Company: Paramount
Tech Info: 16 mm/sound/bw/83 min.
Date/Country: 1940 + USA   Type: Feature
Distr/Arch: uni
Annotation: Story of 2 boys, one black, one white who raise
    an outcast dog into a championship field dog. Cordell
    Hickman is Text; Fred (Snowflake) Toones is "1st and 2nd
    Thessalonians."

BISHOP TURNER--BLACK NATIONALIST
Series: Afro-American History
Producer: Encyclopedia Britannica Educational Corp.
Tech Info: 16 mm/sound/color/1 reel/8 min.
Date/Country: 1968 + USA   Type: Documentary
Distr/Arch: iu
Annotation: Presents the childhood educational experiences
    and political activities of Bishop Henry M. Turner* and
    his influence on the modern civil rights movement.

BITTER MELONS
Producer: John Marshall
Tech Info: 16 mm/sound/color/1 reel/32 min.
Date/Country: 1966 + Botswana   Type: Documentary
Distr/Arch: iu + der + ucemc + psu
Annotation: Focuses on the Bushmen of the Kalahari Desert in
    southern Africa to underscore the difficulty of survival
    in an area where game is scarce because waterholes are dry
    most of the year. Highlights traditional music, dance,
    and children's games.

BLACK AMERICAN DREAM, THE
Producer: BBC
Studio/Company: BBC
Tech Info: 16 mm/color/sound/2 reels/65 min. (Part I: 35
    min; Part II: 30 min.)/videotape version
Date/Country: 1971 + Britain   Type: Documentary
Distr/Arch: tim + cal
Annotation: What is Black Power? The militancy of the six-
    ties is compared to present day Black movements. Featured
    in the film are Stokely Carmichael*, Jesse Jackson*, and
    other black leaders in exclusive interviews.

BLACK AND TAN MIX UP, A
Nar/Cast: Ebony Players*
Producer: Ebony Film Corporation
Date/Country: 1918 + USA

BLACK AND TAN
Nar/Cast: Duke Ellington* and his Cotton Club orchestra +
    Fredi Washington* + Alec Lovejoy*
Screenplay: Dudley Murphy
Producer: Dick Currier   Director: Dudley Murphy
Studio/Company: RKO Radio
Tech Info: 16 mm/bw/sound/20 min.
Date/Country: 1929 + USA   Type: Musical Short
Distr/Arch: kpf + moma
Annotation: Fredi Washington is the ill but courageous
    dancer in this film designed mainly to display the talents
    of Ellington, (his first appearance on film) and his
    music. In love with Ellington, Washington dances as she
    dies, but the last sound she hears is Duke's "Black and
    Tan Fantasy."

BLACK AND WHITE IN COLOR
Nar/Cast: Jacques Spiesser + Jean Carmet + Catherine Rouvel
    + Jacques Dufilho
Screenplay: Jean-Jacques Annaud + Georges Conchon
Producer: Arthur Cohn + Jacques Perrin + Giorgio Silvagni
    Director: Jean-Jacques Annaud
Tech Info: 16 mm/sound/color/91 min./in French with English
    subtitles
Date/Country: 1976 + France + Ivory Coast   Type: Feature
Distr/Arch: crnf
Annotation: Winner of the Academy Award for best foreign
    language film of 1976, the film takes place in 1914 in
    Colonial West Africa and is the story of a small war
    fought between the French Colonials and the German coloni-

als on African soil using African tribesmen as soldiers.
The "war" and its attendant absurdities are ironically
revealed as the two sides blunder toward the Armistice.

BLACK AND WHITE IN SOUTH AFRICA
Series: Commonwealth of Nations
Producer: National Film Board of Canada
Tech Info: 16 mm/sound/bw/1 reel/30 min.
Date/Country: 1958 + Canada   Type: Documentary
Distr/Arch: iu + mghf
Annotation: Reports on the present developments and future
    plans for the program of apartheid in the Union of South
    Africa. Indicates the beliefs which underlie the con-
    flicts among the Bantu, the British, and the Boers. Out-
    lines the present policy of rigid racial separation in the
    Union and projects eventual results of this policy into
    the future.

BLACK AND WHITE TOGETHER?
Producer: NET
Tech Info: 16 mm/sound/bw/2 reels/58 min.
Date/Country: 1969   Type: Documentary
Distr/Arch: iu
Annotation: Describes Project WILL, a plan designed to
    promote racial understanding between black and white high
    school students in Atlantic City. Relates how one staff
    member becomes disillusioned during the federally spon-
    sored project conducted in two six-week sessions, and
    challenges the premise of the experiment. Indicates that
    although the students were supposed to be making their own
    decisions, they actually had no control over the project.

BLACK AND WHITE: UNLESS WE LEARN TO LIVE TOGETHER
Producer: Jesse Sandler
Tech Info: 16 mm/sound/color/16 min.
Date/Country: USA   Type: Documentary
Distr/Arch: aef
Annotation: The study of two men narrated by Leonard
    Nimoy--a black man who lost a great leader and friend, and
    a white man who must deal with the hatred of his black
    neighbors.

BLACK AND WHITE: UPTIGHT
Producer: Avanti Films
Tech Info: 16 mm/color/sound/1 reel/35 min.
Date/Country: 1969   Type: Documentary
Distr/Arch: roa + iu + bfa
Annotation: The beliefs and myths about black people that
    have led to social prejudice and discrimination are ex-
    plored in this film aimed at analyzing the subtle ways in
    which hate and racism are perpetuated in American society.

BLACK AND WHITE
Date/Country: USA   Type: Comedy Short
Annotation: A white girl tries to squelch her rival by
    magically darkening the rival's skin, only to have her
    plan backfire and affect herself also. She then must deal
    with the advances of a black butler.

BLACK ARTISTS
Producer: Paul Highman
Tech Info: 16 mm/sound/color/28 min.
Date/Country: 1969 + USA   Type: Documentary
Distr/Arch: afgr
Annotation: Examination of three black artists: Samella
    Lewis, William Pajaud, and John Riddle.

BLACK AT YALE
Producer: Warrington Hudin
Date/Country: 1977 + USA   Type: Documentary Short
Annotation: A documentary about being black at Yale which
    focuses on the attempt of an outsider to become a member
    of the student body without formal registration, simply by
    attending classes.

BLACK BART
Studio/Company: Warner Brothers
Date/Country: 1973 + USA   Type: Feature

BLACK BEACH
Alt Title(s): see The Love Flower

BLACK BELT JONES
Nar/Cast: Jim Kelly* + Gloria Hendry*
Screenplay: Oscar Williams*
Producer: Fred Weintraub + Paul Heller   Director: Robert
    Clouse
Studio/Company: Warner Brothers
Date/Country: 1973 + USA   Type: Feature
Annotation: Jim Kelly, a Kung Fu and martial arts champion,
    heads a group of young blacks who are pitted against white
    gangsters.

BLACK BOOMERANG, THE
Studio/Company: William H. Clifford Photoplay Co.
Tech Info: 35 mm/silent/bw
Date/Country: 1925 + USA   Type: Feature

BLACK BUNCH
Alt Title(s): Jungle Sex   Director: Henning Schellerup
Tech Info: 67 min.
Date/Country: 1972 + USA   Type: Feature
Annotation: Women use their bodies to fight in this x-rated,
    low budget romp through the jungle with rhetoric of the
    seventies.

BLACK CAESAR
Nar/Cast: Fred Williamson* + Art Lund + Gloria Hendry* +
    Minnie Gentry* + D'Urville Martin* + Julius Harris*
Screenplay: Larry Cohen
Producer: Larry Cohen + Peter Sabiston   Production
    Director: Larry Cohen
Studio/Company: American International
Tech Info: 16 mm/sound/color/92 min.
Date/Country: 1973 + USA   Type: Feature
Distr/Arch: unf

Annotation: Williamson is a gangster who tries to get his
   share of the money squeezed from the ghetto by the Mafia.

BLACK CANADIAN EXPERIENCE
Nar/Cast: Michael Wilkinson*
Producer: Lenny Little-White   Director: Lenny Little-White
Date/Country: 1972 + Canada   Type: Documentary
Annotation: A documentary which examines closely the ex-
   perience of Blacks in Canada from a historical perspec-
   tive.

BLACK CHARIOT
Nar/Cast: Bernie Casey*
Screenplay: Robert L. Goodwin*
Producer: Robert L. Goodwin*   Director: Robert L. Goodwin*
Date/Country: 1971 + USA   Type: Feature

BLACK COP, THE
Producer: NET
Tech Info: 16 mm/bw/sound/1 reel/15 min.
Date/Country: 1968 + USA   Type: Documentary
Distr/Arch: iu
Annotation: Explores the relationship of the black policeman
   to the black community. Interviews representatives of
   both sides in New York City and in Los Angeles. Musical
   accompaniment by the John Coltrane* Quartet.

BLACK COWBOY, THE
Producer: WOW-TV, Omaha, Nebraska
Studio/Company: WOW-TV, Omaha, Nebraska
Tech Info: 16 mm/sound/bw/25 min.
Date/Country: USA
Distr/Arch: adl
Annotation: Historical interpretation of the black cowboy's
   contributions to development of the West is cut-in with
   actual interviews of black men who shared that experience.

BLACK DELTA RELIGION
Producer: Center for Southern Folklore
Tech Info: 16 mm/sound/bw/1 reel/15 min.
Date/Country: 1973 + USA   Type: Documentary
Distr/Arch: iu + csf
Annotation: Documents the evolution of religion from tradi-
   tional rural services to sanctified urban services in the
   Mississippi Delta. Includes preaching and congregation
   reaction, singing, baptism by immersion, and a variety of
   formal and informal black American religious experiences.

BLACK EYE
Nar/Cast: Fred Williamson* + Rosemary Forsyth + Teresa
   Graves* + Bret Morrison
Screenplay: Mark Haggard + Jim Martin
Producer: Pat Rooney   Director: Jack Arnold
Studio/Company: Warner Brothers
Tech Info: 16 mm/technicolor/sound/3 reels/98 min.
Date/Country: 1974 + USA   Type: Feature
Distr/Arch: wsa
Annotation: A private eye (Williamson) investigates the

murder of a silent film star and his investigation leads
him through some modern California scenes of porno filmmaking, drugs, and changing sexual lifestyles. Teresa
Graves, who plays his love interest, also has a female
lover (Rosemary Forsyth).

BLACK FANTASY
Producer: Lionel Rogosin   Director: Lionel Rogosin
Tech Info: 16 mm/sound/color/78 min.
Date/Country: 1974   Type: Feature
Distr/Arch: imp
Annotation: Film mixes reality and fantasy in depicting the
    experiences of Jim Collier, a black musician, married to a
    white woman.

BLACK G.I., THE
Producer: NET
Tech Info: 16 mm/bw/sound/2 reels/55 min.
Date/Country: 1970   Type: Documentary
Distr/Arch: iu
Annotation: Illustrates discrimination against Blacks both
    on and off U.S. military bases. Includes on-location in-
    terviews with black servicemen and Pentagon officials.

BLACK GIRL
Alt Title(s): see La Noire de...

BLACK GIRL
Nar/Cast: Leslie Uggams* + Brock Peters* + Claudia McNeil* +
    Peggy Pettitt* + Gloria Edwards* + Loretta Greene* +
    Louise Stubbs* + Ruby Dee*
Screenplay: Ossie Davis*   Story: J.E. Franklin*
Producer: Lee Savin   Director: Ossie Davis*
Studio/Company: Cinerama Releasing
Tech Info: 16 mm/sound/color/3 reels/107 min.
Date/Country: 1973 + USA   Type: Feature
Distr/Arch: swa
Annotation: Black Girl is the drama of three generations of
    black women. It depicts tensions and conflicts which stem
    from a collective familial sense of inferiority.   At the
    center of the drama, is a young girl named Billie Jean
    (Pettitt) who dreams of becoming a dancer and rejects the
    indolence of her half-sisters. They in turn resent Billie
    Jean's ambition to "make something" of herself.   Louise
    Stubbs is the mother, Claudia McNeil the grandmother,
    Brock Peters the absent father, Leslie Uggams the one who
    escapes to college. Ruby Dee has a cameo role.

BLACK GODFATHER, THE
Nar/Cast: Jimmy Witherspoon*   Director: John Evans
Studio/Company: Penthouse
Date/Country: 1974 + USA   Type: Feature
Annotation: Jimmy Witherspoon plays a black leader in this
    gangster film with blacks pitted against the Mafia.

BLACK GOLD
Nar/Cast: Lawrence Corman* + Kathryn Boyd*
Producer: Norman Film Manufacturing Company

Tech Info: 35 mm/silent/bw/6 reels
Date/Country: 1928 + USA

BLACK_GUNN
Nar/Cast: Jim Brown* + Brenda Sykes* + Vida Blue* +   Martin
   Landau + Gene Washington* + Deacon Jones* + Cookie
   Gilchrist* + Tody Smith* + Clancy Williams* + Bernie
   Casey* + Jim Watkins*
Screenplay: Franklin Coen
Producer: John Heyman + Norman Priggen + Champion Production
   Company   Director: Robert Hartford-Davis
Studio/Company: Columbia Pictures
Tech Info: 16 mm/color/sound/3 reels/94 min.
Date/Country: 1972 + USA   Type: Feature
Distr/Arch: swa
Annotation: Jim Brown plays a slick nightclub owner caught
   in the middle between the Mafia and a group of black
   radicals as they fight for control of the numbers racket.

BLACK_HAS_ALWAYS_BEEN_BEAUTIFUL
Nar/Cast: James Van DerZee*
Producer: NET
Tech Info: 16 mm/sound/bw/17 min./1 reel
Date/Country: 1971 + USA   Type: Documentary
Distr/Arch: iu
Annotation: Capturing the pride and beauty of black people
   are Van DerZee's photographs of Harlem school children,
   the black Yankees, Marcus Garvey, Bill "Bojangles" Robin-
   son and many others.

BLACK_HERITAGE:_A_HISTORY_OF_THE_AFRO-AMERICANS
Producer: WCBS-TV
Tech Info: 16 mm/sound/bw/1 reel/30 min.
Date/Country: 1969 + USA   Type: Documentary
Distr/Arch: tch
Annotation: This award-winning TV series, consisting of 108
   thirty minute film lectures is available from Teachers
   College Library of Columbia University. General   and
   specific topics are listed in the catalogue, Films and
   Videotapes in the Collection of the Teachers College Li-
   brary (see List of Distributors).

BLACK_HISTORY:_LOST,_STOLEN_OR_STRAYED?
Series: Of Black America
Nar/Cast: Bill Cosby*
Producer: CBS   Director: Andrew A. Rooney + Perry Wolff
Tech Info: 16 mm/sound/color/2 reels/55 min.
Date/Country: 1968 + USA   Type: Documentary
Distr/Arch: bfa + kpf + iu + tribu
Annotation: Film focuses on "lost" black history and the
   effect of its absence from the history books. Narrated by
   Bill Cosby.

BLACK_INDIANS_OF_NEW_ORLEANS,_THE
Producer: Maurice M.Martinez
Tech Info: 16 mm/sound/color/33 min./1 reel
Date/Country: 1976 + USA   Type: Documentary
Distr/Arch: cmi

Annotation: First definitive treatment of the Black Indians
    of New Orleans, descendants of North American Indians and
    former African slaves.   The film describes the cultural
    traditions of the Black Indians, popularly known as the
    Mardi Gras Indians, and their evolution in socio-histori-
    cal context.

BLACK_JACK
Nar/Cast: Georg Stanford Brown*   Director: William T.   Naud
Date/Country: 1973 + USA   Type: Feature

BLACK_JESUS
Alt Title(s): see Seduto Alla Sua Destra

BLACK_JEWS
Producer: Avraham Goren
Studio/Company: New Line Cinema
Tech Info: 16 mm/color/sound/25 min.   Type: Documentary
Distr/Arch: nlc
Annotation: A documentary on a group of black Jews living
    semi-communally in New Jersey. Their predicament--facing
    discrimination, from both Jews and Blacks -- provides a
    different viewpoint on being black in America.

BLACK_LEGION,_THE
Nar/Cast: Humphrey Bogart + Dick Foran + Earl O'Brian + Ann
    Sheridan + Robert Barrat + Joseph Sawyer   Director:
    Archie Mays
Studio/Company: Warners
Tech Info: 16 mm/sound/bw/83 min.
Date/Country: 1936 + USA   Type: Feature
Distr/Arch: uas
Annotation: Another film based on the story of the "Black
    Legion," a successor to the Ku Klux Klan, which flourished
    in the Middle West in the 1930's.

BLACK_LIKE_ME
Nar/Cast: James Whitmore + Roscoe Lee Brown* + Al Freeman,
    Jr.* + Will Geer + Eva Jessye* + P.J. Sidney* + Richard
    Ward*
Screenplay: Gerda Lerner + Carl Lern   Story: John Howard
    Griffin
Producer: Julius Fannenbaum   Director: Carl Lerner
Studio/Company: Continental + Walter Reade Sterling
Tech Info: 16 mm/bw/sound/3 reels/110 min.
Date/Country: 1964 + USA   Type: Feature
Distr/Arch: kpf + bud + wrs
Annotation: A white southerner, played by James Whitmore
    manages to change the color of his skin and live "black"
    in this film adaptation of Griffin's Black_Like_Me.   P.J.
    Sidney plays Frank Newcomb and Al Freeman, Jr., his son,
    who represent two opposing black views.

BLACK_MAGIC
Producer: Oscar Micheaux*
Studio/Company: Micheaux Film Corporation
Date/Country: 1932 + USA

BLACK MAMA, WHITE MAMA
Nar/Cast: Pam Grier* + Margaret Makov
Screenplay: H.R. Christian
Producer: John Ashley + Eddie Romero   Director: Eddie
   Romero
Studio/Company: American International
Tech Info: 16 mm/sound/color/87 min.
Date/Country: 1973 + USA   Type: Feature
Distr/Arch: unf

BLACK MEN AND IRON HORSES
Nar/Cast: A. Phillip Randolph*
Tech Info: 16 mm/sound/color/18 min.
Date/Country: USA
Distr/Arch: adl
Annotation: This film documents the historical and
   pioneering work of black engineers and workers who made
   significant contributions to the development of American
   rail travel.   Featured are Elijah McCoy* ("The Real Mc-
   Coy"), Granville T. Woods, and Charles Rickey*.

BLACK MODERN ART
Nar/Cast: Dana Chandler* + Valerie Maynard* + Leroy Clarke*
Producer: Fundacion Juan March   Director: Juan A. Ruiz-
   Anchia
Tech Info: 16 mm/color/22 min./sound/1 reel
Date/Country: 1976 + USA   Type: Documentary
Distr/Arch: tri
Annotation: This documentary focuses on three black American
   artists whose painting and sculpture reflect the "cross-
   fertilization of a unique ethnic heritage with a sensitiv-
   ity to the problems of modern society." The film contains
   examples of their work; each artist comments on his or her
   own artistic philosophy.

BLACK MOON
Nar/Cast: Jack Holt + Fay Wray + Dorothy Burgess + Clarence
   Muse* + Mme. Sul-te-wan* + Lawrence Criner + Juanita Lane
    Story: Clements Ripley   Director: Roy William Null
Studio/Company: Columbia Production
Date/Country: 1934 + USA
Annotation: A tale of voodoo unravels in the West Indies as
   a white goddess is unable to stop Blacks from killing off
   an island's white population.

BLACK MUSIC IN AMERICA: FROM THEN TILL NOW
Producer: Learning Corporation of America   Director: Hugh
   A. Robertson*
Tech Info: 16 mm/color/sound/1 reel/28 min.
Date/Country: 1971 + USA   Type: Documentary
Distr/Arch: iu
Annotation: Introduces renowned black musicians and the con-
   tribution black music has made to America in the forms of
   jazz, blues, spirituals, protest songs, swing, and rock
   and roll.   Gives a history of black music, from the time
   of the introduction of slavery in America to the present
   day, using old engravings and film clips. Includes Louis
   Armstrong*, Mahalia Jackson*, Bessie Smith*, Count Basie*,

Billie Holiday*, Duke Ellington*, and others.

BLACK_MUSIC_IN_TRANSITION
Tech Info: 30 min.
Date/Country: 1969 + USA   Type: Documentary
Annotation: Poet A.B. Spellman* discusses the Harlem Renais-
    sance, the "great migration" of Afro-Americans from the
    South and traces the origin and development of jazz.

BLACK_MUSLIMS_SPEAK_FROM_AMERICA
Nar/Cast: Malcolm Muggeridge
Studio/Company: BBC-TV
Tech Info: 16 mm/bw/sound/33 min.
Date/Country: 1970   Type: Documentary
Distr/Arch: tim
Annotation: Malcolm Muggeridge interviews seven young Black
    Muslims in an attempt to understand the philosophical,
    political and religious implications of the Nation of
    Islam.

BLACK_NETWORK
Nar/Cast: Nina Mae McKinney* + The Nichols Brothers* +
    Amanda Randolf*
Studio/Company: Vitaphone
Tech Info: 16 mm/sound/bw/2 reels/65 min.
Date/Country: 1936 + USA   Type: Feature
Distr/Arch: uas
Annotation: Story about blacks trying to create a radio
    show.

BLACK_ON_WHITE
Nar/Cast: Anita Sanders + Terry Carter* + Nini Seguin
Screenplay: Tinto Brass + Franco Longo
Producer: Radley Metzger   Director: Tinto Brass
Studio/Company: Lion Film
Tech Info: 35 mm/sound/color/89 min.
Date/Country: 1969 + Italy   Type: Feature
Annotation: An X-rated feature about an Italian woman in
    London with her husband, who daydreams incidents about a
    young attractive black man who follows her about town.

BLACK_ORPHEUS
Alt Title(s): Orfeu Negro
Nar/Cast: Breno Melo* + Marpessa Dawn*
Screenplay: Jacques Viot   Story: Vinicius de Moraes
Producer: Sacha Gordine   Director: Marcel Camus
Studio/Company: Lopert Films
Tech Info: 16 mm/35 mm/color/sound/103 min./Portugese with
    English subtitles/also a dubbed version
Date/Country: 1959 + Brazil   Type: Feature
Distr/Arch: jan
Annotation: Camus' film loosely parallels the classic legend
    of Orpheus and Eurydice. The tragic love story unravels
    against the background of carnival in Rio de Janeiro's
    black ghetto. Grand Prix, 1959 Cannes Festival. Marpessa
    Dawn, an American dancer, plays Eurydice.

BLACK_PANTHERS,_THE

Nar/Cast: Eve Crane
Producer: Agnes Varda   Director: Agnes Varda
Tech Info: 16 mm/color/sound/2 reels/29 min.
Date/Country: 1968 + USA   Type: Documentary
Distr/Arch: gro
Annotation: Varda's documentary records conversations with
   Kathleen Cleaver*, Bobby Seale* and Stokely Carmichael*
   about the Black Panther movement. Shot in California, the
   film is set against a "Free Huey (Newton)" rally in an
   Oakland park.

BLACK PEOPLE OF THE SLAVE SOUTH, 1850
Producer: Steve Krantz Films
Tech Info: 16 mm/sound/color/1 reel/10 min.
Date/Country: 1971 + USA   Type: Documentary
Distr/Arch: iu + ebec
Annotation: Examines the relationship between the cotton gin
   and the development of slavery in the South. Uses
   historical prints to describe plantation life in a
   frontier setting. Discusses the attitudes of slave owners
   toward their slaves and the problems that slaves faced
   even after the Emancipation Proclamation.

BLACK PLUS X
Producer: Aldo Tambellini   Director: Aldo Tambellini
Tech Info: bw/8 min.
Distr/Arch: gro
Annotation: A shock-dream interpretation of racism in
   America, Black Plus X uses children to project the
   traumatic consequences of color prejudice

BLACK POLICEMAN: THE WRITING ON THE WALL
Nar/Cast: Dennis Weaver
Producer: Jesse Sandler
Tech Info: 16 mm/sound/color/16 min.
Date/Country: USA   Type: Dramatized Documentary
Distr/Arch: aef
Annotation: A black police officer experiences racism at his
   own station house. Dennis Weaver narrates.

BLACK POWER IN DIXIE
Studio/Company: WCBS
Tech Info: 16 mm/sound/bw/2 reels/60 min.
Date/Country: 1969 + USA   Type: TV Documentary
Distr/Arch: bfa
Annotation: Part I - 1867-1877 How blacks became influential
   in the South. Part II - Black consciousness in the Recon-
   struction Period. Lerone Bennett* narrates.

BLACK POWER: WE'RE GOIN' TO SURVIVE AMERICA
Producer: leonard M. Henry
Tech Info: 16 mm/sound/bw and color/15 min.
Date/Country: USA   Type: Documentary
Distr/Arch: twn
Annotation: Stokely Carmichael addresses the Black Panthers
   after returning from around-the-world trip. Also the
   Uzozi Aro'ho Dancers.

BLACK POWER: THE SPOKESMEN
Series: The Turning Points: America in the 20th Century
Nar/Cast: Martin Luther King, Jr.* + Stokely Carmichael* +
   Muhhamad Ali* + Malcolm X* + Adam Clayton Powell* + Floyd
   McKissick* + H. Rap Brown* + Alexander Allen* + Whitney
   Young* + Dick Gregory* + Eldridge Cleaver*
Producer: Kaplin and Grinker
Tech Info: 16 mm/sound/color/15 min.
Date/Country: 1969 + USA   Type: Documentary
Distr/Arch: pic
Annotation: Black leaders discuss black power.

BLACK POWER, WHITE BACKLASH
Studio/Company: CBS
Tech Info: 16 mm/sound/bw/50 min.
Date/Country: 1966 + USA   Type: TV Documentary
Distr/Arch: cbs
Annotation: Mike Wallace interviews black leaders: Stokely
   Carmichael, Martin Luther King, Jr., and Daniel H. Watts,
   also people from Cicero, Illinois.

BLACK PREVIEW TRAILERS
Tech Info: 16 mm/sound/bw/1 reel/20 min.
Date/Country: 1934-38 + USA
Distr/Arch: kpf
Annotation: Contains original theatrical "preview" trailers
   from the following all black films: Bronze Buckaroo, Dark
   Manhattan, Harlem Rides the Range, Birthright, God's Step-
   children, Juke Joint, Miracle in Harlem, etc.

BLACK PROTEST: THE QUEST FOR CIVIL LIBERTIES
Series: The Turning Points: America in the 20th Century
Producer: Koplin and Grinker
Tech Info: 16 mm/sound/color/15 min.
Date/Country: 1969 + USA   Type: Documentary
Distr/Arch: pic
Annotation: Beginning with Harry Truman's 1947 speech the
   modern-day fight for full emancipation is traced.

BLACK RABBITS AND THE WHITE RABBITS, THE
Producer: The Schloat House
Tech Info: 16 mm/color/sound/1 reel/8 min.
Date/Country: 1970 + USA   Type: Documentary
Distr/Arch: iu
Annotation: Presents the allegory of two groups of rabbits
   who, over a period of time, enslave each other and profess
   the belief that they are superior. Begins with each group
   living on opposite sides of a river with equal prosperity;
   this harmony is destroyed one night when the white rabbits
   invade the black rabbits' territory and enslave those
   captured. But one day the black rabbits revolt and in
   turn subvert their previous masters.

BLACK RODEO
Nar/Cast: Bud Gramwell* + Skeets Richardson* + Woody Strode*
   + Muhammad Ali* + Aretha Franklin* + B.B. King* + Ray
   Charles*
Producer: Jeff Kanew + Utopia Productions   Director: Jeff

Kanew
Studio/Company: Cinerama Releasing
Tech Info: 16 mm/color/sound/87 min.
Date/Country: 1972 + USA   Type: Documentary
Distr/Arch: swa
Annotation: Black Rodeo riders overwhelmed audiences on
    September 4, 1971, at Randalls, New York. Highlights of
    that event are recorded here while the historical role of
    black cowboys in developing the American West is recounted
    by Woody Strode*.

BLACK ROOTS
Producer: Lionel Rogosin   Director: Lionel Rogosin
Studio/Company: Impact Films
Tech Info: 16 mm/sound/color/61 min.
Date/Country: 1970 + USA   Type: Documentary
Distr/Arch: imp + rad
Annotation: Some Blacks prominent in the civil rights move-
    ment relax at a quiet cafe and discuss the movement, how
    racism affects their lives, and several perform blues
    numbers. Included in this group are Flo Kennedy*, Rev.
    Fred D. Kirkpatrick*, Rev. Gary Davis*, Jim Collier*,
    Larry Johnson* and Wende Smith*.

BLACK SAMSON
Nar/Cast: Rockne Tarkington* + William Smith + Carol Speed +
    Connie Strickland + Napolean Whiting*   Director: Charles
    Bail
Studio/Company: Warner Brothers
Tech Info: 16 mm/sound/color/3 reels/88 min.
Date/Country: 1974 + USA   Type: Feature
Distr/Arch: wsa
Annotation: The streets are the backdrop for this story of
    one man's battle to keep his neighborhood free of dope
    pushers and mob influence.

BLACK SHADOWS ON A SILVER SCREEN
Series: The American Document
Nar/Cast: Ossie Davis*
Screenplay: Thomas R. Cripps
Producer: Steven Enrique + William Bowman   Director: Steven
    York
Studio/Company: Post-Newsweek Stations, Inc.
Tech Info: 16 mm/sound/color/2 reels/55 min.
Date/Country: 1976 + USA   Type: Documentary
Distr/Arch: luc
Annotation: The motion picture history of black involvement
    in American films, with scenes from films depicting posi-
    tive and negative black images. Contributions of black
    filmmakers like Oscar Micheaux illustrate the rugged path
    trod by black producers and actors. Highlighted are the
    careers of Paul Robeson*, Josephine Baker*, Fred Washing-
    ton* with narration by Ossie Davis*. Music: Duke Elling-
    ton*, Cab Calloway, others.

BLACK SHERLOCK HOLMES
Studio/Company: Ebony Pictures
Annotation: A black comic rendition of Conan Doyle.

BLACK SIX, THE
Nar/Cast: Gene Washington* + Carl Eller* + Lem Barney* +
    Mercury Morris* + Willie Lanier* + Joe Greene*
Screenplay: George Theakos
Producer: Matt Cimber   Director: Matt Cimber
Studio/Company: Cinemation
Tech Info: 90 min.
Date/Country: 1974 + USA   Type: Feature
Annotation: Six black Viet Nam veterans form a motorcycle
    gang and determine to stay at peace with everything until
    one of the veteran's brothers is killed by a white gang
    plotting to get the six. football pros are hard to beat.

BLACK SOLDIER, THE
Series: Of Black America
Producer: CBS
Tech Info: 16 mm/sound/bw/1 reel/27 min.
Date/Country: 1968 + USA   Type: Documentary
Distr/Arch: iu + bfa
Annotation: Traces the history of the black American's
    participation in the armed forces of the United States,
    from the Revolutionary War to the war in Vietnam. Reveals
    little- known facts about Blacks, such as segregation in
    the military prior to 1947, and points out that black
    soldiers have served in American wars, whether they were
    accepted socially or not.

BLACK THUMB
Producer: King Screen Productions
Tech Info: 16 mm/sound/color/1 reel/7 min.
Date/Country: 1970   Type: Dramatized Documentary
Distr/Arch: iu + hraw + bfa
Annotation: Examines the dramatic realization of internal
    racial prejudice by a white 'liberal' salesman who out-
    wardly has tried to exhibit an unbiased attitude, yet who
    is shocked to find that the black man he sees doing yard
    work is the owner of a house on the route where he is sel-
    ling his wares door to door.

BLACK THUNDERBOLT
Nar/Cast: Jack Johnson*
Studio/Company: A.A. Millman
Tech Info: 35 mm/silent/bw/7 reels
Date/Country: 1922 + USA   Type: Feature
Annotation: Filmed in Spain while Johnson was "in exile."

BLACK TODAY, THE
Series: The Blacks
Producer: BBC
Tech Info: 16 mm/sound/bw/40 min.
Date/Country: 1967 + Britain   Type: Documentary
Distr/Arch: tim
Annotation: Description of black life in Britain, Johannesb-
    urg, South London, Rio de Janeiro, Harlem and Los Angeles.

BLACK VIEWS ON RACE
Nar/Cast: Ralph Abernathy* + Muhammad Ali* + Harry

Belafonte* + Julian Bond* + Edward Brooke* + H. Rap Brown*
   + James Brown* + Jim Brown* + Stokely Carmichael* +
   Shirley Chisholm* + Dick Gregory* + Coretta King* + Martin
   Luther King* + Malcolm X* + Sidney Poitier* + Adam Clayton
   Powell* + Jackie Robinson* + Bayard Rustin* + Bobby Seale*
   + Carl Stokes*
Producer: Merton Koplin + Charles Grinker
Tech Info: 16 mm/sound/color/4 min.
Date/Country: 1970 + USA   Type: Documentary
Distr/Arch: tl
Annotation: A series of actual public comments and diverse
   opinions of outstanding Afro-Americans. Each is a
   separate single-subject film, four minutes in length.

BLACK WATERS
Nar/Cast: John Loder + Lloyd Hamilton + James Kirkwood +
   Noble Johnson*
Studio/Company: British and Dominions + World Wide
Tech Info: 16 mm/sound
Date/Country: 1929 + Britain
Annotation: Reportedly this was Noble Johnson's first sound
   film.

BLACK WIDOW
Nar/Cast: Ginger Rogers + Van Heflin + Hilda Simms* + George
   Raft
Screenplay: Nunnally Johnson
Producer: Nunnally Johnson   Director: Nunnally Johnson
Studio/Company: Twentieth Century Fox
Tech Info: 16 mm/sound/color/3 reels/95 min.
Date/Country: 1954 + USA   Type: Feature
Distr/Arch: fnc
Annotation: Van Heflin portrays a Broadway producer falsely
   accused of murder who searches for information to clear
   himself. Among those he talks to is Ann, a black waitress
   played by Hilda Simms.

BLACK WOMAN, THE
Nar/Cast: Nikki Giovanni* + Lena Horne* + Bibi Amina Baraka*
   + Roberta Flack* + Loretta Abbot*
Producer: NET
Tech Info: 16 mm/bw/sound/2 reels/52 min.
Date/Country: 1970 + USA   Type: TV Documentary
Distr/Arch: iu
Annotation: Nikki Giovanni, Lena Horne, Bibi Amina Baraka,
   and other black women discuss their role in contemporary
   society and the problems they confront. Focusing on the
   relationship of black women to black men, white society,
   and the liberation struggle, the film also includes
   singing by Roberta Flack, a dance by Loretta Abbott, and
   poetry by Nikki Giovanni.

BLACK WORLD
Series: Of Black America
Nar/Cast: Mike Wallace
Studio/Company: CBS
Tech Info: 16 mm/sound/bw/55 min.
Date/Country: 1968 + USA   Type: Documentary

Distr/Arch: bfa
Annotation: Mike Wallace narrates as black Americans and African leaders in the struggle for freedom confer.

BLACK, KING, THE
Alt Title(s): Harlem Hot Shot
Nar/Cast: A.B. Comathiere + Vivianne Baker* + Knolly
  Mitchell* + Dan Michaels* + Mary Jane Watkins* + Harry
  Gray* + Mike Jackson* + Lorenzo Tucker* + Trixie Smith*
  Story: Donald Heywood
Producer: Southland Pictures   Director: Donald Heywood
Studio/Company: Metropolitan Studios (Fort Lee, NJ)
Tech Info: 16 mm/bw/sound/2 reels/70 min.
Date/Country: 1932 + USA   Type: Feature
Distr/Arch: kpf + bud + par
Annotation: "Charcoal" Johnson, through connivance, becomes
  the minister/leader of a Logan, Mississippi, congregation
  from which he attempts to extort money for a Back to
  Africa movement.   The corrupt Johnson proclaims himself
  King of the United States of Africa.

BLACKBOARD JUNGLE, THE
Nar/Cast: Sidney Poitier* + Glenn Ford + Anne Francis
Producer: Pandro S. Berman   Director: Richard Brooks
Studio/Company: MGM
Tech Info: 16 mm/sound/bw/3 reels/101 min.
Date/Country: 1955 + USA   Type: Feature
Distr/Arch: fnc
Annotation: Slum schools and juvenile delinquency are the
  subject of this film. At one point, a high school teacher
  (Glenn Ford) is rescued from teenaged bullies by a black
  student (Sidney Poitier).

BLACKENSTEIN
Date/Country: 1972 + USA   Type: Feature
Annotation: A "black" version of the popular Frankenstein in
  the horror genre.

BLACULA
Nar/Cast: William Marshall* + Vonetta McGee* + Denise
  Nicholas* + Thalmus Rasulala* + Emily Yancy* + Ketty
  Lester*
Screenplay: Raymond Koenig + Joan Torres
Producer: Joseph T. Naar   Director: William Crain
Studio/Company: American International
Tech Info: 16 mm/sound/color/3 reels/92 min.
Date/Country: 1972 + USA   Type: Feature
Distr/Arch: swa
Annotation: Turned into a vampire by the evil Count Dracula,
  Blacula remains sealed until unexpectedly released by art
  collectors in present day Los Angeles.

BLANC ET LE NOIR, LE
Nar/Cast: Raimu + Suzanne Dantes + Fernandel
Screenplay: Sacha Guitry   Story: Sacha Guitry
Producer: Braunberger-Richebe   Director: Robert Florey
Tech Info: 35 mm/bw/sound/108 min.
Date/Country: 1930 + France   Type: Feature

Annotation: Margaret, believing her husband Marcel to be
unfaithful, gets even by haphazardly taking a lover for
the night, who is, unknown to her, a black singer. Before
she sees the newly born infant, Marcel exchanges the baby
for a white infant and the two parents are happily re-
conciled.

BLAZING SADDLES
Nar/Cast: Mel Brooks + Cleavon Little* + Gene Wilder + Count
   Basie* and Band*   Director: Mel Brooks
Studio/Company: Warner Brothers
Tech Info: 16 mm/sound/color/3 reels/93 min.
Date/Country: 1974 + USA   Type: Feature
Distr/Arch: wsa
Annotation: Cleavon Little is the sheriff and Gene Wilder
   his side kick in this parody of all Westerns and other
   assorted Hollywood genres. Opens with Blacks who are
   working on the railroad but who won't sing "them old
   spirituals;" insist on champagne tunes instead.
   Anachronisms abound including Count Basie and his band
   playing in the desert and giving the "Old West" sheriff
   the "right on."

BLIND GARY DAVIS
Producer: Harold Becker
Tech Info: 16 mm/sound/bw/12 min.
Date/Country: 1964 + USA   Type: Documentary
Distr/Arch: mgh
Annotation: Blind, since birth, Reverend Gary Davis*, and
   his mastery of the guitar is depicted.

BLINDFOLD
Nar/Cast: Hari Rhodes* + Rock Hudson + Claudia Cardinale
Screenplay: Phillip Dunne + W.H. Menger
Producer: Marvin Schwartz   Director: Philip Dunne
Studio/Company: Universal
Tech Info: 16 mm/sound/color/102 min.
Date/Country: 1966 + USA   Type: Feature
Distr/Arch: ccc + cou + cwf + uni
Annotation: Hari Rhodes is Captain Davis in this mystery
   comedy about government scientists, kidnapping and army
   intelligence.

BLOCK IN HARLEM, A
Producer: WNBC-TV
Tech Info: 16 mm/sound/color/16 min.
Date/Country: 1969 + USA   Type: TV Documentary
Distr/Arch: fi
Annotation: How one block in Harlem attempted a rehabilita-
   tion project. (114th Street between 7th and 8th Ave.)

BLONDE BOMBSHELL, THE
Alt Title(s): see Bombshell

BLONDE VENUS
Nar/Cast: Hattie McDaniel* + Jean Harlow + Lena Horne* +
   Ralph Cooper* + Dickie Moore + Marlene Dietrich + Herbert
   Marshall + Cary Grant + Evelyn Preer* + John Torrence +

Edna Torrence + The Hall Johnson Choir*   Story: S.K.
  Lauren + Jules Furthman
Producer: Adolph Zuckor   Director: Josef von Sternberg
Studio/Company: Paramount Publix Corporation
Tech Info: 16 mm/sound/3 reels/80 min.
Date/Country: 1932 + USA   Type: Feature
Distr/Arch: moma + uni
Annotation: Blonde__Venus tells the tale of a wife (Marlene
  Dietrich) accused of infidelity. Rejected and penniless,
  she is introduced to the lower classes before she becomes
  a star on the Paris stage. One of the final scenes shows
  a production of Looking__Backward with The Hall Johnson
  Choir. Evelyn Preer listed in the credits as Iola.

BLONDIE
Nar/Cast: Willie Best* + Penny Singleton + Arthur Lake
Screenplay: Richard Flournoy   Director: Frank Strayer
Studio/Company: Columbia
Tech Info: 16 mm/sound/bw/75 min.
Date/Country: 1938 + USA   Type: Feature
Distr/Arch: unf + wcf + mac + cwf
Annotation: Willie Best plays a porter in this comedy
  adapted from the Chic Young comic-strip, using the same
  characters.

BLOOD_KIN
Alt Title(s): see Last of the Mobile Hot Shots

BLOOD_OF_JESUS
Nar/Cast: Spencer Williams* + Cathryn Caviness* + Heavenly
  Choir* + Juanita Riley* + James B. Jones* + Frank H. Mc-
  Clennan* + Eddie DeBuse* + Rogenia Goldthwaite* + Reather
  Hardeman* + Alva Fuller*
Screenplay: Spencer Williams*   Director: Spencer Williams*
Studio/Company: Amegro Films Presents + Sack Amusement En-
  terprises
Tech Info: 16 mm/bw/sound/2 reels/68 min.
Date/Country: 1941 + USA   Type: Feature
Distr/Arch: kpf + fce + sta + par
Annotation: A religious folk-drama, the film concerns the
  accidental shooting of William's wife, Martha, and of the
  faith in Jesus that brings her back. As she lies dying,
  her soul goes on a symbolic journey in which it rejects
  Hell for Zion, Satan for God, at the foot of the cross.
  When she awakens, recovered, the choir of sisters and
  brothers from the church come in to sing and celebrate the
  miracle with Martha and Frank.

BLOOD'S_WAY   Director: Stan Taylor
Studio/Company: Stan Taylor
Tech Info: 16 mm/sound/color/18 min.
Date/Country: 1972 + USA
Distr/Arch: af
Annotation: Examines the emotional dependency and   the
  cultural differences operating in the relationship of a
  young couple.

BLOSSOM

Studio/Company: Cathedral
Tech Info: 16 mm/sound/color/1 reel/10 min.
Date/Country: US   Type: Documentary
Distr/Arch: roa
Annotation: Two children play on a summer afternoon, unaware
    that race can be a bar to a relationship. Their innocence
    impresses the viewer with a poignant awareness of personal
    values in today's society.

BLOSSOMS_IN_THE_DUST
Nar/Cast: Greer Garson + Walter Pidgeon + Clinton Rosemond*
    + Teresa Harris*
Screenplay: Anita Loos
Producer: Irving Aster   Director: Mervyn LeRoy
Studio/Company: MGM
Tech Info: sound/color
Date/Country: 1941 + USA   Type: Feature
Annotation: Clinton Rosemond has a brief role as Zeke,
    Teresa Harris as Cleo, in this drama about the founding of
    an orphanage in Texas. Based on the real life story of
    Edna Gladney (played by Garson).

BLUE_DASHIKI,_THE:_JEFFERY_AND_HIS_CITY_NEIGHBORS
Producer: Encyclopedia Britannica Ed. Corp.
Tech Info: 16 mm/sound/color/1 reel/14 min.
Date/Country: 1969   Type: Dramatized Documentary
Distr/Arch: iu + ebec
Annotation: Follows the adventures of a young boy seeking to
    earn encugh money to buy a dashiki he has seen in a local
    African import shop. Depicts this black child's pride in
    himself and in the artifacts associated with his race.

BLUE_GARDENIA,_THE
Nar/Cast: Anne Baxter + Richard Conte + Ann Southern + Nat
    "King" Cole*
Screenplay: Vera Caspary + Charles Hoffman
Producer: Alex Gottlieb   Director: Fritz Lang
Studio/Company: Warner Brothers
Date/Country: 1953 + USA   Type: Feature
Annotation: Richard Conte plays a newspaper reporter working
    to clear Anne Baxter of a murder charge. Nat (King) Cole
    plays and sings the title song.

BLUE_STREAK_SERIES
Series: Blue Streak
Nar/Cast: James Lowe*
Studio/Company: Universal
Annotation: James Lowe plays a black sidekick to a white
    cowboy.

BLUES_ACCORDING_TO_LIGHTNIN'_HOPKINS,_THE
Nar/Cast: Lightnin' Hopkins*
Producer: Les Blank   Director: Les Blank
Studio/Company: Flower Films
Tech Info: 16 mm/color/1 reel/sound/31 min.
Date/Country: 1968 + USA   Type: Documentary
Distr/Arch: flf + gro
Annotation: This film portrait of Lightnin' Hopkins (one of

the greatest blues guitarists alive today) embodies the black fclk tradition.

BLUES BETWEEN THE TEETH
Alt Title(s): see Le Blues Entre Les Dents

BLUES FOR LOVERS
Alt Title(s): Ballad in Blue
Nar/Cast: Ray Charles* and his orchestra and the Raelets + Tom Bell + Piers Bishop + Mary Peach
Screenplay: Burton Wohl   Story: Burton Wohl + Paul Henried
Producer: Herman Blazer   Director: Paul Henried
Studio/Company: 20th Century Fox
Tech Info: 16 mm/sound/bw/3 reels/89 min.
Date/Country: 1966 + Britain   Type: Feature
Distr/Arch: fnc
Annotation: Ray Charles, playing himself, helps a recently blinded British boy and his widowed mother adjust to his new life. Ray Charles and his orchestra perform ten numbers. Released in England in 1965 as Ballad in Blue.

BLUES IN THE NIGHT
Alt Title(s): Hot Nocturne
Nar/Cast: Richard Whorf + Priscilla Lane + Betty Field + Jimmy Lunceford and his band*
Screenplay: Robert Rossen   Director: Anatole Litvak
Studio/Company: Paramount
Tech Info: sound/88 min.
Date/Country: 1941 + USA   Type: Feature
Annotation: Jimmy Lunceford and his band perform in one sequence in this film about bands and musicians.

BLUES LIKE SHOWERS OF RAIN
Producer: John Jeremy + Silverscreen Productions   Director: John Jeremy
Tech Info: 16 mm/sound/color/30 min.
Date/Country: 1970 + Britain   Type: Documentary
Distr/Arch: imp
Annotation: Briefly documents Paul Oliver's journey South in 1960 to the "land of the Blues" with photographs and film recordings of bluesmen like Lightnin' Hopkins*, Speckled Red, Otis Spann.

BLUES MAKER
Producer: Department of Film Production, Univ. of Mississippi
Tech Info: 16 mm/sound/bw/14 min.
Date/Country: 1968 + USA   Type: Documentary
Distr/Arch: dfp
Annotation: Fred McDowell* plays, sings, and discusses Mississippi Country Blues. Provided by Center for Southern Folklore.

BLUES UNDER THE SKIN
Alt Title(s): see Le Blues Entre Les Dents

BLUES, THE
Producer: Samuel Charters   Director: Samuel Charters

Tech Info: 16 mm/sound/color/21 min.
Date/Country: 1963 + USA   Type: Documentary
Distr/Arch: mac
Annotation: Poverty and discrimination in the South are
    traced through the development of the blues.   Music and
    the environs of songs of such blues men as Sleepy John
    Estes*, J. D. Short* and Furry Lewis* are shown.

BOARDING HOUSE BLUES
Nar/Cast: "Moms" Mabley* + Dusty Fletcher* + Lucky Millinder
    and his band + John Mason and Company* + Johnny Lee, Jr.*
    + Marcellus Wilson* + Marie Cooke* + Emery Richardson* +
    Harold Cramer* + Sidney Easton* + Freddie Robinson*
    Director: Josh Binney
Studio/Company: All American News Inc.
Tech Info: 35 mm/sound/bw/1 reel
Date/Country: 1948 + USA   Type: Feature
Distr/Arch: bud
Annotation: An "evil" landlord intends to evict "Moms" and
    her tenants from her boarding house because she can't pay
    the rent. The tenants are all entertainers who have to
    have a producer for their show. It all works out with
    some fortune- telling assistance from Moms. The beautiful
    heroine Lila (Marie Cooke) is saved from having to cavoch
    with the landlord and all the boarders have parts in the
    successful show.

BODY AND SOUL: BODY, PART I
Series: Of Black America
Producer: CBS
Tech Info: 16 mm/sound/bw/30 min.
Date/Country: 1968 + USA   Type: TV Documentary
Distr/Arch: bfa + uca
Annotation: Contributions to sports by Black Americans is
    traced by Harry Reasoner.

BODY AND SOUL: SOUL, PART II
Series: Of Black America
Producer: CBS
Tech Info: 16 mm/sound/bw/30 min.
Date/Country: 1968 + USA   Type: TV Documentary
Distr/Arch: bfa + uca
Annotation: Soul music in America with Mahalia Jackson*,
    Billie Holiday* and Aretha Franklin*. Ray Charles nar-
    rates.

BODY AND SOUL
Nar/Cast: Paul Robeson* + Julia Thersea Russell* + Mercedes
    Gilbert*
Producer: Oscar Micheaux*   Director: Oscar Micheaux*
Studio/Company: Micheaux Film Corporation
Tech Info: 16 mm/bw/silent
Date/Country: 1924 + USA   Type: Feature
Annotation: In his first film Robeson plays a dual role - a
    preacher who preys on the people and the heroine and his
    brother, a good man. Required to give a balance to his
    theme by the New York Censors, Micheaux changed the
    preacher's role so that he is preacher, then detective,

then finally an uplift-bourgeois future husband for the
heroine who awakens from her nightmare experience to a
happy ending.

BODY DISAPPEARS, THE
Nar/Cast: Jeffrey Lynn + Jane Wyman + Edward Everett Horton
   + Willie Best*
Screenplay: Scott Daris + Erna Lazarns   Director: D. Ross
   Lederman
Studio/Company: Warner Brothers
Tech Info: 16 mm/sound/bw/72 min.
Date/Country: 1942 + USA   Type: Feature
Distr/Arch: uas
Annotation: A typical "who-dunnit" comedy with Willie Best
   supplying the comedy.

BOESMAN AND LENA
Nar/Cast: Athol Fugard + Yvonne Bryceland + Sandy Tube*
   Story: Athol Fugard (play)   Director: Ross Devenish
Tech Info: 16 mm/sound/color/102 min.
Date/Country: 1973 + South Africa   Type: Feature
Distr/Arch: nyf
Annotation: Athol Fugard plays Boesman in this adaptation of
   his play about a Cape "colored" couple who have to take to
   the road. Dialogue in English and Afrikaans.

BOF
Alt Title(s): Anatomie d'un Livreur
Nar/Cast: Julian Negulesco + Paul Crauchet + Marie Dubois +
   Marie Helene Breillat + Mamadou Diop*
Screenplay: Claude Faraldo   Director: Claude Faraldo
Studio/Company: Marianne Films + Filmanthrope + Albina
   Productions
Tech Info: 110 min.
Date/Country: 1971 + France   Type: Feature
Distr/Arch: saf
Annotation: In this satirical comedy, a delivery man, his
   father, Germaine his wife, a woman picked up by chance and
   a black streetsweeper decide to leave the city, towards
   noon. Archived only.

BOMBSHELL
Alt Title(s): The Blonde Bombshell
Nar/Cast: Jean Harlow + Louise Beavers* + Lee Tracy + Frank
   Morgan   Story: Caroline Francke + Mack Crane   Director:
   Victor Fleming
Studio/Company: MGM
Tech Info: 16 mm/sound/bw/3 reels/91 min.
Date/Country: 1933 + USA   Type: Feature
Distr/Arch: fnc
Annotation: Jean Harlow plays an extravagant movie star
   living in Hollywood in this farce about life in the movie
   colony. Louise Beavers plays Loretta, Harlow's maid.

BOOGIE WOOGIE BLUES
Nar/Cast: Hadda Brooks*
Studio/Company: All American News, Inc.
Tech Info: 35 mm/sound/1 reel/10 min.

Date/Country: 1948 + USA   Type: Short
Distr/Arch: lc

BOOGIE WOOGIE DREAM
Nar/Cast: Lena Horne*   +   Albert Ammons* + Pete Johnson* +
    Teddy Wilson*
Producer: Jack Goldberg + Dave Goldberg   Director: Hans
    Burger
Studio/Company: Goldberg + Hollywood Productions
Tech Info: 16mm/ sound/ bw/ 13 min.
Date/Country: 1942 + USA   Type: Musical Short
Distr/Arch: emg
Annotation: Short story set in Cafe Society, New York City.
    Includes title song, others.

BOOK OF NUMBERS, THE
Nar/Cast: Raymond St. Jacques*   +   Freda   Payne*   +   Phillip
    Thomas*
Screenplay: Larry Spiegel   Story: Robert Pfarr*
Producer: Raymond St. Jacques*   Director: Raymond St. Jac-
    ques*
Studio/Company: Brut
Tech Info: 16 mm/sound/color/80 min.
Date/Country: 1973 + USA   Type: Feature
Distr/Arch: swa
Annotation: Two black waiters start a numbers racket in the
    thirties in Arkansas which becomes so lucrative the white
    underworld wants to take it over. Music performed by Son-
    ny Terry* and Brownie McGhee*.

BOOKER T. WASHINGTON
Producer: Vignette
Tech Info: 16 mm/sound/color/11 min.
Date/Country: 1966 + USA   Type: Documentary
Distr/Arch: bfa
Annotation: The   early life of Booker T. Washington, edu-
    cator, leader, founder of Tuskegee Institute is narrated
    by eminent historian John Hope Franklin*.

BOOM TOWN, WEST AFRICA
Producer: BBC-TV
Tech Info: 16 mm/sound/bw/1 reel/26 min.
Date/Country: United Kingdom   Type: Documentary
Distr/Arch: iu
Annotation: Depicts the life of the Kamara family of Sierra
    Leone and shows how it has been affected by industrializa-
    tion. Discusses the dissolution of tribal customs and
    formation of young people's organizations which tend to
    replace tribal organization.

BORDERLINE
Nar/Cast: Paul Robeson* + Eslanda Goode Robeson* + Hilda
    Doolittle   Director: Kenneth Macpherson
Studio/Company: Pool Films
Tech Info: bw/silent
Date/Country: 1929 + Switzerland   Type: Feature
Distr/Arch: ipm + geh
Annotation: Robeson's first foreign film, shot in Swit-

zerland by an independent British film company is an experimental study in visual contrasts as well a a comment
on racism.   Robeson plays Pete, a small town cafe worker
whose wife Adah (Eslanda Robeson) returns from an involvement with a white man (Thorne). Thorne and his wife become estranged over the issue and the town blames Pete and
Adah.   Thorne's wife dies accidentally thereby giving the
town another excuse for making Pete the scapegoat for its
hatreds.

BORED OF EDUCATION
Series: Our Gang
Nar/Cast: Our Gang + Billie Thomas*
Producer: Hal Roach   Director: Gordon Douglas
Studio/Company: MGM
Tech Info: super 8 mm/16 mm/bw/sound/1 reel/11 min.
Date/Country: 1936 + USA   Type: Comedy Short
Distr/Arch: bla
Annotation: First in the new 10 minute format. In this
   short Spanky hatches a scheme whereby he and Alfalfa can
   get out of going back to school. Alfalfa develops a
   phoney toothache, but the scheme is foiled when the kindly
   new teacher treats the class to ice cream and forces the
   boys' return. Billie Thomas stars as Buckwheat.

BOROM SARRET
Nar/Cast: Abdoulaye Ly*
Screenplay: Ousmane Sembene*
Producer: Les Films Domrev (Dakar) + Actualite's Francaises
   (Paris)   Director: Ousmane Sembene*
Tech Info: 16 mm/sound/bw/1 reel/20 min./French voice over/
   English subtitles
Date/Country: 1962 + Senegal   Type: Dramatic Short
Distr/Arch: nyf
Annotation: A young black man in Dakar sets out with his
   horse and cart for a day's work. He encounters many dis-
   appointments, especially unpaid fees; in addition to
   having his cart appropriated because he entered the for-
   bidden "exclusive" quarter of Dakar.

BOSKO AND THE PIRATES
Studio/Company: MGM
Tech Info: 8 min.
Date/Country: 1937 + USA   Type: Animated Short
Annotation: In this cartoon a frog colony impersonates Cab
   Calloway, Louis Armstrong and the Mills Brothers.

BOSTON STRANGLER, THE
Nar/Cast: Tony Curtis + Henry Fonda + William Marshall*
Screenplay: Edward Anhalt   Story: Gerold Frank
Producer: Robert Fryer   Director: Richard Fleischer
Studio/Company: 20th Century Fox
Tech Info: 16 mm/sound/color/120 min.
Date/Country: 1968 + USA   Type: Feature
Distr/Arch: fnc
Annotation: The story of Albert DeSalvo (Tony Curtis), the
   supposed Boston Strangler. William Marshall plays Edward
   W. Brooke, Jr., Massachusetts Attorney General who per-

suades Bottomly (Fonda) to set up a special bureau to
facilitate the investigation of the stranglings.

BOUNCING_BABIES
Series: Our Gang
Nar/Cast: Our Gang + Allen Hoskins*
Screenplay: Robert F. McGowan
Producer: Robert F. McGowan + Hal Roach   Director: Robert
   F. McGowan
Studio/Company: MGM + Roach
Tech Info: super 8 mm/16 mm/sound on disc/1 reel/15-20 min.
Date/Country: 1929 + USA   Type: Comedy Short
Distr/Arch: roa + bla
Annotation: Wheezer feels ignored now that he has a new baby
   brother. Farina tells him a tall tale that he once ex-
   changed an unwanted baby brother for a goat. Wheezer
   tries the same, not knowing he is taking a doll instead.
   Everyone is in on it and when Wheezer tries to get brother
   back he's told the baby's been returned to heaven and can
   only come back if Wheezer prays hard for him. Aside from
   the tale Farina is seen with Wheezer being scared by some
   other kids in Halloween costumes. Allen Hoskins stars as
   Farina.

BOUNDARY_LINES
Studio/Company: International   Type: Documentary
Distr/Arch: roa
Annotation: Animated lines, figures, and scenes, illustrate
   how "a line is an idea". Pleas for tolerance and breaking
   down of barriers between people.

BOWERY_TO_BROADWAY
Nar/Cast: Jack Oakie + Maria Montez + Turhan Bey + Ann Blyth
   + Ben Carter* + Mantan Moreland*
Screenplay: Edmund Joseph + Bart Lytton + Arthur Horman
   Story: Edmund Joseph + Bart Lytton   Director: Charles
   Lamont
Studio/Company: Universal
Tech Info: 16 mm/sound/bw/3 reels/94 min.
Date/Country: 1944 + USA   Type: Feature
Distr/Arch: uni
Annotation: When two Irish cabaret owners compete for
   headlining attractions, their mischievious efforts take
   them both to 42nd Street and Broadway. Albam (Mantan
   Moreland) and No-More (Ben Carter) provide touches of
   comic rivalry.

BOXING_GLOVES
Series: Our Gang
Nar/Cast: Our Gang + Allen Hoskins*
Screenplay: Hal Roach + Robert F. McGowan
Producer: Hal Roach   Director: Anthony Mack
Studio/Company: MGM + Roach
Tech Info: super 8 mm/16 mm/bw/sound/part silent/2 reels/20
   min.
Date/Country: 1929 + USA   Type: Comedy Short
Distr/Arch: roa + bla
Annotation: Joe and Chubby, fighting over Jean, are

volunteered to liven up Manny and Farina's boxing arena.
Each has been promised the other will take a dive, but
there's not much of a fight until Farina tells Chubby to
muss Joe's hair which enrages him. Joe punches everyone
in sight, including Farina. Both fighters are knocked
cold; as Farina announces the decision a fan hits him with
a tomato. Allen Hoskins stars as Farina.

BOY IN THE TREE
Alt Title(s): see Pojken i Tradet

BOY OF TWO WORLDS
Nar/Cast: Jimmy Sterman* + Edwin Adolpson + Asbjorn Anderson
  + Ninja Tholstrup + Karl Stegger   Director: Astrid Hen-
  ning-Jensen
Tech Info: 16 mm/color/sound/dubbed/88 min.
Date/Country: 1960 + Denmark
Distr/Arch: bud + ivy + ker + mac + mod + mot + roa + tfc +
  unf + wcf + wel
Annotation: A West Indian child whose father was a sea
  captain is orphaned and goes to live with his father's
  sister in a small village in Denmark. The boy escapes the
  taunting of his classmates and the indifference of the
  adults by running away to the forest. After a reform
  school experience and a Robinson Crusoel-like retreat, he
  eventually agrees to give the human race another chance.

BOY TEN FEET TALL, A
Alt Title(s): Sammy Going South
Nar/Cast: Edward G. Robinson + Fergus McClelland + Constance
  Cummings + Orlando Martins*
Screenplay: Stuart Douglas
Producer: Hal Mason   Director: Alexander MacKendrick
Studio/Company: Paramount
Tech Info: 16 mm/sound/color/3 reels/117 min.
Date/Country: 1965 + Britain   Type: Feature
Distr/Arch: fnc
Annotation: Set in Africa, this film follows the journey of
  a young English boy's trek from Port Said to Durban, South
  Africa. He walks over 5,000 miles to find his aunt after
  his parents are killed during the bombing of Port Said in
  Egypt's struggle for independence. Orlando Martins plays
  Abu Lubaba. Opened in London in 1963 as Sammy Going
  South.

BOY: AN EXPERIENCE IN THE SEARCH FOR IDENTITY
Series: Study in Color
Tech Info: 16 mm/sound/bw/1 reel/12 min.
Distr/Arch: adl
Annotation: Through imaginative role-playing, a young black
  man indulges in a fantasy which reveals his deep sensitivity to name-calling and stereotyped attitudes toward racial minorities. The dialogue exposes the degradation to
  which a prejudiced person subjects other human beings.

BOYHOOD OF GEORGE WASHINGTON CARVER, THE
Producer: Coronet Films
Tech Info: 16 mm/sound/color/1 reel/13 min.

Date/Country: 1973 + USA   Type: Documentary
Distr/Arch: iu + corf
Annotation: Depicts for children the first thirteen years in
    the life of George Washington Carver. Shows how his inten-
    se desire to learn and his quick, inquisitive mind led him
    to pursue such fields as science, art, and agriculture.

BOYS_IN_THE_BAND,_THE
Nar/Cast: Cliff Gorman + Leonard Frey + Lawrence Luckinbill
    + Kenneth Nelson + Reuben Greene*
Screenplay: Mart Crowley
Producer: Mart Crowley   Director: William Friedkin
Studio/Company: Leo Productions, Ltd + Cinema Center
Tech Info: 16 mm/sound/color/120 min.
Date/Country: 1970 + USA   Type: Feature
Distr/Arch: mac + aim + ics + swa + twy
Annotation: Reuben Greene plays Bernard, the only black
    participant in the birthday party for Harold (Leonard
    Frey). Nine actors of the original stage production
    recreate their roles as homosexual celebrants.

BOYS_TO_BOARD
Series: Our Gang
Nar/Cast: Our Gang + Ernie Morrison* + Allen Hoskins*
Screenplay: Hal Roach
Producer: Hal Roach   Director: Tom McNamera
Studio/Company: Pathe
Tech Info: silent/bw/2 reels
Date/Country: 1923 + USA   Type: Comedy Short
Annotation: This film finds the gang at Mother Malone's
    school, which promises good meals, fresh air recreation
    and various other niceties, while in reality, it's run by
    a shrewish lady who doles out skimpy meals. As a result,
    the gang and the good natured husband of the lady escape
    only to run into a bootlegger's trap. They manage to sub-
    due the culprit, return as heroes and live happily ever
    after. Ernie Morrison stars as Sunshine Sammy and Allen
    Hoskins stars as farina.

BOYS_WILL_BE_JOYS
Series: Our Gang
Nar/Cast: Our Gang + Allen Hoskins*
Screenplay: Hal Roach
Producer: Hal Roach   Director: Robert F. McGowan
Studio/Company: Pathe
Tech Info: silent/bw/2 reels
Date/Country: 1925 + USA   Type: Comedy Short
Annotation: The gang members are told that their amusement
    park will be bulldozed to make way for a new factory, so
    they go see the young at heart president of the company to
    enlist his aid in saving their park. Soon, they have con-
    verted not only the president, but the whole board. Allen
    Hoskins stars as Farina.

BOY!_WHAT_A_GIRL!
Nar/Cast: Duke Williams* + Sheila Guyse* + Warren Patterson*
    + Al Jackson* + Sybil Lewis* + Tim Moore* + Milton Wood* +
    Betti Mays*

Producer: Jack Goldberg + Arthur Leonard   Director: Arthur
    Leonard
Studio/Company: Herald Pictures
Tech Info: 16 mm/sound/bw/70 min.
Date/Country: 1946 + USA   Type: Feature
Distr/Arch: emg + lc
Annotation: Slight story about a show and its would-be
    producers provides a reason for the entertainment which
    features Big Sid Caslett* and his band, the Slam Stewart*
    Trio, and The Harlem Maniacs*; introduces Deek Watson* and
    the Brown Dots*; includes Ann Cornell* and the Interna-
    tional Jitterbugs* and a guest appearance by Gene Krupa.

BRAND OF CAIN, THE
Alt Title(s): Lem Hawkins's confession
Nar/Cast: Clarence Brooks* + Alec Lovejoy* + Dorothy Van
    Engle* + Laura Bowman* + Lionel Monagas* + Eunice Wilson*
    + Sandy Burns* + Henrietta Loveless* + Bee Freeman* +
    Alice B. Russell* + Andrew Bishop*
Studio/Company: Oscar Micheaux Corporation
Tech Info: sound/bw
Date/Country: 1935 + USA   Type: Feature
Annotation: A young writer and law student (Brooks) has a
    book he wishes to sell. A case of mistaken identity oc-
    curs and he falls in love with the person he thinks is the
    buyer of his book.   Classically, they are separated be-
    cause of the mistaken identity then reunited over the
    defense of his lady love's brother.

BRAZIL: THE VANISHING NEGRO
Series: History of the Negro People
Producer: NET
Tech Info: 16 mm/sound/bw/1 reel/30 min.
Date/Country: 1965   Type: TV Documentary
Distr/Arch: iu + uca + uco
Annotation: Depicts the interracial experiences of the Negro
    in Brazil and stresses how they differ markedly from the
    experiences of North American Negroes. Visits the port of
    Salavador and pictures traditional Afro-Brazilian
    religious ceremonies. Includes interviews with Negro
    Brazilians.

BREAKFAST IN HOLLYWOOD
Nar/Cast: Nat "King" Cole and the King Cole Trio   Director:
    Jean-Claude Bonnardot
Tech Info: 91 min.
Date/Country: 1946 + USA   Type: Feature
Annotation: A comedy about an American radio program
    features Nat Cole* and his "King" Cole Trio.

BREAKING POINT, THE
Nar/Cast: John Garfield + Juano Hernandez* + Patricia Neal
Screenplay: Ronald MacDougall   Story: Ernest Hemingway
Producer: Jerry Wald   Director: Michael Curtiz
Studio/Company: Warner Brothers
Date/Country: 1950 + USA   Type: Feature
Annotation: In this second film adaptation of Hemingway's To
    Have and to Have Not, John Garfield and Juano Hernandez

play friends and partners in a charter business pushed
into the grey area of the law by various setbacks.

BREEZING HOME
Nar/Cast: Willie Best*
Date/Country: 1937 + USA   Type: Feature

BREWSTER'S MILLIONS
Nar/Cast: Dennis O'Keefe + Helen Walker + Eddie Anderson* +
    June Havoc + Gail Patrick   Story: George Barr   McCutcheon
    (Novel)
Producer: Edward Small   Director: Alan Dwan
Studio/Company: United Artists
Tech Info: 16mm/ sound/ bw/ 79 min.
Date/Country: 1945 + USA
Distr/Arch: mog
Annotation: Story of a young man whose eccentric relative
    leaves him a fortune which he may inherit, with one
    stipulation -- given $500,000 he must be penniless and
    asset-less in 6 months. Eddie Anderson plays Jackson.

BRIAN'S SONG
Alt Title(s): Pic (book)
Nar/Cast: James Caan + Billy Dee Williams* + Jack Warden +
    Shelly Fabares + Judy Pace*
Screenplay: William Blinn   Story: Gale Sayers
Producer: Paul Junger Witt   Director: Buzz Kulik
Studio/Company: Columbia + Screen Gems
Tech Info: 16 mm/sound/color/3 reels/75 min.
Date/Country: 1972 + USA   Type: TV Feature
Distr/Arch: arg + bud + cwf + mmm + mod + mot + tfc + twy +
    unf + wcf + wel + who + roa + swa
Annotation: A touching story is developed around the friend-
    ship that is created between two professional football
    players for the Chicago Bears--Brian Piccolo and Gale Say-
    ers.   Racial differences are transcended when the two men
    become roommates, a first in the Bears' history.   A true
    story, Brian's Song focuses on the mutual respect and af-
    fection the two men develop for each other.

BRIDE OF HATE, THE
Studio/Company: Triangle-Kay Bee
Tech Info: bw/silent
Date/Country: 1916 + USA
Annotation: Southern doctor seeks revenge on a man by en-
    couraging marriage between this enemy and a light-skinned
    slave of his, won in a card game. The revelation of her
    racial origin later drives the enemy to drink and death.

BRIDE WALKS OUT, THE
Nar/Cast: Barbara Stanwyck + Robert Young + Hattie McDaniel*
    + Ned Sparks   Story: Howard E. Rogers
Producer: Edward Small   Director: Leigh Jason
Studio/Company: RKO Radio
Date/Country: 1936 + USA   Type: Feature
Annotation: Light comedy about a young couple trying to live
    on $35.00 a week, especially difficult with the wife's
    expensive taste.   Hattie McDaniel in one of her almost

dozen film appearances in 1936.

BRIGHT ROAD
Alt Title(s): See How They Run
Nar/Cast: Dorothy Dandridge* + Harry Belafonte* + Philip
   Hepburn* + Maidie Norman*
Screenplay: Emmett Lavery   Story: Mary E. Vroman*
Producer: Sol P. Fielding   Director: Gerald Mayer
Studio/Company: MGM
Tech Info: 16 mm/sound/bw/2 reels/69 min.
Date/Country: 1953 + USA   Type: Feature
Distr/Arch: fnc
Annotation: Dorothy Dandridge plays a young teacher trying
   to help a withdrawn, insecure student played by Philip
   Hepburn.

BRIGHT VICTORY   Story: Baynard Kendrick
Producer: Robert Buckner   Director: Mark Robson
Studio/Company: Universal + International
Tech Info: 16 mm/sound/bw/90 min.
Date/Country: 1951 + USA   Type: Feature
Distr/Arch: uni
Annotation: Concerns prejudice in a hospital for the blind
   once the white patients discover a blind black soldier is
   among them.

BRING HOME THE TURKEY
Series: Our Gang
Nar/Cast: Our Gang + Allen Hoskins* + Jannie Hoskins*
Screenplay: Hal Roach
Producer: Hal Roach   Director: Robert F. McGowan
Studio/Company: Pathe
Tech Info: silent/bw/2 reels
Date/Country: 1927 + USA   Type: Comedy Short
Annotation: Unhappy at Happyland Home, an orphanage, the
   gang's only friend is a black man named 'Uncle Tom' - who
   provides for them when they run away. When the gang is
   finally caught and brought to count, the cruelty of the
   orphanage comes to light, new management is brought in and
   Tom is made chef. Uncle Tom is played by Tom Wilson in
   burnt cork. His three 'children' are Farina, Mango and
   Pleurisy. Allen Hoskins stars as Farina and Jannie
   Hoskins stars as Mango.

BROADWAY BILL
Nar/Cast: Clarence Muse* + Warner Baxter + Myrna Loy +
   Walter Connally   Story: Mark Hellinger   Director: Frank
   Capra
Studio/Company: Columbia
Date/Country: 1934 + USA   Type: Feature
Annotation: Horse race comedy that stars Warner Baxter and
   Clarence Muse, about a couple of down and outers who place
   all their hopes on a nag of a horse.

BROADWAY RHYTHM
Nar/Cast: George Murphy + Ginny Simms + Lena Horne* + Nancy
   Walker + Hazel Scott* + Eddie Anderson*   Story: Jerome
   Kern + Oscar Hammerstein, II

Producer: Jack Cummings   Director: Roy Del Ruth
Studio/Company: MGM
Date/Country: 1944 + USA   Type: Feature
Annotation: An MGM musical loosely based on a Jerome Kern,
    Oscar Hammerstein musical, featuring Lena Horne, Hazel
    Scott, and Eddie Anderson in cameo roles.

BROKEN CHAINS
Nar/Cast: Malcom McGregor + Colleen Moore + Ernest Torrence
    + Claire Widsor + James Marcus + Beryl Mercer + William
    Orlamond + Gerald Prinz
Screenplay: Winifred Kimball   Director: Allen Holubar
Tech Info: 35 mm/silent/bw/7 reels
Date/Country: 1922 + USA   Type: Feature
Annotation: A woman's jewels are stolen and a young man
    believes himself a coward because he was unable to help
    her.   He later beats the man who stole the jewels and
    frees the thief's daughter from the chains by which she
    has been kept.   Blacks are portrayed in The Birth of a
    Nation tradition.

BROKEN EARTH
Nar/Cast: Clarence Muse* + Frieda Shaw Choir*
Date/Country: 194- + USA

BROKEN STRINGS
Nar/Cast: Clarence Muse* + Sybil Lewis* + William Washing-
    ton* + Matthew Beard* + Pete Webster* + Tommivetta Moore*
    + Edward Thompson* + Buck Woods* + Darby Jones* + Jess Lee
    Brooks* + Earl Morris* + Stevens Sisters* + Elliott Car-
    penter*
Screenplay: Berard B. Ray + Clarence Muse* + David Arlen
Producer: L.C. Borden Productions + International Roadshow
    Release   Director: Bernard B. Ray
Studio/Company: International Roadshows + Goldberg Brothers
Tech Info: 16 mm/bw/sound/80 min./35 mm/sound/bw/6 reels/ 72
    min.
Date/Country: 1940 + USA   Type: Feature
Distr/Arch: sta + lc + wma
Annotation: Muse stars as a concert violinist (Arthur Willi-
    ams) who, after an automobile accident and an injury to
    his hands, is reduced to teaching barely talented pupils
    and those who are only interested in jazz and swing.   A
    black doctor, played by Jess Lee Brooks, restores the use
    of his hands through an operation paid for by performances
    by his son and his pupils. The operation is a complete
    success only when he begins to applaud his son's virtuoso
    swing   performance.   Matthew (Stymie) Beard plays a
    teenaged villain.

BROKEN VIOLIN, THE
Nar/Cast: Gertrude Snelson* + J. Homer Tutt* + Daisy Foster*
    + "Boots" Hope* + Ardelle Dabney* + W. Hill* + Ethel
    Smith* + Alce B. Russell* + Ike Paul*
Screenplay: Oscar Micheaux*
Date/Country: 1926 + USA   Type: Feature
Annotation: Based on Micheaux's book House of Mystery, The
    Broken Violin is the story of a talented young woman, the

daughter of an alcoholic father and a poor, hardworking mother. Her musical career is almost aborted when her father in a drunken rage breaks her violin.

BRONZE BUCKEROO
Nar/Cast: Herbert Jeffrey* + Lucius Brooks* + Artie Young* + Flournoy E. Miller* + Clarence Brooks* + Earl J. Morris*
Producer: Jed Buell   Director: R.C. Kahn
Studio/Company: Hollywood Productions
Date/Country: 1938 + USA   Type: Feature
Annotation: Herb Jeffrey is the good guy (Bob Blake) who, with his side kick Dusty (Flournoy Miller), tracks down the villain and aids the heroine in this musical western. Filmed at a black dude ranch in California.

BRONZE CASTING: VINCENT KOFI
Producer: Leo Steiner
Tech Info: 16 mm/sound/bw/18 min.
Date/Country: Ghana   Type: Documentary
Distr/Arch: pic
Annotation: Ghanaian sculptor Kofi* works in clay modeling a figure eventually cast in bronze.

BRONZE VENUS
Alt Title(s): see The Duke Is Tops

BROTHER JOHN
Nar/Cast: Sidney Poitier* + Will Geer + Bradford Dillman + Beverly Todd* + Ramon Bieri + Warren J. Kemmerling + Lincoln Kilpatrick* + P. Jay Sidney* + Richard Ward* + Lynn Hamilton*
Screenplay: Ernest Kinoy
Producer: Joel Glickman   Director: James Goldstone
Studio/Company: Columbia
Tech Info: 16 mm/color/sound/3 reels/94 min.
Date/Country: 1971 + USA   Type: Feature
Distr/Arch: mac + unf + roa + arg + cin + cwf + mod + mot + sel + tfc + wcf + wel + wil + ics + ker
Annotation: John Kane (Poitier) mysteriously arrives in the small Alabama town of his birth just prior to the death of his aunt. The object of suspicion and fear, John, with a grammar school education, speaks a dozen languages and seems to be able to anticipate the future. A black labor strike during the height of the Civil Rights movement portends mass violence and Kane is suspected of engineering the crisis. Music by Quincy Jones*.

BROTHER RAT
Nar/Cast: Pricilla Love + Wayne Morris + Johnnie Davis + Ronald Reagan + Eddie Albert + Jane Wyman + Louise Beavers*
Screenplay: Richard Maculay + Jerry Wald   Story: John Monks + Earl F. Finklehoff
Producer: John Monks + Earl F. Finklehoff   Director: William Keighley
Date/Country: 1938 + USA   Type: Feature
Annotation: The escapades of cadets at a military institute in Virginia. Louise Beavers plays Jenny.

BROTHER
Producer: U.S. Federal Aviation Administration
Tech Info: 16 mm/sound/color/14 min.
Date/Country: 1970 + USA   Type: Documentary
Distr/Arch: nac
Annotation: Covers problems of minorities in getting jobs in
    the field of aviation and how two black men succeeded.

BROTHER
Producer: Bill Foster*
Studio/Company: Foster Photoplay Company
Date/Country: 191- + USA

BROTHERHOOD OF MAN, THE   Story: Ruth Benedict
Producer: United Productions of America + UAW
Tech Info: 16 mm/sound/color/11 min.
Date/Country: 1946 + USA   Type: Animated Short
Distr/Arch: iu + mghf
Annotation: Uses an animated cartoon to prove that dif-
    ferences between the human races are superficial, ac-
    cidental, and environmental. Points out that though there
    are four distinct types of blood, all are found in all
    races, and therefore its difference has no more racial
    relevance than does differing skin color to intellectual
    ability. At the end, all racial groups march forward
    together.

BROTHERS AND SISTERS IN CONCERT
Alt Title(s): Save the Children
Nar/Cast: Curtis Mayfield* + Isaac Hayes* + Roberta Flack* +
    Jackson Five* + Marvin Gaye* + Gladys Knight* and the
    Pips* + The Chi-Lites* + The Temptations* + Staple
    Singers* + Cannonball Adderly* + Jerry Butler* + Sammy
    Davis, Jr.* + Brenda Lee Eager* + Rev. James Cleveland* +
    Nancy Wilson* + Zulema*
Producer: Matt Robinson*   Director: Stan Lathan*
Studio/Company: Paramount
Tech Info: 16 mm/sound/color/90 min.
Date/Country: 1973 + USA   Type: Feature
Distr/Arch: fnc
Annotation: Made originally as a documentary film based on
    the 1972 PUSH Expo theme. The 122 minute version goes
    into depth on the theme of black self-determination; con-
    tains footage of Rev. Jesse Jackson and Black Expo.
    Shorter version places emphasis on the various artists'
    performances.

BROTHERS
Nar/Cast: Bernie Casey* + Vonetta McGee* + Ron O'Neal
Screenplay: Edward Lewis + Mildred Lewis
Producer: Arthur Barron
Studio/Company: Warner Brothers
Tech Info: 16 mm/sound/color/104 min.
Date/Country: 1977 + USA   Type: Feature
Distr/Arch: swa
Annotation: Vonetta McGee plays Angela Davis and Bernie
    Casey plays George Jackson in this fictional rendering of

these two highly controversial political figures. Music
composed and arranged by Taj Mahal*.

BROWN BOMBER, THE
Producer: Harry M. Popkin
Studio/Company: Million Dollar Pictures + Sack Amusement

BROWN GRAVY
Series: Christie Comedy
Nar/Cast: Evelyn Preer* + Spencer Williams* + Edward Thomp-
    son*
Screenplay: Octavus Roy Cohen + Spencer Williams
Producer: Al Christie
Studio/Company: Paramount
Tech Info: 35 mm/bw/sound/2 reels
Date/Country: 1929 + USA   Type: Comedy Short
Annotation: Dialect gags, black religious and fraternal life
    and black music abound in this Christie comedy which also
    has a singing contest between a black chorus is Memphis.

BRUTE, THE
Nar/Cast: Sam Langford* + Evelyn Preer* + Lawrence Chenault*
    + A.B. Comathiere* + Susie Sutton*
Studio/Company: Micheaux Film Corporation
Date/Country: 1920 + USA   Type: Feature
Annotation: Sam Langford, the boxer, battles against
    lynching in the South in this Micheaux melodrama which was
    shut down by Southern police. Evelyn Preer is the beauti-
    ful girl who falls into the clutches of an underworld
    brute.

BUBBLING OVER
Nar/Cast: Ethel Waters* + Frank Wilson*   Director: Leigh
    Jason
Studio/Company: RKO Radio + Van Beuren Corp.
Tech Info: 16 mm/bw/sound/2 reels/20 min.
Date/Country: 1934 + USA   Type: Comedy Short
Distr/Arch: kpf + emg
Annotation: The comings and goings in a Harlem tenement are
    featured in this comedy with music. Ethel Waters attempts
    to get rid of her lazy husband's out-of-work relatives.
    She sings "Darkies Never Dream." Frank Wilson plays the
    mind reader, Swami River.

BUBBLING TROUBLES
Series: Our Gang
Nar/Cast: Our Gang + Billie Thomas*
Screenplay: Hal Law + Robert A. McGowan
Producer: Jack Chertok + Richard Goldstone   Director:
    Edward Cahn
Studio/Company: MGM
Tech Info: bw/sound/1 reel
Date/Country: 1940 + USA   Type: Comedy Short
Annotation: Alfalfa's stomach is twice puffed up by overac-
    tive bicarbonate of soda - the first time his friends
    think he's taken explosive and, by a mix-up believe he's
    exploded. The second time Alfalfa's inflated stomach
    causes an enormous belch that blows the front of his house

down.   Billie Thomas stars as Buckwheat.

BUCCANEERS, THE
Series: Our Gang
Nar/Cast: Our Gang + Ernie Morrison* + Allen Hoskins*
Screenplay: Hal Roach
Producer: Hal Roach   Director: Robert McGowan
Studio/Company: Pathe
Tech Info: silent/bw/2 reels
Date/Country: 1924 + USA   Type: Comedy Short
Annotation: When their would - be pirate ship sinks after
    being christened with a bottle of ketchup, the gang stows
    away on an old scow which drifts out to sea, and has to be
    rescued by the Navy.   Ernie Morrison stars as Sunshine
    Sammy and Allen Hoskins stars as Farina.

BUCK AND THE PREACHER
Nar/Cast: Sidney Poitier* + Harry Belafonte* + Ruby Dee* +
    Cameron Mitchell + James McEachin* + Clarence Muse* + En-
    rique Lucero + Lynn Hamilton*
Screenplay: Ernest Kinoy   Story: Ernest Kinoy + Drake
    Walker
Producer: Joel Glickman   Director: Sidney Poitier*
Studio/Company: E   R (Poitier)-Belafonte Enterprises
    Productions + Columbia Pictures
Tech Info: 16 mm/color/sound/3 reels/102 min.
Date/Country: 1972 + USA   Type: Feature
Distr/Arch: swa + roa + arg + buc + bud + cwf + ics + mac +
    mod + mot + twy + wcf + wel
Annotation: The myth of the West is revised and presented
    from the black and Indian point of view. With the help of
    the Indians, Poitier and Belafonte take a group of Blacks
    to resettle in Mexico.   Music score by Benny Carter*,
    featuring Sonny Terry* and Brownie McGhee*.

BUCK BENNY RIDES AGAIN
Nar/Cast: Eddie Anderson* + Ellen Drew + Jack Benny + Phil
    Harris + Virginia Dale   Story: Mark Sandrich
Producer: Mark Sandrich   Director: Mark Sandrich
Studio/Company: Paramount
Tech Info: 16 mm/sound/bw/86 min.
Date/Country: 1940 + USA   Type: Feature
Distr/Arch: uni
Annotation: The various stars of Benny's hit radio program
    star in this western, including Anderson as "Rochester."

BUCK DANCER
Nar/Cast: Georgia Sea Island Singers* + Ed Young*
Producer: Edmund Carpenter + Bess Lomax Harnes + Alan Lomax
Tech Info: 16 mm/sound/bw/1 reel/6 min.
Date/Country: 1974 + USA   Type: Documentary
Distr/Arch: rad
Annotation: Ed Young is a northern Mississippi fife player
    whose music was popular at country picnics in Mississippi
    until a few decades ago; his "buck dance" was a tradi-
    tional dance of male country Blacks. He is accompanied by
    the Georgia Sea Island Singers. (Filmed in 1966).

BUCKET OF CREAM ALE, A
Studio/Company: Biograph
Date/Country: 1904 + USA   Type: Comedy Short
Annotation: In a moment of victory, a black servant pours a
    bucket of ale over a Dutchman, who threw a glass of ale at
    her first.

BUCKTOWN
Nar/Cast: Fred Williamson* + Pam Grier* + Thalmus Rasulala
    Director: Arthur Marks
Studio/Company: American International
Tech Info: 16 mm/sound/color/94 min.
Date/Country: 1975 + USA   Type: Feature
Distr/Arch: swa
Annotation: Williamson and his friends struggle against a
    corrupt and exploitative police force in a southern city.

BULL DOGGERS, THE
Nar/Cast: Bill Pickett* + Anita Bush* + Steve Reynolds*
Studio/Company: Normal Film Manufacturing Company
Date/Country: 1923 + USA   Type: Feature
Annotation: Bill Pickett demonstrates his great skill at
    "bull dogging" and other cowboy feats; includes trick
    riding by black cowboys and cowgirls.

BULL'S EYE
Nar/Cast: Noble Johnson*
Studio/Company: Universal
Date/Country: USA   Type: Feature
Annotation: A universal B movie with a brief role for Noble
    Johnson.

BULLETS OR BALLOTS
Nar/Cast: Edward G. Robinson + Joan Blondell + Humphrey
    Bogart + Louise Beavers*
Screenplay: Seton Miller
Producer: First National   Director: William Keighley
Studio/Company: Warner Brothers
Tech Info: 16 mm/sound/bw/81 min.
Date/Country: 1936 + USA   Type: Feature
Distr/Arch: uas
Annotation: Louise Beavers as "Madame Nellie La Fleur" i.e.
    Nellie Silvers, plays the founder and head of the Harlem
    numbers game in this film which has Edward G. Robinson
    portraying an undercover cop out to bust the rackets.

BULLITT
Nar/Cast: Georg Stanford Brown* + Steve McQueen + Jacqueline
    Bisset + Robert Vaughn
Screenplay: Alan R. Trustman + Harry Kleiner
Producer: Philip D'Antoni + Solar Productions   Director:
    Peter Yates
Studio/Company: Warners + Seven Arts
Tech Info: 16 mm/sound/color/113 min.
Date/Country: 1968 + USA   Type: Feature
Distr/Arch: arg + bud + ccc + cwf + ics + mac + mot + roa +
    sel + swa + tfc + twy + unf + wcf + wel + who + wil
Annotation: Taut detective tale with Blacks in believable

roles. One is a surgeon in a San Francisco hospital, Dr.
Willard (Brown) who helps Bullitt (McQueen) when the man
he is guarding against Mafia thugs is murdered in the
hospital. Veiled comments about Willard by an ambitious
politician (Vaughn) have racist implications.

BUNDLE OF BLUES, A
Nar/Cast: Duke Ellington* and his orchestra + Ivy Anderson*
Studio/Company: Paramount
Tech Info: 16 mm/bw/sound/1 reel/10 min.
Date/Country: 1933 + USA   Type: Musical Short
Distr/Arch: emg + kpf
Annotation: Among other numbers, Ivy Anderson sings an
   elaborately staged version of "Stormy Weather" in this
   musical short.

BURDEN OF RACE, THE
Nar/Cast: Edna Morton* + Lawrence Chenault* + Elizabeth Williams* + Percy Verwagen* + Mabel Young* + Arthur Ray*
Date/Country: 1921 + USA   Type: Feature
Annotation: A young black man achieves academically and ath-
   letically; then he is faced with the emotional challenge
   of falling in love with a girl "not of his race."

BURIED TREASURE
Series: Our Gang
Nar/Cast: Our Gang + Allen Hoskins*
Screenplay: Hal Roach
Producer: Hal Roach   Director: Robert McGowan
Studio/Company: Pathe
Tech Info: silent/bw/2 reels
Date/Country: 1926 + USA   Type: Comedy Short
Annotation: The gang sets out in search of Captain Kidd's
   treasure - they set out to sea in a makeshift yacht and
   land on an island where a movie crew is Filming - the crew
   throws a scare into the kids but the gang has the last
   laugh. Allen Hoskins stars as Farina.

BURNING CROSS, THE
Nar/Cast: Hank Daniels + Virginia Patton + Joel Fluellen* +
   Maidie Norman*
Screenplay: Aubrey Wisberg
Producer: Walter Colmes   Director: Walter Colmes
Studio/Company: Somerset-Screen Guild
Tech Info: 16 mm/sound/bw/79 min.
Date/Country: 1947 + USA   Type: Feature
Distr/Arch: ivy
Annotation: Joel Fluellen has a leading role as an ex-
   serviceman who is murdered by the Ku Klux Klan in this
   film which attempts to expose the bigotry and brutality of
   the Klan and its efforts to keep Blacks from exercising
   their right to vote.

BURN!
Alt Title(s): Quemada + Queimada
Nar/Cast: Marlon Brando + Evaristo Marquez* + Renato
   Salvatori + Wanani
Screenplay: Franco Solinas + Giorgio Arlorio   Story: Gillo

Pontecorvo + Franco Solinas + Arlorio Giorgio
Producer: Alberto Grimaldi   Director: Gillo Pontecorvo
Studio/Company: P.E.A. + United Artists
Tech Info: 16 mm/sound/color/3 reels/112 min.
Date/Country: 1970 + France + Italy   Type: Feature
Distr/Arch: uas
Annotation: Pontecorvo looks at the problems of neo-coloni-
   alism on the black island of Queimada, a "Portugese" sugar
   colony in the Caribbean. Brando is the English villain
   and Marquez the leader of the Black revolution. Opened in
   Rome, 1969, as Quemada in Paris, 1971, as Queimada.

BUS IS COMING, THE
Nar/Cast: Mike Simms + Burl Bullock + Stephanie Faulkner* +
   Morgan Jones* + Bob Brubaher
Screenplay: Horace Jackson*
Producer: Horace Jackson*   Director: Wendell James Frank-
   lin*
Studio/Company: William Thompson International + K-Calb
   Productions
Date/Country: 1971 + USA   Type: Feature
Annotation: Black Vietnam veteran investigates his brother's
   murder by a racist policeman amid black/white crossfire.
   Selected to be shown at the 1971 San Francisco Film
   Festival, it wa the first film made by the Compton, Cali-
   fornia production company, K-Calb, spelled backwards:
   black.

BUS, THE
Producer: Haskell Wexler
Studio/Company: Harrison
Tech Info: 16 mm/bwsound/62 min.
Date/Country: 1965 + USA   Type: Documentary
Distr/Arch: mac
Annotation: In August of 1963 groups from all over the U.S.
   journeyed to Washington, D.C. for a massive civil rights
   demonstration.   Haskell Wexler (director of Medium Cool)
   joined the San Francisco delegation and produced this
   candid document of their trip.

BUSH MAMA
Screenplay: Haile Gerima*
Tech Info: 16 mm/bw/sound/90 min.
Date/Country: 1976 + USA   Type: Documentary
Distr/Arch: tri
Annotation: Bush Mama is a portrait of the changing con-
   sciousness of a black woman living on welfare in a Los
   Angeles ghetto, trying to raise her young daughter alone.

BUSHBABY, THE
Nar/Cast: Margaret Brooks + Louis Gossett* + Johan Mkopi* +
   Kisesa Mayega* + Tommy Ansah* + Jumoke Dehayo*
Screenplay: Robert Maxwell
Producer: Robert Maxwell + John Trent   Director: John Trent
Studio/Company: Velvet Film Productions + MGM
Tech Info: 16 mm/sound/color/100 min.
Date/Country: 1970 + Britain   Type: Feature
Distr/Arch: fnc

Annotation: Tembo (Gossett) tries to help Jackie (Brooks),
the daughter of his former employer, an East African game
warden. Complications arise when it is assumed he is her
abductor, but all comes right in the end. The Tanzanian
filming of exterior scenes with cooperation of Tanzanian
government.

BUSHMAN OF THE KALAHARI: ABC'S DOCUMENTARY ON AFRICA
Nar/Cast: Gregory Peck
Producer: ABC
Studio/Company: ABC + National Geographic
Tech Info: 16 mm/sound/color
Date/Country: 1974   Type: Documentary
Distr/Arch: aim + nge + con
Annotation: This film discusses the way of life of the
Kalahari Bushmen--how they get their food, educate their
children, limit the size of their families, and cooperate
with each other. Gregory Peck narrates.

BUSHMAN, THE   Director: C. Ernest Cadle
Tech Info: 35 mm/silent/bw
Date/Country: 1927 + Africa   Type: Documentary
Annotation: The lifestyle of African bushmen is shown
through their hunting and dancing and the photographing of
African coastal towns and African animal herds.

BUSHMEN OF THE KALAHARI
Producer: ABC
Tech Info: 16 mm/sound/color/1 reel/12 min.
Date/Country: 1967 + USA   Type: Documentary
Distr/Arch: iu + ueva
Annotation: Presents an overview of the life of the Kalahri
Bushmen. Shows various activities of daily life.
Describes tribal customs, including attitudes toward sex
and family rearing.

BUSTED ROMANCE, A
Nar/Cast: Ebony Players*
Studio/Company: Ebony Film Corporation
Date/Country: 1918 + USA

BUSTING THE SHOW   Director: Dave Fleischer
Tech Info: bw/silent
Date/Country: 1920 + USA   Type: Comedy Short
Annotation: An Our Gang comedy type, this film included a
blackface comedian who entertained in the kids' show with
the descriptive title, "The Grate Nigger Bucking Wing
Dancer."

BUSY BODY, THE
Nar/Cast: Richard Pryor* + Sid Caesar + Robert Ryan + Anne
Baxter + Godfrey Cambridge*
Screenplay: Ben Starr   Story: Donald Westlake
Producer: William Castle   Director: William Castle
Studio/Company: Paramount + 16 + 16 mm/sou + /color/101 min.
+ 17 + 1967 + USA   Type: Feature
Distr/Arch: fnc
Annotation: Comedy farce with Sid Caesar as a mama's boy

accused of murder by a bumbling gangster syndicate. Richard Pryor is Whittaker, Godfrey Cambridge is Mike.

BUTLER, THE
Producer: Bill Foster*
Studio/Company: Foster Photoplay Company
Date/Country: 191- + USA
Annotation: A kidnap and detective melodrama.

BWANA DEVIL
Nar/Cast: Robert Stack + Barbara Britton + Kalu K Sankur* + Miles Clark, Jr.*
Screenplay: Arch Oboler
Producer: Arch Oboler   Director: Arch Oboler
Studio/Company: United Artists
Date/Country: 1953 + USA   Type: Feature
Annotation: First feature length 3 dimensional movie made, it has to do with two man eating lions who terrorize the making of a railroad in Africa.

BWANA TOSHI
Studio/Company: Susumu Hani
Tech Info: 16 mm/sound/color/115 min./Japanese with English subtitles
Date/Country: 1965 + Kenya + Tanzania   Type: Documentary
Distr/Arch: mab
Annotation: Humorous documentary of a Japanese settler in an East African village.

BY HOOK OR BY CROOK
Alt Title(s): see I Dood It

BY RIGHT OF BIRTH
Nar/Cast: Clarence Brooks* + Anita Thompson* + Webb King*
Screenplay: George P. Johnson*
Studio/Company: Lincoln Motion Picture Co.
Tech Info: 16 mm/bw/silent/1 reel
Date/Country: 1921 + USA   Type: Dramatic Short
Annotation: In a very complicated plot a young woman of black and Indian ancestry eventually finds her real mother and grandmother and comes into possession of property which is her "by right of birth", partly through the assistance of a young black lawyer who dispenses with the villain. The happy ending includes a family reunion.

BY STORK DELIVERY   Director: Mack Swain
Date/Country: 1916 + USA   Type: Comedy Short
Annotation: Mixed-baby situation with black parents (whites in blackface) hunting down the kidnappers of their child.

BYE BYE BRAVERMAN
Nar/Cast: George Segal + Jack Warden + Jessica Walter + Phyllis Newman + Godfrey Cambridge*
Screenplay: Herbert Sargent
Producer: Sidney Lumet   Director: Sidney Lumet
Studio/Company: Warner Brothers + Seven Arts
Tech Info: 16 mm/color/sound/3 reels/94 min.
Date/Country: 1968 + USA   Type: Feature

Distr/Arch: mac + arg + bud + cin + mod + mot + roa + sel +
  swa + tfc + twy + unf + wel + wil
Annotation: This is an off-beat comedy about the death of a
  promising author, and the way in which it affects his
  friends and relatives. When the author's four best
  friends get together to drive out to the funeral,
  everything goes wrong. Godfrey Cambridge is the taxicab
  driver.

C-H-I-C-K-E-N SPELLS CHICKEN
Studio/Company: Essany
Date/Country: 1910 + USA   Type: Comedy Short
Annotation: Shows chicken-snatching as a common plot device
  in comedies with Rastus types played by whites in black-
  face.

CAB CALLOWAY'S HI-DE-HO ≤1/≤2
Nar/Cast: Cab Calloway's* Orchestra   Story: Milton Hocky
Producer: E.M. Glucksman   Director: Fred Waller
Studio/Company: Paramount
Tech Info: 16 mm/bw/sound/1 reel/10 min.
Date/Country: 1934 + USA   Type: Musical Short
Distr/Arch: emg + kpf + unf
Annotation: Between swing numbers, Cab finds time to flirt
  with the wife of a Pullman porter, while her husband is
  away at work. Orchestra plays "Rail Rhythm" and "The Lady
  With the Fan." These are two short Calloway films, one
  made in 1934, the other in 1937.

CAB CALLOWAY'S JITTERBUG PARTY
Nar/Cast: Cab Calloway*   Director: Fred Waller
Tech Info: 16 mm/sound/bw/1 reel/10 min.
Date/Country: 1931 + USA   Type: Musical Short
Distr/Arch: emg + kpf
Annotation: More of Cab's special brand of musical zaniness
  in a Harlem nightclub.

CABIN IN THE COTTON, THE
Nar/Cast: Richard Barthelmess + Bette Davis + Clarence Muse*
  + Fred "Snowflake" Toomes*
Screenplay: Paul Green   Story: Henry Kroll   Director:
  Michael Curtiz
Studio/Company: Warners + First National Picture
Tech Info: 16 mm/sound/bw/79 min.
Date/Country: 1932 + USA   Type: Feature
Distr/Arch: uas
Annotation: The plight of southern sharecroppers is the sub-
  ject of this tale adapted for the screen. Clarence Muse
  portrays a blind man reduced to begging. (He was also an
  advisor on the set during the filming.)

CABIN IN THE SKY
Nar/Cast: Lena Horne* + Eddie Anderson* + Ethel Waters* +
  Rex Ingram* + Kenneth Spencer* + Ernest Whitman* + Mantan
  Moreland* + Louis Armstrong* + Oscar Polk* + Buck and Bub-
  bles* (Ford Lee and John Sublett) + Willie Best* + Hall
  Johnson Choir* + Butterfly McQueen* + Ruby Dandridge* +
  Duke Ellington*

Screenplay: Joseph Schrank
Producer: Arthur Freed   Director: Vincente Minnelli
Studio/Company: MGM
Tech Info: 16 mm/sound/sepia tone (bw)/3 reels/100 min.
Date/Country: 1943 + USA   Type: Feature
Distr/Arch: fnc + eas
Annotation: A musical fantasy is the frame for the story of
    Little Joe (Anderson) and his wife Petunia (Waters). Lit-
    tle Joe is a "backslider" and a sweepstakes ticket and
    Georgia Brown (Horne) put his soul in jeopardy. In heaven
    a battle for it goes on between Lucifer, Jr. and a General
    of the Lord. Ethel Waters sings the hit, "Happiness is
    Just a Thing Called Joe,"

CABIRIA
Nar/Cast: Ernesto Pagani + Antonio Branioni
Screenplay: Gabriele D'Annunzio
Producer: Italia Film Company   Director: Giovanni Pastrone
Date/Country: 1914 + Italy   Type: Feature
Annotation: Italian extravaganza about the overthrow of
    Carthage by the Romans during the 2nd Century A.D.   In-
    cludes a Carthaginian hero named Maciste who's "black" as
    Hannibal is "black."

CAIN
Nar/Cast: Thomy Bourdelle + Rama-Take*
Screenplay: Leon Poirier
Producer: Leon Poirier   Director: Leon Poirier
Tech Info: English dialogue
Date/Country: 1932 + France   Type: Feature
Annotation: This modern version of Robinson Crusoe sub-
    stitutes a native maiden, Zouzour (played by Rama-Take)
    for the traditional Friday. Washed up on an island, Cain
    (Bourdelle) fights a group of black islanders for posses-
    sion of Zouzour. After years of apparent bliss with his
    black spouse, Cain is offered rescue by a ship on its way
    back to France, but he demurs, returning to his island
    paradise, off the coast of Madagascar.

CAIRO
Nar/Cast: Robert Young + Jeanette MacDonald + Ethel Waters*
    + Dooley Wilson*
Screenplay: John McClain   Director: W.S. Van Dkyke, III
Studio/Company: MGM
Tech Info: 16 mm/sound/bw/101 min.
Date/Country: 1942 + USA   Type: Feature
Distr/Arch: fnc
Annotation: Jeanette MacDonald plays an American movie queen
    in Cairo suspected by newsman Robert Young of being a Nazi
    spy. Ethel Waters and Dooley Wilson colaborate on "When
    the love you love won't love you anymore."

CALDONIA
Nar/Cast: Louis Jordan* + Nicki O'Daniel* + Roxie Joynes* +
    Richard Huey* + Sam Sporty-O-Dee* + Taylor and Harris* +
    George Wirtshire* + Milton Woods* + Three Suntan Girls*
Producer: Louis Jordan*
Studio/Company: Astor Pictures

Tech Info: 16 mm/sound/bw/18 min.
Date/Country: 1945 + USA   Type: Musical Short
Annotation: Musical comedy short devolving on the conflict
   between Jordan who wants to go to Hollywood with his band
   to make a movie and Caldonia, his sweetheart, who wants to
   keep him in New York so they can be together.

CALHOUN SCHOOL, THE! THE WAY TO A BETTER FUTURE
Series: National Archives Gift Collection
Tech Info: 16 mm/silent/1 reel/bw
Annotation: Training given at this small school in Alabama,
   in agricultural methods, health and skills with the hands.
   (Part of Record Group 200 HF series, Harmon Foundation
   Collection).

CALIFORNIA STRAIGHT AHEAD
Nar/Cast: Tom Wilson + Reginald Denny + Gertrude Olmsted
   Story: Harry Pollard + Byron Morgan   Director: Harry Pol-
   lard
Tech Info: 35 mm/bw/silent
Date/Country: 1926 + USA   Type: Feature
Annotation: Tom Wilson (in blackface) plays Sambo, a valet
   who helps his playboy white boss on his journey to prove
   himself.   Sambo handles everything--including helping his
   boss get the girl.

CALL ME BWANA
Nar/Cast: Bob Hope + Anita Ekberg + Orlando Martins* + Bai
   Johnson* + Mark Heath*
Screenplay: Nate Monaster + Johanna Harwood
Producer: Albert R. Broccoli   Director: Gordon Douglas
Studio/Company: United Artists
Tech Info: 16 mm/sound/color/4 reels/103 min.
Date/Country: 1963 + USA   Type: Feature
Distr/Arch: uas
Annotation: Bob Hope plays a fake African authority, who is
   drafted by the President to retrieve a strategic nose cone
   that has crashed in Africa. Also after the nose cone are
   the Russians, headed by Anita Ekberg. The Africans serve
   as background.

CALL OF DUTY, THE
Nar/Cast: Walter Huston
Studio/Company: Alexander Productions
Date/Country: 1946 + USA   Type: Documentary
Annotation: Experience of Blacks in the Navy. Walter Huston
   narrates.

CALL OF HIS PEOPLE, THE
Nar/Cast: George Brown* + Edna Morton* + Mae Kemp* + James
   Steven* + Lawrence Chenault* + Mercedes Gilbert* + Percy
   Verwayen*   Story: Aubrey Browser
Studio/Company: Reol Motion Picture Corp.
Tech Info: 35 mm/silent/bw/6 reels
Date/Country: 1922 + USA   Type: Feature
Annotation: Filmed at the Irvington-on-the-Hudson, N.Y.
   estate of black millionairess A. Lelia Walker, The Call of
   His People is a story of "passing;" the theme of "it is

the man, not the color, that counts" is emphasized by the
character Weathering.

CALLALOO
Nar/Cast: Ursula Johnson*   Director: Irene Nicholson + Bri-
an Montagu
Tech Info: 16 mm/sound
Date/Country: 1937 + Britain   Type: Documentary
Annotation: A documentary made for the Trinidad Guardian
with songs by Edric Connor*. Ursula Johnson, a worker in
Port of Spain, is one of the Trinidadians in the film.

CALLING ALL KIDS
Series: Our Gang
Nar/Cast: Our Gang + Billie Thomas*
Producer: MGM   Director: Sam Baerwitz
Studio/Company: MGM
Tech Info: bw/sound/1 reel
Date/Country: 1943 + USA   Type: Comedy Short
Annotation: The gang stages a military salute for a radio
and studio audience. Billie Thomas, as Buckwheat, does an
"impression" of the Rochester character with the real
voice of Eddie Anderson* dubbed in.

CALYPSO JOE
Nar/Cast: Herb Jeffries* + Angie Dickinson   Director:
Edward Dein
Tech Info: 16 mm/sound/bw/76 mi
Date/Country: 1957 + USA   Type: Feature
Distr/Arch: cin

CAME THE BRAWN
Series: Our Gang
Nar/Cast: Our Gang + Billie Thomas*
Screenplay: Hal E. Roach
Producer: Hal Roach   Director: Gordon Douglas
Studio/Company: MGM + Roach
Tech Info: super 8 mm/16 mm/bw/sound/1 reel/10 min.
Date/Country: 1938 + USA   Type: Comedy Short
Annotation: At Spanky's arena Alfalfa will fight the Masked
Marvel, just as soon as he can find a marvel he can beat.
Waldo is finally chosen, but Butch pulls a last minute
substitution. Butch is about to go in for the last fall,
when Porky and Buckwheat come to the rescue. Billie
Thomas stars as Buckwheat.

CAMEO KIRBY
Nar/Cast: J. Harold Murray + Stepin Fetchit* + Myrna Loy
Story: Booth Tarkington + Harry L. Wilson   Director:
Irving Cummings
Tech Info: sound/bw
Date/Country: 1930 + USA   Type: Feature
Annotation: Film about riverboat life and New Orleans in the
1850's - complete with the winning of a plantation during
a card game, duels and Mardi Gras balls. Fetchit does his
usual slow comic routine.

CAN THIS BE DIXIE

Nar/Cast: Hattie McDaniel*
Date/Country: 1936 + USA   Type: Feature
Annotation: Hattie McDaniel in one of her many maid roles.

CANARY MURDER CASE, THE
Nar/Cast: Oscar Smith* + William Powell + James Hall +
   Louise Brooks + Jean Arthur
Screenplay: S.S. Van Dine
Producer: Paramount Famous Lasky Corp.   Director: Malcolm
   St. Clair
Tech Info: 35 mm/bw/7 reels
Date/Country: 1928 + USA   Type: Feature
Annotation: A blackmailing musical comedy star is strangled
   and there are 4 suspects. Philo Vance (Powell), wealthy
   amateur detective, is asked by the father of one of the
   suspects to work on the case. Oscar Smith has a small
   role.

CANNED FISHING
Series: Our Gang
Nar/Cast: Our Gang + Billie Thomas*
Producer: Hal Roach   Director: Gordon Douglas
Studio/Company: MGM + Roach
Tech Info: super 8 mm/16 mm/bw/sound/1 reel/10 min.
Date/Country: 1938 + USA   Type: Comedy Short
Distr/Arch: roa + bla
Annotation: When Porky and Buckwheat foul up their playing
   hooky scheme, Spanky and Alfalfa are stuck babysitting
   Junior. Billie Thomas stars as Buckwheat.

CANNIBAL ISLAND
Nar/Cast: Noble Johnson*
Date/Country: 1924 + USA

CANTO PER TE
Nar/Cast: John Kitzmiller*
Date/Country: 1956 + Italy   Type: Feature

CAPTAIN BLOOD
Nar/Cast: Errol Flynn + Olivia DeHavilland + Rex Ingram*
Screenplay: Casey Robinson   Story: Raphael Subutini
   Director: Michael Curtiz
Studio/Company: Warner Brothers
Tech Info: 16 mm/sound/bw/98 min.
Date/Country: 1935 + USA   Type: Feature
Distr/Arch: uas
Annotation: This Subutini film deals romantically with
   Captain Blood, a notorious slave trade in the Carribean.
   The Errol Flynn character is a doctor wrongly accused of
   plotting against King James. Taken to the Carribean as a
   slave, he leads an uprising, steals a Spanish ship, be-
   comes a pirate, and comes to Jamaica's aid against the
   French.

CAPTAIN HENRY'S RADIO SHOW
Nar/Cast: Pat Padget + Pick Malone + Lanny Ross + Muriel
   Wilson
Studio/Company: Paramount

Tech Info: sound/bw/1 reel/30 min.
Date/Country: 1933 + USA   Type: Musical Short
Annotation: A filmed version of the radio show (spinoff of
    stage/film Show Boats) with Padget and Malone as "Molasses
    and January" in blackface, minstrel style.

CAPTAIN SINBAD
Nar/Cast: Bernie Hamilton* + Guy Williams + Pedro Armendariz
Screenplay: Samuel B. West + Harry Relis   Story: Samuel B.
    Wesh + Harry Relis
Producer: Frank King + Herman King   Director: Byron Haskin
Studio/Company: MGM
Date/Country: 1963 + USA   Type: Feature
Distr/Arch: fnc
Annotation: Bernie Hamilton plays Quintus in this Sinbad
    fantasy about monsters, imaginary kingdoms and a princess.

CAPTAIN SPANKY'S SHOW BOAT
Series: Our Gang
Nar/Cast: Our Gang + Billie Thomas*
Screenplay: Hal Law + Robert A. McGowan
Producer: Jack Chertok   Director: edward Cahn
Studio/Company: MGM
Tech Info: bw/sound/1 reel
Date/Country: 1939 + USA   Type: Comedy Short
Annotation: The gang puts on another variety show.

CAPTAINS COURAGEOUS
Nar/Cast: Spencer Tracy + Freddie Bartholomew + Noble John-
    son*   Director: Victor Fleming
Studio/Company: MGM
Tech Info: 16 mm/sound/bw/116 min.
Date/Country: 1937 + USA   Type: Feature
Annotation: Noble Johnson is "Roustan" in this film version
    of the Robert Louis Stevenson classic.

CAR WASH
Nar/Cast: Richard Pryor* + George Carlin + Ivan Dixon* +
    Franklin Ajaye* + DeWayne Jessie* + Tracy Reed* + Garrett
    Morris* + Clarence Muse* + Leonard Jackson* + The Pointer
    sisters* + Antonio Fargas* + Lauren Jones* + Arthur French
        Director: Michael Schultz*
Studio/Company: Universal
Tech Info: 16 mm/sound/color/97 min.
Date/Country: 1976 + USA   Type: Feature
Distr/Arch: swa + uni
Annotation: The drama of one day in the lives of the people
    (black, Chicano, Indian, white) working in a Los Angeles
    car wash. Ivan Dixon is the father figure who helps the
    young Revolutionary in trouble; Pryor is "Daddy Rich," a
    fast-talking preacher whose license plate reads TITHE;
    octogenarian Muse plays a shoeshine man with dignity.

CARDINAL, THE
Nar/Cast: Romy Schneider + John Huston + Ossie Davis* + John
    Saxon
Screenplay: Robert Dozier   Story: Henry Morton Robinson
Producer: Otto Preminger   Director: Otto Preminger

Studio/Company: Columbia Pictures
Tech Info: 16 mm/sound/color/4 reels/175 min.
Date/Country: 1963 + USA   Type: Feature
Distr/Arch: arg + bud + mot + ker + roa + swa + twy
Annotation: Story of the rise of a poor, Boston Irish priest
    to become a prince of the Roman Catholic Church.   Ossie
    Davis plays a priest in Georgia harassed by the KKK.

CARIBBEAN,__THE:__ANTIGUA,__BARBADOS,__MARTINIQUE,_TRINIDAD,
    TOBAGO_AND_JAMAICA
Studio/Company: United World
Tech Info: color/17 min.
Date/Country: 1966   Type: Documentary
Distr/Arch: ueva
Annotation: The Caribbean people are seen through their
    culture, agriculture, and tourism.

CARMEN_JONES
Nar/Cast: Harry Belafonte* + Dorothy Dandridge* + Pearl
    Bailey* + Olga James* + Joe Adams* + Diahann Carroll* +
    Brock Peters* + Alvin Ailey
Screenplay: Harry Kleiner
Producer: Otto Preminger   Director: Otto Preminger
Studio/Company: Twentieth Century Fox
Tech Info: Cinemascope/sound/color/3 reels/107 min.
Date/Country: 1954 + USA   Type: Feature
Distr/Arch: fnc
Annotation: This adaptation of Bizet's opera appeared first
    on Broadway in 1943. The motion picture version, staying
    close to the stage production, exploits the richness of
    southern black folklore in the context of a typical
    romantic   triangle.   The   singing voices of Carmen,
    (Dandridge), Joe (Belafonte) and Husky (Adams) are dubbed
    by vocalists Marilyn Horn, Le Vern Hucherson, and Marvin
    Hayes. Bailey sings "Beat Out That Rhythm on a Drum" in
    her own voice.

CARNIVAL_IN_RHYTHM
Nar/Cast: Katherine Dunham and her troupe* + Archie Savage*
    + Talley Beatty*
Studio/Company: Warners
Date/Country: 1940 + USA   Type: Feature
Annotation: A short film devoted to Katherine Dunham and her
    ballet company; a mixture of classical and Afro-Cuban
    dance.

CAROLINA_BLUES
Nar/Cast: Kay Kyser + Ann Miller + Marie Bryant*   + Harold
    Nicholas* + Step Brothers* + Louise Franklin*
Screenplay: Joseph Hoffman
Producer: Sam Bischoff   Director: Leigh Jason
Studio/Company: Columbia
Date/Country: 1944 + USA   Type: Feature
Annotation: A Kay Kyser vehicle built around the story of
    two young entertainers who try to join Kyser's band as
    they raise money for war bonds. Included in the movie is
    a black dance troupe.

CAROLINA
Alt Title(s): The House of Connelly (play)
Nar/Cast: Janet Gaynor + Lionel Barrymore + Robert Young +
    Stepin Fetchit*   Story: Paul Green   Director: Henry King
Studio/Company: Fox
Date/Country: 1934 + USA   Type: Feature
Annotation: Love story which depicts the difficulties, many
    of them amusing, in matching a northern girl with a
    southern gentleman. Stepin Fetchit clowns as Scipio, a
    combination stable hand and butler.

CARPETBAGGERS, THE
Nar/Cast: Archie Moore* + George Peppard + Caroll Baker
Screenplay: John Michael Hayes   Story: Harold Robbins
Producer: Joseph E. Levine   Director: Edward Dmytryk
Studio/Company: Paramount
Tech Info: 16 mm/sound/color/150 min.
Date/Country: 1964 + USA   Type: Feature
Distr/Arch: fnc
Annotation: George Peppard plays Jonas Cord, Jr., in this
    thinly disguised story about Howard Hughes. The film
    traces Cord's life in the business world and his many
    loves. Archie Moore has a minor role, as Jedediah.

CASABLANCA
Nar/Cast: Humphrey Bogart + Ingrid Bergman + Paul Henreid +
    Claude Rains + Peter Lorre + Dooley Wilson*
Screenplay: Jules Epstein + Philip Epstein + Howard Koch
Producer: Hal Wallis   Director: Michael Curtiz
Studio/Company: Warners
Tech Info: 16 mm/sound/bw/3 reels/102 min.
Date/Country: 1942 + USA   Type: Feature
Distr/Arch: uas
Annotation: Bogart as Rick in this romantic-adventure thril-
    ler set in North Africa just before the outbreak of WWII.
    Dooley Wilson plays Sam who plays again "As Time Goes By."
    He is Rick's friend/confidante and owns 10 percent of the
    club (in one script version).

CASBAH
Nar/Cast: Tony Martin + Yvonne DeCarlo + Peter Lorre +
    Katherine Dunham* and her dancers
Screenplay: L. Bush-Fekete + Arnold Manoff
Producer: Nat G. Goldstone   Director: John Berry
Studio/Company: Universal-International
Tech Info: 16 mm/sound/bw/92 min.
Date/Country: 1948 + USA   Type: Feature
Distr/Arch: ivy
Annotation: Remake of Algiers, this is the story of Pepe
    (Martin), a master thief who leaves the sanctuary of the
    "Casbah" to pursue his lady love only to find death.
    Katherine Dunham plays Odette in her only dramatic role;
    she and her dance troupe also perform.

CASINO ROYALE
Nar/Cast: Tracy Reed* + Peter Sellers + David Niven
Screenplay: Wolf Mankowitz + John Law
Producer: Charles Feldman + Jerry Bresler   Director: John

Huston + Ken Hughes + Val Guest + Robert Parrish + Joseph
   McGrath
Studio/Company: Columbia
Tech Info: 16 mm/sound/color/130 min.
Date/Country: 1967 + Britain   Type: Feature
Distr/Arch: bud + ccc + cha + col + cwf + ics + mac + mod +
   mot + roa + sel + swa + twy + unf + wcf + wel + who + wil
Annotation: Tracy Reed is gang leader in this James Bond
   comedy that parodies James Bond with an international all
   star cast.

CASTLE KEEP
Nar/Cast: Al Freeman Jr* + Bert Lancaster + Patrick O'Neal
Screenplay: Daniel Taradash + David Rayfiel
Producer: Martin Ransohoff + John Calley   Director: Sydney
   Pollack
Studio/Company: Columbia Pictures
Tech Info: 16 mm/sound/color/106 min.
Date/Country: 1969 + USA   Type: Feature
Distr/Arch: arg + bud + cin + cwf + ics + mac + mod + mot +
   roa + swa + twy
Annotation: A group of exhausted, slightly lunatic soldiers
   lead by a one-eyed major played by Bert Lancaster try to
   hold a castle against a German counterattack. Al Freeman,
   Jr., plays a young black private writing a novel of the
   group's experiences; his narrative serves to underline the
   humor and horrors of war.

CAT BALLOU
Nar/Cast: Lee Marvin + Nat King Cole* + Jane Fonda + Lee
   Marvin
Screenplay: Walt Newman + Frank Pierson   Story: Roy Chan-
   slor
Producer: Harold Hecht   Director: Elliot Silverstein
Studio/Company: Columbia
Tech Info: 16 mm/sound/color/96 min.
Date/Country: 1965 + USA   Type: Feature
Distr/Arch: arg + bud + cin + cwf + ics + mac + mod + mot +
   roa + sel + new + tfc + twy + unf
Annotation: Starring Fonda, and Marvin in his Oscar winning
   role, this film is a spoof of the western film genre,
   featuring an innocent school marm whose ranch is about to
   be taken away. She turns to crime and in the end is saved
   by a drunken gunslinger and his cohorts.   Songs by Nat
   King Cole.   Nat King Cole in his last film appearance
   portrays a traveling minstrel who sings the "Ballad of Cat
   Ballou."

CAT, DOG AND CO.
Series: Our Gang
Nar/Cast: Our Gang + Allen Hoskins*
Screenplay: Robert F. McGowan
Producer: Robert F. McGowan + Hal Roach   Director: Anthony
   Mack
Studio/Company: MGM
Tech Info: super 8 mm/16 mm/bw/silent/synchronized music
   track and sound effects, on disc/2 reels
Date/Country: 1929 + USA   Type: Comedy Short

Distr/Arch: bla
Annotation: Joe, Harry and Farina's dog-powered kiddie cars
  provoke a be-kind-to-animals lecture from a humane society
  lady. The gang is eventually won over - all except
  Wheezer who must endure a daydream in which he is dwarfed
  by gigantic animals dressed as humans who put him on trial
  for cruelty to animals. Final sequence has Gang releasing
  all animals in town. Allen Hoskins stars as Farina.

CATCH MY SOUL
Nar/Cast: Richie Havens* + Lance LeGault + Season Hubley +
  Tony Joe White* + Susan Tyrrell
Screenplay: Jack Good
Producer: Richard Rosenbloom + Jack Good   Director: Patrick
  McGoohan
Studio/Company: Cinerama
Tech Info: 95 min.
Date/Country: 1973 + USA   Type: Feature
Annotation: Plot line parallels Shakespeare's Othello, in an
  updated adaptation. Havens is Othello, Lance LeGault is
  Iago, season Hubley is Desdemona, and Tony Joe White is
  Cassio. Music by Tony Joe White.

CAUSE FOR THANKSGIVING
Series: Sonny Jim
Producer: Tefft Johnson   Type: Comedy Short
Annotation: Jim swaps a turkey for black Lily Ann's baby
  brother so Lily Ann's family can have a holiday dinner.

CAVALCADE OF HARLEM
Studio/Company: Harlem Productions
Date/Country: 1937 + USA

CEDDO
Nar/Cast: Tabara Ndiaye* + Moustapha Yade* + Mamdou Ndiaye
  Diagne* + Ousmane Camara* + Alioune Fall*
Screenplay: Ousmane Sembene*   Director: Ousmane Sembene*
Studio/Company: Dakar Films
Tech Info: 16 mm/sound/3 reels/color/ 120 min./in Wolof with
  English subtitles by Carrie Sembene*
Date/Country: 1977 + Senegal   Type: Feature
Distr/Arch: nyf
Annotation: Set in the 18th century, Ceddo depicts the
  struggle of Moslems (east) and Christians (west) to
  dominate Africa. The symbols of the West are embodied in
  a gun runner, alcohol peddling slaver and a missionary
  "bwana" type; of the East in the Iman who unseats the
  King, subverts the village council and exercies exclusive
  authority in the name of Allah. It is a woman who sets
  them free.

CENTENNIAL SUMMER
Nar/Cast: Jeanne Crain + Cornel Wilde + Linda Darnell + Avon
  Long*   Story: Albert Idell
Producer: Otto Preminger   Director: Otto Preminger
Studio/Company: 20th Century Fox
Tech Info: 16 mm/sound/bw/102 min.
Date/Country: 1946 + USA   Type: Feature

Distr/Arch: fnc
Annotation: In a copy of Meet Me In St. Louis, this film
   centers around a family of young ladies in Philadelphia
   during the 1876 exposition. Broadway star Avon Long has
   one number in the film.

CENTRAL AFRICA
Series: ABC's Documentary on Africa
Nar/Cast: Gregory Peck
Producer: ABC-TV
Studio/Company: ABC-TV
Tech Info: 16 mm/sound/color/1 reel/20 min.
Date/Country: 1968 + Angola + Zaire + Mozambique + Zimbabwe
   + Zambia   Type: TV Documentary
Distr/Arch: con + mghf + psu + ucemc
Annotation: The peoples of Central Africa and the complex
   problems of race relations are studied to develop an un-
   derstanding of the social and economic bases of African-
   European tensions in both the free and the colonial areas
   of Central Africa.

CERTAIN SMILE, A
Nar/Cast: Christine Carene + Rossano Brazzi + Bradford Dil-
   lman + Johnny Mathis* + Nat "King" Cole*
Screenplay: Frances Goodrich + Albert Hackett   Story:
   Francoise Sagan
Producer: Henry Ephron   Director: Jean Negulesco
Studio/Company: 20th Century Fox
Tech Info: 16 mm/sound/color/106 min.
Date/Country: 1958 + USA   Type: Feature
Distr/Arch: fnc
Annotation: Film made from Francoise Sagan's novel about
   adultery and its inevitable consequences.   Johnny Mathis
   and Nat King Cole are featured in night club scenes.

CHAMPEEN, THE
Series: Our Gang
Nar/Cast: Our Gang + Ernie Morrison* + Allen Hoskins*
Screenplay: Hal Roach
Producer: Hal Roach   Director: Robert McGowan
Studio/Company: Pathe
Tech Info: silent/bw/2 reels
Date/Country: 1923 + USA   Type: Comedy Short
Annotation: To raise money for some apples he's stolen, Sun-
   shine Sammy (Ernie Morrison) decides to promote a fight
   between Mickey and Jackie, both of whom are vying for the
   same girl.   Allen Hoskins plays Farina.

CHANCE TO LEARN, A
Series: White Paper
Producer: ABC
Tech Info: 16 mm/sound/color/1 reel/21 min.
Date/Country: 1968 + USA   Type: Documentary
Distr/Arch: iu + fnc
Annotation: Shows black dissatisfaction in the schools and
   contrasts black and white demands for local control in New
   York City and in Little Rock, Arkansas.   Interviews
   Charles V. Hamilton* and Daniel P. Moynihan discussing

local school control. Visits Project Unique in Rochester,
New York, a quality inner city school, a demonstration in
a department store, and a pre-school education program.

CHANGE OF HABIT
Nar/Cast: Barbara McNair* + Elvis Presley + Mary Tyler Moore
Screenplay: James Lee + S.S. Schiveitzer + Eric Bercovici
Producer: Joe Connelly   Director: WilliamGraham
Studio/Company: Universal
Tech Info: 16 mm/sound/color/105 min.
Date/Country: 1969 + USA   Type: Feature
Distr/Arch: ccc + cwf + roa + tmc + uni + wcf
Annotation: Presley is a devoted doctor running a clinic in
  a black/ latino slum. His helpers are three not very
  traditional nuns, Barbara McNair, as Sister Irene, among
  them.

CHANGE OF HEART
Alt Title(s): see The Hit Parade of 1943

CHANGE OF MIND
Nar/Cast: Raymond St. Jacques* + Janet MacLachlan* + Susan
  Oliver + Leslie Neilson + David Bailey + Andrew Womble
Screenplay: Seeleg Lester + Richard Weston
Producer: Seeleg Lester + Richard Weston   Director: Robert
  Stevens
Studio/Company: Cinerama Release
Tech Info: 16 mm/color/sound/98 min.
Date/Country: 1969 + USA   Type: Feature
Distr/Arch: cdc
Annotation: When the brain of a white District Attorney is
  transplanted into the body of a black man, complicatins
  arise both professionally and personally. With his wife
  and mother unable to accept him in his black body, David
  Row (Raymond St. Jacques) begins to question his identity.
  Susan Oliver plays his wife Mary, Janet MacLachlan a help-
  ful friend. Score by Duke Ellington*, played by Ellington, et al.

CHAPPAQUA
Nar/Cast: Jean-Louis Barrault + Ornette Coleman* + Conrad
  Rooks + Allen Ginsburg + Ravi Shankar + William S. Bur-
  roughs
Screenplay: Conrad Rooks
Producer: Conrad Rooks   Director: Conrad Rooks
Tech Info: sound/bw/92 min.
Date/Country: 1967 + USA   Type: Feature
Annotation: Autobiographical drama about an alcoholic/drug
  addicted son of a business executive who after his
  father's death decides he wants to be cured.   His
  fantasies include an evil drug pusher, Indian guru, a
  woman, poetry and music. Coleman plays "Peyote Eater."

CHARLES LLOYD: JOURNEY WITHIN
Screenplay: Eric Sherman
Producer: Eric Sherman   Director: Eric Sherman
Tech Info: 16 mm/sound/bw/60 min.
Date/Country: 1968 + USA   Type: Documentary

Distr/Arch: mac
Annotation: The life struggle of the jazz artist, Charles
  Lloyd*.

CHARLESTON
Alt Title(s): see Sur un Air de Charleston

CHARLEY-ONE-EYE
Nar/Cast: Richard Roundtree* + Roy Thinnes + Nigel Davenport
Screenplay: Keith Leonard
Producer: David Frost + James Swann   Director: Don Chaffey
Studio/Company: Paramount
Tech Info: 16 mm/color/sound/3 reels/107 min.
Date/Country: 1973 + USA   Type: Feature
Distr/Arch: fnc
Annotation: Filmed in Spain, Charley-One-Eye attempts to
  examine the exploitation of black freedmen and Indians in
  the old West.

CHARLIE CHAN IN EGYPT
Series: Charlie Chan
Nar/Cast: Stepin Fetchit* + Frank Conroy + Pat Paterson +
  Warner Oland + Rita Hayworth
Screenplay: Helen Logan + Robert Ellis
Producer: Edward T. Lowe   Director: Louis King
Studio/Company: Warner Brothers
Tech Info: 16 mm/sound/bw/2 reels/71 min.
Date/Country: 1935 + USA   Type: Feature
Distr/Arch: roa + bud + sel + twy + mac + wil
Annotation: Charlie Chan investigates the disappearance of
  ancient relics in Egypt. His chauffeur, Snowshoes (Stepin
  Fetchit), becomes aware of his "roots" in between a light
  courtship and an encounter with a ghost in a pyramid.

CHARLIE CHAN IN THE SECRET SERVICE
Series: Charlie Chan
Nar/Cast: Sidney Toler + Mantan Moreland* + Gwen Tenyon
  Director: Phil Rosen
Studio/Company: Monogram
Tech Info: 16 mm/sound/68 min./bw
Date/Country: 1944 + USA   Type: Feature
Distr/Arch: uas + mog
Annotation: Mantan Moreland is Birmingham Brown, Charlie
  Chan's chauffeur and comic foil.

CHASE, THE
Nar/Cast: Joel Fluellen* + Marlon Brando + Jane Fonda +
  Robert Redford + Davis Roberts*
Screenplay: Lillian Hellman   Story: Horton Foote
Producer: Sam Spiegel   Director: Arthur Penn
Studio/Company: Columbia
Tech Info: 16 mm/sound/color/135 min.
Date/Country: 1966 + USA   Type: Feature
Distr/Arch: arg + bud + ccc + cha + cwf + mac + mot + roa +
  swa + twy + unf + wel + who
Annotation: Marlon Brando is the sheriff in a Texas town
  filled with sex, violence and racism. Joel Fluellen plays
  Lester Johnson.

CHASING TROUBLE
Nar/Cast: Frankie Darro* + Mantan Moreland* + Marjorie
    Reynolds + Milburn Stone + Cheryl Walker
Screenplay: Mary McCarthy   Director: Howard Bretherton
Studio/Company: Monogram
Tech Info: 16 mm/sound
Date/Country: 1940 + USA   Type: Feature
Annotation: One of a series of films in which Darro and his
    friend/helper (Moreland) track down the bad guys.

CHATTERBOX
Nar/Cast: Joe E. Brown + The Mills Brothers*   Director:
    Joseph Santley
Studio/Company: Republic
Tech Info: 76 min.
Date/Country: 1943 + USA
Annotation: A comic burlesque about a cowboy movie star
    features the singing of the Mills Brothers.

CHE
Nar/Cast: Frank Silvera* + Woody Strode*   + Omar Sharif +
    Jack Palance
Screenplay: Michael Wilson + Sy Burtlett
Producer: Sy Bartlett Director: Richard Fleischer
Studio/Company: 20th Century Fox
Tech Info: 16 mm/sound/color/96 min.
Date/Country: 1969 + USA   Type: Feature
Distr/Arch: fnc
Annotation: Dramatizes life of Che Guevara (Sharif) from his
    landing in Cuba with Castro (Palance) until his death in
    Bolivia eight years later. Frank Silvera is the Bolivian
    goatherd who turns Che in; Woody Strode is Guillermo.

CHEATERS
Nar/Cast: Bill Boyd + Louise Beavers* + June Collyer + Alan
    Mowbray
Screenplay: Adele Buffington   Director: Phil Rosen
Studio/Company: Liberty Pictures
Tech Info: sound/bw
Date/Country: 1934 + USA   Type: Feature
Annotation: Four crooks plan to separate a millionaire from
    his money, by having the female of the gang marry the mil-
    lionaire, and divorce him for a handsome settlement.
    Things go awry when the head crook discovers he loves the
    girl. Louise Beavers plays Lily.

CHECK AND DOUBLE CHECK
Nar/Cast: Freeman Gosden + Charles Correll + Duke Ellington*
    and his Cotton Club Orchestra* + Sue Carol
Screenplay: J. Walter Ruben   Story: Bert Kalmar + Harry
    Ruby
Producer: William LeBaron   Director: Melville Brown
Studio/Company: RKO Radio Pictures
Tech Info: 16 mm/bw/sound/2 reels/84 min.
Date/Country: 1930 + USA   Type: Feature
Distr/Arch: bud + cfm + kpf + emg + rad + wcf + nat
Annotation: The only Amos and Andy film available stars the

team of Gosden and Correll (white actors in burnt cork) in
the roles they originated for radio. A haunted house, a
wild taxi ride through the streets of New York, and a happy ending for two young lovers are ingredients for this
black comedy set in Harlem and an upper class suburb.
Russell Powell is the Kingfish (also in black face).
Musical sequence with Ellington and orchestra.

CHEZ LES MANGEURS D'HOMME
Alt Title(s): Menchenfresser Der Sudee   Director: Andre
   Paul Antoine + Robert Lugeon
Tech Info: silent/bw/2200 meters
Date/Country: France + 1928
Distr/Arch: saf
Annotation: Film sychronized with Kanak choruses and songs.
   In eight parts. Archived only.

CHICAGO AFTER DARK
Nar/Cast: Lollypop Jones* + Allen McMillen* + Edgar Lewis
   Morton* + James Dunsmore* + Artilbelle McGinty* + Tops and
   Wilda*   Director: Josh Binney
Studio/Company: All American News, Inc.
Tech Info: 35 mm/bw/sound/3 reels
Date/Country: 1946   Type: Musical Short
Distr/Arch: lc

CHICAGO BLUES   Director: Harley Cokliss
Tech Info: 50 min.
Date/Country: 1971 + Britain   Type: Documentary
Annotation: Influence of the rural blues on urban music of
   Chicago examined. Includes Muddy Waters* and others.

CHICKEN FEED
Series: Our Gang
Nar/Cast: Our Gang + Allen Hoskins* + Jannie Hoskins*
Screenplay: Hal Roach
Producer: Hal Roach   Director: Anthony Mack + Charles Oelze
Studio/Company: Pathe
Tech Info: silent/bw/2 reels
Date/Country: 1927 + USA   Type: Comedy Short
Annotation: After watching a magic show, Joe gets some
   'magic powder' which transforms Mango first into a monkey,
   then a cat, a bear and finally a chicken - who they
   believe was eaten by a hobo. They take the bones and
   presto she's back. Allen Hoskins stars as Farina and Jan-
   nie Hoskins stars as Mango.

CHILDREN AND WOMEN IN THE BELGIAN CONGO
Series: National Archives Gift Collection
Tech Info: color cuts/partly edited
Annotation: Part of Record Group 200 HF series, Harmon
   Foundation Collection.

CHILDREN IN THE BALANCE: THE TRAGEDY OF BIAFRA
Producer: NET
Tech Info: 16 mm/sound/bw/1 reel/60 min.
Date/Country: 1969 + USA   Type: Documentary
Distr/Arch: iu

Annotation: Focuses attention upon the Biafran children who
    are dying from starvation and malnutrition. Points out
    that the amount of food delivered to Biafra must be in-
    creased in order to prevent and curtail starvation. Em-
    phasizes the tragedy of the Nigerian Civil War.

CHILDREN OF AFRICA
Series: National Archives Gift Collection
Tech Info: 16 mm/silent/2 reels/color
Annotation: Everyday activities in the Congo, titled especi-
    ally for children. (Part of Record Group 200 HF series,
    Harmon Foundation Collection).

CHILDREN OF CIRCUMSTANCE
Nar/Cast: Catherine Alexander* + Ollington E. Smith*
Studio/Company: Gramercy Pictures
Date/Country: 1937 + USA

CHILDREN OF FATE
Nar/Cast: Lawrence Chenault* + Harry Henderson* + Arline
    Mickey* + Howard Agusta* + Alonzo Jackson* + Shingzie
    Howard* + William A. Clayton*
Studio/Company: Colored Players Film Corporation
Date/Country: 1929 + USA
Annotation: Romanticized tale of a man who makes his fortune
    gambling and gains his health and happiness because of the
    love and inspiration of his childhood sweetheart.

CHILDREN OF THE DAMNED
Nar/Cast: Ian Hendry + Alan Badel + Clive Powell + Barbara
    Ferris + Lee Yoke-Moon + Alfred Burke + Roberta Rex
Screenplay: John Briley   Story: John Wyndham
Producer: Lawrence P. Bachman   Director: Anton M. Leader
Studio/Company: MGM
Tech Info: 16 mm/sound/bw/90 min.
Date/Country: 1964 + Britain   Type: Feature
Distr/Arch: fnc
Annotation: This science fiction drama, the successor to
    Village of the Damned introduces six children (from En-
    gland, Russia, India, China, and the U.S. advanced one
    million years in intelligence. Their knowledge of mass
    destruction weapons threatens the status quo of existing
    governments.

CHILDREN OF THE WORLD: DAHOMEY
Producer: Denis Hargrave + Percy Rodrigues* + Jim Carney +
    M.C. Mann + Eric Lindgren
Studio/Company: Canadian Broadcasting Corp. + NET + United
    Nations
Tech Info: 16 mm/sound/color/1 reel/24 min.
Date/Country: 1968 + Dahomey   Type: Documentary
Distr/Arch: iu + bu
Annotation: Dahomean politics, economics, history, culture
    and religion as explained by 11 year old Nicholas Mignau-
    wande. Tribal wars, and the wearing of tribal scars, no
    longer allowed as now everyone works toward a common goal.

CHILDREN OF THE WORLD: SOMALIA

Studio/Company: NET
Tech Info: 16 mm/color/sound/1 reel/28 min.
Date/Country: 1968   Type: Documentary
Distr/Arch: iu
Annotation: The lifestyle of the nomadic camel herders of
    Africa is viewed through the eyes of Ismel, an eleven year
    old boy in Somalia.

CHILDREN WERE WATCHING: INTERGRATION IN NEW ORLEANS, THE
Producer: Drew Associates + Time-Life
Tech Info: 16 mm/sound/bw/30 min.
Date/Country: 1967 + USA   Type: Documentary
Distr/Arch: tl
Annotation: The feelings of a black child entering the first
    intergrated school of New Orleans.

CHILDREN WERE WATCHING, THE/INTEGRATION IN NEW ORLEANS
Series: Living Camera
Studio/Company: Drew Associates + Time-Life Broadcast
Tech Info: 16 mm/bw/sound/1 reel/30 min.
Date/Country: 1967 + USA   Type: Documentary
Distr/Arch: tim
Annotation: A six-year-old black girl valiantly enters the
    first integrated school in New Orleans. The child's point
    of view is recorded.

CHILDREN
Series: The Family of Man
Producer: BBC-TV
Studio/Company: BBC-TV
Tech Info: 16 mm/sound/color/2 reels/45 min.
Date/Country: 1971 + Botswana + New Guinea + England   Type:
    TV Documentary
Distr/Arch: tim
Annotation: A comparison of how children are raised in the 3
    different societies - in which are the children happier,
    what is the role of mothers, sex.

CHINA GATE
Nar/Cast: Gene Barry + Angie Dickinson + Nat "King" Cole*
Screenplay: Samuel Fuller
Producer: Samuel Fuller   Director: Samuel Fuller
Studio/Company: 20th Century Fox
Tech Info: 16 mm/sound/bw/97 min.
Date/Country: 1957 + USA   Type: Feature
Distr/Arch: ivy + mot + wcf
Annotation: On a dangerous mission to destroy a Communist
    held ammo dump in the Vietnamese jungle, various patrol
    members begin to reveal their emotional problems.   Nat
    "King" Cole stars as Goldie, a WWII and Korean War vet who
    wants international peace and justice.

CHINA SEAS
Nar/Cast: Clark Gable + Jean Harlow + Hattie McDaniel*
    Director: Tay Garnett
Studio/Company: MGM
Tech Info: 16 mm/sound/bw/89 min.
Date/Country: 1935 + USA   Type: Feature

Distr/Arch: fnc
Annotation: Enhanced by an exotic setting, Gable and Harlow
    star in this film about piracy on the high seas, double
    crossing and love. Hattie McDaniel plays Harlow's wise-
    cracking maid.

CHINESE CAT, THE
Series: Charlie Chan
Nar/Cast: Mantan Moreland* + Benson Fong + Joan Woodbury +
    Sidney Toler   Story: Earl Derr Biggers   Director: Phil
    Rosen
Studio/Company: Monogram
Tech Info: 16 mm/sound/bw/70 min.
Date/Country: 1944 + USA   Type: Feature
Distr/Arch: mog + uas
Annotation: Mantan Moreland is Birmingham Brown, Charlie
    Chan's chauffeur and comic foil.

CHINESE RING
Series: Charlie Chan
Nar/Cast: Mantan Moreland* + Roland Winter + Warren Douglas
    + Victor Sen Young   Story: Earl Derr Biggers   Director:
    William Beaudine
Studio/Company: Monogram
Tech Info: 16 mm/bw/sound/2 reels/67 min.
Date/Country: 1947 + USA   Type: Feature
Distr/Arch: cin
Annotation: Mantan Moreland plays Birmingham Brown, Charlie
    Chan's chauffeur and comic relief.

CHINUA ACHEBE
Series: African Writers of Today
Producer: NET
Tech Info: 16 mm/sound/bw/1 reel/29 min.
Date/Country: 1964   Type: Documentary
Distr/Arch: iu
Annotation: Opens with an interview involving Nkosi*, Soy-
    inka*, and featured guest Achebe*. Focuses on the craft
    and work of Achebe himself. Shows him discussing the in-
    fluences which have shaped his artistic life and closes
    with an examination of the traditional novel and a possi-
    ble new African novel form.

CHISHOLM: PURSUING THE DREAM
Producer: Freedonia
Tech Info: 16 mm/sound/color/42 min.
Date/Country: 1973 + USA
Distr/Arch: nlc
Annotation: Shirley Chisholm's attempts to be the first
    black/first woman to get the 1972 Democratic presidential
    nomination.

CHOO CHOO SWING
Studio/Company: Universal
Tech Info: 13 min.
Date/Country: 1943 + USA   Type: Musical Short
Annotation: Count Basie* and his Orchestra play the title
    number and "Swingin' the Blues."

CHOO-CHOO
Series: Our Gang
Nar/Cast: Our Gang + Matthew Beard*
Screenplay: Hal E. Roach
Producer: Hal E. Roach + Robert F. McGowan   Director:
    Robert F. McGowan
Studio/Company: MGM + Roach
Tech Info: super 8 mm/16 mm/bw/sound/2 reels/15-20 min.
Date/Country: 1932 + USA   Type: Comedy Short
Distr/Arch: roa + bla
Annotation: The gang changes places with a group of orphans
    who are being taken by train to their new home. The gang
    puts the entire train in an uproar. Matthew Beard stars
    as Stymie.

CICERO MARCH
Series: New Militants and the Urban Crisis
Producer: The Film Group
Tech Info: 16 mm/sound/bw/8 min.
Date/Country: 1968 + USA   Type: Documentary
Distr/Arch: uca + uco
Annotation: In September, 1966 there was a march through a
    white community by both Blacks and whites, a protest
    against white 'supremacy'.

CINCINNATI KID, THE
Nar/Cast: Cab Calloway* + Steve McQueen + Edward G.   Robin-
    son + Ann-Margret
Screenplay: Ring Lardner, Jr. + Terry Southern   Story:
    Richard Jessup
Producer: Martin Ransohoff   Director: Norman Jewison
Studio/Company: MGM
Tech Info: 16 mm/sound/color/113 min.
Date/Country: 1966 + USA   Type: Feature
Distr/Arch: fnc
Annotation: Calloway as a traveling card shark in a film
    about top-flight poker players. Title song by Ray
    Charles*.

CINDERELLA LIBERTY
Nar/Cast: James Caan + Marsha Mason   Director: Mark Rydell
Date/Country: 1973 + USA
Distr/Arch: fnc
Annotation: Marsha Mason, a Seattle hustler partial to men
    on leave, has an affair with one (Caan) who falls in love
    with her and her mulatto son.

CINDY
Nar/Cast: Charlaine Woodard* and an all-black cast   Story:
    James L. Brooks + Stan Daniels + David Davis + Ed Wein-
    berger
Producer: James L. Brooks + Stan Daniels + David Davis + Ed
    Weinberger for Charles Walters Productions
Date/Country: 1977 + USA   Type: TV Feature
Annotation: This original musical-comedy special is based on
    the Cinderella Story and features an all-black cast. The
    story is set in Harlem during the 1940's.

CIRCE_THE_ENCHANTRESS
Nar/Cast: Mae Murray + James Kirkwood + Tom Ricketts +
  Charles Gerard + William Haines + Lillian Langdon
Screenplay: Vincente Blasco-Ibanez
Producer: Tiffany Prod.   Director: Robert Z. Leonard
Studio/Company: Metro Goldwyn
Tech Info: 35 mm/silent/bw/7 reels
Date/Country: 1924 + USA   Type: Feature
Distr/Arch: mgm
Annotation: Blacks appear as jazz musicians, serving as
  background to the seductive female lead (White).

CIRCUS_FEVER
Series: Our Gang
Nar/Cast: Our Gang + Allen Hoskins* + Eugene Jackson* +
  Ernie Morrison, Sr.*
Screenplay: Hal Roach
Producer: Hal Roach   Director: Robert McGowan
Studio/Company: Pathe
Tech Info: silent/bw/2 reels
Date/Country: 1925 + USA   Type: Comedy Short
Annotation: On the one day of the year that the circus is in
  town, Farina and Gene are sick with speckled fever; Mick-
  ey, Jackie and Joe don't want to go to school so they fake
  the symptoms only to be caught. Allen Hoskins is Farina,
  Eugene Jackson is his brother Gene, and Ernie Morrison,
  Sr. is Dr Royal Sorghum.

CIRCUS,_THE   Director: G.V. Alexandrov
Studio/Company: Mosfilm
Date/Country: 1937 + Russian   Type: Feature
Annotation: Heroine is an American circus star who refuses
  the circus master's attentions. Out of revenge, he shows
  her "secret" to the circus audience - her black child -
  the reason she had left America. However, they neither
  scorn nor abuse her; instead they tenderly pass the child
  from group to group.

CITIES_-_CRIME_IN_THE_STREETS
Producer: NET
Tech Info: 16 mm/bw/sound/2 reels/60 min.
Date/Country: 1966   Type: Documentary
Distr/Arch: iu
Annotation: Two important aspects of the crime problem in
  the United States, police protection and the rehabilitation of juvenile offenders, are examined by police ex-
  perts, criminologists, and others. Training schools are
  visited and their methods contrasted with community programs designed to keep the juvenile from ever becoming
  criminal.

CITIES_AND_THE_POOR,_PART_I
Producer: NET
Tech Info: 16 mm/sound/bw/1 reel/60 min.
Date/Country: 1966   Type: Documentary
Distr/Arch: iu
Annotation: An introduction to the problems of the urban

poor in the United States which explores who the poor are,
where they are, and the reasons for their dilemma. Typical attempts by the poor themselves, as well as the
government and private agencies, to find a way out of
poverty are documented.

CITIES AND THE POOR, PART II
Producer: NET
Tech Info: 16 mm/sound/bw/1 reel/60 min.
Date/Country: 1966   Type: Documentary
Distr/Arch: iu
Annotation: The second of two films on poverty in the cities
    explores the rise of militant groups among the urban poor.
    It documents their methods of organizing for the purpose
    of obtaining better living conditions, jobs, and schools,
    and the effect of these organized efforts upon the federal
    poverty program and established local governmental bodies.
    Neighborhood organizations in Chicago and Los Angeles are
    studied as typical examples.

CITY STATES OF EAST AFRICA
Nar/Cast: Prof. Joseph Harris
Producer: WCBS-TV
Tech Info: 16 mm/sound/bw/1 reel/30 min.
Date/Country: 1969 + East Africa   Type: Documentary
Distr/Arch: hraw
Annotation: Development of city-states of East Africa, the
    relationship of the Somedi, the Arabs, and Bantu to the
    original inhabitants and how it resulted in the growth of
    Swahili culture.

CIVIL DISORDER: THE KERNER REPORT -- I
Producer: Public Broadcasting Library + NET
Tech Info: 16 mm/sound/bw/2 reels/56 min.
Date/Country: 1968   Type: Documentary
Distr/Arch: iu
Annotation: Several examples of what the Kerner Report
    called 'the polarization of the American community' are
    presented. The need for sufficient funds to finance a
    more positive approach is emphasized by the late Dr.
    Martin Luther King*. A project in Brooklyn which success-
    fully eliminated many riot-inciting grievances demon-
    strates what private housing can do.

CIVIL DISORDER: THE KERNER REPORT -- II
Producer: Public Broadcasting Library
Tech Info: 16 mm/sound/bw/2 reels/56 min.
Date/Country: 1968   Type: Documentary
Distr/Arch: iu
Annotation: Continuation of Part I presents examples of ef-
    forts to relieve black underemployment and also includes a
    review of the Kerner Report as a social document by author
    James Baldwin*, Rev. Leon H. Sullivan* and Whitney Young*.
    Baldwin comments that the Kerner Report is honest but in-
    adequate and that racism is a threat to all Americans.

CIVIL DISORDER: THE KERNER REPORT -- III
Producer: Public Broadcasting Library + NET

Tech Info: 16 mm/sound/bw/1 reel/24 min.
Date/Country: 1968   Type: Documentary
Distr/Arch: iu
Annotation: Three prominent black leaders analyze the Kerner
    Report in terms of whether or not they believe anything
    will be done in response to it and if there still is time.
    Charles V. Hamilton*, Bayard Rustin*, and Kenneth Clark*
    are on the panel. The panel members cite earlier reports
    which were never acted on and otherwise indicate their
    pessimism with regard to progress this time.

CIVIL RIGHTS MOVEMENT: HISTORIC ROOTS
Producer: NBC
Tech Info: 16 mm/sound/bw/1 reel/17 min.
Date/Country: 1967 + USA   Type: Documentary
Distr/Arch: iu + ebec
Annotation: Traces the historical background of Blacks in
    the U.S. Shows how Blacks were forced to leave their
    homeland to be sold as slaves, and relates the connection
    between the invention of the cotton gin and the prolifera-
    tion of the slave trade. Shows the effect Uncle Tom's
    Cabin had on the abolitionist movement.

CIVIL RIGHTS MOVEMENT: THE NORTH
Producer: NBC
Tech Info: 16 mm/sound/bw/1 reel/23 min.
Date/Country: 1966   Type: Documentary
Distr/Arch: iu + ebec
Annotation: Surveys some of the problems of discrimination
    against Blacks in the areas of employment and education in
    several North American cities through interviews with a
    number of leaders including Senator Edward Brooke*, Billy
    Martin, Malcom X*, and Senator Robert Kennedy.   Examines
    the purposes of the demonstration, the Black Muslim posi-
    tion, and problem areas in Chicago,   Illinois,   and
    Elizabeth, New Jersey.

CIVIL RIGHTS MOVEMENT: THE PERSONAL VIEW
Producer: NBC
Tech Info: 16 mm/sound/bw/1 reel/22 min.
Date/Country: 1966   Type: Documentary
Distr/Arch: iu + ebec
Annotation: Gives a general overview of social conditions as
    they exist for Blacks and whites.   Relates personal ex-
    periences of whites and Blacks to portray fear, hate, and
    suspicion. Reviews stereotypes which distort the image of
    the Black.

CIVIL WAR AND RECONSTRUCTION, 1861-1876, THE
Series: History of the Negro in America
Producer: Niagara Films
Tech Info: 16 mm/sound/bw/1 reel/19 min.
Date/Country: 1965   Type: Documentary
Distr/Arch: iu + mghf
Annotation: Traces the role of the Negro in American History
    from the outbreak of the Civil War through the reconstruc-
    tion period.   Points out the role of blacks in the fight
    for emancipation: discusses the 'Emancipation Proclama-

tion,' and indicates the provisions of the thirteenth, fourteenth, and fifteenth amendments to the Cconstitution.

CLASH BY NIGHT
Nar/Cast: Barbara Stanwyck + Paul Douglas + Marilyn Monroe + Benny Carter* Band
Screenplay: Alfred Hayes   Story: Clifford Odets
Producer: Harriet Parsons   Director: Fritz Lang
Studio/Company: RKO
Tech Info: 105 min.
Date/Country: 1952 + USA   Type: Feature
Annotation: This adaptation of the Clifford Odets play about an unresolved love triangle features the Benny Carter Band.

CLAUDINE
Nar/Cast: Diahann Carroll* + James Earl Jones* + Ralph Wilcox* + Lawrence Hilton Jacobs*
Screenplay: Les Pines + Tina Pines
Producer: Joyce Selznick + Hannah Weintraub + Third World Film Co.
Studio/Company: 20th Century Fox
Tech Info: 16 mm/color/sound/3 reels/92 min.
Date/Country: 1974 + USA   Type: Feature
Distr/Arch: fnc
Annotation: A romantic tragi-comedy about Manhattan Blacks today. The story revolves around a welfare mother (played by Diahann Carroll) of six who falls in love with a garbage man (played by James Earl Jones). Music and lyrics by Curtis Mayfield*, performed by Gladys Knight* and the Pips*.

CLEAN PASTURES
Studio/Company: Warner Brothers
Tech Info: 16 mm   Type: Animated Short
Distr/Arch: uas
Annotation: A parody of Green Pastures.

CLEF CLUB FIVE MINUTES FOR TRAIN
Studio/Company: Colored and Indian Film Company
Date/Country: 191- + USA

CLEOPATRA JONES AND THE CASINO OF GOLD
Nar/Cast: Tamara Dobson*   Director: Charles Bail
Studio/Company: Warner Brothers
Tech Info: 16 mm/sound/color/96 min.
Date/Country: 1974 + USA   Type: Feature
Distr/Arch: wsa
Annotation: Tamara Dobson is once again the high-style, high-standing Cleo in this espionage thriller. This time she is off to Hong Kong and Macao to rout the Dragon Princess, feared leader of an international narcotics operation.

CLEOPATRA JONES
Nar/Cast: Tamara Dobson* + Esther Rolle* + Bernie Casey* + Brenda Sykes* + Shelley Winters
Screenplay: Max Julien* + Sheldon Keller

Producer: William Tennant   Director: Jack Starrett
Studio/Company: Warner Brothers
Tech Info: 16 mm/sound/color/3 reels/89 min.
Date/Country: 1973 + USA   Type: Feature
Distr/Arch: wsa
Annotation: Cleopatra is an international narcotics agent
    bent on ridding drugs from the black community. Her task
    is made easier by good looks, knowledge of karate, and
    help from the community. Film shows supportive relation-
    ships between black men and black women. Musical score by
    J.J. Johnson*.

CLOWN PRINCES
Series: Our Gang
Nar/Cast: Our Gang + Billie Thomas*
Screenplay: Hal Law + Robert A. McGowan
Producer: Jack Chertok   Director: George Sidney
Studio/Company: MGM
Tech Info: bw/sound/1 reel
Date/Country: 1939 + USA   Type: Comedy Short
Annotation: The gang stages a circus performance to help
    Porky's parents pay their rent. Buckwheat appears as The
    Wild Man from Borneo. Billie Thomas stars as Buckwheat.

COAL BLACK AND DE SEBBEN DWARFS
Series: Merrie Melodies Cartoon
Screenplay: Warren Foster
Producer: Leon Schlesinger
Studio/Company: Warner Brothers
Tech Info: 16 mm/sound/bw
Date/Country: 1942 + USA   Type: Animated Short
Distr/Arch: uas
Annotation: A retelling of "Snow White and the Seven
    Dwarfs", this wartime offering parodies Snow White by
    making her a "luscious chocolate cutie" threatened by the
    Queen (who appears to be "African"). The dwarfs (all en-
    listed men) protect her until the arrival of "Prince Chaw-
    min." Animation by Rod Scribner.

COBBLER, THE
Series: Our Gang
Nar/Cast: Our Gang + Ernie Morrison* + Allen Hoskins*
Screenplay: Hal Roach
Producer: Hal Roach   Director: Tom McNamara
Studio/Company: Pathe
Tech Info: silent/bw/2 reels
Date/Country: 1923 + USA   Type: Comedy Short
Annotation: The gang members and their friend the cobbler
    take off for a picnic which results in various hijinks and
    ends with Farina's raid on a watermelon patch. Ernie Mor-
    rison stars as Sunshine Sammy and Allen Hoskins stars as
    Farina.

COCOTIER (LE)   Director: Jean Rouch
Date/Country: 1962 + France
Distr/Arch: saf
Annotation: Archived only.

COFFY
Nar/Cast: Pam Grier* + Booker Bradshaw* + Allan Arbus +
   Robert DoQui* + William Elliott*
Screenplay: Jack Hill
Producer: Robert A. Papagian
Studio/Company: American International
Tech Info: 16 mm/sound/color/3 reels/91 min.
Date/Country: 1973 + USA   Type: Feature
Distr/Arch: swa
Annotation: Pam Grier stars as a young nurse whose teenage
   sister is hospitalized after being induced to use drugs.
   Coffy embarks upon a personal campaign of vengeance.
   Robert DoQui plays King George, the pimp-pusher; Booker
   Bradshaw is Brunswick, her boyfriend.

COLEMAN HAWKINS QUARTET
Tech Info: 30 min.
Date/Country: 1961 + Belgium   Type: Documentary
Annotation: Coleman Hawkins* Quartet performs in a Brussels
   studio.

COLONIALISM: A CASE STUDY - NAMIBIA
Producer: United Nations
Tech Info: 16 mm/sound/color/1 reel/21 min.
Date/Country: 1975   Type: Documentary
Distr/Arch: iu + jou
Annotation: Discusses the present colonial status of the
   African nation of Namibia (Southwest Africa), tracing the
   historical development of its colonial rule. Attacks the
   present apartheid policy of South Africa and the South
   African refusal to turn the mandated territory of Namibia
   over to the United Nations.

COLOR LINE: THE MIXED RACES IN SOUTH AFRICA
Studio/Company: BBC-TV
Tech Info: 16 mm/bw/sound/1 reel/40 min.
Date/Country: 1971 + South Africa   Type: Documentary
Distr/Arch: tim
Annotation: "Colored" in South Africa is a legal category
   falling between white and black. The film is an analysis
   of this condition and its social implications for these
   persons of mixed blood.

COLOR OF JUSTICE, THE
Producer: Sterling
Tech Info: 16 mm/sound/color/26 min.
Date/Country: 1971 + USA   Type: Documentary
Distr/Arch: sef
Annotation: The Dred Scott case to the school busing situa-
   tion: Black Americans' search for equality and justice.

COLOR US BLACK
Producer: NET
Tech Info: 16 /sound/bw/2 reels/60 min.
Date/Country: 1968   Type: Documentary
Distr/Arch: iu + aim + cal
Annotation: Depicts the black man's struggle for his own
   identity over and above the white norm from the point of

view of the black students at predominantly black Howard
University in Washington, D.C. Traces development of a
four-day takeover of the administration building. Includes a student-made film.

COLORED_AMERICA_ON_PARADE
Series: Colored America on Parade
Studio/Company: All American News
Tech Info: 16 mm/bw/sound/1 reel/10 min.
Date/Country: 1940 + USA   Type: Documentary
Distr/Arch: kpf
Annotation: This was the first of a series of all-black new-
    sreels. Members of fraternal organizations march before
    the camera in various parades across the U.S.

COLORED_AMERICAN_WINNING_HIS_SUIT,_THE
Studio/Company: Frederick Douglass Film Co.
Date/Country: 1916 + USA
Annotation: Melodrama of a family's rise from slavery to
    freedom and success. Not only does the father prosper and
    acquire his former master's homestead, but he also
    provides an education for his daughter and son. He be-
    comes a good enough lawyer to assist the young woman he
    loves to win all, as his name implies (Bob Winall).

COLORED_AMERICANS_IN_THE_NATION'S_CAPITAL
Studio/Company: Toddy Pictures
Date/Country: 194- + USA   Type: Documentary

COLORED_AMERICANS
Studio/Company: Mutual Film Corporation
Date/Country: 1918 + USA

COLORED_CHAMPIONS_OF_SPORT
Nar/Cast: John Borican* + Gil Cruter*
Producer: Edward W. Lewis
Date/Country: 1940 + USA

COLORED_GIRL'S_LOVE,_A   Director: Mack Sennett
Studio/Company: Keystone   Type: Comedy Short
Annotation: Whites in blackface act out the comedy roles.

COLORED_MEN_IN_WHITE
Studio/Company: Toddy Pictures
Date/Country: 194- + USA   Type: Documentary

COLORED_STENGRAPHER,_THE
Studio/Company: Edison
Date/Country: 1909 + USA   Type: Comedy Short
Annotation: A white husband hides his blonde secretary from
    his wife by substituting a black charwoman in her place.

COLORED_TROOPS_AT_CHILLICOTHE
Studio/Company: Finley Film Company

COLORED_VILLAINY
Studio/Company: Keystone
Date/Country: 1915 + USA   Type: Comedy Short

Annotation: A local boy wins the girl from the out-of-towner
in a blackface farmer's daughter/traveling salesman joke.

COLOSSUS: THE FORBIN PROJECT
Alt Title(s): see The Forbin Project

COM-TAC 303
Nar/Cast: Billy Dee Williams* + Henry Fonda + Chad Everett +
Greg Morris* + Corinna Tsopel   Story: William D. Gordon +
James Doherty
Producer: William A. Throwbridge + Joseph Cranston
Director: Robert Totten
Studio/Company: Pinnacle Productions
Date/Country: 1977 + USA

COME BACK, AFRICA
Nar/Cast: Lewis N'Kosi* + Blake Modisane* + Miriam Makeba*
Screenplay: Lionel Rogosin + Lewis N'Kosi* + Blake Modisane*
Producer: Lionel Rogosin   Director: Lionel Rogosin
Tech Info: 16 mm/sound/bw/3 reels/90 min.
Date/Country: 1959 + South Africa   Type: Dramatized Docu-
mentary
Distr/Arch: imp + imr
Annotation: Semi-documentary   about repressive life in
apartheid South Africa. Miriam Makeba* makes a brief ap-
pearance as singer in the slums of Sophiatown outside
Joahannesberg. Won Italian Film Critics Award at Venice
Film Festival (1960).

COME BACK, CHARLESTON BLUE
Nar/Cast: Godfrey Cambridge* + Raymond St. Jacques* + Minnie
Gentry* + Percy Rodrigues*
Screenplay: Bontche Schweig + Pegg Elliott   Story: Chester
Himes
Producer: Samuel Goldwyn, Jr.   Director: Mark Warren*
Studio/Company: Warner Brothers
Tech Info: 16 mm/sound/color/3 reels/100 min.
Date/Country: 1972 + USA   Type: Feature
Distr/Arch: arg + cwf + ics + ker + mod + mac + tfc + twy +
wcf + who + wsa
Annotation: Police detectives Cambridge (Grave Digger Jones)
and St. Jacques (Coffin Ed Johnson) stick their noses
into a war between the Mafia and a black narcotics pusher
for control of the Harlem drug trade. Musical score com-
posed and conducted by Donny Hathaway*, supervised by
Quincy Jones*, of this adaptation of The Heat's On,
Hines's novel.

COME BACK, MISS PIPPS
Series: Our Gang
Nar/Cast: Our Gang + Billie Thomas*
Screenplay: Hal Law + Robert A. McGowan
Producer: MGM   Director: Edward Cahn
Studio/Company: MGM
Tech Info: bw/sound/1 reel
Date/Country: 1941 + USA   Type: Comedy Short
Annotation: When the school board chairman fires beloved
Miss Pipps for giving a birthday party for Mickey at

school - the gang puts on a skit which results in the
chairman being demoted to gardener. Billie Thomas stars
as Buckwheat.

COME BACK
Nar/Cast: Louise Fullen* + K.D. Nollan* + Ellen Ray* + Ethel
   Watson* + Victor Price*
Producer: Leigh Whipper*
Date/Country: 1922 + USA

COME DAY, GO DAY, GOD SEND SUNDAY
Producer: Niklason/Platt Educational Films
Tech Info: 16 mm/sound/color/52 min.
Date/Country: 1974 + USA   Type: Documentary
Distr/Arch: ngs
Annotation: Focuses on black church members in Rappahannock
   County, Virginia. Provided by Center for Southern
   Folklore.

COME ON COWBOY
Nar/Cast: Mantan Moreland* + Mauryne Brent* + Johnny Lee*
Studio/Company: Goldmax Productions
Date/Country: 1948 + USA

COMEDIANS, tHE
Nar/Cast: Richard Burton + Elizabeth Taylor + Alec Guiness +
   Peter Ustinov + Georg Stanford Brown* + Roscoe Lee Brwone*
   + Gloria Foster* + James Earl Jones* + Raymond St. Jac-
   ques* + Cicely Tyson*
Screenplay: Graham Greene   Story: Graham Greene
Producer: Peter Glenville   Director: Peter Glenville
Studio/Company: MGM
Tech Info: color/sound/5 reels/160 min./cinemascope availa-
   ble
Date/Country: 1967 + USA   Type: Feature
Distr/Arch: fnc
Annotation: Shot in Dahomey, West Africa, The Comedians at-
   tempts to depict a reign of terror under black
   dictatorship in the Caribbean.

COMES MIDNIGHT
Nar/Cast: Eddie Green* + James Baskett* + Elinor Seagures* +
   Bonnie Skeet* + Amanda Rudolph*
Studio/Company: Sepia Art Picture Company
Date/Country: 1940   Type: Feature

COMIC, THE
Nar/Cast: Dick Van Dyke + Michele Lee + Mickey Rooney +
   Mantan Moreland* + Isabell Sanford*
Screenplay: Carl Reiner
Producer: Carl Reiner + A. Ruben   Director: Carl Reiner
Studio/Company: Columbia
Tech Info: 16 mm/sound/color/3 reels/94 min.
Date/Country: 1969 + USA   Type: Feature
Distr/Arch: arg + bud + ccc + cha + cwf + ics + ker + mac +
   mod + new + roa + sel + wcf + wel + who + wil
Annotation: Mantan Moreland has a minor role in this movie
   about comedy stars of the silent film era.

COMING HOME
War/Cast: Jane Fonda + Jon Voight + Bruce Dern + Olivia
  Cole*
Screenplay: Waldo Salt + Robert C.Jones
Producer: Jerome Hellman   Director: Hal Ashby
Studio/Company: United Artists
Date/Country: 1977 + USA   Type: Feature
Annotation: Olivia Cole is a nurse (small role) at the
  Veterans Hospital in which Voight, a disabled veteran of
  the Viet Nam War, meets Jane Fonda, the wife of an officer
  serving in Viet Nam. Opening scene has black and white
  disabled men, who are nonprofessionals, discussing the
  meaning of the war. The impact of the war on the lives of
  these young people and on all Americans is examined in
  this film.

COMMENCEMENT DAY
Series: Our Gang
War/Cast: Our Gang + Ernie Morrison* + Jannie Hoskins* +
  Allen Hoskins*
Screenplay: Hal Roach
Producer: Hal Roach   Director: Robert McGowan
Studio/Company: Pathe
Tech Info: silent/bw/2 reels
Date/Country: 1924 + USA   Type: Comedy Short
Annotation: Though it may be the last day of the school, it
  is not any less hectic: saxophones filled with pepper,
  Mickey playing a violin with a frog down his back, and a
  beehive let loose in the classroom. Ernie Morrison stars
  as Sunshine Sammy, Jannie Hoskins stars as Mango and Allen
  Hoskins stars as Farina.

CONDEMNED MEN
Alt Title(s): Four Shall Die

CONDOR, EL
War/Cast: Jim Brown* + Lee Van Cleef + Patricia O'Neal +
  Mariana Hill
Screenplay: Larry Cohen + Steven Carahatsos   Story: Steven
  Carahatsos
Producer: Andre de Toth   Director: John Guillermin
Studio/Company: National General
Tech Info: 16 mm/sound/color/102 min./dubbed
Date/Country: 1970 + USA   Type: Feature
Distr/Arch: fnc + swa
Annotation: Jim Brown gets involved in storming a fabled
  fortress (El Condor) with Lee Van Cleef and some motley
  apaches thinking to find the buried gold of Maximillion.
  Things do not work out as planned even after much sex and
  slaughter.

CONFEDERATE SPY, THE
Tech Info: silent/bw
Date/Country: 1910 + USA   Type: Dramatic Short
Annotation: Uncle Daniel a Negro spy for the Confederacy
  dies in front of a Northern squad happy to have done it
  for his "massa's sake."

CONFORMITY_AND_THE_CRUTCH
Nar/Cast: Dr. Thomas Pettigrew
Producer: NET Network
Studio/Company: NET Network
Tech Info: 16 mm/bw/sound/30 min.
Date/Country: 1961 + USA   Type: Short
Distr/Arch: adl
Annotation: The psychology of bigotry and the difference
   between pathological bigotry and bigotry due to social
   conformity are discussed in relationship to research in
   sociology. Thomas Pettigrew narrates.

CONFRONTATION_IN_COLOR
Producer: Greater Philadelphia Movement
Tech Info: 16 mm/sound/color/40 min.
Date/Country: 1968 + USA   Type: Documentary
Distr/Arch: afr
Annotation: 'Who is human' is discussed by Blacks and
   whites.

CONFRONTATION_IN_WASHINGTON:_RESURRECTION_CITY
Producer: Koplin and Grinker
Tech Info: 16 mm/sound/color/15 min.
Date/Country: 1970 + USA   Type: Documentary
Distr/Arch: pic
Annotation: In May, 1968, the nation's poor (including Afro-
   Americans, native Americans, Mexican-Americans, and Ap-
   palachian whites) arrived in Washington by mule train,
   truck, bus, rail and on foot. Their trip as well as their
   building of Resurrection City is shown.

CONFRONTATION:_DIALOGUE_IN_BLACK_AND_WHITE
Producer: PBL + NET
Tech Info: 16 mm/bw/sound/1 reel/35 min.
Date/Country: 1967 + USA   Type: Documentary
Distr/Arch: iu
Annotation: Presents a dialogue of one hundred citizens in-
   vited to a studio to confront each other with their views
   on the racial situation following a tense summer in Chi-
   cago. Screening of a film of Chicago's west side to an
   interracial audience is followed by canded discussion.

CONFRONTED
Producer: NET
Tech Info: 16 mm/sound/bw/1 reel/50 min.
Date/Country: 1955 + USA   Type: Documentary
Distr/Arch: iu
Annotation: The issue of integration in schools, jobs, and
   housing confronts several Northern communities: in Queens,
   a New York City borough; in St. Louis, in Chicago, and in
   Folcroft, Penn.

CONGO_CROSSING
Nar/Cast: Virginia Mayo + Rex Ingram* + George Nadar + Peter
   Lorre
Screenplay: Rich Simmons
Producer: Howard Christie   Director: Joseph Pevney

Studio/Company: Universal-International
Tech Info: 16 mm/sound/color/87 min.
Date/Country: 1956 + USA   Type: Feature
Distr/Arch: uni
Annotation: Various fugitive types (including Rex Ingram as
   Gorman) come together in a mythical West African state,
   Congotanga, where they are free from extradition.

CONGO MAISIE
Nar/Cast: Ann Southern + John Carroll + Ernest Whitman* +
   Martin Wilkins* + Nathan Curry*
Screenplay: Mary McCall, Jr.   Story: Wilson   Collison
   Director: H.C. Potter
Studio/Company: MGM
Date/Country: 1940 + USA   Type: Feature
Annotation: Female magician (Southern as Maisie Ravier)
   stranded at a lonely medical outpost in the Congo, solves
   marital problems, turns back native attack with tricks,
   and falls in love. Blacks in movie seen mostly as na-
   tives, uneducated, etc. easily tricked by magical Maisie.
   Whitman is Varnoi; Wilkins is Zia, Curry is Laemba.

CONGO
Nar/Cast: Truman Bradley
Screenplay: John La Touche + Frank La Touche   Director:
   Andre Cavvin
Studio/Company: Warner Brothers
Date/Country: 1944   Type: Feature
Distr/Arch: wsa + moma

CONJURE WOMAN, THE
Nar/Cast: Evelyn Preer* + Percy Verwayen*
Studio/Company: Micheaux Film Corporation
Tech Info: 35 mm/silent/bw
Date/Country: 1926 + USA   Type: Feature

CONNECTION, THE
Nar/Cast: Warren Finnerty + Garry Goodrow + Carl Lee* +
   Roscoe Lee Brown* + William Redfield   Story: Jack Geeber
Producer: Shirley Clarke + Lewis Allen   Director: Shirley
   Clarke
Studio/Company: The Connection Co + Allen   Hodgdon   Produc-
   tions + Films Around the World
Tech Info: 16 mm/sound/bw/102 min.
Date/Country: 1961 + USA   Type: Feature
Distr/Arch: nyf
Annotation: Filmed in documentary style, this movie focuses
   on various drug addicts waiting for their "connection" in
   a New York loft. Roscoe Lee Brown plays J.J. the photo-
   grapher and Carl Lee stars as "Cowboy." Jazz by Freddie
   Redd* and quartet.

CONQUEROR, THE
Studio/Company: Fox
Date/Country: 1917   Type: Feature
Annotation: The plot of this screen "biography" of Sam
   Houston, future hero of the Battle of San Jacinto,
   devolves on the malapropism of a Mammy (white, in black-

face) whose mistress is a young woman Sam Houston calls
on.   When he is told that she can not see him until he
"strained to be Constable" (instead of that she was "con-
strainedly unable" to see him), he launches into a
political career.

CONRACK
Nar/Cast: Jon Voight + Paul Winfield* + Hume Cronyn + Madge
   Sinclair*   Story: Pat Conroy
Producer: Martin Ritt + Harriet Frank, Jr.   Director:
   Martin Ritt
Studio/Company: Twentieth Century Fox
Tech Info: 16 mm/sound/color/3 reels/107 min.
Date/Country: 1974 + USA   Type: Feature
Distr/Arch: fnc
Annotation: Conrack tells the true story of a white school
   teacher's experiences teaching and living among black
   children on one of the Sea Islands off the coast of South
   Carolina. Adapted from the novel, The Water Is Wide.

CONTEMPORARY EDUCATION: GHANA
Tech Info: 16 mm/sound/bw/30 min.
Date/Country: 1962 + Ghana   Type: Documentary
Distr/Arch: ueuwis
Annotation: An interview with headmasters of secondary
   schools in Ghana.

CONTINENT OF AFRICA: LAND BELOW THE SAHARA
Series: Africa in Change
Producer: Encyclopedia Britannica Films, Inc.
Tech Info: 16 mm/sound/color/1 reel/21 min.
Date/Country: 1966   Type: Documentary
Distr/Arch: iu + ebec
Annotation: Pictures the great diversty of physical geo-
   graphy of Africa,   and points out early European settle-
   ments and the influence of the colonial powers on the con-
   tinent. Surveys the continent's rich resources and con-
   cludes with an orientation concerning current social and
   political problems.

CONVICTS 4
Alt Title(s): Reprieve
Nar/Cast: Sammy Davis, Jr.* + Ben Gazzara + Vincent Price
Screenplay: Millard Kaufman
Producer: A. Ronald Lubin   Director: Millard Kaufman
Studio/Company: Allied Artists
Tech Info: sound/bw/105 min.
Date/Country: 1962 + USA   Type: Feature
Annotation: Davis Is Wino, The "Halloween Bandit," in this
   biographical drama of John Resko (Gazzara) who, during the
   depression, killed a storekeeper who tried to prevent him
   from stealing a toy for his child. Wino is one of the
   prisoners at Dannemora with whom the belligerant Resko is
   in constant trouble before his rehabilitation through
   painting takes place.

COOGAN'S BLUFF
Nar/Cast: James Edwards* + Clint Eastwood + Susan Clark

Screenplay: Herman Miller + Dean Riesner + Howard Rodman
Producer: Don Siegal   Director: Don Siegal
Studio/Company: Universal
Tech Info: 16 mm/sound
Date/Country: 1968 + USA   Type: Feature
Distr/Arch: ccc + cwf + roa + swa + tmc + twy + uni
Annotation: Clint Eastwood as Coogan goes east to extradite
  a criminal. James Edwards plays Jackson.

COOL BREEZE
Nar/Cast: Raymond St. Jacques* + Judy Pace* + Thalmus
  Rasulala* + Jim Watkins* + Lincoln Kilpatrick* + Sam Laws
Screenplay: Barry Pollack   Story: W.R. Burnett
Producer: Gene Corman   Director: Barry Pollack
Studio/Company: MGM
Tech Info: 16 mm/sound/color/3 reels/101 min.
Date/Country: 1972 + USA   Type: Feature
Distr/Arch: fnc
Annotation: A remake of The Asphalt Jungle, Cool Breeze is a
  crime caper about a super cool con artist who masterminds
  a three million dollar jewel robbery, presumably to set up
  a Black People's Bank.

COOL WORLD, THE
Nar/Cast: Hampton Clanton* + Yolanda Rodriguez* + Bostic
  Felton* + Carl Lee* + Clarence Williams, III* + Gloria
  Foster* + Georgia Burke* + Marilyn Cox + Mul Waldron +
  Dizzy Gillespie* + Yusef Lateef* + Arthur Taylor + Richard
  Ward* + Jay Brooks*
Screenplay: Shirley Clarke + Carl Lee*   Story: Warren Mil-
  ler
Producer: Frederick Wiseman   Director: Shirley Clarke
Studio/Company: Wiseman Film Productions + Cinema 5 Distrib-
  uting Cc.
Tech Info: 16 mm/bw/sound/3 reels/104 min.
Date/Country: 1964 + USA   Type: Feature
Distr/Arch: zph
Annotation: The Cool World is a film about the human condi-
  tion in Harlem. It focuses on Duke Curtis' life. Gloria
  Foster plays Duke's mother, left alone to head the family,
  who takes part of her frustrations (re men) out on her
  boy. Duke (Clarence Williams III) wants to be a "cool"
  killer, the biggest man on the street.

COOLEY HIGH
Nar/Cast: Glynn Turman* + Lawrence-Hilton Jacobs* + Garrett
  Morris* + Cynthia Davis* + Corin Rogers*
Screenplay: Eric Monte
Producer: Samuel Z. Arkoff   Director: Michael Schultz*
Studio/Company: American International
Tech Info: 16 mm/sound/color/107 min.
Date/Country: 1975 + USA   Type: Feature
Distr/Arch: swa
Annotation: This film is an unflinching look at ghetto life
  and dreams. The transition from teenager to young adult
  is a trying, sometimes brutal experience which some
  survive and some do not.

COON TOWN SUFFRAGETTES
Producer: Sigmund Lubin
Studio/Company: Independent
Date/Country: c. 1914 + USA
Annotation: Southern "Mammies" try to keep their no-good
    husbands out of saloons in this variant of Lysistrata.

COONSKIN
Nar/Cast: Betty White* + Charles Gordone + Scatman Crothers*
    + Philip Thomas*
Screenplay: Ralph Bakshi
Producer: Albert S. Ruddy   Director: Ralph Bakshi
Studio/Company: Bryanston Release
Tech Info: 16 mm/sound/color/83 min.
Date/Country: 1975 + USA   Type: Feature
Distr/Arch: swa
Annotation: With animation and live action, Bakshi again
    attempts satirically to convey violence and frustration in
    urban America. Cartoon characters: Brother Bear, Brother
    Fox, Old Man Bone, Brother Rabbit. Voices by Barry White,
    Charles Gordone, Scatman Crothers, and Philip Thomas.

COQUETTE
Nar/Cast: Louise Beavers* + Mary Pickford + Johnny Mack
    Brown
Screenplay: John Grey + Allen McNeill
Producer: Pickford Corp.   Director: Sam Taylor
Studio/Company: United Artists
Tech Info: sound/bw/9 reels/6,993 ft.
Date/Country: 1929 + USA   Type: Feature
Annotation: Beavers is Julia in this melodrama about a
    father who kills a man he thinks is beneath his southern
    belle daughter (Pickford) to keep them from marrying.

CORNBREAD, EARL AND ME
Nar/Cast: Moses Gunn* + Rosalind Cash* + Bernie Casey* +
    Keith Wilkes* + Madge Sinclair* + Lawrence Fishburne, III*
Screenplay: Leonard Lamesdorf   Story: Ronald F. Fair
Producer: Joe Manduke   Director: Joe Manduke
Studio/Company: American International
Tech Info: 16 mm/color/sound/3 reels/99 min.
Date/Country: 1975 + USA   Type: Feature
Distr/Arch: swa
Annotation: Cornbread (Keith Wilkes) tragically copes with
    the pressures of the inner-city while relying on his
    basketball talents to make a better life for himself and
    his family. His friend, Young Wilford, played by Lawrence
    Fishburne, III, sets the moral tone for the adult world in
    the city which butchers human beings as well as hogs
    (adapted from the novel Hog Butcher). Musical score by
    Donald Byrd*, performed by the Blackbyrds*.

CORNER, THE
Producer: Robert Ford
Tech Info: 16 mm/sound/bw/26 min.
Date/Country: 1963 + USA   Type: Documentary
Distr/Arch: mac
Annotation: 'The Vice Lords' describe their way of life in

Chicago.

CORPSE ACCUSES, THE
Studio/Company: Toddy Pictures
Date/Country: 1946   Type: Feature
Annotation: A mystery-comedy.

COTTON COMES TO HARLEM
Nar/Cast: Raymond St. Jacques* + Godfrey Cambridge* + Redd
   Foxx* + Calvin Lockhart* + Judy Pace* + John Anderson +
   J.D. Cannon + Emily Yancy* + Frederick O'Neal*
Screenplay: Ossie Davis* + Arnold Perl Story: Chester
   Himes*
Producer: Samuel Goldwyn, Jr.   Director: Ossie Davis* +
   Sam Bennerson*
Studio/Company: United Artists
Tech Info: 16 mm/color/sound/3 reels/97 min.
Date/Country: 1970 + USA   Type: Feature
Distr/Arch: uas
Annotation: A comedy about life in Harlem based on the novel
   by black author Chester Himes. A shady back-to-Africa
   movement, syndicate money, and a bale of cotton turn
   Harlem upside down.

COTTON-PICKIN' DAYS
Nar/Cast: Forbes Randolph Kentucky Jubilee Singers*
Studio/Company: Tiffany
Tech Info: 1 reel
Date/Country: 1930 + USA   Type: Musical Short
Annotation: The Forbes Randolph choir sings, among other
   things, "Camptown Races" and "Way Down Upon the Swanee
   River," with background of Southern cabins and singing
   field hands.

COUNT OF MONTE CRISTO, THE
Nar/Cast: Clarence Muse* + Robert Donat + Elissa Landi
   Director: Rowland V. Lee
Studio/Company: United Artists
Tech Info: 16 mm/bw/sound/127 min.
Date/Country: 1934 + Britain   Type: Feature
Distr/Arch: alb + bud + mog + sel + who + wil + wrs
Annotation: Third remake of Dumas's classic novel, with
   Clarence Muse in the role of Ali, one of Dante's faithful
   lieutenants.

COUNTDOWN AT KUSINI
Nar/Cast: Ruby Dee* + Greg Morris* + Ossie Davis* + Jab Adu*
   + Yomi Obileye* + Funso Adeolu* + Elsie Olusola* + Michael
   Henderson + Rasheed Onikoyi* + Thomas Baptiste* + Manu
   Dibango* + Kola Ogunnaike* + Ibidun Allison* + Cheryl
   Borde* + John Chukwa* + Joseph Loyode* + Nguba Aspinal* +
   Helen Okorodudu* + Nathlyn Flowers*
Screenplay: Ossie Davis* + Al Freeman, Jr.*
Producer: Ladi Ladibo* + Lillian Benhow* + Delta Sigma Theta
   Sorority Director: Ossie Davis*
Studio/Company: Independent
Tech Info: 16 mm/sound/color/3 ree
Date/Country: 1975 + USA   Type: Feature

Distr/Arch: swa
Annotation: Shot in Lagos, Nigeria, <u>Countdown</u>--the first
    entertainment film financed primarily by a black women's
    organization--is a romantic adventure about revolution and
    political intrigue in Africa. Set in the fictitious
    African country Fahari, the film shows the growing aware-
    ness of an Afro-American musician Red Salter (Morris) and
    his identification with the aspirations and struggle for
    independence of his African brothers and sisters, in the
    persons of Motapo (Davis) and Leah Matanzima (Dee).

<u>COUNTY CHAIRMAN, THE</u>
Nar/Cast: Will Rogers + Evelyn Venable + Mickey Rooney +
    Stepin Fetchit*
Producer: Edward W. Butcher   Director: John Blystone
Studio/Company: Fox
Date/Country: 1935 + USA   Type: Feature
Annotation: Will Rogers plays a party chariman in Tomahawk,
    County, Wyo., trying to get a political neophyte elected.
    Film has many amusing insights into American politics and
    has Stepin Fetchit as Rogers' foil on various escapades

<u>COURTSHIP OF MILES STANDISH, THE</u>
Nar/Cast: Noble Johnson* + Charles Ray + Enid Bennett + E.
    Alyn + Warren Joseph Dowling + Sam Grosse + Norval Mac-
    Gregor
Producer: Charles Ray Prod.   Director: Frederick Sullivan
Tech Info: 35 mm/silent/bw/9 reels
Date/Country: 1923 + USA   Type: Feature
Annotation: Noble Johnson has a small role in this histori-
    cal romance.

<u>COUSIN WILBUR</u>
Series: Our Gang
Nar/Cast: Our Gang + Billie Thomas*
Screenplay: Hal Law + Robert A. McGowan
Producer: Jack Chertok   Director: George Sidney
Studio/Company: MGM
Tech Info: bw/sound/1 reel
Date/Country: 1939 + USA   Type: Comedy Short
Annotation: An accident insurance scheme, suggested by Al-
    falfa's prissy cousin Wilbur to help the club nearly
    wrecks them until Wilbur beats up the local bullies who
    had emptied the club's 'accident' insurance treasury by
    punchng out the neighborhood. Billie Thomas stars as
    Buckwheat.

<u>COWARD, THE</u>
Nar/Cast: Charles Ray + Frank Keenan + Gertrude Claire
    Director: Thomas H. Ince
Studio/Company: Triangle
Tech Info: slent/bw
Date/Country: 1915 + USA   Type: Feature
Annotation: The coward in this melodrama about the Civil War
    is a young southerner who disgraces his planter family by
    deserting the Confederate army. He later acquits himself
    properly by escaping to give overheard Yankee information
    to the Confederates. He is aided and abetted by a Negro

servant who shoots one of the Yankee soldiers. The
servant is played on "darkened down" makeup, not in blackface.

COWBOY CANTEEN
Nar/Cast: Charles Starrett + Mills Brothers*   Director: Lew
   Landers
Tech Info: 72 min.
Date/Country: 1944 + USA   Type: Feature
Annotation: Musical western features the Mills Brothers and
   other groups.

COWBOYS, THE
Nar/Cast: Roscoe Lee Brown* + John Wayne + Bruce Dern
   Director: Mark Rydell
Studio/Company: Warners
Tech Info: 16 mm/sound/color/128 min.
Date/Country: 1972 + USA   Type: Feature
Distr/Arch: arg + bud + con + ics + ker + mac + mod + mot +
   roa + swa + tfc + twy + wcf + wel
Annotation: Brown is a cook on the trail in yet another John
   Wayne western.

COWS OF DOLO KEN PAYE, THE
Producer: Holt, Rinehart and Winston
Tech Info: 16 mm/sound/color/1 reel/31 min.
Date/Country: 1970 + USA   Type: Documentary
Distr/Arch: iu + hraw
Annotation: Identifies conflicts within the Kpelle tribe in
   Fokwele, Liberia, regarding the traditional and modern
   adaptations of farming and law. Illustrates the complex
   conflicts between the prosperous, cattle-owning chief and
   the ordinary farmers.

CRADLE ROBBERS
Series: Our Gang
Nar/Cast: Our Gang + Ernie Morrison* + Allen Hoskins*
Screenplay: Hal Roach
Producer: Hal Roach   Director: Robert McGowan
Studio/Company: Pathe
Tech Info: silent/bw/2 reels
Date/Country: 1924 + USA   Type: Comedy Short
Annotation: Forced to babysit, the gang members come up with
   an ingenious way to baby sit and fish. They also hold a
   baby contest which ends with the police chasing them and a
   gypsy.   Ernie Morrison stars as Sunshine Sammy and Allen
   Hoskins stars as Farina.

CRASH DIVE
Nar/Cast: Tyrone Power + Anne Baxter + Dana Andrews + Dame
   May Whitty + Ben Carter*   Story: W.R. Burnett
Producer: Milton Sperling   Director: Archie Mayo
Studio/Company: Twentieth Century-Fox
Date/Country: 1943 + USA   Type: Feature
Annotation: Typical war story with commanding officer and
   his exec both in love with same nurse. Ben Carter plays
   Oliver Cromwell Jones, a navy messman probably modeled on
   Dorie Miller, who manned a machine gun, downing enemy

planes during the Japanese attack on Pearl Harbor.

CRAZY_HORSE
Series: Our Gang
Nar/Cast: Our Gang + Allen Hoskins*
Producer: Hal Roach + Robert F. McGowan   Director: Robert
   F. McGowan
Studio/Company: MGM + Roach
Tech Info: super 8 mm/bw/silent/2 reels
Date/Country: 1928 + USA   Type: Comedy Short
Distr/Arch: bla
Annotation: A bored little rich girl lets the gang into her
   mansion which her father has wired for an April Fool's
   party. Mayhem breaks loose when the gang is led around
   setting off all the booby-traps. Allen Hoskins stars as
   Farina.

CRAZY_HOUSE/FUNZAPOPPIN'
Nar/Cast: Olsen and Johnson + Count Basie and his band* +
   Delta Rhythm Boys*   Director: Edward F. Cline
Tech Info: 80 min.
Date/Country: 1943 + USA   Type: Feature
Annotation: Sequel to Hellzapoppin' includes Count Basie and
   the Delta Rhythm Boys performing.

CRAZY_HOUSE
Nar/Cast: Louise Franklin* + Olson and Johnson + Count Basie
   and his Band*
Screenplay: Robert Lees + Frederic Renaldo   Director:
   Edward F. Cline
Studio/Company: Universal
Tech Info: 16 mm/sound/bw/80 min
Date/Country: 1943 + USA   Type: Feature
Distr/Arch: tmc + uni
Annotation: Basie and his band perform along with many
   others in this Olson and Johnson style musical-comedy with
   a thin story line.

CRIME_AND_PUNISHMENT,_U.S.A.
Nar/Cast: Frank Silvera* + George Hamilton
Screenplay: Walter Newman   Story: Feodor Dostoevski
Producer: Denis Sanders   Director: Denis Sanders
Studio/Company: Allied Artists
Tech Info: 16 mm/sound/bw/96 min.
Date/Country: 1959 + USA   Type: Feature
Distr/Arch: cin
Annotation: Silvera is police lieutenant A.D. Porter, the
   pursuer of modern-dress Raskolinkov (Hamilton), who is
   highly conversant with abnormal psychology as well as con-
   temporary law enforcement tactics.

CRIME_SMASHER
Nar/Cast: Frank Graham + Mantan Moreland* + Richard Cromwell
     Director: James Tinling
Studio/Company: Monogram
Date/Country: 1943 + USA   Type: Feature
Annotation: Mantan Moreland co-stars with Frank Graham in
   this gangster film.

CRIME STREET
Studio/Company: Toddy Pictures
Tech Info: 66 min.
Date/Country: 194- + USA   Type: Feature
Annotation: An action film about juvenile delinquency.

CRIMSON FOG, THE
Nar/Cast: Thomas   Moseley* + Inez Clough* + Lawrence
   Chenault* + Vera Temple* + Billy Andrews* + Kitty Ar-
   blanche* + Billy Sheppard* + Alvin Childress*
Producer: Charles Allman White
Studio/Company: Paragon Pictures
Date/Country: 1932 + USA

CRIMSON SKULL, THE
Alt Title(s): Scarlet Claw
Nar/Cast: Anita Bush* + Lawrence Chenault* + Bill Pickett* +
   Steve Reynolds*
Tech Info: 30mm/ silent/ bw/ 6 reels
Date/Country: 1921 + USA   Type: Feature
Annotation: Filmed on location in Boley, Oklahoma (all black
   town), this mystery western, as it was billed, is about
   outlaws who threaten the peace of law-abiding citizens,
   and who are bested by the good guys. The real champion
   rodeo rider, Bill Pickett, appears, as well as the one-
   legged cowboy Steve Reynolds, along with thirty black cowboys.

CRISIS IN LEVITTOWN, P.A.
Nar/Cast: Dr. Dan W. Dodson
Producer: Dynamic Films   Director: Lee R. Bobker + Lester
   Becker
Studio/Company: Dynamic Films
Tech Info: 16 mm/bw/sound/30 min.
Date/Country: 1957 + USA   Type: Documentary
Distr/Arch: mac + kpf
Annotation: Crisis in Levittown shows a series of interviews
   by a New York University sociologist with residents of a
   white Pennsylvania community shortly after a black family
   with three children move in.   The spectrum of white
   responses to this event is analyzed by Dan Dodson.

CRISIS IN MEDICINE, A
Producer: NET
Tech Info: 16 mm/sound/bw/1 reel/15 min.
Date/Country: 1969 + USA   Type: Documentary
Distr/Arch: iu
Annotation: Most black people are being provided with inadequate medical and dental care and today there are fewer
   black doctors graduating from Medical schools than there
   were in 1955. In black communities there is one black
   doctor for every 5,000 people compared to a ratio of one
   physician to 670 people in white communities.

CROIX DU SUD
Studio/Company: Pathe
Date/Country: 1932 + French   Type: Feature

Annotation: An African king spurns his white wife for a
   black one. Shot in Africa and Joinville.

CROOKED MONEY
Alt Title(s): see While Thousands Cheer

CROWNING EXPERIENCE, THE
Nar/Cast: Muriel Smith* + Louis Byles* + Ann Buckles* + Anna
   Marie McCurdy* + Phyllis Konstam Austin* + Robert An-
   derson* + George McCurdy* + William Pawley, Jr.*
Screenplay: Alan Thornhill
Producer: Moral Rearmament   Director: Rickard Tegstrom
Studio/Company: Moral Rearmament
Tech Info: 16 mm/sound/color/3 reels/102 min.
Date/Country: 1960   Type: Feature
Distr/Arch: aim
Annotation: All black cast in the screen version of the life
   of Mary McLeod Bethune, black woman educator, advisor to
   four U.S. presidents and founder of Bethune-Cookman Col-
   lege.

CRUISE OF THE HELLION, THE
Nar/Cast: Martin Turner* + Donald Keith + Edna Murphy
Screenplay: George W. Pyper
Producer: Duke Worne Productions   Director: Duke Worne
Studio/Company: Rayart-Imperial Photoplay
Tech Info: 35 mm/silent/bw/7 reels/6,089 ft.
Date/Country: 1927 + USA   Type: Feature
Annotation: A romantic melodrama with a young man shanghied
   to sea where he helps to quell a mutiny and gets the girl.
   No specific information about Turner's role available.

CRY OF JAZZ   Director: Edward Bland
Tech Info: 33 min.
Date/Country: 1959 + USA   Type: Documentary
Annotation: Discussion of jazz and the role of Blacks in
   America. Includes music played by Sun Ra* and his
   orchestra.

CRY, THE BELOVED COUNTRY
Nar/Cast: Canada Lee* + Sidney Poitier* + Charles Carson +
   Michael Goodliffe + Lionel Ngakane* + Edric Connor* + Al-
   bertina Temba*
Screenplay: Alan Paton   Story: Alan Paton
Producer: Zoltan Korda   Director: Zoltan Korda
Studio/Company: United Artists
Tech Info: 16 mm/color/sound/3 reels/105 min.
Date/Country: 1952 + Britain   Type: Feature
Distr/Arch: bud + cal + mac + twy + wrs
Annotation: British, American, and South African filmmakers
   and actors collaborated in filming the drama in authentic
   locations. It focuses on Stephen Kumalo (Canada Lee), an
   African minister, who journeys to Johannesburg to find his
   wayward son. The tragedy of the South African experience
   unfolds during his search. Poitier is a young priest.

CURSE OF THE CAT PEOPLE, THE
Nar/Cast: Simone Simon + Ann Carter + Sir Lancelot*

Screenplay: DeWitt Bodeen
Producer: Val Lewton   Director: Gunther Fritsch + Robert
   Wise
Studio/Company: RKO Radio
Tech Info: 16 mm/sound/bw/70 min.
Date/Country: 1944 + USA   Type: Feature
Distr/Arch: mac
Annotation: A sensitive little girl creates an imaginary
   playmate who turns out to be her dead mother. Sir
   Lancelot as Edward offers sympathy and understanding to
   the lonely child played by Ann Carter.

CURTAIN POLE, THE
Nar/Cast: Mack Sennett + Linda Arvidson + Florence Lawrence
   + Harry Salter
Producer: D.W. Griffith + Biograph   Director: D.W. Griffith
Studio/Company: Biograph
Tech Info: 35 mm/silent/bw/765 ft.
Date/Country: 1909 + USA   Type: Comedy Short
Annotation: Film depicts a Frenchman who tries to help his
   hostess hang a curtain pole, breaks the pole and sets out
   to replace it. His inebriated misadventures include a
   trip through "Darky" town where the victims of his revel-
   ries are black (whites in black face).

CUSTARD NINE
Producer: Clarence Muse* (assistant Producer)
Studio/Company: Harris Dickson Film Company for Pathe
Date/Country: 1911 + USA
Annotation: A sketch of Virgil Custard leading Vicksburg's
   black baseball team through assorted farcical adventures.

DAD FOR A DAY
Series: Our Gang
Nar/Cast: Our Gang + Billie Thomas*
Screenplay: Hal Law + Robert A. McGowan
Producer: Jack Chertok   Director: Edward Cahn
Studio/Company: MGM
Tech Info: bw/sound/1 reel
Date/Country: 1939 + USA   Type: Comedy Short
Annotation: The gang prevails on Mr. Henry to be Mickey's
   'dad for a day' at their Father and Son picnic. At the
   end he asks Mickey's mother to marry him. Billie Thomas
   stars as Buckwheat.

DAKAR FESTIVAL OF NEGRO ARTS
Alt Title(s): See The First World Festival of Negro Arts

DANCE: ECHOES OF JAZZ
Producer: NET
Tech Info: 16 mm/sound/bw/1 reel/30 min.
Date/Country: 1966 + USA   Type: Documentary
Distr/Arch: iu
Annotation: Traces the development of American jazz dance,
   from tap dancing through the stylized theatrical forms of
   the 1900's and orchestrated jazz of the thirties, to the
   cool, abstract music of the sixties. Music by Jelly Roll
   Morton*, Duke Ellington*, and Gunther Schuller (on a theme

by John Lewis*).

DANCERS IN THE DARK
Nar/Cast: Duke Ellington* + Adelaide Hall*   Story: James A.
    Creelman (play)
Tech Info: 76 min.
Date/Country: 1932 + USA   Type: Feature
Annotation: Film about the romance between a taxi driver
    (Adelaide Hall) and a jazz musician.

DANCING NIG, THE
Studio/Company: Essanay
Date/Country: 1907   Type: Short
Annotation: The company's film note attests to the "well
    known fact" that a "darky" has trouble keeping his feet
    still when he hears the sound of music. This film ap-
    parently means to demonstrate that "fact."

DANCING ROMEO
Series: Our Gang
Nar/Cast: Our Gang + Billie Thomas*
Screenplay: Hal Law + Robert A. McGowan
Producer: MGM   Director: Cyril Endfield
Studio/Company: MGM
Tech Info: bw/sound/1 reel
Date/Country: 1944 + USA   Type: Comedy Short
Annotation: Helped by a wire and pulley apparatus manned by
    Mickey and Buckwheat, Froggy is able to dance his way into
    Marilyn's heart. Billie Thomas stars as Buckwheat.

DANDY IN ASPIC, A
Nar/Cast: Calvin Lockhart* + Laurence Harvey + Tom Courtenay
    + Mia Farrow
Screenplay: Derek Marlowe
Producer: Anthony Mann   Director: Anthony Mann
Studio/Company: Columbia
Tech Info: 16 mm/sound/color/107 min.
Date/Country: 1968 + Britain   Type: Feature
Distr/Arch: bud + cha + col + con + cwf + mac + mot + roa +
    sel + wel + who + wil
Annotation: Calvin Lockhart has the small part of Brogue in
    this drama of spies and counterspies.

DANIEL WATTS
Producer: NET
Tech Info: 16 mm/bw/sound/1 reel/30 min.
Date/Country: 1967   Type: Documentary
Distr/Arch: iu
Annotation: Presents an interview with Daniel H. Watts,
    editor of the Liberator. Relates Watts' position on such
    issues as urban riots, anti-semitism, origins of 'Black
    Power' leaders, and religion in the Afro-American commun-
    ity.

DARING GAME
Nar/Cast: Lloyd Bridges + Brock Peters* + Nico Minardos +
    Michael Ansara
Screenplay: Andy White

Producer: Gene Levitt   Director: Laslo Benedek
Studio/Company: Paramount
Tech Info: 16 mm/sound/color/103 min.
Date/Country: 1968 + USA   Type: Feature
Distr/Arch: ivy
Annotation: When a noted political scientist and his
    daughter are held captive by a Caribbean dictator, Lloyd
    Bridges and his group of aviator-Frogmen-karate experts
    are called in with their various gadgets to free the pair.
    Brock Peters plays Jonah Hunt.

DARK ALIBI, THE
Series: Charlie Chan
Nar/Cast: Sidney Toler + Mantan Moreland* + Ben Carter* +
    Benson Fong
Screenplay: George Callahan
Producer: James S. Burkett   Director: Phil Karlson
Studio/Company: Monogram
Tech Info: 16 mm/sound/bw/2 reels/61 min.
Date/Country: 1946 + USA   Type: Feature
Distr/Arch: cin
Annotation: Mantan Moreland as Birmingham Brown has an en-
    counter with a skelton in this Charlie Chan mystery.

DARK AND CLOUDY
Nar/Cast: Lillian Biron* + George Ovey*
Studio/Company: Gaiety Comedies
Tech Info: 35 mm/silent/bw/2 reels
Date/Country: 1919 + USA   Type: Comedy Short
Distr/Arch: lc

DARK LOVER'S PLAY, A
Studio/Company: Keystone
Date/Country: 1915 + USA   Type: Comedy Short
Annotation: Mack Sennett uses a pair of "coontown lovers" to
    elicit the humor in this comedy short.

DARK MANHATTAN
Nar/Cast: Ralph Cooper* + Cleo Herndon* + Clarence Brooks* +
    Sam McDaniels* + Jess Lee Brooks* + Corny Anderson* +
    Rubeline Glover* + James Abamson* + Nicodemus Stewart* +
    Jack Liney*
Screenplay: Arthur Brooks   Story: George Randol
Producer: George Randol + Ben Rinaldo   Director: Harry
    Fraser + Ralph Cooper
Studio/Company: Million Dollar Pictures + Renaldo Films +
    Cooper-Randol productions
Tech Info: 16 mm/bw/sound/2 reels/70 min.
Date/Country: 1937 + USA   Type: Feature
Distr/Arch: lc
Annotation: Dark Manhattan is about the numbers racket in
    Harlem and the rise of "Curly" Thorpe (Ralph Cooper) to a
    position of eminence.

DARK OF THE SUN
Nar/Cast: Rod Taylor + Jim Brown* + Yvette Mimieux + Kenneth
    More + Peter Carsten + Calvin Lockhart* + Bloke Modisane*
Screenplay: Quentin Werty + Adrian Spies

Producer: George England   Director: Jack Cardiff
Studio/Company: MGM
Tech Info: 16 mm/sound/color/3 reels/100 min.
Date/Country: 1968 + Britain   Type: Feature
Distr/Arch: fnc
Annotation: Rod Taylor and Jim Brown (Sgt. Ruffo) play
    mercenaries sent into the Congo to rescue inhabitants and
    recover $50 million of diamonds at a remote outpost before
    the Simba's attack. The Nazi-type, played by Carsten,
    murders Brown for the diamonds, and is likewise eliminated
    by Taylor. Calvin Lockhart plays Ubi, an African politi-
    cal leader who wants the diamonds; Modisane is Kataki, an
    African committed to his people as was Sgt. Ruffo.

DARK ROMANCE OF A TOBACCO CAN, THE
Date/Country: 1911 + USA   Type: Comedy Short
Annotation: A young man must produce a wife in order to lay
    claim to a fortune. He proposes by mail to a woman whose
    name he finds in a tobacco can, and is horrified to find
    that she is black.

DARK SANDS
Alt Title(s): see Jericho

DARK TOWN JUBILEE
Nar/Cast: Bert Williams*
Studio/Company: Biograph
Tech Info: 16 mm/sound
Date/Country: 1914 + USA   Type: Comedy Short
Annotation: Bert Williams, famous comedian, actor, singer
    and mime starred in this, his first film, which reportedly
    caused a race riot in Brooklyn.

DARK WATERS
Nar/Cast: Merle Oberon + Franchot Tone + Rex Ingram* + Nina
    Mae McKinney*   Director: Andre de Toth
Studio/Company: United Artists
Tech Info: 16mm/ sound/ bw/ 90 min.
Date/Country: 1945 + USA   Type: Feature
Distr/Arch: ivy + mac + mog
Annotation: In the mysterious Louisiana bayous, Merle Oberon
    gets caught up in various strange goings-on and thinks
    she's going insane. McKinney plays opposite Ingram who is
    cast as Pearson Jackson.

DARKER THAN AMBER
Nar/Cast: Rod Taylor + Suzy Kendall + Janet MacLachlan*
Screenplay: John McDonald   Story: Ed Waters
Producer: Robert Clouse   Director: Frank Phillips
Studio/Company: National General Pictures
Tech Info: sound/color/97 min.
Date/Country: 1970 + USA   Type: Feature
Annotation: Based on the Travis McGee mystery novel series,
    Rod Taylor as McGee goes after the killers of a girl whom
    he saved and fell in love with. Janet MacLachlan plays
    Noreen Walker, the girl's maid, who gives McGee important
    information that helps him solve the murder.

DARKTOWN AFFAIR
Studio/Company: Mount Olympus
Date/Country: 1921 + USA

DARKTOWN REVUE   Director: Oscar Micheaux*
Studio/Company: Micheaux Film Corporation
Date/Country: 1931 + USA   Type: Feature

DARKTOWN STRUTTERS BALL   Director: George Randol*

DARKTOWN STRUTTERS
Nar/Cast: Trina Parks* + Roger E. Mosley* + Edna Richardson
   + Bettye Sweet + Shirley Washington* + Christopher Joy +
   Stan Shaw + DeWayne Jesse + Charles Knapp + Edward
   Marshall + Dick Miller + Milt Kogan + Norman Bartold +
   Gene Simms + Sam Laws + Frankie Crocker + Della Thomas +
   Ed Bakey + Puddle Bagley + Frances Nealy + Barbara Mor-
   rison + Raymond Allen + Charles Woolf + Alvin Childress* +
   Zara Cully
Screenplay: George Armitage   Director: William Witney
Studio/Company: New World Pictures
Tech Info: 16 mm/sound/color/90 min.
Date/Country: 1975 + USA   Type: Feature
Distr/Arch: fnc
Annotation: A black female singing group tries for fame and
   fortune. The film spoofs the minstrel tradition with con-
   temporary social satire.

DATE WITH DUKE, A
Nar/Cast: Duke Ellington*
Producer: George Pal
Studio/Company: Paramount
Tech Info: 16 mm/color/sound/1 reel/10 min.
Date/Country: 1946 + USA   Type: Animated Short
Distr/Arch: emg + kpf
Annotation: Duke Ellington plays his composition, "Perfume
   Suite," in this George Pal "puppetoon."

DAUGHTER OF SHANGHAI
Nar/Cast: Anna May Wong + Phillip Ahn + Charles Bickford +
   Ernest Whitman*   Story: Garnett Weston   Director: Robert
   Florey
Studio/Company: Paramount
Tech Info: 16 mm/sound/bw/63 min.
Date/Country: 1937 + USA   Type: Feature
Distr/Arch: uni
Annotation: After her father is killed, Anna May Wong and
   Phillip Ahn go after the gang that did it, and uncover an
   alien smuggling racket. Ernest Whitman has a minor role
   as Sam Tsillce.

DAUGHTER OF THE CONGO
Nar/Cast: Kathleen Noisette* + Lorenzo Tucker* + Clarence
   Reed* + Willor Lee Guilford* + Joe Byrd* + Alice B. Rus-
   sell* + Gertrude Selson* + Percy Verwayen* + Salem Tutt
   Whitney*
Producer: Oscar Micheaux*   Director: Oscar Micheaux*
Studio/Company: Micheaux Film Corporation

Tech Info: 35 mm/silent with talking sequences and music
   score/9 reels
Date/Country: 1930 + USA   Type: Feature
Annotation: A black cavalry officer rescues a young mulatto
   girl from Arab slave hunters in a small country in West
   Africa.

DAVID HARUM
Nar/Cast: Will Rogers + Louise Dresser + Evelyn Venoble +
   Stepin Fetchit* + Kent Taylor
Screenplay: Walter Woods   Story: Edward Noyes Wescott
   Director: James Cruze
Studio/Company: Fox Film Corp.
Tech Info: 16 mm/sound/bw/3 reels/82 min.
Date/Country: 1934 + USA   Type: Feature
Distr/Arch: moma
Annotation: Will Rogers plays a country slicker double-
   dealing with a blind race horse. Stepin Fetchit also
   stars in the cast.

DAVID LIVINGSTONE-HIS LIFE AND ACHIEVEMENTS
Series: National Archives Gift Collection
Tech Info: 16 mm/silent/6 reels/bw
Annotation: Authentically set, the film follows Living-
   stone's life and achievements in England and Africa.
   (Part of Record Group 200 HF series, Harmon Foundation
   Collection).

DAVID PORTER - NEGRO ARTIST
Series: National Archives Gift Collection
Tech Info: 16 mm/1 reel/silent/cuts/color
Annotation: Part of Record Group 200 HF series, Harmon
   Foundation Collection.

DAVID RUBADIRI, LEOPOLO SEDAR SENGHOR, BERNARD FONLON, WOLE
   SOYINKA
Series: African Writer of Today
Producer: NET
Tech Info: 16 mm/sound/bw/1 reel/29 min.
Date/Country: 1964 + USA   Type: Documentary
Distr/Arch: iu
Annotation: Visits a classroom in Nyasaland, where the
   teacher-poet Rubadiri* discusses Soyinka's poem 'Telephone
   Conversation.' Presents President Senghor* of Senegal,
   also an admired poet, who speaks on the concept of 'ne-
   gritude.' Closes with an interview with Dr. Fonlon* in
   Cameroon, who discusses dangers facing African literature.

DAVID RUBADIRI
Series: African Writers of Today
Producer: NET
Tech Info: 16 mm/sound/bw/1 reel/29 min.
Date/Country: 1964 + USA   Type: Documentary
Distr/Arch: iu
Annotation: Presents Mr. Nkosi* interviewing poet and edu-
   cator David Rubadiri* of Nyasaland and Kenyan poet Joseph
   Kariuki. Describes native oral tradition involved in
   African writing, discusses possible future forms, and ex-

amines how African literature is taught in the schools.

DAY_AT_THE_RACES,_A
Nar/Cast: Marx Brothers + Ivie Anderson* + Crinoline Choir
Screenplay: Robert Pirosh + George Seaton + George Op-
   penheimer   Story: Robert Pirosh + George Seaton
   Director: Sam Wood
Studio/Company: MGM
Tech Info: 16 mm/sound/bw/109 min.
Date/Country: 1937 + USA   Type: Feature
Distr/Arch: fnc
Annotation: In   Ivie Anderson's "All God's Children Got
   Rhythm" number, the Lindy dancers, including Leon James*
   perform. Dorothy Dandridge* (as a child) has reportedly
   been identified in one of the production numbers in this
   Marx Brothers' take over of the racetrack.

DAY_IN_AN_AFRICAN_VILLAGE,_A
Series: National Archives Gift Collection
Tech Info: 16 mm/silent/2 1-reel units/bw
Annotation: Tribal customs in Central Africa--hunting, food
   preparation, crafts, recreation. (Part of Record Group
   200 HF series, Harmon Foundation Collection).

DAY_THE_EARTH_MOVED,_THE
Nar/Cast: Jackie Cooper + Cleavon Little* + Stella Stevens
Studio/Company: ABC-TV
Date/Country: 1974 + USA   Type: TV Feature
Annotation: Cooper and Little star as a team of aerial
   photographers who accidentally discover a new method of
   predicting earthquakes. Their discovery leads to the
   prediction of the imminent destruction of the town of
   Bates, which ignores the warning.

DAYBREAK_IN_UDI
Producer: British Information Service
Tech Info: 16 mm/sound/bw/1 reel/40 min.
Date/Country: Britain   Type: Documentary
Distr/Arch: iu + bris
Annotation: Shows the political awakening of a Nigerian vil-
   lage during the building of a maternity home there.

DAYTON'S_DEVILS
Nar/Cast: Georg Stanford Brown* + Rory Calhoun + Leslie
   Nielsen
Screenplay: Fred De Gorter   Story: Fred De Gorter
Producer: Robert W.Stahler   Director: Jack Shea
Studio/Company: Commonwealth United
Tech Info: 16 mm/sound/color/101 min.
Date/Country: 1968 + USA   Type: Feature
Distr/Arch: ivy + mac + mod + mot + sel + tmc + unf + wcf +
   wel + wil
Annotation: Brown plays Theon Gibson in this adventure
   melodrama about an ex-Air Force Colonel who puts together
   a "crack" semi-military unit out of a group of misfits for
   the purpose of grand theft. Gibson is a member of the
   group.

DEAD ENDS AND NEW DREAMS
Producer: Robert Ornstein
Tech Info: 16 mm/sound/color/25 min.   Type: Documentary
Distr/Arch: mgh
Annotation: The works of a young black poet, Norman Jordan.

DEAD HEAT ON A MERRY-GO-ROUND
Nar/Cast: Roy Glenn* + James Coburn + Camilla Sparv
Screenplay: Bernard Girard
Producer: Carter De Haven, III   Director: Bernard Girard
Studio/Company: Columbia
Tech Info: 16 mm/sound/color/104 min.
Date/Country: 1966   Type: Feature
Distr/Arch: arg + buc + bud + ccc + cha + con + ics + mac +
   mod + mct + swa + twy + wcf + who
Annotation: Super con man Eli Kotch (Coburn) pulls off a
   string of robberies by seducing and/or marrying assorted
   females, and taking on a series of identities, but out-
   wits himself in the end. Among those who unwittingly
   aid/abet him is Sgt. Elmer K. Coxe (Glenn).

DEAD OF NIGHT
Nar/Cast: Michael Redgrave + Mervyn Johns + Sally Anne Howes
   + Elizabeth Welch*   Director: Alberto Cavalcanti +
   Charles Crichton + Basil Dearden + Robert Hamer
Studio/Company: Ealing
Tech Info: 16mm/ sound/ bw/ 104 min.
Date/Country: 1945 + Britain   Type: Feature
Distr/Arch: bud + ccc + jan + tnf
Annotation: Elizabeth Welch is a popular Parisian night club
   owner (Beulah) adept at singing the blues in this four
   episode thriller.

DEADLINE AT 11   Director: Louis DeBulger

DEATH OF A GUNFIGHTER
Nar/Cast: Lena Horne* + Richard Widmark
Screenplay: Allen Smithee
Producer: Richard E. Lyons   Director: Allen Smithee
Studio/Company: Universal
Tech Info: 16 mm/sound/color/2 reels/97 min.
Date/Country: 1969 + USA   Type: Feature
Distr/Arch: uni
Annotation: A western with an interracial love/marriage
   theme. Involves a town marshal (Widmark) who kills too
   easily and alienates his town. Claire Quintana (Horne) is
   the woman he marries.

DEATH
Series: Family of Man
Producer: BBC-TV
Studio/Company: BBC-TV
Tech Info: 16 mm/sound/color/2 reels/45 min.
Date/Country: 1971 + Botswana + New Guinea + Hong Kong +
   England   Type: TV Documentary
Distr/Arch: tim
Annotation: How the various societies mentioned deal with
   death - a surrey crematorium, Botswanian witch doctor, a

New Guinean sorcerer fights a ghost and incense and paper are burned in Hong Kong.

DEBT, THE
Tech Info: 35 mm/bw/silent/2 reels
Date/Country: 1912 + USA   Type: Dramatic Short
Annotation: Early example of the "tragic Mulatto" theme in which the offspring of a white father/white mother and the same white father/Mulatto mistress meet and fall in love. As they are about to marry, they discover the awful inter-racial, almost incestuous truth.

DECEIT
Nar/Cast: Evelyn Preer* + William E. Fountaine* + George Lucas* + Norman Johnstone* + Cleo Desmond* + A.B. Comathiere*
Producer: Oscar Micheaux*   Director: Oscar Micheaux*
Studio/Company: Micheaux Film Corporation
Date/Country: 1921 + USA   Type: Feature
Annotation: Dramatization of censorship pressure by civic groups and censor boards on filmmakers. "The Hypocrite" is the film-within-the- film which apparently demonstrates or symbolizes Micheaux's own experiences, with his film, Within Our Gates.

DECKS RAN RED, THE
Nar/Cast: Dorothy Dandridge* + James Mason + Stuart Whitman + Broderick Crawford + Curt Jurgens + Joel Fluellen*
Screenplay: Andrew Stone
Producer: Andrew Stone   Director: Andrew Stone
Studio/Company: MGM
Tech Info: 16 mm/sound/bw/3 reels/84 min.
Date/Country: 1958 + USA   Type: Feature
Distr/Arch: fnc
Annotation: Story of a mutiny on an American freighter in the Pacific, with Dorothy Dandridge playing the flirtatious female.

DEEP IS THE WELL
Alt Title(s): see The Well

DEEP, THE
Nar/Cast: Robert Shaw + Jacqueline Bisset + Nick Nolte + Lou Gossett*
Screenplay: Peter Benchley + Tracy Keenan Wynn   Story: Peter Benchley (novel)
Producer: Peter Guber   Director: Peter Yates
Studio/Company: Columbia + EMI
Tech Info: 16 mm/sound/color/123 min.
Date/Country: 1977 + USA   Type: Feature
Distr/Arch: swa
Annotation: Louis Gossett is a villain in this suspense mystery of treasure and terror which takes place mainly underwater.

DEFIANT ONES, THE
Nar/Cast: Sidney Poitier* + Tony Curtis + Theodore Bikel
Screenplay: Nathaniel E. Douglas + Harold Jacob Smith

Producer: Stanley Kramer   Director: Stanley Kramer
Studio/Company: United Artists
Tech Info: 16 mm/bw/sound/3 reels/97 min.
Date/Country: 1958 + USA   Type: Feature
Distr/Arch: uas
Annotation: Two escaped convicts from a Southern prison
  farm, one white and one black, find themselves shackled
  together in their bid for freedom. Racial hostilities
  attenuate when they are both faced with the challenge to
  survive.

DELIGHTFULLY DANGEROUS
Nar/Cast: Jane Powell + Ralph Bellamy + Arthur Treacher +
  Louise Beavers*
Screenplay: Walter DeLeon + Arthur Phillips
Producer: Charles Rogers   Director: Arthur Lubin
Studio/Company: United Artists
Tech Info: 16mm/ sound/ bw/
Date/Country: 1945 + USA   Type: Feature
Distr/Arch: scie + ncs
Annotation: Louise Beavers is Hannah who, along with Arthur
  Treacher and Ralph Bellamy, assists Jane Powell in her
  attempts to straighten out the adult world.

DELITTO AL LUNA PARK
Nar/Cast: John Kitzmiller*
Date/Country: 1952 + Italy   Type: Feature

DELTA BLUES SINGER: JAMES "SONNY FORD" THOMAS
Producer: Bill Ferris + Josette Rossi + Center for Southern
  Folklore
Tech Info: 16 mm/sound/bw/45 min.
Date/Country: 1970 + USA   Type: Documentary
Distr/Arch: csf
Annotation: The life and art of Delta Blues musician James
  Thomas. Provided by Center for Southern Folklore.

DEMETRIUS AND THE GLADIATORS
Nar/Cast: Victor Mature + Susan Hayword + William Marshall*
  + Michael Rennie
Producer: Frank Ross   Director: Delmer Daves
Studio/Company: 20th Century Fox
Tech Info: 16 mm/sound/color/101 min.
Date/Country: 1953 + USA   Type: Feature
Distr/Arch: cwf + fnc
Annotation: This sequel to The Robe mixes equal parts
  spectacle, action, sex and reverence. William Marshall
  plays King Glycon.

DEMOCRACY, OR A FIGHT FOR RIGHT
Nar/Cast: Sidney P. Dones*
Studio/Company: Democracy Photoplay Corporation
Date/Country: 1929 + USA   Type: Feature
Annotation: A story of race heroes.

DER LEONE HAVE SEPT CABEZAS
Alt Title(s): Der Leone Have Sept Cabezas   Director:
  Glauber Rocha

Tech Info: 16 mm/color/sound/3 reels/97 min./French, Itali-
   an, Portuguese, Spanish, German, with English subtitles
Date/Country: 1970   Type: Feature
Distr/Arch: nyf
Annotation: A black revolutionary, a Portugese mercenary, an
   American CIA agent, a French missionary (Jean-Pierre
   Leaud) and a voluptuous nude woman called Golden Temple of
   Violence are among the characters in Rocha's allegory.
   Filmed on location in the Congo.

DERBY DAY
Series: Our Gang
Nar/Cast: Our Gang + Ernie Morrison* + Allen Hoskins*
Screenplay: Hal Roach
Producer: Hal Roach   Director: Robert McGowan
Studio/Company: Pathe
Tech Info: silent/bw/2 reels
Date/Country: 1923 + USA   Type: Comedy Short
Annotation: After watching a horse race, the gang decides to
   stage one of its own, with various noble steeds, like
   mules, cows, goats and dogs. Ernie Morrison stars as Sun-
   shine Sammy and Allen Hoskins stars as Farina.

DESIDERIO 'E SOLE
Nar/Cast: John Kitzmiller*
Date/Country: 1954 + Italy   Type: Feature

DESORDRE ET LA NUIT, LE
Alt Title(s): Night Affair
Nar/Cast: Jean Gabin + Nadja Tiller + Hazel Scott*
Screenplay: Michael Andiard + Gilis Grangier + Jacques
   Robert   Story: Jacques Robert
Producer: Lucien Vraid   Director: Gilles Grangier
Studio/Company: President Films
Date/Country: 1961 + France   Type: Feature
Annotation: While trying to solve a murder, Jean Gabin takes
   up with the dead man's drug-addicted mistress. Hazel
   Scott appears in a minor role as Valentine Horse. The
   film released abroad in 1958.

DETECTIVE, THE
Nar/Cast: Frank Sinatra + Lee Remick + Ralph Meeker + Al
   Freeman, Jr.* + Sugar Ray Robinson*
Screenplay: Abby Mann   Story: Roderick Thorp
Producer: Aaron Rosenberg   Director: Gordon Douglas
Studio/Company: Fox
Tech Info: 16 mm/sound/color/114 min.
Date/Country: 1968 + USA   Type: Feature
Distr/Arch: fnc
Annotation: Sinatra plays a New York City detective who
   railroads an innocent man to the electric chair for a
   homosexual murder. Freeman is Robbie Loughren; Robinson
   is Kelly.

DETROIT 9000
Nar/Cast: Hari Rhodes* + Vonetta McGee* + Alex Rocco
Screenplay: Matt Robinson*
Producer: Matt Robinson*   Director: Stan Lathan* + Arthur

Marks
Studio/Company: General Film
Tech Info: 16 mm/sound/color/106 min.
Date/Country: 1973 + USA
Distr/Arch: bac

DEVIL AT FOUR O'CLOCK, THE
Nar/Cast: Spencer Tracy + Frank Sinatra + Gregoire Aslan +
   Bernie Hamilton*
Screenplay: Liam O'Brian   Story: Max Cutto
Producer: Fred Kohlmar   Director: Mervyn LeRoy
Studio/Company: Columbia
Tech Info: 16 mm/sound/color/127 min.
Date/Country: 1961 + USA   Type: Feature
Distr/Arch: alb + arg + buc + ccc + cha + cwf + mac + mod +
   mot + new + roa + tfc + twy + wcf + wel
Annotation: Three convicts, including Frank Sinatra (Harry)
   and Bernie Hamilton (Charlie) help Spencer Tracy (Father
   Doonan) move a children's leper hospital out of the way of
   a reactivated volcano.

DEVIL IS DRIVING, THE
Nar/Cast: Frank Wilson* + Edmund Lowe + Dickie Moore
   Story: Frank Mitchell Dazey
Producer: Charles H. Rogers   Director: Benjamin Stoloff
Studio/Company: Paramount
Date/Country: 1932 + USA   Type: Feature
Annotation: Automobile theft, accident and murder give rise
   to the action in which Frank Wilson has a small part.

DEVIL'S DAUGHTER, THE
Nar/Cast: Nina Mae McKinney* + Jack Carter* + Ida James* +
   Hamtree Harington*   Director: Arthur Leonard
Studio/Company: Goldberg Productions
Tech Info: 16 mm/sound/bw/2 reels/70 min.
Date/Country: 1939 + USA   Type: Feature
Distr/Arch: kpf + bud + emg
Annotation: Love and hate set in Jamaica with Nina Mae McK-
   inney as a young woman who comes to the island to take
   over her father's plantation. Includes a voodoo ceremony.

DEVIL'S DISCIPLE, THE
Nar/Cast: Evelyn Preer* + Lawrence Chenault* + Edward Thomp-
   son*
Studio/Company: Micheaux Film Corporation
Tech Info: 35 mm/silent/bw
Date/Country: 1926 + USA   Type: Feature
Annotation: Alludes to prostitution in New York City.

DEVILED HAMS
Nar/Cast: The Erskine Hawkins* Orchestra + Wilbur Bascomb*
   Director: Milton Schwarzwald
Tech Info: 10 min.
Date/Country: 1937 + USA   Type: Musical Short
Annotation: The Erskine Hawkins Orchestra displays its
   musical skill. amid a satanic scene.

DEVILS OF DARKNESS

Nar/Cast: Tracy Reed* + William Sylvester
Screenplay: Lyn Fairhurst   Story: Lyn Fairhurst
Producer: Tom Blakeley   Director: Lance Comfort
Studio/Company: Fox
Tech Info: 16 mm/sound/bw/85 min.
Date/Country: 1965 + Britain   Type: Feature
Distr/Arch: fnc
Annotation: Tracy Reed is Karen, a model who is abducted by
    Count Sinistre, an updated Dracula, but is saved by Paul
    (Sylvester) who unmasks the evil count.

DIANKHA-BI
Alt Title(s): Young Woman, The
Nar/Cast: Aida Toure* + Aissatou Dieng* + Fifi Diallo* +
    Berthe Basse* + Yves Diagne* + Eddje Diop* + N'Diaga N'Di-
    aye + Saly Kane* + Awa Gueye*
Screenplay: Mahama Traore*
Producer: UNESCO Pilot Project   Director: Mahama Traore*
Studio/Company: Sunu Films
Tech Info: 50 min.
Date/Country: 1968 + Senegal
Annotation: This early film of Traore's (neither short nor
    feature) is a dramatic tale about the pressures of tradi-
    tion and modern life on three young women.

DIARY OF A HARLEM FAMILY
Nar/Cast: Gordon Parks*
Screenplay: Gordon Parks*
Producer: PBL + NET   Director: Joseph Filipowic
Tech Info: 16 mm/bw/sound/1 reel/20 min.
Date/Country: 1968 + USA   Type: Documentary
Distr/Arch: ind + kpf
Annotation: Parks' photo essay on film reveals the plight of
    a black family living in the poverty of Harlem. The
    award-winning photographer spends a brutal winter with the
    family focusing on the problems of inadequate education,
    lack of employment and income. The attendant social and
    personal crises reveal themselves.

DIARY OF A MAD HOUSEWIFE
Nar/Cast: Hilda Haynes* + Richard Benjamin + Carrie Snod-
    gress
Screenplay: Gleanor Perry
Producer: Frank Perry   Director: Frank Perry
Studio/Company: Universal
Tech Info: 16 mm/sound/color/100 min.
Date/Country: 1970 + USA   Type: Feature
Distr/Arch: ccc + cwf + swa + tmc + twf + uni
Annotation: Hilda Haynes is Lottie in this domestic drama
    about a New York housewife who rebels against her
    chauvinistic husband and their middle class, upwardly
    mobile lifestyle.

DIGGING FOR BLACK PRIDE
Producer: NET
Tech Info: 16 mm/sound/bw/1 reel/19 min.
Date/Country: 1971   Type: Documentary
Distr/Arch: iu

Annotation: Shows children in Brooklyn's Bedford-Stuyvesant
   section learning about their African heritage through
   classroom activities and 'digs' in vacant lots and urban
   renewal areas to locate artifacts linking them to their
   19th century ancestors.

DIMPLES
Nar/Cast: Stepin Fetchit* + Hall Johnson Choir* + Shirley
   Temple + Frank Morgan + Helen Westley + Robert Kent + John
   Carradine
Screenplay: Arthur Sherkman + Nat Perrin
Producer: Nunnally Johnson   Director: William A. Seiter
Studio/Company: 20th Century Fox
Tech Info: 16 mm/sound/bw/78 min.
Date/Country: 1936 + USA   Type: Feature
Distr/Arch: fnc
Annotation: The Bowery in New York just before the Civil War
   is the setting. Conflict arises over a production of Un-
   cle Tom's Cabin in which Shirley is to play "Little Eva."
   Stepin Fetchit is Cicero.

DINGAKA
Nar/Cast: Stanley Baker + Juliet Prowse + Ken Gamper* + Al-
   fred Jabulan* + John Sithebe* + Paul Makgoba*
Screenplay: James Uys
Producer: James Uys   Director: James Uys
Studio/Company: Embassy Pictures
Tech Info: 16 mm/color/sound/3 reels/96 min.
Date/Country: 1965 + South Africa   Type: Documentary
Distr/Arch: mac
Annotation: The story is set in modern Africa where the con-
   trasts of two ways of life--the modern and the tradi-
   tional--are in conflict. The differences between tradi-
   tional life and law are pointed up in the story of a suc-
   cessful white Johannesburg Lawyer's defense of a black
   villager who stands accused of murder under white law.
   Filmed on location in South Africa.

DINK: A PRE-BLUES MUSICIAN
Producer: Cecilia Conway + Cheyney Hales
Tech Info: 16 mm/sound/bw/25 min.
Date/Country: 1975 + USA   Type: Documentary
Distr/Arch: cc
Annotation: Focuses on 80-year-old Dink Roberts, black banjo
   player from Haw River, North Carolina, and his family.
   Provided by Center for Southern Folklore.

DINKY DOODLE IN UNCLE TOM'S CABIN   Director: Walter Lantz
Tech Info: 1 reel
Date/Country: 1925 + USA   Type: Animated Short
Annotation: Suggested by the novel Uncle Tom's Cabin.

DIRIGIBLE
Nar/Cast: Jack Holt + Fay Wray + Clarence Muse*   Story: Lt.
   Com. Frank + Wilber Wead   Director: Frank Capra
Studio/Company: Columbia
Tech Info: 16 mm/sound/bw/102 min.
Date/Country: 1931 + USA   Type: Feature

Distr/Arch: col
Annotation: Muse plays Clarence in this melodrama about the
   rivalry between the pilots of heavier-than-air and
   lighter-than-air craft, and their adventures in the
   Antarctic.

DIRTY_DOZEN, THE
Nar/Cast: Jim Brown* + Lee Marvin + Donald Sutherland + Tel-
   ly Savalas + John Cassavetes + Charles Bronson + Ben Car-
   ruthers*
Screenplay: Nunnally Johnson + Lukas Heller
Producer: Kenneth Hyman   Director: Robert Aldrich
Studio/Company: MGM
Tech Info: 16 mm/sound/color/4 reels/149 min.
Date/Country: 1967 + USA + Britain   Type: Feature
Distr/Arch: fnc
Annotation: Jim Brown is part of a tough team of court-
   martialed soldiers who are released from a military prison
   to carry out a dangerous mission during World War II.

DIRTY_GERTY_FROM_HARLEM, USA
Nar/Cast: Francine Everette* + Don Wilson* + Katherine
   Moore* + "Piano" Frank* + Spencer Williams* + July Jones*
   + Howard Gallaway* + Six Harlem Beauties* + Alfred
   Hawkins* + David Boykin* + Lee Lewis* + Inez Newell* +
   John King* + Shelly Ross* + Hugh Watson* + Don Gilbert*
Story: True T.Thompson
Producer: Bert Goldberg   Director: Spencer Williams*
Studio/Company: Alfred R. Sack release
Tech Info: 16 mm/sound/bw/60 min.
Date/Country: 1946 + USA   Type: Feature
Distr/Arch: emg + thu + imp
Annotation: In this remake of Rain, Gerty La Rue (Francine
   Everette) and her troup arrive at the Paradise Hotel
   (Kingston, Jamaica), but Gerty is actually on the run from
   one of the men she has jilted. Larry does find her by the
   end of the film and shoots her "becuase he loves her."
   Spencer Williams appears briefly as "Old Hager," a fortune
   teller who foreshadows Gerty's demise.

DISAPPEARANCE_OF_MARY_JANE, THE
Nar/Cast: Chicago Bathing Girls* + Jimmie Cox*
Studio/Company: Acme Film Distribution Company
Date/Country: 1921 + USA

DISCOVERING_AMERICAN_FOLK_MUSIC
Series: Discovering Music
Producer: Bernard Wilets
Tech Info: 16 mm/sound/color/1 reel/21 min.
Date/Country: 1969   Type: Documentary
Distr/Arch: iu + bfa
Annotation: Introduces the viewer to American folk music,
   emphasizing the great influence which British and African
   folk music have had upon it.

DISCOVERING_JAZZ
Series: Discovering Music
Producer: BFA

Tech Info: 16 mm/sound/color/1 reel/22 min.
Date/Country: 1969 + USA   Type: Documentary
Distr/Arch: iu + bfa
Annotation: Presents an historical overview of jazz as an
    American musical form. Discusses the combination of
    African rhythms and European harmony into Dixieland and
    blues. Also traces the evoloution of jazz.

DISCOVERY_AND_BETRAYAL
Series: Search for the Nile
Nar/Cast: James Mason
Producer: Michael Hastings + Derek Marlowe + BBC-TV
Tech Info: 16 mm/sound/color/2 reels/52 min.
Date/Country: 1972 + East Africa   Type: Documentary
Distr/Arch: tim
Annotation: The adventures of Burton and Speke as they
    search for the source of the Nile. Speke does discover
    Lake Victoria.

DISNEYLAND_AFTER_DARK   Director: H.S. Luske + W. Beaudine
Tech Info: 46 min.
Date/Country: 1962 + USA   Type: Documentary
Annotation: Features Louis Armstrong* and His Band with Kid
    Ory and Buddy St. Cyr.

DISORDERLY_ORDERLY
Nar/Cast: Sammy Davis, Jr.* + Jerry Lewis
Screenplay: Frank Tashlin
Producer: Paul Jones   Director: Frank Tashlin
Studio/Company: Paramount
Tech Info: 16 mm/sound/bw/color/101 min.
Date/Country: 1964 + USA   Type: Feature
Distr/Arch: fnc
Annotation: A Jerry Lewis farce, this time in a hospital

DISTANT_SOUNDS,_THE
Tech Info: 58 min.
Date/Country: 1967 + USA   Type: Documentary
Annotation: Two black jazz musicians explain the roots of
    the Afro-American music they play.

DIVORCE_IN_THE_FAMILY
Nar/Cast: Jackie Cooper + Lewis Stone + Lois Wilson + Louise
    Beavers*   Story: Delmar Daves   Director: Charles F.
    Riesner
Studio/Company: MGM
Date/Country: 1932 + USA   Type: Feature
Annotation: Louise Beavers plays her maid's role in this
    admonishment about divorce and its effect on the young,
    particularly the young one played by Jackie Cooper.

DIVOT_DIGGERS
Series: Our Gang
Nar/Cast: Our Gang + Billie Thomas*
Producer: Hal Roach   Director: Robert F. McGowan
Studio/Company: MGM + Roach
Tech Info: super 8 mm/16 mm/bw/sound/2 reels/15-20 min.
Date/Country: 1936 + USA   Type: Comedy Short

Distr/Arch: roa + bla
Annotation: Buckwheat caddies for Darla and Spanky, Porky
   for Alfalfa as the gang has a blissful day of 'golf.' But
   the caddies walk off the job at the club protesting low
   rates and the gang is rounded up to substitute. The gang
   and their pet chimp totally disrupt the game.   Billie
   Thomas stars as Buckwheat.

DIXIANA
Nar/Cast: Bebe Daniels + Bill Robinson* + Everett Marshall +
   Bert Wheeler
Screenplay: Luther Reed   Story: Anne Caldwell   Director:
   Luther Reed
Studio/Company: Radio Pictures Corp.
Date/Country: 1930 + USA   Type: Feature
Annotation: Bebe Daniels in her first film role plays Dixi-
   ana, a performer in a circus theater with whom Everett
   Marshall, the local rich boy, falls in love.   The
   scoundrel played by Robert Woolsey and Everett's mother
   try to thwart the romance to no avail. Bill Robinson has
   a tap dancing routine during the film, and is credited as
   "Specialty Dancer."

DIXIE HANDICAP
Nar/Cast: Claire Windsor + Frank Keenan + Lloyd Hughes +
   John Sainpolis + Otis Harlan
Screenplay: Gerald Beaumont   Director: Reginald Baker
Studio/Company: Metro-Goldwyn Pictures
Tech Info: 35 mm/silent/bw
Date/Country: 1924 + USA   Type: Feature
Annotation: A "stupid colored man" is a part of the scenery
   in this film about a judge who has fallen on hard times,
   his daughter, his filly and the Kentucky Derby.

DIXIE JAMBOREE
Nar/Cast: Frances Langford + Eddie Quillan + Guy Kibbee +
   Louise Beavers* + Ben Carter* + Cab Calloway* + Adelaide
   Hall*
Screenplay: Sam Neumann   Director: Christy Cabanne
Studio/Company: PRC
Tech Info: 16 mm/sound/bw/80 min.
Date/Country: 1945 + USA
Distr/Arch: ivy + mog
Annotation: Musical comedy set aboard the last surviving
   Mississippi showboat.

DIXIE LOVE
Nar/Cast: Lucille Poe* + Richard Gregg* + Alvin Childress*
Studio/Company: Paragon Pictures
Tech Info: silent/bw
Date/Country: 1933 + USA

DIXIE
Nar/Cast: Bing Crosby + Dorothy Lamour + Billy de Wolfe
   Story: Karl Tunbert + Darrell Ware   Director: A. Edward
   Sutherland
Studio/Company: Paramount
Tech Info: 16 mm/sound/color/90 min.

Date/Country: 1943 + USA   Type: Feature
Distr/Arch: uni
Annotation: A film "biography" of Daniel Emmett, the
  original "Virginia man" and the composer of "Dixie" with
  numerous blackface routines.

DIXIELAND_JAMBOREE
Nar/Cast: Cab Calloway* + Adelaide Hall* + The Nicholas
  Brothers* + Eunice Wilson*
Studio/Company: Warner Brothers + Vitaphone
Tech Info: 16 mm/sound/1 reel/9 min.
Date/Country: 1935 + USA   Type: Musical Short
Distr/Arch: uas

DIZZY_GILLESPIE_QUINTET
Producer: Ralph J. Gleason + Richard Christian
Tech Info: 29 min.
Date/Country: 1964 + USA   Type: TV Documentary
Annotation: A program of music and discussion with Dizzy
  Gillespie and others, in KQED's Jazz Casual Series.

DIZZY_GILLESPIE
Nar/Cast: Dizzy Gillespie*
Producer: Les Blanc
Tech Info: 16 mm/bw/sound/1 reel/22 min.
Date/Country: 1965 + USA   Type: Documentary
Distr/Arch: flf
Annotation: Dizzy, his band and his theories about music are
  in this musical short.

DO_THE_DEAD_TALK?
Nar/Cast: Ebony Players*
Studio/Company: Ebony Film Corporation
Tech Info: silent/bw
Date/Country: 1918 + USA

DO_YOU_THINK_A_JOB_IS_THE_ANSWER?
Producer: Public Broadcasting Library of NET
Tech Info: 16 mm/bw/sound/2 reels/68 min.
Date/Country: 1969 + USA   Type: Documentary
Distr/Arch: iu
Annotation: Illustrates the campaign initiated by businessmen to hire the hard-core unemployed, but reveals that
  often the trainees view these as 'dead-end' jobs.   Explains that private industries in Detroit are move concerned with social consciousness than in filling bottom-
  level jobs.   Relates how Detroit Blacks are challenging
  these policies as they seek programs with better opportunities for advancement.

DOCKS_OF_NEW_ORLEANS,_THE
Series: Charlie Chan
Nar/Cast: Roland Winters + Victor Sen Young + Mantan
  Moreland*
Screenplay: W. Scott Darling
Studio/Company: Monogram
Tech Info: 16 mm/sound/bw/2 reels/64 min.
Date/Country: 1948 + USA   Type: Feature

Distr/Arch: cin
Annotation: Mantan Moreland plays Chan's chauffeur
   Birmingham Brown as Charlie's foil.

DOCTOR DOOLITTLE
Nar/Cast: Geoffrey Holder* + Rex Harrison + Samantha Eggar +
   Anthony Newley
Screenplay: Leslie Bricusse   Story: Hugh Lofting
Producer: Arthur P. Jacobs + APJAC Productions   Director:
   Richard Fleisher
Studio/Company: 20th Century Fox Release
Tech Info: 16 mm/sound/color/152 min.
Date/Country: 1967 + USA   Type: Feature
Distr/Arch: fnc
Annotation: Holder plays tribal chieftan Willie Shakespeare
   in this musical fantasy based on a series of stories
   bearing the same title. Rex Harrison stars in title role.

DOCTOR GEORGE WASHINGTON CARVER AND DR. CRUMP
Series: National Archives Gift Collection
Tech Info: 16 mm/1 color print
Annotation: Part of Record Group 200 HF series, Harmon
   Foundation Collection.

DOCTOR RHYTHM
Nar/Cast: Bing Crosby + Mary Carlisle + Beatrice Lillie +
   Louis Armstrong*
Screenplay: Jo Swerling + R. Connell   Story: O. Henry
Producer: Emanuel Cohen   Director: Frank Tuttle
Studio/Company: Paramount
Tech Info: 16 mm/sound/bw/81 min.
Date/Country: 1938 + USA   Type: Feature
Distr/Arch: uni
Annotation: This film adaptation of O. Henry's short story
   "The Badge of Policeman O'Roon," features Louis Armstrong
   and his band in various numbers.

DOCTOR'S WIVES
Nar/Cast: Dyan Cannon + Richard Crenna + Diana Sands*
Screenplay: Daniel Taradash   Story: Frank G. Slaughter
Producer: M.J. Frankovich   Director: George Schaefer
Studio/Company: Columbia
Tech Info: 16 mm/sound/color/95 min.
Date/Country: 1971 + USA   Type: Feature
Distr/Arch: ccc + ker + mod + mot + wel + who
Annotation: Diana Sands plays a nurse who is having an af-
   fair with one of the doctors in this melodrama which has
   very little to do with the medical profession.

DOG DAYS
Series: Our Gang
Nar/Cast: Our Gang + Allen Hoskins*
Screenplay: Hal Roach
Producer: Hal Roach   Director: Robert McGowan
Studio/Company: Pathe
Tech Info: silent/bw/2 reels
Date/Country: 1925   Type: Comedy Short
Annotation: The gang members compete against each other with

their trained pet dogs. Allen Hoskins stars as Farina.

DOG DAZE
Series: Our Gang
Nar/Cast: Our Gang + Billie Thomas*
Screenplay: Alfred Giebler
Producer: MGM   Director: George Sidney
Studio/Company: MGM
Tech Info: bw/sound/1 reel
Date/Country: 1939 + USA   Type: Comedy Short
Annotation: The gang gets into trouble trying to raise money
    to pay back Butch's loan by gathering up 'stray' animals
    and hoping they'll be rewarded. Billie Thomas stars as
    Buckwheat.

DOG HEAVEN
Series: Our Gang
Nar/Cast: Our Gang + Allen Hoskins*
Screenplay: Robert F. McGowan
Producer: Robert F. McGowan + Hal Roach   Director: Anthony
    Mack
Studio/Company: MGM
Tech Info: super 8 mm/bw/silent/2 reels
Date/Country: 1927 + USA   Type: Comedy Short
Distr/Arch: bla
Annotation: Pete the Pup, despondent because Joe seems to
    have abandoned him in favor of a flirtatious young girl,
    tries to hang himself. As Pete explains to a dog friend,
    Joe has even gone so far as to accuse Pete of pushing the
    girl into a lake when Pete had in fact been trying to save
    her.   Before Pete and his friend can collaborate in Pete's
    suicide, a tearful Joe arrives and the two are reconciled.
    Allen Hoskins stars as Farina.

DOGS IS DOGS
Series: Our Gang
Nar/Cast: Our Gang + Matthew Beard*
Screenplay: H. M. Walker
Producer: Robert F. McGowan + Hal Roach   Director: Robert
    F. McGowan
Studio/Company: MGM + Roach
Tech Info: super 8 mm/16 mm/bw/sound/2 reels/15-20 min.
Date/Country: 1931 + USA   Type: Comedy Short
Distr/Arch: roa + bla
Annotation: Stymie, although outside of the plot which in-
    cludes conflict between Wheezer, his stepmother, and her
    son Sherwood, helps wheezer to rescue Sherwood from the
    well he has been pushed into. Later, with an elaborate
    con, Stymie manages to supply a magnificent ham and egg
    breakfast for all, for the happy ending.   Matthew Beard
    plays Stymie.

DOGS OF WAR
Series: Our Gang
Nar/Cast: Our Gang + Ernie Morrison* + Allen Hoskins*
Screenplay: Hal Roach
Producer: Hal Roach   Director: Robert McGowan + Ernie Mor-
    rison, Sr.*

Studio/Company: Pathe
Tech Info: silent/bw/2 reels
Date/Country: 1923 + USA   Type: Comedy Short
Annotation: The gang invades a movie studio and makes a
    shambles out of the sets and a movie in production before
    being chased out. Ernie Morrison stars as Sunshine Sammy
    and Allen Hoskins stars as Farina.

DOIN' THEIR BIT
Series: Our Gang
Nar/Cast: Our Gang + Billie Thomas
Producer: MGM   Director: Herbert Glazer
Studio/Company: MGM
Tech Info: bw/sound/1 reel
Date/Country: 1942 + USA   Type: Comedy Short
Annotation: The gang puts on its own local USO show. Billie
    Thomas stars as Buckwheat.

DOING THEIR BIT
Studio/Company: Toussaint Motion Picture Company
Tech Info: silent/bw
Date/Country: 1918 + USA   Type: Documentary
Annotation: Depicts World War I black soldiers in battle.

DON REDMAN AND HIS ORCHESTRA   Director: Joseph Henabery
Studio/Company: Warners + Vitaphone
Tech Info: 16 mm/sound/1 reel/10 min.
Date/Country: 1934 + USA   Type: Musical Short
Distr/Arch: uas
Annotation: Music of Don Redman and his orchestra in a
    nightclub setting, includes "Nagasuki," "Yeah Man," and
    others.

DON'T LIE
Series: Our Gang
Nar/Cast: Our Gang + Billie Thomas*
Screenplay: Hal Law + Robert A. McGowan
Producer: MGM   Director: Edward Cahn
Studio/Company: MGM
Tech Info: bw/sound/1 reel
Date/Country: 1942 + USA   Type: Comedy Short
Annotation: Since Buckwheat is given to lying, the gang
    doesn't believe him when he says he's seen a 'monkey-
    spook' near the haunted house. They dress Froggy as a
    chimp and take Buckwheat to the haunted house for a good
    scare, but when the real monkey shows up, they are ter-
    rified. Billie Thomas stars as Buckwheat.

DON'T PLAY US CHEAP   Director: Melvin Van Peebles*
Studio/Company: Yeah Inc.
Date/Country: 1973 + USA   Type: Feature
Annotation: A film version of Melvin Van Peebles' Broadway
    play. This is a story of two imps who try to break up a
    Saurday night party in Harlem. Filmed on location in New
    Mexico.

DOUBLE DEAL
Nar/Cast: Jeni LeGon* + Monte Hawley* + Florence O'Brian* +

Edward Thompson* + Maceo Sheffield* + F.E. Miller* + Edgar
Washington* + Freddie Jackson* + Charles Hawkins* +
Shelton Brooks*
Screenplay: Arthur Hoerl + Fluornoy E. Miller*
Producer: Bert Goldberg + Jack Goldberg   Director: Arthur
Dreifuss
Studio/Company: International Road Show
Date/Country: 1939 + USA   Type: Feature
Annotation: A gangster, played by Edward Thompson, double
deals his boss (Sheffield) and tries to put the blame on a
rival (Jackson) for his girl friend's (Jeni) affections.
He is double crossed by Jeni and ends up on the wrong end
of a policeman's gun.

DOUBLE TROUBLE
Alt Title(s): See Swingin' Along

DOWN ARGENTINE WAY
Nar/Cast: Don Ameche + Betty Grable + Carmen Miranda +
Nicholas Brothers*
Screenplay: Darrell Ware + Karl Tunberg   Story: Rian James
+ Ralph Spence
Producer: Darryl F. Zanuck   Director: Irving Cummings
Studio/Company: 20th Century Fox
Tech Info: 16 mm/sound/color/88 min.
Date/Country: 1940 + USA   Type: Feature
Distr/Arch: fnc
Annotation: Lively 40's musical about a young American girl
who falls in love with older gaucho played by Don Ameche.
The film features dance routines with the Nicholas
Brothers.

DR. GEORGE WASHINGTON CARVER
Nar/Cast: Clinton Rosemond*
Studio/Company: MGM
Date/Country: 1945 + USA   Type: Documentary
Annotation: Documentary based on the life and work of the
Negro scientist.

DR. JAMES WELDON JOHNSON
Series: National Archives Gift Collection
Tech Info: 16 mm/1 reel
Annotation: Part of Record Group 200 HF series, Harmon
Foundation Collection.

DR. MABUSE DER SPIELER
Nar/Cast: Rudolph Klein-Rogge + Aude Egede Nissen + Gertrude
Welcker + Alfred Abel
Producer: UFA   Director: Fritz Lang
Tech Info: silent/bw/10 reels
Date/Country: 1922 + Germany   Type: Feature
Annotation: Story of Dr. Mabuse, hypnotist who baffles
everyone with his disguises and his ability to control the
minds of others in order to carry on his dreadful busi-
ness. The 1950's version has a brief black scene.

DR. STRANGELOVE OR: HOW I LEARNED TO STOP WORRYING AND LOVE
THE BOMB

Nar/Cast: Peter Sellers + George C. Scott + James Earl
   Jones* + Tracy Reed* + Sterling Hayden
Screenplay: Stanley Kubrick + Terry Southern + Peter George
   Story: Peter George
Producer: Stanley Kubrick   Director: Stanley Kubrick
Studio/Company: Hawk Films Dist. + Columbia Pictures
Tech Info: 16 mm/bw/sound/93 min.
Date/Country: 1964 + Britain   Type: Feature
Distr/Arch: swa
Annotation: A maniacal Air Force general orders a nuclear
   attack on the Soviet Union; the film focuses on the in-
   eptitude of high government and military officials to deal
   with the situation. James Earl Jones is Lt. Lothar Zogg,
   air force bombadier. (Lothar, from the comic strip
   "Mandrake the Magician," is the name of a burly, black
   character.)

DRAWING THE COLOR LINE
Studio/Company: Edison
Date/Country: 1909 + USA   Type: Comedy Short
Annotation: Comedy in which the main character has his face
   blackened with burnt cork while drunk and becomes just
   another black man unrecognizable to friends or family.

DREAM OF THE WANDERER, THE
Series: Search for the Nile
Producer: M. Hastings + D. Marlowe + BBC-TV
Tech Info: 16 mm/sound/color/2 reels/52 min.
Date/Country: 1972 + East Africa   Type: Documentary
Distr/Arch: tim
Annotation: The story of how Richard Barton, John Hanning
   Speke, and Livingstone all started looking for the source
   of the Nile.

DREAM STREET
Nar/Cast: Porter Strong + Carol Dempster + Ralph Graves
Screenplay: Roy Sinclair   Story: Thomas Burke
Producer: D.W. Griffith   Director: D.W. Griffith
Studio/Company: United Artists
Tech Info: 35 mm/silent/bw/10 reels
Date/Country: 1921 + USA   Type: Feature
Distr/Arch: moma
Annotation: Porter Strong plays Samuel Jones (a blackface
   role) in this melodrama with a happy ending.

DREAMER, THE
Nar/Cast: Mantan Moreland* + June Richmond* + Mabel Lee* +
   Pat Rainey*
Studio/Company: Astor Pictures
Tech Info: sound/bw
Date/Country: 1948 + USA   Type: Feature

DRESS REHEARSAL
Nar/Cast: Eddie Green*
Studio/Company: Sepia Art Picture Company
Date/Country: 1939 + USA   Type: Comedy Short
Annotation: Eddie Green plays the star performer of a stage
   company who is late for the dress rehearsal. The comedy

devolves on his problems getting to the theatre.

DRUM IS A WOMAN, A
Nar/Cast: Duke Ellington*
Producer: U.S. Steel
Annotation: Ellington on the United States Steel Hour.

DRUMS O'VOODOO
Alt Title(s): Voodoo Drums + Louisiana
Nar/Cast: J. Augustus Smith* + Laura Bowman* + Chick McKin-
    ney* + Lionel Monagas* + Edna Barr* + A.B. Comathiere* +
    Fred Bonny* + Alberta Perkins* + Paul Johnson*   Story: J.
    Augustus Smith*
Producer: Robert Mintz + Louis Weiss   Director: Arthur
    Hoerle
Studio/Company: International Stage Play Pictures
Date/Country: 1933 + USA   Type: Feature
Annotation: Set in Louisiana, this melodrama is adapted from
    a play by J. Augustus Smith who also plays the lead.
    brothel dancing, aggravated assault and Christian revival.

DRUMS OF AFRICA
Nar/Cast: Frankie Avalon + Marietta Hartley + Hari Rhodes* +
    Lloyd Bochner
Screenplay: Robin Estridge
Producer: Alfred Zimbalist   Director: James B. Clark
Studio/Company: MGM
Tech Info: 16 mm/color/sound/3 reels/92 min.
Date/Country: 1963 + USA   Type: Feature
Distr/Arch: fnc
Annotation: A railroad engineer and his nephew try to finish
    a new rail route in turn-of-the-century East Africa, beset
    by various problems, including Arab slave traders.   Hari
    Rhodes is Kasongo.

DRUMS OF FATE
Nar/Cast: Mary Miles Minter + Maurice B. Flynn + George Faw-
    cett + Noble Johnson*   Director: Charles Maigne
Studio/Company: Paramount Films
Date/Country: 1923 + USA   Type: Feature
Annotation: Blacks appear as jungle natives ("savages") who
    capture the white man in this adventure melodrama partly
    set in Africa. Noble Johnson plays the native king.

DRUMS OF THE CONGO
Nar/Cast: Ona Munson + Stuart Erwin + Ernest Whitman* +
    Dandridge, Dorothy* + Jules Bledsoe* + Jesse Lee Brooks*
    Director: Christy Cabanne
Studio/Company: Universal
Tech Info: 16 mm/sound/bw/70 min.
Date/Country: 1942 + USA   Type: Feature
Distr/Arch: tfcr
Annotation: Opposing secret agents race to tribal back
    country on a secret mission. Among the natives are Jules
    Bledsoe as Kalu, Dorothy Dandridge as Malimi, Ernest Whit-
    man as King Malaba and Jess Lee Brooks as Chief Majeduka.

DRUMS OF THE JUNGLE

Alt Title(s): Ouanga
Nar/Cast: Fredi Washington* + Sheldon Leonard + Philip
    Brandon + Marie Paxton + Winifred Harris   Director: Ge-
    orge Terwillerger
Studio/Company: Paramount
Date/Country: 1935 + USA   Type: Feature

DRY WOOD AND HOT PEPPER
Producer: Les Blanc
Tech Info: 16 mm/color/total 91 min./Dry Wood (37 min.), Hot
    Pepper (54 min.)
Date/Country: 1973 + USA   Type: Documentary
Distr/Arch: flf
Annotation: Two part documentary about creole life and
    Louisiana Bayou music; Hot Pepper gives the viewer insight
    into the music (and life) of creole bluesman Clifton
    Chenier*.

DU TAM-TAM AU JAZZ   Director: Philippe Brunet
Tech Info: 70 min.
Date/Country: 1969 + France   Type: Documentary
Annotation: Included in this three-part documentary are sec-
    tions on Afro-Cuban music, spirituals, gospels, blues and
    jazz, showing the influence of African and Afro-American
    tradition on American culture.

DUBARRY WAS A LADY
Nar/Cast: Louise Beavers* + Red Skelton + Lucille Ball +
    Gene Kelly + Virginia 'Brian + "Rags" Ragland + Zero
    Mostel
Screenplay: Nancy Hamilton + Wilkie Mahoney   Story: H.
    Fields + B.G. DeSylva
Producer: Arthur Freed   Director: Roy Del Ruth
Studio/Company: MGM
Tech Info: color
Date/Country: 1943 + USA   Type: Feature
Annotation: This musical film is about a hat-check boy (Red
    Skelton) who has a dream that he is Louis XVI and his
    DuBarry is the nightclub's singing star (Ball).   Louise
    Beavers plays Niagara.

DUCHESS OF IDAHO
Nar/Cast: Esther Williams + Van Johnson + Lena Horne*
Screenplay: Dorothy Cooper + Jerry Davis
Producer: Joe Pasternak   Director: Robert Z. Leonard
Studio/Company: MGM
Tech Info: 16 mm/sound/color/98 min.
Date/Country: 1950 + USA   Type: Feature
Distr/Arch: fnc
Annotation: Esther Williams plays a swimming star out to
    help her friend snare a playboy. Lena Horne sings a song
    in her "specialty" appearance.

DUE PROCESS OF LAW DENIED
Nar/Cast: Leigh Whipper*
Studio/Company: 20th Century Fox + Teaching Film Custodians
Tech Info: 16 mm/sound/bw/1 reel/30 min.
Date/Country: 1943 + USA   Type: Dramatic Short

Distr/Arch: iu
Annotation: Abridged from the feature film The__Ox-Bow__In-cident. Shows a posse following three supposed cattle rustlers, capturing them, and lynching them in spite of their protests that they are innocent. Leigh Whipper acts as the Christian conscience of the group which learns too late that it is always dangerous to take the law into one's own hands.

DUE_SELVAGGI_A_CORTE
Nar/Cast: John Kitzmiller*
Date/Country: 1959 + Italy   Type: Feature

DUEL_AT_DIABLO
Nar/Cast: James Garner + Dennis Weaver + Sidney Poitier* + Bill Travers + Bibi Andersson
Screenplay: Marvin Albert + Michael Grilikhes   Story: Marvin Albert
Producer: Fred Engel   Director: Ralph Nelson
Studio/Company: United Artists
Tech Info: 16 mm/color/sound/3 reels/103 min.
Date/Country: 1966 + USA   Type: Feature
Distr/Arch: uas + mac
Annotation: A violent tale filmed in the badlands of Southern Utah, Duel__at__Diablo reenacts the cavalry's bloody conquest over the Apache nation. Toller (Poitier) is a sophisticated ex-calvary sergeant who wants to put the past behind him and open his own gambling casino, but has to become a part of the battle to get paid by the Army for the horses he breaks into service.

DUEL_IN_THE_SUN
Nar/Cast: Butterfly McQueen* + Jennifer Jones + Gregory Peck + Joseph Cotter + Lionel Barrymore + Lillian Gish
Producer: David O. Selznick   Director: King Vidor
Studio/Company: Selznick
Tech Info: 35 mm/16 mm/sound/color/4 reels/130 min.
Date/Country: 1947 + USA   Type: Feature
Distr/Arch: mac + aim + bud + ccc + ker + mot + roa + sel + twy + unf + who + wil
Annotation: On a feudal Texas ranch two brothers fight over a "half- breed" Indian girl, and the railroad which wants to push across the ranch. Butterfly McQueen is Vashti in a poignant yet typical maid role.

DUEL_PERSONALITIES
Series: Our Gang
Nar/Cast: Our Gang + Billie Thomas*
Screenplay: Hal Law + Robert A. McGowan
Producer: Jack Chertok   Director: George Sidney
Studio/Company: MGM
Tech Info: bw/sound/1 reel
Date/Country: 1939 + USA   Type: Comedy Short
Annotation: A hypnotist convinces Alfalfa he's D'Artagnan. Alfalfa challenges Butch to a duel for Darla's hand, but Butch convinces Alfalfa they should both just play dead and wait to see to whom Darla runs. Darla has overheard, however, and at the duel lets the two lie there and walks

off with Waldo instead. Billie Thomas stars as Buckwheat.

DUFFY_OF_SAN_QUENTIN
Nar/Cast: Joel Fluellen* + Louis Hayward + Joanne Dru
Screenplay: Walter Doniger
Producer: Walter Doniger + Berman Swartz   Director: Walter
   Doniger
Studio/Company: Warner Brothers
Date/Country: 1954 + USA   Type: Feature
Annotation: Joel Fluellen is Bill, one of the inmates in
   this prison drama about a vengeful con (Hayward) who is
   reclaimed by the love of a good nurse (Dru).

DUKE_ELLINGTON_-_LOVE_YOU_MADLY
Nar/Cast: Duke Ellington*   Director: Richard Moore
Tech Info: 59 min.
Date/Country: 1966 + USA   Type: Documentary
Annotation: Filmed by Ralph Gleason, Duke is seen on the
   road, with friends and with his orchestra. Includes
   footage of the Monterey Jazz Festival and other per-
   formances.

DUKE_ELLINGTON_AND_HIS_ORCHESTRA
Nar/Cast: Duke Ellington*
Producer: Mike Bryan
Tech Info: 25 min.
Date/Country: 1962 + USA   Type: Musical Short
Annotation: Duke Ellington and his orchestra perform "Take
   the A Train," "Things Ain't What They Used to Be," "Kinda
   Dukish," and others, in this production for the Goodyear
   Tire Company, recorded in New York.

DUKE_ELLINGTON_AND_HIS_ORCHESTRA
Nar/Cast: Johnny Hodges* + Ben Webster* + Ray Nance* +   Taft
   Jordan* + Duke Ellington*   Director: Jay Bonafield
Tech Info: 9 min.
Date/Country: 1943 + USA
Annotation: One of the RKO Jamboree series. Numbers in-
   clude: "Mood Indigo" and "Sophisticated Lady."

DUKE_ELLINGTON_AT_THE_WHITE_HOUSE
Producer: Sidney J. Stiber
Tech Info: 18 min.
Date/Country: 1969 + USA   Type: Documentary
Annotation: Film record of a reception given at the White
   House for President Nixon and his guests on the occasion
   of Duke Ellington's* 70th birthday.

DUKE_ELLINGTON_SWINGS_THROUGH_JAPAN
Producer: CBS
Tech Info: 16 mm/sound/bw/26 min.
Date/Country: 1964 + USA   Type: Documentary
Distr/Arch: asf + mac
Annotation: America's "grand old" jazz man and his musicians
   on tour through Japan. Provided by Center for Southern
   Folklore.

DUKE_IS_TOPS,_THE

Alt Title(s): Bronze Venus
Nar/Cast: Lena Horne* + Ralph Cooper* + Lawrence Criner* + Monte Hawley* + Vernon McCalla* + Edward Thompson* + Neva Peoples* + Everett Brown*
Studio/Company: Toddy Pictures + Million Dollar Studios
Date/Country: 1938 + USA   Type: Feature
Distr/Arch: lc
Annotation: Musical romance with Lena Horne as the success-
    ful performer who almost loses her man because his career
    as a producer is failing. They are reunited for the
    finale.

DUNGEON, THE
Nar/Cast: William Fountaine* + Shingzie Howard* + J. Kenneth
    Goodman* + W.B.F. Crowell* + Earle Browne Cook* + Blanche
    Thompson* + Evelyn Preer*   Story: Oscar Micheaux
Producer: Oscar Micheaux*   Director: Oscar Micheaux*
Studio/Company: Micheaux Film Corporation
Tech Info: bw/silent
Date/Country: 1922 + USA   Type: Feature
Annotation: About a man who has murdered eight of his
    previous wives and is about to murder the ninth. The
    dungeon is where the women meet their fate, but the ninth,
    Myrtle, is rescued and the villain eliminated.

DURO LADIPO
Producer: NET
Tech Info: 16 mm/sound/bw/1 reel/30 min.
Date/Country: 1967 + Nigeria   Type: Documentary
Distr/Arch: iu + ucemc
Annotation: An introduction to Duro Ladipo who is founder,
    director, playwright, composer, and principal male actor
    of the Duro Ladipo traveling Theatre Company of Oshogbo,
    Nigeria. Ladipo explains his interest in drama and music.
    Several examples of his folk operas are shown during a
    tour of Yoruba villages.

DUSKY VIRGIN, THE
Producer: Charles Allman White
Studio/Company: Paragon Pictures
Tech Info: silent/bw
Date/Country: 1932 + USA   Type: Feature

DUTCHMAN
Nar/Cast: Al Freeman, Jr.* + Shirley Knight
Screenplay: Imamu Baraka (LeRoi Jones)*   Story: Imamu
    Baraka (LeRoi Jones)*
Producer: Gene Persson   Director: Anthony Harvey
Studio/Company: Continental Films
Tech Info: 16 mm/bw/sound/2 reels/55 min.
Date/Country: 1967 + Britain   Type: Feature
Distr/Arch: bud + wrs
Annotation: Clay (Al Freeman, Jr.) is teased and abused by a
    young white female passenger on a New York subway.
    Adapted from the play, the slightly expanded film version
    allegorically depicts black vulnerability to white treat-
    ment in America.

EAGLE_IN_A_CAGE
Nar/Cast: Moses Gunn* + John Gielgud + Ralph   Richardson   +
   Kenneth Haigh
Screenplay: Millard Lampell   Director: Fielder Cook
Studio/Company: Group W Films Production + National General
   Pictures
Tech Info: 98 min.
Date/Country: 1972 + USA   Type: Feature
Annotation: Moses Gunn has a   supporting   role   (as   General
   Gourgaud) in this film about Napoleon's exile on St.
   Helena and his attempts to escape.

EARL_"FATHA"_HINES
Producer: Ralph J. Gleason   Director: Richard Moore
Tech Info: 30 min.
Date/Country: 1963 + USA   Type: Documentary
Annotation: Part of Gleason's jazz casual series   for   KQED,
   features pianist Earl Hines*.

EAST_AFRICA_(KENYA,_TANGANYIKA,_UGANDA)
Series: Africa in Change
Producer: Encyclopedia Britannica Films, Inc.
Tech Info: 16 mm/sound/color/1 reel/21 min.
Date/Country: 1963   Type: Documentary
Distr/Arch: iu + unebr + uill + iowa + ebec
Annotation: Pictures East   Africa as a region of diversity
   both in physical geography and people. Contrasts   ancient
   tribal   life with metropolitan activities.   Emphasizes the
   importance of education in the future unification   of   the
   people of East Africa.

EAST_AFRICA_(1962)
Alt Title(s): East Africa, Second Edition
Studio/Company: Paul Hoefler
Tech Info: 16 mm/sound/color/1 reel/22 min.
Date/Country: 1962 + Kenya + Tanzania + Uganda   Type: Docu-
   mentaryShort
Distr/Arch: cox + ebec + wasu + suf + umavec + bfa
Annotation: The effects of British rule on the   cities,   pe-
   ople, trade, education and legal system of East Africa.

EAST_AFRICA:_ENDS_AND_BEGINNINGS
Producer: NET
Tech Info: 16 mm/sound/bw/2 reels/48 min.
Date/Country: 1970 + Kenya + Tanzania   Type: Documentary
Distr/Arch: iu + ucemc
Annotation: An investigative report on the political,
   economic, and social development in Kenya and Tanzania,
   including an extensive interview with Tanzanian President
   Julius K. Nyerere*. Also included is   a   brief   interview
   with a field commander of the Mozambique Liberation Front.

EAST_AFRICA:_KENYA,_TANGANYIKA,_UGANDA
Screenplay: Paul Bohannan
Studio/Company: Encyclopedia Britannica Films
Tech Info: 16 mm/sound/color/1 reel/25 min.
Date/Country: 1963 + Kenya + Tanganyika   +   Uganda   Type:
   Documentary

Distr/Arch: uill + psu + ebec + msu + umavec + kent + ucemc
    + iowa + fsu + bu + mp
Annotation: While showing the beauty of the area, this film
    shows how topography influenced settlement and economic
    development.   Also featured are   the   lifestyles   and
    cultures of the Africans, Asians and Europeans during this
    transitional period.

EAST_OF_BORNEO
Nar/Cast: Charles Bickford + Rose Hobart + Lupita Tovar +
    Noble Johnson*   Story: Dale Van Every   Director: George
    Melford
Studio/Company: Universal
Tech Info: 16 mm/sound/bw/77 min.
Date/Country: 1932 + USA   Type: Feature
Distr/Arch: imp
Annotation: Jungle thriller that has Rose Hobart trying to
    save her   doctor husband, Charles Bickford, from the evil
    clutches of a Sorbonne-educated, psychopathic rajah.   No-
    ble Johnson also stars in this movie made in the Trader
    Horn genre.

EAST_SIDE,_WEST_SIDE:_NO_HIDING_PLACE
Producer: Talen Associates + Paramount Ltd.
Tech Info: 16 mm/sound/bw/2 reels/50 min.
Date/Country: 1968   Type: Dramatized Documentary
Distr/Arch: iu + carouf
Annotation: Dramatizes the reactions of neighbors when a
    black family moves into a white, suburban neighborhood and
    one white family decides to prevent the neighbors from
    panicking.

EASY_MONEY
Nar/Cast: S.H. Dudley* + Evelyn Ellis*
Studio/Company: Reol Productions
Tech Info: silent/bw
Date/Country: 1921 + USA

EASY_STREET
Nar/Cast: Richard B. Harrison* + Willor Lee Guilford* +
    Lorenzo Tucker*
Producer: Oscar Micheaux*
Studio/Company: Micheaux Film Corporation
Date/Country: 1930 + USA   Type: Feature

EASY_TO_GET
Nar/Cast: Paul Robeson* + Joe Louis* + Ralph Metcalfe*
Date/Country: USA   Type: Documentary
Distr/Arch: nars
Annotation: Army training film (TF 8-1423), narrated by Paul
    Robeson, with direct appeals made by Sgt. Joe Louis and
    Lt. Ralph Metcalfe to the Negro soldier to avoid venereal
    disease either by abstinence or by the use of contracep-
    tive devices. Dramatic incidents are used along with some
    animated segments. Emphasis is on the desirability of
    improving the health and mental status of the race.

EDDIE_GREEN'S_LAUGH_JAMBOREE

Nar/Cast: Eddie Green* + Ernestine Jones*
Studio/Company: Toddy Pictures
Tech Info: bw/50 min.
Date/Country: 194- + USA   Type: Feature

EDGE_OF_THE_ARENA:_PORTRAIT_OF_A_BLACK_CANDIDATE
Producer: Rediscovery
Tech Info: 16 mm/sound/color/28 min.
Date/Country: 1972 + USA   Type: Documentary
Distr/Arch: nacc + sef
Annotation: Georgia's first black candidate for national
  office since reconstruction days, Andrew Young.

EDGE_OF_THE_CITY
Alt Title(s): A Man is Ten Feet Tall
Nar/Cast: Sidney Poitier* + John Cassavetes + Ruby Dee*
Screenplay: Robert A. Arthur   Story: Robert A. Arthur
Producer: David Susskind   Director: Martin Ritt
Studio/Company: MGM + United Artists
Tech Info: 16 mm/bw/sound/3 reels/85 min.
Date/Country: 1957 + USA   Type: Feature
Distr/Arch: fnc
Annotation: In this story of the waterfront two stevedores,
  Axel North (John Cassavetes) and Tommy Tyler (Sidney
  Poitier) Become friends. Tyler helps North find con-
  fidence in himself--"standing up to life can make a man
  ten feet tall" - and is killed protecting the younger man
  from a violent and aggressive bigot.

EDISON,_MARCONI_AND_CO.
Series: Our Gang
Nar/Cast: Our Gang + Allen Hoskins*
Producer: Hal Roach   Director: Anthony Mack
Studio/Company: MGM
Tech Info: bw/silent/2 reels
Date/Country: 1928 + USA   Type: Comedy Short
Annotation: The Gang as a band of inventors led by Jay. The
  action centers around Wheezer's hair raising ride at the
  wheel of the Gang's 8-portholed car. Allen Hoskins stars
  as Farina.

EDUCATION_AND_CULTURE_IN_EAST_AFRICA
Studio/Company: EWICAN
Tech Info: 16 mm/sound/color/1 reel/20 min.
Date/Country: 1970 + East Africa   Type: Documentary
Distr/Arch: osu
Annotation: This film emphasizes the many ways that old
  Africa is still present in East Africa, in things like
  religion, dance, schools, etc.

EDUCATION_OF_SONNY_CARSON,_THE
Nar/Cast: Rony Clanton* + Don Gordon* + Paul Benjamin +
  Joyce Walker* + Thomas Hicks
Screenplay: Fred Hudson   Story: Sonny Carson*
Producer: Irwin Yablans + David Golden   Director: Michael
  Campus
Studio/Company: Paramount
Tech Info: 16 mm/color/sound/3 reels/104 min.

Date/Country: 1974 + USA   Type: Feature
Distr/Arch: fnc
Annotation: Campus has recruited directly from the community
    in his documentary style look at young Blacks with dreams
    of escaping their ghetto situation. Professional actor
    Rony Clanton plays Sonny Carson whose life, in reality,
    has been reshaped by the lessons he learned trying to stay
    alive in Brooklyn's Bedford-Stuyvesant area.

EE BABA LEBA
Nar/Cast: Dizzy Gillespie* + Helen Humes* + Ralph Brown*
Tech Info: sound/bw/10 min.
Date/Country: 1947 + USA   Type: Musical Short
Annotation: Dizzy Gillespie and his Bebop Orchestra perform
    "Salt Peanuts" and "Ee Baba Leba" with Helen Humes doing
    the vocal on the latter. They also play the musical sup-
    port for Ralph Brown's tap dance number.

EEOC STORY
Nar/Cast: Ruby Dee*
Screenplay: William Greaves*
Producer: William Greaves*   Director: William Greaves*
Tech Info: 16 mm/color/sound/38 min.   Type: Documentary
Distr/Arch: wgp
Annotation: An informal, yet systematic, look at the
    machinery of the Equal Employment Opportunity Commission
    showing how it serves both the minority community and
    women. Ruby Dee narrates.

ELDRIDGE CLEAVER
Screenplay: William Klein
Producer: William Klein   Director: William Klein
Studio/Company: ONCIC + Cinema 5
Date/Country: 1970 + Algeria   Type: Documentary
Annotation: Filmed while Cleaver was in exile in Algeria,
    this is a thoughtful documentary of the man and his
    political and personal beliefs at that period of his life.
    Produced, written and directed in collaboration with
    Eldridge Cleaver* and Robert Scheer. Also features Kath-
    leen Cleaver*.

ELECTION DAY
Series: Our Gang
Nar/Cast: Our Gang + Allen Hoskins* + Louise Beavers* +
    Clarence Muse*
Screenplay: Anthony Mack
Producer: Hal Roach   Director: Anthony Mack
Studio/Company: MGM + Roach
Tech Info: super 8 mm/16 mm/bw/silent/1 reel
Date/Country: 1929 + USA   Type: Comedy Short
Distr/Arch: bla
Annotation: Farina and his little sister, Pleurisy, can't
    leave their farmyard until election votes are counted, but
    their mother wants them to deliver laundry. Finally they
    get downtown, but are caught in a battle between the
    police and a crooked group of gangster- politicians trying
    to loot the ballot boxes. During the shoot-out Farina and
    Pleurisy foil the crooks by finding the 'missing' ballots

in their laundry wagon and turning them in. But Mom
spanks them anyway for not delivering the laundry.

ELECTION DAZE
Series: Our Gang
Nar/Cast: Our Gang + Billie Thomas*
Screenplay: Hal Law + Robert A. McGowan
Producer: MGM   Director: Herbert Glazer
Studio/Company: MGM
Tech Info: bw/sound/1 reel
Date/Country: 1943 + USA   Type: Comedy Short
Annotation: After two tie votes, the gang decides to split
    and operate in two groups under separate leaders, Mickey
    and Froggy. Chaos reigns and Buckwheat reminds them of
    the Civil War. A new election puts Janet in command with
    promise of Saturday morning visiting day for dolls. Bil-
    lie Thomas stars as Buckwheat.

ELEPHANTS NEVER FORGET
Nar/Cast: Stepin Fetchit*   Director: Gordon Douglas
Date/Country: 1939 + USA   Type: Feature

ELEVEN P.M.
Nar/Cast: Marion H. Williams* + Sammie Fields* + Leo Pope* +
    Richard Maurice*
Screenplay: Richard Maurice*
Producer: Richard Maurice*   Director: Richard Maurice*
Studio/Company: Richard D. Maurice Productions
Tech Info: 16 mm/bw/silent/6 reels
Date/Country: 1928 + USA   Type: Feature
Distr/Arch: sta + lc
Annotation: A writer falls asleep and dreams the plot for a
    new drama which includes a strange element of reincarna-
    tion.

ELLERY QUEEN'S PENTHOUSE MYSTERY
Nar/Cast: Ralph Bellamy + Margaret Lindsay + Mantan
    Moreland*
Screenplay: Eric Taylor   Director: James Hogan
Studio/Company: Columbia
Date/Country: 1941 + USA   Type: Feature
Annotation: Mantan Moreland is Roy to Bellamy's Ellery Queen
    in this mystery about ventriloquists and Chinese
    treasures.

ELMER GANTRY
Nar/Cast: Rex Ingram* + Burt Lancaster + Jean Simmons + Dean
    Jagger   Story: Sinclair Lewis
Producer: Bernard Smith   Director: Richard Brooks
Studio/Company: United Artists
Tech Info: 16 mm/sound/color/146 min.
Date/Country: 1960 + USA   Type: Feature
Distr/Arch: uas
Annotation: Film adaptation of Sinclair Lewis' novel of a
    religious opportunist, his colleagues and times. Lan-
    caster is Gantry, Simmons a female evangelist through whom
    he gets his start and Ingram plays a black preacher.

EMBASSY
Nar/Cast: Max Von Sydow + Richard Roundtree* + Ray Milland +
    Chuck Connors
Date/Country: 1972   Type: TV Feature
Annotation: Roundtree is featured as Dick Shannon in love
    with   a   woman doctor and involved in international
    diplomacy. Milland is an American ambassador, Connors the
    man trying to kill Von Sydow, a Russian defector.

EMPEROR JONES, THE
Nar/Cast: Paul Robeson* + Dudley Diggs + Frank Wilson* +
    Fredi Washington* + Ruby Elzy + George Haymind Stamper* +
    Jackie Mayble* + Blueboy O'Connor* + Brandon Evans + Rex
    Ingram* + Gordon Taylor*
Screenplay: DuBose Heyward   Story: Eugene O'Neil
Producer: John Krimsky + Gifford Cochran   Director: Dudley
    Murphy
Studio/Company: United Artists Corp.
Tech Info: 16 mm/bw/sound/2 reels/73 min.
Date/Country: 1933 + USA   Type: Feature
Distr/Arch: rad + kpf + jan + bud + emg + cfm + lc
Annotation: Brutus Jones (Paul Robeson), a Pullman porter,
    manages to usurp the throne of the ruler of a Caribbean
    island. His lust for power leads to disastrous conse-
    quences. Frank Wilson is Jeff; Fredi Washington, Undine;
    Ruby Elzy, Dolly.

EN REMONTANT LE MISSISSIPPI
Alt Title(s): Out of the Blacks, into the Blues
Nar/Cast: Ted Joans* + Louis Armstrong* + Arthur "Big Boy"
    Crudup* + Willie Dixon* + B.B.King* + Walter "Furry"
    Lewis* + Mance Lipscomb* + Brownie McGhee* + Roosevelt
    Sykes* + Sonny Terry* + Bukka White* + Junior Wells* +
    Robert Pete Williams*   Director: Robert Manthoulis
Tech Info: 106 min.
Date/Country: 1971 + France + West Germany   Type: Docu-
    mentary
Annotation: Ted Joans narrates and the musicians perform in
    a Mississippi River journey (in two parts) rediscovering
    the origin of the Blues.

END OF THE DIALOGUE
Producer: Morena Films + Pan-African Congress   Director:
    Nana Mahomo*
Tech Info: 16 mm/bw/45 min.
Date/Country: 1970 + South Africa   Type: Documentary
Distr/Arch: adf
Annotation: The difference in living standards between
    whites and Blacks in modern day South Africa are dramati-
    cally pointed to in this secretly shot documentary. Made
    in association with Morena Films by a group of black and
    white South African exiles.

END OF THE RIVER, THE
Nar/Cast: Sabu + Bibi Ferreira + Robert Douglas +.Raymond
    Lovell + Orlando Martins*
Screenplay: Wolfgang Wilheim   Story: Desmond Holdridge
Producer: m. Powel + E. Pressberger   Director: Derek Twist

Studio/Company: Archers
Date/Country: 1947 + Britian

END OF THE ROAD
Nar/Cast: Stacy Keach + Harris Yulin + Dorothy Tristan +
  James Earl Jones*
Screenplay: Dennis McGuire + Terry Southern + Aram Avakian
  Story: John Barth
Producer: Terry Southern + Stephen F. Kesten   Director:
  Aram Avakian
Studio/Company: Allied Artists
Tech Info: 16 mm/color/sound/3 reels/114 min.
Date/Country: 1970 + USA   Type: Feature
Distr/Arch: cin
Annotation: James Earl Jones plays Doctor D, Keach's
  therapist in an (x-rated) adaptation of John Barth's novel
  of the "academic-intellectual" fifties, complete with as-
  sistant professor, faculty wife, small town college. This
  one adds novel psychiatric methods, abortion and ac-
  cidental death.

ENSIGN PULVER
Nar/Cast: Al Freeman, Jr.* + Diana Sands* + Burl Ives +
  Robert Walker, Jr.
Screenplay: Joshua Logan + Peter Flibleman
Producer: Joshua Logan   Director: Joshua Logan
Studio/Company: Warner Bros.
Tech Info: 16 mm/sound/color/104 min.
Date/Country: 1964 + USA   Type: Feature
Distr/Arch: arg + ccc + cwf + mac + mod + mot + roa + sel +
  swa + tfc + wcf + wel + who + wil
Annotation: In this comedy-drama sequel to Mister Roberts
  Burl Ives is the hated Captain who gets his comeuppance,
  via Ensign Pulver and a bit of blackmail. Freeman plays
  Taru and Sands, Mila.

ENTER THE DRAGON
Nar/Cast: Jim Kelly* + Bruce Lee
Studio/Company: Warner Brothers
Date/Country: 1970 + USA

EPHESUS
Producer: Fred Padula
Tech Info: 16 mm/sound/bw/25 min.
Date/Country: 1965 + USA   Type: Documentary
Distr/Arch: mac + uca + can
Annotation: Sunday evening services at a black Holiness
  church in Berkeley, California.

EQUAL PROTECTION OF THE LAWS
Producer: Paul Burnford
Tech Info: 16 mm/sound/color/1 reel/30 min.
Date/Country: 1967 + USA   Type: Documentary
Distr/Arch: iu + bfa
Annotation: Relates the difficulties encountered in attem-
  pting to integrate a California school system. Portrays
  the conflicts engendered when previously de facto se-
  gregated schools for non-white Americans are required to

desegregate.   Highlights opposition to open housing laws
and underlying racial and cultural animosities.

ESEQUALITY UNDER LAW: THE LOST GENERATION OF PRINCE EDWARD
COUNTY
Producer: Encyclopedia Britannica Films
Tech Info: 16 mm/sound/color/1 reel/25 min.
Date/Country: 1964   Type: Documentary
Distr/Arch: iu + ebec
Annotation: Documents the racial strife in Prince Edward
County, Virginia. Explains how schools were closed during
a four- year period to avoid racial integration until Su-
preme Court action forced their reopening under integrated
conditions in 1964.

ESCAPADES OF ESTELLE
Producer: Harry Palmer
Studio/Company: Mutual Pictures
Tech Info: 35 mm/silent/bw/1 reel   Type: Animated Short
Distr/Arch: lc
Annotation: A "Komic Kartoon," reference print only.

ESCAPE FROM DEVIL'S ISLAND
Nar/Cast: Victor Jory + Florence Rice + Norman Foster +
Daniel Haynes* + Noble Johnson*
Screenplay: Earle Snell + Fred Niblo, Jr.   Story: Fred De
Gresac   Director: Albert Rogell
Studio/Company: Columbia
Date/Country: 1935 + USA
Annotation: A motley assortment of convicts attempt to
escape from the notorious French prison fortress.   Daniel
Haynes plays Djikki, Noble Johnson is Bisco.

ET LA NEIGE N'ETAIT PLUS
Alt Title(s): And There Was Snow No Longer
Screenplay: Samb Makharam* + Jacques Janvier
Producer: Ababacar Samb-Makharam*   Director: Ababacar
Samb-Makharam*
Tech Info: sound/22 min./French commentary
Date/Country: 1965 + Senegal   Type: Dramatic Short
Annotation: Highly discussed film about the return of an
African student from Europe to his village and his read-
justment to his family and African tradition. At first he
retains his European attitudes but in a symbolic shift,
rejects his westernized girlfriend for a simple, beautiful
seller of peanuts.

ETHIOPIA (1956)
Producer: Encyclopedia Britannica Films
Tech Info: 16 mm/sound/bw/24 min.
Date/Country: Ethiopia   Type: Documentary
Distr/Arch: ebec
Annotation: The political events of the past 50 years are
reviewed.

ETHIOPIA (1972)
Producer: Darer International Corp. + Stanley Darer + Peter
Whittle

Tech Info: 16 mm/sound/bw/40 min.
Date/Country: Ethiopia   Type: Documentary
Distr/Arch: cmsls
Annotation: A day in the life of 80 year old Haile Selassie.

ETHNIC DANCE - ROUNDTRIP TO TRINIDAD
Series: A Time To Dance
Nar/Cast: Geoffrey Holder* + Carmen de Lavallade*
Producer: NET
Tech Info: 16 mm/sound/bw/1 reel/29 min.
Date/Country: 1960 + USA   Type: Documentary
Distr/Arch: iu
Annotation: Explores the significance of ethnic dance in the
    field cf formal dance. Presents a variety of West Indian
    dances including Bele, Yanvallou, and Banda, a Haitian
    dance about death.

ETHNOLOGICAL CRIMINAL
Series: Criminal Man
Producer: KQED + NET
Tech Info: 16 mm/sound/bw/1 reel/30 min.
Date/Country: 1958   Type: Documentary
Distr/Arch: iu
Annotation: Discusses the relationship of crime to race,
    national origin, and minority groups. Points out patterns
    of belief and the misconceptions that exist. Relates
    living conditions and geographical distribution of crime.
    Concludes that race is irrelevant to criminality.

EUBIE BLAKE PLAYS
Nar/Cast: Eubie Blake*
Studio/Company: Lee DeForest Phonofilms
Tech Info: 35 mm/sound/bw/1 reel   Type: Musical Short
Distr/Arch: lc
Annotation: Eubie Blake plays and sings "Way Down Upon the
    Swanee River."

EVAN'S CORNER   Story: Elizabeth Starr Hill
Producer: Bosustow Productions
Tech Info: 16 mm/sound/color/1 reel/23 min.
Date/Country: 1969 + USA   Type: Dramatic Short
Distr/Arch: iu + bfa
Annotation: Shows how a young black boy copes with a need
    for privacy in an over-crowded ghetto home by claiming a
    corner for his own. Reveals his own feelings when he
    realizes that he cannot live alone in a "corner" but has
    to be willing to step out and help others.

EVERBODY WORKS BUT FATHER
Nar/Cast: Lew Dockstader
Studio/Company: Biograph
Date/Country: 1905 + USA   Type: ComedyShort
Annotation: Two versions (one version white, the other
    black); in both the family battles against its father who
    dominates from his rocking chair.

EVERY DAY'S A HOLIDAY
Nar/Cast: Mae West + Edmund Lowe + Lloyd Nolan + Louis Arm-

strong*
Screenplay: Mae West
Producer: Emanuel Cohn   Director: A. Edward Sutherland
Studio/Company: Paramount
Tech Info: 16 mm/sound/bw/79 min.
Date/Country: 1938 + USA   Type: Feature
Distr/Arch: uni
Annotation: Mae West is Peaches O'Day, a singer who passes
    herself off as Mlle. FiFi, the singing rage of "Paree,"
    who in her spare time sells the Brooklyn Bridge to various
    suckers. The film features Louis Armstrong and his band
    in a night club scene.

EVERY MAN FOR HIMSELF
Series: Our Gang
Nar/Cast: Our Gang + Allen Hoskins*
Screenplay: Hal Roach
Producer: Hal Roach   Director: Robert McGowan
Studio/Company: Pathe
Tech Info: silent/bw/2 reels
Date/Country: 1924 + USA   Type: Comedy Short
Annotation: To support its athletic club, the gang runs a
    shoeshine stand and also scraps with the new twins in
    town. Allen Hoskins stars as Farina.

EVERY MAN NEEDS ONE
Nar/Cast: Henry Gibson + Ken Berry + Connie Stevens + Gail
    Fisher*
Screenplay: Carl Kleinschmitt
Producer: Jerry Paris   Director: Jerry Paris
Studio/Company: Spelling/Goldberg Production
Date/Country: 1972 + USA   Type: TV Feature
Annotation: Gail Fisher makes a cameo appearance in this
    romantic comedy about a swinging bacheolor who hires a
    female assistant.

EVERYBODY'S PREJUDICE
Producer: National Film Board of Canada
Tech Info: 16 mm/sound/bw/1 reel/21 min.
Date/Country: 1961   Type: Documentary
Distr/Arch: con
Annotation: The characteristics of the bigot are ultimately
    isolated in this educational film treating prejudices
    based on fact and those completely divorced from reason.

EX-FLAME
Nar/Cast: Neil Hamilton + Marian nixon + Norman Kerry +
    Louis Armstrong*   Director: Victor Halperin
Tech Info: sound/bw/73 min.
Date/Country: 1931 + USA   Type: Feature
Annotation: A set of misunderstandings in an affluent family
    leads to the wife leaving home after being accused of
    having an affair with a recently deceased friend. All
    works out in the end. Louis Armstrong first worked in
    films with his band in this film, supposedly a modernized
    version of East Lynne.

EXILE, THE

Nar/Cast: Eunice   Brooks*   +   Charles   Moore*   +   A.B.
  Comathiere* + Carl Mahon* + Lou Vernon* + Katherine
  Noisette* + Louise Cook* + Roland Holder + George Randol*
  + Donald Haywood's band*   Director: Oscar Micheaux*
Studio/Company: Micheaux Film Corporation
Date/Country: 1931 + USA   Type: Feature
Annotation: A young man, disenchanted with his fiancee,
  leaves Chicago for the West and settles in South Dakota.
  There he meets and becomes very attached to a young woman
  he believes is white, but all works out well for them when
  he discovers she is of mixed blood.

EXPERT, THE
Nar/Cast: Charles Sale + Louise Beavers* + Dickie Moore +
  Lois Wilson   Story: Edna Ferber   Director: Archie Mayo
Studio/Company: Warner Brothers
Tech Info: 16 mm/sound/bw/69 min.
Date/Country: 1932 + USA   Type: Feature
Distr/Arch: uas
Annotation: Story of an elderly man who comes to live with
  his son's family and the complications that arise. Louise
  Beavers is Lulu.

EXPRESS YOURSELF: REVENGE
Producer: Afram
Tech Info: 16 mm/sond/color/50 min.   Type: Documentary
Distr/Arch: afr
Annotation: Black prisoners' view of treatment in a New
  Jersey prison controlled by whites.

EXTRAORDINARY SEAMAN, THE
Nar/Cast: Juano Hernandez* + Faye Dunaway
Screenplay: Phillip Rock + Hal Dresner
Producer: Edward Lewis   Director: John Frankenheimer
Studio/Company: MGM
Tech Info: 16 mm/sound/color/80 min.
Date/Country: 1969 + USA   Type: Feature
Distr/Arch: fnc
Annotation: Comedy About four American sailors in World War
  II and a whiskey-drinking ghost, and his attempt to redeem
  his family honor ater having lost it when he got drunk
  before battle in 1914 (WWI). Juano Hernandez plays Ali
  Shar.

EYE OF THE STORM, THE
Producer: ABC
Tech Info: 16 mm/sound/color/1 reel/26 min.
Date/Country: 1970 + USA   Type: Documentary
Distr/Arch: iu + xex
Annotation: Presents an experiment in prejudice and dis-
  crimination conducted by a Riceville, Iowa, teacher with
  her third grade class. Indicates that prejudice and dis-
  crimination are learned attitudes, a key to their elimina-
  tion in society.

EYES IN THE NIGHT
Nar/Cast: Edward Arnold + Ann Harding + Mantan Moreland*
Screenplay: Guy Trosper + Howard E. Rogers

Producer: Jack Chertok   Director: Fred Zinnimann
Studio/Company: MGM
Date/Country: 1942 + USA   Type: Feature
Annotation: Mantan Moreland is Alistair in this suspense
    melodrama about a blind detective (Arnold) who uncovers
    spies and solves murders with scarcely any concern for his
    handicap.

EYES_OF_YOUTH
Nar/Cast: Abbie Mitchell*
Studio/Company: Quality Amusement Company
Date/Country: 1920 + USA

EZEKIEL_MPHAHLELE
Producer: NET
Tech Info: 16 mm/sound/bw/1 reel/29 min.
Date/Country: 1964 + USA   Type: Documentary
Distr/Arch: iu
Annotation: Presents an interview with exiled South African
    essayist and short story writer, Mphahlele*, who discusses
    the advantages and disadvantages of a writer in exile.

FABULOUS_HARLEM_GLOBETROTTERS
Nar/Cast: Harlem Globetrotter Team*
Studio/Company: Castle
Tech Info: 16 mm/sound/color/10 min.   Type: Sport Short
Distr/Arch: roa
Annotation: The "magicians" of basketball are featured in
    this comedy short displaying their basketball talent.

FACE_TO_FACE
Series: Epitaph for Jim Crow
Producer: NET Network + Harvard University
Tech Info: 16 mm/bw/sound/30 min.
Date/Country: 1961 + USA   Type: Documentary
Distr/Arch: adl
Annotation: Dr. Pettigrew explores the problems of bringing
    diverse groups together and the value of various kinds of
    contact in attempts to better intergroup relations.

FACTS_OF_LIFE,_THE
Nar/Cast: Louise Beavers* + Bob Hope + Lucille Ball + Ruth
    Hussey
Screenplay: Norman Panama + Melvin Frank
Producer: Norman Panama   Director: Melvin Frank
Studio/Company: United Artists
Tech Info: sound/103 min.
Date/Country: 1961 + USA   Type: Feature
Annotation: Bob Hope and Lucille Ball play a couple each
    married to another who decide to have an affair, and their
    various escapades in trying to consumate it. Louise
    Beavers has a minor role as Hope's maid in her last film
    appearance.

FAIR_AND_MUDDY
Series: Our Gang
Nar/Cast: Our Gang + Allen Hoskins*
Producer: Hal Roach   Director: Charley Oelze

Studio/Company: MGM
Tech Info: bw/silent/2 reels
Date/Country: 1928 + USA   Type: Comedy Short
Annotation: The gang wins the heart of a stuffy matron by
    involving her in a mud throwing battle with a rival gang.
    Allen Hoskins stars as Farina.

FALL GUY
Producer: William Foster*
Studio/Company: Foster Photoplay Company
Tech Info: silent/bw
Date/Country: 1913 + USA

FAMILY HONEYMOON
Nar/Cast: Claudette Colbert + Fred McMurray + Hattie Mc-
    Daniel* + Rita Johnson
Screenplay: Dane Lussier
Producer: John Beck + Z. Wayne Griffin   Director: Claude
    Binyon
Studio/Company: Universal International
Tech Info: 16 mm/sound/bw/94 min.
Date/Country: 1948 + USA   Type: Feature
Distr/Arch: uni
Annotation: The various trials and tribulations when newly-
    wed Fred McMurray goes on his honeymoon with his new wife
    Claudette Colbert and her 3 children. Hattie McDaniel
    plays Phyllis in a minor role.

FAMILY NOBODY WANTED, THE
Nar/Cast: Shirley Jones + James Olson + Katherine Helmond +
    Sherry Lynn Kupahu*
Screenplay: Suzanne Clauser
Producer: William Kayden   Director: Ralph Senensky
Studio/Company: Universal City Studios + Groverton Produc-
    tions, Ltd.   Type: TV Feature
Annotation: Story of the Doss family, based on the novel by
    Helen Doss, and their twelve racially mixed children.

FAMILY OF GHANA
Producer: National Film Board of Canada
Tech Info: 16 mm/sound/bw/1 reel/30 min.
Date/Country: 1958   Type: Documentary
Distr/Arch: iu + mghf
Annotation: Experiences of a family in Ghana illustrate the
    culture of that country. Includes sequences of Accra and
    of native music and dancing.

FAMILY SECRET, THE
Nar/Cast: Martin Turner* + Baby Peggy Montgomery + Gladys
    Hulette + Edward Earle
Screenplay: Lois Zellner   Director: William Seiter
Studio/Company: Universal Pictures
Tech Info: 35 mm/silent/bw/6 reels
Date/Country: 1924 + USA   Type: Feature
Annotation: Martin Turner plays Uncle Rose in a melodrama
    about a secret marriage, a lost baby and a burglary.

FAMILY TROUBLES

Series: Our Gang
Nar/Cast: Our Gang + Billie Thomas*
Screenplay: Hal Law + Robert A. McGowan
Producer: MGM   Director: Herbert Glazer
Studio/Company: MGM
Tech Info: bw/sound/1 reel
Date/Country: 1943 + USA   Type: Comedy Short
Annotation: When Janet runs away from home, the gang tries
    to get the kindly Joneses to adopt her.   They do, but
    decide to turn mean to teach her a lesson. She runs away
    again and hides out with the gang in a cave, until life
    gets too hard and she returns home. Billie Thomas stars
    as Buckwheat.

FANNIE BELL CHAPMAN: GOSPEL SINGER
Producer: Judy Peiser + Bill Ferris + Center for Southern
    Folklore
Tech Info: 16 mm/sound/color/42 min.
Date/Country: 1975 + USA   Type: Documentary
Distr/Arch: csf
Annotation: Fannie Chapman's* life, family and religion are
    described. She is a faith healer and gospel singer in
    Centreville, Mississippi. Provided by Center for Southern
    Folklore.

FANNIE LOU HAMER: CHRONICLE OF A MOVEMENT
Series: Portrait in Black
Producer: Rediscovery
Tech Info: 16 mm/sound/color/10 min.
Date/Country: 1972   Type: Documentary
Distr/Arch: red + sef
Annotation: Documentary of Fannie Lou Hamer and her struggle
    for political representation for Blacks in Mississippi.

FAREWELL TO FAME
Nar/Cast: Frankie Darro + Mantan Moreland*   Director: Jean
    Yarborough
Date/Country: 1941 + USA   Type: Feature
Annotation: See annotation for Chasing Trouble.

FAREWELL UNCLE TOM
Alt Title(s): seeAdieu Oncle Tom

FARM HANDS
Series: Our Gang
Nar/Cast: Our Gang + Billie Thomas*
Screenplay: Hal Law + Robert A. McGowan
Producer: MGM   Director: Herbert Glazer
Studio/Company: MGM
Tech Info: bw/sound/1 reel
Date/Country: 1943 + USA   Type: Comedy Short
Annotation: The city bred gang runs into various misad-
    ventures when they are invited for a stay on a farm. Bil-
    lie Thomas stars as Buckwheat.

FAST COMPANY
Series: Our Gang
Nar/Cast: Our Gang + Ernie Morrison* + Allen Hoskins*

Screenplay: Hal Roach
Producer: Hal Roach   Director: Robert McGowan
Studio/Company: Pathe
Tech Info: silent/bw/2 reels
Date/Country: 1924 + USA   Type: Comedy Short
Annotation: On the way to a swimming expedition, the gang
  runs into a rich kid, whereupon Mickey trades places with
  him and goes back to the hotel where the rich kid lives.
  The rest of the gang tags along and tears up the hotel.
  Ernie Morrison stars as Sunshine Sammy and Allen Hoskins
  stars as Farina.

FAST FREIGHT
Series: Our Gang
Nar/Cast: Our Gang + Allen Hoskins*
Screenplay: Robert F. McGowan
Producer: Robert F. McGowan + Hal Roach   Director: Anthony
  Mack
Studio/Company: MGM + Roach
Tech Info: super 8 mm/16 mm/bw/silent/2 reels
Date/Country: 1929 + USA   Type: Comedy Short
Distr/Arch: bla
Annotation: Riding the rails with Pete, Farina meets a gang
  of kids who want to join him on his trip to California
  where he wants to be a street sweeper on streets paved
  with gold. Bees eventually chase them from the train, to
  a deserted house in some woods, where as night falls the
  kids think they're seeing ghosts. A policeman arrives to
  'rescue' them, but Farina goes back to the train - only
  this time he finds himself locked inside a car full of
  skeltons and cadavers heading for a medical school.

FEAR AND DESIRE
Nar/Cast: Frank Silvera* + Kenneth Harp + Paul Mazursky
Screenplay: Howard O. Sackles
Producer: Stanley Kubrick   Director: Stanley Kubrick
Date/Country: 1953 + USA   Type: Feature
Annotation: Frank Silvera, the only one of the small cast
  with major film experience, plays Mac, the sergeant, one
  of four (World War II) soldiers trapped behind enemy lines
  after their plane has been shot down. As second in command, he is tough, outwardly unaffected by the hardships
  they face and driven by a compulsion to capture the enemy
  general whom they identify at an outpost.

FEAR WOMAN
Nar/Cast: Alistair Cooke
Producer: United Nations
Tech Info: 16 mm/sound/color/28 min.
Date/Country: 1971 + Ghana   Type: Documentary
Distr/Arch: mghf + ueuwis + ucemc + umavec + untv
Annotation: Shows how women run a large proportion of the
  nation's retail trade in this West African country.

FEARLESS FRANK
Alt Title(s): Frank's Greatest Adventure
Nar/Cast: Ben Carruthers* + Jon Voight + Monique Van Vooren
  + Nelson Algren

Screenplay: Philip Kaufman
Producer: Philip Kaufman   Director: Philip Kaufman
Studio/Company: American International
Tech Info: 16 mm/sound/color/79 min.
Date/Country: 1969 + USA   Type: Feature
Distr/Arch: unf
Annotation: Carruthers is "The Cat", one of the gangsters
    who kills Frank, half of the Jon Voight character, in this
    satire cn urban life which includes monsters, supermen,
    seduction and Nelson Algren as Needles.

FEATHERED SERPENT, THE
Series: Charlie Chan
Nar/Cast: Sidney Toler + Roland Winters + Keye Luke + Mantan
    Moreland*
Screenplay: Oliver Drake
Producer: James S. Burkett   Director: William Beaudine
Studio/Company: Monogram
Tech Info: 16 mm/sound/bw/2 reels/61 min.
Date/Country: 1948 + USA   Type: Feature
Distr/Arch: cin
Annotation: Mantan Moreland is Birmingham Brown, Charlie
    Chan's chauffeur and comic foil.

FESTIVAL
Producer: Patchke Productions   Director: Murray Lerner
Tech Info: 16 mm/sound/bw/98 min.
Date/Country: 1967 + USA   Type: Documentary
Annotation: Scenes of Newport Folk Festivals from 1963-66.
    Includes, among others, Staple Singers*, Mississippi John
    Hurt*, Fred McDowell*, Georgia Sea Island Singers*.

FEUD AND THE TURKEY, THE   Director: D.W. Griffith
Studio/Company: Biograph
Tech Info: 35 mm/silent/bw/904 ft.
Date/Country: 1908 + USA   Type: Dramatic Short
Annotation: Old Aunt Dinah and Uncle Daniel, the "colored"
    servants are active participants in this "romance of the
    Kentucky Mountains." In fact, Aunt Dinah's prayers for a
    Christmas turkey for the young folk eventually bring about
    a family reconciliation and an end to the feud.

FIERCEST HEART, THE
Nar/Cast: Rafer Johnson* + Hari Rhodes* + Stuart Whitman +
    Juliet Prowse
Screenplay: Edmund North
Producer: George Sherman   Director: George Sherman
Studio/Company: Fox
Tech Info: 16 mm/sound/color/91 min.
Date/Country: 1961 + USA   Type: Feature
Distr/Arch: mod + ics + wsa
Annotation: Rafer Johnson is Nzobo, an African friend of
    Steve Bates (Whitman), with whom he breaks out of a prison
    garrison in South Africa. They join a group of Boers
    escaping from British oppression and eventually Nzobo
    slays a Zulu chief when the Zulus raid the Boer settle-
    ment, in this mid 19th century melodrama.

FIFTY ROADS TO TOWN
Nar/Cast: Don Ameche + Ann Southern + Slim Summerville +
   Jane Darwell + Stepin Fetchit*
Screenplay: George Marion, Jr. + William Conselman   Story:
   Louis Frederick Nebel
Producer: Raymond Griffith   Director: Norman Taurog
Studio/Company: Twentieth Century Fox
Tech Info: sound/bw
Date/Country: 1937 + USA   Type: Feature
Annotation: Mistaken identity provides much of the humor in
   this farce about the goings-on at an out of the   way cot-
   tage. Stepin Fetchit is Percy in a not unusual role.

FIGHT AGAINST SLAVERY, THE
Nar/Cast: Stanley Irons* + Patrick Barr + David Collings +
   Ronald Pickup + Ronald Lacey + Gareth Thomas + Dinsdale
   Landon + John Castle
Screenplay: Evan Jones*
Producer: BBC + Time-Life Films + Christopher Ralling
Studio/Company: BBC
Tech Info: 16 mm/film or videocassette/color/sound/six 52
   minute episodes
Date/Country: 1976 + Great Britain   Type: TV Dramatized
   Documentary
Distr/Arch: tim
Annotation: A six-part dramatization of the history of
   slavery filmed on location in Africa, England and the West
   Indies. Beginning ,in 1750, when the shipping of slaves to
   the New World was at its height, each episode follows the
   development of public attitudes and legal opinion that led
   to emancipation in the British Empire in 1834.   Stanley
   Irons plays the black martyr Daddy Sharp.

FIGHT NEVER ENDS, THE
Nar/Cast: Joe Louis* + Ruby Dee* + The Mills Brothers* +
   William Greaves* + Emmett "Babe" Wallace* + Harrell Til-
   lman* + Elwood Smith* + Gwendolyn Tynes*
Producer: William Alexander*
Studio/Company: Alexander Productions
Date/Country: 1947 + USA   Type: Feature
Annotation: Joe Louis, as himself, fights juvenile deli-
   quency in a film billed as "a story as powerful as the
   Brown Bomber himself."

FIGHT THAT GHOST
Nar/Cast: Dewey "Pigmeat" Markham* + John "Rastus" Murray* +
   Sidney Easton*
Studio/Company: Toddy Pictures
Tech Info: sound/bw/62 min.
Date/Country: 1946 + USA   Type: Feature
Annotation: A comedy mystery feature replete with ghosts.

FIGHTER, THE
Nar/Cast: Richard Conte + Lee J. Cobb + Vanessa Brown +
   Frank Silvera*
Screenplay: Aben Kandel + Herbert Kline
Producer: Alex Gottlieb   Director: Herbert Kline
Studio/Company: United Artists

Date/Country: 1952 + USA   Type: Feature
Annotation: Frank Silvera plays Paulino, father of the
    Mexican boxer-revolutionary (Conte), who uses his success-
    ful boxing career to finance the struggle of his people
    against the repressive regime in Mexico.

FIGHTERS, THE
Nar/Cast: Muhammad Ali* + Joe Frazier*
Screenplay: William Greaves*
Producer: William Greaves*   Director: William Greaves*
Tech Info: 16 mm/sound/color/3 reels/114 min.
Date/Country: 1974 + USA   Type: Documentary
Annotation: Records the first Muhammad Ali-Joe Frazier bout
    in March 1971 and shows every moment of every round, re-
    corded by cameras stationed all over Madison Square
    Garden.

FIGHTIN' FOOLS
Series: Our Gang
Nar/Cast: Our Gang + Billie Thomas*
Screenplay: Hal Law + Robert McGowan
Producer: MGM   Director: Edward Cahn
Studio/Company: MGM
Tech Info: bw/sound/1 reel
Date/Country: 1941 + USA   Type: Comedy Short
Annotation: The gang defeats Slicker and his bunch in a
    tomato, cheese and watermelon throwing battle.   Billie
    Thomas stars as Buckwheat.

FIGHTING AMERICANS
Tech Info: 50 min.
Date/Country: 1943   Type: Newsreel
Annotation: Shows black air cadets from Tuskegee Army Air
    Field, Alabama and black WACS from Ft. Devens, Mass.

FIGHTING DEACON, THE
Studio/Company: Tiger Flowers and Walt Miller
Date/Country: 1925 + USA   Type: Dramatized Documentary
Annotation: Depicts the rise of boxer Tiger Flowers*, known
    as the "Fighting Deacon," to big money in the ring in the
    1920's.

FIGHTS OF NATIONS, THE
Studio/Company: Biograph
Tech Info: bw/silent/1 reel/8 min.
Date/Country: 1907 + USA   Type: Dramatic Short
Annotation: The film shows a series of ethnic pairs who
    fight each other in stereotypical ways. Jews, Scots,
    Blacks, etc.; e.g. Blacks cut each other with razors, in
    "Sunny Africa, Eighth Avenue," fighting over a woman. The
    finale includes reconciliation of all the combatants ex-
    cept the Blacks.

FINAL COMEDOWN, THE
Nar/Cast: Billy Dee Williams* + Pamela Jones* + Maidie
    Norman* + Raymond St. Jacques* + D'Urville Martin* + R.G.
    Armstrong + Celia Kaye
Screenplay: Oscar Williams*

Producer: Oscar Williams*   Director: Oscar Williams*
Studio/Company: New World
Tech Info: sound/color/84 min.
Date/Country: 1972 + USA   Type: Feature
Annotation: A black youth is forced through injustice and
    circumstances to lead a violent rebellion.

FINALLY GOT THE NEWS
Producer: Stewart Bird + Peter Gessner + Rene Lichtman +
    John Louis, Jr. + League of Revolutionary Black Workers
Tech Info: 16 mm/color/bw/sound
Date/Country: 1970 + USA   Type: Documentary
Distr/Arch: tri
Annotation: A documentary offering the workers' view of con-
    ditions inside Detroit's auto factories and the develop-
    ment of a black revolutionary movement.

FINCHO
Nar/Cast: Patrick Akponu* + Comfort Ajilo* + Gordon Parry-
    Hobroyd + Harry Belafonte*
Producer: Sam Zebba*   Director: Sam Zebba*
Tech Info: 16 mm/color/sound/3 reels/75 min.
Date/Country: 1958 + Nigeria   Type: Dramatized Documentary
Distr/Arch: mac
Annotation: Set in Nigeria, Fincho raises the problems of
    industrialization and modernization in emerging African
    nations. The cast is composed of non-professional Nigeri-
    an actors. Introduction by Harry Belafonte.

FIND LIVINGSTONE
Series: Search for Nile
Nar/Cast: James Mason
Producer: Michael Hastings   Director: Derek Marlowe
Studio/Company: BBC-TV
Tech Info: 16 mm/sound/color/2 reels/52 min.
Date/Country: 1972 + East Africa   Type: Documentary
Distr/Arch: timlif
Annotation: Stanley is sent by James Bennet to find Living-
    stone, which he does on November 3, 1871; together they
    explore Lake Tanganyika's north shore.

FINDERS KEEPERS, LOVERS WEEPERS
Nar/Cast: Lavelle Roby* + Anne Chapman + Paul Lockwood
Screenplay: Richard Zachary   Story: Russ Meyer
Producer: Russ Meyer   Director: Russ Meyer
Studio/Company: 16 mm/sound/color/71 min. + 17 + 1969 + USA
    Type: Feature
Distr/Arch: bac
Annotation: another x-rated Meyer film with characters,
    especially female, who have enormous sexual appetites.
    Lavelle Roby plays Claire, the keeper of the house and
    long time sexual parner of Paul's (Paul Lockwood) whose
    bar she plans to rob. Complications multiply.

FINIAN'S RAINBOW
Nar/Cast: Al Freeman, Jr.* + Fred Astaire + Petula Clark +
    Tommy Steele + Frederick O'Neal + Roy Glenn* + Avon Long*
Screenplay: E.Y. Harburg + Fred Saidy

Producer: Fred Landor   Director: Francis Ford Coppola
Studio/Company: Warner Bros. + Seven Arts
Tech Info: 16 mm/sound/color/160 min.
Date/Country: 1968 + USA   Type: Feature
Distr/Arch: arg + bud + ccc + cha + cwf + ics + mac + mod +
   mot + new + roa + sel + tfc + tmc + twy + unf + wcf +   who
   + wil
Annotation: The story deals with an Irishman who has buried
   his gold and a bigoted white Southern senator who is
   turned black by Sharon (Clark)'s wish that he would understand the plight of the sharecropper.

FIRE_FIGHTERS
Series: Our Gang
Nar/Cast: Our Gang + Ernie 'Booker T.' Morrison* + Allen
   Hoskins* + Ernie Morrison, Sr.* + George Rowe
Screenplay: Hal Roach + Robert F. McGowan
Producer: Hal Roach   Director: Robert McGowan
Studio/Company: Pathe
Tech Info: silent/bw/2 reels
Date/Country: 1922 + USA   Type: Comedy Short
Annotation: The Our Gangers, inspired by the Fire Depart-
   ment's new boiler tank, turn themselves into a miniature
   Fire Department who aid in the capture of moonshiners.
   Allen Hoskins stars as Farina.

FIRED_WIFE
Nar/Cast: Louise Allbritton + Diana Barrymore + Walter Abel
   + Rex Ingram*
Screenplay: Michael Resier + Ernest Pagano   Director:
   Charles Lamont
Studio/Company: Universal
Date/Country: 1943 + USA   Type: Feature
Annotation: A couple want to keep their marriage secret for
   business reasons; the film records their many escapades in
   trying to do so. Rex Ingram plays Charles.

FIRST_BABY,_THE
Nar/Cast: Hattie McDaniel*
Date/Country: 1936 + USA   Type: Feature
Annotation: One of the many films Hattie McDaniel appeared
   in as maid/servant in 1936.

FIRST_ROUND-UP,_THE
Series: Our Gang
Nar/Cast: Our Gang + Matthew Beard* + Billie Thomas*
Producer: Hal Roach   Director: Gus Meins
Studio/Company: MGM + Roach
Tech Info: super 8 mm/16 mm/bw/sound/2 reels/20 min.
Date/Country: 1934 + USA   Type: Comedy Short
Distr/Arch: roa + bla
Annotation: The gang goes on a camping trip, but only Scotty
   and Spanky seem to be prepared.   They hitchhike to the
   spot while the others walk, have food where the others
   don't, and are perfectly happy in the dark while the
   others are scared to death. Matthew Beard stars as Stymie
   and Billie Thomas stars as Buckwheat.

FIRST SEVEN YEARS, THE
Series: Our Gang
Nar/Cast: Our Gang + Allen Hoskins*
Screenplay: Robert F. McGowan
Producer: Robert F. McGowan + Hal Roach   Director: Robert
  F. McGowan
Studio/Company: MGM
Tech Info: bw/sound/2 reels
Date/Country: 1930 + USA   Type: Comedy Short
Annotation: Jackie and Speck battle for the affections of
  Mary Ann. Allen Hoskins stars as Farina.

FIRST WORLD FESTIVAL OF NEGRO ARTS, THE
Alt Title(s): Dakar Festival of Negro Arts
Producer: Alexandra Sahia Studios for UNESCO + William
  Greaves*
Tech Info: 16 mm/sound/color/1 reel/20 min.
Date/Country: 1968 + Senegal   Type: Documentary
Distr/Arch: iu + mghf
Annotation: Discloses the purpose of the First World
  Festival of Negro Arts held in Dakar as an attempt to
  create an awareness of Negro art and culture. Surveys the
  contributions in music, dance, textiles, poetry,
  sculpture, and painting.

FIRST YEAR, THE
Nar/Cast: Matt Moore + Kathryn Perry + Carolynne Snowden*
  Story: Frank Cravens   Director: Frank Borzage
Studio/Company: Fox
Date/Country: 1926 + USA   Type: Feature
Annotation: This film deals with a couple learning to adjust
  to each other during their first year of marriage.
  Carolynne Snowden plays their nonchalant maid.

FISH HOOKY
Series: Our Gang
Nar/Cast: Our Gang + Bobbie Beard* + Allen Hoskins*
Producer: hal Roach   Director: Robert F. McGowan
Studio/Company: MGM + Roach
Tech Info: super 8 mm/16 mm/bw/sound/1 reel/19 min.
Date/Country: 1933 + USA   Type: Comedy Short
Distr/Arch: bla
Annotation: When the gang plays hooky, they miss out on a
  school trip to an amusement park and have a run-in chase
  with the truant officer instead. Allen Hoskins stars as
  Farina.

FISH
Nar/Cast: Bert Williams*
Studio/Company: Biograph
Tech Info: silent/bw
Date/Country: 1916 + USA   Type: Comedy Short
Annotation: Bert Williams stars as a country boy who among
  other things, fishes and hawks his catch to white folks.

FISHY TALES
Series: Our Gang
Nar/Cast: Our Gang + Billie Thomas*

Producer: Hal Roach   Director: Gordon Douglas
Studio/Company: MGM
Tech Info: super 8 mm/16 mm/bw/sound/1 reel/11 min.
Date/Country: 1937 + USA   Type: Comedy Short
Distr/Arch: bla
Annotation: Alfalfa gets into a fight with Butch. Spanky
    helps Alfalfa fake a broken leg, but Butch gets wise and
    goes after Alfalfa. The fight begins while Alfalfa is
    playing William Tell with Buckwheat as his target holder.
    Billie Thomas stars as Buckwheat.

FIVE ON THE BLACK HAND SIDE
Nar/Cast: Clarice Taylor* + Leonard Jackson* + Virginia
    Capers* + Glynn Turman* + D'Urville Martin* + Richard
    Martin*   + Sony Jim* + Bonnie Banfield* + Ja'Net Dubois +
    Carl Mikal Franklin
Screenplay: Charlie L. Russell*   Story: Charlie L. Russell*
    (play)
Producer: Brock Peters* + Michael Tolan   Director: Oscar
    Williams*
Studio/Company: United Artists
Tech Info: 16 mm/color/sound/3 reels/96 min.
Date/Country: 1973 + USA   Type: Feature
Distr/Arch: uas
Annotation: Black nationalism and women's liberation battle
    against middle class conventionality as the younger son
    and later the wife of a black barbershop owner form third
    world protest against the patriarch's conservative and
    anglophile values in this sometimes serious comedy.   God-
    frey Cambridge appears in a cameo role.

FIVE PENNIES, THE
Nar/Cast: Danny Kaye + Barbara Bel Geddes + Louis Armstrong*
Producer: Jack Rose   Director: Melville Shavelson
Studio/Company: Paramount
Tech Info: 16 mm/sound/color/114 min.
Date/Country: 1959 + USA   Type: Feature
Distr/Arch: fnc
Annotation: Film based on the life of Loring (Red) Nichols,
    features Louis Armstrong both musically and dramatically.

FIVE
Nar/Cast: Charles Lampkin* + William Phipps + Susan Douglas
    + Earl Lee + James Anderson
Screenplay: Arch Oboler
Producer: Arch Oboler   Director: Arch Oboler
Studio/Company: Columbia
Date/Country: 1951 + USA   Type: Feature
Annotation: Five people - a racist mountain climber, a gent-
    le black man, a pregnant young woman, a dying banker, and
    a sensitive young man - are the only survivors of a nu-
    clear holocaust. The banker dies; the mountain climber
    kills the black man (Lampkin) and then dies of radiation
    burns; the young woman loses her baby; but she and the
    young man are, Adam/Eve-like, left together at the fade.

FLAME IN THE STREETS
Nar/Cast: Earl Cameron* + Sylvia Sims + John Mills + Johnny

Sekka*
Screenplay: Ted Willis
Producer: Roy Baker   Director: Roy Baker
Studio/Company: Atlantic
Tech Info: 35 mm/sound/bw/93 min.
Date/Country: 1962 + Britain   Type: Feature
Annotation: Set in London, the story of the tensions in a
    middle class family when the daughter wants to marry a
    black man, a West Indian, Peter Lincoln, played by Sekka.
    Earl Cameron plays Lincoln's friend, Gabriel Gomez, who is
    badly burned during a racist riot.

FLAME OF NEW ORLEANS
Nar/Cast: Marlene Dietrich + Teresa Harris* + Bruce Cabot
    Director: Rene Clair
Studio/Company: Universal
Tech Info: 16 mm/sound/bw/79 min.
Date/Country: 1941 + USA   Type: Feature
Distr/Arch: uni
Annotation: Harris is maid to Dietrich, a putative countess,
    who, like her, is well traveled and overly wise.

FLAMES OF WRATH, THE
Nar/Cast: Roxie Mankins* + John Burton* + Charles Pearson* +
    Anna Kelson* + John Lester Johnson* + Frank Colbert*
Studio/Company: Western Film Productions
Tech Info: 35 mm/bw/silent/5 reels
Date/Country: 1923 + USA   Type: Feature
Annotation: A melodrama about the planned theft of a valua-
    ble diamond. A young woman, (played by Roxie Mankins)
    acting the role of a shrewd detective, takes care of ex-
    posing and prosecuting the proper villains.

FLAMING CRISIS, THE
Nar/Cast: Dorothy Dunbar* + Calvin Nicholson* + Henry Dixon*
    + Talford White*
Studio/Company: Monarch Productions
Date/Country: 1924 + USA   Type: Feature
Annotation: Melodrama about a newspaperman who is unfairly
    convicted of a murder he did not commit, but spends 2
    years in jail before he escapes to the cattle lands of the
    southwest. There he meets a young woman, Tex Miller, with
    whom he falls in love, but he must go through a series of
    adventures before he can settle down with her and live
    happily ever after.

FLAMING FRONTIER, THE
Nar/Cast: Noble Johnson* + Hoot Gibson + Dustin Farnum
    Director: Edward Sedgwick
Studio/Company: Universal
Tech Info: 35 mm/silent/bw/9 reels
Date/Country: 1926 + USA
Annotation: Johnson is chief Sitting Bull in this filmic
    depiction of Custer's last stand.

FLAMINGO ROAD
Nar/Cast: Joan Crawford + Zachary Scott + Sydney Greenstreet
    + Sam McDaniel*

Screenplay: Robert Wilder
Producer: Jerry Wald   Director: Michael Curtiz
Studio/Company: Warner Brothers
Tech Info: 16 mm/sound/bw/96 min.
Date/Country: 1949 + USA   Type: Feature
Distr/Arch: uas
Annotation: Love and political corruption figure in this
    melodrama set in a small southern town, as Joan Crawford
    struggles to leave her mean beginnings. Sam McDaniel
    plays Boatright.

FLAMINGO
Nar/Cast: Herbert Jeffrey* + Dorothy Dandridge*
Producer: Stillman Pond Productions
Date/Country: 1947 + USA

FLANIO
Screenplay: Gordon Parks*
Producer: Elektra   Director: Gordon Parks*
Tech Info: 16 mm/sound/bw/12 min.
Date/Country: 1964 + Brazil   Type: Documentary
Distr/Arch: mgh
Annotation: How a 12-year-old boy sees slum life in Rio de
    Janeiro. Also photographed by Parks.

FLESH AND FLAME
Alt Title(s): see The Night of the Quarter Moon

FLICKER UP
Nar/Cast: Billy Eckstine* + May Lou Harris*
Producer: Alexander Productions
Date/Country: 1946 + USA

FLOAT LIKE A BUTTERFLY, STING LIKE A BEE
Nar/Cast: Muhammad Ali*
Producer: William Klein   Director: William Klein
Studio/Company: Delpire Productions + Grove Films
Tech Info: 16 mm/bw/sound/3 reels/94 min.
Date/Country: 1969 + USA   Type: Docuumentary
Distr/Arch: gro
Annotation: A factual biography of Ali's ring career,
    covering 15 months, from February, 1964 bout with Sonny
    Liston, when he won the heavyweight title to May of 1965
    when he won the rematch.

FLORIAN SLAPPEY SERIES, THE
Screenplay: Octavus Roy Cohen
Producer: Octavus Cohen
Date/Country: 1925-26   Type: Comedy Shorts
Annotation: A series of all black comedies produced by Cohen
    during 1925-26.

FLORIDA CRACKERS
Producer: Bill Foster*
Studio/Company: Kalem
Date/Country: USA
Annotation: A film which contained a graphic lynching scene
    and which was a source of real controversy. Made by

pioneer black filmmaker, Bill Foster.

FLORIDA ENCHANTMENT, A
Studio/Company: Vitagraph
Tech Info: silent/bw
Date/Country: 1914 + USA   Type: Feature
Annotation: Comedy about sex changes caused when two maids
   swallow "magic" seeds. Only one actual Black appears in
   the film.

FLY MY KITE
Series: Our Gang
Nar/Cast: Our Gang + Allen Hoskins* + Matthew Beard*
Screenplay: H. M. Walker
Producer: Robert F. McGowan   Director: Robert F. McGowan
Studio/Company: MGM
Tech Info: super 8 mm/16 mm/bw/sound/1 reel/21 min.
Date/Country: 1931 + USA   Type: Comedy Short
Distr/Arch: bla
Annotation: The no-good son-in-law tries to swindle kindly
   grandma out of her suddenly valuable gold bonds which she
   has loaned to the kids to use on one of their kites. The
   gang joins together to save the bonds and vanquish the
   evil son-in-law. Allen Hoskins stars as Farina and Matthew Beard stars as Stymie.

FLYING ACE, THE
Nar/Cast: Kathryn Boyd* + Lawrence Criner* + B. DeLegg* +
   Harry Platter* + Lyons Daniels* + Sam Jordan* + George
   Calvin* + Dr. R.I. Brown* + Steve Reynolds*
Producer: Norman Film Manufacturing Company
Date/Country: 1926 + USA

FLYING DOWN TO RIO
Nar/Cast: Dolores del Rio + Fred Astaire + Ginger Rogers +
   Etta Moten* + Clarence Muse*   Story: Louis Brock
   Director: Thornton Freeland
Studio/Company: RKO Radio
Tech Info: 16 mm/sound/bw/100 min.
Date/Country: 1933 + USA   Type: Feature
Distr/Arch: fnc
Annotation: Musical comedy in which playboy-aviator Gene
   Raymond romances Dolores Del Rio while flying down to Rio.
   Etta Moten sings "Flying Down to Rio" in a segregated seg-
   ment.

FLYING FISTS SERIES
Nar/Cast: Benny Leonard
Date/Country: 1924 + USA
Annotation: Flying Fists, a B series, starred Benny Leonard,
   light heavyweight champion. In each film a "black shadow"
   (uncredited) appears; he shares the fighter's bad moments,
   helps in plotting ring strategy, and in Jazz Bout (No. 6
   in the series), his drum playing infuses Leonard, in the
   late rounds, with new spirit so that he not only wins the
   bout but also the girl.

FLYING WILD

Nar/Cast: Ernie Morrison* + East Side Kids
Screenplay: Al Martin
Producer: Sam Katzman   Director: William West
Studio/Company: Monogram
Tech Info: 16 mm/sound/bw/63 min.
Date/Country: 1941 + USA   Type: Feature
Distr/Arch: cie
Annotation: "Sunshine" Sammy, the first black to appear in
   Our Gang (silents), joins the East Side Kids who are
   sleuthing out saboteurs in an airplane plant.

FOLKS, THE
Producer: James Mannas, Jr.* + American Film Institute
   Director: James Mannas, Jr.*
Tech Info: 16 mm/sound/bw/50 min.
Date/Country: 1968 + USA   Type: Documentary
Distr/Arch: gro
Annotation: A documentary portrait of black residents of the
   Bedford-Stuyvesant area of Brooklyn. A wide variety of
   people come before the camera and speak for themselves
   about their hopes, and about their problems of living in
   the inner city.

FOLLOW THE BOYS
Nar/Cast: Louis Jordan* + Louise Beavers* + Nicodemus
   Stewart* + George Raft + Vera Zorina + W.C. Fields
Screenplay: Lou Breslow + Gertrude Purcell
Producer: Charles K. Feldman   Director: Eddie Sutherland
Studio/Company: Universal
Tech Info: 16 mm/sound/bw/109 min.
Date/Country: 1944 + USA   Type: Feature
Distr/Arch: uni
Annotation: Film is basically a talent show put on by the
   Hollywood Victory Committee to spread cheer during WWII.

FOLLOW THE NORTH STAR
Producer: Gerber and Beckwith
Studio/Company: ABC
Tech Info: 16 mm/color/sound/1 reel/47 min.
Date/Country: 1975 + USA   Type: TV Feature
Distr/Arch: tim

FOLLOW YOUR HEART
Nar/Cast: Clarence Muse* + Marion Talley + Michael Bartlett
   + Nigel Bruce + Luis Alberni + Hall Johnson Choir*
Screenplay: Nathaniel West + Sam Ornitz + Lester Cole
   Story: Dana Burnet
Producer: Nat Levine   Director: Aubrey Scotto
Studio/Company: Republic Pictures
Tech Info: 16 mm/sound/bw/80 min.
Date/Country: 1936 + USA   Type: Feature
Distr/Arch: ivy
Annotation: An operetta set in the blue grass land of
   Kentucky mixes classical operatic fare with contemporary
   melodies. The Hall Johnson Choir provides background
   music; the choir leader is played by Clarence Muse.

FOOL AND FIRE

Studio/Company: Foster Photoplay Company
Date/Country: 191- + USA

FOOL'S_ERRAND,_A
Nar/Cast: William Fountaine + Shingzie Howard

FOOLISH_LIVES
Nar/Cast: Frank Chatman* + Henry Harris* + Frank Carter* +
   Jewell Cox* + Marguerite Patterson* + Jonella Patton*
Studio/Company: Young Producers Filming Company
Tech Info: 35 mm/silent/bw
Date/Country: 1922 + USA   Type: Feature
Annotation: A story of "Negro life."

FOOLS_FOR_SCANDAL
Nar/Cast: Carole Lombard + Fernand Gravet + Ralph Bellamy +
   Allen Jenkins + Les Hite* and Orchestra + Jeni LeGon*
Screenplay: Herbert Fields + Joseph Fields
Producer: Mervyn LeRoy   Director: Mervyn LeRoy
Studio/Company: Warner Brothers
Tech Info: 16 mm/sound/bw/81 min.
Date/Country: 1938 + USA   Type: Feature
Distr/Arch: uas
Annotation: An Amercan film star falls in love with a mar-
   quis. Les Hite and his orchestra are back ground; Jeni
   LeGon does a specialty dance number.

FOOTBALL_ROMEO
Series: Our Gang
Nar/Cast: Our Gang + Billie Thomas*
Screenplay: Hal Law + Robert A. McGowan + Jack White
Producer: Jack Chertok   Director: George Sidney
Studio/Company: MGM
Tech Info: bw/sound/1 reel
Date/Country: 1938 + USA   Type: Comedy Short
Annotation: Lovelorn Darla successfully plots to get Alfalfa
   to   play   in   the   big   game against Butch's team by
   threatening to make public a poem Alfalfa has written to
   her.   Alfalfa is the game's hero. Billie Thomas stars as
   Buckwheat.

FOOTLIGHT_SERENADE
Nar/Cast: Betty Grable + John Payne + Victor Mature + Mantan
   Moreland*
Screenplay: Robert Ellis + Helen Logan + Lynn Starling
Producer: William Le Baron   Director: Gregory Ratoff
Studio/Company: Fox
Tech Info: 16 mm/sound/bw/80 min.
Date/Country: 1942 + USA   Type: Feature
Distr/Arch: fnc
Annotation: Mantan Moreland has a bit part as a dresser in
   this Fox backstage musical

FOR_ALL_MY_STUDENTS
Producer: Bonnie Sherr
Tech Info: 16 mm/sound/bw/36 min.
Date/Country: 1968 + USA   Type: Documentary
Distr/Arch: uca

Annotation: Discussion of why many black students fail in
   school.

FOR HIS MOTHER'S SAKE
Nar/Cast: Jack Johnson* + Matty Wilkens* + Adrian Joyce* +
   Jack Hopkins* + Jack Newton* + Dick Lee* + Hank West* +
   Everett Godfrey* + Edward McMowan* + Ruth Walker*
Studio/Company: Blackburn Velde Productions
Date/Country: 1921 + USA   Type: Feature
Annotation: Jack Johnson plays the older brother in this
   film about filial loyalty. He saves his younger brother
   from a petty crimial act, does some boxing in Mexico and
   sees that all comes out well for his mother's sake.

FOR LOVE OF IVY
Nar/Cast: Sidney Poitier* + Abbey Lincoln* + Leon Bibb* +
   Carroll O'Connor + Beau Bridges + Hugh Hurd* + Stanley
   Green
Screenplay: Robert Alan Arthur   Story: Sidney Poitier*
Producer: Edgar J.Scherick + Jack Wetson   Director: Daniel
   Mann
Studio/Company: Cinerama Releasing Corp. + ABC Pictures
   Corp.
Tech Info: 16 mm/color/sound/3 reels/102 min.
Date/Country: 1968 + USA   Type: Feature
Distr/Arch: fnc
Annotation: A young and attractive black domestic worker
   (Abbey Lincoln), Ivy, is swept off her feet by a suave,
   professional black gambler, Jack Parks, played by Sidney
   Poitier. Quincy Jones* composed the music for this
   romantic comedy, which shows a white family doing
   everything possible to keep its "jewel" of a maid happy,
   including manipulating her life.

FOR MASSA'S SAKE
Nar/Cast: Crane Wilbur
Studio/Company: Pathe
Date/Country: 1911 + USA   Type: Dramatic Short
Annotation: Devoted former slave tries to sell himself to
   pay his ex-master's gambling debts.

FOR PETE'S SAKE
Nar/Cast: Al Freeman, Jr.* + Billy Graham
Screenplay: James F. Collier
Producer: Frank R. Jacobson   Director: James F. Collier
Studio/Company: World Wide Pictures
Tech Info: sound/color/90 min.
Date/Country: 1966 + USA   Type: Feature
Annotation: Billy Graham plays himself in this melodrama
   built around the religious conversion of a gasoline sta-
   tion attendant and his wife.

FOR PETE'S SAKE
Series: Our Gang
Nar/Cast: Our Gang + Matthew Beard* + Carolina Beard*
Producer: Hal Roach   Director: Gus Meins
Studio/Company: MGM + Roach
Tech Info: super 8 mm/16 mm/bw/sound/20 min.

Date/Country: 1934 + USA   Type: Comedy Short
Distr/Arch: roa + bla
Annotation: A running gag in this film involves Stymie's
    sister, Buckwheat (played here by Carolina Beard) getting
    stuck in awkward places, with Scotty and Spanky alerting
    Stymie to the problem each time.

FOR PETE'S SAKE
Nar/Cast: Barbra Streisand + Michael Sarrazin + Estelle
    Parsons + Richard Ward*
Screenplay: Stanley Shapiro + Maurice Richlin
Producer: Martin Erlichman + Stanley Shapiro   Director:
    Peter Yates
Studio/Company: Columbia Pictures
Date/Country: 1974 + USA   Type: Feature
Annotation: Richard Ward plays the role of Bernie in this
    comedy about a young housewife (Streisand) who gets into
    endless difficulties trying to help her husband, a young
    cab driver (Sarrazin), who wants to go to college.

FORBIDDEN ADVENTURE
Nar/Cast: Louise Glaum + Charles Ray
Studio/Company: Mutual
Tech Info: bw/silent
Date/Country: 1915 + USA
Annotation: Blacks are used as background in this "African"
    adventure.

FORBIN PROJECT, THE
Alt Title(s): Colossus! The Forbin Project
Nar/Cast: Georg Stanford Brown* + Eric Brolden + Susan Clark
Screenplay: James Bridges
Producer: Stanley Chase   Director: Joseph Sargent
Studio/Company: Universal Pictures
Tech Info: 16 mm/sound/color/100 min.
Date/Country: 1970 + USA   Type: Feature
Distr/Arch: cwf + mac + swa + tmc + twy + uni
Annotation: Georg Stanford Brown is Fisher in this science
    fiction drama about computers taking over the world.
    Colossus,   the   project brainchild of Charles Forbin
    (Brolden) becomes father to the man.

FOREST PEOPLE OF CENTRAL AFRICA
Producer: Dept. of Anthropology, Harvard University
Tech Info: 16 mm/silent/bw/1 reel/20 min.
Date/Country: 1920 + Central Africa   Type: Documentary
Distr/Arch: fce
Annotation: Shows the daily activities of central African
    pygmies; includes iron-making and dances.

FORGOTTEN BABIES
Series: Our Gang
Nar/Cast: Our Gang + Matthew Beard* + Bobbie Beard*
Producer: Robert F. McGowan + Hal Roach   Director: Robert
    F. McGowan
Studio/Company: MGM + Roach
Tech Info: super 8 mm/16 mm/bw/sound/2 reels/17 min.
Date/Country: 1933 + USA   Type: Comedy Short

Distr/Arch: roa + bla
Annotation: The gang gets Spanky to babysit all their
    brothers and sisters so they can go swimming. The infants
    systematically demolish Spanky's house and when the gang
    returns they discover Spanky's put the whole bunch into
    cages. Matthew Beard stars as Stymie.

FORMULA FOR LOVE
Alt Title(s): see Kaerlighedens Melodi

FORTUNE COOKIE, THE
Nar/Cast: Jack Lemmon + Walter Mathau + Archie Moore* + Judy
    Pace* + Ron Rich*
Screenplay: Billy Wilder + I.A.L. Diamond
Producer: Billy Wilder   Director: Billy Wilder
Studio/Company: United Artists + 16 + 16 mm/sound/bw/125
    min. + 17 + 1966 + USA   Type: Feature
Distr/Arch: uas
Annotation: Harry Hinkle, a TV cameraman (Lemmon) is ac-
    cidentally knocked down by 220 pounds of halfback, Luther
    "Boom Boom" Jackson (Ron Rich), during a pro football
    game. Convinced by his brother-in-law to sue, weak-willed
    Harry carries out the charade until the quiet and the
    decency of Boom Boom changes his mind. Archie Moore is
    Mr. Jackson, Judy Pace is Elvira.

FOUR FEATHERS, THE
Nar/Cast: Richard Arlen + Clive Brooks + Fay Wray + Noble
    Johnson* + Zack Williams*   Story: A.E.W. Mason
Producer: Marian Cooper + Ernest Schoedsack + Lothar Mendes
Date/Country: 1929 + USA   Type: Feature
Annotation: Melodrama about a coward who becomes a hero
    (Arlen) and subsequently returns the four symbolic white
    feathers. This after many harrowing adventures and ex-
    citing battles with the Fuzzy Wuzzies. Blacks are seen in
    numerous bellicose poses, Johnson and Williams among them.

FOUR HORSEMEN OF THE APOCALYPSE, THE
Nar/Cast: Noble Johnson* + Rudolph Valentino + Alice Terry +
    Pomeroy Cannon   Director: Rex Ingram
Studio/Company: Metro Pictures
Tech Info: 35 mm/silent/bw/11 reels
Date/Country: 1921 + USA   Type: Feature
Annotation: Story of Julio, W.W. I soldier, and how he comes
    to join the army because of the lover who rejects him and
    a stranger who inspires him to invoke the Four Horsemen
    (War, Conquest, Famine and Death) to distinguish himself.
    Noble M. Johnson plays Conquest.

FOUR SHALL DIE
Alt Title(s): Condemned Men
Nar/Cast: Mantan Moreland* + Dorothy Dandridge* + Pete Web-
    ster* + Jesse Lee Brooks* + John Thomas* + Edward Thomp-
    son* + Alfred Grant* + Reginald Fenderson*
Studio/Company: Million Dollar Studios, Hollywood
Date/Country: 1946 + USA   Type: Feature
Distr/Arch: cfi
Annotation: Dandridge plays a young heiress, who is beseiged

by two young men, both of whom want to marry her. In addition to the love triangle is the mystery of four deaths which Mantan Moreland, as the detective, tries to solve.

FOURTH ALARM, THE
Series: Our Gang
Nar/Cast: Our Gang + Allen Hoskins* + Jannie Hoskins*
Screenplay: Hal Roach
Producer: Hal Roach   Director: Robert McGowan
Studio/Company: Pathe
Tech Info: silent/bw/2 reels
Date/Country: 1926 + USA   Type: Comedy Short
Annotation: After being befriended by the local fire chief, the gang builds a replica of the fire station in a barn. When there's a fire at a chemical lab both groups answer, but the police chase the gang away. When Farina and Mary discover the fire may reach some explosives, they battle the fire saving everyone from being blown into the next state. Allen Hoskins stars as Farina and Jannie Hoskins stars as Mango.

FOX MOVIETONE FOLLIES
Nar/Cast: Stepin Fetchit* + Carolynne Snowden* + Lola Lane + Sue Carol   Story: David Butler   Director: David Butler
Studio/Company: Fox
Date/Country: 1929 + USA   Type: Feature
Annotation: Slight story line strings together a series of song and dance and variety numbers. Fetchit and Snowden are principals in song and dance numbers and also perform specialty dances.

FOXES OF HARROW, THE
Nar/Cast: Rex Harrison + Kenny Washington* + Maureen O'Hara + Victor McLaglen + Helen Crozier + Sam McDaniel* + Libby Taylor* + Renee Beard* + Suzette Harbin*
Screenplay: Wanda Tuchock   Story: Frank Yerby*
Producer: William Bacher   Director: John M. Stahl
Studio/Company: Twentieth Century Fox
Tech Info: 16 mm/bw/sound/4 reels/110 min.
Date/Country: 1947 + USA   Type: Feature
Distr/Arch: fnc
Annotation: The Fox dynasty and its plantation, Harrow represent a dramatic model for a social and historical view of slavery in Louisiana. Some dramatic moments with Suzette Harbin, a proud African slave woman unwilling to have her infant grow into slavery.

FOXY BROWN
Nar/Cast: Pam Grier* + Peter Brown + Terry Carter*
Screenplay: Jack Hill
Producer: Buzz Feitshans   Director: Jack Hill
Studio/Company: American International
Tech Info: 16 mm/sound/color/94 min.
Date/Country: 1974 + USA   Type: Feature
Distr/Arch: swa
Annotation: When her boyfriend is murdered, a nurse (Grier) sets out to get revenge on the killers and does. She ends up preying on the the gangsters and dope pushers as well.

FRAME-UP! THE IMPRISONMENT OF MARTIN SOSTRE
Producer: Pacific Street Film Collective
Tech Info: 16 mm/sound/color/30 min.
Date/Country: 1974 + USA   Type: Documentary
Distr/Arch: psfc
Annotation: Experiences of a politically active black book-
   store owner who claims he was framed on drug charges and
   is serving time in prison.

FRAMED
Nar/Cast: Joe Don Baker + Brock Peters* + Conny Van Dyke +
   John Marley + Brenton Banks*
Screenplay: Mort Briskin
Producer: Mort Briskin + Joel Briskin   Director: Phil
   Karlson
Studio/Company: Paramount
Tech Info: 16 mm/sound/color
Date/Country: 1974 + USA   Type: Feature
Annotation: Ron Lewis (Joe Don Baker) is a nightclub owner-
   gambler who, after a big win, is framed by a corrupt state
   senator. He does four years in prison and when he comes
   out to find the guilty ones the only help he gets is from
   Sgt. Sam Perry (Brock Peters). After he collects all the
   damaging evidence, he turns it over to Sgt. Perry so that
   Perry can clean up the state. Brenton Banks plays Jeremiah, a black musician in Lewis's nightclub who is a friend
   of Sam's.

FRAMING OF THE SHREW, THE
Series: Christie Comedy
Nar/Cast: Evelyn Preer* + Spencer Williams* + Roberta Hyson*
   + Edward Thompson*
Screenplay: Octavus Roy Cohen + Spencer Williams*
Producer: Al Christie + Octavus Roy Cohen
Studio/Company: Paramount
Tech Info: sound/bw/2 reels
Date/Country: 1929 + USA   Type: Comedy Short
Annotation: An obstreporous wife (Preer) is tamed and
   trained by her smaller but wily husband.

FRAMING YOUTH
Series: Our Gang
Nar/Cast: Our Gang + Billie Thomas*
Producer: Hal Roach   Director: Gordon Douglas
Studio/Company: MGM + Roach
Tech Info: super 8 mm/16 mm/bw/sound/1 reel/10 min.
Date/Country: 1937 + USA   Type: Comedy Short
Distr/Arch: bla + roa
Annotation: Threatened by Butch, Spanky persuades Alfalfa
   not to enter a radio talent contest. But Spanky and Al-
   falfa finally win out against Butch the bully. Billie
   Thomas is Buckwheat.

FRANK'S GREATEST ADVENTURE
Alt Title(s): see Fearless Frank

FRANKIE "SUGAR CHILE" ROBINSON - BILLIE HOLIDAY - COUNT

BASIE AND HIS SEXTET
Nar/Cast: Count Basie* + Billie Holiday* + Frankie "Sugar
    Chile" Robinson* + Basie Sextet*   Director: Will Cowan
Studio/Company: Universal-International
Tech Info: 15 min.
Date/Country: 1950 + USA   Type: Musical Short
Annotation: The above listed artists perform such numbers as
    "God Bless the Child," "Now Baby, or Never," "After School
    Boogie," and "One O'Clock Jump."

FRAULEIN
Nar/Cast: James Edwards* + Mel Ferrer + Dana Wynter
Screenplay: Leo Townsend
Producer: Walter Reisch   Director: Henry Koster
Studio/Company: Fox
Tech Info: 16 mm/sound/color/98 min.
Date/Country: 1958 + USA   Type: Feature
Distr/Arch: fnc
Annotation: James Edwards plays Corporal Hanks, a bit part,
    in this melodrama about a young German woman's trials and
    tribulations at the hands of both the Nazis and the Russi-
    ans.

FRED McDOWELL
Producer: Seattle Folklore Society
Studio/Company: KCTS-TV
Tech Info: 16 mm/sound/bw/15 min.
Date/Country: 1969 + USA   Type: Documentary
Annotation: Film biography of Mississippi Fred McDowell*
    includes his bottleneck blues style in such numbers as
    "John Henry" and "Louisiana Blues."

FREDERICK DOUGLASS" THE HOUSE ON CEDAR HILL
Producer: Carlton Moss*
Tech Info: 16 mm/bw/sound/1 reel/17 min.
Date/Country: 1953   Type: Documentary
Distr/Arch: con
Annotation: A filmed biography of Frederick Douglass (1817-
    1895), eminent leader in the struggle against slavery.
    Narration from Douglass' writings; musical score based on
    Afro-American folk songs.

FREDERICK DOUGLASS
Series: Afro-American History
Producer: Encyclopedia Britannica Educational Corp.
Tech Info: 16 mm/sound/color/1 reel/8 min.
Date/Country: 1971 + USA   Type: Documentary
Distr/Arch: iu + ebec
Annotation: Depicts the accomplishments of Frederick
    Douglass, who, after escaping from slavery, became an
    agent for the Underground Railroad. Records his recruit-
    ment of black civilians for the Union army and examines
    his later career as author, advisor to presidents, and
    champion of freedom.

FREDERICK DOUGLASS
Nar/Cast: Robert Hooks*   Director: Sherman Marks
Studio/Company: Sandek

Tech Info: 16 mm/sound/bw/50 min.*spanish dubbed version
   also available
Date/Country: 1965 + USA
Distr/Arch: cal + iqf
Annotation: Hooks plays the great abolitionist, ex-slave
   Frederick Douglass.

FREE_AND_EQUAL
Nar/Cast: Jack Richardson
Producer: Thomas H. Ince
Date/Country: 1915 + USA   Type: Feature
Annotation: Free_and_Equal, was premiered in New York in
   1925. Intended to prove that the Negro is naturally corrupt as well as inferior, the film is an exhortation
   against the "mixing of the races." Richardson (in black
   face) plays Alexander Marshall, the black character who
   after being taken into the home of a liberal Northern
   judge, pursues the judge's daughter, then rapes and
   strangles the maid.

FREE_AT_LAST
Series: History of the Negro People
Producer: NET
Tech Info: 16 mm/sound/bw/1 reel/30 min.
Date/Country: 1965   Type: Documentary
Distr/Arch: iu
Annotation: Uses dramatic readings from the works of
   Frederick Douglass*, Booker T. Washington*, W.E.B DuBois*,
   and Marcus Garvey* to trace the history of the American
   Negro from emancipation to the end of World War II.   Dis-
   cusses the influence of Washington, DuBois, and Garvey on
   the present black-white position in the United States.

FREE_EATS
Series: Our Gang
Nar/Cast: Our Gang + Matthew Beard*
Screenplay: H. M. Walker
Producer: Robert F. McGowan + Hal Roach   Director: Raymond
   McCarey
Studio/Company: MGM + Roach
Tech Info: super 8 mm/16 mm/bw/sound/2 reels/15-20 min.
Date/Country: 1932 + USA   Type: Comedy Short
Distr/Arch: roa
Annotation: Two midgets, disguised as babies aid some crooks
   by crashing a party thrown by a wealthy patron for poor
   children. Stymie catches on, but no one believes him un-
   til the end when he clears the implicated gang members by
   "unmasking" the midgets. Matthew Beard stars as Stymie.

FREE_PEOPLE_OF_GUINEA-BISSAU   Director: Axel Lohmann + Rudi
   Spee
Tech Info: 16 mm/bw/sound/50 min./Portugese dialog with En-
   glish subtitles and narration
Date/Country: 1970 + Sweden   Type: Documentary
Distr/Arch: tri
Annotation: Free_People_in_Guinea-Bissau sketches the
   historical background of the independence movement in
   Guinea-Bissau and then examines the process of reconstruc-

tion and education in one of the areas of the country
liberated during the guerilla war.

FREE_WHEELING
Series: Our Gang
Nar/Cast: Our Gang + Matthew Beard*
Producer: Hal Roach   Director: Robert McGowan
Studio/Company: MGM + Roach
Tech Info: super 8 mm/16 mm/bw/sound/2 reels/20 min.
Date/Country: 1932 + USA   Type: Comedy Short
Distr/Arch: roa
Annotation: Stymie is called away from the gang's newly con-
    structed, mule powered 'taxi' to deliver laundry to the
    'big house' where Dickie sits in bed with a stiff neck
    kept there by an overly protective mother. Stymie gets
    Dickie out of the house, cures his stiff-neck and gets him
    a ride in the taxi which ends with a wild ride down a
    steep hill. Matthew Beard stars as Stymie.

FREE,_WHITE_AND_21
Nar/Cast: Frederick O'Neal* + Annalena Lund + George Edgely
Screenplay: Harold Darwin + Larry Buchannan   Director: Lar-
    ry Buchanan
Studio/Company: American International
Tech Info: 16 mm/sound/bw/102 min.
Date/Country: 1964 + USA   Type: Feature
Distr/Arch: mac
Annotation: A courtroom drama in which a black man (O'Neal)
    is accused of raping a blond Swedish Freedom Rider (Lund).

FREEDOM_FOR_GHANA
Producer: Ghana Information Service
Tech Info: 16 mm/sound/color/35 min.
Date/Country: 1957 + Ghana   Type: Documentary
Distr/Arch: gis
Annotation: The anniversary celebration of Ghana's in-
    dependence.

FREEDOM_MOVEMENT,_1877-tODAY
Series: History of the Negro in America
Producer: Niagara
Tech Info: 16 mm/sound/bw/1 reel/21 min.
Date/Country: 1965   Type: Documentary
Distr/Arch: iu + mghf
Annotation: Traces attempts of Afro-Americans to acquire
    basic freedoms from 1877 to the present. Indicates how
    segregation laws, especially in the South, have tended to
    humiliate and degrade black people. Prsents a brief over-
    view of the present struggle to attain equal rights.

FRENCH-ENGLISH_QUESTION,_THE
Series: New Africa
Producer: Canadian Broadcasting Corp. + UNESCO
Tech Info: 16 mm/sound/bw/1 reel/24 min.
Date/Country: 1967 + West Africa   Type: Documentary
Distr/Arch: mghf
Annotation: Shows how colonial languages affect the culture
    of new countries. Cameroun, with its two official

languages (English-French), is shown as well as Senegal and Nigeria.

FRIDAY FOSTER
Nar/Cast: Pam Grier* + Yaphet Kotto* + Godfrey Cambridge* + Eartha Kitt*   Director: Arthur Marks
Studio/Company: American International
Tech Info: 16 mm/sound/color/90 min.
Date/Country: 1977 + USA   Type: Feature
Distr/Arch: swa
Annotation: An ex-model turned photographer (Grier) joins with a private investigator (Kotto) to avenge the murder of her best friend. They encounter more murder, as well as political intrigue.

FRIENDLY GAME, THE
Producer: Chronicle Productions
Tech Info: 16 mm/sound/bw/1 reel/15 min.
Date/Country: 1967   Type: Dramatic Short
Distr/Arch: iu + mmm
Annotation: Presents an allegorical chess game between a white man and a black man to show their interpersonal exchange and tension. Shows that the white man allows the Black to compete because he feels that the Black man has to lose; the Black plays only so that he can beat the white man and take what he has.

FRIENDLY PERSUASION
Nar/Cast: Gary Cooper + Dorothy McGuire + Anthony Perkins + Joel Fluellen*   Story: Jessamyn West
Producer: William Wyler   Director: William Wyler
Studio/Company: Allied Artists
Date/Country: 1956 + USA   Type: Feature
Annotation: Joel Fluellen has a small character role as Enoch in this story of an amiable, gentle Indiana Quaker family whose happy life is interrupted by their son's breaking of faith and joining Morgan's Raiders.

FRINI, CORTIGIANA D'ORTANTE
Nar/Cast: John Kitzmiller*
Date/Country: 1953 + Italy   Type: Feature

FRITZ THE CAT   Director: Ralph Bakshi
Studio/Company: Warner Brothers
Tech Info: 16 mm/sound/color/2 reels/78 min.
Date/Country: 1972 + USA   Type: Feature
Distr/Arch: wsa
Annotation: An animated adult cartoon in which the drawings of underground comics artist Robert Crumb come alive on the commercial screen. The hero of the satire a '60s college dropout who unwittingly causes disaster wherever he goes without realizing the consequences of his acts. Blacks figure prominently in Harlem sequences. Billie Holiday* on the sound track.

FROM COTTON PATCH TO CONGRESS
Studio/Company: M.W. Baccus Films Company
Date/Country: 191- + USA

FROM_FETISHES_TO_FAITH
Series: National Archives Gift Collection
Tech Info: 16 mm/silent/1 reel/bw
Annotation: Primitive rites and work of Protestant missions
   in developing native leadership. (Part of Record Group
   200 HF series, Harmon Foundation Collection).

FROM_HELL_TO_HEAVEN
Nar/Cast: Clarence Muse* + Carole Lombard + Jack Oakie
Screenplay: Lawrence Hazard   Director: Erle Kenton
Studio/Company: Paramount
Date/Country: 1933 + USA   Type: Feature
Annotation: The goings on at a hotel, in the Grand_Hotel
   tradition, with Clarence Muse playing a wily elevator
   operator.

FROM_THE_INSIDE_OUT
Producer: Contemporary
Tech Info: 16 mm/sound/bw/24 min.
Date/Country: 1967 + USA   Type: Dramatic Short
Distr/Arch: mgh + uca
Annotation: Black ghetto life as described by black
   teenagers in California. Written and directed by them.

FROM_THESE_ROOTS
Producer: William Greaves* Productions, Inc.
Tech Info: 16 mm/bw/1 reel/sound/28 min.
Date/Country: 1974 + USA   Type: Dramatized Documentary
Distr/Arch: wgp
Annotation: Depicts the social, cultural and political
   facets of the period known as the Harlem Renaissance.

FROM_WHENCE_COMETH_MY_HELP
Nar/Cast: Sidney Poitier*
Date/Country: 1949 + USA   Type: US Army Documentary
Annotation: Poitier plays a distraught soldier being com-
   forted by a chaplain in this training film for Army
   chaplains which demonstrates how to assist servicemen with
   their problems.

FRONTIER_SCOUT
Nar/Cast: Mantan Moreland*
Producer: Franklyn Warner Prod.
Date/Country: 1938 + USA   Type: Feature

FRUSTRATIONS_OF_A_BLACK_POLICEMAN,_THE
Series: Six American Families
Producer: Travelers Insurance Co.
Studio/Company: PBS
Tech Info: 16 mm/color/sound/2 reels/60 min.
Date/Country: 1977 + USA   Type: Documentary
Annotation: Complicated problems of black policemen, their
   personal experiences and relationships with the public
   both black and white.

FURY_OF_THE_JUNGLE
Nar/Cast: Clarence Muse*

Date/Country: 1934 + USA   Type: Feature
Annotation: Muse plays Malango.

FUTURE_AND_THE_NEGRO,_THE
Series: History of the Negro People
Producer: NET
Tech Info: 16 mm/sound/bw/3 reels/75 min.
Date/Country: 1965   Type: Documentary
Distr/Arch: iu
Annotation: Presents a panel discussion on the subject of
    the Negro's future.   Discusses the economic plight of
    black people in the United States and abroad.   Emphasizes
    racism, which is felt to be deeply ingrained in people in
    the world over.

FUTURE_OF_1,000,000_AFRICANS
Tech Info: 16 mm/sound/1 reel/21 min.   Type: Documentary
Distr/Arch: ueuwis
Annotation: Future of Bechuanaland, Basutoland and Swaziland
    are discussed.

FUZZ
Nar/Cast: James McEachin* + Burt Reynolds + Raquel Welch
    Director: Richard A. Colla
Studio/Company: United Artists
Tech Info: 16 mm/sound/color/93 min.
Date/Country: 1972 + USA   Type: Feature
Distr/Arch: uas
Annotation: James Mac Eachin as Artie is a detective on the
    Boston police force and is actively involved in tracking
    down a mysterious killer sending ransom notes.   Other
    Blacks as detectives, hustlers in assorted roles, in-
    cluding one supposedly brainless female in the killer's
    employ.

GAMBLER_FROM_NATCHEZ,_THE
Nar/Cast: Dale Robertson + Debra Puget + Woody Strode*
Screenplay: Gerald D. Adams + Irving Wallace
Producer: Leonard Goldstein   Director: Henry Levin
Studio/Company: 20th Century Fox
Tech Info: 16 mm/sound/color/83 min.
Date/Country: 1954 + USA   Type: Feature
Distr/Arch: fnc
Annotation: Returning home to New Orleans from the army,
    Vance Colby (Dale Robertson) finds that his father has
    been killed by gamblers who were cheating him. Since the
    law won't do anything, he sets out to get revenge.   Woody
    Strode plays Josh.

GAME,_THE   Story: George Houston Bass
Producer: Roberta Hodes + Mobilization for Youth
Studio/Company: Independent
Tech Info: 16 mm/1 reel/bw/17 min.
Date/Country: 1966 + USA   Type: Dramatic Short
Distr/Arch: gro
Annotation: Prejudice and violence experienced by black and
    Puerto Rican youth is rendered dramatically in this film,
    acted and filmed by Mobilization for Youth.

GAME
Producer: Abigail Child + Jon Child   Director: Jon Child
Tech Info: 16 mm/bw/sound/1 reel/38 min.
Date/Country: 1972 + USA   Type: Dramatized Documentary
Distr/Arch: rad
Annotation: The film depicts two street hustlers, Tina and
   Yogi Slim, both black and middle class, who are playing
   their game with some awareness of the dangers. They
   present their case, disagree about women's liberation, and
   opt for continuing their lifestyle outside the law.

GAMES, THE
Nar/Cast: Rafer Johnson* + Michael Crawford + Ryan O'Neal
Screenplay: Erich Segal
Producer: Lester Lensk   Director: Michael Winnes
Studio/Company: Fox
Tech Info: 16 mm/sound/color/95 min.
Date/Country: 1970 + Britain   Type: Feature
Distr/Arch: fnc
Annotation: Rafer Johnson is one of the commentators in this
   drama about four long distance runners and the Olympic
   marathon in Rome.

GANG SMASHERS
Alt Title(s): Gun Moll
Nar/Cast: Nina Mae McKinney* + Lawrence Criner* + Monte Haw-
   ley* + Edward Thompson* + Mantan Moreland* + Vernon McCal-
   la* + Reginald Fenderson* + Arthur Ray* + John Criner* +
   Charles Hawkins* + Neva Peoples*
Screenplay: Ralph Cooper*
Studio/Company: Million Dollar Productions
Date/Country: 1938 + USA   Type: Feature
Annotation: A woman rules the Harlem rackets.

GANG WAR
Nar/Cast: Ralph Cooper* + Gladys Snyder* + Lawrence Criner*
   + Reginald Fenderson* + Monte Hawley* + Jesse Lee Brooks*
   + Maceo Sheffield*
Producer: Leo Popkin + Harry Popkin
Studio/Company: Million Dollar Productions
Date/Country: 1939 + USA   Type: Feature
Annotation: Two rival gangs, one led by Cooper, the other by
   Criner, struggle control the juke box machines in Harlem.
   loses and, like Cagney, he ends up bullet riddled with
   Jesse Lee Brooks as the policeman uttering the crime
   doesn't pay moral. struggle to control the juke box
   machines in Harlem. Cooper

GANGSTERS ON THE LOOSE
Alt Title(s): see Bargain with Bullets

GANJA AND HESS
Alt Title(s): Double Possession
Nar/Cast: Duane Jones* + Marlene Clark* + Bill Gunn* + Sam
   Waymon* + Leonard Jackson*
Screenplay: Bill Gunn*   Director: Bill Gunn*
Studio/Company: Kelly-Jordan

Tech Info: 16 mm/sound/color/90 min.
Date/Country: 1973 + USA   Type: Feature
Distr/Arch: kje
Annotation: Symbolic portrayal of a Europeanized black man.
  Cameraman is James E. Hinton*.

GANZA ZUMBA
Nar/Cast: Antonio Pitanga* + Lea Garcia* + Eliezer Gomes* +
  Luiza Maranhas* + Jorge Coutinho*
Screenplay: Leopoldo Serran + Ruben Rocha Filho   Story:
  Carlos Diegues
Producer: Carlos Diegues + Jarhas Barbosa   Director: Carlos
  Diegues
Tech Info: 16 mm/sound/bw/99 min./3 reels/in Portugese with
  English subtitles.
Date/Country: 1963 + Brazil   Type: Feature
Distr/Arch: nyf
Annotation: The film depicts the escape of a group of black
  slaves from the sugar cane plantations in northwestern
  Brazil in 1641.   Their refuge, the "guilombo dos
  Palmares," lasted for more than fifty years (until about
  1697), withstanding onslaughts by the Portugese and the
  Dutch. It became a symbol of freedom for all enslaved
  blacks.

GARCONS ET FILLES
Alt Title(s): Boys and Girls
Producer: French Ethnological Film Committe + Pierre Vidal +
  Phillippe Luzuy
Tech Info: 16 mm/sound/bw/1 reel/30 min./French with English
  subtitles
Date/Country: 1965 + Central Africa Republic + Gbaya   Type:
  Documentary
Distr/Arch: ueuwis + hfsc
Annotation: This film shows young Gbaya girls and boys of
  the Bouar-Baboua region going through initiation rites.
  Shot earlier, in 1961-62. Anthropology research by Michel
  Brunet.

GARGA M'BOSSE
Alt Title(s): Cactus
Nar/Cast: Oumou M'Baye* + Abou Camara*
Screenplay: Mahama Traore* + Pathe Diagne
Producer: Sunu Film + Swedish Broadcasting   Director:
  Mahama Traore*
Tech Info: sound/color/80 min./Wolof with French subtitles
Date/Country: 1974 + Senegal   Type: Feature
Annotation: A peasant couple, driven from their "farm" by
  drought, are forced to go to the city for help from a
  friend and a rich distant relative. Along the way their
  son dies and when they arrive in the city it is a long
  search before they find their friend, who welcomes them,
  but their distant relative, a doctor, does not. Under
  these unpleasant circumstances they begin a new life in
  the city.

GATEWAY OF THE MOON
Nar/Cast: Noble Johnson* + Dolores Del Rio + Walter Pigeon

Screenplay: Clifford Bax   Director: John Griffith Way
Studio/Company: Fox
Date/Country: 1928 + USA
Annotation: Dolores Del Rio plays a half-caste girl who
    saves a young engineer (Pigeon) from villainy in the
    tropics of Bolivia. Noble Johnson has a bit role.

GATLING_GUN,_THE
War/Cast: Woody Strode* + Guy Stockwell   Director: Robert
    Gordon
Tech Info: 16 mm/sound/color/93 min.
Date/Country: 1973 + USA   Type: Feature
Distr/Arch: unf

GATOR_AND_THE_PICKANINNY,_THE
Studio/Company: Edison
Date/Country: 1903 + USA   Type: Comedy Short
Annotation: A black man (in makeup) chops open an alligator
    and rescues a black child who was swallowed by the al-
    ligator.

GENERAL_SPANKY
Series: Our Gang
War/Cast: Our Gang + Billie Thomas* + Louise Beavers* + Wil-
    lie Best*
Screenplay: John Guedel + Richard Flournoy + Carl Harbaugh +
    Hal Yates
Producer: Hal Roach   Director: Fred Newmeyer + Gordon
    Douglas
Studio/Company: MGM
Tech Info: bw/sound/71 min./6,426'
Date/Country: 1936 + USA   Type: Comedy Short
Annotation: A civil war period piece which finds Buckwheat
    as a lost slave who teams up with Spanky. The two, joined
    by the gang, eventually become responsible for defending a
    plantation against an attack by Northerners. There are
    references to 'slave masters', 'pickaninnies' and the
    like. Discovering that he's lost, Buckwheat attaches him-
    self to Spanky, knowing that a slave without a master is
    likely to be shot. Billie Thomas stars as Buckwheat.

GENERAL,_THE
War/Cast: Buster Keaton + Helen Mack
Screenplay: Charles Smith   Director: Buster Keaton + Clyde
    Bruckman
Studio/Company: Allied Artists
Date/Country: 1927 + USA   Type: Feature
Annotation: Farcical rendition of the Civil War with Keaton
    as a Southern train driver who outwits the stupid Yankee
    "Nigger lovers" who are the villains of the piece.

GENERATION_OF_HOPE
Series: New African
Producer: Canadian Broadcasting Corporation + UNESCO + Leo
    Rampen
Tech Info: 16 mm/sound/bw/23 min.
Date/Country: 1967 + Ghana + Senegal   Type: Documentary
Distr/Arch: usunesco + mghf

Annotation: The difficulty of searching for an identity and an education by the new generation of post-independence Africans is examined.

GENGHIS_KHAN
Nar/Cast: Woody Strode* + Omar Sharif + Stephen Boyd
Screenplay: Clarke Reynolds + Beverly Cross
Producer: Irving Allen   Director: Henry Levin
Studio/Company: Columbia
Tech Info: 16 mm/sound/color/124 min.
Date/Country: 1965 + USA + Britain + West Germany + Yugoslavia   Type: Feature
Distr/Arch: arg + cha + ics + mod + mot + roa + twf + wcf
Annotation: Woody Strode is Sengal the mute in this adventure melodrama of the growth and development of young prince Temujen into the powerful Genghis Khan. Sengal accompanies the young man when he escapes from Jamuga who has enslaved his people.

GENIUS_AT_WORK
Nar/Cast: Bela Lugosi + Lionel Atwill + Ann Jeffries + Wally Brown + Alan Carney   Director: Leslie Goodwins
Studio/Company: RKO
Tech Info: 16 mm/sound/bw/61 min.
Date/Country: 1946 + USA   Type: Feature
Distr/Arch: fnc
Annotation: Alan Carney of the comedy team Brown and Carney, has an accident which singes him black in this film which has Lugosi near the end of his career, playing butler to a villainous Atwill.

GENTLE_JULIA
Nar/Cast: Jane Withers + Tom Brown + Marsha Hunt + Jackie Searl + Francis Ford + George Meeker + Hattie McDaniel*
Screenplay: Lamar Trotti   Story: Booth Tarkington
Producer: Sol M. Wertzel   Director: John Blystone
Studio/Company: Twentieth Century Fox
Date/Country: 1936 + USA   Type: Feature
Annotation: Child star Jane Withers employs impish tricks to save her Aunt Julia (Marsha Hunt) from an ill-fated engagement. Hattie McDaniel plays Kitty Silvers.

GENTLEMAN_FROM_DIXIE
Nar/Cast: Jack La Rue + Marian Marsh + Clarence Muse* + John Holland + Phyllis Barry + Monte Blue   Story: Fred Myton
Director: Al Herman
Studio/Company: Monogram
Date/Country: 1942 + USA   Type: Feature

GEORGE_WASHINGTON_CARVER
Producer: Vignette
Tech Info: 16 mm/sound/bw/11 min.
Date/Country: 1966 + USA   Type: Documentary
Distr/Arch: bfa
Annotation: Accomplishments of the slave who became a famous scientist. Includes some actual footage of Dr. Carver in his lab.

GEORGE WASHINGTON CARVER
Nar/Cast: Dr. George Washington Carver* + Booker T.
    Washington, III* + Ralph Edwards* + Milton Sprage* + Tim
    Campbell* + Raye Gilbert*
Studio/Company: Bryant Productions
Date/Country: 1940 + USA   Type: Dramatized Documentary
Annotation: Former slave, eminent scientist Dr. George
    Washington Carver (76 years old) tells the story of his
    struggles and successes to a young boy pondering his op-
    tions for the future.

GEORGE WASHINGTON SLEPT HERE
Nar/Cast: Jack Benny + Ann Sheridan + Hattie McDaniel*
Screenplay: Everett Freeman
Producer: Jerry Wald   Director: William Keighley
Studio/Company: Warner Brothers
Tech Info: sound/bw/90 min.
Date/Country: 1942 + USA   Type: Feature
Annotation: Hattie McDaniel is Hester who, along with
    others, adds to the amusement as Jack Benny painfully ad-
    justs to living in a historical Pennsylvania shack to
    please his wife (Ann Sheridan).

GEORGIA ROSE
Nar/Cast: Clarence Brooks* + Evelyn Preer* + Dora Dean John-
    son* + Edward Thompson* + Roberta Hyson* + Spencer Willi-
    ams* + Irene Wilson* + Webb King* + Allegretti Anderson*
Screenplay: Harry A. Gant   Director: Harry A. Gant
Studio/Company: Aristo Films
Tech Info: 35 mm/sound/bw/7 reels
Date/Country: 1930 + USA   Type: Feature
Annotation: A musical about Rose, a young woman who is saved
    from the sinful cabaret and city life by the man she
    loves, but not before several musical numbers including
    "Your're Just a Rosebud from a Garden in Georgia," which
    is where she came from, with her minister-father because
    his crops were destroyed by the boll weevil.

GEORGIA SEA ISLAND SINGERS, THE
Screenplay: Arthur Goodwin + Edmund Carpenter + Bess Lomax
    Hawes + Alan Lomax + Stanley Croner + Isidore Mankofsky +
    Fred Hudson +
Tech Info: 16 mm/sound/bw/1 reel/12 min.
Date/Country: 1974 + USA   Type: Documentary
Distr/Arch: fnc
Annotation: This film is a record of a performance of some
    of the traditional religious activities and music of
    Southern blacks as performed by the Georgia Sea Island
    Singers, filmed in 1963.

GEORGIA, GEORGIA
Nar/Cast: Diana Sands* + Minnie Gentry* + Dirk Benedict +
    Terry Whitmore* + Roger Furman*
Screenplay: Maya Angelou*
Producer: Jack Jordan* + Quentin Kelly   Director: Stig
    Bjorkman
Studio/Company: Cinerama
Tech Info: 16 mm/color/sound/3 reels/91 min.

Date/Country: 1972 + Sweden   Type: Feature
Distr/Arch: swa
Annotation: Georgia Martin (Diana Sands) is an international
    singing star searching for answers about being black and
    female. In Sweden she meets Michael, a white American
    expatriate. The problems surrounding this affair and
    "white fever" result in dramatic confrontations between
    Georgia and her putative mother/companion (Minnie Gentry).
    Filmed on location in Sweden. Songs by Maya Angelow*.

GHOST_BREAKERS,_THE
Nar/Cast: Bob Hope + Willie Best* + Paulette Goddard + Noble
    Johnson* + Virginia Brissac
Screenplay: Walter DeLeon   Story: Dickey and Goddard
Producer: Arthur Hornblow, Jr.   Director: George Marshall
Studio/Company: Paramount Pictures
Tech Info: 16 mm/bw/sound/3 reels/85 min.
Date/Country: 1940 + USA   Type: Feature
Distr/Arch: uni
Annotation: A haunted castle in Cuba is the site of a buried
    treasure. Willie Best plays valet to Bob Hope's sleuth
    and is thoroughly frightened by ghosts and goblins. Noble
    Johnson (Zombie) is voodoo assistant to Virginia Brissac
    (Mother Zombie). Remake of 1922 Ghost_Breakers.

GHOST_OF_TOLSTON'S_MANOR
Nar/Cast: Andrew Bishop* + Lawrence Chenault* + Edna Morton*
    + Monte Hawley*
Studio/Company: Micheaux Film Corporation*
Date/Country: 1934 + USA

GHOST_RIDER,_THE
Nar/Cast: Martin Turner* + Pete Morrison
Screenplay: Bob Williamson
Studio/Company: William Steiner Productions
Tech Info: 35 mm/silent/bw/5 reels
Date/Country: 1925 + USA   Type: Feature
Annotation: Pete Morrison western, with Morrison as Jim
    Poevers, Turner as Felix, his sidekick.

GHOST_TALKS,_THE
Nar/Cast: Helen Twelvetrees + Charles Eaton + Stepin
    Fetchit*   Story: Max Marcin + Edward Hammond   Director:
    Lew Seiler
Studio/Company: Fox
Date/Country: 1929 + USA
Annotation: An early feature length talkie which has various
    criminals looking for a million dollars worth of bonds
    hidden in an old hotel while a ghost tries to scare them
    away. Stepin Fetchit plays one of the workers at the
    hotel.

GIANT_OF_HIS_RACE,_A
Nar/Cast: Mabel Homes* + Walter Holeby* + Walter Long + Ruth
    Freeman*
Studio/Company: North State Film Corporation
Date/Country: 1921 + USA
Annotation: A young man, son of the slave Munga, becomes a

doctor and devotes himself to the service of his race. He
is even able to find a cure for a disease that is plaguing
his people, with the assistance of a courageous young
teacher who is willing to sacrifice herself. He is
awarded a tidy sum for his discovery, and he and the
teacher marry.

GIANTS VS. YANKS
Series: Our Gang
Nar/Cast: Our Gang + Ernie Morrison* + Allen Hoskins*
Screenplay: Hal Roach
Producer: Hal Roach   Director: Robert McGowan
Studio/Company: Pathe
Tech Info: silent/bw/2 reels
Date/Country: 1923 + USA   Type: Comedy Short
Annotation: Though there are a few baseball scenes, the film
    basically revolves around the gang being quarantined in a
    wealthy couple's home, which they tear up with reckless
    abandon. Allen Hoskins stars as Farina.

GIFT OF THE BLACK FOLK, THE
Producer: Carlton Moss*
Tech Info: 16 mm/sound/color/12 min.
Date/Country: 1974 + USA   Type: Documentary
Distr/Arch: pyr
Annotation: Stories about the humanistic contributions of
    black people; e.g. Harriet Tubman, Frederick Douglas, Den-
    mark Vesey. Includes music by Fisk University Orchestra.

GIFTS IN RHYTHM
Nar/Cast: Bob Howard + The Cabin Kids*
Producer: Al Christie
Studio/Company: Educational Pictures
Tech Info: 16 mm/sound/bw/1 reel/10 min.
Date/Country: 1936 + USA   Type: Musical Short
Distr/Arch: kpf
Annotation: The "Cabin Kids" along with Uncle Happy (Bob
    Howard) put on a musical revue at the Fairmont Foundling
    Home.

GIRL CAN'T HELP IT, THE
Nar/Cast: Tom Ewell + Jayne Mansfield + Fats Domino* + Abbey
    Lincoln* + Juanita Moore* + Little Richard*
Screenplay: Frank Tashlin + Herbert Baker
Producer: Frank Tashlin   Director: Frank Tashlin
Studio/Company: Fox
Tech Info: sound/color/97 min.
Date/Country: 1956 + USA   Type: Feature
Annotation: Fats Domino, Little Richard and Abbey Lincoln
    are among the entertainers in this film about the
    theatrical progress of a woman with a phenomenal figure
    (Mansfield). Juanita Moore plays the maid.

GIRL FROM CHICAGO, THE
Alt Title(s): The Spider's Web
Nar/Cast: Carl Mahon* + Starr Calloway* + Grace Smith* +
    Frank Wilson* + Eugene Brooks* + Minta Cato* + Juano
    Hernandez* + Erwin Gary* + John Everett* + Alice B. Rus-

sell* + Cherokee Thornton* + Chick Evans* + Bud Harris* +
Rhythm Rascals Orchestra*
Producer: Oscar Micheaux*   Director: Oscar Micheaux*
Studio/Company: Micheaux Film Corporation*
Tech Info: 16 mm/bw/sound/6 rels/69 min.
Date/Country: 1932   Type: Feature
Distr/Arch: sta + lc
Annotation: A crime melodrama about a young secret service
    agent, Alonzo Smith (Mahon), who gets romantically in-
    volved with a pretty young schoolteacher, Norma (Cal-
    loway), in a small town in Mississippi.   Later, in New
    York, Alonzo has to extricate Norma's friend Mary (Eunice
    Brooks) from serious trouble involving the numbers game
    and is accused of murdering a numbers banker. A slightly
    different, silent version of this film was released in
    1926, entitled The Spider's Web.

GIRL IN ROOM 20, THE
Nar/Cast: Spencer Williams* + July Jones* + Geraldine Brock*
    Director: Spencer Williams*
Studio/Company: United Films
Tech Info: 35 mm/bw/sound/6 reels/64 min.
Date/Country: 194-   Type: Feature
Distr/Arch: lc

GIRL IN THE SHOW, THE
Nar/Cast: Bessie Love
Studio/Company: MGM
Date/Country: 1929 + USA
Annotation: Bessie Love plays Hattie Hartley, the female
    lead in an Uncle Tom's Cabin troupe. Her role is Little
    Eva.

GIRL MISSING
Nar/Cast: Ben Lyon + Glenda Farrell + Louise Beavers* + Lyle
    Talbot
Screenplay: Carl Erickson + Don Mullaly   Director: Robert
    Florey
Studio/Company: Warner Brothers
Tech Info: 16 mm/sound/bw/69 min.
Date/Country: 1933 + USA   Type: Feature
Distr/Arch: uas
Annotation: Story about murder and kidnapping on the wedding
    night of a girl who is not what she appears to be. Louise
    Beavers plays Julie in this mystery-melodrama.

GIRL NOBODY KNEW, THE
Nar/Cast: Ena Hartman*
Studio/Company: Universal Studios
Date/Country: 1966 + USA   Type: Feature
Annotation: Hartman as a sophisticated New Yorker who moves
    in top social circles.

GIRL, A GUITAR AND A TRUMPET, A
Alt Title(s): see Kaerlighedens Melodi

GIRLS ABOUT TOWN
Nar/Cast: Louise Beavers* + Joel McCrea + Kay Francis

Screenplay: Zoe Akins   Director: George Cukor
Studio/Company: Paramount
Tech Info: 16 mm/sound/bw/82 min.
Date/Country: 1931 + USA   Type: Feature
Distr/Arch: uni
Annotation: Story of two attractive gold diggers obtaining
    gifts from susceptible provincial men of means.   Louise
    Beavers has a minor role as a maid.

GLAD RAG DOLL
Nar/Cast: Dolores Costello + Ralph Graves + Louise Beavers*
    Director: Michael Curtiz
Studio/Company: Fox
Tech Info: sound/bw
Date/Country: 1929 + USA   Type: Feature
Annotation: A comedy melodrama about an actress   (Costello),
    her rich admirer and his snobbish family. Louise Beavers
    has a bit role.

GLENN MILLER STORY, THE
Nar/Cast: Louis Armstrong* + James Stewart + June Allyson
Screenplay: Valentine Davies + Oscar Brodney
Producer: Aaron Rosenberg   Director: Anthony Mann
Studio/Company: Universal
Tech Info: 16 mm/sound/color/116 min.
Date/Country: 1954 + USA   Type: Feature
Distr/Arch: uni
Annotation: Film biography of band leader Glenn Miller with
    a jazz sequence featuring Louis Armstrong.

GLI AVVENTURIERI DEI TROPICI
Nar/Cast: John Kitzmiller*
Date/Country: 1960 + Italy   Type: Feature

GLORIOUS FOURTH, THE
Series: Our Gang
Nar/Cast: Our Gang + Allen Hoskins* + Jannie Hoskins*
Screenplay: Hal Roach
Producer: Hal Roach   Director: Robert McGowan
Studio/Company: Pathe
Tech Info: silent/bw/2 reels
Date/Country: 1927 + USA   Type: Comedy Short
Annotation: Farina's sky rocket lands in a fireworks stand
    and the gang's dog swallows capsules that are more power-
    ful than nitro. Allen Hoskins stars as Farina.

GLORY ALLEY
Nar/Cast: Ralph Meeker + Leslie Caron + Louis Armstrong*
Screenplay: Art Cohn
Producer: Nicholas Nayfack   Director: Raoul Walsh
Studio/Company: MGM
Tech Info: 16 mm/sound/bw/79 min.
Date/Country: 1952 + USA   Type: Feature
Distr/Arch: fnc
Annotation: Louis Armstrong plays a jazz singer, who clowns
    as well as plays his horn, in this story about a boxer who
    runs away from a championship fight and has to prove to
    everyone he is not a coward.

GLOVE TAPS
Series: Our Gang
Nar/Cast: Our Gang + Billie Thomas*
Producer: Hal Roach   Director: Gordon Thomas
Studio/Company: MGM
Tech Info: super 8 mm/16 mm/bw/sound/1 reel/11 min.
Date/Country: 1937 + USA   Type: Comedy Short
Distr/Arch: bla
Annotation: Spanky volunteers Alfalfa to fight the new
    neighborhood tough, Butch. Spanky's enthusiastic training
    regimen, of course, isn't enough to make Alfalfa a boxer,
    but at the critical moment in the fight, Porky and Buck-
    wheat knock Butch out with a loaded glove attached to a
    big club. Billie Thomas stars as Buckwheat.

GO DOWN DEATH
Nar/Cast: Myra D. Hemmings* + Samuel H. James* + Eddye L.
    Houston* + Spencer Williams* + Ames Droughan* + Walter
    McMillion* + Irene Campbell* + Charlie Washington* + Helen
    Butler* + Dolly Jones*
Screenplay: Sam Elljay   Story: Jean Roddy
Producer: Spencer Williams*   Director: Spencer Williams*
Studio/Company: Harlemwood Studios + Sack Amusement Co.
Tech Info: 16 mm/sound/2 reels/bw/54 min.
Date/Country: 1944 + USA   Type: Feature
Distr/Arch: bud + kpf + lc
Annotation: Folk-like drama, inspired by James Weldon John-
    son's poem, depicts the faith of Sister Caroline whose
    prayers are answered even after death. The preacher who
    is implicated in immoral activities by Jim, the barowner,
    is proved innocent and Jim is hounded to death by his con-
    science for causing Caroline's death.

GO INTO YOUR DANCE
Nar/Cast: Al Jolson + Ruby Keeler + Glenda Farrell + Fred
    "Snowflake" Toones
Screenplay: Earl Baldwin   Story: Bradford Ropes   Director:
    Archie L. Mayo
Studio/Company: Warners
Tech Info: 16 mm/sound/bw/89 min.
Date/Country: 1935 + USA   Type: Feature
Distr/Arch: uas
Annotation: Al Jolson plays an Ex-Broadway star trying to
    make a comeback. In the movie he has a black valet listed
    in the credits as "Snowflake."

GO WEST, YOUNG MAN
Nar/Cast: Mae West + Nicodemus Stewart* + Warren William +
    Randolph Scott + Lyle Talbot
Screenplay: Mae West   Story: Lawrence Riley
Producer: Emanuel Cohen   Director: Henry Hathaway
Studio/Company: Paramount
Date/Country: 1936 + USA   Type: Feature
Annotation: Nicodemus plays himself in this Mae West vehicle
    which has her acting out the role of Mavis Arden, actress,
    during one of her personal appearances.

GO, MAN, GO
Nar/Cast: Sidney Poitier* + Dane Clark + Harlem Globetrotters* + Pat Breslin
Screenplay: Arnold Becker
Producer: Anton M. Leader   Director: James Wong Howe
Studio/Company: United Artists
Tech Info: 16 mm/sound/bw/82 min.
Date/Country: 1954 + USA   Type: Feature
Distr/Arch: bud + ccc + cha
Annotation: The story of how the Harlem Globetrotters rose from obscure barnstorming days, to prominence as a major box office attraction. Sy Oliver* is responsible for some of the music.

GOD'S LITTLE ACRE
Nar/Cast: Robert Ryan + Aldo Ray + Tina Louise + Michael Landon + Rex Ingram*
Screenplay: Phillip Yordan   Story: Erskine Caldwell
Producer: Sidney Harmon   Director: Anthony Mann
Studio/Company: United Artists
Tech Info: 16 mm/sound/bw/118 min.
Date/Country: 1958 + USA   Type: Feature
Distr/Arch: nil
Annotation: Based on Erskine Caldwell's best seller, the film tells the tale of Ty, a poor white farmer, and his family as they alternate between looking for gold and just trying to live in their meager way. Rex Ingram plays Uncle Felix, Ty's dignified farmhand.

GOD'S STEPCHILDREN
Alt Title(s): All God's Stepchildren
Nar/Cast: Alice B. Russell* + Carmen Newsome* + Jacqueline Lewis* + Alice Lovejoy* + Ethel Moses* + Gloria Press*
Screenplay: Oscar Micheaux*
Producer: Oscar Micheaux*
Tech Info: 16 mm/bw/sound/2 reels/65 min.
Date/Country: 1937 + USA   Type: Feature
Distr/Arch: bud
Annotation: A light-skinned child abandoned by her mother, Naomi doesn't want to acknowledge her race. Forced by her foster mother to attend a black school, she causes so much difficulty she is sent to a convent for 12 years. On her return Naomi is pressed to marry a dark-skinned man, has a child by him whom she abandons and "passes" into the white world. Later when she is rejected by that world, she commits suicide.

GODDESS, THE
Nar/Cast: Louise Beavers* + Kim Stanley + Betty Lou Holland + Joan Copeland   Story: Paddy Chayefsky
Producer: Milton Perlman   Director: John Cromwell
Studio/Company: Columbia Pictures
Tech Info: 16 mm/sound/bw/104 min.
Date/Country: 1958 + USA   Type: Feature
Distr/Arch: mac
Annotation: The rise and fall of a lovely Hollywood star played by Kim Stanley and how she affects the lives of those around her. Louise Beavers plays her cook.

GODS AND THE DEAD, THE
Alt Title(s): see Os Deuses E os mortos

GOIN' FISHIN'
Series: Our Gang
Nar/Cast: Our Gang + Billie Thomas*
Screenplay: Hal Law + Robert A. McGowan
Producer: Jack   Chertok   +   Richard Goldstone   Director:
   Edward Cahn
Studio/Company: MGM
Tech Info: bw/sound/1 reel
Date/Country: 1940 + USA   Type: Comedy Short
Annotation: One thing after another delays the start of the
   gang's camping trip until it's too late to go, while their
   antics have delayed a bus load of passengers. Billie
   Thomas stars as Buckwheat.

GOING PLACES
Nar/Cast: Dick Powell + Anita Louise + Louis Armstrong*
Screenplay: Sig Herzig + Jerry Wald + Maurice Leo   Story:
   Victor Mapes + William Collier, Jr.   Director: Ray En-
   right
Studio/Company: Warner Brothers
Tech Info: 16 mm/sound/bw/84 min.
Date/Country: 1939 + USA   Type: Feature
Distr/Arch: uas
Annotation: Dick Powell stars in this musical as a horse shy
   man who poses as a famous steeple chase rider, with Louis
   Armstrong coming to the rescue.

GOING TO PRESS
Series: Our Gang
Nar/Cast: Our Gang + Billie Thomas*
Screenplay: Hal Law + Robert A. McGowan
Producer: MGM   Director: Edward Cahn
Studio/Company: MGM
Tech Info: bw/sound/1 reel
Date/Country: 1942 + USA   Type: Comedy Short
Annotation: The gang publishes a neighborhood newspaper and
   works to track down the mysterious leader of a tough guys'
   gang. But the mystery leader is helping the gang out and
   their plans are nearly foiled until they set a trap and
   catch the guy redhanded.

GOLD DIGGERS OF 1933
Nar/Cast: Warren William + Joan Blondell + Etta Moten* +
   Dick Powell + Ruby Keeler
Screenplay: Avery Hopwood   Director: Mervyn LeRoy
Studio/Company: Warner Brothers
Tech Info: 16 mm/sound/bw/98 min.
Date/Country: 1933 + USA   Type: Feature
Distr/Arch: uas
Annotation: The problems faced by Dick Powell, Ruby Keeler
   and Joan Blondell in putting together a Broadway show are
   musically brought to the screen. Etta Moten stands out in
   her rendition of "Remember My Forgotten Man."

GOLD IS WHERE YOU FIND IT
Nar/Cast: George Brent + Olivia de Haviland + Claude Rains +
  Margaret Lindsey + John Litel + Tim Holt + Sidney Toler +
  Henry O'Neal + Willie Best*
Screenplay: Warren Duff + Robert Buckner   Story: Clemento
  Ripley   Director: Michael Curtiz
Studio/Company: Warner Brothers
Tech Info: Technicolor
Date/Country: 1938 + USA   Type: Feature
Annotation: Post-Civil War feud between ranchers and miners
  in California reveals greed and exploitation with semi-
  historical flavor. Willie Best in bit role as Joshua.

GOLD WEST, THE
Nar/Cast: Hattie McDaniel*
Date/Country: 1932 + USA   Type: Feature
Annotation: An early film for Hattie McDaniel in which she
  plays a small, unobtrusive servant role.

GOLDEN BOY
Nar/Cast: Barbara Stanwyck + William Holden + Lee J.Cobb +
  Joseph Calleia + Sam Levene + Clinton Rosemond*   Story:
  Clifford Odets   Director: Reuben Mamoulin
Studio/Company: Columbia
Date/Country: 1939 + USA   Type: Feature
Distr/Arch: bud + mod + tfc + wcf
Annotation: Story of a promising concert violinist who for-
  sakes musical career to become a boxer until he ac-
  cidentally kills someone in the ring. Rosemond has a bit
  part.

GOLDEN EYE, THE
Series: Charlie Chan
Nar/Cast: Roland Winters + Wanda McKay + Mantan Moreland*
Screenplay: W. Scott Darling
Producer: James Burkett   Director: William Beaudine
Studio/Company: Monogram
Tech Info: 16 mm/sound/bw/2 reels/69 min.
Date/Country: 1948 + USA   Type: Feature
Distr/Arch: cin
Annotation: Mantan Moreland is Birmingham Brown, Charlie
  Chan's chauffeur and comic foil.

GOLDEN PEARLS OF PROGRESS
Studio/Company: Exquisite Productions
Date/Country: 191-

GOLDILOCKS AND THE JIVIN' BEARS
Series: Merrie Melodies   Director: Fritz Freland
Studio/Company: Warner Brothers
Tech Info: 16 mm/technicolor/sound/1 reel/10 min.
Date/Country: 1944 + USA   Type: Animated Short
Distr/Arch: kpf
Annotation: A typical 1940's cartoon with blacks portrayed
  as boogie-woogie bears.

GOLDSTEIN
Nar/Cast: Ben Carruthers* + Lou Gilbert

Screenplay: Philip Kaufman + Benjamin Manaster
Producer: Philip Kaufman + Benjamin Manaster   Director:
    Philip Kaufman + Benjamin Manaster
Studio/Company: Actura Films International
Tech Info: 16 mm/sound/bw/85 min.
Date/Country: 1965 + USA   Type: Feature
Distr/Arch: mac
Annotation: Carruthers is Jay, a beatnik friend of a young
    sculptor, who, after being rejected by his pregnant
    girlfriend, goes searching the streets of Chicago for the
    prophet Elijah in this satire on urban life. Nelson Al-
    gren appears as himself.

GONE ARE THE DAYS
Alt Title(s): The Man From C.O.T.T.O.N.
Nar/Cast: Ossie Davis* + Ruby Dee* + Godfrey Cambridge* +
    Sorrell Brooke + Hilda Haynes* + Alan Alda + Beah
    Richards*
Screenplay: Ossie Davis*   Story: Ossie Davis*
Producer: Nicholas Webster   Director: Nicholas Webster
Studio/Company: Trans Flux
Tech Info: 16 mm/bw/sound/3 reels/97 min.
Date/Country: 1963 + USA   Type: Feature
Distr/Arch: mac + bud + mod + tfc
Annotation: Rev. Purlie (Ossie Davis) enlists the aid of
    Lutibelle (Ruby Dee) to trick Cap'n Cotchipee out of $500
    to pay for a real church for Blacks in a small southern
    town.   The comedy satirizes southern behavior during the
    Civil Rights movement of the sixties.

GONE HARLEM
Nar/Cast: Jimmy Baskett* + Ethel Moses* + Florence Hill* +
    Chuck Thompson* + The Plantation Club Chorus*
Studio/Company: Creative Cinema
Date/Country: 1939

GONE WITH THE WIND
Nar/Cast: Vivian Leigh + Clark Gable + Leslie Howard +
    Olivia de Havilland + Thomas Mitchell + Hattie McDaniel* +
    Oscar Polk* + Ben Carter* + Eddie Anderson* + Butterfly
    McQueen*
Screenplay: Sidney Howard   Story: Margaret Mitchell
Producer: David Selznick   Director: Victor Fleming
Studio/Company: MGM
Tech Info: 16 mm/color/sound/6 reels/222 min.
Date/Country: 1939 + USA   Type: Feature
Distr/Arch: fnc
Annotation: A dramatic love story between a roguish Yankee
    gambler and a pampered Southern belle is set against the
    background of the Civil War and post-war reconstruction
    periods.   It co-stars Hattie McDaniel who won an Oscar as
    best supporting actress, features McQueen as Prissy.

GOOD BAD BOYS
Series: Our Gang
Nar/Cast: Our Gang + Billie Thomas*
Screenplay: Hal Law + Robert A. McGowan
Producer: Jack Chertok + Richard Goldstone   Director:

Edward Cahn
Studio/Company: MGM
Tech Info: bw/sound/1 reel
Date/Country: 1940 + USA   Type: Comedy Short
Annotation: Alfalfa plans to start a life of crime after
   he's wrongly accused of stealing and the gang's with him,
   all except Spanky who contrives to teach them all a lesson
   about stealing. Billie Thomas stars as Buckwheat.

GOOD CHEER
Series: Our Gang
Nar/Cast: Our Gang + Allen Hoskins* + Jannie Hoskins*
Screenplay: Hal Roach
Producer: Hal Roach   Director: Robert McGowan
Studio/Company: Pathe
Tech Info: silent/bw/2 reels
Date/Country: 1926 + USA   Type: Comedy Short
Annotation: It's the day before Christmas, and though poor,
   the kids hit upon an idea to raise money to get presents
   for their friends. With that and a reward from catching
   bootleggers, a better Christmas is had by all. Allen
   Hoskins stars as Farina.

GOOD GUYS WEAR BLACK, THE
Nar/Cast: Lloyd Haynes*

GOODBYE AGAIN
Nar/Cast: Diahann Carroll* + Ingrid Bergman + Yves Montand
Screenplay: Samuel Taylor
Producer: Anatole Litvak   Director: Anatole Litvak
Studio/Company: United Artists
Tech Info: 16 mm/sound/bw/120 min.
Date/Country: 1961 + USA + France   Type: Feature
Distr/Arch: uas
Annotation: Diahann Carroll is a singer in this adaptation
   of Francoise Sagan's novel, Aimez-vous Brahms? about a
   Parisian woman and her lovers.

GOODBYE AND GOOD LUCK
Producer: PBL + NET
Tech Info: 16 mm/sound/bw/1 reel/30 min.
Date/Country: 1967   Type: Documentary
Distr/Arch: iu
Annotation: Documents an encounter between advocates of
   Black Power and a black Vietnam veteran. Shows veteran's
   concern as he tries to adjust to civilian life.   Shows
   militants trying to persuade him that he has been duped by
   "whitey" and his confusion as he attempts to choose sides.

GOODBYE, MY LADY
Nar/Cast: Sidney Poitier* + Brandon DeWilde + Phil Harris +
   Ethel Barrymore + Walter Brennan
Studio/Company: Warner Brothers
Date/Country: 1956 + USA   Type: Feature
Annotation: Poitier in a supporting role as a young farmer
   who is involved in the problems confronting sharecroppers
   in the Louisiana swamp country.

GOODBYE, UNCLE TOM
Alt Title(s): see Adieu Oncle Tom

GORDON'S WAR
Nar/Cast: Paul Winfield* + Carl Lee* + Gilbert Lee* + Nathan
   C. Heard* + Gilbert Lewis + David Dowling* + Tony King* +
   Ralph Wilcox*
Screenplay: Howard Friedlander + Ed Spielman
Producer: Robert L. Schaffel   Director: Ossie Davis*
Studio/Company: Twentieth Century Fox
Tech Info: 16 mm/color/sound/3 reels/90 min.
Date/Country: 1973 + USA   Type: Feature
Distr/Arch: fnc
Annotation: Paul Winfield is Gordon, Vietnam veteran, who
   returns home to find that his wife, addicted to heroin
   while he was away, has died from an overdose.   To avenge
   her death, Gordon sets out to rid the ghetto of pushers.
   The three friends who join his personal army are Carl Lee
   (Bee), David Dowling (Otis) and Tony King (Roy)>

GOT TO TELL IT: A TRIBUTE TO MAHALIA JACKSON
Producer: CBS
Tech Info: 16 mm/sound/color/33 min.
Date/Country: 1974 + USA   Type: TV Documentary
Distr/Arch: pho
Annotation: The life story of Mahalia Jackson with her per-
   sonal comments.

GOUMBE (LA) DES JEUNES NOCEURS   Director: Jean Rouch
Date/Country: 1965 + France
Distr/Arch: saf

GOVERNOR, THE
Alt Title(s): see The Nigger

GRAFTER AND THE MAID, THE
Alt Title(s): The Grafter and the Girl
Screenplay: Jerry Mills*
Producer: Bill Foster*
Studio/Company: Foster Photoplay Company
Date/Country: 191- + USA

GRAND MAGAL A TOUBA
Alt Title(s): Pilgrimage to Touba
Screenplay: Blaise Senghor* + Thomas Diop*   Director:
   Blaise Senghor*
Tech Info: color/20 min.
Date/Country: 1962 + Senegal   Type: Documentary
Annotation: The film records the 1961 pilgrimage of the
   Mourides, one of the two major Islamic sects in Senegal,
   to Touba, the cradle of the sect.

GRASSHOPPER, THE
Nar/Cast: Jacqueline Bisset + Jim Brown* + Joseph Cotton
Screenplay: Jerry Belson + Garry Marshall   Story: Mark Mc-
   Shane
Producer: Jerry Belson + Garry Marshall   Director: Jerry
   Paris

Studio/Company: National General Pictures
Tech Info: 16 mm/sound/color/95 min.
Date/Country: 1970 + USA   Type: Feature
Distr/Arch: swa
Annotation: The film traces the downfall of a young girl
    from bank clerk to prostitute. During one part of the
    downfall, she's married to a former football player, play-
    ed by Jim Brown.

GRATER AND THE GIRL, THE
Alt Title(s): see The grafter and the Maid

GRAVEL SPRINGS FIFE AND DRUM
Producer: Ferris, Evans, Peiser + Center for Southern
    Folklore
Tech Info: 16 mm/color/sound/10 min.
Date/Country: 1971 + USA   Type: Documentary
Distr/Arch: cal + csf
Annotation: Documents the survival of fife and drum folk
    music, suggestive of West Arican tribal music, which is
    still played in the black community of Gravel Springs in
    northern Mississippi. Among the songs sung and played are
    "Levee Camp Blues" and "Shimmy She Wobble."

GREASED LIGHTNING
Nar/Cast: Richard Pryor* + Cleavon Little* + Pam Grier* +
    Julian Bond* + Beau Bridges
Screenplay: Kenneth Vose + Lawrence Du Kore + Melvin Van
    Peebles* + Leon Capetanos   Director: Michael Schultz*
Date/Country: 1977 + USA   Type: Feature
Annotation: Fictional biography of Wendell Scott, the first
    black man to cross the color line in auto racing. Richard
    Pryor plays Scott who perseveres against numerous odds,
    getting his start on dirt tracks in the South among the
    KKK-minded. Pam Grier is his supportive wife, Beau
    Bridges a white driver who becomes his mechanic and
    friend.

GREAT AMERICAN BROADCAST, THE
Nar/Cast: Alice Faye + John Payne + Jack Oakie + Ink Spots*
    + Nicholas Brothers*   Director: Archie Mayo
Studio/Company: Fox
Tech Info: 16 mm/sound/bw/80 min.
Date/Country: 1941 + USA
Distr/Arch: sel + wcf + who + wil + wsa
Annotation: The four Ink Spots and the Nicholas Brothers
    perform in this musical comedy entertainment.

GREAT AMERICAN DREAM -- THREE VIEWS, THE
Producer: NET
Tech Info: 16 mm/sound/bw/1 reel/36 min.
Date/Country: 1971 + USA   Type: Documentary
Distr/Arch: iu
Annotation: Presents three views of life in black America
    which focus on the dreams, problems, and changing at-
    titudes of black Americans. Includes black freshman Re-
    presentative Ron Dellums, who sees the great American
    dream as a nightmare for millions of blacks, and discusses

the frustrations he encountered during his first   year   in
Washington.

GREAT_DEBATE,_THE
Series: Search for the Nile
Nar/Cast: James Mason
Producer: Michael Hastings   Director: Derek Marlow
Studio/Company: BBC-TV
Tech Info: 16 mm/sound/color/2 reels/52 min.
Date/Country: 1972 + East Africa   Type: Documentary
Distr/Arch: timlif
Annotation: Livingstone has returned to England in 1864 to
    challenge Speke's theory of the origin of the Nile, while
    the Bakers are in Africa searching.

GREAT_LIE,_THE
Nar/Cast: Bette Davis + George Brent + Hattie McDaniel* +
    Sam McDaniel*
Screenplay: Lenore Coffe   Story: Polus Banks   Director:
    Edmund Goulding
Studio/Company: Warner Brothers
Tech Info: 16 mm/sound/bw/107 min.
Date/Country: 1941 + USA   Type: Feature
Distr/Arch: uas
Annotation: Sam and Hattie McDaniel play loyal servants to
    Bette Davis. Davis matches her wits and will with Mary
    Astor as they struggle for the man they both love.

GREAT_TREE_HAS_FALLEN,_A
Producer: Robert Long Productions
Tech Info: 16 mm/sound/color/1 reel/22 min.
Date/Country: 1973   Type: Documentary
Distr/Arch: iu
Annotation: Explains that in Ghana, West Africa, the King of
    the Ashanti Nation, Sir Osei Agyeman Prempeh II, has died
    and records the Nation's chiefs and other followers as
    they gather at the capital, Kumasi, to pay respects to him
    and welcome his successor. Documents the traditional
    practices, dances, music, dress, and symbols of position
    which bind the Nation together.

GREAT_WHITE_HOPE,_THE
Nar/Cast: James Earl Jones* + Jane Alexander + Lou Gilbert +
    Joel Fluellen* + Roy Glenn* + Beah Richard* + Moses Gunn*
    + Scatman Crothers* + Virginia Capers* + Roy Glenn* +
    Marlene Warfield*
Screenplay: Howard Sackler   Story: Howard Sackler
Producer: Howard Turman   Director: Martin Ritt
Studio/Company: Twentieth Century Fox
Tech Info: 16 mm/color/sound/3 reels/103 min.
Date/Country: 1970 + USA   Type: Feature
Distr/Arch: fnc
Annotation: James Earl Jones brings heavyweight champion
    Jack Johnson's controversial life and career to film
    audiences, in the guise of Jack Jefferson.

GREATEST_QUESTION,_THE
Nar/Cast: Tom Wilson + Lillian Gish + Robert Harron

Screenplay: S.E.V. Taylor   Story: William Hale   Director:
   D.W. Griffith
Studio/Company: First National Pictures
Tech Info: 35 mm/silent/bw/6 reels
Date/Country: 1919 + USA   Type: Feature
Distr/Arch: moma
Annotation: Film features Tom Wilson (in blackface) as Zeke,
   an Uncle Remus type who tells ghost stories to children,
   but when he has to go to the graveyard he is frightened by
   the idea of ghosts, real or imagined.

GREATEST SIN
War/Cast: Mae Evlyn Lewis* + Victor Nix*
Studio/Company: Trio Productions
Tech Info: 35 mm/silent/bw/4 reels
Date/Country: 1922 + USA   Type: Dramatic Short
Annotation: A story of Negro life.

GREATEST STORY EVER TOLD, THE
War/Cast: Sidney Poitier* + Max Von Sydow + Charlton Heston
   + Jose Ferrer + Frank Silvera*
Screenplay: James Lee Barrett + George Stevens
Producer: George Stevens   Director: George Stevens
Studio/Company: United Artists
Tech Info: 16 mm/sound/color/193 min.
Date/Country: 1965 + USA   Type: Feature
Distr/Arch: mac + uas
Annotation: The story of the ministry of Christ. Poitier
   plays the Ethiopian (Simon of Cyrene) who is converted to
   Christianity, Silvera is Casper.

GREATEST THING IN LIFE, THE
War/Cast: Lillian Gish + Robert Harron + Elmo Lincoln +
   "Peaches" Jackson
Screenplay: D.W. Griffith + S.E.V. Taylor   Director: D.W.
   Griffith
Studio/Company: Artcraft Pictures
Tech Info: 35 mm/silent/bw/6,062 ft.
Date/Country: 1918 + USA   Type: Feature
Annotation: The greatest thing in life is love and it is
   manifested in this film in numerous ways.   In the most
   famous scene (reel 6) the selfish and condescending young
   Southern hero, played by Harron, shows that he has learned
   respect for all mankind, when he kisses the cheek of a
   dying black soldier who, on the battlefield, (World War I)
   is calling for his "Mammy."

GREATEST, THE
War/Cast: Muhammad Ali* + James Earl Jones* + Lloyd Haynes*
   + Anazette Chase* + Ernest Borgnine + Paul Winfield*
Screenplay: Ring Lardner, Jr.   Director: Tom Gries
Studio/Company: Columbia
Tech Info: color/sound
Date/Country: 1977 + USA   Type: Feature
Annotation: The Greatest traces the life of Mohammad Ali
   from his small town beginnings, through the influence of
   Malcolm X (James Earl Jones) and eventually the Muslim
   faith.   The road to the World heavyweight championship is

shown in footage of the old fights with Joe Frazier, Ken
Norton and Sonny Liston. Anazette Chase plays Belinda;
Ali plays himself; Paul Winfield is his lawyer.

GREEN BERETS, THE
Nar/Cast: Raymond St. Jacques* + John Wayne + David Janssen
Screenplay: James Lee Barrett   Story: Robin Moore
Producer: Michael Wayne   Director: John Wayne + Ray Kellogg
Studio/Company: Warner Bros.
Tech Info: 16 mm/color/sound/4 reels/141 min.
Date/Country: 1968 + USA   Type: Feature
Distr/Arch: bud + ccc + cha + cwf + ics + ker + mac + mod +
   mot + rca + swa + tfc + tmc + unf + wcf
Annotation: This war melodrama traces the actions of the
   Green Berets in Vietnam from the U.S. Military point of
   view. St. Jacques is Doc McGee.

GREEN EYES
Nar/Cast: Paul Winfield* + Rita Tushingham + Jonathan Lippe
   + Victoria Racineo + Lemi
Screenplay: Eugene Logen + David Seltzer
Producer: David Seltzer   Director: John Erman
Studio/Company: Loumier Productions
Date/Country: 1976 + USA   Type: Feature
Annotation: Paul Winfield plays a disabled veteran who
   returns to Viet Nam to find the Vietnamese girl who was
   carrying his child when he left. What he finds is
   hundreds of children, left parent-less and homeless, the
   human waste of war.

GREEN PASTURES, THE
Nar/Cast: Rex Ingram* + Oscar Polk* + Eddie Anderson* +
   Frank Wilson* + Ernest Whitman* + William Cumby* + Edna
   Mae Harris* + Al Stokes* + David Bethea* + George Reed* +
   Clinton Rosemond* + Myrtle Anderson*   Story: Marc Connel-
   ly   Director: William Keighley + Marc Connelly
Studio/Company: Warners
Tech Info: 16 mm/bw/sound/3 reels/110 min.
Date/Country: 1936 + USA   Type: Feature
Distr/Arch: con + fnc + sta + twy + uas
Annotation: A Hollywood attempt to depict black folk life,
   The Green Pastures is a fantasy drawn from the Bible
   presenting a so-called black point of view. Heavenly
   choirs and fish-frys become metaphors for black culture.
   An adaptation of Connelly's play.

GREEN PASTURES
Studio/Company: Warner Brothers
Tech Info: 16 mm/sound/7 min./1 reel
Date/Country: USA   Type: Animated Short
Distr/Arch: uas
Annotation: Cartoon counterparts of Cab Calloway, Fats Wal-
   ler, and Louis Armstrong perform.

GREEN-EYED MONSTER, THE
Nar/Cast: Jack Austin* + Louise Dunbar*
Studio/Company: Norman Film Manufacturing Company
Date/Country: 1921 + USA

Annotation: The green-eyed monster is jealousy and the love
   triangle is settled in this film by a train race.

GREENWICH_VILLAGE_STORY
Nar/Cast: Robert Hogan + Melinda Plank + Toni Seitz
Screenplay: Jack O'Connell
Producer: JackO'Connell   Director: Jack O'Connell
Studio/Company: Shawn International, Inc.
Tech Info: 16 mm/sound/bw/95 min.
Date/Country: 1963   Type: Feature
Distr/Arch: mac
Annotation: Features Blacks as background presences in party
   sequences, street and restaurant scenes and, in general,
   as part of the Village milieu.

GRIDIRON_GRAFT
Alt Title(s): see While Thousands Cheer

GROWING_PAINS
Series: Our Gang
Nar/Cast: Our Gang + Allen Hoskins
Screenplay: Robert F. McGowan
Producer: Robert F. McGowan + Hal Roach   Director: Anthony
   Mack
Studio/Company: MGM
Tech Info: bw/silent/2 reels
Date/Country: 1928 + USA   Type: Comedy Short
Annotation: Mary Ann is a neighborhood brat who pesters the
   gang until they are roused to repay her in kind.   She
   chooses Wheezer to defend her honor and plans to have
   Wheezer drink cod liver oil so that he'll become a giant.
   A circus giant comes to board, learns of the plan, and
   substitutes for Wheezer. The giant is 'vanquished' in the
   end.   Allen Hoskins stars as Farina.

GUESS_WHO'S_COMING_TO_DINNER
Nar/Cast: Spencer Tracy + Katherine Hepburn + Sidney
   Poitier* + Cecil Kellaway + Beah Richards* + Katherine
   Houghton + Roy S. Glenn* + Isabell Sanford* + D'Urville
   Martin*
Screenplay: William Rose
Producer: Stanley Kramer   Director: Stanley Kramer
Studio/Company: Columbia Pictures
Tech Info: 16 mm/color/sound/3 reels/108 min.
Date/Country: 1967 + USA   Type: Feature
Distr/Arch: mac + bud + ccc + con + cwf + mod + sel + tfc +
   twy + wcf + wel + who + wil + arg + buc + roa + ics + swa
Annotation: A young woman from a socially prominent family
   brings home a famous doctor, John Prentice (Sidney
   Poitier) and introduces him to her family as her fiance.
   The parents of the mixed couple are forced to test their
   convictions about equality and human rights.

GUINEA_LOOKS_WEST
Producer: CBS-TV
Tech Info: 16 mm/sound/bw/28 mi
Date/Country: 1963 + Guinea   Type: Documentary
Distr/Arch: cbsf

Annotation: The history of the Republic of Guinea from   1958
   to 1963.

GUN MOLL
Alt Title(s): see Gang Smashers

GUNS AT BATASI
Nar/Cast: Richard Attenborough +   Jack   Hawkins +   Earl
   Cameron* + Mia Farrow + Errol John*
Screenplay: Leo Marks + Marshall Rugh + Robert Holles
Producer: George . Brown   Director: John Guillerman
Studio/Company: 20th Century Fox
Tech Info: 16 mm/sound/color/103 min.
Date/Country: 1964 + Britain   Type: Feature
Distr/Arch: fnc
Annotation: Story about a group of British soldiers trapped
   between two groups of warring Africans. Captain Abraham
   (Cameron) is on one side, Lieutenant Boniface (John) is on
   the other.

GUNS OF THE MAGNIFICENT SEVEN
Nar/Cast: George Kennedy + Bernie Casey* + Monte Markham +
   James Whitmore + Frank Silvera*
Screenplay: Herman Hoffman
Producer: Vincent M. Fennelly   Director: Paul Wendkos
Studio/Company: United Artists
Tech Info: 16 mm/sound/color/106 min.
Date/Country: 1969 + USA   Type: Feature
Distr/Arch: uas
Annotation: Third in the Magnificent Seven western melodrama
   series has "the seven" trying to liberate some revolu-
   tionaries from a fortress in 19th century Mexico.   This
   film marks Bernie Casey's film debut (as Cassie), Silvera
   is the bandit chief, Carlos Lobero.

GUNS OF THE TREES
Nar/Cast: Ben Carruthers* + Frances Stillman + Argus Julli-
   ard + Judie Bond*
Screenplay: Jonas Mekas
Producer: Jonas Mekas   Director: Jonas Mekas
Studio/Company: Filmmakers' Cooperative
Tech Info: 16 mm/bw/sound/75 min.
Date/Country: 1961 + USA
Distr/Arch: fmc
Annotation: This experimental film juxtaposes the lives of
   two couples, one white, one black. Allen Ginsberg reads
   selections of his poetry.

GUNS, THE
Alt Title(s): see Os Fuzis

GUNSAULUS MYSTERY
Nar/Cast: Evelyn Preer* + Lawrence Chenault* + Edward
   Abrams* + Mabel Young* + Eddie Brown* + Hattie Christian*
   + George Russel + W.D. Sindle
Studio/Company: Micheaux Film Corporation
Date/Country: 1921 + USA   Type: Feature
Annotation: Remake of Micheaux's **Within Our Gates**, the film

is based on the Leo Frank case in Georgia. Frank allegedly raped and murdered a young factory girl and apparently tried to implicate the janitor at the factory. The Gunsaulus Mystery is a dramatization of the janitor's story.

GWENDOLYN BROOKS
Producer: NET
Tech Info: 16 mm/bw/sound/1 reel/30 min.
Date/Country: 1966 + USA   Type: Documentary
Distr/Arch: iu
Annotation: An introduction to the poetry and personality of Gwendolyn Brooks and the Chicago environment which provided the sources for most of her materials.   Between poetry readings she describes her method of working, the things she finds most pleasant in life, and the thrill of winning the 1950 Pulitzer Prize for poetry.

HAIL CAESAR: GODFATHER OF HARLEM

HAITI
Series: National Archives Gift Collection
Tech Info: 16 mm/2 reels/color
Annotation: Unedited but excellent color, photographed in good sequence. (Part of Record Group 200 HF series, Harmon Foundation Collection).

HALL JOHNSON CHOIR IN A SYCOPATED SERMON, THE
Studio/Company: Warner Brothers
Tech Info: 16 mm/sound/1 reel
Date/Country: 1935 + USA   Type: Feature
Distr/Arch: uas
Annotation: Storyline surrounding such spirituals as "City Called Heaven," "Certainly Lord," and "Wade in the Water."

HALLELUJAH, I'M A BUM
Alt Title(s): Heart of New York
Nar/Cast: Al Jolson + Edgar Connor* + Madge Evans + Harry Langdon + Chester Conklin
Screenplay: S.N. Behrman   Story: Ben Hecht   Director: Lewis Milestone
Studio/Company: United Artists
Tech Info: 16 mm/bw/sound/82 min.
Date/Country: 1933 + USA   Type: Feature
Distr/Arch: fce + mac + mog + roa + tfc
Annotation: Al Jolson plays the leader of the Central Park hoboes in this film about life among the lowly, which includes Langdon, Conklin and Edgar Connor as Acorn, Jolson's first lieutenant. Acorn does denote dwarf size. Set during the depression.

HALLELUJAH
Nar/Cast: Daniel Haynes* + Nina Mae McKinney* + Victoria Spivey + William Fountaine* + Harry Gray* + Fannie Belle de Knight* + Everett McGarrity* + Milton Dickerson* + Robert Couch* + Walter Tait* + Dixie Jubilee Singers*
Story: Wanda Tuchock   Director: King Vidor
Studio/Company: MGM

Tech Info: 16 mm/sound/bw/107 min.
Date/Country: 1929 + USA   Type: Feature
Distr/Arch: fnc + moma + eas
Annotation: Hollywood's second all-black cast film. Zeke
   (Daniel Haynes) becomes an evangelist after his brother is
   killed in a brawl, but he falls in with beautiful Chick
   (Nina Mae McKinney) and wanders from the path for a time.
   After much travail, including a stint on the chain gang,
   he returns to family and the "good" woman, Missy Rose
   (Victoria Spivey).

HALLS OF ANGER
Nar/Cast: Calvin Lockhart* + Janet MacLachlan* + James A.
   Watson, Jr.* + Davis Roberts* + DeWayne Jesse*
Screenplay: John Shaner + Al Remrus
Producer: Herbert Hirschman   Director: Paul Bogart
Studio/Company: United Artists
Tech Info: 16 mm/color/sound/3 reels/100 min.
Date/Country: 1970 + USA   Type: Feature
Distr/Arch: uas
Annotation: Violence and anger surface in this film when 60
   white students are bussed to an all black high school.
   Calvin Lockhart and Janet MacLachlan are dedicated to
   achieving racial understanding and to improving the lives
   of the students.

HAM AND EGGS AT THE FRONT
Nar/Cast: Myrna Loy + Tom Wilson
Studio/Company: Warner Brothers
Tech Info: silent/bw
Date/Country: 1927 + USA
Annotation: One of Warner's last silent movies has Myrna Loy
   playing a Senegalese seductress in blackface, along with a
   number of other actors in burnt cork in a World War I
   farce.

HAMMER
Nar/Cast: Fred Williamson* + Bernie Hamilton* + Vonetta Mc-
   Gee* + Mel Stewart* + Mawama Davis*
Screenplay: Charles Johnson
Producer: Al Adamson   Director: Bruce Clark
Studio/Company: United Artists
Tech Info: 16 mm/sound/color/3 reels/91 min.
Date/Country: 1972 + USA   Type: Feature
Distr/Arch: uas
Annotation: B.J. Hammer (Williamson), a young boxer on his
   way up, will not throw a fight as he is ordered to do by
   the syndicate and so his troubles begin. Bernie Hamilton
   is Davis the cop, Mawama Davis a noisy prostitute and
   Vonetta McGee, the heroine.

HAMMERHEAD
Nar/Cast: Terry Reed* + Vince Edwards + Diana Dors
Screenplay: William Bast + Herbert Baker
Producer: Irving Allen   Director: David Miller
Studio/Company: Columbia
Tech Info: 16 mm/sound/color/99 min.
Date/Country: 1968 + Britain   Type: Feature

Distr/Arch: mod + mot + wcf + wel
Annotation: Tracy Reed is Miss Hull in this melodrama about
   espionage, hired killers, hippies and kidnapping.

HAMPTON INSTITUTE PRESENTS ITS PROGRAM OF EDUCATION FOR LIFE
Series: National Archives Gift Collection
Tech Info: 16 mm/silent/3 reels/bw or color
Annotation: An overall view of the philosophy behind one of
   the first five schools in this country for Negroes. (Part
   of Record Group 200 HF series, Harmon Foundation Collection).

HANG 'EM HIGH
Nar/Cast: Roy Glenn* + Clint Eastwood* + Ingrid Stevens
Screenplay: Leonard Freeman + Mel Goldberg
Producer: Leonard Freeman   Director: Ted Post
Studio/Company: United Artists
Tech Info: 16 mm/sound/color/114 min.
Date/Country: 1968 + USA   Type: Feature
Distr/Arch: uas
Annotation: Roy Glenn plays a prison guard in this Clint
   Eastwood western melodrama about rustling, rape, and
   revenge in 19th century Oklahoma.

HANG UP
Nar/Cast: Lynn Hamilton*

HANS WESTMAR
Alt Title(s): Horst Wessel
Nar/Cast: Emil Lohkamp + Irmgard Willers + Siegmund Nunberg
   Story: Hans Heinz Ewers
Studio/Company: Volksdeutsche Film Company
Date/Country: 1934 + Germany   Type: Feature
Annotation: Growing decadence of Berlin shown by Negro jazz
   band swinging the martial rhythms of "Die Wacht am Rhein."
   The hero, Hans Westmar, phonetic substitute for Horst Wes-
   sel, sees the way of combating such "degeneracy" by em-
   bracing concepts of National Socialism.

HARD WAY
Producer: NET
Tech Info: 16 mm/sound/bw/2 reels/59 min.
Date/Country: 1965 + USA   Type: Documentary
Distr/Arch: iu
Annotation: Looks at the problem of poverty in the richest
   country in the world and emphasizes how today's poor are
   different from those of past generations. Focuses on
   slums, housing projects, public schools, and settlement
   houses in the St. Louis area.

HARDER THEY COME, THE
Nar/Cast: Jimmy Cliff* + Janet Barkley* + Carl Bradshaw* +
   Ros Daniel Hartman* + Bobby Charlton
Screenplay: Perry Henzell + Trevor D. Rhone*
Producer: Perry Henzel + Island Films   Director: Perry Hen-
   zel
Studio/Company: New World Pictures
Tech Info: 16 mm/sound/color/100 min.

Date/Country: 1973 + Jamaica   Type: Feature
Distr/Arch: fnc + pru
Annotation: First feature film made by Jamaicans stars Jimmy
    Cliff (who also wrote the music) as Ivan, a young black
    man from the country with musical ambitions and talent who
    runs up against the police in Kingston after being th-
    warted by the corruption of the city. Based on the career
    of Rhygin, a criminal-hero who terrorized and fascinated
    Jamaica in the fifties, the film captures the plight of a
    people with little hope for the future, whose economy and
    government are controlled by foreign investment interests.

HARDER THEY FALL, THE
Nar/Cast: Humphrey Bogart + Rod Steiger + Jersey Joe Wol-
    cott* + Jan Sterling
Screenplay: Phillip Yordan   Story: Budd Schulberg
Producer: Phillip Yordan   Director: Mark Robinson
Studio/Company: Columbia
Tech Info: 16 mm/sound/bw/110 min.
Date/Country: 1956 + USA   Type: Feature
Distr/Arch: bud + con + mac + mot + swa + wcf + wel + who
Annotation: Story of corruption in the boxing world as a
    greedy fight promoter (Rod Steiger) pushes a fighter to
    the championship through fixed fights. Jersey Joe is
    among the fighters whose presence seems intended to add a
    note of authenticity.

HARLEM AFTER MIDNIGHT
Nar/Cast: Billy Eckstine* and his orchestra + Ann Baker* +
    Micky O'Daniel* + Al Guster*
Date/Country: 1947 + USA   Type: Musical Short
Annotation: Billy Eckstine and Ann Baker sing with his
    orchestra; O'Daniel and Guster dance.

HARLEM AFTER MIDNIGHT
Nar/Cast: Lorenzo Tucker + Alfred "Slick" Chester*
    Director: Oscar Micheaux*
Studio/Company: Micheaux Film Corporation
Date/Country: 1934 + USA   Type: Feature

HARLEM BIG SHOT
Nar/Cast: A.B. Comathiere* + Lorenzo Tucker*

HARLEM DYNAMITE
Date/Country: 1947 + USA   Type: Musical Short
Annotation: Three numbers are performed by Dizzy Gillespie*
    and His Orchestra

HARLEM FOLLIES
Nar/Cast: Savannah Churchill* + Sheila Guyse* + John Kirby
    and his Band* + Laveda Carter* + Anna Cornell* + Deek Wat-
    son* and the Brown Dots* + Sid Catlett's Band* + Juanita
    Hall* + Stepin Fetchit* + Slam Stewart Trio* + Paterson*
    and Jackson* + Rubel Blakey* + Basil Spears* + Leonardo*
    and Zolo* + Apus* and Estellita* + Al Young* + Norma
    Shepard*
Studio/Company: Herald Pictures
Date/Country: 1950 + USA

HARLEM GLOBETROTTERS, THE
Nar/Cast: Dorothy Dandridge* + Bill Walker* + Angela Clark +
   Thomas Gomez + Peter Thompson + The Globetrotter Team*
Screenplay: Alfred Palka
Producer: Buddy Adler   Director: Phil Brown
Studio/Company: Columbia
Tech Info: 16 mm/sound/bw/2 reels/80 min.
Date/Country: 1951 + USA   Type: Feature
Distr/Arch: arg + buc + bud + cha + cwf + mac + roa + mod +
   mot + tfc + twy + wel + who
Annotation: A college student leaves school to tour with the
   famous Globetrotters basketball team.

HARLEM GLOBETROTTERS
Nar/Cast: Harlem Globetrotter Team*
Studio/Company: Castle
Tech Info: 16 mm/sound/color/1 reel/10 min.   Type: Sports
   Short
Distr/Arch: roa
Annotation: An amusing short in which the Globetrotters per-
   form some of their famous routines.

HARLEM HOT SHOT
Alt Title(s): see The Black King

HARLEM HOTSHOTS
Nar/Cast: Lena Horne* + Leon Gross* + The Core Harris*
   Orchestra + The Red Lilly Chorus* + Teddy Wilson*
Producer: Metropolitan
Tech Info: 16 mm/sound/bw/20 min.
Date/Country: 1940 + United States   Type: Musical Short
Distr/Arch: bud + kpf
Annotation: A short musical film featuring Lena Horne and
   Teddy Wilson. May be a re-title.

HARLEM IN THE TWENTIES
Producer: Encyclopedia Britannica Educational Corporation
Tech Info: 16 mm/sound/color/10 min.
Date/Country: 1970 + USA   Type: Documentary
Distr/Arch: ebec
Annotation: The development of Harlem in the 20's.

HARLEM IS HEAVEN
Alt Title(s): Harlem Rhapsody
Nar/Cast: Bill Robinson* + John Mason* + Putney Dandridge* +
   James Baskett* + Anise Boyer* + Henri Wressell* + Alma
   Smith* + Bob Sawyer* + Eubie Blake and his orchestra*
Studio/Company: Lincoln Productions
Date/Country: 1932 + USA   Type: Feature
Annotation: Bill Robinson's first film is a musical comedy
   in which he plays the role of director and star of a
   Harlem theatre who altruistically helps along the romance
   of Henri Wressell, as Chummy Walker, and Anise Boyer, as
   Jean Stratton.

HARLEM JAZZ FESTIVAL
Nar/Cast: Lionel Hampton and His Orchestra* + Quincy Jones*

+ Sarah Vaughan* + Count Basie Septet* + Dinah Washington*
+ Nat "King" Cole*   Director: Joseph Kohn
Tech Info: 51 min.
Date/Country: 1955 + USA
Annotation: Musical revue including: the Count Basie Septet
   playing "I Cried For You," Dinah Washington singing "My
   Lean Baby" and Nat "King" Cole singing "For Sentimental
   Reasons,"

HARLEM_ON_PARADE
Nar/Cast: Lena Horne*
Producer: Jack Goldberg + Dave Goldberg

HARLEM_ON_THE_PRAIRIE
Nar/Cast: Herb Jeffries* + Mantan Moreland* + Spencer Willi-
   ams* + Connie Harris* + George Randol* + Maceo Sheffield*
   + Flournoy E. Miller*
Producer: Jed Buell   Director: Jed Buell
Studio/Company: Associated Pictures
Date/Country: 1939 + USA   Type: Feature
Annotation: A western with music about Doc Clayburn (Williams) who returns to the scene of his outlaw days to find
   the gold he helped steal twenty years earlier and return
   it to its rightful owners. Shot down before he can accomplish his task, he gives the map to a trustworthy young
   rider (Jeffries) who has to battle the villains in order
   to carry out the old man's wishes.

HARLEM_RENAISSANCE:_THE_BLACK_POETS
Series: Tell It Like It Was
Producer: WCAI-TV   Director: Dick D'Anjoltell
Tech Info: 16 mm/sound/color/1 reel/20 min.
Date/Country: 1970 + USA   Type: Dramatized Documentary
Distr/Arch: iu + carouf + kpf
Annotation: Portrays the emergence of black poets, es-
   sayists, and novelists in the 1920's and 30's through
   dramatic vignettes. Includes excerpts from the works of
   Countee Cullen*, Warren Cuney*, Georgia Douglass Johnson*,
   Fenton Johnson*, W.E.B. DuBois*, and Langston Hughes*.

HARLEM_RHAPSODY
Alt Title(s): see Harlem is Heaven

HARLEM_RHYTHM
Nar/Cast: Dizzie Gillespie and his Orchestra*
Date/Country: 1947 + USA   Type: Musical Short
Annotation: The band is shown playing 3 numbers with dances
   created by Audrey Armstrong and Johnny and Henney.

HARLEM_RIDES_THE_RANGE
Nar/Cast: Herb Jeffries* + Lucius Brooks* + Flournoy E.
   Miller* + Artie Young* + Spencer Williams* + Clarence
   Brooks* + Tom Southern* + The Four Tones*
Screenplay: Spencer Williams* + Flournoy E. Miller*
Studio/Company: Hollywood Productions
Date/Country: 1939 + USA
Annotation: A western musical with the hero (Jeffries)
   struggling to keep the villain (Brooks) from getting con-

trol of a radium mine which belongs to his girl friend's
father.

HARLEM WEINESDAY
Producer: JohnHuhley
Tech Info: 16 mm/sound/color/10 min.
Date/Country: 1959 + USA   Type: Documentary
Distr/Arch: mac
Annotation: An ordinary day in Harlem depicted with jazz by
    Benny Carter*.

HARLEMANIA
Nar/Cast: Ethel Moses* + Jimmy Baskett* + Count Basie*
Studio/Company: Creative Cinema Corporation
Date/Country: 1938 + USA

HARMONY LANE
Nar/Cast: Douglas Montgomery + Evelyn Venable + Clarence
    Muse*
Screenplay: Joseph Santley + Elizabeth Meehan   Director:
    Joseph Santley
Studio/Company: Mascot Productions
Tech Info: 16 mm/sound/bw/89 min.
Date/Country: 1935 + USA   Type: Feature
Distr/Arch: alb + new + thu
Annotation: Film chronicles the life of Stephen Foster, with
    Clarence Muse as "Old Joe."

HARRIET TUBMAN AND THE UNDERGROUND RAILROAD
Series: Great Adventure
Producer: CBS
Tech Info: 16 mm/sound/bw/2 reels/54 min.
Date/Country: 1964 + USA   Type: TV Dramatized Documentary
Distr/Arch: con
Annotation: Harriet Tubman, born a slave in the decades be-
    fore the Civil War, grew up to become one of the most
    daring conductors of the Underground Railroad, with slave
    owner offering $40,000 for her capture. This film
    portrays the first nineteen harrowing trips Mrs. Tubman
    made into slave territory between 1850-1860.

HARRY WILLS IN TRAINING
Nar/Cast: Harry Wills*
Studio/Company: ACME Film Distributors
Date/Country: 1924 + USA
Annotation: Shows Harry Wills the prize fighter in training.

HARVEST: 3,000 YEARS
Nar/Cast: Harege-Weyn Tafere*
Screenplay: Haile Gerima*
Tech Info: 16 mm/bw/sound/150 min./with English subtitles
Date/Country: 1975 + Ethiopia   Type: Dramatized Documentary
Distr/Arch: tri
Annotation: A "docu-drama" on life in contemporary Ethiopia;
    the story of a peasant family's struggle for survival on
    the farm of a rich and tyrannical landlord. Received
    numerous Inernational awards.

HARVEY GIRLS, THE
Nar/Cast: Judy Garland + John Hodiak + Ray Bolger + Ben
    Carter*
Screenplay: Ed Beloin + Nat Curtis + Harvey Crane + James
    O'Hanlon   Story: Samuel Hopkins
Producer: Arthur Freed   Director: George Sidney
Studio/Company: MGM
Tech Info: 16 mm/sound/color/104 min.
Date/Country: 1946 + USA   Type: Feature
Distr/Arch: fnc
Annotation: Musical comedy about the Harvey waitresses who
    followed the building of the Santa Fe railroad, setting up
    Fred Harvey resturants. Ben Carter plays "Old" John-Hen-
    ry.

HAT, THE
Screenplay: Dizzy Gillespie* + Dudley Moore   Director: John
    Hubley + Faith Hubley
Tech Info: 18 min.
Date/Country: 1964 + USA   Type: Animated Short
Distr/Arch: kpf + emg + bud
Annotation: Gillespie and Moore wrote the dialogue and music
    for this cartoon which depicts the origins of interna-
    tional conflict.

HAUNTS OF THE VERY RICH
Nar/Cast: Lloyd Bridges + Cloris Leachman + Edward Asner +
    Moses Gunn*
Studio/Company: ABC-TV
Date/Country: 1972 + USA   Type: TV Feature
Annotation: Moses Gunn plays reticent host to seven people
    especially invited to a beautiful island paradise from
    which they all eventually want to escape.

HAUSA VILLAGE
Producer: British Information Service
Tech Info: 16 mm/sound/bw/1 reel/22 min.
Date/Country: 1947   Type: Documentary
Distr/Arch: iu + bris
Annotation: Shows in detail the life of the Moslem people of
    Hausa Village in northern Nigeria.

HE RIDES TALL
Nar/Cast: Joel Fluellen* + Dan Duryea
Screenplay: Charles W. Irwin
Producer: Gordon Kay   Director: R.G. Springsteen
Studio/Company: Universal
Tech Info: 16 mm/sound/bw/84 min.
Date/Country: 1964 + USA   Type: Feature
Distr/Arch: cou + tmc + uni
Annotation: Joel Fluellen plays Dr. Sam whom Thorne (Duryea)
    forces to operate on and cripple the hand of the Marshal.
    Dr. Sam outwits Thorne by faking the operation so the
    Marshal is able to wipe out Thorne and his gang using his
    perfectly healed hand.

HE'S MY GUY
Nar/Cast: Dick Foran + Irene Hervey + Mills Brothers*

Screenplay: M. Coates + Webster Garrett + Grant Garrett
   Director: Edward F. Cline
Studio/Company: Universal
Tech Info: 65 min.
Date/Country: 1943 + USA   Type: Feature
Annotation: The Mills Brothers are featured in this wartime
   musical set in a defense plant.

HEAD START IN MISSISSIPPI
Producer: NET
Tech Info: 16 mm/sound/bw/1 reel/60 min.
Date/Country: 1966 + USA   Type: Documentary
Distr/Arch: iu
Annotation: Focuses on the controversial Head Start program
   in Mississippi. Shows, through scenes of the children in
   their schools and interviews with the black people who run
   the program, the progress which has been made. Explains
   why the funds for this program are being stopped and
   presents the rebuttal to these charges.

HEADLESS HORSEMAN, THE
Nar/Cast: Will Rogers + Lois Meredith
Screenplay: Carl Sterns   Story: Washington Irving
   Director: Edward Venturini
Studio/Company: Hodkinson
Tech Info: 16 mm/super 8 mm/silent (musical score on-
   ly)/bw/50 min.
Date/Country: 1922 + USA   Type: Feature
Distr/Arch: emg + fce + mog + ivy + bla
Annotation: A young black boy embarks upon a daring ride
   that saves schoolmaster Ichabod Crane from being tarred
   and feathered by villagers who believe that he has abused
   their children.

HEAR US O LORD
Producer: Public Broadcasting Library for NET
Tech Info: 16 mm/sound/bw and color/1 reel/51 min.
Date/Country: 1968
Distr/Arch: iu
Annotation: Examines responses of families in School Dis-
   trict 151, Cook County, Ill., to school desegration order.
   Presents the responses of the Dan Langs and their neigh-
   bors in South Holland, Illinois, the first incorporated
   suburb in the nation ordered to desegregate its schools by
   bussing.

HEART IS A LONELY HUNTER, THE
Nar/Cast: Aln Arkin + Cicely Tyson* + Stacey Keach + Percy
   Rodriguez* + Johnny Popwell*
Screenplay: Thomas C. Ryan   Story: Carson McCullers
Producer: T.C. Ryan + Marc Merson   Director: Robert Ellis
   Miller
Studio/Company: Warner Brothers + Seven Arts
Tech Info: 16 mm/color/sound/4 reels/124 min.
Date/Country: 1968 + USA   Type: Feature
Distr/Arch: mac + roa + arg + buc + bud + con + cwf + ics +
   mod + mot + twy + wcf + wel + who
Annotation: This film is a story of loneliness in a small

southern town, with each character trying desperately to overcome his/her individual hurdle. Cicely Tyson plays Portia as an articulate militant black maid. Percy Rodriguez plays her father, Dr. Copeland, an embittered separatist, who is disappointed that his educated daughter is married to a field hand (Popwell) and is a domestic. Their reconciliation is one of the many strands that weave the story together.

HEART OF MARYLAND, THE
Nar/Cast: Myrna Loy + Mrs. Leslie Carter   Director: David Belasco
Date/Country: 1915 + USA
Annotation: Myrna Loy plays a mulatto role in this Civil War melodrama adapted from the play. Mrs. Carter plays her original role of Maryland Culvert.

HEART OF NEW YORK
Alt Title(s): see Hallelujah, I'm a Bum

HEARTS AND FLAGS
Studio/Company: Edison
Tech Info: silent/bw
Date/Country: 1916 + USA
Annotation: Uncle Wash (played by a white actor in black-face) is the loyal servant who protects his master's daughters from Yankee ruin and then watches when, after the war, a Union Captain returns to marry one of those daughters.

HEARTS ARE THUMPS
Series: Our Gang
Nar/Cast: Our Gang + Billie Thomas*
Producer: Hal Roach   Director: Gordon Douglas
Studio/Company: MGM + Roach
Tech Info: super 8 mm/16 mm/bw/sound/1 reel/10 min.
Date/Country: 1937 + USA   Type: Comedy Short
Distr/Arch: roa + bla
Annotation: Valentine's Day brings out the woman hater in Spanky, Buckwheat and Alfalfa, until Darla winks at Alfalfa. Spanky gets revenge by putting soap in Alfalfa's sandwich which makes him foam at the mouth when he sings for Darla and the entire class. Billie Thomas stars as Buckwheat.

HEARTS DIVIDED
Nar/Cast: Marion Davies + Dick Powell + Hattie McDaniel* + Hall Johnson Choir*
Screenplay: Laid Doyle + Casey Robinson   Story: Rida Johnson Young   Director: Frank Borzage
Studio/Company: Warner Brothers
Tech Info: 16 mm/sound/bw/76 min.
Date/Country: 1936 + USA   Type: Feature
Distr/Arch: uas
Annotation: Story of the love affair between a Baltimore girl and Napoleon's brother. Features the singing of the Hall Johnson Choir.

HEARTS_IN_DIXIE
Nar/Cast: Clarence Muse* + Stepin Fetchit* + Mildred
  Washington* + Eugene Jackson* + Vivian Smith* + A. C. Bil-
  brew Choir* + Zack Williams* + Bernice Pilot* + Gertrude
  Howard* + Clifford Ingram*
Screenplay: Walter Weems
Producer: William Fox   Director: Paul Sloane
Studio/Company: Fox
Tech Info: 35 mm/bw/sound/8 reels/6,444 ft.
Date/Country: 1929 + USA   Type: Feature
Distr/Arch: moma
Annotation: Fetchit plays shiftless Gummy, whose wife Chloe
  must work especially hard because of his laziness to care
  for their two children, the house, the fields, where she
  helps her aging father Nappus (Clarence Muse).   When she
  becomes ill and dies, in spite of the ministrations of the
  Voodo woman for whom Gummy has sent, old Nappus sells
  everything to send his grandson (Jackson) North to study
  medicine in hopes that the boy will eventually return to
  help his people. (Clarence Muse aided in the direction.)

HEARTS_OF_THE_WOODS
Nar/Cast: Clifford Harris* + Lawrence McGuire* + Don
  Pierson* + Anna Lou Allen*
Studio/Company: Superior Arts Production
Date/Country: 1921 + USA   Type: Feature
Annotation: The plot of the film is centered on the attem-
  pted seduction of a young woman into a false marriage by a
  married philanderer.

HEAT'S_ON,_THE
Nar/Cast: Mae West + Victor Moore + William Gaxton + Hazel
  Scott*   Director: Gregory Ratoff
Studio/Company: Columbia
Tech Info: 16mm/sound/bw/79 min.
Date/Country: 1943 + USA   Type: Feature
Distr/Arch: swa
Annotation: Typical Mae West movie, this time with rival
  producers trying to secure Ms. West's talents. Hazel
  Scott makes a brief cameo appearance.

HEAVEN_CAN_WAIT
Nar/Cast: Clarence Muse* + Gene Tierney + Don Ameche +
  Charles Coburn
Screenplay: Samson Raphaelson   Story: Lazlo Bus-Fekete
Producer: Ernest Lubitsch   Director: Ernest Lubitsch
Studio/Company: 20th Century Fox
Date/Country: 1943 + USA   Type: Feature
Annotation: Don Ameche stars in this comedy of manners,
  about a womanizer, who having died applies for admission
  to hell and has to show why he's eligible. Clarence Muse
  has a bit role as Jasper.

HEAVEN_ON_EARTH
Nar/Cast: Madame Sul-te-Wan* + Lew Ayres + Anita Louise
  Story: Ben Lucien Burman (novel, Mississippi)   Director:
  Russell Mack
Studio/Company: Universal

Date/Country: 1931 + USA   Type: Feature
Annotation: A story about poor whites who live in floating
    shantees on the lower Mississippi and are extremely super-
    stitious. Madame Sul-te-Wan plays Voodoo Sue.

HEAVENS ABOVE
Nar/Cast: Peter Sellers + Brock Peters* + Ian Carmichael
    Director: Roy Boulting + John Boulting
Tech Info: 16 mm/sound/color/118 min.
Date/Country: 1963 + Britain   Type: Feature
Distr/Arch: mac + roaf + twy + ccc + col + unf + who
Annotation: The story of a minister in a new vicarage who
    practices the religious life he preaches about, including
    the hiring of a black man (Peters*) as a church employee,
    an act which is quite a surprise to his middle class
    parishioners.

HEAVY TRAFFIC
Screenplay: Ralph Bakshi   Director: Ralph Bakshi
Studio/Company: American International
Tech Info: 16 mm/sound/color/3 reels/76 min.
Date/Country: 1973 + USA   Type: Animated Feature
Distr/Arch: swa
Annotation: An X-rated animation (set in a live-action
    frame), Heavy Traffic is about the violence and moral cor-
    ruption of New York. The film follows Michael and his
    black girlfriend, Carol, through the ugliness of "The Big
    Apple."

HEEBEE JEEBEES
Series: Our Gang
Nar/Cast: Our Gang + Allen Hoskins*
Producer: Robert F. McGowan + Hal Roach   Director: Anthony
    Mack
Studio/Company: MGM
Tech Info: bw/silent/2 reels
Date/Country: 1927 + USA   Type: Comedy Short
Annotation: A hypnotist casts his spell over the gang and
    assigns each some animal characteristic which comes out
    during an afternoon tea at the home of a society leader.
    Allen Hoskins stars as Farina.

HELL CATS
Nar/Cast: Dewey "Pigmeat" Markham*
Studio/Company: Toddy Pictures
Date/Country: 194- + USA

HELL UP IN HARLEM
Nar/Cast: Fred Williamson* + Gloria Hendry* + Julius W.
    Harris*
Screenplay: Larry Cohen
Producer: Larry Cohen + Janell Cohen   Director: Larry Cohen
Studio/Company: American International
Tech Info: 16 mm/sound/color/96 min.
Date/Country: 1973 + USA   Type: Feature
Distr/Arch: swa
Annotation: A sequel to Black Caesar.

HELL'S ALLEY
Nar/Cast: Thomas Moseley* + Jean Webb* + Fay Miller*
Screenplay: Hattie Watkins* + Jean Webb*
Studio/Company: Paragon Features
Date/Country: 1931 + USA

HELL'S HIGHWAY
Nar/Cast: Richard Dix + Tom Brown + Rochelle Hudson +
    Clarence Muse*
Screenplay: Rowland Brown   Director: Rowland Brown
Studio/Company: RKO Radio
Tech Info: 16 mm/sound/bw/80 min.
Date/Country: 1933 + USA   Type: Feature
Distr/Arch: fnc
Annotation: Life on a chain gang is depicted in this film
    that features Clarence Muse in the role of "Rascal" who
    comments on the lot of prisoners and their relative im-
    portance to mules.

HELLDORADO
Nar/Cast: Richard Arlen + Madge Evans + Ralph Bellamy +
    James Gleason + Henry B. Walthall + Stepin Fetchit* +
    Lucky Hurlic*
Producer: Jesse L. Lusky   Director: James Cruze
Studio/Company: Fox
Date/Country: 1935 + USA   Type: Feature
Annotation: A group of motorists and hitchhikers get
    stranded in a ghost town in the California gold country
    and hear there may be a lost vein of gold. Comedy is
    provided by Stepin Fetchit and Lucky Hurlic, the former
    doing his scared-of-ghosts routines.

HELLO BILL
Nar/Cast: Bill Robinson* + Billy Higgins* + Joe Byrd* + Per-
    cy Verwayen* + Floyd Hunter* + Sarah Martin* + Josephine
    Heathman* + Marian Maris*
Studio/Company: Famous Artists Company
Date/Country: 1929 + USA

HELLO, DOLLY
Nar/Cast: Louis Armstrong* + Barbra Streisand + Walter Mat-
    thau + James McEachin*
Screenplay: Ernest Lehman
Producer: Ernest Lehman   Director: Gene Kelly
Studio/Company: 20th Century Fox
Tech Info: 16 mm/sound/color/148 min.
Date/Country: 1969 + USA   Type: Feature
Distr/Arch: fnc
Annotation: Director Kelly did the screen adaptation of this
    well-known Broadway play. The story hasn't changed; Dol-
    ly, still plies her skillful mate-matching trade.   Arms-
    rong does his special "Hello Dolly" rendition.

HELPING GRANDMA
Series: Our Gang
Nar/Cast: Our Gang + Matthew Beard* + Allen Hoskins*
Screenplay: H. M. Walker
Producer: Robert F. McGowan + Hal Roach   Director: Robert

F. McGowan
Studio/Company: MGM + Roach
Tech Info: super 8 mm/16 mm/bw/sound/1 reel/21 min.
Date/Country: 1931 + USA   Type: Comedy Short
Distr/Arch: roa + bla
Annotation: The gang helps kindly Grandma run her general
    store although they nearly aid a chain store operator in
    his attempt to pay much less for the store than it's
    worth. Allen Hoskins stars as Farina and Matthew Beard
    stars as Stymie.

HELPING HANDS
Series: Our Gang
Nar/Cast: Our Gang + Billie Thomas*
Screenplay: Hal Law + Robert A. McGowan
Producer: MGM   Director: Edward Cahn
Studio/Company: MGM
Tech Info: bw/sound/1 reel
Date/Country: 1941 + USA   Type: Comedy Short
Annotation: The lads form the Our Gang Army and begin
    training for combat until a real army major drops by with
    suggestions on how the gang might better serve on the home
    front. Billie Thomas stars as Buckwheat.

HEMINGWAY'S ADVENTURES OF A YOUNG MAN
Nar/Cast: Juano Hernandez* + Richard Beymer + Diane Baker +
    Paul Newman
Screenplay: A.E.Hotchner   Story: Ernest Hemingway
Producer: Jerry Wald   Director: Martin Ritt
Studio/Company: Fox
Tech Info: 16 mm/sound/color/145 min.
Date/Country: 1962 + USA   Type: Feature
Distr/Arch: fnc
Annotation: Hernandez is "Brigs", manager of a punch-drunk
    ex-fighter (Newman), in this adaptation of Hemingway's
    Nick Adams' stories.

HENRY BROWN, FARMER
Nar/Cast: Canada Lee*
Producer: U.S. Department of Agriculture   Director: Roger
    Barlow
Studio/Company: U.S. Department of Agriculture
Date/Country: 1942 + USA   Type: Documentary
Annotation: A documentary on the life of a black farmer in
    Alabama. Ties the farmer to the war effort (WWII). Nar-
    ration by Canada Lee.

HENRY O. TANNER: PIONEER BLACK AMERICAN ARTIST
Producer: Corsair
Tech Info: 16 mm/sound/color/12 min.
Date/Country: 1971   Type: Dramatized Documentary
Distr/Arch: dis
Annotation: The early life of America's first international-
    ly recognized black painter.

HERE COMES ELMER
Alt Title(s): Hitch-Hike to Happiness
Nar/Cast: The "King" Cole Trio*   Director: Joseph Santley

Tech Info: 74 min.
Date/Country: 1943 + USA   Type: Feature
Annotation: A comedy featuring some musical diversion in-
cluding the song "Straighten Up and Fly Right."

HERE COMES THE GROOM
Nar/Cast: Bing Crosby + Jane Wyman + Francot Tone + Louis
Armstrong*
Screenplay: Virginia Van Upp + Liam O'Brien + Myles Connolly
Producer: Frank Capra   Director: Frank Capra
Studio/Company: Paramount
Tech Info: 16 mm/sound/bw/116 min.
Date/Country: 1951 + USA   Type: Feature
Distr/Arch: fnc
Annotation: Bing Crosby as a bachelor reporter who brings
back a couple of French orphans and in order to keep them,
must marry within 5 days. The only hitch, the girl most
likely is about to get married to a millionaire. Music by
Louis Armstrong and others.

HERE IS THE GOLD COAST
Producer: British Information Service
Tech Info: 16 mm/sound/bw/1 reel/37 min.
Date/Country: 1948 + USA   Type: Documentary
Distr/Arch: iu + bris
Annotation: Portrays the life of the people of the Gold
Coast of Africa and contrasts the activities in its chief
city, Accra, with those characteristic of the interior.
Their natural habitat and their educational and health
problems are depicted.

HERITAGE IN BLACK
Producer: Encyclopedia Britannica Educational Corp.
Tech Info: 16 mm/sound/color/1 reel/27 min.
Date/Country: 1969 + USA   Type: Documentary
Distr/Arch: iu + ebec
Annotation: Examines the contributions of black people to
every area of American culture from the discovery of
America to modern times. Includes references to Harriet
Tubman*, George Washington Carver*, Sojourner Truth*, and
Jesse Owens*, among many others, and tells of their
specific contributions.

HERITAGE OF SLAVERY
Series: Of Black America
Producer: CBS
Tech Info: 16 mm/sound/color/2 reels/56 min.
Date/Country: 1968 + USA   Type: Documentary
Distr/Arch: iu + bfa
Annotation: Discusses the arrival of the first slaves in
America and their importance in the economic development
of the South. Discusses the many slave revolts, the un-
derground railways, and the effects of the 1850 Fugitive
Slave Law. Contrasts the heritage of Blacks and whites in
the United States.

HERITAGE OF THE NEGRO
Series: History of the Negro People

Producer: NET
Tech Info: 16 mm/sound/bw/1 reel/30 min.
Date/Country: 1965   Type: Documentary
Distr/Arch: iu
Annotation: Explores the heritage of the Negro by examining
   the civilization and achievements of ancient Africa and
   their significance today. Emphasizes that African history
   as recorded by white historians has traditionally ignored
   the old civilizations of sub-Saharan Africa. Explores the
   art, sculpture, and present-day pageantry which reflect
   the old cultures.

HERO AIN'T NOTHIN BUT A SANDWICH, A
Nar/Cast: Cicely Tyson* + Paul Winfield* + Larry Scott +
   Glynn Turman* + Harold Sylvester + David Groh + Kenneth
   Green* + Helen Martin* + Kevin Hooks*
Screenplay: Alice Childers*   Story: Alice Childers*
Producer: Robert B. Radnitz   Director: Ralph Nelson
Studio/Company: Radnitz + Mattel Productions
Date/Country: 1977 + USA   Type: Feature
Annotation: Benjie (13 years old) who lives in the Watts
   area of Los Angeles with his mother (Cicely Tyson) suffers
   from resentment of his mother's live-in friend (Paul
   Winfield). Major problems arise when Benjie (Larry Scott)
   turns to drugs.

HEROIC BLACK SOLDIERS OF THE WAR, THE
Studio/Company: Frederick Douglass Film Company
Date/Country: 1919 + USA

HEY DOC
Studio/Company: Carousel

HEY MAMA
Producer: Vaughn Ohern
Tech Info: 16 mm/sound/color/18 min.
Date/Country: 1968 + USA   Type: Documentary
Distr/Arch: obe + une + can
Annotation: Black experiences in Venice, California.

HEY, CAB!
Screenplay: Bob Teague*, based on "Letters to a Black Boy"
Producer: King Screen
Tech Info: 16 mm/sound/color/10.5 min.
Date/Country: 1970 + USA   Type: Documentary
Distr/Arch: bfa + uut
Annotation: Depiction of Bob Teague's experience of trying
   to get a cab at night in the ghetto.

HI-DE-HO HOLIDAY
Nar/Cast: Lena Horne*
Date/Country: 194- + USA

HI-DE-HO
Nar/Cast: Cab Calloway and his Orchestra* + Ida   James* +
   Jeni Le Gon* + The Miller Brothers and Lois*   Director:
   Josh Binney
Studio/Company: All-American

Tech Info: 16 mm/sound/bw/2 reels
Date/Country: 1947   Type: Musical Short
Distr/Arch: lc
Annotation: Cab Calloway does his scat song "Hi-de-ho,"
    specialty numbers by the dancers and other musical
    routines.

HI'-NEIGHBOR
Series: Our Gang
Nar/Cast: Our Gang, Matthew Beard* + Bobbie Beard*
Producer: Hal Roach   Director: Gus Meins
Studio/Company: MGM + Roach
Tech Info: Super 8 mm/16 mm/sound/2 reels/18 min.
Date/Country: 1934 + USA   Type: Comedy Short
Distr/Arch: roa + bla
Annotation: Jane passes by Wally for a chance to ride in the
    rich kid's toy fire engine, so the gang decides to build
    one that will hold everyone. The kid challenges the gang
    to a race which ends with Jane being thrown from the rich
    kid's engine, and the gang triumphant. Matthew Beard
    stars as Stymie.

HI, MOM
Nar/Cast: Robert DeNiro + "Be Black, Baby" Troupe* + Jenni-
    fer Salt
Screenplay: Brian De Palma + Charles Hirsch
Producer: Charles Hirsch   Director: Brian De Palma
Studio/Company: Sigma III
Tech Info: sound/color/87 min.
Date/Country: 1970 + USA   Type: Feature
Annotation: A movie about life in the sixties that includes
    a young Vietnam vet, a heroine who's into bombs and an
    all-black troup that performs in white face and blackens
    the faces of the audience during the performance.

HICKEY AND BOGGS
Nar/Cast: Bill Cosby* + Robert Culp + Rosalind Cash* +
    Sheila Sullivan
Screenplay: Walter Hill   Director: Robert Culp
Studio/Company: United Artists
Tech Info: 16 mm/color/sound/4 reels/111 min.
Date/Country: 1972 + USA   Type: Feature
Distr/Arch: uas
Annotation: Cosby and Culp are not quite the run-of-the-mill
    pair of movie detectives. The film shows them as human
    beings whose lives are as meaningful and as absurd as any-
    one else's: they are subject to the same passions, the
    same pleasures, and the same vices.

HIDDEN AFRICA: THE KAPSIKE
Producer: American Economic Foundation
Tech Info: 16 mm/sound/color/1 reel/26 min.
Date/Country: 1969 + Central Africa   Type: Documentary
Distr/Arch: suf
Annotation: Film shows the ritualistic simplicity in which
    the Kapsike live. Shows them as they journey across the
    Sahara to their mountain homes and tells of the diversity
    of life and expression.

HIDDEN HAND, THE
Nar/Cast: Craig Stevens + Elisabeth Fraser + Willie Best*
Screenplay: Anthony Coldeway + Raymond Schrock   Story:
   Rufas King   Director: Ben Stoloff
Studio/Company: Warner Brothers
Tech Info: 16 mm/sound/bw/67 min.
Date/Country: 1942 + USA   Type: Feature
Distr/Arch: uas
Annotation: Plot and counterplot serve up numerous murders
   in this tale of greed set in a sinister mansion. Features
   Willie Best as comic relief.

HIDE AND SHRIEK
Series: Our Gang
Nar/Cast: Our Gang + Billie Thomas*
Producer: Hal Roach   Director: Gordon Douglas
Studio/Company: MGM + Roach
Tech Info: super 8 mm/16 mm/bw/sound/1 reel/10 min.
Date/Country: 1938 + USA   Type: Comedy Short
Distr/Arch: roa + bla
Annotation: Sleuthing for the crook who stole Darla's candy,
   Alfalfa gets his assistants, Porky and Buckwheat into
   trouble in the haunted house at an amusement pier. Billie
   Thomas stars as Buckwheat.

HIDING PLACE, THE
Nar/Cast: George C. Scott + Ruby Dee*
Producer: CBS-TV
Studio/Company: CBS-TV
Tech Info: 16 mm/bw/sound/2 reels/50 min.   Type: TV Documentary
Distr/Arch: adl
Annotation: The film expresses the evils of "block busting"
   perpetrated by unscrupulous real estate dealers upon sub-
   urban home owners. It traces the events in a neighborhood
   into which a black family has just moved, and reveals how
   "block busting" tactics create panic and tension in a community.

HIGH COMMISSIONER
Nar/Cast: Rod Taylor + Christopher Plummer + Calvin Lock-
   hart* + Lilli Palmer
Screenplay: Wilford Greatorex
Producer: Betty Box   Director: Ralph Thomas
Studio/Company: Rank
Tech Info: 16 mm/sound/color/101 min.
Date/Country: 1968 + USA + Britain   Type: Feature
Distr/Arch: fnc
Annotation: Calvin Lockhart is Jamaican in this melodrama of
   murder and intrigue in London.

HIGH NOON
Alt Title(s): see Home of the Brave

HIGH SCHOOL GIRL
Nar/Cast: Helen MacKellar + Mahlon Hamilton + Cecelia Parker
   + Mildred Gover* + Crane Wilbur   Story: Wallace Thurman*

Producer: Bryan Foy   Director: Crane Wilbur
Studio/Company: Foy Productions
Tech Info: sound/bw/55 min.
Date/Country: 1935 + USA
Annotation: An argument for better understanding of the
   young, the film discusses the complications of pre-marital
   sex. Mildred Gover is the maid in the family with pro-
   blems.

HIGH SCHOOL RISING
Studio/Company: Third World Newsreel
Tech Info: 16 mm/sound/bw/15 min.
Date/Country: 1969   Type: Documentary
Distr/Arch: twn
Annotation: Discusses how education perpetuates class dif-
   ferences in IQ tests, tracking systems, vocational shops,
   with the omission of black, brown, Asian, and poor white
   struggles from history texts.

HIGH SOCIETY
Series: Our Gang
Nar/Cast: Our Gang + Allen Hoskins*
Screenplay: Hal Roach
Producer: Hal Roach   Director: Robert McGowan
Studio/Company: Pathe
Tech Info: silent/bw/2 reels
Date/Country: 1924 + USA   Type: Comedy Short
Annotation: Mickey, separated from his uncle and the gang by
   a rich aunt, lives a proper but miserable life till the
   gang comes to visit one day. In typical fashion, they
   make a shambles of the aunt's mansion, and the aunt, una-
   ble to cope, releases Mickey to his uncle. Allen Hoskins
   stars as Farina.

HIGH SOCIETY
Nar/Cast: Bing Crosby + Grace Kelly + Frank Sinatra + Louis
   Armstrong*
Screenplay: John Patrick   Story: Phillip Barry
Producer: Sol C. Siegal   Director: Charles Walters
Studio/Company: MGM
Tech Info: 16 mm/sound/color/107 min.
Date/Country: 1956 + USA   Type: Feature
Distr/Arch: fnc
Annotation: Musical remake of "The Philadelphia Story"
   features Louis Armstrong and his band.

HIGH TENSION
Nar/Cast: Brian Donlevy + Glenda Farrell + Hattie McDaniel*
Screenplay: Lou Breslow + Ed Elisar   Story: J. Robert Bren
   + Norman Houston   Director: Allan Dwan
Studio/Company: 20th Century Fox
Date/Country: 1936 + USA   Type: Feature
Annotation: Comedy and melodrama are mixed in this movie
   about the laying of cable between Honolulu and San
   Francisco. Hattie McDaniel is featured.

HIGH WIND IN JAMAICA, A
Nar/Cast: Anthony Quinn + Lila Kedrova + Ben Carruthers*

Screenplay: Stanley Mann + Ronald Harwood + Denis Dannan
Producer: John Craydon   Director: Alexander MacKendrick
Studio/Company: Fox
Tech Info: 16 mm/color/sound/104 min.
Date/Country: 1965 + USA   Type: Feature
Distr/Arch: fnc
Annotation: Anthony Quinn, commander of a pirate ship in
    Jamaican waters (1870's) gets into incalculable trouble
    when he insists on keeping five captured English children
    aboard ship. Carruthers plays the role of Alberto.

HIGH_YELLOW
Date/Country: 1971 + USA   Type: Feature
Annotation: Story of the trials of a light black woman who
    tries to find a middle ground for herself, not in the
    white world or the black.

HIGHEST_TRADITION,_THE
Studio/Company: Alexander Productions
Date/Country: 1946 + USA   Type: Documentary
Annotation: Documentary depicting Blacks in the U.S. Army.

HILL_WITH_HEROES,_THE
Nar/Cast: William Marshall* + Rod Taylor + Claudia Cardinale
Screenplay: Halsted Welles + Harold Livingston
Producer: Stanley Chase   Director: Joseph Sargent
Studio/Company: Universal
Tech Info: 16 mm/sound/color/102 min.
Date/Country: 1968 + USA   Type: Feature
Distr/Arch: ccc + tmc + uni
Annotation: Post World War II black marketing by two former
    Air-Force officers between Paris and Orans results in more
    complex smuggling operations. William Marshall is Al
    Poland.

HILL,_THE
Nar/Cast: Ossie Davis* + Sean Connery + Harry Andrews
Screenplay: Ray Rigby
Producer: Kenneth Hyman   Director: Sidney Lumet
Studio/Company: MGM + Seven Arts
Tech Info: 16 mm/sound/bw/122 min.
Date/Country: 1965 + Britain   Type: Feature
Distr/Arch: fnc
Annotation: Davis is a West Indian soldier-prisoner known as
    Jacko King in this drama about a British detention camp in
    North Africa during WWII.

HIS_DARKER_SELF
Nar/Cast: Lloyd Hamilton + Tom Wilson + Kate Bruce + Lucille
    LaVerne   Story: Arthur Caesar
Producer: G and H pictures   Director: John W. Noble
Studio/Company: United Artists
Tech Info: 35 mm/silent/bw/2 reels
Date/Country: 1924 + USA   Type: Dramatic Short
Annotation: Jolson originally was to star but walked out; he
    was replaced by Lloyd Hamilton who plays a writer of
    detective fiction who puts on blackface in order to
    capture black bootleggers (played by black actors) in the

Black Cat saloon. Lucille LaVerne plays "Darktown's Cleopatra" in this Griffith supervised comedy.

HIS_GREAT_CHANCE
Nar/Cast: Sandy Burns* + Bobbie Smart* + Tim Moore* + Gertrude Moore* + Walter Long* + Fred Hart* + Mark Slater* + Fannette Burns* + Sam Russell*
Producer: Ben Strasser
Studio/Company: North State Film Corporation
Date/Country: 1923 + USA   Type: Feature
Annotation: Two country boys leave home, make good on the stage, but return to the old folk at home at Christmas time with happy holiday gifts.

HIS_HARLEM_WIFE
Alt Title(s): see Life Goes On

HIS_TRUST_FULFILLED
Nar/Cast: Wilfred Lucan + Claire McDowell + Dorothy West
    Director: D.W. Griffith
Studio/Company: Biograph
Tech Info: 35mm/ silent/ bw/ 2 reels/ 999 feet/ 10-15 min.
Date/Country: 1910 + USA   Type: Dramatic Short
Distr/Arch: moma
Annotation: A continuation of His Trust. See annotation for that film.

HIS_TRUST
Nar/Cast: Wilfred Lucan + Claire McDowell + Dorothy West
    Director: D.W. Griffith
Studio/Company: Biograph
Tech Info: 35mm/ silent/ bw/ 2 reels/ 996 feet/ 10-15 min.
Date/Country: 1910 + USA   Type: Dramatic Short
Distr/Arch: moma
Annotation: Wilfred Lucan plays George, the faithful retainer (in blackface), in a story of the Civil War. For his great loyalty to his departed master, saving his widow and daughter, protecting them from assorted evils, turnng over his house and savings to them, George is at the end of the film rewarded with a handshake from a white man. His Trust and His Trust Fulfilled are shown together. See His Trust Fulfilled entry.

HISTORY_OF_THE_BLACKS
Series: The Blacks
Tech Info: 16 mm/sound/bw/40 min.
Date/Country: 1971 + USA   Type: Documentary
Distr/Arch: bbc + tl
Annotation: Black history for the past three hundred years.

HIT_MAN
Nar/Cast: Bernie Casey* + Pamela Grier* + Lisa Moore* + Bhetty Waldron + Sam Laws*
Screenplay: George Armitage   Story: Ted Lewis
Producer: Gene Corman   Director: George Armitage
Studio/Company: MGM
Tech Info: 16 mm/color/sound/3 reels/93 min.
Date/Country: 1972 + USA   Type: Feature

Distr/Arch: fnc
Annotation: Bernie Casey stars in this remake of Get Carter,
   as the killer out to avenge the death of his brother who
   was involved in porno movies. Set in East Los Angeles,
   the film makes visual use of the area--from the surreal
   Watts Towers to cheap motels.

HIT PARADE OF 1937, THE
Alt Title(s): I'll Reach for a Star
Nar/Cast: Frances Langford + Duke Ellington* + Phil Regan
Screenplay: Bradford Ropes + Samuel Ornitz
Producer: Nat Levine   Director: Gus Meins
Studio/Company: Republic Pictures
Tech Info: 16 mm/sound/bw/83 min.
Date/Country: 1937   Type: Feature
Distr/Arch: ivy
Annotation: Duke Ellington and his band are featured in this
   movie musical about a radio producer looking for a new
   star for his program.

HIT PARADE OF 1943, THE
Alt Title(s): Change of Heart
Nar/Cast: John Carroll + Susan Hayward + Dorothy Dandridge*
   + Count Basie*
Screenplay: Frank Gill   Director: Albert S. Rogell
Studio/Company: Republic
Tech Info: 16 mm/sound/bw/67 min.
Date/Country: 1943 + USA   Type: Feature
Distr/Arch: ivy
Annotation: Story of a slick Tin Pan Alley song writer (John
   Carroll) who romances a girl fresh from the Midwest,
   helped along by various black performers like Dorothy
   Dandridge, Count Basie, and The Harlem Sandman.

HIT
Nar/Cast: Billy Dee Williams* + Richard Pryor* + Paul Hamp-
   pton + Gwen Welles
Screenplay: Alan R. Trustman + David M. Wolf
Producer: Harry Korshak   Director: Sidney J. Furie
Studio/Company: Paramount
Tech Info: 16 mm/color/sound/4 reels/134 min.
Date/Country: 1973 + USA   Type: Feature
Distr/Arch: fnc
Annotation: Williams plays a federal agent who organizes a
   group of people to kill the leaders of the French drug
   syndicate because of his daughter's drug-related death.

HOLD THAT BLONDE
Nar/Cast: Eddie Bracken + Veronica Lake + Willie Best + Al-
   bert Dekker   Story: Paul Armstrong (Play)
Producer: Paul Jones   Director: George Marshall
Studio/Company: Paramount
Tech Info: 16mm/ sound/ bw/ 76 min.
Date/Country: 1945 + USA   Type: Feature
Annotation: Professional jewel thieves mistake Eddie Bracken
   for an interloper from another gang and the chase is on.
   Film co-stars Willie Best as Willie Shelley.

HOLD YOUR MAN
Nar/Cast: Jean Harlow + Clark Gable + George Reed* + Teresa
    Harris*   Story: Anita Loos   Director: Sam Wood
Studio/Company: MGM
Tech Info: sound/color
Date/Country: 1933 + USA   Type: Feature
Annotation: George Reed plays the Reverend Crippen and
    Teresa Harris is Ruby Lee Crippen in this Gable-Harlow
    romance.

HOLE, THE
Nar/Cast: Dizzy Gillespie*
Producer: Storyboard, Inc.
Tech Info: 16 mm/sound/color/1 reel/16 min.
Date/Country: 1962 + USA   Type: Animated Short
Distr/Arch: iu + mghf
Annotation: Uses animation to show how two construction
    workers in New York City view today's world.   Discusses
    accidents, Their causes and consequences, and questions
    the likelihood of preventing all accidents, including nu-
    clear ones.

HOLIDAY INN
Nar/Cast: Bing Crosby + Fred Astaire + Louise Beavers*
Screenplay: Claude Binyon
Producer: Mark Sandrich   Director: Mark Sandrich
Studio/Company: Paramount
Date/Country: 1942 + USA   Type: Feature
Annotation: Louise Beavers is Mamie in this Irving Berlin
    musical with patriotic overtones.   Among Bing Crosby's
    numbers is a song in blackface, "Abraham."

HOLIDAYS...HOLLOW DAYS
Screenplay: Rhozier T. 'Roach' Brown*
Producer: NPACT, Washington, D.C.
Tech Info: 16 mm/sound/bw/1 reel/59 min.
Date/Country: 1973 + USA   Type: Drama
Distr/Arch: iu
Annotation: Presents an original drama about Christmas in
    prison written by Rhozier T. 'Roach' Brown, a convicted
    murderer, and performed by eight black inmates of the D.C.
    Lorton Reformatory.   Reflects on the law and penal system
    and contrasts white, middle-class conceptions of Christmas
    with that of ghetto Blacks serving time in prison.

HOLLYWOOD CANTEEN
Nar/Cast: Joan Leslie + Robert Hutton + Louise Franklin* +
    and a cast of stars from A to Z
Screenplay: Delmer Daves
Producer: Alex Gottlieb   Director: Delmer Daves
Studio/Company: Warner Brothers
Tech Info: 16mm/ sound/ bw/ 125 min.
Date/Country: 1946 + USA   Type: Feature
Distr/Arch: uas
Annotation: A tribute to the real Hollywood Canteen where
    stars entertained the troops during World War II.   Louise
    Franklin has a small role.

HOLLYWOOD HOTEL
Nar/Cast: Dick Powell + Rosemary Lane + Benny Goodman
    Quartet with Teddy Wilson* and Lionel Hampton*
Screenplay: Jerry Wald + Leo Macauley + Richard Macauley
    Director: Busby Berkeley
Studio/Company: Warner Brothers
Tech Info: 110 min.
Date/Country: 1937 + USA   Type: Feature
Annotation: Benny Goodman's Quartet, including Teddy Wilson
    and Lionel Hampton, is featured in this Berkeley musical
    bonanza.

HOLY TERROR, THE
Series: Our Gang
Nar/Cast: Our Gang + Allen Hoskins*
Producer: Robert F. McGowan + Hal Roach   Director: Anthony
    Mack
Studio/Company: MGM
Tech Info: bw/silent/2 reels
Date/Country: 1929 + USA   Type: Comedy Short
Annotation: Opening title reads 'The story of a little girl
    (Mary Ann) who was bad on Monday, naughty on Tuesday, and
    terrible on Wednesday - Thursday they called out the
    marines.' Allen Hoskins stars as Farina.

HOMBRE
Nar/Cast: Frank Silvera* + Frederic March + Paul Newman
Screenplay: Irving Ranetch + Harriet Frank
Producer: Ronetch and Ritt   Director: Martin Ritt
Studio/Company: Twentieth Century Fox
Tech Info: 16 mm/sound/color/111 min.
Date/Country: 1967 + USA   Type: Feature
Distr/Arch: fnc
Annotation: Frank Silvera plays a Mexican bandit in this
    western tale about a stage coach traveling across the
    plains.

HOME BREW
Date/Country: 1920 + USA

HOME IN INDIANA
Nar/Cast: Jeanne Crain + June Haver + Willie Best* + George
    Reed*
Screenplay: Winston Miller
Producer: Andre Daven   Director: Henry Hathaway
Studio/Company: Fox
Tech Info: 16mm/sound/color/103 min.
Date/Country: 1944 + USA   Type: Feature
Distr/Arch: fnc
Annotation: Willie Best is "Mo" and George Reed "Tuppy",
    stable hands in this Hoosier harness racing film.

HOME OF THE BRAVE
Alt Title(s): High Noon
Nar/Cast: Frank Lovejoy + James Edwards* + Lloyd Bridges
Screenplay: Carl Foreman   Story: Arthur Laurents
Producer: Stanley Kramer   Director: Mark Robson
Studio/Company: Independent

Tech Info: 16 mm/bw/souund/2 reels/85 min.
Date/Country: 1949 + USA   Type: Feature
Distr/Arch: bud + mac + twy + roa + cha + fce + ivy + kpf +
    nat + sel + tfc + tmc + unf + wcf + who + wil
Annotation: While on a special mission, Peter Moss (James
    Edwards), the only black soldier in a U.S. army patrol,
    becomes psychologically disabled as a result of his   best
    friend being killed. Through flashbacks and analysis, the
    various nuances of racism are examined.

HOMESTEADER, THE
Nar/Cast: Evelyn Preer* + Lawrence Chenault* + Charles Lu-
    cas* + Iris Hall* + Charles S. Moore* + Vernon S. Duncan*
    + Trevy Woods* + William George
Studio/Company: Micheaux Film Corporation
Tech Info: bw/silent
Date/Country: 1919 + USA   Type: Feature
Annotation: The story of a unique black homesteader in the
    Dakotas, Jean Baptiste (Lucas). After a tragically unhap-
    py marriage with Orleans (Preer) and dreadful complica-
    tions with her family, he eventually is reunited with his
    first love Agnes (Hall) who is not white, as he thought,
    but a very light-skinned mulatto.

HONEY BABY, HONEY BABY
Nar/Cast: Diana Sands* + Calvin Lockhart* + Seth Allen and
    Bricktop + J. Eric Bell
Studio/Company: Kelly-Jordan
Date/Country: 1973 + USA   Type: Feature
Annotation: A black girl from Harlem wins a "Trip-around-
    the-world", but her problem is how to stay alive.

HONKY DONKEY
Series: Our Gang
Nar/Cast: Our Gang + Matthew Beard* + Willie Mae Taylor*
Producer: Hal Roach   Director: Gus Meins
Studio/Company: MGM
Tech Info: bw/sound/2 reels
Date/Country: 1934 + USA   Type: Comedy Short
Annotation: Rich-kid Wally teams up with the gang and their
    pet mule; the latter creates terrible problems for   chauf-
    feur Don Barclay and for Wally's doting mother. Matthew
    Beard stars as Stymie.

HONKY
Nar/Cast: William Marshall* + Brenda Sykes*   Story: Gunard
    Solberg   Director: William A. Graham
Studio/Company: Mahler
Tech Info: 16 mm/sound/92 min.
Date/Country: 1971 + USA   Type: Feature
Annotation: Adaptation of Gunard Solberg's novel Sheila
    about an interracial romance between a young black woman
    and a young white man. Score by Quincy Jones*.

HONOR OF HIS FAMILY, THE
Producer: D.W. Griffith + Biograph   Director: D.W. Griffith
Studio/Company: Biograph
Tech Info: 35 mm/silent/bw/988 ft.

Date/Country: 1910 + USA   Type: Dramatic Short
Annotation: Civil War melodrama with blacks as faithful
    retainers.

HOOK AND LADDER
Series: Our Gang
Nar/Cast: Our Gang + Matthew Beard*
Screenplay: Hal E. Roach + Robert F. McGowan
Producer: Hal Roach   Director: Robert McGowan·
Studio/Company: MGM + Roach
Tech Info: super 8 mm/16 mm/bw/sound/2 reels/20 min.
Date/Country: 1932 + USA   Type: Comedy Short
Distr/Arch: roa + bla
Annotation: The gang forms a volunteer fire company. They
    do get to a warehouse fire, where Stymie ends up tossing
    boxes of dynamite out the window. The explosions attract
    real firemen, but by the time they arrive, Dickie and
    Breezy have managed to put the fire out. Matthew Beard
    stars as Stymie.

HOORAY FOR LOVE
Nar/Cast: Bill Robinson* + Ann Southern + Gene Raymond +
    Fats Waller*
Screenplay: Lawrence Hazard + Ray Harris   Director: Walter
    Lang
Studio/Company: RKO Radio
Date/Country: 1935 + USA   Type: Feature
Annotation: The misfortunes of a struggling producer are
    brought out in this musical comedy which features Bill
    "Bojangles" Robinson and Fats Waller.

HORSE SOLDIERS, THE
Nar/Cast: John Wayne + Constance Towers + William Holden +
    Althea Gibson*
Screenplay: John Lee Mahin + Martin Rackin   Story: Harold
    Sinclair
Producer: John Lee Mahin   Director: John Ford
Studio/Company: United Artists
Tech Info: 16 mm/sound/color/119 min.
Date/Country: 1959 + USA   Type: Feature
Distr/Arch: uas
Annotation: Story of a union cavalry expedition deep into
    confederate territory to cut rail lines to Vicksburg.
    Along the way, southern belle (Towers) and her maid
    (Althea Gibson) are coerced into going along so they won't
    give the expedition away.

HORST WESSEL
Alt Title(s): see Hans Westmar

HOT BISCUITS
Producer: Spencer Williams*

HOT DOGS
Studio/Company: White Film Company
Date/Country: 1921 + USA

HOT HOOFS

Nar/Cast: Moran and Mack (The "Two Black Cows")   Director:
  Harry J. Edwards
Studio/Company: Educational Pictures
Tech Info: 16 mm/sound/bw/20 min.
Date/Country: 1932 + USA   Type: Animated Short

HOT ROCK, THE
Nar/Cast: Moses Gunn* + Robert Redford + George Segal
Screenplay: William Goldman   Story: Donald E. Westlake
Producer: Hal Landers + Bobby Roberts   Director: Peter
  Yates
Studio/Company: 20th Century Fox
Tech Info: 16 mm/sound/color/101 min.
Date/Country: 1972 + USA   Type: Feature
Distr/Arch: fnc
Annotation: A spoof on jewel thievery in which no one seems
  to be able to hold onto an African diamond - including its
  various thieves (Segal and Redford). Moses Gunn plays Dr.
  Amusa; music by Quincy Jones*.

HOTEL
Nar/Cast: Davis Roberts* + Rod Taylor + Melvyn Douglas +
  Carmen McRae*
Screenplay: Wendell Mayes   Story: Arthur Hailey
Producer: Wendell Mayes   Director: Richard Quine
Studio/Company: Warner Bros.
Tech Info: 16 mm/sound/color/124 min.
Date/Country: 1966 + USA   Type: Feature
Distr/Arch: arg + bud + ccc + cwf + ker + mac + mod + mot +
  roa + swa + tfc + unf + wcf + wel + wsa
Annotation: The goings on behind the scenes and counter of a
  large hotel include a civil rights issue - the barring of
  a black couple.   Davis Roberts plays Dr. Adams; Carmen
  McRae, Christine.

HOUNDS OF ZAROFF, THE
Alt Title(s): see The Most Dangerous Game

HOUSE BEHIND THE CEDARS, THE
Nar/Cast: Andrew S. Bishop* + Shingzie Howard* + William
  Crowell* + Lawrence Chenault* + Douglas Griffin*
Screenplay: Charles Chesnutt   Director: Charles W. Chesnutt
Studio/Company: Micheaux Film Corporation
Tech Info: 35 mm/silent/bw/9 reel
Date/Country: 1927 + USA   Type: Feature
Annotation: Adaptation of Chesnutts's novel of passing with
  Shingzie Howard as Rena, and a happy ending with Frank
  Fowler (Griffin) her black lover.

HOUSE OF CONNELLY, THE
Nar/Cast: Janet Gaynor + Robert Young + Richard Cromwell +
  Lionel Barrymore + Stepin Fetchit*   Story: Paul Green
  Director: Henry King
Studio/Company: Fox
Date/Country: 1934 + USA   Type: Feature
Annotation: Fetchit has a bit role in this film about a
  Carolina family who, having fallen on evil days, carry on
  a feud with a northern family who come South to grow

tobacco.

HOUSE_ON_SKULL_MOUNTAIN,_THE
Studio/Company: Columbia
Date/Country: 1973 + USA   Type: Feature

HOUSE_RENT_PARTY
Nar/Cast: Dewey "Pigmeat" Markham* + John Murray* + Mac-
   beth's Calypso Band*
Studio/Company: Toddy Pictures
Date/Country: 1946 + USA

HOUSE_WITH_CLOSED_SHUTTERS,_THE
Nar/Cast: Dorothy West   Director: D.W. Griffith
Studio/Company: Biograph
Tech Info: 35 mm/silent/bw/1 reel/998 ft./10 min.
Date/Country: 1910 + USA   Type: Dramatic Short
Distr/Arch: moma
Annotation: Civil War melodrama about a young woman who dies
   fighting in her cowardly brother's place. He hides him-
   self behind closed shutters to protect the family name.
   Blacks (whites in blackface) appear as faithful servants.

HOW_A_BRITISH_BULLDOG_SAVED_THE_UNION_JACK
Date/Country: 1906 + Britain   Type: Feature
Annotation: Tale of the Zulu War.

HOW_AFRICA_LIVES
Series: National Archives Gift Collection
Tech Info: 35 mm/silent/1 reel/bw
Annotation: Primitive life and how it is affected by the
   coming of the white man. (Part of Record Group 200 HF
   series, Harmon Foundation Collection).

HOW_AN_AFRICAN_TRIBE_IS_RULED_UNDER_COLONIAL_GOVERNMENT
Series: National Archives Gift Collection
Tech Info: 16 mm/silent/2 reels/bw
Annotation: Belgian Congo ruling as it employs tribal
   methods. (Part of Record Group 200 HF series, Harmon
   Foundation Collection).

HOW_HIGH_IS_UP
Nar/Cast: Moss* and Fry* + Corrine Smith*
Studio/Company: Seminole Film Company
Tech Info: silent/bw/2 reel
Date/Country: 1922 + USA   Type: Comedy Short
Annotation: The comedy is built around Moss and Frey's ef-
   forts to fly a plane.

HOWARD_UNIVERSITY
Series: National Archives Gift Collection
Tech Info: partly edited/1 reel
Annotation: Part of Record Group 200 HF series, Harmon
   Foundation Collection.

HOWARD-LINCOLN_FOOTBALL_GAME
Studio/Company: Monumental Pictures Corporation
Date/Country: 1921 + USA

HOWARD'S HOUSE PARTY
Nar/Cast: Bob Howard* + Noble Sissle*
Studio/Company: Century Films
Tech Info: 10 min.
Date/Country: 1947 + USA   Type: Musical Short

HUCKLEBERRY FINN, THE ADVENTURES OF
Nar/Cast: Tony Randall + Eddie Hodges + Archie Moore* + Pat-
ty McCormack + Neville Brand
Producer: Sam Goldwyn, Jr.   Director: Michael Curtiz
Studio/Company: MGM
Tech Info: 16 mm/color/sound/3 reels/107 min.
Date/Country: 1960 + USA   Type: Feature
Distr/Arch: fnc
Annotation: Eddie Hodges as Huckleberry Finn yearns to go
   where the riverboats go. He does just that to get away
   from the Widow Douglas.   Archie Moore, the boxing cham-
   pion, makes his screen debut as Jim, with whom Huck floats
   down the Mississippi.

HUCKLEBERRY FINN, THE ADVENTURES OF
Nar/Cast: Mickey Rooney + Walter Connolly + William Frawley
   + Rex Ingram*
Screenplay: Hugo Butler   Story: Mark Twain
Producer: Joseph L. Mankiewicz   Director: Richard Thorpe
Studio/Company: MGM
Tech Info: 16 mm/sound/bw/3 reels/91 min.
Date/Country: 1939 + USA   Type: Feature
Distr/Arch: fnc
Annotation: This 1939 version, made mainly as a Mickey
   Rooney vehicle, wanders from the original story. In this
   one, Huck is an abolitionist to Rex Ingram's strong, loyal
   Jim.   While slavery is attacked, basic racial attitudes
   are never challenged.

HUCKLEBERRY FINN
Nar/Cast: Paul Winfield* + Jeff East + Harvey Korman + David
   Wayne + Odessa Cleveland*
Screenplay: Robert B. Sherman + Richard M. Sherman   Story:
   Mark Twain   Director: J. Lee Thompson
Studio/Company: United Artists
Tech Info: 16 mm/color/sound/3 reels/118 min.
Date/Country: 1974 + USA   Type: Feature
Distr/Arch: uas + cwf
Annotation: An updated version in updated language and at-
   titudes: Huck's struggle with his conscience is neither
   agonizing nor lengthy.   This new version stars Paul
   Winfield as Jim, Odessa Cleveland as his wife. Roberta
   Flack* sings the theme song "Freedom."

HUCKLEBERRY FINN
Producer: Encyclopedia Britannica
Tech Info: 16 mm/sound/color/78 min.
Date/Country: 1965   Type: Feature
Distr/Arch: oks + ebec

HUCKLEBERRY FINN

Nar/Cast: Jackie Coogan + Clarence Muse* + Jane Darwell +
    Mitzi Green + Eugene Paulette   Director: Norman Taurog
Studio/Company: Paramount
Tech Info: 16 mm/sound/bw/2 reels/71 min.
Date/Country: 1931 + USA   Type: Feature
Distr/Arch: uni + cwf
Annotation: A completely different Huck Finn who ends up
    "sivilized": he saves Maryjane's money, goes back to
    school, even kisses the Widow Douglas. Jim (Muse) is
    forgotten; Huck never faces his conscience; questions of
    slavery, racism never engaged.

HUCKLEBERRY FINN
Nar/Cast: Lewis Sargent + Gordon Griffith + George Reed* +
    Orral Humphrey   Story: Mark Twain   Director: William D.
    Taylor
Tech Info: silent/bw
Date/Country: 1920 + USA   Type: Feature
Annotation: This silent version of Mark Twain's novel of
    life on the Mississippi river features George Reed as
    "Nigger Jim," a slave owned by Huck's aunts, who becomes
    his friend. In this adaptation Huck becomes enamoured of
    Mary Wilks and intends to return to her at the end of the
    film.

HUCKLEBERRY FINN
Nar/Cast: Weyland Rudd   Director: Weyland Rudd
Date/Country: 1937 + Soviet Union

HUEY!
Producer: American Documentary Films in collaboration with
    the Black Panther Party
Tech Info: 16mm/ bw/ sound/ 33 min.
Date/Country: 1968 + USA   Type: Documentary
Distr/Arch: adf
Annotation: Focuses on the death of Bobby Hutton in a police
    raid on the Oakland Panther Headquarters. Shows a rally
    featuring speeches by H. Rapp Brown*, Stokely Carmichael*,
    Congressman Ronald Dellums*, and lawyer Charles Garry.

HUNGER IN AMERICA
Studio/Company: CBS
Tech Info: 16 mm/sound/bw/45 min.
Date/Country: 1968 + USA   Type: Documentary
Distr/Arch: car + imp + uca
Annotation: Documents poor conditions of various ethnic
    groups: black sharecroppers in Alabama, Navajo Indians in
    Arizona, and straining tenant farmers near Washington,
    D.C.

HUNTERS, THE
Producer: Harvard Universty Film Study Center
Tech Info: 16 mm/sound/color/2 reels/76 min.
Date/Country: 1958 + USA   Type: Documentary
Distr/Arch: iu + msu + con
Annotation: Depicts the life and culture of bushmen living
    in the Kalahari Desert of Africa. Illustrates the village
    life and the hunting practices of the bushmen. Reveals

the bare subsistance level of their lives.

HURDLER, THE
Producer: Sterling
Tech Info: 16 mm/sound/color/16 min.
Date/Country: 1970 + USA   Type: Documentary
Distr/Arch: sef
Annotation: A biographical view of Dr. Charles Drew* who
    developed the first blood bank system.

HURRICANE
Nar/Cast: Larry Hagman + Barry Sullvan + Jessica Walter +
    Charles Lampkin*
Screenplay: Jack Turley   Story: William C. Anderson
Producer: Edward J. Montagne   Director: Jerry Jameson
Studio/Company: Metromedia Producers Corporation
Date/Country: 1974 + USA   Type: TV Feature
Annotation: Charles Lampkin plays Wyn Stokey in this TV dis-
    aster film about Hurricane Hilda and the lives affected by
    it.

HURRY SUNDOWN
Nar/Cast: Robert Hooks* + Diahann Carroll* + Rex Ingram* +
    Michael Caine + Jane Fonda + John Phillip Law + Beah
    Richards*
Screenplay: Thomas C. Ryan + Hoorton Foote
Producer: Otto Preminger   Director: Otto Preminger
Studio/Company: Paramount
Tech Info: 16 mm/sound/color/146 min.
Date/Country: 1967 + USA   Type: Feature
Distr/Arch: fnc
Annotation: Robert Hooks and John Phillip Law star as war
    veterans who join forces to thwart unscrupulous land
    developers lead by Michael Caine. Rex Ingram is Professor
    Thurlow.

HUSTLE
Nar/Cast: Paul Winfield* + Burt Reynolds + Catherine Deneuve
    + Ben Johnson
Screenplay: Steve Shagon
Producer: Robert Aldrich   Director: Robert Aldrich
Studio/Company: Paramount
Tech Info: 16 mm/sound/color/120 min.
Date/Country: 1975 + USA   Type: Feature
Distr/Arch: fnc
Annotation: Reynolds is a nostalgic romantic policeman out
    of place in an unprincipled world. Paul Winfield is a
    friend of his on the police force.

HYPNOTIZED
Nar/Cast: George Moran + Charlie Mack + Ernest Torrance +
    Wallace Ford + Maria Alba + Hattie McDaniel*
Screenplay: Mack Sennett + Arthur Ripley
Producer: Mack Sennett   Director: Mack Sennett
Studio/Company: Sono Art-World Wide Pictures
Tech Info: 16 mm/sound/bw/58 min.
Date/Country: 1933 + USA   Type: Feature
Distr/Arch: aim + csv + man + ncs

Annotation: Hypnotized is the last feature film made by the
well-known blackface comedy team, the "Two Black Crows."
The original George Moran is back with his partner,
Charlie Mack, and they cavort with a lion and an elephant
in this adventure comedy.

HYPOCRITE, THE
Nar/Cast: Evelyn Preer* + Cleo Desmond*
Tech Info: silent/bw
Date/Country: 1917 + USA

I AIN'T LYIN': FOLKTALES FROM MISSISSIPPI
Producer: Bill Perris + Yale Univ. Media Design Studio +
Center for Southern Folklore
Tech Info: 16 mm/sound/color/20 min.
Date/Country: 1975 + USA   Type: Documentary
Distr/Arch: csf
Annotation: A film about rural life in Mississippi. (Edited
version available without performances of the dozens and
toasts). Provided by Center for Southern Folklore.

I AIN'T PLAYIN' NO MORE
Tech Info: 16 mm/sound/bw/61 min.
Date/Country: 1970 + USA   Type: Documentary
Distr/Arch: afr
Annotation: Positive interaction of parents, teachers and
students in a community-controlled situation in Washing-
ton, D.C., Morgan Community School.

I AM A FUGITIVE FROM A CHAIN GANG
Nar/Cast: Paul Muni + Glenda Farrell + Helen Vinson +
Preston Foster + Everett Brown*
Screenplay: Robert E. Burns   Director: Mervyn Le Roy
Studio/Company: Warner Brothers
Tech Info: 16 mm/sound.bw/90 min.
Date/Country: 1932 + USA   Type: Feature
Distr/Arch: uas
Annotation: Story of a victim of circumstance's experiences
with the horrors of a chain gang.   This film has sym-
pathetic, realistic portrayals of black prisoners, in-
cluding Brown who is instrumental in the jail break.

I AM SOMEBODY
Producer: American Foundation of Non-Violence   Director:
Madeline Anderson*
Studio/Company: American Foundatin of Non-Violence
Tech Info: 16 mm/color/sound/1 reel/30 min.
Date/Country: 1970 + USA   Type: Documentary
Distr/Arch: mhf + ind
Annotation: The story of the successful hospital workers'
strike of 1969 in Charleston, South Carolina, is docu-
mented.   Interviewed are many of the strikers attempting
to form an AFL-CIO affiliation as well as national figures
like Ralph Abernathy* (SCLC), Leon David (New York Local
1199), and Coretta King*.

I DOOD IT
Alt Title(s): By Hook or By Crook

Nar/Cast: Red Skelton + Eleanor Powell + Lena Horne* + Hazel
   Scott* + Butterfly McQueen*
Screenplay: Sig Herzig + Fred Suidy
Producer: Jack Cummings   Director: Vincente Minnelli
Studio/Company: MGM
Tech Info: 16 mm/sound/bw/102 min.
Date/Country: 1943 + USA   Type: Feature
Distr/Arch: fnc
Annotation: Red Skelton musical comedy in which he plays a
   pants presser married to a glamorous stage star; also
   features Lena Horne and Hazel Scott in musical numbers.

I_DREAM_OF_JEANNIE
Nar/Cast: Louise Beavers* + Ray Middleton + Bill Shirly
Screenplay: Alan LeMay   Director: Alan Devan
Studio/Company: Republic
Tech Info: 16 mm/sound/bw/90 min.
Date/Country: 1952 + USA   Type: Feature
Annotation: A version of the composer Stephen Foster's youth
   with Ray Middleton as Edwin Christy the minstrel man who
   introduced Foster's "Oh Susanna" to the public.

I_ESCAPED_FROM_DEVIL'S_ISLAND
Nar/Cast: Jim Brown* + Christopher George + Rick Ely
   Director: William Witney
Studio/Company: United Artists
Tech Info: 16 mm/color/sound/3 reels/87 min.
Date/Country: 1973 + USA   Type: Feature
Distr/Arch: uas
Annotation: Jim Brown plays Le Bras in this adventurous tale
   of an escape from the notorious Devil's Island.

I_HEARD
Series: Betty Boop cartoon
Nar/Cast: Don Redman* orchestra
Producer: Max Fleischer   Director: Dave Fleischer
Studio/Company: Warner Brothers
Tech Info: 16 mm/bw/sound/1 reel/6-8 min.
Date/Country: 1932 + USA   Type: Animated Short
Distr/Arch: emg + kpf
Annotation: Redman's band is seen live and furnishes the
   music on the sound track.

I_LOVE_A_BANDLEADER
Nar/Cast: Eddie Anderson*
Date/Country: 1945 + USA   Type: Feature
Annotation: Reputedly Eddie Anderson's most lucrative film
   role up to this point (1945) in his career.

I_LOVE_YOU,_ALICE_B._TOKLAS
Nar/Cast: Roy Glenn* + Peter Sellers + Jo Van Fleet
Screenplay: Paul Mazursky + Larry Tucker
Producer: Charles McGuire   Director: Hy Anertack
Studio/Company: Warners
Tech Info: 16 mm/sound/color/93 min.
Date/Country: 1968 + USA   Type: Feature
Distr/Arch: arg + bud + ccc + cha + cwf + ics + mac + med +
   mot + rca + sel + swa + tmc + twf + unf + wcf + wel + who

+ wil
Annotation: Roy Glenn plays a gas station attendant in this
   comedy about marriage, social conformity, hippies and
   marijuana cookies.

I_MISTERI_DI_PARIGI
Nar/Cast: John Kitzmiller*
Date/Country: 1958 + Italy   Type: Feature

I_PASSED_FOR_WHITE
Nar/Cast: Sonya Wilde + James Franciscus + Pat Michon
Screenplay: Fred M. Wilcox   Story: Mary Hastings (book)
Producer: Fred Wilcox   Director: Fred Wilcox
Studio/Company: Allied Artists
Tech Info: 16 mm/sound/bw/92 min.
Date/Country: 1960 + USA   Type: Feature
Distr/Arch: cin
Annotation: Story of a light-skinned girl (played by white
   actress Sonya Wilde) who travels North, passes for white,
   and marries into a snobbish, wealthy white family. The
   various problems she faces, especially with her pregnancy
   are depicted.

I_PIRATI_DELLA_COSTA
Nar/Cast: John Kitzmiller*
Date/Country: 1960 + Italy   Type: Feature

I_TAKE_THIS_WOMAN
Nar/Cast: Spencer Tracy + Willie Best* + Veree Teasdale
Screenplay: James K. McGuiness   Story: Charles McArthur
   Director: W.S. Van Dyke
Studio/Company: MGM
Date/Country: 1940 + USA   Type: Feature
Annotation: Heddy Lamar plays the wife of Spencer Tracy who
   leaves him for another man, only to discover she really
   loves Tracy after all. Willie Best plays the part of
   "Sambo."

I_WALKED_WITH_A_ZOMBIE
Nar/Cast: James Ellison + Frances Dee + Teresa Harris* +
   Darby Jones* + Sir Lancelot* + Jeni LeGon*
Screenplay: Curt Diodmak + Ardel Wray   Story: Inez Wallace
Producer: Val Lewton   Director: Jacques Tourneur
Studio/Company: RKO Radio
Tech Info: 16 mm/sound/color/2 reels/68 min.
Date/Country: 1943 + USA   Type: Feature
Distr/Arch: fnc
Annotation: Black actors are mainly "death's slaves" in this
   horror film derived from Jane Eyre, although Teresa Harris
   as Alma has a more impressive role. Jeni LeGon is a
   dancer, Sir Lancelot a calypso singer.

I_WANT_A_DIVORCE
Nar/Cast: Joan Blondell + Dick Powell + Louise Beavers*
Screenplay: Frank Butler
Producer: George Arthur   Director: Ralph Murphy
Studio/Company: Paramount
Date/Country: 1940 + USA   Type: Feature

Annotation: Louise Beavers plays Celestine in this drama
    about the heartbreak of divorce, a lesson Blondell and
    Powell learn before the end of the film.

I_WISH_I_KNEW_HOW_IT_WOULD_FEEL_TO_BE_FREE
Producer: Peter Rosen + Yale Universty
Tech Info: 16 mm/sound/bw/20 min.
Date/Country: 1968   Type: Documentary
Distr/Arch: uca
Annotation: A typical American ghetto viewed close up, with
    Billy Taylor's* song (sung by Nina Simone*) as sound track
    and title.

I_WONDER_WHY
Nar/Cast: Alexander Scourby
Producer: Robert M. Rosenthal
Tech Info: 16 mm/sound/bw/6 min./1 reel
Date/Country: 1965 + USA   Type: Short Documentary
Distr/Arch: roa + mgh
Annotation: Portrays the thoughts of a young black girl who
    wonders 'why people don't like me.' Music by Don Elliot.
    Alexander Scourby is the narrator.

I'LL_BE_GLAD_WHEN_YOU'RE_DEAD_YOU_RASCAL_YOU
Series: Betty Boop cartoon
Nar/Cast: Louis Armstrong* orchestra
Producer: Max Fleischer   Director: Dave Fleischer
Tech Info: 16 mm/sound/1 reel/6-8 min.
Date/Country: 1932 + USA   Type: Animated Short
Distr/Arch: emg + kpf
Annotation: Betty Boop is on an island captured by can-
    nibals. She is helped by Bimbo and Koko. Armstrong ap-
    pears in the background (as Betty flees) singing "I'll be
    glad when you're dead, you rascal you."

I'LL_REACH_FOR_A_STAR
Alt Title(s): see The Hit Parade of 1937

I'M_A_MAN
Nar/Cast: John Barber*   Director: Peter Rosen
Studio/Company: Contemporary McGraw Hill
Tech Info: 16 mm/sound/color; bw/1 reel/20 min.
Date/Country: 1970 + USA   Type: Documentary
Distr/Arch: mhf
Annotation: This film examines why years of racial strife
    and years of non-violent pleas for understanding have con-
    verted John Barber and his fellow black professionals to
    radical black militancy.

I'M_NO_ANGEL
Nar/Cast: Mae West + Cary Grant + Gertrude Howard* + Kent
    Taylor + Louise Beavers*
Screenplay: Mae West   Story: Mae West   Director: Wesley
    Ruggles
Studio/Company: Paramount
Tech Info: 16 mm/bw/sound/2 reels/70 min.
Date/Country: 1933 + USA   Type: Feature
Distr/Arch: uni

Annotation: Mae West as Tira of the circus makes it to the
   big time with her head-in-the-lion's mouth acts and into
   the hearts of various men. Confusion in her love affair
   with Cary Grant brings about a breach of promise suit with
   Tira representing herself and Gertrude Howard as Beulah
   (of "peel me a grape" fame), helping out. A dressing room
   scene includes Louise Beavers and other unnamed black
   actresses.

I'M_SORRY
Producer: Communication Arts
Tech Info: 16 mm/sound/bw/30 min.
Date/Country: 1966 + USA   Type: Dramatic Short
Distr/Arch: uca
Annotation: How forces in society influence a young black
   man to take up radical politics.

I'M_THE_PRETTIEST_PIECE_IN_GREECE
Nar/Cast: Billie Haywood*
Producer: Richard Wedler
Tech Info: 16 mm/sound/bw/1 reel/29 min.
Date/Country: 1973 + USA   Type: Documentary
Distr/Arch: iu
Annotation: Billie Haywood, songstress and comedienne of the
   1930's and 40's, interviewed. As she reflects on her
   past, she discusses various stories, including her rela-
   tionships with Billie Holiday and Mae West.

I,_A_WOMAN,_PART_III:_THE_DAUGHTER
Nar/Cast: Inger Sundh + Tom Scott* + Ellen Faison
Screenplay: Peer Guldbrandsen   Story: Siv Holm
Producer: Peer Guldbrandsen   Director: Mac Ahlberg
Studio/Company: Productions Unlimited + Chevron Pictures
Tech Info: 16 mm/sound/color/86 min.
Date/Country: 1973 + Sweden   Type: Feature
Distr/Arch: fnc + pru
Annotation: An interracial love story set in present day
   Copenhagen, this film treats several contemporary themes:
   racism, narcotics and lesbianism.

ICE_STATION_ZEBRA
Nar/Cast: Rock Hudson + Patrick McGoohan + Jim Brown*
Screenplay: Douglas Heyes
Producer: Martin Ransohoff + John Calley   Director: John
   Sturges
Studio/Company: MGM
Tech Info: 16 mm/color/sound/5 reels/152 min.
Date/Country: 1968 + USA   Type: Feature
Distr/Arch: fnc
Annotation: Nuclear sub captain Ferraday has orders to run
   beneath theArctic ice-cap to rescue weather station
   scientists who have been radioing for help. With him are
   three men whose missions are unknown: Jones, a British
   agent; Vaslov, a Russian defector; and Anders, an over-
   zealous Marine Captain, played by Jim Brown.

IDI_AMIN_DADA   Director: Barbet Schroeder
Tech Info: 16 mm/sound/color/90 min./English narration

Date/Country: 1960 + France   Type: Documentary
Distr/Arch: civ
Annotation: Documentary "self portrait" of the controversial
    leader of Uganda.

IDOL DANCER, THE
Nar/Cast: Richard Barthelmess + Clarine Seymour + Porter
    Strong + Adolphe Lestina + Walter James + Ben Grauer +
    Walter Kolomoku + Florence Short
Screenplay: S.E.V. Taylor   Story: Gordon Ray Young
    Director: D.W. Griffith
Studio/Company: First National
Tech Info: 35 mm/silent/bw/7 reels/75 min.
Date/Country: 1920 + USA   Type: Featur
Distr/Arch: moma
Annotation: Natives played by whites in black face have a
    number of stock roles in this South Seas romance which
    also includes Christianizing the natives. Florence Short
    and Walter Kolomoku provide the dark-skinned romance;
    Porter Strong is Peter, a native minister; James, Lestina
    and Grauer are also islanders.

IF HE HOLLERS, LET HIM GO
Nar/Cast: Barbara McNair* + Dana Wynter + Raymond St.   Jac-
    ques* + Kevin McCarthy + James McEachin* + Don Newsome*
Screenplay: Charles Martin   Story: Chester Himes* (novel)
Producer: Charles Martin   Director: Charles, Martin
Studio/Company: Cinerama Releasing
Tech Info: 16 mm/color/sound/3 reels/111 min.
Date/Country: 1968 + USA   Type: Feature
Distr/Arch: swa
Annotation: A man, falsely convicted of rape and murder, who
    tries desperately to prove his innocence only to find him-
    self trapped into an attempt to murder the wife of a man
    who could save his life. St. Jacques is James Lake, the
    innocent man, McNair is Lily, the night club singer with
    whom he was in love but who marries his brother while he
    is in prison; Newsome is Williams, his brother; McEachin,
    the defense counsel.

IF THERE WEREN'T ANY BLACKS--YOU'D HAVE TO INVENT THEM
Screenplay: Johnny Speight   Director: Charles Jarrot
Tech Info: 16 mm/sound/2 reels/58 min.
Date/Country: 1969 + Britain   Type: TV Feature
Distr/Arch: kpf + imp
Annotation: Set in a cemetery, the film uses sharp satire to
    demonstrate the conspiracy that prevails between bigotry,
    hypocrisy, unenlightened self-interest, fear and indif-
    ference.   Looking for a scapegoat, various groups blacken
    an officious white man and arrange to eliminate him.

IL EST MINUIT, DOCTEUR SCHWEITZER
Nar/Cast: Pierre Fresnay + Jeanne Moreau + Raymond Rouleau
Screenplay: H. Andre Legrand + Andre Haguet   Story: Gilbert
    Cesbron
Producer: Georges Bernier   Director: Andre Haguet
Studio/Company: Nordia Films
Tech Info: sound/95 min.

Date/Country: 1952 + France   Type: Feature
Distr/Arch: saf
Annotation: In this psychological drama, Albert Schweitzer,
    a pastor who has become a doctor, leaves for Gabon in
    order to care for its native population, decimated by
    malaria. Amidst the opposition of the witch doctors and
    numerous difficulties, Schweitzer does accomplish his
    task. In 1914, war breaks out in Europe and Schweitzer,
    who is Alsatian and therefore German, is arrested.

IL FIGLIO DI CAPITAN BLOOD
Nar/Cast: John Kitzmiller*
Date/Country: 1962 + Italy   Type: Feature

IL GRANDE ADDIO
Nar/Cast: John Kitzmiller*
Date/Country: 1957 + Italy   Type: Feature

IL GRANDE APPELLO
Alt Title(s): The Last Roll-Call   Director: Mario Camerini
Date/Country: 1939 + Italy   Type: Feature
Annotation: Father and son find themselves on opposite sides
    during Italy's war with Ethiopia. Scenes depict Ethiopian
    warriors fighting Italians armed with heavy artillery.

IL NOSTRO CAMPIONE
Nar/Cast: John Kitzmiller*
Date/Country: 1955 + Italy   Type: Feature

IL RIBELLE DI CASTELLAMONTE
Nar/Cast: John Kitzmiller*
Date/Country: 1965 + Italy   Type: Feature

IL SANGUE E LA SFIDA
Nar/Cast: John Kitzmiller*
Date/Country: 1962 + Italy   Type: Feature

ILL WIND
Studio/Company: Toddy Pictures
Tech Info: 68 min.
Date/Country: 194- + USA   Type: Feature

IMITATION OF LIFE
Nar/Cast: Claudette Colbert + Warren William + Ned Sparks +
    Louise Beavers* + Fredi Washington* + Rochelle Hudson +
    Alan Hale + Hazel Washington*
Screenplay: William Hurlbut   Story: Fannie Hurst
Producer: Carl Laemmle, Jr.   Director: John M. Stahl
Studio/Company: Universal
Tech Info: 16 mm/sound/bw/3 reels/90 min.
Date/Country: 1934 + USA   Type: Feature
Distr/Arch: uni
Annotation: This film deals the problem of a light-skinned
    black girl who, because she resents being treated as an
    inferior, makes a desperate bid to pass for white. Fredi
    Washington plays the "tragic Mulatto", Louise Beavers her
    mother, Delilah who makes her employer Claudette Colbert)
    rich by giving her the secret of her pancake flour.

IMITATION OF LIFE
Nar/Cast: Juanita Moore* + John Gavin + Sandra Dee + Susan
  Kohner + Dan O'Herlihy + Ann Robeson + Lana Tuner + Robert
  Alda + Mahalia Jackson* + Troy Donahue
Screenplay: Fannie Hurst
Producer: Ross Hunter   Director: Douglas Serk
Studio/Company: Universal
Tech Info: 16 mm/color/sound/4 reels/124 min.
Date/Country: 1959 + USA   Type: Feature
Distr/Arch: uni
Annotation: A remake of the 1934 version of Fannie Hurst's
  novel features Susan Kohner, a white actress, in the role
  of the young mulatto who tries to pass for white. Black
  actress Fredi Washington played the role in the earlier
  film. Juanita Moore plays the rejected mother who becomes
  the maid of aspiring and struggling actress Lora Meredith
  (Lana Turner).

IMMIGRATION IN THE CITIES
Producer: Granada Television, Ltd.
Tech Info: 16 mm/sound/bw/13 min.
Date/Country: 1972 + USA   Type: Documentary
Distr/Arch: fnc
Annotation: Documents the arrival of new immigrants from the
  rural areas to the cities immediately after the Civil War.
  Provided by Center for Southern Folklore.

IMPACT OF ABE LINCOLN AND MARTIN LUTHER KING, THE
Series: A Better World
Producer: Koplin and Grinker
Tech Info: 16 mm/sound/color/26 min.
Date/Country: USA   Type: Documentary
Distr/Arch: pic
Annotation: How both King and Lincoln fought for unity of
  the nation against great opposition.

IMPACT OF JACKIE ROBINSON, THE
Series: A Better World
Producer: Koplin and Grinker
Tech Info: 16 mm/sound/color/26 min.
Date/Country: USA   Type: Documentary
Distr/Arch: pic
Annotation: How Jackie Robinson* fought for a better world.

IMPACT OF JERSEY JOE WOLCOTT/SHERIFF ARNOLD CREAM, THE
Producer: Koplin and Grinker
Tech Info: 16 mm/sound/color/26 min.
Date/Country: USA   Type: Documentary
Distr/Arch: pic
Annotation: How Joe Wolcott* became heavyweight champion of
  the world and then the first black sheriff of Camden, New
  Jersey.

IN AFRICAN HANDS
Producer: International Film Bureau
Tech Info: 16 mm/sound/color/20 min.
Date/Country: 1971 + Africa

Distr/Arch: texfilm + ifb
Annotation: The creation of a new cultural and political
   synthesis from borrowed influences and their   own   values.

IN_HUMANITY'S_CAUSE
Date/Country: 1911 + USA
Annotation: A Confederate officer is saved from death on the
   battlefield by a blood transfusion from a black   man,   but
   when he sinks to the depths ("blood will tell") disgusting
   his sweethert, he tracks down his donor and they   go   over
   the cliff together.

IN_OLD_CHICAGO
Nar/Cast: Mme. Sul-te-Wan* + Tyrone Power + Alice Faye
Screenplay: Lamar Trotti + Sonya Levien   Story: Nivea Busch
Producer: Darryl F. Zanuck   Director: Henry King
Studio/Company: Fox
Tech Info: 16 mm/souund/bw/111 min.
Date/Country: 1938 + USA   Type: Feature
Distr/Arch: fnc
Annotation: Madame Sul-te-Wan plays Hattie in this   saga   of
   the O'Learys, their cow and the great Chicago fire.

IN_OLD_KENTUCKY
Nar/Cast: Stepin Fetchit* + Carolynne Snowden* + James Murray + Helene Costello   Story: Charles Dazey   Director:
   John Stahl
Date/Country: 1927 + USA   Type: Feature
Annotation: A post-World War I horseracing tale which includes the peccadillos of a young major returned South
   from the wars, his family-of-little-funds, and several
   Blacks to add the proper regional touch. Carolynne Snowden, who apparently believes in the efficacy of pies,
   especially in winning wars, and Stepin Fetchit, who is
   himself more than highly appreciative of such culinary
   art, actually have a love affair.

IN_OLD_KENTUCKY
Nar/Cast: Will Rogers + Bill Robinson* + Nina Mae McKinney*
Screenplay: Sam Hellman + Gladys Lehman   Story: Charles T.
   Dazey
Producer: Edward Butcher   Director: George Marshall
Studio/Company: 20th Century Fox
Tech Info: 16 mm/sound/bw/86 min.
Date/Country: 1935 + USA   Type: Feature
Annotation: Will Rogers plays Steve Tapley, a horse   trainer
   who tries to patch up a feud between the Shattucks and the
   Martingales, in his last film Bill Robinson as Wash Jack-
   son "taps away the duller moments."

IN_OLD_KENTUCKY
Nar/Cast: Mary Pickford + Henry B. Walthall + Linda Arvidson
   + Mack Sennett   Director: D.W. Griffith
Studio/Company: Biograph + Cuddebackville
Tech Info: 35 mm/silent/bw/1 reel/983 ft./10-15 min.
Date/Country: 1909 + USA   Type: Dramatic short
Distr/Arch: moma
Annotation: The film depicts a conflict between two brothers

who serve on opposite sides during the Civil War. Blacks
(whites in blackface) appear as faithful servants: the
film opens and closes with a scene with the loyal butler.

IN SEARCH OF A PAST
Series: Of Black America
Producer: CBS
Tech Info: 16 mm/sound/color/2 reels/53 min.
Date/Country: 1968 + USA   Type: Documentary
Distr/Arch: iu + bfa
Annotation: Documents responses of three teen-aged black
   American students traveling in Ghana in search of their
   African heritage. Reveals their surprise at discovering
   both similarities and differences in African and American
   lifestyles. Shows dialogue between the visiting American
   students and three African students as the Americans
   defend their struggle for racial equality.

IN SEARCH OF MYSELF
Tech Info: 16 mm/sound/bw/1 reel/30 min.
Date/Country: 1965   Type: Documentary
Distr/Arch: con
Annotation: People of the emerging nations of Africa are
   living through a conflict in which the battlegrounds are
   their own minds and feelings. The conflict between
   modernization and tradition becomes significant for
   artists and musicians seen at work in Nigeria's Mbari Art
   Center.

IN SLAVERY DAYS
Nar/Cast: Robert Z. Leonard + Margarita Fischer   Director:
   Otis Turner
Date/Country: 1913 + USA   Type: Dramatic Short
Annotation: The mulatto (played by white actress Margarita
   Fisher) is depicted as a depraved and evil character, tor-
   mented by "black blood." Substituted for the daughter of
   the house during childhood, later as an adult, she sells
   the white girl into slavery. But her plan is foiled by
   the girl's lover.

IN THE BORDER STATES   Director: D.W. Griffith
Studio/Company: Biograph
Tech Info: 35 mm/silent/bw/1 reel/990 ft./10-15 min.
Date/Country: 1910 + USA   Type: Dramatic Short
Distr/Arch: moma
Annotation: Blacks are used as atmosphere in this Civil War
   melodrama.

IN THE COMPANY OF MEN
Screenplay: William Greaves*
Producer: William Greaves*   Director: William Greaves*
Tech Info: 16 mm/bw/sound/2 reels/52 min.
Date/Country: 1969 + USA   Type: Documentary
Distr/Arch: wgp
Annotation: Greaves' film examines the conflicting attitudes
   between the so-called hard-core unemployed and a company
   foreman.

IN THE COOL OF THE DAY
Nar/Cast: Nat "King" Cole* + Jane Fonda + Peter Finch
Screenplay: Meade Roberts
Producer: John Houseman   Director: Robert Stevens
Studio/Company: MGM
Tech Info: 16 mm/sound/color/89 min.
Date/Country: 1963 + USA   Type: Feature
Distr/Arch: fnc
Annotation: Songs by Nat "King" Cole in this melodrama about
  marriage and infidelity.

IN THE DEPTHS OF OUR HEARTS
Nar/Cast: Herman De La Valades* + Agusta Williams* + Irene
  Conn* + Virgil Williams*
Studio/Company: Royal Garden Film Company
Tech Info: bw/silent
Date/Country: 1920 + USA   Type: Feature
Annotation: Story of color caste and how it affects the
  lives cf two light-skinned young people brought up by
  their mother to avoid dark-skinned members of the race.
  The son rebels, is later reunited with his former (dark
  skinned) sweetheart and finally changes his mother's and
  sister's color conscious, hypocritical attitudes.

IN THE FALL OF '64
Date/Country: 1914 + USA
Annotation: An entire slave quarter fights to hide a Con-
  federate officer from the Union soldiers.

IN THE HEAT OF THE NIGHT
Nar/Cast: Sidney Poitier* + Rod Steiger + Beah Richards* +
  Lee Grant
Screenplay: Sterling Silliphant   Story: John Ball
Producer: Walter Mirisch   Director: Norman Jewison
Studio/Company: Mirisch Corp. + United Artists
Tech Info: 16 mm/color/sound/3 reels/109 min.
Date/Country: 1967 + USA   Type: Feature
Distr/Arch: uas
Annotation: Drama of racial hatred and prejudice set in a
  little Mississippi town. This is the first of the Virgil
  Tibbs series with Sidney Poitier as the smart Yankee
  detective, Rod Steiger as the southern sheriff with
  limited intelligence and unlimited prejudice. Music by
  Quincy Jones*; Ray Charles* sings the title song.

IN THE MONEY
Nar/Cast: Louise Beavers*   Director: Frank Strayer
Tech Info: sound/bw
Date/Country: 1933 + USA

IN THE NIGHT
Nar/Cast: Frankie Darro + Mantan Moreland*   Story: Edmond
  Kelso   Director: Jean Yarborough
Date/Country: 1941 + USA   Type: Feature
Annotation: See annotation for Chasing Trouble.

IN THE RAPTURE
Nar/Cast: Gwendolyn Parrish* + Clifford Hatcher* + Joe

Folson* + Andy Crim
Screenplay: Margerine Hatcher*
Producer: William C. Hatcher*   Director: William H. Wig-
gins, Jr.*
Tech Info: 16 mm/sound/color/90 min./3 reels
Date/Country: 1976 + USA   Type: Dramatized Documentary
Distr/Arch: ind
Annotation: Cast is comprised of choir members from the
Church of God in Christ, Temple, ≤18, Northside New Era
Baptist Church and Operation Bread Basket of Indianapolis,
Indiana. In the Rapture is an Afro-American religious
folk drama which depicts the eternal moral struggle of man
to shun evil and do good.

IN THIS OUR LIFE
Nar/Cast: Bette Davis + Olivia de Havilland + Hattie Mc-
Daniel* + George O'Brien + Dennis Morgan + Ernest An-
derson* + Billie Burke + Frank Craven
Screenplay: Howard Koch   Story: Ellen Glasgow
Producer: Hal Wallace   Director: John Huston
Studio/Company: Warners
Tech Info: 16 mm/bw/sound/3 reels/96 min.
Date/Country: 1942 + USA   Type: Feature
Distr/Arch: uas
Annotation: Adaptation of Ellen Glasgow's novel in which the
"wicked" sister Stanley Timberlake (Bette Davis) makes off
with the "good" sister's (de Havilland) husband. Other
deeds include an accident (hit-and-run) in which she im-
plicates Parry (Ernest Anderson), the decent educated
young black son of Minerva Clay (McDaniel), long-time family domestic. A few memorable scenes with Minerva and
Parry, whose career as an aspiring lawyer is almost
aborted.

INCIDENT, THE
Nar/Cast: Tony Musante + Martin Sheen + Brock Peters* + Ruby
Dee* + Beau Bridges
Screenplay: Nicholas E. Baehr
Producer: Monroe Sachson   Director: Larry Peerce
Studio/Company: 20th Century Fox
Tech Info: 16 mm/sound/bw/106 min.
Date/Country: 1967 + USA   Type: Feature
Distr/Arch: fnc
Annotation: A cross-section of America including a black
couple played by Brock Peters and Ruby Dee are trapped
aboard a subway car by two thugs. How they react to the
various indignities heaped upon them is the basis of this
film.

INDIOS A NORD-OVEST
Nar/Cast: John Kitzmiller*
Date/Country: 1964 + Italy   Type: Feature

INDUSTRIAL DEVELOPMENT IN GHANA
Producer: Ghana Information Service
Tech Info: 16 mm/sound/color/bw/30 min.
Date/Country: Ghana   Type: Documentary
Distr/Arch: gis

Annotation: The   industrial situation in Ghana is examined.

INFORMER, THE   Director: D.W. Griffith
Studio/Company: Biograph
Tech Info: 35 mm/silent/bw/1 reel/1080 ft./10-15 min.
Date/Country: 1912 + USA   Type: Dramatic Short
Distr/Arch: moma
Annotation: Civil War melodrama in which a black family
    guards the plantation from Yankee troops.

INGAGI
Studio/Company: Congo Pictures Ltd.
Tech Info: silent/bw
Date/Country: 1930   Type: Feature
Annotation: Silent   film supposedly depicting a safari in
    gorilla country of the then Belgian Congo. Ingagi was the
    legendary gorilla who supposedly abducted a white woman.
    This ritual sacrifice of the female to the beast in order
    to protect the village is a "fact" seemingly acceptable to
    the "ignorant and superstitous" Africans.

INK SPOTS, THE
Nar/Cast: Georgie Auld and His Auld Stars* + Joy Lane* + The
    Barry Sisters* + The Ink Spots*   Director: Will Cowan
Studio/Company: Universal-International
Tech Info: 15 min.
Date/Country: 1955 + USA   Type: Musical Short
Annotation: Georgie Auld and His Auld Stars are featured in
    a nightclub setting with numbers including "If I Didn't
    Care."

INNER CITY DWELLER: HEALTH CARE
Producer: IU-AVC
Tech Info: 16 mm/sound/color/1 reel/23 min.
Date/Country: 1971 + USA   Type: Documentary
Distr/Arch: iu
Annotation: In a simulated portrayal designed to give the
    perspective of an inner city resident, a young mother at-
    tempts to recieve routine medical treatment for her child
    and enccunters red tape, long periods of waiting, and
    other dehumanizing procedures that a welfare parent must
    go through. Animated charts show that although the urban
    center cf a city is most densely populated it is the out-
    lying areas which have most of the health care facilities.

INNER CITY DWELLER: WORK
Producer: Indiana University Audio-Visual Center
Tech Info: 16 mm/sound/color/1 reel/19 min.
Date/Country: 1972 + USA   Type: Documentary
Distr/Arch: iu
Annotation: A young unemployed black man who must provide
    for his wife and children enters a job-training program,
    acquires a decent paying job, and is soon laid-off placing
    him back into the same position from which he started.

INNER-CITY SCHOOL: MY FIRST TEACHING ASSIGNMENT
Series: Human Relations: One Dimension of Teaching
Producer: IU-AVC

Tech Info: 16 mm/sound/bw/1 reel/20 min.
Date/Country: 1973 + USA   Type: Documentary
Distr/Arch: iu
Annotation: Follows Rose Brady, a first-year teacher,
    through a typical day with her racially mixed sixth-grade
    class. Observes the teacher and students going about
    their activities which reflect a text book-oriented, in-
    flexible program. Notes that the school is old with
    limited services and facilities.

INNOCENTS_IN_PARIS
Nar/Cast: Alistair Sim + Ronald Shiner + Claire Bloom +
    James Edwards*
Screenplay: Anatole de Grunwald
Producer: Anatole de Grunwald   Director: Gordon Parry
Studio/Company: Favorite Pictures
Date/Country: 1955 + Britain   Type: Feature
Annotation: The comedic adventures of a planeload of British
    tourists over 'the course of a week in Paris. James
    Edwards, as George spends most of his time in a neigh-
    borhood bar.

INSTITUTE_FOR_SEX_RESEARCH_FILM_COLLECTION
Tech Info: 8 mm/16 mm/average length 15 min.
Date/Country: 1922-1972 + USA + Britain + France + Germany +
    Japan + Denmark + Sweden + Mexico + Cuba
Distr/Arch: isr + iu
Annotation: Brief descriptions of each film, dealing with
    some aspect of sexuality, can be found in the Institute
    card file. Collection includes about 140 films of inter-
    racial or intra-racial contact. See instructions for ac-
    cess in Archives Section.

INTERNATIONAL_HOUSE
Nar/Cast: W.C. Fields + Peggy Joyce + Cab Calloway* + Bela
    Lugosi
Screenplay: Lou Heifetz + Neil Brant   Director: Edward
    Sutherland
Studio/Company: Paramount
Tech Info: 16 mm/sound/bw/72 min.
Date/Country: 1933 + USA   Type: Feature
Distr/Arch: swa + twy + uni
Annotation: Comedy which features Cab Calloway singing "Ree-
    fer Man."

INTERNATIONAL_JAZZ_FESTIVAL
Nar/Cast: Julian "Cannonball" Adderley and his Group*
    Director: Patrick Ledoux
Tech Info: 18 min.
Date/Country: 1962 + Belgium
Annotation: Glimpses of the jazz festival in the Ardennes at
    Comblain-la-Tour in 1962.

INTERRUPTED_CRAP_GAME
Studio/Company: Selig Company
Date/Country: 1905 + USA   Type: Comedy Short
Annotation: "Darkies" leave their crap game in order to
    chase a chicken.

INTERVIEW WITH BOBBY SEALE
Producer: Third World Newsreel
Tech Info: 16 mm/sound/bw/15 min.
Date/Country: 1969 + USA   Type: Documentary
Distr/Arch: twn
Annotation: The chairman of the Black Panther Party is in-
    terviewed in a San Francisco jail.

INTERVIEW WITH BRUCE GORDON
Producer: Harold Becker
Tech Info: 16 mm/sound/bw/17 min.
Date/Country: 1964 + USA   Type: Documentary
Distr/Arch: con
Annotation: A young black man working on the voter registra-
    tion drive with the Student Non-Violent Coordinating Com-
    mettee in Selma, Alabama, discusses his beliefs and his
    personal history in the civil rights movement.

INTOLERANCE
Nar/Cast: Lillian Gish + Mae Marsh + Walter Long + Elmo
    Lincoln + Wallace Reid + Eric Von Stroheim
Screenplay: D.W. Griffith
Producer: Wark Producing Corporation   Director: D.W. Grif-
    fith
Studio/Company: WARK
Tech Info: original 35 mm/silent/bw/14 reels/16 mm/silent/bw
    (and tinted version)/180 min.
Date/Country: 1916 + USA   Type: Feature
Distr/Arch: bud + con + cwf + emg + ivy + kpf + mma + sel +
    unf + wil + cie + csv + gme + ncs + nil + thu + moma
Annotation: Ethiopians are part of the socially/racially
    heterogeneous forces of Cyrus (George Seigmann) and his
    "hordes" of barbarians, in the Babylonian segment of In-
    tolerance. William Dark Cloud plays an Ethiopian Chief-
    tain, Charles Eagle Eye, a barbarian chieftain.

INTRODUCING EAST AFRICA
Producer: Editorial Film Productions
Tech Info: 35 mm/bw/1758 ft./20 min.
Date/Country: 1950 + Britain   Type: Documentary
Distr/Arch: iwm
Annotation: Informational film on East Africa.

INTRUDER IN THE DUST
Nar/Cast: Juano Hernandez* + David Brian + Elzie Emmanuel +
    Elizabeth Patterson + Claude Jarman
Screenplay: Ben Maddow   Story: William Faulkner
Producer: Dore Schary   Director: Clarence Brown
Studio/Company: MGM
Tech Info: 16 mm/bw/sound/3 reels/87 min.
Date/Country: 1949 + USA   Type: Feature
Distr/Arch: fnc + eas
Annotation: Racial and social resentments are revealed in
    this story of a barely averted lynching in a small
    Southern town. Even more it is the story of Lucas
    Beauchamp (Juano Hernandez), a black man who would rather
    be lynched for a crime he didn't commit than give up his

dignity.

INTRUDER, THE
Nar/Cast: William Shatner + Charles Barnes* + Jeanne Cooper
    + Beverly Lundsford + Frank Maxwell
Screenplay: Charles Beaumont   Story: Charles Beaumont
Producer: Corman, Roger + Corman, Gene   Director: Roger
    Corman
Studio/Company: Pathe-America
Tech Info: 16 mm/bw/sound/3 reels/87 min.
Date/Country: 1962 + USA   Type: Feature
Annotation: Concerns a racist rabole rouser who goes to a
    small Southern town and arouses the townspeople against
    integration in the local schools.   Charles Barnes plays
    Joey Green, the young man, who is almost a lynch victim.

INVISIBLE GHOST, THE
Nar/Cast: Bela Lugosi + Polly Ann Young + Clarence Muse*
Screenplay: Helen Martin + Al Martin
Producer: Sam Katzman   Director: Joseph Lewis
Studio/Company: Monogram
Date/Country: 1941 + USA   Type: Feature
Annotation: Clarence Muse is Evans in this mystery which has
    Bela Lugosi choking at least one member of his household
    to death in a fit of monomania.

IRISH LUCK
Nar/Cast: Mantan Moreland*
Date/Country: 1938 + USA   Type: Feature
Annotation: Mantan Moreland plays a "faithful righthand man"
    role.

IS MY FACE RED
Nar/Cast: Clarence Muse* + Zazu Pitts + Ricardo Cortez
Screenplay: Ben Markson + Allen Rivkin   Director: William
    Seiter
Studio/Company: RKO
Date/Country: 1932 + USA   Type: Feature
Annotation: Clarence Muse has a bit role as Horace in this
    comedy about a scandal mongering columnist.

ISLAND IN THE SUN
Nar/Cast: Harry Belafonte* + James Mason + Dorothy
    Dandridge* + Joan Fontaine + John Justin
Screenplay: Alfred Hayes   Story: Alec Waugh
Producer: Darryl F. Zanuck   Director: Robert Rossen
Studio/Company: Twentieth Century Fox
Tech Info: 16 mm/color/sound/4 reels/119 min.
Date/Country: 1957 + USA   Type: Feature
Distr/Arch: fnc
Annotation: The Fleurys, an old colonial family in the West
    Indies, are caught up is a political scandal when it's
    discovered that the family has mixed blood.   A conflict
    thus arises between factions for power: the black
    (Belafonte) and the apparently white (Mason). The murder
    of an Englishman and interacial affairs contribute to the
    complexity of relationships in the film. The Dorothy
    Dandridge and John Justin affair works out, the

Belafonte-Fontaine affair does not.

ISN'T IT ROMANTIC?
Nar/Cast: Veronica Lake + Mona Freeman + Pearl Bailey*
Screenplay: Theodore Strauss + Joseph Michel + Richard Breen
Producer: Daniel Dare   Director: Norman Z. McLeod
Studio/Company: Paramount
Tech Info: 87 min.
Date/Country: 1948 + USA   Type: Feature
Annotation: Pearl Bailey plays Addie, the maid, and does
    several comedy songs in this film set in turn-of-the-
    century Indiana.

ISTANBUL
Nar/Cast: Errol Flynn + Cornell Borchers + John Bently + Nat
    King Cole*
Screenplay: Seton Miller + Barbara Gray + Richard Simmons
Producer: Albert J Cohen   Director: Joseph Pevney
Studio/Company: Universal International
Tech Info: 16 mm/sound/color/84 min.
Date/Country: 1957   Type: Feature
Distr/Arch: uni
Annotation: Errol Flynn stumbles onto a cache of stolen
    jewels and runs the tightrope between the police and the
    thieves who want the jewels back. Nat "King" Cole (as
    Danny Rice) contributes background music.

IT_HAPPENED_AT_LAKEWOOD_MANOR
Nar/Cast: Suzanne Somers + Robert Foxworth + Myrna Loy +
    Lynda Day George + Bernie Casey*
Screenplay: Gordon Trueblood + Peter Nelson
Producer: Peter Nelson   Director: Robert Scheerer
Studio/Company: Alan Landsburg Production
Date/Country: 1977 + USA   Type: TV Feature
Annotation: Suspenseful tale of a deadly threat from the
    earth's depths that hits a group of people at a plush sum-
    mer resort. Bernie Casey plays Vince.

IT_HAPPENED_IN_HARLEM
Nar/Cast: Slick and Slack* + Phil Gomez* + Dotty Rhodes* +
    Juanita Pitts* + George Wiltshire* + Mickey O'Daniel* +
    Milton Woods*   Director: Bud Pollard
Studio/Company: All American News, Inc.
Tech Info: 35 mm/sound/bw/3 reels
Date/Country: 1945 + USA   Type: Feature
Distr/Arch: lc

IT_HAPPENED_ONE_SUNDAY
Nar/Cast: Robert Beatty + Barbara White + Judy Kelly + Mar-
    jorie Rhodes + Ernest Butcher + Robert Adams*   Director:
    Karel Lamac
Studio/Company: Associated British
Date/Country: 1945 + Britain   Type: Feature

IT_WON'T_RUB_OFF,_BABY
Alt Title(s): see Sweet Love, Bitter

IT'S_A_BEAR

Series: Our Gang
Nar/Cast: Our Gang + Allen Hoskins* + Ernie Morrison*
Screenplay: Hal Roach
Producer: Hal Roach   Director: Robert McGowan
Studio/Company: Pathe
Tech Info: silent/bw/2 reels
Date/Country: 1924 + USA   Type: Comedy Short
Annotation: With air gun, lasso, sling shot and bow and ar-
    row the gang members head out to Mickey's farm to do some
    big game hunting. Things get out of hand when a bear
    shows up at the end of Ernie's lasso. Allen Hoskins stars
    as Farina.

IT'S_A_BIG_COUNTRY
Nar/Cast: Ethel Barrymore + Keith Brassule
Screenplay: Dore Schary
Producer: Dore Schary   Director: Richard Thorpe + John
    Sturges + Charles Vidor + Don Weis + Clarence Brown + Wil-
    liam A. Wellman + Don Hartman
Studio/Company: MGM
Tech Info: 16 mm/sound/bw/88 min.
Date/Country: 1951 + USA   Type: Feature
Distr/Arch: fnc
Annotation: Film anthology portrays contributions to na-
    tional effort in wartime (World War I), of all ethnic
    groups in America.

IT'S_A_MAD,_MAD,_MAD,_MAD_WORLD
Nar/Cast: Eddie Anderson* + Spencer Tracy + Milton Berle +
    Sid Caeser + Buddy Hackett + Ethel Merman
Screenplay: William Rose + Tania Rose
Producer: Stanley Kramer   Director: Stanley Kramer
Studio/Company: United Artists
Tech Info: 16 mm/sound/color/192 min.
Date/Country: 1963 + USA   Type: Feature
Distr/Arch: uas
Annotation: Zany comedy about various people who hear a dy-
    ing man gasp where a large amount of money was hidden and
    their race to get to it first. Eddie Anderson is the
    first cab driver.

IT'S_GOOD_TO_BE_ALIVE
Nar/Cast: Ruby Dee* + Paul Winfield*
Annotation: The story of baseball great Roy Campanella,
    whose diamond career came to a sudden halt after he was
    crippled in an automobile accident. Dee portrays Cam-
    panella's agonized first wife; and Winfield plays the tit-
    le role.

IT'S_NATION_TIME
Nar/Cast: Jesse Jackson* + Imamu Amiri Baraka* + Julien
    Bond* + Richard Hatcher* + Minister Tours Farrakan*
Producer: NET
Tech Info: 16 mm/sound/bw/1 reel/21 min.
Date/Country: 1970 + USA
Distr/Arch: iu
Annotation: Discusses the themes of nationalism and Pan-
    Africanism at the Congress of African People in Atlanta,

Georgia.   Shows   workshops   on   political   liberation,
creativity, education, and history.   Presents performances
by the Challengers* of Philadelphia, the Pharoah Sanders
Quartet*, and the Last Poets* who do 'Die Nigger Die.'

ITALIAN JOB, THE
Nar/Cast: Michael Caine + Noel Coward
Screenplay: Troy Kennedy Martin
Producer: Michael Delley   Director: Peter Collinson
Studio/Company: Paramount
Tech Info: 16 mm/sound/color/100 min.
Date/Country: 1969 + Britain   Type: Feature
Distr/Arch: fnc
Annotation: Quincy Jones* does the music score and songs for
   this crime thriller.

ITS YOUR THING
Nar/Cast: Jackie "Moms" Mabley* + Ike Turner* + Tina Turner*
   + Isley Brothers* + Clara Ward Singers*
Producer: Ronald Isley   Director: Mike Gargiulo
Studio/Company: Medford Film Corp.
Tech Info: 35 mm/sound/color/108 min.
Date/Country: 1970 + USA   Type: Documentary
Annotation: Soul music concert in Yankee Stadium, June 21,
   1969.

IVANHOE DONALDSON
Producer: Harold Becker + Warren Forma
Tech Info: 16 mm/sound/bw/57 min.
Date/Country: 1964 + USA   Type: Documentary
Distr/Arch: mac
Annotation: Civil Rights work in the South: Core and SNCC
   projects, freedom walks, etc.

IVORY HUNTERS
Nar/Cast: Anthony Steel + Dinah Sheridan + Orlando Martins*
   + Jafeth Ananda* + Johanna Kitou*
Screenplay: W.P. Lipscomb + Ralph Smart + Leslie Norman
Producer: Michael Balcon   Director: Harry Watt
Studio/Company: Arthur Rank Organization
Tech Info: sound/color
Date/Country: 1952 + Britain   Type: Feature
Annotation: A romanticized fictional version of how the Na-
   tional Parks of Kenya were created.   Martins, Ananda,
   Kitou are native to the terrain.

J.D.'S REVENGE
Nar/Cast: Glynn Turman* + Lou Gossett* + Joan Pringle*
   Director: Arthur Marks
Studio/Company: American International
Tech Info: 16 mm/sound/color/95 min.
Date/Country: USA   Type: Feature
Distr/Arch: swa
Annotation: A hoodlum, long dead is reincarnated in the body
   of a young law student whose personality undergoes a hor-
   rible metamorphosis as the spirit of the dead man seeks
   vengeance.

J.T.
Series: CBS Children's Hour
Screenplay: Jane Wagner
Producer: CBS
Studio/Company: Carousel Films, Inc,
Tech Info: 16 mm/bw/sound/2 reels/50 min.
Date/Country: 1969 + USA   Type: Feature
Distr/Arch: iu + roa + carouf
Annotation: J.T. Gambel, a black boy in Harlem does not
  relate well to his hostile environment until he finds a
  friend.   J.T. learns about love, responsibility, honesty,
  and sharing after befriending an alley cat.   Neighborhood
  bullies torment the cat; the cat escapes only to be killed
  in the street traffic, but J.T.'s family and the neighborhood grocer console him.

J'IRAI CRACHER SUR VOS TOMBES
Nar/Cast: Antonella Lualdi + Christian Marquand + Fernand
  Ledoux + Paul Guers
Screenplay: J. Dopagne
Producer: Andre Labrousse   Director: Michael Gast
Studio/Company: C.T.I.
Tech Info: 107 min.
Date/Country: 1959 + France   Type: Feature
Distr/Arch: af
Annotation: In the southern United States, accused of having
  raped a young white girl, a black man is hanged. His
  brother escapes North vowing revenge. He decides to hang
  a young white woman to avenge his brother, but she tells
  him that does not prevent her from loving him.   They
  decide then to flee to Canada, but the police kill them.

JACK JOHNSON
Nar/Cast: Brock Peters*
Screenplay: Al Bodlan
Producer: Jim Jacobs   Director: William Cayton
Tech Info: 16 mm/color/sound/3 reels/90 min.
Date/Country: 1970 + USA   Type: Documentary
Distr/Arch: mac
Annotation: This award winning documentary, nominated for an
  Oscar, captures the excitement of Johnson's flamboyant
  career. (The filmmakers use actual footage from his
  famous ring bouts.) The film portrays Johnson as a man who
  faces difficult struggles and prejudice with humor, pride
  and courage. Music by Miles Davis*.

JACK LONDON
Nar/Cast: Louise Beavers* + Michael O'Shea + Susan Hayward +
  Ossa Massen
Screenplay: Ernest Pascal + Isaac Don Levine
Producer: Samuel Bronston   Director: Alfred Santell
Studio/Company: United Artists
Tech Info: 16 mm/sound/bw/93 min.
Date/Country: 1943 + USA   Type: Feature
Distr/Arch: alb + buc + bud + cfm + fce + fnc + mog + sel +
  tfc + wcf + wil
Annotation: Film biography of Jack London, with Louise
  Beavers playing the type of role which made her famous.

JACKIE ROBINSON STORY, THE
Nar/Cast: Louise Beavers* + Jackie Robinson* + Ruby Dee* +
    Joel Fluellen* + Minov Watson + Bernie Hamilton* + Kenny
    Washington* + Howard Louis McNeely*
Screenplay: Lawrence Taylor + Arthur Mann
Producer: Mort Briskin   Director: Alfred E. Green
Studio/Company: Eagle-Lion Prod.
Tech Info: 16 mm/sound/bw/76 min.
Date/Country: 1950 + USA   Type: Feature
Distr/Arch: bud + fnc + lew + mog
Annotation: The story of Robinson's breakthrough to the
    major leagues and his early playing career. Louise
    Beavers plays Robinson's mother; Ruby Dee plays his
    sweetheart-then-wife Rae.

JACKIE ROBINSON
Producer: Sterling
Tech Info: 16 mm/sound/bw/27 min.
Date/Country: 1965 + USA   Type: Documentary
Distr/Arch: sef
Annotation: A study of the first black player in major
    league baseball.

JACOB LAWRENCE, NEGRO ARTIST
Series: National Archives Gift Collection
Tech Info: 16 mm/color
Annotation: Part of Record Group 200 HF series, Harmon
    Foundation Collection.

JADE MASK, THE
Series: Charlie Chan
Nar/Cast: Mantan Moreland* + Sidney Toler + Edwin Luke +
    Janet Warren   Story: Earl Derr Biggers   Director: Phil
    Rosen
Studio/Company: Monogram
Tech Info: 16 mm/sound/bw/66 min.
Date/Country: 1945 + USA   Type: Feature
Distr/Arch: uas
Annotation: Mantan Moreland is Birmingham Brown, Charlie
    Chan's chauffeur and comic foil.

JAGUAR
Producer: Jean Rouch   Director: Jean Rouch
Tech Info: 16 mm/sound/color/3 reels/93 min. (French narra-
    tion with English subtitles)
Date/Country: 1971   Type: Documentary
Distr/Arch: iu + mghf + cal
Annotation: Follows three young men in pre-independence West
    Africa on their journey of discovery from Niger to the
    Gold Coast and shows each finding employment and adventure
    in either Accra or Kumasi. Concludes with their return
    home where they settle down after having become 'jaguars,'
    or men-of-the-world.

JAILHOUSE BLUES
Nar/Cast: Mamie Smith*   Director: Basil Smith
Studio/Company: Columbia

Tech Info: 9 min.   Type: Musical Short
Annotation: Mamie Smith is featured artist.

JAM SESSION
Nar/Cast: Louis Armstrong* and his orchestra + Charlie
    Barnet and orchestra + Clarence Muse*   Director: Charles
    Barton
Studio/Company: Columbia
Tech Info: 16 mm/bw/sound/74 min.
Date/Country: 1944 + USA   Type: Feature
Distr/Arch: kpf
Annotation: Musical feature with loosely sketched story
    line. Clarence Muse has a comic relief role.

JAMAICANS IN LONDON
Producer: Derrick Knight   Director: Robert Angell
Studio/Company: Company Vukane Ventures Productions
Tech Info: 16 mm/bw/sound/1 reel/30 min.
Date/Country: 1970 + Britain   Type: Dramatic Short
Distr/Arch: con + iu
Annotation: The five-year-old son of an anti-Negro organizer
    and the young daughter of a black Jamaican family meet and
    tour London together. The two children become trapped in
    a condemned building giving the two fathers an opportunity
    to re-examine their racial attitudes.

JAMBOREE
Alt Title(s): Disc Jockey Jamboree
Nar/Cast: Count Basie* + Joe Williams* + Fats Domino*
    Director: Roy Lockwood
Tech Info: 86 min.
Date/Country: 1957 + USA   Type: Feature
Annotation: Popular entertainers are introduced through a
    sketchy story line and apperances are made by jazz
    artists. Numbers include "One O'Clock Jump" and "Wait and
    See."

JAMES BALDWIN FROM ANOTHER PLACE
Nar/Cast: James Baldwin*
Producer: Sedat Pakay   Director: Sedat Pakay
Tech Info: 16 mm/bw/sound/1 reel/11 min.
Date/Country: 1975 + Istanbul + Turkey   Type: Documentary
Distr/Arch: rad
Annotation: Baldwin is shown in the visually exotic environ-
    ment of Turkey, far from the United States and at home
    among the people of a foreign culture. Baldwin discusses
    his personal life, his role as artist and his American
    past.

JAMES BROWN: THE MAN
Producer: NBC
Tech Info: 16 mm/sound/color/15 min.
Date/Country: 1974 + USA   Type: Documentary
Distr/Arch: ste
Annotation: The life and career of James Brown*. Includes
    some musical performances. Provided by Center for
    Southern Folklore.

JAMES WELDON JOHNSON
Series: Poetry by Americans
Producer: Oxford
Tech Info: 16 mm/sound/color/12 min.
Date/Country: 1972 + USA   Type: Documentary
Distr/Arch: oxf
Annotation: Portrait of James Weldon Johnson, executive
    secretary of the NAACP, poet, diplomat, musician, teacher.
    Raymond St. Jacques*, reads Johnson's 'The Creation' from
    God's Trombones.

JAMMIN' THE BLUES
Nar/Cast: Harry Edison* + Lester Young* + Illinois Jacquet*
    + Philly Jo Jones* + Sidney Catlett* + Red Callender* +
    Marie Bryant* + Barney Kessel
Producer: Norman Granz   Director: Gjon Mili
Studio/Company: Warner Brothers
Tech Info: 16 mm/bw/sound/1 reel/10 min.
Date/Country: 1944 + USA   Type: Musical Short
Distr/Arch: kpf
Annotation: Photographed by Gjon Mili, this film is a semi-
    documentary of a "jam session" in a black nightclub.
    Barney Kessel (white) is shot in silhouette.

JANIE
Nar/Cast: Joyce Reynolds + Robert Hutton + Hattie McDaniel*
    + Alan Hale
Screenplay: Agnes C. Johnston + Charles Hoffman
Producer: Alex Gottlieb   Director: Michael Curtiz
Studio/Company: Warner Brothers
Tech Info: 16 mm/sound/bw/102 min.
Date/Country: 1944 + USA   Type: Feature
Distr/Arch: uas
Annotation: Story of how precocious children can keep the
    home in a constant uproar, with Hattie McDaniel playing
    the maid.

JASPER LANDRY'S WILL
Alt Title(s): Uncle Jasper's Will
Nar/Cast: William E. Fontaine* + Shingzie Howard*
Studio/Company: Micheaux Film Corporation
Date/Country: 1923 + USA   Type: Feature

JASPER SERIES
Producer: George Pal
Studio/Company: Paramount
Tech Info: 16 mm/sound/color/10 min.
Date/Country: 1946 + USA   Type: Animated Short
Distr/Arch: kpf
Annotation: George Pal's series produced in the forties with
    Jasper as a Negro boy "puppetoon" - animated puppet, com-
    plete with bug eyes and a penchant for watermelon. He has
    a protective "Mammy" and together they have innumerable
    experiences, usually some confrontation with a black
    scarecrow hustler and his sidekick, a fast talking crow.
    Jasper in a Jam and Jasper in a Haunted House are two cur-
    rently available for rental.

JAVA_HEAD
Nar/Cast: Anna May Wong + Elizabeth Allan + Ralph Richardson
    + Herbert Lomas + Orlando Martins*
Screenplay: Martin Brown + Gordon Wellesley
Producer: Basil Dean   Director: J. Walter Ruben
Studio/Company: 1st Division Exchange
Date/Country: 1935 + Britain   Type: Feature
Annotation: Martin has a small role in this adaptation of
    Joseph Hergesheimer's novel which on the screen is sim-
    plified into a story about the son of a famous shipping
    family who brings home a Manchu lady (Wong) as his wife
    and shocks the neighbors.

JAZZ_DANCE:_CHICAGO_STYLE
Producer: WTTW-TV, Chicago
Tech Info: 16 mm/sound/bw/27 min.
Date/Country: 1970 + USA   Type: Documentary
Distr/Arch: orr
Annotation: The background of jazz dancing in Chicago.
    Provided by Center for Southern Folklore.

JAZZ_FESTIVAL
Nar/Cast: Lionel Hampton* + Ruth Brown* + Larry Darnell* +
    Cab Calloway* + The Clovers* + Herb Jeffries* + Bill
    Bailey* + Dinah Washington* + Nipsey Russell* + Mantan
    Moreland* + Duke Ellington* + The Larks* + Count Basie* +
    Sarah Vaughan*
Producer: Ben Frye   Director: Joseph Kohn
Studio/Company: Studio Films, Inc.
Tech Info: 35 mm/bw/sound/7 reels
Date/Country: 1955 + USA   Type: Feature
Distr/Arch: lc

JAZZ_FESTIVAL
Nar/Cast: Mantan Moreland* + Nipsy Russell* + Duke Elling-
    ton* + The Larks* + Ames Milburn* + Cab Calloway* + Sarah
    Vaughan* + Count Basie*
Producer: Ben Frye   Director: Joseph Kohn
Studio/Company: Studio Films, Inc.
Tech Info: 35 mm/tinted/sound/4 reels
Date/Country: 1955 + USA   Type: Musical Short
Distr/Arch: lc
Annotation: This is a short version of the film listed as
    Jazz Festival above.

JAZZ_IS_MY_RELIGION
Producer: John Jeremy   Director: John Jeremy
Tech Info: 16 mm/sound/bw/50 min.   Type: Documentary
Distr/Arch: imp
Annotation: Music by: Johnny Griffin*; jazz poems by Lang-
    ston Hughes*, Ted Joans*, read by Joans. Uses voices of:
    Sunny Murray*, Johnny Griffin*, Jon Hendricks*, Julio
    Finn*, Guy Warren*, Dewey Redman*, Blue Mitchell*, Jo
    Jones*, Dizzy Gillespie*, Jimmy Garrison*, Bill Evans*,
    Andrew Cryille*, Kenny Clarke*, Marion Brown*, Art
    Blakey*, Rashied Ali*. Traces the jazz roots of blues and
    other contemporary music.

JAZZ_IS_OUR_RELIGION
Nar/Cast: Johnny Griffin + Dizzy Reece + Ignatius Quail + Coleridge Goode + Terri Quaye + Rudi Henderson + Jon Hendricks* + The Clarke-Boland Band + Ted Joans*
Director: John Jeremy
Tech Info: 50 min.
Date/Country: 1972 + Britain
Annotation: A compilation of the place jazz has in the lives of its performers through words and music. Ted Joans reads his poem, "Jazz is My Religion."

JAZZ_ON_A_SUMMER'S_DAY
Nar/Cast: Louis Armstrong* + Jimmy Giuffre Trio + Thelonious Monk* + Henry Grimes + Sonny Stitt* + Sal Salvador + Anita O'Day + George Shearing Quartet + Dinah Washington* + Gerry Mulligan + Big Maybelle* + Chuck Berry* + Chico Hamilton Quintet* + Mahalia Jackson* + Jack Teagarden
Screenplay: Arnold Perl + Albert D'Anniable
Producer: Bert Stern   Director: Bert Stern
Studio/Company: Raven Films, Inc.
Tech Info: 16 mm/color/sound/3 reels/85 min.
Date/Country: 1960 + USA   Type: Feature
Distr/Arch: nyf
Annotation: Newport Jazz Festival artists are featured in this record of Newport, Rhode Island in the summer of 1958.

JAZZ_SINGER,_THE
Nar/Cast: Al Jolson + May McAvory + Warner Oland + Eugenie Besserer + Otto Lederer
Screenplay: Alfred A. Cohn   Story: Samson Raphaelson
Director: Alan Crosland
Studio/Company: Warner Brothers
Tech Info: 16 mm/bw/sound/3 reels/89 min.
Date/Country: 1927 + USA   Type: Feature
Distr/Arch: uas
Annotation: Sam Warner's vitaphone found its first voice on screen in The Jaz Singer. Al Jolson plays Jack Rabinowitz, a cantor's son, who is caught between his devotion to family and tradition and his deep love for the jazz his father feels is sacriligious. Jolson dons blackface in the famous rendition of "Mammy."

JAZZ,_THE_INTIMATE_ART
Nar/Cast: Louis Armstrong* + Dizzy Gillespie* + Dave Brubeck + James Moody
Producer: Robert Drew + Mike Jackson
Tech Info: sound/color/53 min.
Date/Country: 1968 + USA   Type: Documentary
Annotation: Four jazzmen are interviewed by Dan Morrow; they are also seen in concert.

JEFFRIES-JOHNSON_1910   Director: William Kimberlin
Studio/Company: Contemporary + McGraw Hill
Tech Info: 16 mm/sound/bw/1 reel/21 min.   Type: Documentary
Distr/Arch: con
Annotation: The film is a powerful re-creation of this un-

forgettable championship match, which made Jack Johnson
the first black heavyweight champion of the world. Shot
from rare old footage, with narration and an original ragtime score, the film documents the historic fight, the
racist campaign which preceded it, and the anxious world
that awaited its results.

JERICHO
Alt Title(s): Dark Sands
Nar/Cast: Paul Robeson* + Henry Wilcoxen + Wallace Ford +
   Princess Kouka* + James Carew + Lawrence Brown + Ike Hatch
   + Rufus Fennell + Frank Cochrane + George Barraud +
   Orlando Martins* + Eslanda Goode Robeson*   Director:
   Thornton Freeland
Studio/Company: Buckingham
Tech Info: 16 mm/bw/sound/2 reels/75 min.
Date/Country: 1937 + Britain   Type: Feature
Distr/Arch: kpf
Annotation: Robeson portrays Jericho a falsely convicted
   soldier who flees from war time France to Africa where he
   lives as a desert sheik, saving an Arab caravan and being
   saved by his white Gunga Din, Wallace Ford. Jericho's
   pursuer finds him and attempts to take him back to stand
   trial.

JESSE "LONE CAT" FULLER
Producer: Seattle Folklore Society
Tech Info: 25 min.
Date/Country: 1968 + USA   Type: Documentary
Annotation: Jesse Fuller* performs his blues and includes
   some favorites like "John Henry" and "Red River Blues."

JESSE FROM MISSISSIPPI
Series: Newcomers to the City
Producer: Encyclopedia Britannica Educational Corp.
Tech Info: 16 mm/sound/color/1 reel/14 min.
Date/Country: 1971 + USA   Type: Documentary
Distr/Arch: iu + ebec
Annotation: Discusses the problems encountered by a black
   couple who move with their son Jesse from a farm in Mis-
   sissippi, to a northern city, in adjusting to city life.

JESSE JAMES
Nar/Cast: Ernest Whitman* + Tyrone Power + Henry Fonda +
   Nancy Kelly
Screenplay: Nunnally Johnson
Producer: Darryl F. Zanuck   Director: Henry King
Studio/Company: Fox
Tech Info: sound/color
Date/Country: 1939 + USA   Type: Feature
Annotation: Ernest Whitman plays Pinkie, strong black role
   as confidant, in this fictional biography of the famous
   outlaw Jesse James (Power).

JESSIE OWENS RETURNS TO BERLIN
Producer: Cappy
Tech Info: 16 mm/sound/bw/54 min. (also available in two 27
   min. films)

Date/Country: 1965   Type: Documentary
Distr/Arch: mgh
Annotation: The 1936 Olympics as viewed by Jessie Owens*.
    Some actual footage of the games in Berlin.

JESUS CHRIST SUPERSTAR
Nar/Cast: Carl Anderson* + Yvonne Elliman + Ted Neely
Screenplay: Melvyn Braggs + Norman Jewison   Story: Tim
    Price
Producer: Norman Jewison + Robert Stigwood   Director:
    Norman Jewison
Studio/Company: Universal
Tech Info: 16 mm/sound/color (available in Cinemascope)/3
    reels/108 min.
Date/Country: 1973 + USA   Type: Feature
Distr/Arch: cwf + swa + twy + uni
Annotation: A rock-musical version of the life and death of
    Jesus features a black man in the role of Judas Iscariot
    (Carl Anderson).

JEZEBEL
Nar/Cast: Bette Davis + Henry Fonda + George Brent +
    Margaret Lindsay + Donald Crisp + Fay Bainter + Richard
    Cromwell + Lew Payton* + Eddie Anderson* + Matthew Beard*
    + Theresa Anderson*
Screenplay: Clements Ripley + Aben Finkel + John Houston
    Story: Owen Davis, Sr.   Director: William Wyler
Studio/Company: Warner Brothers
Tech Info: 16 mm/bw/sound/3 reels/104 min.
Date/Country: 1938 + USA   Type: Feature
Distr/Arch: uas
Annotation: Jezebel is a melodrama of a vengeful woman
    scorned in antebellum Louisiana. Naturalistic treatment
    of Blacks as servants and slaves, romance of ante-bellum
    New Orleans with its atmosphere of mystery and foreboding,
    provide the setting.

JIM COMES TO JO'BURG
Producer: John Swanson   Director: John Swanson
Date/Country: 1949 + South Africa
Annotation: Jim* is a country boy who goes to the big city
    of Johannesburg. Filmed in Praetoria, South Africa, the
    story shows how Jim is victimized by the city's harsh
    values and later is redeemed through the patronage of
    benevolent whites.

JIMI HENDRIX
Nar/Cast: Jimi Hendrix* + Eric Clapton + Peter Townshend
Producer: Joe Boyd + John Head + Gary Weis
Studio/Company: Warner Brothers
Tech Info: 16 mm/sound/color/102 min.
Date/Country: 1973   Type: Documentary
Distr/Arch: wsa
Annotation: Covered in this documentary about rock star Jimi
    Hendrix who died at age 27 of overdose of barbituates such
    prominent musicians as Eric Clapton and Peter Townshend as
    well as Hendrix's friends and business associates. Inter-
    views are interspersed with performances.

JIMI PLAYS BERKELEY
Nar/Cast: Jimi Hendrix*
Producer: Peter Pilafian + Eric Saarinen + Joan Churchill +
  Baird Bryant
Studio/Company: Dor Jamm Productions
Tech Info: 55 min.
Date/Country: 1971 + USA   Type: Documentary
Annotation: Film of Jimi Hendrix's 1970 Memorial Day concert
  at Berkeley, California. Includes short interview seg-
  ments with "Hendrix assoc."

JIMMIE LUNCEFORD AND HIS DANCE ORCHESTRA   Director: Joseph
  Henabery
Tech Info: 10 min.
Date/Country: 1936 + USA   Type: Musical Short
Annotation: Features the band with The Three Brown Jacks*
  and vocalist Myra Johnson*.

JIMTOWN SPEAKEASY
Nar/Cast: Aubrey Lyles* + Flournoy E. Miller*
Studio/Company: MGM
Date/Country: 192- + USA
Annotation: Miller and Lyles do a comedy bootlegger routine
  and add much of the stage business from their successful
  Shuffle Along (1921) Broadway production to this MGM
  comedy.

JITTERING JITTER-BUGS
Nar/Cast: Hamtree Harrington* + Lee Norman's* Orchestra +
  Arthur White's* Lindy Hoppers   Director: Walter Graham
Tech Info: 16 mm/bw/sound/1 reel/12 min.
Date/Country: 1938 + USA   Type: Musical Short
Distr/Arch: kpf
Annotation: Hamtree, et. al., are the stars in this musical
  comedy which takes place in Harlem.

JIVIN IN BE BOP
Nar/Cast: Dizzy Gillespie* + Helen Humes* + Ray Sneed* +
  Sahji* + Freddie Carter* + Ralph Brown* + Dan Durley* +
  Johnny Taylor* + Phil and Audrey* + Jonny* and Henny* +
  Daisy Richardson* + Panch and Dolores*
Producer: William D.Alexander   Director: Leonard Anderson +
  Spencer Williams*
Studio/Company: William D. Alexander Presents
Tech Info: 16 mm/bw/sound/2 reels/60 min.
Date/Country: 1947 + USA   Type: Feature
Distr/Arch: kpf + emg
Annotation: One of the greatest of all jazz stars appears in
  this feature length show playing most of his Bop hits of
  the forties. A number of other black entertainers,
  dancers, and singers appear as well.

JOANNA
Nar/Cast: Glenna Foster Jones* + Genevieve Waite + Calvin
  Lockhart* + Don Sutherland
Screenplay: Michael Sarne
Producer: Michael S. Laughlin   Director: Michael Sarne

Studio/Company: 20th Century Fox
Tech Info: 16 mm/cinemascope available/color/sound/3 reels/
   107 min.
Date/Country: 1968 + Britain   Type: Feature
Distr/Arch: fnc
Annotation: Calvin Lockhart plays Gordon, husband of Joanna,
   in this story of her disjointed odyssey through life.
   She's an art student, he, the owner of a nightclub who
   gets into difficulty with the protection racket and
   eventually kills one of the gangsters to get revenge for
   the vicious beating they gave him.

JOB, THE
Series: A Study In Color
Tech Info: 16 mm/sound/bw/29 min.
Distr/Arch: adl
Annotation: A sophisticated approach to the problem of raci-
   al prejudice, this humorous satire attacks the hypocrisy
   of using race as an angle to promote movies, plays or
   books.

JOE LOUIS STORY, THE
Nar/Cast: Coley Wallace* + Paul Stewart + Hilda Simms* +
   James Edwards*
Screenplay: Robert Sylvester
Producer: Sterling Silliphant   Director: Robert Gordon
Studio/Company: United Artists
Tech Info: 16 mm/bw/sound/3 reels/87 min.
Date/Country: 1953 + USA   Type: Feature
Distr/Arch: roa + aim + bud + cwf + mac + new + twy + wcf
Annotation: A fictional dramatization of Louis' career in
   the ring features actual sequences of his ring battles
   with Braddock, Baer, Carnera, and others.

JOE PALOOKA IN THE KNOCKOUT
Nar/Cast: Clarence Muse*
Date/Country: 1947 + USA   Type: Feature
Annotation: Muse plays a small role.

JOEY
Nar/Cast: Carla Pinza + Jean Paul Delgado + Niger Akoni*
   Director: Luis San Andres
Tech Info: 16 mm/sound/color/2 reels/54 min.
Date/Country: USA   Type: Feature
Distr/Arch: ics
Annotation: Story of a young Puerto Rican boy befriended by
   a black karate instructor who helps him master the wisdom
   as well as the techniques of karate.

JOHN AND MARY
Nar/Cast: Dustin Hoffman + Mia Farrow
Screenplay: John Mortimer
Producer: Ben Kadish   Director: Peter Yates
Studio/Company: Fox
Tech Info: sound/color/192 min.
Date/Country: 1969 + USA   Type: Feature
Annotation: Romantic comedy in the sixties live-in/roomate
   tradition. Music and song by Quincy Jones*.

JOHN COLTRANE QUARTET, THE
Series: Jazz Casual
Producer: Ralph Gleason + KQED
Tech Info: 30 min.
Date/Country: 1963 + USA   Type: TV Documentary
Annotation: Thirty minutes of performance by the Coltrane*
    Quartet includes "Afro Blues."

JOHN HENRY
Producer: Jerry Weiss + BFA Educational Media
Tech Info: 16 mm/sound/color/11 min.
Date/Country: 1972 + USA
Distr/Arch: bfa
Annotation: Documents the legend of John Henry the railroad
    worker. Provided by Center for Southern Folklore.

JOHN OUTERBRIDGE: BLACK ARTIST
Producer: Lewis-Wong
Tech Info: 16 mm/sound/color/21 min.
Date/Country: 1971   Type: Documentary
Distr/Arch: aci
Annotation: Shows how a metal sculptor works and how Outer-
    bridge's ideas are reflected in his work.

JOHNNY COME LATELY
Alt Title(s): See Johnny Vagabond

JOHNNY COOL
Nar/Cast: Sammy Davis, Jr.* + Henry Silva + Elizabeth Mont-
    gomery
Screenplay: Joseph Landon
Producer: William Asher   Director: William Asher
Studio/Company: United Artists
Date/Country: 1964 + USA   Type: Feature
Annotation: Davis as "Educated," a sophisticated "hanger-on"
    in the underworld's gambling casinos. Plot turns on un-
    derworld life and intra-gang rivalry.

JOHNNY VAGABOND
Alt Title(s): Johnny Come Lately
Nar/Cast: James Cagney + Grace George + Hattie McDaniel*
Screenplay: John Van Druten
Producer: William Cagney   Director: William K. Howard
Studio/Company: United Artists
Date/Country: 1943 + USA   Type: Feature
Annotation: Hattie McDaniel plays Aida in this adaptation of
    Louis Bromfield's story, "McLeod's Folly," with Cagney as
    a vagrant newspaper man who helps an aging woman publisher
    of a small town newspaper battle the "bad guys."

JOINT IS JUMPING, THE
Nar/Cast: John Mason* + Charles Ray + J. Patrick Patterson* +
    Hattie Weaver*   Director: Josh Binney
Studio/Company: All American News, Inc.
Tech Info: 35 mm/bw/silent (later sound)/4 reels
Date/Country: 1948 + USA
Distr/Arch: lc

JOINT
Alt Title(s): see Baks

JOMO KENYATTA
Producer: ABC-TV
Tech Info: bw/29 min./sound
Date/Country: 1965 + Kenya   Type: TV Documentary
Annotation: Interviews and discussions with Jomo Kenyatta,
    president of Kenya and Bruce McKenzie, the one white
    cabinet member of Kenyatta's cabinet. Includes scenes of
    Kikuyu and Masai life.

JOSHUA
Producer: Bert Salzman
Tech Info: 16 mm/bw/sound/1 reel/16 min.
Date/Country: 1968
Distr/Arch: iu + aci
Annotation: Examines the personal encounters that Joshua, a
    black ghetto teenager, has with three people on the day
    before he leaves for college on a track scholarship. In-
    dicates Joshua's moods through the use of visual images
    and a changing background of either hard-rock music or
    silence.

JOURNEY TO SHILOH
Nar/Cast: Charles Lampkin* + Rex Ingram* + James Caan
Screenplay: Gene Coon
Producer: Howard Christie   Director: William Hale
Studio/Company: Universal
Tech Info: 16 mm/sound/color/92 min.
Date/Country: 1968 + USA   Type: Feature
Distr/Arch: ccc + cwf + tmc + uni
Annotation: Ingram is Jacob and Lampkin is Edward in this
    Civil War melodrama about six young men and their dream of
    glory which turns into a nightmare early when they witness
    the execution of a runaway slave.

JOY SCOUTS
Series: Our Gang
Nar/Cast: Our Gang + Billie Thomas*
Screenplay: Hal Law + Robert A. McGowan
Producer: Jack Chertok   Director: Edward Cahn
Studio/Company: MGM
Tech Info: bw/sound/1 reel
Date/Country: 1939 + USA   Type: Comedy Short
Annotation: Told they are too young to join the Boy Scouts,
    the gang goes off on a disastrous camping trip of its own
    and needs to be rescued by the Scouts. Billie Thomas
    stars as Buckwheat.

JUBILO, JR.
Series: Our Gang
Nar/Cast: Our Gang + Allen Hoskins* + Will Rogers
Screenplay: Hal Roach
Producer: Hal Roach   Director: Robert McGowan
Studio/Company: Pathe
Tech Info: silent/bw/2 reels

Date/Country: 1924 + USA   Type: Comdey Short
Annotation: Jubilo (Will Rogers) reminisces back to when he
  was young and wanted to get his mother a birthday present.
  In the flashback sequences, Mickey plays Jubilo, Jr., who
  tries various schemes to raise money, and finally, with
  the gang's help, puts on a circus performance to do so.
  Allen Hoskins stars as Farina.

JUDGE HORTON AND THE SCOTTSBORO BOYS
Nar/Cast: Arthur Hill + Vera Miles
Date/Country: USA   Type: TV Feature
Annotation: Drama of the notorious Scottsboro case from the
  point of view of the judge, played by Arthur Hill.

JUDGE PRIEST
Nar/Cast: Will Rogers + Henry B. Walthall + Rochelle Hudson
  + Hattie McDaniel* + Stepin Fetchit*
Screenplay: Dudley Nichols + La Mar Trotti
Producer: Sol Wurtzel   Director: John Ford
Studio/Company: Fox
Tech Info: 16 mm/bw/sound/3 reels/80 min.
Date/Country: 1934 + USA   Type: Feature
Distr/Arch: fnc
Annotation: Will Rogers movie about a homespun judge in a
  small southern town, highlighted by give and take between
  Rogers and Fetchit, the putative chicken thief. McDaniel
  is Aunt Dilsey; she and the Judge duet together on "My Old
  Kentucky Home."

JUDGE'S STORY, THE
Studio/Company: Thanhauser
Date/Country: 1911 + USA
Annotation: A young black worker is saved by a judge who in
  effect repays a debt of gratitude to the young man.   The
  story is told in a flashback by a "Mammy" character.

JUKE JOINT
Nar/Cast: Spencer Williams* + July Jones* + Mantan Moreland*
Producer: Alfred Sack   Director: Spencer Williams*
Studio/Company: Harlemwood + Sack Attractions
Tech Info: 35 mm/bw/sound/7 reels
Date/Country: 1947 + USA   Type: Feature
Distr/Arch: lc
Annotation: Williams, Moreland and Jones in a backstage plot
  set in Texas; includes a jitterbug contest, a staple of
  the forties.

JULY DAYS
Series: Our Gang
Nar/Cast: Our Gang + Ernie Morrison* + Allen Hoskins*
Screenplay: Hal Roach
Producer: Hal Roach   Director: Robert McGowan
Studio/Company: Pathe
Tech Info: silent/bw/2 reels
Date/Country: 1923 + USA   Type: Comedy Short
Annotation: Mickey falls for the new girl on the block and
  goes to extremes to show her, even to the extent of having
  a suit of armor made out of pots and pans. Allen Hoskins

stars as Farina.

JUNCTION 88
Nar/Cast: Noble Sissle* + Bob Howard* + Dewey "Pigmeat"
  Markham* + Wyatt Clark*
Tech Info: 35 mm/sound/bw/6 reels
Date/Country: 194-
Distr/Arch: lc

JUNGLE FREAKS
Alt Title(s): see Macunaima

JUNGLE GENTS
Nar/Cast: The Bowery Boys + Robert "Smokey" Whitfield*
  Director: Edward Bernds
Studio/Company: Allied Artists
Tech Info: 16 mm/sound/bw/64 min.
Date/Country: 1954 + USA   Type: Feature
Distr/Arch: cin

JUNGLE QUEEN
Nar/Cast: Dorothy Dandridge*   Director: Ray Taylor + Lewis
  Collins
Date/Country: 1946 + USA   Type: Feature

JUNGLE SEX
Alt Title(s): see Black Bunch

JUNGLE TRAIL, THE
Studio/Company: Fox
Date/Country: 1919 + USA   Type: Feature
Annotation: A white man's "great strength" begets him the
  worshipful obeisance of a black tribe over whom he then
  rules.

JUNGLE, THE
Producer: 12th Oxford Street Film-makers Corp.
Tech Info: 16 mm/sound/bw
Date/Country: 1968 + USA   Type: Dramatized Documentary
Distr/Arch: uca
Annotation: A study of gang life in the Philadelphia ghetto,
  made by the 12th and Oxford Street gang.

JUST AROUND THE CORNER
Nar/Cast: Bill Robinson* + Shirley Temple + Joan Davis +
  Bert Lahr + Charles Farrell
Screenplay: Ethel Hill + J.P. McEvoy + Darrell Ware   Story:
  Paul G. Smith
Producer: Darryl F. Zanuck Director: Irving Cummings
Studio/Company: 20th Century Fox
Tech Info: 16 mm/sound/bw/70 min.
Date/Country: 1938 + USA   Type: Feature
Distr/Arch: fnc
Annotation: Shirley Temple sets out to end the depression by
  having a talent show and sending the proceeds to Uncle Sam
  to start jobs programs. The film contains a performance
  by Robinson.

JUSTICE?
Producer: NET
Tech Info: 16 mm/sound/bw/59 min./2 reels
Date/Country: 1971 + USA   Type: Documentary
Distr/Arch: iu
Annotation: This examination of black justice in American
    courts and prisons includes interviews with prisoners,
    students, defense attorneys, and others with emphasis upon
    the cases of Angela Davis and the Soledad Brothers.

KADDU BEYKAT
Screenplay: Safi Faye*
Producer: Safi Faye*   Director: Safi Faye*
Tech Info: 95 min./in Wolof with some French commentary
Date/Country: 1975 + Senegal   Type: Dramatized Documentary
Annotation: Monitors the daily life of an agricultural
    peasant. Depicts poverty and governmental policies that
    seem to perpetuate it through the efforts of a peasant to
    marry despite the money he lacks to support a wife and pay
    for the traditional marriage ritual.

KAERLIGHEDENS MELODI
Alt Title(s): Formula for Love + A Girl, a Guitar, and a
    Trumpet   Director: Bent Christensen
Tech Info: 87 min.
Date/Country: 1959 + Denmark   Type: Feature
Annotation: Features Louis Armstrong* and Velma Middleton*
    in a jazz cellar sequence in this Danish musical film.

KAFFIR'S GRATITUDE, THE
Studio/Company: Biograph
Date/Country: 1915 + USA   Type: Dramatic Short
Annotation: Loyalty is the reason behind the "Kaffir," a
    black man, saving a white man's diamond fortune.

KALAHARI, THE
Producer: Don Meier Productions + Mutual of Omaha
Studio/Company: Don Meier Productions
Tech Info: 16 mm/sound/color/1 reel/25 min.
Date/Country: 1964 + Botswana   Type: Documentary
Distr/Arch: nbcee
Annotation: Briefly documents the land, people and wildlife
    of the Kalahari Desert.

KARIM
Screenplay: Ousame Soce Diop*   Director: Momar Thiam*
Date/Country: 1970 + Senegal   Type: Feature
Annotation: Complicated story of a young bookkeeper's aide,
    Karim, who loses out in the traditional courtship of
    Mareme when another, more affluent suitor, Bodara, claims
    her hand. Leaving St. Louis for Dakar, he becomes in-
    volved with the distractions of the city, other women,
    young French speaking intellectuals; finally he loses his
    job and returns home. There he finds that his rival has
    been sent to jail for embezzlement and he is able to marry
    Mareme.

KEEP ON ROCKIN'

Nar/Cast: Bo Diddley* + Little Richard* + Chuck Berry*
Producer: D.A. Pennebaker
Tech Info: 16 mm/sound/color/90 min.
Date/Country: 1969 + USA   Type: Documentary
Distr/Arch: pen
Annotation: Performances at the Toronto Rock and Roll
  Revival. Provided by Center for Southern Folklore.

KEEP PUNCHING
Nar/Cast: Henry Armstrong* + Canada Lee* + Dooley Wilson* +
  Alvin Childress* + Francine Everett* + Lionel Monagas* +
  Willie Bryant* + Mae Johnson* + Hamtree Harrington*
  Director: John Clein
Tech Info: bw/sound
Date/Country: 1939 + USA   Type: Feature
Annotation: A fight film with the prone to womanize-and-gam-
  ble boxer (Armstrong) almost seduced by the fast life and
  an equally fast woman (Johnson) but keeps his equilibrium,
  wins the bout and ends up happily with the "good" woman
  (Everett).

KEEP WEST
Nar/Cast: Woody Strode* + Stephen Boyd + Sheree North
Screenplay: Anthony S. Martin
Producer: Anthony S. Martin   Director: Ralph Leacock
Studio/Company: Warner Brothers
Date/Country: 1972 + USA   Type: TV Feature
Annotation: Strode plays Candy Rhodes, ex-fighter, right
  hand man to Steve (Boyd) retired CIA/Justice Department
  man who has to defend himself against a dead man's in-
  genious revenge plan.

KEITH TURNS 18
Producer: John Friedman
Tech Info: 16 mm/sound/color/18 min.
Date/Country: 1974 + USA   Type: Documentary
Distr/Arch: edc
Annotation: The interest in classical ballet by a young
  black man and his participation in his own dance group.

KENNER
Nar/Cast: Jim Brown* + Madlyn Rhue + Robert Coote
Screenplay: Harold Clemins + John P. Loring
Producer: Mary P. Murray   Director: Steve Sekely
Studio/Company: MGM
Tech Info: 16 mm/sound/color/92 min.
Date/Country: 1964 + USA   Type: Feature
Distr/Arch: fnc
Annotation: Brown is cast as Kenner, a foot loose American
  sailor of fortune, who has a brief affair with Madlyn Rhue
  in Bombay and befriends her fatherless son.

KENTUCKY KERNALS
Nar/Cast: Willie Best* + Bert Wheeler + Spanky McFarland +
  Paul Page
Screenplay: Bert Kalmar + Harry Ruby + Fred Guiol
  Director: George Stevens
Studio/Company: RKO Radio Pictures

Tech Info: 16 mm/sound/bw
Date/Country: 1934 + USA   Type: Feature
Distr/Arch: fnc
Annotation: Bert Wheeler and Robert Woodsey take former Our
    Ganger "Spanky" McFarland to claim his estate and get
    caught up in family feuds.   This movie features Willie
    Best, listed on the credits as Sleep 'n' Eat.

KENTUCKY MINSTRELS
Alt Title(s): Life is Real
Nar/Cast: Scott and Whaley + C. Denier Warren + Wilson
    Coleman + Norman Green
Studio/Company: Gaumont
Date/Country: 1934 + Britain   Type: Feature
Annotation: Released in the United States as *Life is Real*,
    this British film depicts the career of a blackface En-
    glish stage minstrel duo (Scott and Whaley) with some
    Blacks in the cast.

KENTUCKY
Nar/Cast: Loretta Young + Walter Brennan + George Reed* +
    Madame Sul-te-Wan* + Eddie Anderson*
Screenplay: Lamar Trotti + John Taintor Foote   Story: John
    Taintor Foote
Producer: Darryl F. Zanuck   Director: David Butler
Studio/Company: Twentieth Century Fox
Tech Info: 16 mm/sound/color/96 min.
Date/Country: 1938 + USA   Type: Feature
Distr/Arch: fnc
Annotation: George Reed is Ben and Madame Sul-te-Wan is Lily
    in this horseracing tale which includes a feud, a fore-
    closure on the old plantation, a love affair, and a happy
    ending.

KENYA BORAN
Series: Faces of Change
Producer: American University Field Staff
Tech Info: 16 mm/sound/color/2 reels/65 min.
Date/Country: 1974 + USA   Type: Documentary
Distr/Arch: iu + aufs
Annotation: Documents, focusing on two fathers and their
    sons, the effects of mechanization, modern education, and
    the central government as they reach a formerly isolated
    village in northern Kenya. Shows the conflict between old
    and new ways and leads to speculation on the outcome of
    the society's choices.

KENYA: THE MULTI-RACIAL EXPERIMENT
Nar/Cast: Gregory Peck
Producer: ABC
Studio/Company: ABC
Tech Info: 16 mm/color/sound/1 reel/19 min.
Date/Country: 1968 + Kenya   Type: Documentary
Annotation: The different forms of black-white relations in
    Africa are studied by examining in turn the Atlantic slave
    trade, the position of white settlers in Kenya, and
    Kenya's current race policies.

KENYATTA
Series: Kenya Trilogy
Producer: Anthony-David Productions
Tech Info: 16 mm/sound/color/51 min.; 28 min. (edited
    version)
Date/Country: 1973 + Kenya   Type: Documentary
Distr/Arch: fnc
Annotation: A filmed biography of Jomo Kenyatta, President
    of Kenya. Uses interviews, photographs, old film footage
    to show Kenyatta's experiences: mission school education,
    colonial service, political exile, emergence as leader in
    the fight for independence.

KEY WITNESS
Nar/Cast: Jeffrey Hunter + Johnny Nash* + Dennis Hopper +
    Frank Silvera*
Screenplay: Alfred Brenner + Sidney Michaels
Producer: Pandro S. Berman   Director: Phil Karlson
Studio/Company: MGM
Date/Country: 1960 + USA   Type: Feature
Annotation: Hunter plays a man who witnesses a murder by a
    street gang, volunteers to testify and is hounded by them
    until he almost loses his family and his life. Johnny
    Nash plays a brave young boy with a conscience.

KID 'N' AFRICA
Nar/Cast: Shirley Temple
Tech Info: 16 mm/bw/sound/1 reel/10 min.
Date/Country: 1933 + USA   Type: Comedy Short
Distr/Arch: nil
Annotation: Shirley Temple on a child-sized African mis-
    sionary safari is captured by "mini-cannibals" (real black
    children). She is rescued from the cooking pot by a
    junior Tarzan (Diaperzan) and his friendly elephant.

KID FROM BORNEO, THE
Series: Our Gang
Nar/Cast: Our Gang + Matthew Beard*
Producer: Hal Roach + Robert F. McGowan   Director: Robert
    McGowan
Studio/Company: MGM + Roach
Tech Info: super 8 mm/16 mm/bw/sound/1 reel/20 min.
Date/Country: 1933 + USA   Type: Comedy Short
Distr/Arch: roa + bla + kpf
Annotation: Spanky's uncle has gotten up a Wild Man from
    Borneo side show act, but when the kids go to the show to
    meet the uncle they've never seen, they mistake Bumbo the
    wild man for Uncle George. The wild man only looks
    fierce, but he has a craving for candy and chases Stymie
    (who's just taken out some candy) and the gang back to
    Spanky's house, all the time yelling 'Yum-yum, eat 'em
    up.'

KID FROM SPAIN, THE
Nar/Cast: Eddie Cantor + Edgar Connor* + Robert Young
    Story: William McGuire + Bert Kalmar + Harry Ruby
Producer: Sam Goldwyn   Director: Leo McCarey
Studio/Company: Goldwyn-United Artists

Tech Info: 16 mm/sound/bw/96 min.
Date/Country: 1932 + USA   Type: Feature
Distr/Arch: mac
Annotation: Connor is a bullfighter's assistant in this
    musical comedy with Eddie Cantor having to assume the role
    of "Don Sebastion the Second," the greatest bullfighter of
    all time.

KID_MILLIONS
Nar/Cast: Eddie Cantor
Producer: Sam Goldwyn   Director: Roy Del Ruth
Studio/Company: MGM
Tech Info: 16 mm/sound/bw/90 min.
Date/Country: 1934 + USA   Type: Feature
Distr/Arch: mac
Annotation: Cantor treats a group of black children to a
    celebration in an ice cream plant in this musical comedy.

KIDDIE_CURE
Series: Our Gang
Nar/Cast: Our Gang + Billie Thomas*
Screenplay: Hal Law + Robert A. McGowan
Producer: Jack Chertok + Richard Goldstone   Director:
    Edward Cahn
Studio/Company: MGM
Tech Info: bw/sound/1 reel
Date/Country: 1940 + USA   Type: Comedy Short
Annotation: A hypochondriac learns his doctor has suggested
    he adopt some kids as a cure. When the gang shows up to
    retrieve a baseball, the sick man chases them and creates
    general mayhem planning to blame all on the children. He
    learns he's a hypochondriac at the same moment he dis-
    covers a concern for the children's safety. Billie Thomas
    stars as Buckwheat.

KILLER_DILLER
Nar/Cast: Dusty Fletcher* + George Wiltshire* + Butterfly
    McQueen* + Nellie Hill* + King Cole Trio* + Andy Kirk and
    Orchestra + Clark Brothers* + 4 Congaroos* + Varieties
    Dance Girls* + Jackie "Moms" Mabley* + Beverly White* +
    Patterson and Jackson*
Screenplay: Hal Sieger
Producer: E.M. Glucksman   Director: Josh Binney
Studio/Company: All American
Tech Info: 16 mm/bw/sound/2 reels/80 min.
Date/Country: 1948 + USA   Type: Feature
Distr/Arch: kpf + emg
Annotation: The story of a magician who does disappearing
    acts ties together a variety program of musical numbers
    including an act by Jackie "Moms" Mabley.

KILLER_FORCE
Nar/Cast: Telly Savalas + Peter Fonda + Hugh O'Brian + O.J.
    Simpson*
Producer: Nat Wachsberger + Patrick Wachsberger   Director:
    Val Guest
Studio/Company: American International
Date/Country: 1975 + USA   Type: TV Feature

Annotation: Jewel thieves plot to steal 20 million dollars in diamonds from an African mine. Webb (Savalas), who's hired to catch the thieves, unwittingly trusts the gang's leader (Fonda) with the information that makes it possible for the gang to steal the jewels. Webb pursues the robbers across the desert.

KILLERS, THE
Nar/Cast: Burt Lancaster + Ava Gardner + Edmund O'Brien + Bill Walker* + Davis Roberts*
Screenplay: Anthony Veiler   Story: Ernest Hemingway
Producer: Mark Hellinger   Director: Robert Siodmak
Studio/Company: Universal
Tech Info: 16mm/ sound/ bw/ 102 min.
Date/Country: 1946 + USA   Type: Feature
Distr/Arch: uni
Annotation: In one of Burt Lancaster's first movies, he plays a young boxer who tosses away his career for the love of Ava Gardner only to be double-crossed and killed. Bill Walker plays Sam; Davis Roberts has a bit part.

KILLING, THE
Nar/Cast: Sterling Hayden + Coleen Gray + James Edwards*
Screenplay: Stanley Kubrick   Story: Lionel White
Producer: James B. Harris   Director: Stanley Kubrick
Studio/Company: United Artists
Tech Info: 16 mm/sound/bw/83 min.
Date/Country: 1956 + USA   Type: Feature
Distr/Arch: uas
Annotation: Assorted low life types get together to rob a race track. James Edwards plays a parking attendant.

KING AND I, THE
Nar/Cast: Yul Brynner + Deborah Kerr + Rita Moreno + Martin Benson
Screenplay: Ernest Lehman   Story: Margaret Landon
Producer: Charles Brackett   Director: Walter Lang
Studio/Company: 20th Century Fox
Tech Info: 16 mm/sound/color/133 min.
Date/Country: 1956   Type: Feature
Distr/Arch: fnc
Annotation: Dramatization of Uncle Tom's Cabin in the film; however not in blackface.

KING COTTON
Date/Country: USA   Type: Documentary
Annotation: Blacks filmed in Rome, Georgia.

KING FOR A DAY
Nar/Cast: Bill Robinson* + Muriel Rahn* + Hattie Noel* + Dusty Fletcher* + Babe Matthews*
Date/Country: 1934 + USA   Type: Musical Short
Annotation: Musical short with a variety of song and dance numbers.

KING GUN
Nar/Cast: Woody Strode* + Robert Fuller + Guy Stockwell
Studio/Company: Universal

Tech Info: 16 mm/color/sound/97 min./3 reels
Date/Country: 1970 + USA   Type: Feature
Distr/Arch: roa + unf

KING KONG
Nar/Cast: Fay Wray + Robert Armstrong + Bruce Cabot + Noble
   Johnson* + Rex Ingram*
Screenplay: James Creelman + Ruth Rose   Story: Edgar Wal-
   lace + M.C. Cooper
Producer: Merian Cooper + Ernest B. Schoedsack   Director:
   Merian Cooper + Ernest B. Schoedsack
Studio/Company: RKO Radio
Tech Info: 16 mm/35 mm/bw/sound/3 reels/110 min.
Date/Country: 1933 + USA   Type: Feature
Distr/Arch: jan + fnc + moma
Annotation: The Hollywood classic of the beauty and the
   beast features Noble Johnson as the black chief and Rex
   Ingram as part of the ship's crew attempting to capture
   Kong.

KING OF BURLESQUE
Nar/Cast: Warner Baxter + Fats Waller* + Alice Faye
Screenplay: Gene Markey + Harry Tugend
Producer: Darryl F. Zanuck   Director: Sidney Lanfield
Studio/Company: 20th Century Fox
Tech Info: sound/bw
Date/Country: 1936 + USA   Type: Feature
Annotation: Story of a burlesque producer who tries to make
   it on Broadway only to fail and have his high class wife
   leave him. Then with the aid of his burlesque friends, he
   puts on a succesful Broadway production. Fats Waller as
   Ben adds to the musical part of this comedy musical.

KING OF KINGS, THE
Nar/Cast: Noble Johnson* + H.B. Warner + Ernest Torrence +
   Rex Ingram* + Joseph Shildkraut
Screenplay: Cecil B. DeMille
Producer: Cecil B. DeMille   Director: Cecil B. DeMille
Studio/Company: Pathe
Tech Info: 16 mm/music and sound effects only/bw/115 min.
Date/Country: 1927 + USA   Type: Feature
Distr/Arch: fnc + bud + byu + ccc + cwf + emg + ker + kpf +
   mod + nat + new + sel + tfc + twy + unf + wel + who + wil
Annotation: Noble Johnson is a dashing chariot driver in
   this original film version of the life of Christ (H.B.
   Warner). Joseph Schildkraut plays Judas Iscariot.

KING OF THE JUNGLE
Nar/Cast: Buster Crabbe + Frances Dee + Sam Baker* + Sidney
   Toler
Screenplay: Charles Thurley Stoncham   Director: H. Bruce
   Humberstone + Max Marcin
Studio/Company: Paramount
Tech Info: 16 mm/sound/bw/75 min.
Date/Country: 1933 + USA   Type: Feature
Distr/Arch: uni
Annotation: Tarzan-like story about a young boy brought up
   by lions after his parents are killed by wild animals.

When grown, he (Buster Crabbe) and elephants are captured and brought to civilization as a circus animal act. He works until he can buy their way back to Africa. Sam Baker is Gwana, one of the African natives.

KING OF ZOMBIES
Nar/Cast: Dick Purcell + Mantan Moreland* + John Archer + Henry Victor + Joan Woodbury + Marguerite Whitten + Leigh Whipper*
Screenplay: Edmond Kelso   Director: Jean Yarborough
Studio/Company: Monogram
Tech Info: 16 mm/sound/bw/67 min.
Date/Country: 1941 + USA   Type: Feature
Distr/Arch: ncs
Annotation: Mantan Moreland was co-starred with white actor Purcell in this "zombie comedy."

KING SOLOMON'S MINE
Nar/Cast: Stewart Granger + Deborah Kerr + Kimursi* + Siria-que*
Screenplay: Helen Deutsch
Producer: Sam Zimbalist   Director: Compton Bennett + Andrew Marton
Studio/Company: MGM
Tech Info: 16 mm/sound/bw and color/102 min.
Date/Country: 1950 + USA   Type: Feature
Distr/Arch: fnc
Annotation: Another remake of Rider Haggard's King Solomon's Mines; this one with Africans in the African roles.

KING SOLOMON'S MINES
Nar/Cast: Paul Robeson* + Cedric Hardwicke + Roland Young + Anna Lee + John Loder + Arthur Sinclair + Robert Adams* + Arthur Goullett + Makubalo Hlubi* + Sydney Fairbrother + Ecco Homo Toto* + Frederick Leister
Screenplay: Ralph Spence + Roland Pertwee   Story: Sir H. Rider Haggard   Director: Robert Stevenson
Studio/Company: Gaumont-British
Tech Info: 16 mm/bw/sound/2 reels/80 min.
Date/Country: 1937 + Britain   Type: Feature
Distr/Arch: jan + cfm
Annotation: Robeson plays Umbopa, an African porter to a group of hunters and adventurers in South Africa. Falling upon a map to King Solomon's mines, they find the site of the treasure which is guarded by a fierce tribe. As it turns out Umbopa is in reality the true chief of the tribe; a fight ensues and the victorious Umbopa permits his white friends entrance to the mines. Robert Adams is Twala, Makubalo Hlubi is Kapsie.

KING: A FILMED RECORD, MONTGOMERY TO MEMPHIS
Nar/Cast: Harry Belafonte* + Ruby Dee* + Ben Gazzara + James Earl Jones* + Burt Lancaster + Elaine May + Mike Nichols + Anthony Quinn + Clarence Williams, III*
Producer: Ely Landau + Martin Luther King Foundation
Tech Info: 35 mm/16 mm/sound/bw/3 hours/103 min. (abridged)/ 81 min.-short
Date/Country: 1970 + USA   Type: Documentary

Distr/Arch: rad
Annotation: The biography of a movement from the Montgomery
    bus boycott to the assassination of Dr. King. Nothing is
    contrived and no narrator imposes comments. Newsreel and
    television footage reveal the civil rights campaigns as
    they actually happened (1955-1968).   Songs by Mahalia
    Jackson*, Odetta, and Nina Simone*.

KING'S ACCORDION, THE   Director: Paul Martin* + Odile
    Martin*
Tech Info: 16 mm/22 min.*french dialogue/English subtitles
Date/Country: 1971 + Madascar + France
Distr/Arch: nyf
Annotation: An exploration of how primitive ritual relates
    to present-day Madascar--whether entertainment, retreat
    into past, or an expression of cultural identity.

KINGS GO FORTH
Nar/Cast: Frank Sinatra + Tony Curtis + Natalie Wood
Screenplay: Merle Miller   Story: Joe David Brown
Producer: Frank Ross   Director: Delmer Daves
Studio/Company: United Artists
Tech Info: 16 mm/sound/bw/109 min.
Date/Country: 1958 + USA   Type: Feature
Distr/Arch: uas
Annotation: Natalie Wood plays a mulatto wooed by both Frank
    Sinatra and Tony Curtis until they find out about her an-
    cestry, then only one comes back.

KISENGA, MAN OF AFRICA
Alt Title(s): see Men of Two Worlds

KISMET
Nar/Cast: Noble Johnson* + Otis Skinner + Loretta Young +
    David Manners
Screenplay: Howard Estabrook
Producer: Robert North   Director: John Francis Dillon
Studio/Company: First National Pictures
Tech Info: 65 mm/sound/bw/10 reels
Date/Country: 1930 + USA   Type: Feature
Annotation: Hajj (Skinner) finds his way in and out of
    prison in order to kill his enemy and save his daughter
    from harm in a harem. Noble Johnson has a small role.

KISS ME DEADLY
Nar/Cast: Ralph Meeker + Albert Dekker + Juano Hernandez*
    Director: Robert Aldrich
Studio/Company: United States
Tech Info: 16 mm/sound/bw/105 min.
Date/Country: 1955 + USA   Type: Feature
Distr/Arch: uas

KISS OF DEATH
Nar/Cast: Victor Mature + Richard Widmark + Jo Jones*
Screenplay: Ben Hecht + Charles Lederer
Producer: Fred Kohlmar   Director: Henry Hathaway
Studio/Company: Fox
Tech Info: 99 min.

Date/Country: 1947 + USA   Type: Feature
Annotation: Jo Jones plays drums in a jazz combo which per-
    forms in a nightclub sequence in this chilling tale of a
    reformed   gangster   (Victor Mature)   who tries to go
    straight.

KISS THE BOYS GOOD-BYE
Nar/Cast: Don Ameche + Mary Martin + Oscar Levant + Eddie
    Anderson*
Screenplay: Harry Tugend + Dwight Taylor   Story: Clare
    Booth
Producer: Paul Jones   Director: Victor Schertzinger
Studio/Company: Paramount
Date/Country: 1941 + USA   Type: Feature
Annotation: Film adaptation of Clare Booth's play about
    movie talent searchers, made into a musical comedy with
    Eddie "Rochester" Anderson in a featured role.

KISSES FOR MY PRESIDENT
Nar/Cast: Fred McMurray + Polly Bergan + Arlene Dahl + Bill
    Walker* + Eli Wallach
Screenplay: Claude Binyon + Robert G. Kane
Producer: Curtis Bernhardt   Director: Curtis Bernhardt
Studio/Company: Warner Bros.
Tech Info: 16 mm/sound/bw/113 min.
Date/Country: 1964 + USA   Type: Feature
Distr/Arch: arg + ccc + ics + mac + mod + tfc + wel
Annotation: Story of what happens when the first woman
    president is elected. Bill Walker is in the minor role of
    Joseph.

KLANSMAN, THE
Nar/Cast: Richard Burton + Lee Marvin + Cameron Mitchell +
    Lola Falana* + Luciana Paluzzi + David Huddleston + Linda
    Evans + O.J. Simpson*
Screenplay: Millard Kaufman + Samuel Fuller   Story: William
    Bradford Huie
Producer: William Alexander* + Bill Shiffin   Director:
    Terence Young
Studio/Company: Paramount
Tech Info: 16 mm/color/sound/3 reels/112 min.
Date/Country: 1974 + USA   Type: Feature
Distr/Arch: fnc
Annotation: Set in a backwoods Alabama town, The Klansman
    focuses on harassed Blacks, a raped white woman, an ec-
    centric southern gentleman living in the past and the ir-
    rational bigotry of white-hooded Ku Kluxers. O.J.   Simp-
    son is Garth.

KNOCKOUT KID, THE
Nar/Cast: Martin Turner* + Jack Perrin + Molly Malone
Screenplay: Sheldon Forrest   Director: Albert Rogell
Studio/Company: Harry Webb Productions
Tech Info: 35 mm/silent/bw/5 reels/4,901 ft
Date/Country: 1925 + USA
Annotation: A western comedy with Jack Perrin as Jack Lan-
    ning, son of a millionaire who is disowned by his father
    because he has become a boxer. With his valet Snowball

(Martin Turner) he goes to Texas, is suspected of cattle
rustling and is almost lynched. Jack solves everything by
saving the payroll of a widow's ranch from bandits and
gets the widow's niece after some amorous complications.

KODOU
Nar/Cast: Fatou Fall* + Madeline Kiallo* + El Hadji Seck* +
     Mohamed Latyr Seck* + Nar Sene* + Daouda Seck*
Producer: Paulin Soumanou Vieyra*   Director: Ababacar
     Samb-Makharam*
Tech Info: 16 mm/bw/sound/80 min.
Date/Country: 1971 + Senegal   Type: Feature
Annotation: With a cast of mainly non-professional actors,
     Samb-Makharam's film depicting the daily life of an Afri-
     can village can also be viewed as an allegory of the
     struggle between tradition and modernity. In the story of
     Kodou, a young woman who rebels against the painful lip
     tatooing ritual and is therefore ostracized, the struggle
     is dramatized.

KOINONIA
Producer: Philip Garvin + WGBH-TV, Boston
Tech Info: 16 mm/sound/color/28 min.
Date/Country: 1974 + USA
Distr/Arch: yal
Annotation: Black Baptist religion as seen by a female
     member of the church (Gary, Indiana). Provided by Center
     for Southern Folklore.

KONGI'S HARVEST
Nar/Cast: Wole Soyinka* + Oha Danlola*   Story: Wole Soyinka
     Director: Ossie Davis*
Studio/Company: Calpenny Productions
Tech Info: 16 mm/35 mm/85 min.
Date/Country: 1970 + USA   Type: Feature
Distr/Arch: nlc
Annotation: This film vesion of Wole Soyinka's highly
     political play about the abuses of power was shot on loca-
     tion in Nigeria and directed by American actor/director
     Ossie Davis. Soyinka plays Kongi, a tyrannical ruler.

KONGO
Nar/Cast: Walter Huston + Lupe Velez + Virginia Bruce
     Story: Chester DeVonde + Kilbourn Tordon (Play)
     Director: William Cowan
Studio/Company: MGM
Tech Info: 16mm/ sound/ bw/ 85 min.
Date/Country: 1932 + USA   Type: Feature
Distr/Arch: fnc
Annotation: Natives used as backdrop in this melodrama which
     is set in the Congo and is meant to horrify. Walter
     Huston, as the vengeance wracked cripple Flint, shoots a
     black man who threatens to tell a local chieftain about
     Flint's villainy. He covers himself by saying that the
     man had been caught stealing.

KRAKATOA, EAST OF JAVA
Nar/Cast: Geoffrey Holder* + Maximillian Schell + Diane

Baker
Screenplay: Clifford Newton Gould
Producer: William R. Forman   Director: Bernard L. Kowalski
Studio/Company: ABC
Tech Info: 16mm/ sound/ color/ 148 min
Date/Country: 1969 + USA   Type: Feature
Distr/Arch: fnc
Annotation: Holder   is Bazooki Man in this adventure
   melodrama about the search for a treasure of pearls sup-
   posedly on a ship sunk off the coast of a volcanic island
   -- Krakatoa.

KU KLUX KLAN--THE INVISIBLE EMPIRE
Nar/Cast: Charles Kuralt
Producer: CBS
Tech Info: 16 mm/sound/bw/46 min.
Date/Country: 1965 + USA   Type: Documentary
Distr/Arch: iu + carsl
Annotation: Examines the aims and mentality of the Knights
   of the Ku Klux Klan from their beginnings in Tennessee
   over a hundred years ago to their still active, prejudici-
   al treatment of Black, Jewish, and Catholic communities.
   Employs rare film footage of a 1915 Klan ritual and shows
   many excerpts from actual meetings and secret ceremonies.
   Filmed by CBS.

KWACHA: THE STRUGGLE FOR ANGOLA
Producer: Kwadwo Oluwale Akpan
Tech Info: 16 mm/sound/color/1 reel/30 min.
Date/Country: 1975 + Angola   Type: Documentary
Distr/Arch: acusa + fa
Annotation: Revolution and   reconstruction   in Angola.
   Depicts the struggle of UNITA (National Union for the
   Total Independence of Angola) against Portugese rule.

L-SHAPED ROOM, THE
Nar/Cast: Leslie Caron + Brock Peters* + Tom Bell
Screenplay: Brian Forbes   Story: Lynn Reid Banks
Producer: James Wolf + Richard Attenborough   Director: Bri-
   an Forbes
Studio/Company: Romulus
Tech Info: 16 mm/sound/bw/124 min.
Date/Country: 1963 + Britain   Type: Feature
Distr/Arch: swa + colu
Annotation: Brock Peters plays a jazz musician, living in
   the same London digs as Leslie Caron and her lover, and
   who gets involved in their complicated affair.

L'ALIBI
Alt Title(s): The Alibi
Nar/Cast: Erich   von Stroheim + Johnny Russell*; + Valaida
   Snow*   Story: Marcel Achard   Director: Pierre Chenal
Tech Info: 82 min.
Date/Country: 1938 + France   Type: Feature
Annotation: Jazzman Johnny Russell is featured and Valaida
   Snow appears in this melodrama about a dance hall hostess
   in Paris who unwittingly provides an alibi for a murder.
   Von Stroheim is the villain.

L'AMITIE NOIRE
Producer: Jean Cocteau + Francois Villiers
Tech Info: 16 mm/sound/color/1 reel/20 min./French narration
Date/Country: 1944 + Chad   Type: Documentary
Distr/Arch: facsea + moma
Annotation: A film showing French Equatorial African arts,
   handicrafts and ceremonial dances.

L'AVENTURE DU JAZZ   Director: Louis Pannasie + Claudine
   Pannasie
Date/Country: 1969 + France   Type: Documentary
Annotation: Blues and swing musicians (vocal and instru-
   mental) filmed in New York over a ten year period include,
   among others, Sister Rosetta Tharp*, Memphis Slim*, and
   John Lee Hcoker*.

L'INSPECTEUR CONNAIT LA MUSIQUE
Alt Title(s): Blues
Nar/Cast: Claude Luter + Sidney Bechet*   Director: Jean
   Josipovici
Tech Info: 90 min.
Date/Country: France + 1955   Type: Feature
Annotation: Sidney Bechet has a leading role in this
   melodrama about a blues singer.

LA FORZA DEL DESTINO
Nar/Cast: Nelli Corradi + Tito Gobbi + Gino Sinimberghi +
   John Kitzmiller*
Producer: Carmine Gallone   Director: Carmine Gallone
Studio/Company: Union Film-Gallone Productions
Date/Country: 1950 + Italy   Type: Feature
Annotation: Kitzmiller has a small role in this adaptation
   of Verdi's opera based on the drama by Angelo Saavedra.

LA MORT DU CYGNE   Director: Jean Benoit-Levy
Studio/Company: Kosmo
Date/Country: 1937 + France   Type: Feature
Annotation: A light-skinned Italian-looking apprentice bal-
   lerina appears in this film.

LA NOIRE DE...
Alt Title(s): Black Girl
Nar/Cast: Mbissine Therese Diop* + Robert Fontaine + Momar
   Nar Sene* + Anne-Marie Jelinek + Ousmane Sembene*
Screenplay: Ousmane Sembene*   Story: Ousmane Sembene*
Producer: Les Films Domireew, Dakar + Actualites Francaises
   Director: Ousmane Sembene*
Tech Info: 16 mm/bw/sound/60 min./French with English sub-
   titles
Date/Country: 1969 + France + Senegal   Type: Feature
Distr/Arch: nyf
Annotation: Sembene's first feature length film (his fourth
   film) tells the story of a young African girl from Dakar
   enticed into taking a job as a domestic for a French fam-
   ily in Antibes. Enslaved in her new situation the girl
   commits suicide. The film won the Prix Jean Vigo for Best
   Direction. Sembene appears as the writer. (A longer

version with ten-minute color sequence exists.) Opened in
Paris, 1967; in Senegal 1969.

LA PALOMA
Nar/Cast: The Kessler twins + Louis Armstrong*   Director:
  Paul Martin
Tech Info: 100 min.
Date/Country: 1959 + West Germany   Type: Feature
Annotation: Mainly German entertainers are featured in this
  film revue which does, however, have an appearance by
  Louis Armstrong.

LA PECCATRICE DELL' ISOLA
Nar/Cast: John Kitzmiller*
Date/Country: 1953 + Italy   Type: Feature

LA PERMISSION
Alt Title(s): see The Story of a Three Day Pass

LA RAGAZZA DI TRIESTA
Nar/Cast: John Kitzmiller*
Date/Country: 1953 + Italy   Type: Feature

LA RIVOLTA DEI MERCENARI
Nar/Cast: John Kitzmiller*
Date/Country: 1961 + Italy   Type: Feature

LA ROUTE DU BONHEUR
Nar/Cast: Louis Armstrong and His Orchestra* + Sidney
  Bechet*   Director: Maurice Labro + Giorgio Simonelli
Tech Info: 92 min.
Date/Country: 1952 + France + Italy   Type: Feature
Annotation: Musical comedy with performances by Sidney
  Bechet, Armstrong and his orchestra.

LA TIGRE DEI SETTE MARI
Nar/Cast: John Kitzmiller*
Date/Country: 1963 + Italy   Type: Feature

LA VALLE DELLA PACE
Nar/Cast: John Kitzmiller*   Director: F. Stiglic
Date/Country: 1957 + Italy   Type: Feature

LACRIME D' AMORE
Nar/Cast: John Kitzmiller*
Date/Country: 1956 + Italy   Type: Feature

LAD AN' A LAMP, A
Series: Our Gang
Nar/Cast: Our Gang + Matthew Beard* + Bobbie Beard*
Producer: Robert F. McGowan + Hal Roach   Director: Robert
  F. McGowan
Studio/Company: MGM + Roach
Tech Info: super 8 mm/16 mm/bw/sound/1 reel/17 min.
Date/Country: 1932 + USA   Type: Comedy Short
Distr/Arch: bla
Annotation: People and events conspire to make the gang
  believe they've found Alladin's lamp. Stymie wishes for a

watermelon, Spanky wishes Cotton would be turned into a
monkey ('all he needs is a tail'). Both appear to get
their wishes. Matthew Beard stars as Stymie.

LADIES_OF_THE_BIG_HOUSE
Nar/Cast: Sylvia Sidney + Gene Raymond + Louise Beavers*
   Story: Ernest Booth   Director: Marion Gering
Studio/Company: Paramount-Publix
Date/Country: 1931 + USA   Type: Feature
Annotation: Louise Beavers is Ivory, one of the occupants of
   the prison to which Sylvia Sidney as Kathleen Storm is
   remanded after being convicted of murder on circumstantial
   evidence.

LADIES_THEY_TALK_ABOUT
Nar/Cast: Barbara Stanwyck + Preston Foster + Madame Sul-
   te-Wan*
Screenplay: Dorothy Mackaye + Carlton Miles   Director:
   Howard Bretherton + William Keighley
Studio/Company: Warner Brothers
Tech Info: 16 mm/sound/bw/69 min.
Date/Country: 1933 + USA   Type: Feature
Distr/Arch: uas
Annotation: Film about life in a woman's prison with a sup-
   ply of black inmates including Sul-te-Wan.

LADY_BY_CHOICE
Nar/Cast: Carole Lombard + May Robson + Roger Pryor + Fred
   "Snowflake" Toones*
Screenplay: Jo Swerling   Story: Dwight Taylor   Director:
   David Burton
Studio/Company: Columbia Pictures
Date/Country: 1934 + USA   Type: Feature
Annotation: Carole Lombard stars as a fan dancer who
   "adopts" a mother for a publicity gag only to have "mom"
   turn her world upside down. Fred Toones, billed as "Snow-
   flake," plays Mose, the usual domestic.

LADY_FARE,_THE
Series: Christie Comedy
Nar/Cast: Spencer Williams* + Evelyn Preer* + Edward Thomp-
   son*
Screenplay: Octavus Roy Cohen + Spencer Williams*
Producer: Al Christie
Studio/Company: Paramount
Tech Info: bw/2 reels/sound
Date/Country: 1929 + USA   Type: Comedy Short
Annotation: One of the Christie comedy series which like the
   others, uses "Negro dialect."

LADY_FOR_A_NIGHT
Nar/Cast: Joan Blondell + John Wayne + Lew Payton* + Hattie
   Noel + Hall Johnson Choir*
Screenplay: Isabel Down + Boyce DeGaw   Story: Garrett Fort
      Director: Leigh Jason
Studio/Company: Republic Pictures
Tech Info: 16 mm/sound/bw/88 min.
Date/Country: 1941 + USA   Type: Feature

Distr/Arch: ivy
Annotation: Joan Blondell plays a Memphis gambling queen who
    marries a high society type to gain respectability, only
    to be accused of murder when her husband downs the
    poisoned drink he meant for her. Lew Payton plays
    "Napoleon," and the Hall Johnson Choir sing "Ezekiel Saw
    de Wheel."

LADY FROM LOUISIANA
Alt Title(s): Lady From New Orleans
Nar/Cast: John Wayne + Ona Munson + Dorothy Dandridge*
Screenplay: Vera Caspary + Michael Hogan + Guy Endere
    Director: Bernard Vorhaus
Studio/Company: Republic
Tech Info: 16 mm/sound/bw/84 min.
Date/Country: 1941 + USA   Type: Feature
Distr/Arch: ivy
Annotation: John Wayne, as a reformer out to get political
    grafters, falls in love with the chief villain's daugher
    (Ona Munson) and when the chief is killed by his own men,
    Wayne is accused. Dandridge plays lady's maid to Munson.

LADY FROM NEW ORLEANS
Alt Title(s): see Lady from Louisiana

LADY FROM PHILADELPHIA, THE
Studio/Company: CBS
Tech Info: 16 mm/sound/bw/55 min.
Date/Country: 1958 + Asia   Type: Documentary
Distr/Arch: mgh
Annotation: Marian Anderson* tours Asia.

LADY IN A CAGE
Nar/Cast: Olivia de Havilland + Ann Southern + James Caan +
    Jeff Corey + Scatman Crothers*
Screenplay: Luther Davis
Producer: Luther Davis   Director: Walter Grauman
Studio/Company: Paramount
Tech Info: 16 mm/sound/color/94 min.
Date/Country: 1964 + USA   Type: Feature
Distr/Arch: fnc
Annotation: Trapped in an elevator, Mrs. Hilliard (de Havil-
    land) is helpless, as she watchs strangers taunt, destroy,
    rob, torture and kill while destroying her house.
    Crothers is a junkyard proprietor's assistant.

LADY IN THE LINCOLN MEMORIAL
Producer: Sterling
Tech Info: 16 mm/sound/color/18 min.
Date/Country: 1971   Type: Documentary
Distr/Arch: sef + nacc
Annotation: The early career of Marian Anderson* and the
    development of her international fame.

LADY OF THE HAREM
Nar/Cast: Noble Johnson* + Ernest Torrence + William Col-
    lier, Jr.
Screenplay: James T. O'Donohue

Producer: Famous Players-Lasky   Director: Raoul Walsh
Tech Info: 35 mm/silent/bw/6 reels
Date/Country: 1926 + USA   Type: Feature
Annotation: A greedy sultan captures the daughter of a con-
    fectioner's friend.   When the father tries to buy her
    back, she's abducted and a trap is set by the sultan to
    capture the father and the confectioner and kill them.
    They all escape and kill the evil sultan.   Noble Johnson
    has a small role as a tax collector.

LADY SINGS THE BLUES
Nar/Cast: Diana Ross* + Billy Dee Williams* + Richard Pryor*
    + Virginia Capers* + Scatman Crothers* + Lynn Hamilton*
Screenplay: Terence McClay + Chris Clark + Suzanne de Passe
    Story: Billie Holiday* (autobiography) with William Duf-
    fy
Producer: Jay Weston + James White + Motown-Weston-Furie
    Production   Director: Sidney Furie
Studio/Company: Paramount
Tech Info: 16 mm/color/sound/4 reels/144 min.
Date/Country: 1972 + USA   Type: Feature
Distr/Arch: rbc
Annotation: Critics have acclaimed Diana Ross' film debut in
    this fictionalized biography of blues singer Billie
    Holiday.   Prison, withdrawal, reunion, than a triumphant
    comeback are handled by Miss Ross in this film.   Richard
    Pryor is Piano Man, Billy Dee Williams the man she loves.
    Joseph Wilcots* was cinematographer.

LADY'S FROM KENTUCKY, THE
Nar/Cast: George Raft + Ellen Drew + Louise Beavers* + Lew
    Payton*
Screenplay: Malcom Boyd   Story: Rowland Brown
Producer: Jeff Lazarus   Director: Alexander Hall
Studio/Company: Paramount
Date/Country: 1938 + USA   Type: Feature
Annotation: A New York bookie inherits half interest in a
    race horse and while looking after his inheritence he
    falls in love with the South and a Southern belle. Louise
    Beavers is Aunt Tina and Lew Payton is Sixty.

LAMB
Producer: Ministry of Information   Director: Paulin
    Soumanou Vieyra*
Date/Country: 1963 + Senegal   Type: Documentary
Annotation: Lamb, Wolof word for wrestling, is the highly
    popular national sport/ritual of Senegal. The film com-
    mentary is done humorously by two voices, one criticizing
    the film for not emphasizing the ritual aspects, the other
    criticizing the film for over emphasizing the rituals.
    Ousmane Sembene* appears briefly.

LAMBAAYE
Nar/Cast: Lamadou Fall* + Makhouredia Gueye* + Isseu Niang*
    + Mody Gueye*
Screenplay: Mahama Traore* + Pathe Diagne*   Story: Sonar
    Senghor*   Director: Mahama Traore*
Studio/Company: Sunu Film + Secma Prod.

Tech Info: sound/color/80 min./in French
Date/Country: 1972 + Senegal   Type: Feature
Annotation: Government officials are expecting an Inspector
    General to come and monitor them incognito. All of them
    guiltily and desperately try to discover which of the new-
    comers in town might be he. An adaptation of Gogol's The
    Inspector General.

LAND OF PROMISE
Producer: Information Service of South Africa
Tech Info: 16 mm/sound/color/1 reel/22 min.
Date/Country: 1974 + South Africa   Type: Documentary
Distr/Arch: sm
Annotation: Overview of modern South African society.   In-
    cludes history and development of apartheid policy from
    the government point of view.

LANDLORD, THE
Nar/Cast: Pearl Bailey* + Diana Sands* + Lou Gossett* + Beau
    Bridges + Lee Grant + Mel Stewart* + Marki Bey* + Carl
    Lee*
Screenplay: Bill Gunn*   Story: Kristin Hunter*
Producer: Norman Jewison   Director: Hal Ashby
Studio/Company: United Artists
Tech Info: 16 mm/color/sound/3 reels/113 min.
Date/Country: 1970 + USA   Type: Feature
Distr/Arch: uas
Annotation: A boy, attempting to assert his independence
    buys an apartment house occupied by Blacks in a Brooklyn
    slum. Diana Sands is Fanny Coppee; Lou Gosset her na-
    tionalist-minded husband; Pearl Bailey is world wise Marge
    - all are the landlord's (Beau Bridges) non-paying
    tenants.

LANDMARK SPIRITUAL TEMPLE
Producer: Ethnographic
Tech Info: 16 mm/sound/bw/25 min.
Date/Country: 1968 + USA   Type: Documentary
Distr/Arch: uca
Annotation: A black San Francisco church and its various
    members.

LANGSTON HUGHES
Series: Tell It Like It Was
Nar/Cast: Dallie* + Kevin Brooks* + Walter Delegall* + Don
    Allen*
Producer: CBS   Director: Jerry Chamberlain
Studio/Company: WCAU-TV
Tech Info: 16 mm/color/sound/28 min.
Date/Country: 1970 + USA   Type: TV Documentary
Distr/Arch: kpf
Annotation: Film biography of the "poet laureate" of Harlem.

LAST ANGRY MAN, THE
Nar/Cast: Claudia McNeil* + Cicely Tyson* + Godfrey Cam-
    bridge* + Billy Dee Williams* + Paul Muni + David Wayne +
    Betsy Palmer + Luther Adler   Story: Gerald Green
Producer: Fred Kohlmar   Director: Daniel Mann

Studio/Company: Columbia Pictures
Tech Info: 16 mm/bw/sound/3 reels/100 min.
Date/Country: 1959 + USA   Type: Feature
Distr/Arch: arg + bud + ccc + cha + con + cwf + mod + mot +
   roa + twy + mac + wcf + wel + who
Annotation: Paul Muni plays Dr. Sam Abelman who tirelessly
   treats the sick, the poor and the unfortunate in a slum
   neighborhood. Billy Dee Williams (Josh Quincy) appears as
   one of the doctor's patients with Claudia McNeil as his
   mother. Godfrey Cambridge plays a delinquent, Cicely
   Tyson a victim of assault.

LAST_DETAIL,_THE
Nar/Cast: Otis Young* + Jack Nicholson + Randy Quaid
Screenplay: Robert Towne   Story: Darryl Ponicsan
Producer: Gerald Ayres   Director: Hal Ashby
Studio/Company: Columbia
Tech Info: 16 mm/sound/color/3 reel/102 min.
Date/Country: 1973 + USA   Type: Feature
Distr/Arch: swa
Annotation: Two Navy career men (Nicholson and Young) escort
   a young sailor from Norfolk to Portsmouth where he'll be
   placed in the brig for a year for having stolen $40.00
   from charity contributions. Along the way the two, more
   experienced sailors try to introduce the boy to a good
   time and raise him to maturity in what could be called the
   "serviceman's way."

LAST_GANGSTER,_THE
Nar/Cast: Louise Beavers* + Edward G. Robinson + James
   Stewart + John Carradine
Screenplay: John L. Mahin   Story: William Wellman
   Director: Edward Ludwig
Studio/Company: MGM
Date/Country: 1937 + USA   Type: Feature
Annotation: Gangster Robinson and reporter Stewart battle
   for Robinson's son (played by Douglas Scott) after the
   former is released from prison. Robinson wants to make
   the boy into Public Enemy Number 1, Jr. Stuart, now the
   adopted father, wants the straight and narrow for the son.
   Louise Beavers is Gloria in one of her maid roles.

LAST_GRAVE_AT_DIMBAZA
Screenplay: Nana Mahomo*
Tech Info: 16 mm/color/sound/2 reels/55 min.
Date/Country: 1974 + South Africa   Type: Documentary
Distr/Arch: tri + cal
Annotation: A documentary on apartheid in South Africa and
   its everyday reality for the majority of South Africa's
   population, the Blacks and other "colored" peoples. The
   film examines the harsh living and working conditions of
   Blacks, and the inequities to which they are subjected in
   white-ruled South Africa. Shot secretly by a black South
   African filmmaker and critic of that country's policies in
   1973-4.

LAST_GRENADE,_THE
Nar/Cast: Stanley Baker + Honor Blackman + Rafer Johnson* +

Richard Attenborough + Alex Cord
Screenplay: Kenneth Ware
Producer: Joseph Shaftel   Director: Gordon Fleming
Studio/Company: Cinerama Corp.
Tech Info: 16 mm/sound/color/94 min.
Date/Country: 1970 + Britain   Type: Feature
Annotation: Treachery and intrigue are highlighted in this
    movie that has two mercenaries (Stanley Baker and Alex
    Cord) seeking to eliminate each other. Rafer Johnson
    plays Joe Jackson.

LAST MILE, THE
Nar/Cast: Daniel Haynes* + Preston Foster
Screenplay: John Wexley
Producer: World Wide   Director: Sam Bischoff
Tech Info: 16 mm/sound/bw/70 min.
Date/Country: 1932 + USA   Type: Feature
Annotation: Daniel Haynes is Sonny Jackson, in cell 2, one
    of the condemned murderers in this film about prison, at-
    tempted escape, and capital punishment.

LAST OF THE MOBILE HOT SHOTS
Alt Title(s): Blood Kin
Nar/Cast: Robert Hooks* + Lynn Redgrave + James Coburn
Screenplay: Gore Vidal
Producer: Sidney Lumet   Director: Sidney Lumet
Studio/Company: Warner Bros. + Sidney Lumet Production
Tech Info: 16 mm/sound/color/108 min.
Date/Country: 1970 + USA   Type: Feature
Distr/Arch: wsa
Annotation: Film version of The Seven Descents of Myrtle, a
    play by Tennesse Williams. The story is of two brothers
    one white, one black (Chicken, played by Robert Hooks) and
    the women they both love. Myrtle (Lynn Redgrave) the one
    Jeb (James Coburn) marries, is the lone survivor of the
    "Mobile Hot-Shots," a topless, all girl band. (Music by
    Quincy Jones*.)

LAST PARADE
Nar/Cast: Clarence Muse* + Jack Holt + Tom Moore + Constance
    Cummings   Director: Erle C. Kenton
Studio/Company: Columbia
Tech Info: sound/bw
Date/Country: 1931   Type: Feature
Annotation: Life on death row, with Clarence Muse featured
    as one of the tenants.

LAST TOLL-CALL, THE
Alt Title(s): see Il Grande Appello

LAST VOYAGE, THE
Nar/Cast: Robert Stack + Dorothy Malone + Woody Strode* +
    George Sanders
Screenplay: Andrew L. Stone
Producer: Andrew L. Stone   Director: Andrew L. Stone
Studio/Company: MGM
Tech Info: 16 mm/sound/color/91 min.
Date/Country: 1960 + USA   Type: Feature

Distr/Arch: fnc
Annotation: On this last voyage Dorothy Malone is trapped
     beneath a steel beam on a sinking ship. Robert Stack and
     Woody Strode struggle to free her in time.

LAUGHING AT DANGER
Nar/Cast: Mantan Moreland*   Director: James W. Herne
Date/Country: 1940 + USA   Type: Feature

LAUGHING IRISH EYES
Nar/Cast: Phil Regan + Walter C. Kelly + Clarence Muse*
Screenplay: Olive Cooper + Ben Ryan + Stanley Rauh
     Director: Joseph Santley
Studio/Company: Republic Pictures
Tech Info: 16 mm/sound/bw/54 min.
Date/Country: 1936 + USA   Type: Feature
Distr/Arch: alb + ivy
Annotation: Story of an Irish tenor who, while fighting his
     way to the middleweight championship, would rather sing
     than fight. Clarence Muse plays Deacon.

LAUGHING POLICEMAN, THE
Nar/Cast: Walter Matthau + Bruce Dern + Lou Gossett*
Producer: Stuart Rosenberg   Director: Stuart Rosenberg
Studio/Company: 20th Century-Fox Presentation
Date/Country: 1973 + USA   Type: TV Feature
Annotation: Detectives (Matthau, Dern, Gossett) pursue the
     slayer of 9 victims killed on a bus. Emphasis here is on
     detective-work, not violence.

LAUGHTER IN HELL
Nar/Cast: Pat O*brien + Merna Kennedy + Gloria Stuart + Tom
     Brown + Noel Madison + Clarence Muse*   Director: Edward
     L. Cahn
Studio/Company: Universal
Date/Country: 1933 + USA   Type: Feature
Annotation: Pat O'Brien in a chain gang film complete with
     evil and murder. Clarence Muse is one of the chain gang
     members.

LAW OF NATURE, THE
Nar/Cast: Noble Johnson* + Clarence Brooks* + Albertine
     Pickens*
Studio/Company: Lincoln Motion Picture Company*
Tech Info: silent/bw
Date/Country: 1917 + USA   Type: Feature
Annotation: Story of a young governess who marries the
     father of the children in her charge. Although he is a
     wealthy western cattleman, he cannot live up to her
     Eastern societal standards, and she becomes involved with
     a former admirer when her husband returns to his ranch.
     Left alone, she comes to regret her behavior and returns
     to her husband.

LAW OF THE JUNGLE
Nar/Cast: Mantan Moreland*   Director: Jean Yarborough
Date/Country: 1942 + USA   Type: Feature

LAWLESS NINETIES, THE
Nar/Cast: John Wayne + Ann Rutherford + Etta McDaniel* +
   Fred "Snowflake" Toones*
Screenplay: Joseph Poland   Director: Joseph Kane
Studio/Company: Republic
Tech Info: 16 mm/sound/bw/56 min.
Date/Country: 1936 + USA   Type: Feature
Distr/Arch: ivy
Annotation: The story of the violence which preceded Wy-
   oming's entering the union. Etta McDaniel is Mandy Lou
   and Fred Toones (billed as "Snowflake") is Mose.

LAWYER, THE
Nar/Cast: James McEachin* + Barry Newman
Screenplay: Sidney Furie + Harold Buchman
Producer: Brad Dexter   Director: Sidney Furie
Studio/Company: Paramount
Tech Info: 16 mm/sound/color/117 min.
Date/Country: 1970   Type: Feature
Distr/Arch: rbc
Annotation: McEachin is Stuker in this drama about an
   ambitious young lawyer (Newman) Petrocelli who defends a
   physician accused of murdering his wife.

LAY MY BURDEN DOWN
Producer: Jack Willis + NET
Tech Info: 16 mm/bw/sound/2 reels/60 min.
Date/Country: 1966 + USA   Type: Documentary
Distr/Arch: iu + nef
Annotation: Documents the economic and educational plight of
   black tenant farmers in the southern United States. In
   spite of hard work in the fields, the tenant farmer can
   provide his family with only the most meager existence.

LAZY DAYS
Series: Our Gang
Nar/Cast: Our Gang + Allen Hoskins*
Screenplay: Robert F. McGowan
Producer: Robert F. McGowan + Hal Roach   Director: Robert
   F. McGowan
Studio/Company: MGM + Roach
Tech Info: super 8 mm/16 mm/bw/sound on disc/2 reels
Date/Country: 1929 + USA   Type: Comedy Short
Distr/Arch: roa
Annotation: Lazy Farina just barely manages to rouse himself
   when Joe reports that there's a baby contest in town in
   which he might win $50. Farina gives his infant brother a
   bath and dresses him but rests under a tree after a while,
   until Joe and the gang come by and tell him the show hap-
   pened a month ago. Allen Hoskins stars as Farina.

LE BLUES ENTRE LES DENTS
Alt Title(s): Blues Between the Teeth + Blues Under the Skin
Nar/Cast: Mance Lipscomb* + Sonny Terry* + Brownie McShee* +
   B.B. King* + Furry Lewis* + Roosevelt Sykes*
Screenplay: Robert Manthoulis
Producer: Neyrac Films   Director: Robert Manthoulis
Tech Info: 16 mm/sound/color/188 min.

Date/Country: 1972 + France   Type: Feature
Annotation: The story of a black ghetto couple and their
   troubles. With blues music interludes.

LEADBELLY
Nar/Cast: Roger E. Mosley* + Paul Benjamin + Madge Sinclair*
   + Alan Manson + Art Evans*
Screenplay: Ernest Kinoy
Producer: Mark Merson + David Frost   Director: Gordon Park-
   s*
Studio/Company: Paramount
Tech Info: 16 mm/color/sound/3 reels/126 min.
Date/Country: 1976 + USA   Type: Drama/Biography
Distr/Arch: fnc
Annotation: Drama about the legendary blues composer-singer
   Huddie Ledbetter, better known as Leadbelly, the great
   American folk singer and 12-string guitarist who died in
   1949 at the age of 60. The story is told in the context
   of the visit John Lomax, the musicologist and collector of
   folk songs, made to a Louisiana prison in 1933 to record
   for the Library of Congress the repertoire of this black
   man renowned for his back-country songs.

LEARNING TREE, THE
Nar/Cast: Kyle Johnson* + Alex Clarke* + Estelle Evans* +
   Dand Elcar + Mira Waters + Joel Fluellen* + Malcom Atterb-
   uy + Richard Ward*   Story: Gordon Parks*
Producer: Gordon Parks*   Director: Gordon Parks*
Studio/Company: Warner Brothers + Seven Arts
Tech Info: 16 mm/color/sound/3 reels/107 min.
Date/Country: 1969 + USA   Type: Feature
Distr/Arch: mac + bud + ccc + con + cwf + ics + ker + kpf +
   mod + mct + new + roa + sel + tfc + twy + unf + wcf + wel
   + who + wil
Annotation: The Learnin Tree is based on the autobiographical novel by photo-journalist Gordon Parks. The film
   treats the lives of black teenagers growing up in Kansas
   in the 1920's. Joseph Wilcots* was cinematographer; Parks
   composed the music score.

LEGACY OF A DREAM
Nar/Cast: James Earl Jones* + Coretta Scott King* + Ambas-
   sador Andrew Young*
Producer: Richard Kaplan + Martin Luther King Foundation
   Director: Richard Kaplan
Tech Info: 16 mm/color/sound/1 reel/29 min.
Date/Country: 1970 + USA   Type: Documentary
Distr/Arch: rad
Annotation: Legacy of a Dream conveys the drama and
   historical perspective of the 50's and 60's and shows the
   influence of those events on today. Earlier voter
   registration campaigns are contrasted to recent elections
   of Black mayors, officials and congressmen. Blue Ribbon
   Award American Film Festival, New York (citizenship
   category); First Prize Gold Medal and Special Jury award,
   Atlanta Film Festival.

LEGACY OF BLOOD

Nar/Cast: Clifton Davis* + Moses Gunn* + Jonelle Allen* + Frances Foster*
Date/Country: 1974 + USA   Type: TV Feature
Annotation: To pay off a loan shark (Davis), an honest man (Gunn) turns to a desperate plot to kill his wife's niece (Foster) for the inheritance his wife (Allen) would receive.

LEGACY_OF_THE_DRUM,_THE
Nar/Cast: Dizzy Gillespie* + Durke Mitchell* + The Mitchell-Ruff Duo* + Miles Davis*   Director: Sam Weiss
Date/Country: 1970 + USA   Type: Documentary
Annotation: Gillespie talks with Mitchell and the Mitchell-Ruff Duo and Miles Davis.

LEGEND_OF_JIMMY_BLUE_EYES,_THE
Tech Info: 16 mm/color/sound/1 reel/22 min.
Date/Country: 1964 + USA   Type: Dramatic Short
Distr/Arch: mac
Annotation: Award winning short combines color effects, graphic arts, and live action to tell this Faustian legend of a New Orleans jazz trumpeter who sells his soul to the devil to reach that "high note".

LEGEND_OF_JOHN_HENRY,_THE
Nar/Cast: Roberta Flack*
Producer: Pyramid   Director: Sam Weiss
Tech Info: 16 mm/sound/color/11 min.
Date/Country: 1973 + USA   Type: Animated Short
Distr/Arch: pyr
Annotation: Roberta Flack narrates/sings the legend of the great railroad man John Henry, black folk hero.

LEGEND_OF_NIGGER_CHARLEY,_THE
Nar/Cast: Fred Williamson* + D'Urville Martin* + Don Pedro Colley*
Screenplay: Martin Goldman + Larry G. Spangler   Story: James Bellah
Producer: Larry G. Spangler   Director: Martin Goldman
Studio/Company: Paramount
Tech Info: 16 mm/color/sound/4 reels/115 min.
Date/Country: 1972 + USA   Type: Feature
Distr/Arch: fnc
Annotation: This soul western about three runaway slaves was one of the first films to show the black man as a rebellious figure in the Old West. Freedom, manhood, and most importantly a set of values independent of whites is what the violence and racial conflict are about.

LEGION_OF_TERROR
Nar/Cast: Bruce Cabot + Marguerite Churchill + Ward Bond + Arthur Loft + John Tyrell + Charles Wilson
Screenplay: Bert Granet   Director: C.C. Coleman
Studio/Company: Columbia
Date/Country: 1937 + USA   Type: Feature
Annotation: The film concerns the revival of the secret society, Ku Klux Klan type, which menaced the USA in the middle nineteen-thirties.

LEGIONE STRANIERA
Nar/Cast: John Kitzmiller*
Date/Country: 1953 + Italy   Type: Feature

LEM HAWKIN'S CONFESSION
Alt Title(s): see The Brand of Cain

LEO THE LAST
Nar/Cast: Marcello Mastroianni + Billie Whitelaw + Calvin
    Lockhart* + Glenna Foster Jones* + Ram John Holder* + Lou
    Gossett*
Screenplay: Bill Stair + John Boorman
Producer: Irwin Winkler + Robert Chartoff   Director: John
    Boorman
Studio/Company: United Artists
Tech Info: 16 mm/sound/color/100 min.
Date/Country: 1970 + Britain   Type: Feature
Distr/Arch: uas
Annotation: Rich, isolated Leo (Mastroianni), the last in
    the line of a deposed European monarchy, gets slowly drawn
    into the lives of a black family he observes from his
    window (in London) which looks out onto a black ghetto.
    Foster Jones is Salambo, Lockhart (Roscoe) the man who
    loves her and is sent to jail for beating up a shopkeeper
    who tries to rape her.

LEOPARD WOMAN, THE
Nar/Cast: Louise Glaum + Noble Johnson*
Date/Country: 1920 + USA
Annotation: A Negro dies in the place of the Leopard woman's
    lover, whom she had ordered killed. She regrets the order
    to kill him and is happy to learn her lover didn't die.

LEOPOLD SEDAR SENGHOR
Producer: NET
Tech Info: 16 mm/sound/bw/1 reel/30 min.
Date/Country: 1967
Distr/Arch: iu
Annotation: An introduction to the poet laureate and the
    President of Senegal, Leopold Sedar Senghor, his poetry,
    and the environment which his poems reflect.   President
    Senghor discusses his philosophy concerning the blending
    of the African and the Western cultural traditions, and
    Maurice Sonnar Senghor, director of the National Theater
    of Senegal, reads five of President Senghor's poems in
    English.

LES LACHES VIVANT D'ESPOIR
Alt Title(s): My Baby Is Black + The Colour of Love
Nar/Cast: Gordon Heath* + Francoise Giret
Screenplay: Claude Bernhard Aubert
Producer: Claude Bernhard Aubert   Director: Claude Bernhard
    Aubert
Tech Info: sound/bw/75 min.
Date/Country: 1961 + France   Type: Feature
Annotation: Daniel an African student falls in love with a
    French girl, also a student, and fathers her child. They

are beset by problems but plan to build a future together.
Released in U.S., 1965.

LES PERLES DE LA COURONNE
Alt Title(s): The Pearls of the Crown
Nar/Cast: Sacha Guitry + Jacqueline Delubac + Jean Louis
   Barroult + Arletty
Screenplay: Sacha Guitry   Director: Sacha Guitry + Christi-
   an Jaque
Date/Country: 1937 + France   Type: Feature
Annotation: The four pearls which supposedly adorned the
   English crown is told as a fairy tale spanning four
   centuries, among royalty like Francis I, Mary Queen of
   Scots, Henry VIII and Pope Clement VII, is the Queen of
   Abyssinia in a segment with black courtiers and temple
   dancers.

LES PRINCES NOIRS DE SAINT-GERMAIN DES PRES
Alt Title(s): The Black Princes of St.-Germain
Nar/Cast: Aziz Diop-Mambety* + Muriel Dovaz* + Moussa Sarr*
   + Aurelia Crawford* + Moussa Coulibalz* + Christiane
   Gibelin*
Producer: Societe Nationale de Cinematographie   Director:
   Ben Diogaye Beye*
Tech Info: sound/color/15 min./in French
Date/Country: 1974 + Senegal   Type: Dramatic Short
Annotation: Many young Africans visit Paris for the "vie en
   rose" (the good life) and some are prone to telling
   stories of wealth and royal blood to achieve it. The film
   examines this tendency on the Boulevard Saint-Germain.

LET MY PEOPLE LIVE
Nar/Cast: Rex Ingram* + Erostine Coles* + Peggy Howard* +
   Wilbert Smith*
Producer: National Anti-Tuberculosis Association   Director:
   Edgar G. Ulmer
Studio/Company: Motion Picture Service Corp.
Tech Info: 35 mm/sound/bw/14 min.
Date/Country: 1944 + USA   Type: Dramatized Documentary
Distr/Arch: nars
Annotation: A plea to wipe out tuberculosis among rural
   Blacks; dramatizes the necessity for early diagnosis.
   Made in cooperation with Tuskegee Institute, National Ur-
   ban League, WPA, Veterans Administration. Ingram plays
   the doctor. Tuskegee choir, under the direction of Willi-
   am Dawson* performs; Tuskegee Little Theatre students take
   part in the dramatization.

LET NO MAN WRITE MY EPITAPH
Nar/Cast: Bernie Hamilton* + Ella Fitzgerald* + Shelley
   Winters + Burl Ives + James Darren
Screenplay: Robert Presnell, Jr.   Story: Willard Motley*
Producer: Boris D. Kaplan   Director: Phillip Leacock
Studio/Company: Columbia
Date/Country: 1960 + USA   Type: Feature
Annotation: James Darren struggles against slum conditions
   and a step-father who has hooked his mother on drugs.
   Ella Fitzgerald plays a night club singer hooked on drugs;

she also sings one number.

LET THE CHURCH SAY AMEN
Producer: St. Clair Bourne*
Studio/Company: Chamba
Tech Info: 16 mm/sound/color/2 reels/78 min.
Date/Country: 1972 + USA   Type: Documentary
Distr/Arch: bfc
Annotation: Focuses on the role of the contemporary black
    church from the viewpoint of a young man from his seminary
    experience to the pastorate.   Received bronze medal in
    International Film and Television festival in N.Y.

LET THE GOOD TIMES ROLL
Nar/Cast: Chuck Berry* + Little Richard* + Chubby Checker* +
    Bo Diddley* + The Shirelles* + The Coasters* + Fats
    Domino*   Director: Sid Levin
Studio/Company: Columbia
Tech Info: 16 mm/color/sound/3 reels/99 min.
Date/Country: 1973 + USA   Type: Documentary
Distr/Arch: swa
Annotation: Old favorites of the fifties like Chuck Berry
    and Chubby Checker are showcased as they performed then
    and now; numerous artists are included.

LET THE RAIN SETTLE IT
Producer: St. Francis Productions
Tech Info: 16 mm/sound/color/1 reel/13 min.
Date/Country: 1970 + USA   Type: Dramatized Documentary
Distr/Arch: iu + roa
Annotation: Presents the experiences of a white man and his
    eleven- year-old son as car trouble forces them into a
    rural southern black family environment. Shows the white
    boy's reactions, experiences, and attitudes during his
    stay, and relates his feelings to those of the Afro-
    American boy and his grandparents.

LET THEM COME WITH RAIN
Series: U.N. International Zone
Nar/Cast: Alistair Cooke
Producer: United Nations
Tech Info: 16 mm/sound/color
Date/Country: Botswana   Type: Documentary
Distr/Arch: jou + kent + uill + untv
Annotation: Since the Kalahari desert comprises much of Bot-
    swana, the country's leaders look toward the desert's
    natural resources to build an industrial future.

LET'S DO IT AGAIN
Nar/Cast: Bill Cosby* + Denise Nichols* + Sidney Poitier* +
    J.J. Walker* + Billy Eckstine*   Director: Sidney Poitier*
Studio/Company: Warner Brothers
Tech Info: 16 mm/color/soundd/112 min.
Date/Country: 1975 + USA   Type: Feature
Distr/Arch: swa
Annotation: Walker is "boxer" Bootney Farnsworth who is set
    up by Cosby and Poitier in a title match and the trouble
    begins when the bets are laid with mobsters.   Billy Eck-

stine has a small acting role.

LET'S SWITCH
Nar/Cast: Barbara Eden + Barbara Feldon + Pat Harrington +
    Ron Glass*
Screenplay: Peter Lefcourt + Ruth Brooks Flippen + Andy
    Chubby Williams + Sid Arthur
Producer: Bruce Johnson   Director: Alan Rafkin
Studio/Company: Universal City Studios Production
Date/Country: 1974 + USA   Type: TV Feature
Annotation: Ron Glass plays LaRue Williams in this comedy
    about two friends who decide to exchange roles and ways of
    life; one is a women's magazine editor (Feldon), the other
    a suburban housewife/mother (Eden).

LIBERATION OF L.B. JONES, THE
Nar/Cast: Roscoe Lee Brown* + Brenda Skyes* + Lola Falana* +
    Yaphet Kotto* + Lee Majors + Lee J. Cobb + Fayard
    Nicholas*
Screenplay: Sterling Silliphant + Jesse Hill Ford
Producer: Ronald Lubill   Director: William Wyler
Studio/Company: Columbia
Tech Info: 16 mm/sound/color/102 min.
Date/Country: 1970 + USA   Type: Feature
Distr/Arch: swa
Annotation: L.B. Jones a black undertaker (Brown) sues his
    wife (Falana) for divorce when he discovers she is having
    an affair with a redneck policeman, but the only libera-
    tion he is allowed is death - and gratuitous castration -
    in the racist town of Somerton, Tennessee, where blacks
    are unsafe no matter what their class or financial status.

LIBERTE UN
Nar/Cast: Maurice Ronet + Croinne Marchand + Iba Gueye* +
    Nanette Senghor* + Assane Fall* + Rose Basse + Frederique
    Andrew + Regine Reyre + Alain Le Layec + Sonar Senghor* +
    Absoulaye Diof* + Douta Seck + Diouf Malik + Pierre Cazes
    + Michel caussades + J.P. Loubet
Screenplay: Charles Tacchella + R.M. Arlaud   Story: Yves
    Ciampi + Jean Campistron
Producer: Jean Cotet   Director: Yves Ciampi
Studio/Company: P.A.t. Films-Sorafilms + Ucina
Tech Info: 35 mm/bw/sound/90 min.
Date/Country: 1962 + France + Senegal   Type: Feature
Distr/Arch: saf
Annotation: Presented at the 15th Cannes Festival, 1962.
    Ronet plays Michel; Marchand, Anne; Iba Gueye, Malik;
    Senghor, Aminata; Assane Fall, Abdoulaye. No further in-
    formation available.

LIEBALALA
Nar/Cast: Margaret Cameron Hubbard
Studio/Company: University of Calif.
Tech Info: 16 mm/bw/sound/2 reels/58 min.
Date/Country: 1935 + Zambia   Type: Dramatized Documentary
Distr/Arch: cal
Annotation: Originally filmed in 1935 by Margaret Cameron
    Hubbard in Barotseland, the film has recently been

"rediscovered." It is basically a travelogue which includes a melodrama of Lozi social life (with Lozi actors
directed by visiting westerners). Interesting are sequences on fishing, iron-making and Chokwe masquerading.
Sound track of authentic Lozi music taped by ethnomusi-
cologist Hugh Tracey has been added.

LIFE_GOES_ON
Alt Title(s): His Harlem Wife
Nar/Cast: Louise Beavers* + Edward Thompson* + Reginald
    Fenderson* + Lawrence Criner* + Monte Hawley* + Hope Ben-
    nett* + Jesse Lee Brooks* + May Turner* + Artie Brandon* +
    Edward Robertson* + Oliver Farmer* + Eloise Witherspoon* +
    Lillian Randolph*
Screenplay: Paul Dunham
Studio/Company: Million Dollar Studios Production
Date/Country: 1938 + USA   Type: Feature
Annotation: Louise Beavers, a widow from the South, has joy
    from one son (Edward Thompson) who becomes a prosperous
    lawyer but anxiety from the other (Reginald Fenderson),
    who is accused of a murder he did not commit. Courtroom
    drama ensues when one brother defends the other.

LIFE_IN_HARLEM
Series: Colored America on Parade
Nar/Cast: E.W. Lewis   Director: Edward W. Lewis
Studio/Company: Sack Amusement Corp.
Tech Info: 16 mm/bw/sound/1 reel/10 min.
Date/Country: 1940 + USA   Type: Documentary
Distr/Arch: kpf
Annotation: Life_in_Harlem is part of the documentary
    series, "Colored America on Parade" produced for all-black
    theatres.

LIFE_IN_SENEGAL
Producer: Gaumont
Date/Country: 1910   Type: Documentary
Annotation: Black school boys working hard on their studies.

LIFE_IS_REAL
Nar/Cast: Nina Mae McKinney*
Date/Country: 1934 + USA

LIFE_OF_BOOKER_T._WASHINGTON
Date/Country: 1940

LIFE_OF_FLORENCE_MILLS
Studio/Company: Duo Art Pictures
Date/Country: 1940

LIFE_OF_GEORGE_WASHINGTON_CARVER
Date/Country: 1940

LIFEBOAT
Nar/Cast: Tullulah Bankhead + John Hodiak + Henry Hull +
    Walter Slezak + Canada Lee* + Hume Cronyn
Screenplay: Jo Swerling   Story: John Steinbeck
Producer: Kenneth Macgowan   Director: Alfred Hitchcock

Studio/Company: Twentieth Century Fox
Tech Info: 16 mm/bw/sound/3 reels/97 min.
Date/Country: 1944 + USA   Type: Feature
Distr/Arch: fnc + ime
Annotation: Nine victims of a torpedoed American vessel
    during World War II find themselves afloat on the Atlantic
    in a tiny lifeboat. Eight of the survivors represent a
    broad cross-section of American society, including a black
    steward, Joe (Canada Lee), who has just saved a drowning
    woman and her child.

LIFTING_AS_WE_CLIMB
Producer: Artisan Production + National Association of
    Colored Women
Tech Info: 16 mm/sound/bw/1 reel/15 min.
Date/Country: 1953 + USA   Type: Documentary
Distr/Arch: iu
Annotation: Discusses the activities and the program of the
    National Association of Colored Women. Traces the growth
    of the organization from 1896 to 1953. Points to the past
    achievements of the organization and outlines its program
    for the future.

LIGHT_OF_ETHIOPIA
Producer: Educational Film Enterprise, Inc.
Tech Info: 16 mm/sound/bw/26 min.
Date/Country: 1956 + Ethiopia   Type: Documentary
Distr/Arch: efe
Annotation: The annexation of Ethiopia by Mussolini's army
    is told.

LIGHT_SHINES_IN_BAKUBALAND,_THE
Series: National Archives Gift Collection
Tech Info: 16 mm/silent/3 reels/bw
Annotation: A true story. A missionary evangelist wins over
    one of the last remaining independent tribes. (Part of
    Record Group 200 H.F. series, Harmon Foundation Collec-
    tion).

LIGHTNING   Story: Zane Grey
Studio/Company: Tiffany Productions, Inc.
Tech Info: 7 reels
Date/Country: 1926   Type: Feature
Annotation: In this film, the female leads do a Topsy and
    Eva act a la Uncle Tom's Cabin.

LIKE_A_BEAUTIFUL_CHILD
Producer: John Schultz
Tech Info: 16 mm/sound/bw/27 min.
Date/Country: 1967 + USA   Type: Documentary
Distr/Arch: mac
Annotation: Drug and hospital employees struggle for dignity
    and adequate wages. Presented by Local 1199, Drug and
    Hospital Employees Union, AFL-CIO.

LILITH
Nar/Cast: Ben Carruthers* + Jean Seberg + Warren Beatty
    Director: Robert Rossen

Studio/Company: Columbia
Tech Info: 16 mm/sound/bw/114 min.
Date/Country: 1964 + USA   Type: Feature
Distr/Arch: ccc + cha + con + cwf + mac + mod + mot + swa +
    twy + whc
Annotation: Ben Carruthers is Benito in this drama about a
    Korean war veteran (Beatty) who falls in love with a
    beautiful mentally ill patient in the mental institution
    where he works.

LILLIES_OF_THE_FIELD
Nar/Cast: Sidney Poitier* + Lilia Skala
Screenplay: James Poe   Story: William E. Barrett
Producer: Ralph Nelson   Director: Ralph Nelson
Studio/Company: United Artists
Tech Info: 16 mm/bw/sound/3 reels/97 min.
Date/Country: 1963 + USA   Type: Feature
Distr/Arch: mac + uas
Annotation: Poitier won an Oscar for his role as a traveling
    vagabond who befriends a group of immigrant nuns and helps
    them build a missionary school.

LIMIT,_THE
Nar/Cast: Yaphet Kotto* + Quinn Redeher + Pamela Jones*
Screenplay: Sean Cameron   Story: Yaphet Kotto*
Producer: Frank Roh   Director: Yaphet Kotto*
Studio/Company: Cannon
Tech Info: 90 min.
Date/Country: 1972 + USA   Type: Feature
Annotation: Black motorcycle policeman makes friends with
    the leader of a motorcycle gang thereby incurring the
    wrath of the gang who seeks revenge.

LINCOLN_THE_LOVER
Annotation: Portrays Lincoln's love for Ann Rutledge and has
    a scene where a "darkey servant" ponders affectionately
    over Lincoln in his sleep by the fire.

LINCOLN'S_DREAM
Alt Title(s): see Birth of a Race

LION_HUNTERS,_THE
Producer: Jean Rouch
Studio/Company: Films de la Pleiade
Tech Info: 16 mm/sound/color/2 reels/68 min.
Date/Country: 1965   Type: Documentary
Distr/Arch: iu + cal + con + mac + tfc
Annotation: Follows Gao hunters on a lion hunt near the
    border of Mali and Niger. Explains in the words of the
    hunters the meanings and reasons for many of their
    procedures, beliefs, and rituals.   Includes visual and
    narrated ethnography of the Gao and the Fulani, the
    Tuareg, and the Belie with whom they come in contact.

LION_OF_JUDAH,_THE:_HAILE_SELASSIE_OF_ETHIOPIA
Producer: BBC-TV
Tech Info: 16 mm/sound/color/50 min.
Date/Country: 1972 + Ethiopia   Type: Dramatized Documentary

Distr/Arch: timlif
Annotation: The past and present history of Ethiopia plus
   the life of Haile Selassie.

LION, THE
Nar/Cast: Rafer Johnson* + William Holden + Trevor Howard +
   Makara Kwaiha* + Ramadhani Zakee* + Paul Oduor* +
   Christopher Agunda* + Pamela Franklin*
Screenplay: Louis Kamp + Irene Kamp
Producer: Samuel Engel   Director: Jack Cardiff
Studio/Company: Fox
Tech Info: 16mm/ sound/ color/ 96 min.
Date/Country: 1962 + USA   Type: Feature
Distr/Arch: fnc
Annotation: Filmed in South Africa, this adventure melodrama
   deals only peripherally with an African tribal chief,
   whose life is saved by an American lawyer visiting his
   ex-wife and daughter at a game reserve supervised by the
   wife's new husband. Complications arise because the lawy-
   er has interfered with tribal custom.

LIONEL HAMPTON AND HERB JEFFRIES
Nar/Cast: Lionel Hampton and his band* + Vicky Lee* + Lolsy
   White* + The Four Hamptons*   Director: Will Cowan
Studio/Company: Universal International
Tech Info: 15 min.
Date/Country: 1955 + USA   Type: Musical Short
Annotation: Focuses on the artists above performing, for
   example, "Baby, Don't Love Me" and "Black Coffee."

LIONEL HAMPTON AND HIS ORCHESTRA
Alt Title(s): Negro Marches On   Director: Will Cowan
Studio/Company: Universal-International
Tech Info: 14 min.
Date/Country: 1949 + USA   Type: Musical Short

LISBON STORY, THE
Nar/Cast: Walter Rilla + David Farrar + Patricia Burke +
   Lawrence O'Madden + Austin Trevor + Paul Bonifas + Ralph
   Truman + Harry Welchman + Esme Percy + Allan Jeayes + Fela
   Sowande*
Screenplay: Harold Purcell + Harry Parr-Davies
Producer: Louis H. Jordan   Director: Paul L. Stein
Studio/Company: Four Continents Films, Inc.
Tech Info: 16 mm/sound/bw/98 min.
Date/Country: 1946 + Britain   Type: Feature
Distr/Arch: ivy

LISTEN WHITEY
Producer: Granada
Tech Info: 16 mm/sound/bw/30 min.
Date/Country: USA   Type: Documentary
Distr/Arch: imp
Annotation: The black ghetto of Washington, D.C. responds to
   the assassination of Martin Luther King.

LITTLE BLACK SAMBO
Producer: Celebrity Pictures   Director: U.B. Iwerks

Studio/Company: Celebrity Pictures Cartoon
Tech Info: 16 mm/color/sound/1 reel/10 min.
Date/Country: 1933 + USA   Type: Animated Short
Annotation: This film is an animated version of the old
    story with Sambo as a black child with a dog, and a mother
    who seems to be part of the American scene. This tiger
    doesn't turn to butter but is outwitted and physically
    beaten by Sambo and his dog.

LITTLE COLONEL, THE
War/Cast: Shirley Temple + Lionel Barrymore + John Lodge +
    Evelyn Venable + Bill Robinson* + Hattie McDaniel*
Screenplay: William Conselman   Story: Anne Fellows Johnston
    Director: David Butler
Studio/Company: Twentieth Century Fox
Tech Info: 16 mm/bw/sound/2 reels/80 min.
Date/Country: 1935 + USA   Type: Feature
Distr/Arch: fnc
Annotation: Elizabeth leaves her father (Barrymore), unre-
    constructed Colonel Lloyd, to marry Jack, a Yankee
    soldier. She and their child Laura, the "Little Colonel"
    (Shirley Temple) later return South to await Jack's return
    but live poorly, helped only by the black folk - Hattie
    McDaniel as Mom Beck and Bill Robinson as Walker, the but-
    ler who teaches the Little Colonel some of his best dance
    steps. All problems are solved when the irascible Colonel
    is won over by Laura, Walker and Mom Beck.

LITTLE DAIDY
Series: Our Gang
War/Cast: Our Gang + Matthew Beard* + Allen Hoskins*
Screenplay: H.M. Walker
Producer: Robert F. McGowan + Hal Roach   Director: Robert
    F. McGowan
Studio/Company: MGM
Tech Info: super 8 mm/16 mm/sound/1 reel/21 min.
Date/Country: 1931 + USA   Type: Comedy Short
Distr/Arch: bla
Annotation: Farina is Stymie's guardian in this film which
    involves a farewell party for Stymie before he's to be
    sent off to an orphanage. Stymie manages to eat all the
    party food before the gang arrives but everyone unites to
    drive off the orphanage official. A strong vehicle for
    Matthew Beard who stars as Stymie. Allen Hoskins* stars
    as Farina.

LITTLE DARK ANGELS
Alt Title(s): see Angelitos Negroes

LITTLE EVA ASCENDS   Director: George Baker
Date/Country: 1922 + USA
Annotation: Has a sequence in which a play version of Uncle
    Tom's Cabin is performed. From a story in the Saturday
    Evening Post.

LITTLE FOXES, THE
War/Cast: Bette Davis
Screenplay: Lillian Hellman + Arthur Kober + Dorothy Parker

Producer: Samuel Goldwyn   Director: William Wyler
Tech Info: 16 mm/sound/bw/116 min.
Date/Country: 1941 + USA   Type: Feature
Distr/Arch: aim + mac
Annotation: blacks are background, occasional commentators
    on, but peripheral to the action in this adaptation of
    Hellman's play about a southern family in decay in the
    early 1900's.

LITTLE_LADIES_OF_THE_NIGHT
Nar/Cast: David Soul + Lou Gossett* + Linda Purl + Clifton
    Davis*
Screenplay: Hal Sitowitz
Producer: Hal Sitowitz   Director: Marvin Chomsky
Studio/Company: Spelling-Goldberg Production
Date/Country: 1977 + USA   Type: TV Feature
Annotation: A young girl runs away from her parents after
    being rejected by them and finds immediate acceptance in a
    prostitution ring. Two New York cops (Soul and Gossett)
    work to get her away from that lifestyle but her pimp
    (Davis), her own fears, and governmental red tape hamper
    her escape.

LITTLE_MEN
Nar/Cast: Ralph Morgan + Phyllis Fraser + Hattie McDaniel* +
    Dickie Moore
Screenplay: Gertrude Orr   Story: Louisa May Alcott
    Director: Phil Rosen
Studio/Company: Mascot
Tech Info: 16 mm/sound/bw/80 min.
Date/Country: 1934 + USA   Type: Feature
Distr/Arch: fce
Annotation: Film adaptation of Ms. Alcott's book with Hattie
    McDaniel playing her usual maid part.

LITTLE_MISS_MARKER
Nar/Cast: Shirley Temple + Willie Best* + Charles Bickford +
    Adolph Menjou   Story: Damon Runyan
Studio/Company: Paramount
Tech Info: 16 mm/bw/sound/2 reels
Date/Country: 1934 + USA   Type: Feature
Distr/Arch: uni
Annotation: Willie Best plays nursemaid to Shirley Temple
    who dubs him "The Black Knight" in this sentimental drama
    about an orphaned child being raised by gamblers.

LITTLE_MISS_PINKERTON
Series: Our Gang
Nar/Cast: Our Gang + Billie Thomas*
Screenplay: Hal Law + Robert A. McGowan
Producer: MGM   Director: Herbert Glazer
Studio/Company: MGM
Tech Info: bw/sound/1 reel
Date/Country: 1943 + USA   Type: Comedy Short
Annotation: The gang wants a chance to solve a $100 murder
    mystery promotion and is helped by a kindly janitor who is
    later killed by real crooks who take most of the gang
    hostage. Of course, they are eventually saved. Billie

Thomas plays Buckwheat.

LITTLE_MOTHER
Series: Our Gang
Nar/Cast: Our Gang + Allen Hoskins*
Screenplay: Robert F. McGowan
Producer: Robert F. McGowan + Hal Roach   Director: Robert
    F. McGowan
Studio/Company: MGM
Tech Info: super 8 mm/bw/silent/1 reel
Date/Country: 1929 + USA   Type: Comedy Short
Distr/Arch: bla
Annotation: Since their mother has died, Mary Ann must take
    care of her brothers Wheezer and Beezer while father works
    as a night watchman. Between gags the children hope for
    the return of mother from heaven - and one day she appears
    - in the form of mother's twin sister who decides to let
    them go on believing mother has returned.   Allen   Hoskins
    stars as Stymie.

LITTLE_PAPA
Series: Our Gang
Nar/Cast: Our Gang + Billie Thomas*
Producer: Hal Roach   Director: Gus Meins
Studio/Company: MGM + Roach
Tech Info: super 8 mm/16 mm/bw/sound/1 reel/20 min.
Date/Country: 1935 + USA   Type: Comedy Short
Distr/Arch: roa + bla
Annotation: Spanky tries to make his baby brother sleepy so
    that he can skip out to play football. Billie   Thomas
    stars as Buckwheat.

LITTLE_RANGER,_THE
Series: Our Gang
Nar/Cast: Our Gang + Billie Thomas*
Screenplay: Hal Law + Robert McGowan
Producer: Jack Chertok   Director: Gordon Douglas
Studio/Company: MGM
Tech Info: bw/sound/1 reel
Date/Country: 1938 + USA   Type: Comedy Short
Annotation: Alfalfa   and   Butch's rivalry for Darla's affec-
    tions is partly resolved when Alfalfa dreams in a   movie
    house, transferring the screen characters into the gang.
    Alfalfa's date, Muggsy, saves the day in the dream and
    becomes Alfalfa's new girl when he awakens. Billie Thomas
    stars as Buckwheat.

LITTLE_RASCALS,_THE
Alt Title(s): See Our Gang Series (individual titles listed)

LITTLE_ROBINSON_CRUSOE
Nar/Cast: Jackie Coogan + Daniel J. O'Brian + Noble Johnson*
    + Tote Dulrow*
Screenplay: Willard Mack
Studio/Company: Jackie Coogan Prod.
Date/Country: 1924
Annotation: Orphan Jackie Coogan sets sail for Australia to
    live with relatives, but gets shipwrecked on an island

inhabited by cannibals - who worhip him as a war god.   He
saves a neighboring settlement and is returned to San
Francisco a hero. Noble Johnson plays a cannibal chief.

LITTLE SINNER
Series: Our Gang
Nar/Cast: Our Gang + Billie Thomas*
Producer: Hal Roach   Director: Gus Meins
Studio/Company: MGM + Roach
Tech Info: super 8 mm/16 mm/bw/sound/2 reels/17 min.
Date/Country: 1935 + USA   Type: Comedy Short
Distr/Arch: roa + bla
Annotation: Skipping Sunday school to go fishing, Spanky,
   accompanied by Porky and Buckwheat, risks divine punish-
   ment.   A series of coincidences (including an eclipse of
   the sun) convinces him he's getting it and he dashes back
   to church.   Also involved is a black baptism with chorus
   and a brief encounter by Spanky with two Blacks in white
   clothing, shouting 'Halleliujah'. Billie Thomas stars as
   Buckwheat.

LITTLEST REBEL, THE
Nar/Cast: Shirley Temple + Jack Holt + Bill Robinson* +
   Guinn Williams + Willie Best* + Hannah Washington*
   Director: David Butler
Studio/Company: Twentieth Century Fox
Tech Info: 16 mm/bw/sound/2 reels/80 min.
Date/Country: 1936 + USA   Type: Feature
Distr/Arch: fnc
Annotation: Civil War picture, in which the "good" Con-
   federate folk are set upon by the "bad" Yankees. Shirley
   Temple puts on blackface to save herself but when that
   fails, she calls on Uncle Billy (Robinson) to protect her.
   He becomes guardian when her father is taken North to a
   prison camp and her mother dies. Uncle Billy and Shirley
   then tap dance their fare (Willie Best passes the hat) to
   Mr. Lincoln to importune the President for the release of
   her father.

LIVE AND LET DIE
Nar/Cast: Yaphet Kotto* + Geoffrey Holder* + Brock Peters* +
   Gloria Hendry* + Roger Moore + Julius Harris*   Story: Ian
   Fleming   Director: Guy Hamilton
Studio/Company: United Artists
Tech Info: 16 mm/sound/color/125 min.
Date/Country: 1973 + USA   Type: Feature
Distr/Arch: uas
Annotation: In the eighth James Bond film with Roger Moore
   in the starring role, the villains are overwhelmingly
   black. Bond tracks down a drug smuggling operation from
   Harlem to the Caribbean islands to New Orleans; Yaphet
   Kotto and Julius Harris are the criminal operators who are
   wiped out by Bond in the name of justice. Holder plays
   the voodoo prince.

LIVES OF A BENGAL LANCER, THE
Nar/Cast: Gary Cooper + Franchot Tone + Noble Johnson*
Screenplay: Grover Jones + William S. McNutt + Waldemer

Young
Producer: Louis D. Lighton   Director: Henry Hathaway
Studio/Company: Paramount
Tech Info: 16 mm/sound/bw/110 min.
Date/Country: 1935 + USA   Type: Feature
Distr/Arch: mma + uni
Annotation: Blood and guts melodrama about the British who
   patroled India's northern frontier. Noble Johnson plays
   Ram Singh, one of the turbaned "Indians."

LIVING BETWEEN TWO WORLDS
Nar/Cast: Maye Henderson* + Anita Poree* + Mami Dillard* +
   Horace Jackson* + Napoleon Whiting*
Producer: Horace Johnson   Director: Robert Johnson
Studio/Company: Empire Films
Tech Info: sound/ b w/ 78 min.
Date/Country: 1963 + USA   Type: Feature
Annotation: Ivan Dixon* was assistant director of this film
   about a young man who, although strongly devoted to his
   mother (Henderson), has difficulty deciding on the voca-
   tion he has trained for (the ministry) after his fiancee
   (Dillard) is raped by two whites. He makes his decision
   and is highly successful.

LOADED DOOR, THE
Nar/Cast: Noble Johnson* + Hoot Gibson
Studio/Company: Universal
Tech Info: silent/bw
Date/Country: 1922 + USA
Annotation: Johnson is "Blackie Lopez" in this Gibson
   western.

LOBOLA
Producer: Jan M. Perold
Tech Info: 16 mm/sound/bw/1 reel/26 min.
Date/Country: 1954 + South Africa   Type: Documentary
Distr/Arch: iu + con + ccunesco + uill + ucemc
Annotation: Pictures some of the personal and social pro-
   blems arising out of cultural differences between two
   tribes and also the movement of Blacks into the urban
   areas of the white man. Uses photography and a narration
   frequently interposed with native proverbs.

LODGE NIGHT
Series: Our Gang
Nar/Cast: Our Gang + Ernie Morrison* + Allen Hoskins* +
   Ernie Morrison Sr.*
Screenplay: Hal Roach
Producer: Hal Roach   Director: Robert McGowan
Studio/Company: Pathe
Tech Info: super 8 mm/16 mm/silent/bw/1 reel
Date/Country: 1923 + USA   Type: Comedy Short
Distr/Arch: bla
Annotation: Our Gang parodies of the KKK, by having a club
   called the Cluck Cluck Klams. This time the gang is in-
   strumental in bringing car thieves to justice. A subplot
   has a black professor addressing a group which ends up
   shooting craps. Allen Hoskins stars as Farina.

LONG NIGHT, THE   Story: Julian Mayfield*   Director: Woodie
    King*
Date/Country: 1976 + USA   Type: Feature
Annotation: A family film about a young boy's attempt to
    recover $27.00 of his mother's money that was stolen from
    him. Analyzed in the film are the pressures on black fam-
    ily life in America.

LONG SHIPS, THE
Nar/Cast: Sidney Poitier* + Richard Widmark + Rosanna Schi-
    affino
Screenplay: Berkeley Mather + Beverly Cross
Producer: Irving Allen   Director: Jack Cardiff
Studio/Company: Columbia
Tech Info: 16 mm/color/sound/4 reels/125 min.
Date/Country: 1964 + Britain + Yugoslavia   Type: Feature
Distr/Arch: arg + bud + mac + mot + roa + tfc + twy
Annotation: Poitier plays powerful Moorish sheik El Mansuh,
    a romanticized villain, in this adventure melodrama about
    a Viking Thane (Widmark) searching for the lost Golden
    Bell of St. James.

LONGEST YARD, THE
Nar/Cast: Burt Reynolds + Eddie Albert + Dino Washington* +
    Ray Nitschke + Sonny Sixkiller
Screenplay: Tracy Keenan Wynn
Producer: Albert S. Ruddy   Director: Robert Aldrich
Studio/Company: Paramount
Tech Info: color/121 min.
Date/Country: 1974 + USA   Type: Feature
Distr/Arch: fnc
Annotation: Blacks play some of the inmates in this story of
    an ex-pro football player who gets sent to a Southern
    jail. The key scene in the film is when the inmates,
    coached by Reynolds, play competitive football against the
    guards.

LONNIE'S DAY
Producer: Coronet Films
Tech Info: 16 mm/sound/bw/1 reel/14 min.
Date/Country: 1969 + USA   Type: Dramatized Documentary
Distr/Arch: iu + corf
Annotation: Depicts one day in the life of an eight-year-old
    Black who lives in a high-rise ghetto apartment building.
    Shows him at school, at home, and in his social group.
    Illustrates the contrast between the child's dream world
    of rock-and-roll singers and the harsh reality of conflict
    in his home.

LOOK OUT, SISTER
Nar/Cast: Louis Jordan* and his "Caledonia" Tympany Band* +
    Betty Scott* + Monte Hawley*
Screenplay: John Gordon
Producer: R.M. Savini   Director: Bud Pollard
Studio/Company: Astor Pictures + Leo Film
Tech Info: 16 mm/bw/sound/2 reels/67 min.
Date/Country: 1946 + USA   Type: Feature

Distr/Arch: bud + emg + lc
Annotation: Musical with a minor plot.

LOOKING FOR MR. GOODBAR
Nar/Cast: Diane Keaton + LeVar Burton*   Director: Richard
  Brooks
Date/Country: 1977 + USA
Annotation: LeVar Burton has a small role in this adaptation
  of Judith Rossner's novel about a sexually starved woman.

LORD SHANGO   Director: Raymond Marsh
Tech Info: 91 min.
Date/Country: 1975 + USA
Annotation: Displays the conflicts between tribal traditions
  and old southern gospel traditions.

LORRAINE HANSBERRY: THE BLACK EXPERIENCE IN THE CREATION OF
  DRAMA
Nar/Cast: Sidney Poitier* + Ruby Dee* + Diana Sands* + Roy
  Scheider + Al Freeman, Jr.* + Claudia McNeil*
Tech Info: 16 mm/sound/color/35 min.
Date/Country: USA   Type: Dramatized Documentary
Distr/Arch: aof
Annotation: Traces life of Lorraine Hansberry, leading black
  playwright from childhood to her early death at the age of
  34. Excerpts from her plays included: A Raisin in the
  Sun, The Sign in Sidney Brustein's Window, Les Blancs.
  Claudia McNeil narrates.

LOSERS, THE
Nar/Cast: Bernie Hamilton* + Adam Roarke
Screenplay: Alan Caillou
Producer: Joe Solomon   Director: Jack Starrett
Studio/Company: Fanfare Film Production
Tech Info: 16 mm/sound/color/90 min.
Date/Country: 1971 + USA   Type: Feature
Distr/Arch: bud + wcf + pru
Annotation: Five former motorcycle gang members turned Army
  men attempt to rescue a Presidential advisor from the Viet
  Cong. Bernie Hamilton plays Army Captain Jackson.   Side
  plot has him reunited with a native girl and their child
  whom he had deserted.

LOSING JUST THE SAME
Producer: NET
Tech Info: 16 mm/bw/sound/2 reels/60 min.
Date/Country: 1966   Type: Documentary
Distr/Arch: iu + cal
Annotation: Illustrates the hope and despair of Blacks in
  urban America through the life of a single family. Shows
  the the mother in spite of all their poverty, dreams of
  her children's success. Focuses on her 17-year-old son
  who drops out of school and gets a job in order to fulfill
  his dream of owning a fine car and shows the dreams of
  both mother and son being shattered when he is accused of
  arson and sent to jail.

LOST BOUNDARIES

Nar/Cast: Bill Greaves* + Canada Lee* + Beatrice Pearson +
  Mel Ferrer   Story: William L. White
Producer: Louis de Rochemont   Director: Alfred L. Werker
Tech Info: 16 mm/bw/sound/3 reels/99 min.
Date/Country: 1949 + USA   Type: Feature
Distr/Arch: wsa
Annotation: Concerns a New Hampshire physician "passing" for
  white and his children who are unaware of their "Negro"
  blood. Mel Ferrer and Beatrice Pearson play the mulatto
  physician and his wife.

LOST CONTINENT, THE
Nar/Cast: Ben Carruthers* + Eric Porter + Hildegard Knef
Screenplay: Michael Nash
Producer: Michael Carreras   Director: Michael Carreras
Studio/Company: Fox
Tech Info: 16 mm/sound/bw/89 min.
Date/Country: 1968 + Britain   Type: Feature
Distr/Arch: fnc
Annotation: Carruthers is Ricaldi who is an agent sent to
  recover money stolen by Eva, ex-mistress of a Latin
  dictator, in this science fiction drama which takes place
  mainly on board a freighter sailing from Africa to South
  America.   Ricaldi is, however, carried off by an octopus
  during a hurricane.

LOST EXPRESS, THE
Nar/Cast: Martin Turner* + Henry Barrows + Helen holmes
Producer: Morris R. Schlank   Director: J.P. McGowan
Tech Info: 35 mm/silent/bw/5 reels
Date/Country: 1926 + USA   Type: Feature
Annotation: Martin Turner plays George Washington Jones in
  this melodrama about trains, kidnapping, family problems
  and reconciliation.

LOST HORIZON
Nar/Cast: Ronald Colman + Jane Wyatt + Hall Johnson Choir*
  Director: Frank Capra
Studio/Company: Columbia
Tech Info: 16 mm/sound/bw/120 min.
Date/Country: 1937   Type: Feature
Distr/Arch: con + ics + mac + mod + new + swa + twy + wcf +
  wel + who
Annotation: Hall Johnson Choir sings its spirituals in the
  classic film of Shangri-La.

LOST IN THE STARS
Nar/Cast: Brock Peters* + Melba Moore* + Raymond St. Jac-
  ques* + Clifton Davis* + Paul Rogers + Paulene Myers +
  Paula Kelly* + H.B. Barnum, III + Jitu Cumbuka*
Screenplay: Alfred Hayes + Walt Hannemann   Story: Kurt
  Weill + Maxwell Anderson
Producer: Ely Landau + Edward Lewis   Director: Daniel Mann
Studio/Company: American Express Films, Inc. + Ely Landau
  Independent Organization Inc. + Cinevision LTEE
Tech Info: 16 mm/color/sound/3 reels/105 min.
Date/Country: 1973 + USA   Type: Feature
Distr/Arch: aft + rbc

Annotation: Musical version of Cry, the Beloved Country by
Alan Paton, stars Brock Peters as Stephen Kumalo in search
of his son Absalom who has left his home for Johannesburg.
The tragedy of two families dramatizes the tragedy of
South Africa. Much of the film was shot in Jamaica.

LOST_IN_THE_STRATOSPHERE
Nar/Cast: Hattie McDaniel* + Eddie Nugent   Director:
   Melville Brown
Studio/Company: Monogram
Tech Info: 16 mm/sound/bw/70 min.
Date/Country: 1934 + USA   Type: Feature
Distr/Arch: mog
Annotation: Hattie McDaniel plays a non-docile maid role.

LOST_LADY,_THE
Alt Title(s): see Safe in Hell

LOST_MAN,_THE
Nar/Cast: Sidney Poitier* + Cathy Ellis* + Al Freeman, Jr.*
   + Leon Bibb* + Joanna Shimkus + Bernie Hamilton* + Beverly
   Todd* + Paul Winfield* + Virginia Capers* + Vonetta McGee*
   + Lincoln Kilpatrick*
Screenplay: Robert Alan Aurthur
Producer: Edward Muhl + Melville Tucker   Director: Robert
   Alan Aurthur
Studio/Company: Universal
Tech Info: 16 mm/color/sound/3 reels/105 min.
Date/Country: 1969 + USA   Type: Feature
Distr/Arch: cwf + twy + uni
Annotation: Sidney Poitier as Jacob Higgs is uncompromising
   in his desire to provide a decent future for children of
   the ghetto. (Based on the film Odd_Man_Out, 1947, about
   the IRA--Irish Revolutionary Army).

LOST_WORLD,_THE
Nar/Cast: Bessie Love + Lloyd Hughes + Lewis Stone + Wallace
   Beery + Arthur Hoyt + Margaret McWade + Finch Smiles +
   Jules Cowles   Story: Sir Arthur Conan Doyle
Studio/Company: First National Pictures
Tech Info: 35 mm/silent/bw/10 reels
Date/Country: 1925 + USA   Type: Feature
Annotation: Prof. Challenger hypothesizes the existence of a
   lost world in South America and in order to prove himself
   he forms an expedition. The expedition includes, among
   others a "game and loyal black" and several "half-breeds."
   They return having found the lost world, with a
   brontosaurus that escapes in London, falls through the
   London Bridge and returns to the sea.

LOUIS_ARMSTRONG_AND_THE_ALL_STARS
Nar/Cast: Louis Armstrong* + Trummy Young* + Joe Darens-
   bowig* + Billy Kyle* + Billy Cronk* + Danny Barcelona* +
   Jewell Brown*
Producer: Mike Bryan
Studio/Company: Goodyear Tire Co.
Tech Info: color/sound/25 min.
Date/Country: 1961 + USA

Annotation: Performance by the above musicians includes the
   numbers: "C'est si bon," "Nobody Knows the Trouble I've
   Seen," "The Saints."

LOUIS ARMSTRONG: CHICAGO STYLE
Nar/Cast: Ben Vereen* + Red Buttons + Janet MacLachlan* +
   Ketty Lester*
Screenplay: James Le
Producer: Lee Philips   Director: Lee Philips
Studio/Company: Stonehenge-Charles Fries Productions
Date/Country: 1976 + USA   Type: TV Feature
Annotation: Dramatic portrayal of one of the greatest men of
   jazz. Ben Vereen plays Louis Armstrong.

LOUIS ARMSTRONG
Nar/Cast: Louis Armstrong*   Director: Richard Moore
Tech Info: 30 min.
Date/Country: 1963 + USA   Type: TV Documentary
Annotation: Armstrong performs his music and discusses it
   with Ralph J. Gleason, jazz music critic.

LOUIS ARMSTRONG
Nar/Cast: Louis Armstrong*
Tech Info: 9 min.
Date/Country: 1971 + USA   Type: Musical Short
Annotation: Short biography including a personal interview
   and a clip of him singing "I Can't Give You Anything but
   Love."

LOUIS ARMSTRONG
Nar/Cast: Louis Armstrong* + Jewell Brown* + Tommy Young +
   Billie Kyle + Joe Darensbourg + Danny Barcelona + Billy
   Cronk
Studio/Company: United Artists
Tech Info: 16 mm/color/sound/1 reel/28 min.
Date/Country: 1962 + USA   Type: Musical Short
Distr/Arch: kpf
Annotation: Armstrong performs his songs for the camera in
   this musical film.

LOUISE
Producer: Philip Gainin + WGBH-TV, Boston
Tech Info: 16 mm/sound/color/28 min.
Date/Country: 1973 + USA   Type: Documentary
Distr/Arch: yal
Annotation: Religious services in a small Mississippi Delta
   town focusing on two men and two women. Includes a
   baptism, church service and personal prayers. Provided by
   Center for Southern Folklore.

LOUISIANA DIARY
Producer: NET
Tech Info: 16 mm/sound/bw/2 reels/59 min.
Date/Country: 1963   Type: Documentary
Distr/Arch: iu
Annotation: Documents special efforts by a CORE (Congress of
   Racial Equality) group to assist Blacks in the Sixth Con-
   gressional District in Louisiana to register to vote. One

march results in the use of tear gas by the police and in
the arrest of CORE officials.

LOUISIANA PURCHASE
Nar/Cast: Bob Hope + Vera Zorina + Sam McDaniel*
Screenplay: Jerome Chodorov + Joseph Fields
Producer: B.G. De Sylva   Director: Irving Cummings
Studio/Company: Paramount
Tech Info: 16 mm/sound/color/98 min.
Date/Country: 1941 + USA   Type: Feature
Distr/Arch: uni
Annotation: Sam McDaniel has a bit role in this Bob Hope
   musical comedy, adapted from the Broadway stage hit.

LOUISIANA
Alt Title(s): see Drums O'Voodoo

LOVE AND UNDERTAKERS
Studio/Company: Colored and Indian Film Company
Date/Country: 1918 + USA

LOVE BUG, THE
Series: Our Gang
Nar/Cast: Our Gang + Allen Hoskins* + Eugene Jackson* +
   Ernie Morrison Sr.*
Screenplay: Hal Roach
Producer: Hal Roach   Director: Robert McGowan
Studio/Company: Pathe
Tech Info: silent/bw/2 reels
Date/Country: 1925 + USA   Type: Comedy Short
Annotation: After getting advice on their love lives, the
   gang heads for a deluxe beauty parlor where they find in-
   genious new uses for the various items there. Allen
   Hoskins stars as Farina and Eugene Jackson stars as
   Pineapple.

LOVE BUG, THE
Studio/Company: Norman Film Manufacturing Company
Date/Country: 1920 + USA

LOVE BUSINESS
Series: Our Gang
Nar/Cast: Our Gang + Matthew Beard* + Allen Hoskins*
Screenplay: H. M. Walker
Producer: Robert F. McGowan + Hal Roach   Director: Robert
   F. McGowan
Studio/Company: MGM + Roach
Tech Info: super 8 mm/16 mm/bw/sound/1 reel/20 min.
Date/Country: 1931 + USA   Type: Comedy Short
Distr/Arch: roa + kpf + bla
Annotation: Jackie and Chubby are both in love with Miss
   Crabtree, the teacher. Matthew Beard stars as Stymie and
   Allen Hoskins stars as Farina.

LOVE FLOWER, THE
Alt Title(s): Black Beach
Nar/Cast: Richard Barthelmess + Carol Demster + Adolphe
   Lestina

Screenplay: D.W. Griffith   Story: Ralph Stock   Director:
    D.W. Griffith
Studio/Company: First National + United Artists
Tech Info: 35 mm/silent/bw/7 reels
Date/Country: 1920 + USA   Type: Feature
Annotation: South sea adventure film with "Blacks" as na-
    tives. Previewed in New York under the title Black Beach,
    the title of the story from which it was adapted.

LOVE IN A BUNGALOW
Nar/Cast: Louise Beavers*
Date/Country: 1937 + USA   Type: Feature
Annotation: Louise Beavers plays a small role as
    maid/servant.

LOVE IN SYNCOPATION
Nar/Cast: Ruby Dee + Maxine Johnson* + Harrel Tillman* +
    Powell Lindsay* + June Eckstine* + Tops* and Wilda* + Ron-
    nel* and Edna* + The Woods Orchestra* + Henri Woods*
Producer: William Alexander
Studio/Company: Alexander Productions + Astor Pictures
Date/Country: 1947 + USA   Type: Feature
Annotation: During World War II some navy See Bees formed
    the Henri Woode Band; the film depicts their fight to gain
    recognition in the entertainment industry.

LOVE IS AN AWFUL THING
Nar/Cast: Douglas Carter* + Owen Moore + Thomas Guise + Mar-
    jorie Dcw
Studio/Company: Owen Moore Film Corp.
Tech Info: 35 mm/silent/bw/7 reels
Date/Country: 1922 + USA
Annotation: Douglas Carter plays a porter with some light
    humorous touches in this film about a young man who is
    about to get married. His plans are thwarted by an old
    flame who says he promised to marry her. All is
    ultimately explained and the marriage takes place.

LOVE MART, THE
Nar/Cast: Gilbert Roland + Raymond Turner* + Billie Dove +
    Noah Beery   Director: George Fitzmaurice
Studio/Company: First National Pictures, Inc.
Tech Info: 35 mm/silent/bw/8 reels
Date/Country: 1927 + USA   Type: Feature
Annotation: The so-called belle of the south is rumored to
    have Negro ancestry and is sold as a slave. Her owner
    does not believe the rumor and forces the person who
    started the rumor to confess and then marries the girl.
    Raymond Turner plays Poupet, servant to Gilbert Roland as
    Jallot.

LOVE MY DOG
Series: Our Gang
Nar/Cast: Our Gang + Allen Hoskins*
Screenplay: Hal Roach
Producer: Hal Roach   Director: Robert McGowan
Studio/Company: Pathe
Tech Info: silent/bw/2 reels

Date/Country: 1927 + USA   Type: Comedy Short
Annotation: There's a hydrophobia epidemic, so all the dogs
    are being rounded up and will be killed unless the $5.00
    vaccination fee can be paid - Farina's dog is captured and
    how he raises the money to save his dog is this short's
    story. Allen Hoskins stars as Farina.

LOVE THY NEIGHBOR
Nar/Cast: Eddie Anderson* + Jack Benny + Fred Allen   +   Mary
    Martin
Screenplay: Will Morrow + Ed Beloin   Director: Mark
    Sandrich
Studio/Company: Paramount
Tech Info: 16 mm/sound/bw/82 min.
Date/Country: 1940 + USA   Type: Feature
Distr/Arch: uni
Annotation: Cinematic portrayal of the Benny-Allen radio
    rivalry with Eddie Anderson stealing the film from the
    principals as the character he made famous, "Rochester."

LOYAL HEARTS
Nar/Cast: Sidney Preston Dohnes* + Thais Nehli Kalana*
Studio/Company: Democracy Film Company
Tech Info: silent/bw/7 reels/35 mm
Date/Country: 1919 + USA   Type: Feature
Annotation: A young well-to-do woman who has been "passing"
    has her secret discovered. To avoid disgrace she goes to
    France to nurse the soldiers (World War I).   While at-
    tending the wounded she is attacked by villainous Germans,
    but is saved by a man who turns out to be her former but-
    ler. Romance ensues.

LOYALTY OF JUMBO, THE
Studio/Company: Selig
Date/Country: 1914 + USA   Type: Feature
Annotation: White mother holds off African natives while her
    daughter's pet elephant goes for help in this melodrama.

LUCI DEL VARIETA
Alt Title(s): Variety Lights
Nar/Cast: Giuletta Masina + Peppino De Filippo + John Kitz-
    miller*
Producer: Federico Fellini + Alberto Lattuada   Director:
    Federico Fellini + Alberto Lattuada
Tech Info: 16 mm/sound/bw/93 min./Italian with English sub-
    titles
Date/Country: 1951 + Italy   Type: Feature
Distr/Arch: con
Annotation: Kitzmiller plays Johnny the trumpet player in
    this comedy-drama about the life and times of a traveling
    vaudeville troupe. Shown in U.S., 1965.

LUCK IN OLD CLOTHES
Studio/Company: Ebony Film Corporation
Date/Country: 1918 + USA

LUCKY GAMBLERS
Nar/Cast: Lollypop Jones* + Edith Graves* + Augustus Smith*

+ Frederick Johnson
Producer: All American News   Director: Josh Binney
Studio/Company: All American News
Tech Info: 16 mm/bw/sound/1 reel/20 min.
Date/Country: 1946 + USA   Type: Comedy Short
Distr/Arch: kpf

LUCKY GHOST
Nar/Cast: Mantan Moreland* + F.E. Miller* + Eddie Anderson*
Producer: Jed Buell   Director: Jed Buell
Studio/Company: Buell + Dixie National Pictures
Date/Country: 1941 + USA   Type: Feature
Annotation: Mantan Moreland does a bug-eyed bit in this
  comedy successor to Mr. Washington Goes to Town.

LUCKY CORNER, THE
Series: Our Gang
Nar/Cast: Our Gang + Billie Thomas*
Producer: Hal Roach   Director: Gus Meins
Studio/Company: MGM + Roach
Tech Info: super 8 mm/16 mm/sound/1 reel/20 min.
Date/Country: 1936 + USA   Type: Comedy Short
Distr/Arch: roa + bla
Annotation: The gang comes to the aid of Grandpa in his
  fight to keep his lemonade stand in business over the op-
  position of a mean store owner and his bratty son. At one
  point Buckwheat's father, a bootblack, offers to share his
  space with Grandpa's lemonade stand. Billie Thomas stars
  as Buckwheat.

LURE OF A WOMAN, THE
Nar/Cast: Regina Cohee* + Dr. A. Porter Davis* + Charles
  Allen*
Producer: Progress Picture Assoc.   Director: J.M. Simms
Studio/Company: Afro-American Exhibitors Company
Tech Info: 35 mm/silent/bw/5 reels
Date/Country: 1921 + USA
Annotation: The first black film produced in Kansas City.

LURE OF THE WOODS
Date/Country: 1922 + USA

LYDIA BAILEY
Nar/Cast: Dale Robertson + Ann Francis + William Marshall* +
  Ken Renard* + Juanita Moore* + Martin Wilkens* + Alvin
  Ailey*
Screenplay: Michael Blankfort + Philip Dunne   Story: Ken-
  neth Roberts
Producer: Jules Schermer   Director: Jean Negulsco
Studio/Company: 20th Century Fox
Tech Info: 16 mm/sound/color/89 min.
Date/Country: 1952 + USA   Type: Feature
Distr/Arch: mac + mog + sel + wcf + wel + wil
Annotation: Tale of a young Baltimore lawyer caught up in
  the internal strife and intrigue of Haiti in the early
  1880's. William Marshall is King Dick, a follower of
  Toussaint L'Ouverture, the liberator- generals who has a
  minimal role in this romantic melodrama.

LYING LIPS
Nar/Cast: Edna Mae Harris* + Carmen Newsome* + Amanda
  Randolph* + Frances Williams* + Frank Costell* + J. Louis
  Johnson* + Teddy Hall* + Slim Thompson* + Juano Hernandez*
  + Robert Earl Jones* + Cherokee Thornton* + Gladys Willi-
  ams + Henry Gives* + Don Delese* + Charles Latorre* +
  Robert Paqiun* + George Reynolds*
Producer: Hubert Julian* + Oscar Micheaux*   Director: Oscar
  Micheaux*
Studio/Company: Micheaux Film Corporation
Tech Info: 16 mm/sound/bw/60 min.
Date/Country: 1939 + USA   Type: Feature
Distr/Arch: kpf
Annotation: Elsie Ballwood, a young nightclub singer (Har-
  ris) is convicted and sent to prison for the murder of her
  aunt. Benjamin (Newsome) who is in love with Elsie and
  Detective Wanzer (Jones) set out to prove her innocence.
  They do and Elsie and Benjamin are married after she is
  pardoned and released from prison.

McCABE AND MRS. MILLER
Nar/Cast: Warren Beatty + Julie Christie + Keith Carradine +
  Lilly Franks* + Rodney Gage*   Story: Robert Altman
Producer: Robert Altman
Distr/Arch: wsa
Annotation: Gage and Franks play Mr. and Mrs. Washington in
  the film.

M*A*S*H*
Nar/Cast: Fred Williamson* + Donald Sutherland + Elliot
  Gould + Sally Kellerman
Screenplay: Ring Lardner, Jr.   Story: Richard Hooker
Producer: Ingo Preminger   Director: Robert Altman
Studio/Company: 20th Century Fox
Tech Info: 16 mm/color/sound/116 min.
Date/Country: 1970 + USA   Type: Feature
Distr/Arch: fnc
Annotation: Irreverent movie about doctors at an Army
  hospital near the front lines during the Korean war. Fred
  Williamson plays "Spearchucker," the doctor who is an ac-
  complished passer on the football field.

MACK, THE
Nar/Cast: Max Julien* + Don Gordon* + Richard Pryor* +
  Juanita Moore*
Screenplay: Robert J. Poole
Producer: Harvey Bernard   Director: Michael Campus
Studio/Company: Cinerama
Tech Info: 16 mm/color/sound/3 reels/110 min.
Date/Country: 1973 + USA   Type: Feature
Distr/Arch: swa
Annotation: The Mack is a film that portrays the lifestyle
  and experience of a black pimp as he struggles to stay on
  top, battling both black and white mobsters.

MACKENNA'S GOLD
Nar/Cast: Gregory Peck + Omar Sharif

Screenplay: Carl Foreman
Producer: Carl Foreman + Dmitri Tiomkin   Director: J.   Lee
   Thompson
Studio/Company: Columbia
Tech Info: 16 mm/sound/color/136 min.
Date/Country: 1969 + USA   Type: Feature
Distr/Arch: bud + ccc + cha + cwf + ics + mac + mod + mot +
   roa + swa + twy + unf + wcf + wel + who
Annotation: A Western melodrama with the music scored by
   Quincy Jones*.

MACUNAIMA
Alt Title(s): Jungle Freaks   Director: Joaquim Pedro de
   Andrade
Studio/Company: New Line Cinema
Tech Info: 16 mm/35 mm/color/sound/3 reels/95 min.
Date/Country: 1971 + Brazil   Type: Feature
Distr/Arch: nlc
Annotation: Macunaima is a political comedy from Brazil.
   The central character is born a full grown black man who
   miraculously changes to white and encounters   modern
   "civilization" in a series of hilarious adventures.

MAD MISS MANTON, THE
Nar/Cast: Barbara Stanwyck + Henry Fonda + Sam Levene + Hat-
   tie McDaniel*
Screenplay: Philip G. Epstein   Story: Wilson Collinson
Producer: P.J. Wolfson   Director: Leigh Jason
Studio/Company: RKO-Radio
Tech Info: 16 mm/sound/bw/80 min.
Date/Country: 1938 + USA   Type: Feature
Distr/Arch: fnc
Annotation: Suspense-comedy about a Park Avenue socialite
   turned detective (Barbara Stanwyck) with help from able
   Hilda (Hattie McDaniel).

MADAGASCAR - TROUBADOURS ET MENESTRELS NOIRS
Tech Info: 35 mm/bw/372 meters
Date/Country: France   Type: Documentary
Distr/Arch: saf
Annotation: Part I shows musicians, singers, dancers,
   professional wrestlers and a seance. The frenetic move-
   ment of the dancers is shown in the dance of the kite
   (bird).   Part II shows wrestlers who are challenged, who
   struggle and then, as winners, are carried in triumph.
   (Archived only.)

MADE FOR EACH OTHER
Nar/Cast: Louise Beavers* + Carol Lombard + Jimmy Stewart +
   James Coburn
Screenplay: Jo Swerling
Producer: David O. Selznick   Director: John Cromwell
Studio/Company: United Artists
Tech Info: 16 mm/sound/bw/97 min.
Date/Country: 1939 + USA   Type: Feature
Distr/Arch: alb + bud + cfm + ima + mac + mog + wcf + cie +
   csv
Annotation: Story of a young couple and their trials as they

adjust to each other, their baby and social pressures.
Louise Beavers is Lily.

MADE IN MISSISSIPPI: BLACK FOLK ART AND CRAFTS
Producer: Bill Ferris + Yale University Media Design Studios
   + Center for Southern Folklore
Tech Info: 16 mm/sound/color/20 min.
Date/Country: 1975 + USA   Type: Documentary
Distr/Arch: csf
Annotation: Presents folk art, crafts, and architecture in
   rural Mississippi through interviews. Provided by Center
   for Southern Folklore.

MADIGAN
Nar/Cast: Raymond St. Jacques* + Richard Widmark + Henry
   Fonda
Screenplay: Henri Simorin + Abraham Polonsky
Producer: Frank P. Rosenberg   Director: Don Siegal
Studio/Company: Universal
Tech Info: 16 mm/sound/color/101 min.
Date/Country: 1968 + USA   Type: Feature
Distr/Arch: ccc + swa + tmc + uni
Annotation: Raymond St. Jacques plays Dr. Taylor, a
   clergyman in this drama about a manhunt in Manhattan with
   Widmark as Detective Madigan.

MADINA BOE
Producer: Jose Massip
Tech Info: 16 mm/sound/bw/40 min.*spanish with English sub-
   titles
Date/Country: 1967 + Guinea-Bissau
Distr/Arch: twn + ohn
Annotation: The liberation movement of Guinea-Bissau for
   freedom from the Portugese is documented. Some efforts to
   meet the needs of the people--food, health, education--is
   also shown.

MAGGOT, THE
Producer: Topper Carew   Type: Animated Short
Annotation: Animated,   anti-heroin/anti-pusher film for
   children.

MAGIC GARDEN, THE
Nar/Cast: Tommy Ramokgopa* + Dolly Rathebe* + Harriet
   Qubeka* + David Mukwanazi*
Screenplay: Ferdinand Webb + Donald Swanson + C. Pennington
   Richards
Producer: Donald Swanson   Director: Donald Swanson
Studio/Company: Swan Films
Tech Info: 16 mm/sound/bw/63 min.
Date/Country: 1952 + South Africa   Type: Feature
Distr/Arch: csv
Annotation: The misadventures of a thief who steals forty
   pounds from an old man who has just donated it to the
   church. How the money affects the various people who come
   in contact with it is the core of this light comedy.

MAGIC TREE, THE

Producer: Landmark Educational Media
Tech Info: 16 mm/sound/color/1 reel/11 min.
Date/Country: 1970   Type: Animated Short
Distr/Arch: iu + tex
Annotation: Presents, through animation, a folk tale from
    the Congo about an unloved son who leaves home, finds love
    and wealth, and loses it. Observes him encountering a
    magic tree; concludes with the boy reavealing the secret
    of the magic tree to his family.

MAGICIANS OF THE BLACK HILLS
Series: Africa
Nar/Cast: Lowell Thomas
Producer: BBC-TV + Odyssey Productions
Studio/Company: Odyssey Productions
Tech Info: 16 mm/sound/color/1 reel/25 min.
Date/Country: 1965 + Cameroun   Type: Documentary
Distr/Arch: tim
Annotation: The power of the tribal blacksmiths of the
    Matakams of the Mandara Mountains is depicted. The black-
    smiths protect the power by handing down this knowledge to
    their sons only; they in turn can marry only daughters of
    blacksmiths.

MAGNUM FORCE
Nar/Cast: Clint Eastwood + Hal Holbrook + Felton Perry*
Screenplay: John Milus + Michael Cimino
Producer: Robert Daley   Director: Ted Post
Studio/Company: Warners
Tech Info: 16 mm/sound/color/124 min.
Date/Country: 1973 + USA   Type: Feature
Distr/Arch: wsa
Annotation: Felton Perry plays a black policeman who works
    with Dirty Harry Callahan (Eastwood) on the force in San
    Francisco.   A black prostitute is killed by her pimp for
    "holding out" on him. The pimp is eliminated by a "death
    squad"   within   the police force, masterminded by a
    lieutenant (Hal Holbrook) who doesn't see the system work-
    ing to eliminate crime and violence. Harry eliminates the
    death squad and a number of others but is unable to save
    his partner who becomes one of the "death squad's"
    victims.

MAHALIA JACKSON
Date/Country: 1961 + USA
Annotation: A compilation of numbers from a series of
    television performances. Numbers include "Down By the
    Riverside," "He's Got the World in His Hand," "Precious
    Lord," "Somebody Bigger Than You and I," and many others.

MAHOGHANY
Nar/Cast: Diana Ross* + Billy Dee Williams* + Anthony Perk-
    ins + Jean-Pierre Aumont
Producer: Rob Cohen + Jack Ballard   Director: Berry Gordy*
Studio/Company: Paramount
Tech Info: 16 mm/color/sound/3 reels/105 min.
Date/Country: 1975 + USA   Type: Feature
Distr/Arch: fnc

Annotation: The story of a poor black girl from Chicago who
   becomes a top international fashion model only to give it
   up for an honest black politician (Billy Dee Williams),
   for "success is nothing without someone you love to share
   it with you." Diana Ross received an Oscar nomination for
   costume design.

MAID OF SALEM
Nar/Cast: Madame Sul-te-Wan* + Claudette Colbert + Fred Mc-
   Murray   Director: Frank Lloyd
Studio/Company: Paramount
Tech Info: 16 mm/sound/bw/86 min.
Date/Country: 1937 + USA   Type: Feature
Distr/Arch: uni + tmc
Annotation: Sul-te-Wan plays Tituba in this film about New
   England Puritans.

MAIL AND FEMALE
Series: Our Gang
Nar/Cast: Our Gang + Billie Thomas*
Producer: Hal Roach   Director: Fred Newmeyer
Studio/Company: MGM + Roach
Tech Info: super 8 mm/16 mm/bw/sound/1 reel/10 min.
Date/Country: 1937 + USA   Type: Comedy Short
Distr/Arch: roa + bla
Annotation: Alfalfa gets into trouble being both woman-hater
   and lover. Billie Thomas is Buckwheat.

MAIN CHANCE, THE
Nar/Cast: Tracy Reed* + Edward De Souza + Gregoire Aslan
Screenplay: Richard Harris
Producer: Jack Greenwood   Director: John Knight
Studio/Company: Merton Park Studios + Embassy
Tech Info: sound/bw/61 min.
Date/Country: 1966 + Britain   Type: Feature
Annotation: Christine (Tracy Reed), secretary to supposed
   wine merchant Potter (Aslan), is not only responsible for
   getting Blake (DeSouza), former RAF pilot, to carry a
   package of diamonds from France to England for Potter, she
   also warns Blake, after he has double-crossed Potter, of
   the bomb Potter has placed aboard his plane.

MAITRES (LES) FOUS
Alt Title(s): Maitres (Les) Fous "Hauka"   Director: Jean
   Rouch
Studio/Company: Films de la Pleiade
Tech Info: 16 mm/color/1 reel/30 min.
Date/Country: 1954-55 + France
Distr/Arch: con + saf
Annotation: Provocative study of Haouka section in Accra,
   West Africa. (Archived only).

MAJOR DUNDEE
Nar/Cast: Brock Peters* + Charlton Heston + Richard Harris
Screenplay: Harry Julien + Oscar Saul + Sam Peckinpah
Producer: Jerry Bresher   Director: Sam Peckinpah
Studio/Company: Columbia
Tech Info: 16 mm/sound/color/134 min.

Date/Country: 1965 + USA   Type: Feature
Distr/Arch: arg + buc + bud + ccc + cwf + ker + kpf + mac +
   mod + mot + nat + tfc + unf + wcf + wel + who
Annotation: Western set in Civil War era with Brock Peters
   as Aesop, a member of U.S. cavalry.

MAKE WAY FOR A LADY
Nar/Cast: Herbert Marshall + Ann Shirley + Willie Best* +
   Margot Grahame
Screenplay: Gertrude Purcell
Producer: Zion Myers   Director: David Burton
Studio/Company: RKO Radio
Tech Info: bw/sound
Date/Country: 1936 + USA   Type: Feature
Annotation: Film about a young girl, who besides being
   mistaken for nobility, tries to marry off her widowed
   father to a lady novelist whom they both despise. Willie
   Best has his usual role.

MAKE WAY FOR TOMORROW
Nar/Cast: Fay Bainter + Victor Moore + Louise Beavers*
   Director: Leo McCarey
Studio/Company: Paramount
Tech Info: 16 mm/sound/bw/91 min.
Date/Country: 1937 + USA   Type: Feature
Distr/Arch: mma + uni
Annotation: Louise Beavers plays her smiling maid role.

MALAGA
Nar/Cast: Trevor Howard + Dorothy Dandridge* + Edmund Purdom
Screenplay: David Osborn + Donald Ogden Stewart
Producer: Clyde Thomas   Director: Laslo Benedek
Studio/Company: Warner Brothers
Tech Info: sound/ b w/ 97 min.
Date/Country: 1962 + Britain   Type: Feature
Distr/Arch: abpc
Annotation: Dandridge plays Gianni, Carran's ex-mistress,
   who makes an uneasy alliance with Bain, Carran's partner
   in crime who has been done out of his share of the jewels
   they stole. Gianni falls in love with Bain, and after he
   turns himself over to the police offers to make a new life
   with him.

MALCOLM X SPEAKS
Nar/Cast: Gil Noble*
Producer: ABC
Studio/Company: ABC
Tech Info: 16 mm/bw/sound/55 min.
Date/Country: 1971 + USA   Type: Documentary
Distr/Arch: gro
Annotation: Gil Noble reviews the life and teachings of
   Malcolm X beginning with an interview with friends of the
   Muslim activist from his early days. It moves into docu-
   mentary footage of Malcolm leading protests and making
   speeches, revealing his growth from that of a professed
   racist to an understanding that through Islam whites were
   also a part of the human family.

MALCOLM X: STRUGGLE FOR FREEDOM
Producer: Lebert Bethune + Don Taylor   Director: Lebert
   Bethune + Don Taylor
Tech Info: 16 mm/bw/sound/1 reel/22 min.
Date/Country: 1967 + USA   Type: Documentary
Distr/Arch: gro
Annotation: This brief portrait of Malcolm was filmed during
   his trip to Europe and Africa three months before his as-
   sassination; gives concrete details about this period in
   his life.

MALCOLM X
Studio/Company: Carousel
Tech Info: 16 mm/color/sound/1 reel/23 min.
Date/Country: USA   Type: Documentary
Distr/Arch: fnc
Annotation: This film biography of Malcolm X explores the
   formation and growth of his beliefs and values, as well as
   how his life changed from that of a drug-dealing criminal
   to an inspirational leader for thousands of young Blacks.

MALCOLM X
Nar/Cast: Ossie Davis* + James Earl Jones*
Producer: Martin Worth + Arnold Perl
Studio/Company: Warner Brothers
Tech Info: 16 mm/sound/color/3 reels/92 min.
Date/Country: 1972 + USA   Type: Dramatized Documentary
Annotation: A film biography of Malcolm X composed of actual
   film footage of his speeches (black and white), photo-
   graphs, interviews up to including his death and post
   mortem scenes. Betty Shabazz was consultant. Music: Bil-
   lie Holliday*, Duke Ellington*, Slim and Slam*.

MALE ANIMAL, THE
Nar/Cast: Henry Fonda + Olivia De Haviland + Hattie Mc-
   Daniel*
Screenplay: James Thurber + Elliot Nugent
Producer: Hal Wallis   Director: Elliot Nugent
Studio/Company: Warner Brothers
Tech Info: 101 min./bw/16 mm/sound
Date/Country: 1942 + USA   Type: Feature
Distr/Arch: uas
Annotation: Hattie McDaniel plays a bit role as Cleota the
   maid in the household of Professor and Mrs. Turner.   Em-
   phasis, in the play, is on academic freedom, and the in-
   tegrity of the professor-student relationship. Cleota is
   an appendage to the household but McDaniel's few appearances are filled with acerbic comments mixed with some
   malapropisms.

MAMA'S LITTLE PIRATE
Series: Our Gang
Nar/Cast: Our Gang + Billie Thomas* + Matthew Beard*
Producer: Hal Roach   Director: Gus Meins
Studio/Company: MGM + Roach
Tech Info: super 8 mm/16 mm/bw/sound/1 reel/20 min.
Date/Country: 1934 + USA   Type: Comedy Short
Distr/Arch: roa + bla

Annotation: Spanky and the gang go treasure hunting and find
a cave with mounds of treasure watched over by a giant who
captures the gang one by one. Then Spanky wakes up. Billie Thomas stars as Buckwheat and Matthew Beard stars as
Stymie.

MAMBO
Nar/Cast: Dino De Laurentis + Silvana Mangano + Michael Ren-
nie + Katherine Dunham*
Screenplay: Ernio De Concini + Guido Piovene + Ivo Perille +
Robert Rossen
Producer: Carlo Ponti   Director: Robert Rosser
Studio/Company: Paramount
Date/Country: 1955 + Italy   Type: Feature
Annotation: Katherine Dunham plays herself in this story of
a love triangle which ends tragically for one of the
three.

MAME
Nar/Cast: Lucille Ball + Beatrice Arthur + Robert Preston
Screenplay: Paul Zindel
Producer: Robert Fryer + James Cresson   Director: Gene Saks
Studio/Company: American Broadcasting Companies
Tech Info: 131 min.
Date/Country: 1974 + USA   Type: Feature
Annotation: Adaptation of the musical play, this story
revolves around Auntie Mame who wants to adopt her nephew
and raise him and ultimately does. A black band is
featured in one of the sequences with Mame (Ball) party-
ing.

MAMMY'S CHILD
Studio/Company: Crystal Films
Date/Country: 1913 + USA   Type: Comedy Shot
Annotation: A young white girl decides to trade her doll for
a real black baby until she receives the sinister stare of
the baby's mother.

MAMMY'S GHOST
Annotation: Mammy (white in blackface) instructs her young
white ward in the art of chain-rattling (simulating a
ghost), a ruse to keep the Yankee soldiers from discovering the attic sanctuary.

MAMMY
Alt Title(s): Mr. Bones (play)
Nar/Cast: Al Jolson + Louise Dresser + Lois Moran + Lowell
Sherman
Screenplay: L.G. Rigby   Story: Irving Berlin   Director:
Michael Curtiz
Studio/Company: Warner Brothers
Tech Info: 16 mm/sound/bw/84 min.
Date/Country: 1930 + USA   Type: Feature
Distr/Arch: uas
Annotation: Al Jolson movie about a traveling minstrel show,
with Jolson doing blackface. Louise Dresser is the "mam-
my."

MAMPRUSI_VILLAGE
Producer: British Information Service   Director: John Page
Tech Info: 16 mm/sound/bw/1 reel/20 min.   1729 ft.
Date/Country: 1944 + Britain   Type: Documentary
Distr/Arch: iu + bris + iwm
Annotation: Shows self-government of an African tribal
   society in the late 1940's. Depicts village life in an
   agricultural community of the African Gold Coast where the
   governing body composed of native chiefs must handle such
   complex matters as flood control, taxes, education,
   police, and transportation - all carried out in spite of
   the fact that very few of the populace can read and write.

MAMY_WATER   Director: Jean Rouch
Date/Country: 1954-5 + France
Distr/Arch: saf
Annotation: No further information available. (Archived
   only).

MAN_ABOUT_TOWN
Nar/Cast: Jack Benny + Dorothy Lamour + Eddie Anderson* +
   Binnie Barnes + Edward Arnold + Monty Wooley + Theresa
   Harris*
Screenplay: Morrie Ryskind
Producer: Arthur Hornblow   Director: Mark Sandrich
Studio/Company: Paramount
Tech Info: 16 mm/sound/bw/85 min.
Date/Country: 1939 + USA   Type: Feature
Distr/Arch: uni
Annotation: Benny is the "man about town" who gets himself
   into trouble wooing two wealthy women in spite of
   Rochester's (Anderson) warnings. Rochester, who does an
   eccentric dance in this film, is the one who has to ex-
   tricate his boss from his self-made difficulties.

MAN_AND_BOY
Nar/Cast: Bill Cosby* + Gloria Foster* + Leif Erikson + Ge-
   orge Spell* + Douglas Turner Ward* + John Anderson +
   Yaphet Kotto*
Screenplay: Harry Essex + Oscar Saul
Producer: Marvin Miller   Director: E.W. Swackhamer
Studio/Company: Levitt-Pickman Corp.
Tech Info: 16 mm/35 mm/color/sound/3 reels/98 min.
Date/Country: 1971 + USA   Type: Feature
Distr/Arch: fnc + luc
Annotation: Bill Cosby portrays a former Union soldier who
   has moved his family to a homestead in the Old West at the
   end of the Civil War. When a valuable horse is stolen,
   father and son set out in search of the thieves. They
   learn from each other in the hostile, violent West of the
   1870's. Musical score by J.J. Johnson*, supervised by
   Quincy Jones*.

MAN_CALLED_ADAM,_A
Nar/Cast: Sammy Davis, Jr.* + Louis Armstrong* + Ossie
   Davis* + Cicely Tyson* + Roy Glenn*
Screenplay: Les Pine + Tina Rome
Producer: Ike Jones + Jim Waters   Director: Leo Penn

Studio/Company: Embassy Pictures
Tech Info: 16 mm/sound/bw/3 reels/99 min.
Date/Country: 1966 + USA   Type: Feature
Distr/Arch: mac + mod
Annotation: Explores the world and inner-struggles of the
    black jazz musician and suggests relations between the
    black musician, civil rights, and the white musician.
    Music by Benny Carter*.

MAN FRIDAY
Nar/Cast: Richard Roundtree* + Peter O'Toole   Director:
    Jack Gold
Studio/Company: Avco Embassy
Tech Info: 16 mm/color/sound/3 reels/109 min.
Date/Country: 1970 + USA   Type: Feature
Distr/Arch: swa
Annotation: An interpretation of Daniel Defoe's classic
    Robinson Crusoe, the story is told from Friday's (Round-
    tree) point of view. The film depicts Crusoe (O'Toole) as
    a fanatical white supremist, Friday as the servant who
    becomes the master.

MAN FROM C.O.T.T.O.N., THE
Alt Title(s): see Gone Are the Days

MAN FROM MOROCCO, THE
Nar/Cast: Anton Walbrook + Margaretta Scott + Mary Morris +
    Harley Power + Harold Lang + Peter Noble + Orlando
    Martins*
Screenplay: Edward Dryhurst   Story: Rudolph Cartier
    Director: Max Greene
Date/Country: 1945 + Britain   Type: Feature
Annotation: Martins plays Jeremiah, an African volunteer
    with the International Brigade fighting against Franco and
    facism in Spain in 1937. A story of suspense and intrigue
    which stars Walbrook as a Loyalist officer.

MAN FROM C.R.G.Y., THE
Nar/Cast: Slappy White* + Robert Walker + Steve Rossi
Screenplay: Ted Mark   Story: Ted Mark
Producer: Sidney Pink   Director: James H. Hill
Tech Info: sound/192 min.
Date/Country: 1970 + USA   Type: Feature
Annotation: Slappy White and Steve Rossi do a comedy routine
    in this R-rated film spoof of X-rated films.

MAN FROM TEXAS, THE
Studio/Company: Ben Roy Productions
Date/Country: 1921 + USA
Annotation: A black film with no further information availa-
    ble.

MAN IN THE MIDDLE
Producer: John Jay College of Criminal Justice
Tech Info: 16 mm/bw/sound/1 reel/22 min.
Date/Country: USA
Distr/Arch: adl
Annotation: A professional police training film, the subject

focuses on how cooperation between the community and the
police force can be achieved. The setting is a precinct
in a lower middle class black neighborhood.

MAN IS TEN FEET TALL, A
Alt Title(s): see Edge of the City

MAN NAMED CHARLIE SMITH, A
War/Cast: James Whitmore
Producer: N. H. Cominos   Director: N. M. Cominos
Tech Info: 16 mm/sound/1 reel/16 min.
Date/Country: 1962 + USA   Type: Dramatized Documentary
Distr/Arch: mac + fnc
Annotation: History of slavery and the Black man in America
  through memory of one man named Charlie Smith, 120 years
  old. The period is reconstructed through the use of
  photographs and old newsreels. James Whitmore is the nar-
  rator.

MAN OF TWO WORLDS
Alt Title(s): Kisenga, Man of Africa
War/Cast: Robert Adams* + Eric Portman + Orlando Martins* +
  Sam Blake* + Napolean Florent* + Viola Thompson* + Eseza
  Makumbi* + Tunji Williams* + Phyllis Calvert + Rudolph
  Evans* + Uriel Porter*
Screenplay: Joyce Cary + Herbert Victor + Thorold Dickison
  Director: Thorold Dickinson
Studio/Company: Two Cities Film Co.
Date/Country: 1946 + Britain   Type: Feature
Annotation: The film depicts the struggle against fear and
  superstition that an educated black African faces upon his
  return to his country--then Tanganyika. Robert Adams
  plays Kisenga, Orlando Martins, the witch doctor. Filmed
  mainly in a London studio. Man of Two Worlds was released
  in the United States as Kisenga, Man of Africa, 1952.

MAN ON AMERICA'S CONSCIENCE, THE
Alt Title(s): see Tennessee Johnson

MAN WHO SHOT LIBERTY VALANCE, THE
War/Cast: James Stewart + John Wayne + Vera Miles + Lee
  Marvin + Woody Strode*
Screenplay: James Warner Bellah + Willis Goldbeck
Producer: Willis Goldbeck   Director: John Ford
Studio/Company: Paramount
Tech Info: 16 mm/sound/bw/122 min.
Date/Country: 1962 + USA   Type: Feature
Distr/Arch: rbc
Annotation: Strode plays Pompey in this western drama about
  a senator from a western state (Stewart) whose reputation
  rests on his having shot a notorious gunfighter, Liberty
  Valance (Marvin).

MAN WITH THE GOLDEN GUN, THE
War/Cast: Roger Moore + Christopher Lee + Britt Ekland +
  Clifton James*
Screenplay: Richard Maibaum + Tom Mankiewicz
Producer: Albert A. Broccoli + Harry Saltzman   Director:

Guy Hamilton
Studio/Company: United Artists
Date/Country: 1974 + USA   Type: Feature
Annotation: Bond (Moore) aided by two ladies and a bumbling
  sheriff (James), manages to escape the gold bullet meant
  for him just in time to rescue an energy machine from
  malevolent Scaramanga (Christopher Lee).

MAN_WITHOUT_MERCY
Nar/Cast: Sammy Davis, Jr.*   Director: Bernard Girard
Date/Country: 1969 + USA   Type: Feature

MAN'S_DUTY,_A
Nar/Cast: Clarence Brooks*
Producer: George P. Johnson*
Studio/Company: Lincoln Motion Picture Company
Date/Country: 1919 + USA   Type: Feature
Annotation: Melodrama dealing with black family life.

MAN,_THE
Nar/Cast: James Earl Jones* + Martin Balsam + Burgess
  Meredith + Barbara Rush + Janet MacLachlan*
Screenplay: Rod Serling   Story: Irving Wallace
Producer: Lee Rich   Director: Joseph Sargent
Studio/Company: Paramount
Tech Info: 16 mm/color/sound/3 reels/93 min.
Date/Country: 1972 + USA   Type: Feature
Distr/Arch: aim + bud + fnc + mac + mod + unf + who
Annotation: James Earl Jones is a black senator who has ac-
  ceded to the presidency through a series of mishaps.
  Struggling to keep an unprepared nation together, he
  fights both politicians and his radical daughter (MacLach-
  lan). The end shows him on top for the moment, but alone.

MAN,_WOMAN_AND_SIN
Nar/Cast: Gilbert Roland   Director: Monta Bell
Studio/Company: MGM
Tech Info: silent/bw
Date/Country: 1927 + USA
Annotation: A vignette showing three black children playing
  around a fire-hydrant and an old black man strumming a
  banjo establishes the fact of Gilbert Roland's far from
  affluent beginnings since he lives behind the rich folk
  and in close proximity to those of modest means.

MANCHURIAN_CANDIDATE,_THE
Nar/Cast: Frank Sinatra + Laurence Harvey + James Edwards* +
  Angela Lansbury
Screenplay: George Axelrod
Producer: George Axelrod + John Frankenheimer   Director:
  Richard Condon
Studio/Company: United Artists
Tech Info: 16 mm/sound/bw/126 min.
Date/Country: 1962 + USA   Type: Feature
Distr/Arch: uas
Annotation: Story about a P.O.W. brainwashed to become an
  assassin and returned to the U.S.   James Edwards is
  Corporal Melvin.

MANDABI
Alt Title(s): The Money Order
Nar/Cast: Mamadou Guye* + Ynousse N'Diaye* + Issa Niang* +
   Serigne N'Diayes*
Screenplay: Ousmane Sembene*   Story: Ousmane Sembene*
Producer: Jean Maumy   Director: Ousmane Sembene*
Studio/Company: Domireve (Dakar) + C.F.P.C. (Paris)
Tech Info: 16 mm/color/sound/2 reels/90 min./Wolof with En-
   glish subtitles
Date/Country: 1968 + Senegal + France   Type: Feature
Distr/Arch: fnc + gro + ucemc
Annotation: Mandabi is the story of Ibrahim Dieng, who after
   being unemployed for 4 years, receives a money order from
   a nephew. The money totally disrupts his life as he
   spends wildly and goes into debt. When he learns that he
   can't cash the money order due to a lost I.D., he loses
   everything because of red tape.

MANDINGO
Nar/Cast: James Mason + Susan George + Perry King + Richard
   Ward* + Brenda Sykes* + Ken Norton* + Lillian Heyman
Screenplay: Norman Wexler   Story: Kyle Onstott + Jack Kirk-
   land
Producer: Dino de Laurentis   Director: Richard Fleischer
Studio/Company: Paramount
Tech Info: 16 mm/technicolor/sound/4 reels/127 min.
Date/Country: 1970 + USA   Type: Feature
Distr/Arch: fnc
Annotation: Mandingo is a violent view of slavery that at-
   tempts to show the degradations which many slaves were
   forced to live through. Ken Norton plays Mede.

MANGROVE NINE
Producer: Monument Films
Tech Info: 16 mm/color/sound/40 min.
Date/Country: 1973 + Britain   Type: Documentary
Distr/Arch: odeo
Annotation: The film focuses on what happens to nine black
   people- two women, seven men - who are arrested by police
   and charged with assault and riot after a demonstra-
   tion/protest against harrassment of the Mangrove
   Restaurant, their social center in the Notting Hill Gate
   area of London.

MANHANDLED
Nar/Cast: Dorothy Lamour + Dan Duryea + James Edwards*
Screenplay: Lewis Foster + Whitman Chambers
Producer: William Pine + William Thomas   Director: Lewis R.
   Foster
Studio/Company: Paramount
Tech Info: 16 mm/sound/bw/97 min.
Date/Country: 1944 + USA   Type: Feature
Distr/Arch: sel + tmc + unf + wcf + wil
Annotation: James Edwards is a butler in this melodrama
   which features Duryea, a private investigator pushing
   Lamour around as well as trying to pin a murder and a rob-
   bery on her.

MANHATTAN_MERRY-GO-ROUND
Nar/Cast: Phil Regan + Leo Carnillo + Cab Calloway*
Screenplay: Harry Sauber
Producer: Harry Sauber   Director: Charles F. Riesner
Studio/Company: Republic
Tech Info: 16 mm/sound/bw/89 min.
Date/Country: 1937 + USA   Type: Feature
Distr/Arch: ivy
Annotation: Musical picture which features Cab Calloway and
    his band.

MANON_LESCAUT
Nar/Cast: Noble Johnson*
Date/Country: 1926   Type: Feature
Annotation: Noble Johnson has a small role in this adapta-
    tion of Massenet's opera.

MANTAN_MESSES_UP
Nar/Cast: Mantan Moreland* + Monte Hawley* + Lena Horne*
Producer: Ted Toddy
Studio/Company: Toddy Pictures
Annotation: Mantan stars in this musical comedy.

MANTAN_RUNS_FOR_MAYOR
Nar/Cast: Mantan Moreland* + Flournoy E. Miller* + John Lee
Studio/Company: Toddy Films + Lucky Star Productions
Date/Country: 194- + USA

MARCH_OF_TIME
Series: Music in America
Tech Info: 22 min.
Date/Country: 1935 + USA   Type: Newsreel
Annotation: "Leadbelly" Huddie Ledbetter's prison sentence
    and pardon are included in this March of Time chapter No
    2, 1935, Music in America Series.

MARCH_OF_TIME
Series: Music in America
Nar/Cast: Benny Goodman and His Band + The Original
    Dixieland Jazz Band* + Art Tatum* + The Eddie Condon All
    Stars + George Gershwin
Tech Info: 16 min.
Date/Country: 1944 + USA   Type: Newsreel
Annotation: This chapter shows various types of music in-
    cluding opera and popular music as well as jazz.

MARCH_OF_TIME
Series: Music in America
Nar/Cast: The Original Dixieland Jazz Band*
Tech Info: 20 min.
Date/Country: 1937 + USA   Type: Newsreel
Annotation: A sequence entitled "The Birth of Swing" shows
    the Original Dixieland Jazz Band playing "Tiger Rag," in
    this March of Time, chapter No. 7, 1937, Music in America
    series.

MARCHING_ON   Director: Spencer Williams*

Annotation: Documentary in style, William's film depicts
  black soldiers in a fictional story against the background
  of Army life in the all black 25th infantry. Showing all
  of the pressures of segregation, it stresses patriotism
  and the contribution of Blacks to the war effort.

MARCUS_GARLAND   Director: Oscar Micheaux*

MARGIE
Nar/Cast: Jeanne Crain + Glenn Langan + Hattie McDaniel*
Screenplay: F. Hugh Herbert   Story: Ruth McKenney + Richard
  Bronsten
Producer: Walter Morosco   Director: Henry King
Studio/Company: 20th Century Fox
Tech Info: 16 mm/sound/color/94 min.
Date/Country: 1946 + USA   Type: Feature
Annotation: Story of a high school girl in the late
  twenties, before the crash, with Hattie McDaniel as the
  maid.

MARIAN_ANDERSON
Series: Concerts on Film
Producer: World Artists, Inc.
Tech Info: 16 mm/sound/bw/1 reel/27 min.
Date/Country: 1953 + USA   Type: Documentary
Distr/Arch: iu
Annotation: Presents Marian Anderson* as she sings a program
  of songs in rehearsal as well as on concert stage.
  Provides details of her life, including her birthplace,
  friends that have helped her, her farm home in Con-
  necticut, and the honors bestowed upon her.

MARIE_GALANTE
Nar/Cast: Spencer Tracy + Ketti Gallian + Stepin Fetchit* +
  Ned Sparks
Screenplay: Reginald Berkeley
Producer: Winifield Sheehan   Director: Henry King
Studio/Company: Fox Film Corp.
Tech Info: sound/bw
Date/Country: 1934 + USA   Type: Feature
Annotation: Story of a young French girl who gets shanghaied
  and ends in the Panama Canal Zone, where she innocently
  gets involved in various spy factions. Fetchit plays a
  bartender in a Panama cafe and provides some amusing mo-
  ments, along with Ned Sparks and Helen Morgan.

MARION_BROWN
Nar/Cast: Marion Brown* + Leo Smith*
Tech Info: 23 min.
Date/Country: 1971 + West Germany   Type: Documentary
Annotation: A studio workout and talk about their "free"
  music is given in this film study of Marion Brown, Leo
  Smith and "assistants."

MARK_OF_THE_HAWK,_THE
Nar/Cast: Sidney Poitier* + Eartha Kitt* + Juano Hernandez*
  + Clifton MacKlin
Screenplay: Ward Jarvis   Story: Lloyd Young

Producer: Lloyd Young   Director: Michael Audley
Studio/Company: Universal-International
Tech Info: 16 mm/color/sound/3 reels/85 min.
Date/Country: 1958 + USA   Type: Feature
Distr/Arch: uni
Annotation: Sidney Poitier is at first sympathetic to a
    liberation movement, then he fights against the group only
    to be accused of being a member of the movement and put on
    trial for murder. Finally, after being cleared, Poitier
    gives a speech supporting colonial forces.

MAROC 7
Nar/Cast: Tracy Reed* + Cyd Charisse + Gene Barry
Screenplay: David Osborn
Producer: John Gale + Leslie Phillips   Director: Gerry
    O'Hara
Studio/Company: Paramount
Tech Info: 16 mm/sound/color/92 min.
Date/Country: 1968 + Britain   Type: Feature
Distr/Arch: rbc
Annotation: Tracy Reed is Vivienne in this crime melodrama
    about an ambitious plan to steal an ancient Arabian medal-
    lion from Morocco.

MARSE COVINGTON
Studio/Company: Metro
Date/Country: 1915 + USA   Type: Feature
Annotation: A slave of "Marse Covington" is so loyal to his
    master that he refuses to take advantage of his legal
    right to freedom after Emancipation.

MARTE, DIO DELLA QUERRA
Nar/Cast: John Kitzmiller*
Date/Country: 1962 + Italy   Type: Feature

MARTIN LUTHER KING: THE MAN AND THE MARCH
Producer: Public Broadcasting Laboratory of NET
Tech Info: 16 mm/bw/sound/3 reels/85 min.
Date/Country: 1968 + USA   Type: Documentary
Distr/Arch: iu
Annotation: Records the history of the late Dr. Martin
    Luther King's 'Poor Peoples March.' Shows him conferring
    with aides, traveling to solicit support and developing
    the operational details of the March.

MARTIN LUTHER KING, JR.: FROM MONTGOMERY TO MEMPHIS
Producer: Bailey-Film Associates
Tech Info: 16 mm/sound/bw/1 reel/26 min.
Date/Country: 1969 + USA   Type: Documentary
Distr/Arch: iu + bfa + adl
Annotation: Surveys the career of Dr. Martin Luther King,
    Jr., and the anti-violent Civil Rights Movement under his
    leadership, from the 1955-56 bus boycott in Montgomery
    Birmingham, Washington, Selma, Chicago, and Memphis, to
    convey the essence of the man and the movement.

MARTIN LUTHER KING, JR.
Producer: Steve Krantz Films

Tech Info: 16 mm/sound/color/1 reel/9 min.
Date/Country: 1971 + USA   Type: Documentary
Distr/Arch: iu + ebec
Annotation: Presents the life of Martin Luther King, Jr., as
    a social activist who helped to initiate social change in
    the United States while serving as the spokesman for mil-
    lions of black people. Describes the bus boycotts in
    Montgomery, Alabama, the years of the sit-ins, voter
    registration drives, and King's assassination in 1968.

MARTIN LUTHER KING
Studio/Company: BBC-TV
Tech Info: 16 mm/bw/sound/1 reel/30 min.
Date/Country: 1970 + USA   Type: Documentary
Distr/Arch: tim
Annotation: In this filmed interview, Dr. King discusses his
    hopes, philosophies, the Montgomery Boycott which brought
    him fame, and the depth of his religious convictions.

MARY, QUEEN OF TOTS
Series: Our Gang
Nar/Cast: Our Gang + Allen Hoskins*
Screenplay: Hal Roach
Producer: Hal Roach   Director: Robert McGowan
Studio/Company: Pathe
Tech Info: super 8 mm/16 mm/bw/silent/1 reel
Date/Country: 1925 + USA   Type: Comedy Short
Distr/Arch: bla
Annotation: Mary, a sheltered rich girl has a set of dolls
    that are replicas of the gang. When they 'come to life',
    she tries to kiss them all. Farina is not the only one
    who is horrified, but he looks the most incensed. (The
    only ethnic slur reference to the 'Wop' who made the
    dolls.)

MARYLAND
Nar/Cast: Walter Brennan + Fay Bainter + Charlie Ruggles +
    Hattie McDaniel* + Marjorie Weaver + Sydney Blackmer +
    Clarence Muse* + George Reed* + Ben Carter* + Ernest Whit-
    man* + Zack Williams* + Thaddeus Jones* + Clinton
    Rosemond* + Jesse Graves + Madame Sul-te-Wan*
Screenplay: Ethel Hill + Jack Andrews
Producer: Darryl F. Zanuck   Director: Henry King
Studio/Company: 20th Century Fox
Tech Info: 16 mm/sound/color/91 min.
Date/Country: 1940   Type: Feature
Distr/Arch: fnc
Annotation: Story of the hunt society of Maryland complete
    with a large black supporting cast. Ben Carter is Hattie
    McDaniel's husband and they have domestic quarrels about
    such things as gambling and burial society premiums.

MASHER, THE
Date/Country: 1907 + USA   Type: Comedy Short
Annotation: A would-be lady's man has little success with
    his amorous overtures until a lady with a veil responds
    favorably. Much to his chagrin, she turns out to be
    black; he turns tail and runs.

MASSACRE
Nar/Cast: Richard Barthelmess + Ann Dvorak + Dudley Diggs +
    Sidney Tola + Clarence Muse*   Story: Robert Gessner +
    Ralph Block   Director: Alan Crosland
Studio/Company: First National Productions
Date/Country: 1934 + USA
Annotation: Corrupt federal agents cheat Indians on the
    Spotted Eagle Reservation until Joe Thunder Horse (Richard
    Barthelmess) gives up fame and wealth as a rodeo attrac-
    tion to set mattters straight.   He takes up with Muse
    (Sam) when the Indians turn on him becuase he is too edu-
    cated.

MATT HELM
Nar/Cast: Tony Franciosa + Val Bisoglio + Hari Rhodes*
Screenplay: Sam H. Rolfe
Producer: Irving Allen   Director: Buzz Kulik
Studio/Company: Columbia Pictures
Date/Country: 1975 + USA   Type: TV Feature
Annotation: While investigating a threat on a beautiful
    movie star's life, Matt Helm (Tony Franciosa) finds him-
    self involved in black market munitions market.

MAU MAU
Series: Kenya Trilogy
Producer: Anthony-David Productions
Date/Country: 1973 + Kenya   Type: Documentary
Distr/Arch: fnc
Annotation: Depicts a Mau Mau movement in historical per-
    spective as response to colonial repression.   Uses news-
    reels, photographs and interviews to authenticate.

MAURIE
Alt Title(s): see Big Mo

MAYBE NEXT WEEK, SOMETIME
Producer: David Boatwright
Tech Info: 16 mm/sound/color/30 min.
Date/Country: 1974 + USA   Type: Documentary
Distr/Arch: rad
Annotation: Black music as a way of life.   The film features
    such local southern artists as: Juanita Green, Albert
    Smith, and Big Betty and The Spiritualities.

MAYBE TOMORROW
Producer: Public Television Library
Tech Info: 16 mm/sound/color/1 reel/19 min.
Date/Country: 1970   Type: Dramatic Short
Distr/Arch: iu
Annotation: Explores a romance between a black, eighth-grade
    girl and a white, high school boy in terms of its implica-
    tions in the black community.   Reveals that the girl feels
    intimidated by youths her own age and finally decides that
    she is no longer free to see the boy.   Written and
    produced for a course in film production at Spring Hill-
    College.

MAYOR OF HELL, THE
Nar/Cast: James Cagney + Madge Evans + Allen Hoskins* + Dudley Diggs
Screenplay: Islin Auster   Director: Archie Mayo
Studio/Company: Warner Brothers
Tech Info: 16 mm/sound/bw/90 min.
Date/Country: 1933 + USA   Type: Feature
Distr/Arch: uas
Annotation: James Cagney stars as a new warden of a re-
    formatory who institutes self-government, better food, and
    less punishment in order to help prisoners truly reform.
    Hoskins is billed as Farina (his "Our Gang" character) who
    plays the role of "Smoke", one of the boys.

MAYOR OF JIMTOWN
Nar/Cast: Aubrey Lyles* + Flournoy E. Miller*
Screenplay: Aubrey Lyles* + Flournoy E. Miller*
Studio/Company: MGM
Date/Country: 192- + USA
Annotation: Miller and Lyles are the mayor and police chief,
    respectively, of Jimtown with dialect-dialogue in this MGM
    musical comedy.

MCMASTERS, THE
Nar/Cast: Brock Peters* + Jack Palance + Burl Ives + Nancy
    Kwan
Screenplay: Harold Jacob Smith
Producer: Monroe Sackson   Director: Alf Kjellin
Studio/Company: Chevron
Tech Info: 16 mm/color/sound/3 reels/89 min.
Date/Country: 1970 + USA   Type: Feature
Distr/Arch: unf + mod + wcf + pru
Annotation: Brock Peters plays Benji, a former slave and
    union army veteran, who returns from the war to an assort-
    ment of complicated problems in this post-bellum western.
    Burl Ives is his benevolent former master with good inten-
    tions, Jack Palance the racist-villain, and Nancy Kwan,
    Benjie's gift from the Indians, who rescue him from
    hostile whites. The original version (97 minutes) was
    approved by the producer, screen writer and leading man;
    the 89 minute version by the distributor.

MEAN MOTHER

MEANEST MAN IN THE WORLD, THE
Nar/Cast: Eddie Anderson* + Jack Benny + Priscilla Lane +
    Edmund Gwen
Screenplay: George Seaton + Allan House   Story: George M.
    Cohan
Producer: William Perberg   Director: Sidney Lanfield
Studio/Company: 20th Century Fox
Tech Info: 16 mm/sound/bw/57 min.
Date/Country: 1943 + USA
Distr/Arch: sel + wil
Annotation: Jack Benny as a heart-of-gold lawyer who
    develops the reputation of meanness to gain clients - with
    comedic results. Anderson plays his Rochester role.

MEDICAL MISSIONS IN AFRICA
Series: National Archives Gift Collection
Tech Info: 35 mm/silent/1 reel/bw
Annotation: Witch doctor methods are contrasted with medical
    science. (Part of Record Group 200 HF series, Harmon
    Foundation Collection.)

MEDICINE MAN
Series: U.N. International Zone
Nar/Cast: Alistair Cooke
Producer: United Nations
Tech Info: 16 mm/sound/color
Date/Country: Gambia   Type: TV Documentary
Distr/Arch: untv
Annotation: Lenri Peters* (poet/surgeon) returns to Gambia
    after years in a British hospital. Working in a poorly
    equipped hospital in Bansang, Dr. Peters tries to combine
    modern medicine and traditional native healing techniques.
    Also, reflects in his poetry, the African experience.

MEDIUM COOL
Nar/Cast: Robert Forster + Verna Bloom + Felton Perry*
Screenplay: Haskell Wexler
Producer: Wexler, Jerrold + Wexler, Haskell   Director:
    Haskell Wexler
Studio/Company: Paramount
Tech Info: 16 mm/sound/color/110 min.
Date/Country: 1969 + USA   Type: Feature
Distr/Arch: rbc
Annotation: Drama about a news cameraman for a Chicago TV
    station who covers a number of diverse events in his
    "medium cool" uninvolved way: car crashes, assassination
    of Robert Kennedy, a human interest story in a black
    neighborhood where the residents are hostile and accuse
    him of irresponsibility. Perry is one of the residents.

MEDIUM, THE
Nar/Cast: Leo Coleman* + Marie Powers + Anna Maria Al-
    berghetti
Screenplay: Gian-Carlo Menotti
Producer: Walter Lowenthal   Director: Gian-Carlo Menotti
Studio/Company: Trans Film
Date/Country: 1951   Type: Feature
Annotation: Leo Coleman plays a mute gypsy boy who is
    maltreated and finally murdered by "The Medium" (Powers),
    a false spiritualist driven to distraction by her own
    mental trickery. An adaptation of the Broadway musical
    drama.

MEET ME IN LAS VEGAS
Nar/Cast: Dan Dailey + Cyd Charisse + Lena Horne*
Screenplay: Isobel Lennart
Producer: Joe Pasternak   Director: Roy Rowland
Studio/Company: MGM
Tech Info: 16 mm/sound/color/112 min.
Date/Country: 1956 + USA   Type: Feature
Distr/Arch: fnc
Annotation: Musical comedy with Las Vegas backdrop featuring

Lena Horne and the voice of Sammy Davis, Jr.

MEET THE MAESTROS
Nar/Cast: Cab Calloway* + Isham Jones and His Orchestra*
Studio/Company: Paramount
Tech Info: 9 min.
Date/Country: 1938 + USA   Type: Musical Short
Annotation: This music short features the above musicians.
   Cab Calloway plays "Zah-zuh-zag."

MEETING THE MAN
Nar/Cast: James Baldwin*   Director: Terence Dixon
Tech Info: 16 mm/sound/color/27 min.
Date/Country: 1971 + France   Type: Documentary
Annotation: A self-portrait of the writer and his conflicts.
   Baldwin demands to be seen as he is: a black man and wit-
   ness to the world.

MELANCHOLY DAME
Series: Christie Comedy
Nar/Cast: Evelyn Preer* + Edward Thompson* + Spencer Willi-
   ams* + Roberta Hyson*
Screenplay: Octavus Roy Cohen
Producer: Al Christie   Director: Octavus Roy Cohen +
   Spencer Williams*
Studio/Company: Paramount + Famous Laskey Corp.
Tech Info: 35 mm/bw/sound/2 reels
Date/Country: 1928 + USA   Type: Comedy Short
Annotation: Jonquil, the wife of "Permanent" Williams, owner
   of a nightclub, is jealous of his attentions to one of his
   entertainers, Sappho. The complications of this triangle
   are the source of comedy in this burlesque of the black
   bourgeoisie of Birmingham. First black sound film.

MELINDA
Nar/Cast: Calvin Lockhart* + Rosalind Cash* + Vonetta McGee*
   + Paul Stevens + Rockne Tarkington + Jim Kelley*
Screenplay: Lonnie Elder, III
Producer: Pervis Atkins   Director: Hugh A. Robertson
Studio/Company: MGM
Tech Info: 16 mm/color/sound/3 reels/100 min.
Date/Country: 1972 + USA   Type: Feature
Distr/Arch: fnc
Annotation: A Black D.J. (Calvin Lockhart) falls is love
   with Melinda (Vonetta McGee) in this movie, but their
   romance is short-lived when she is ordered murdered by a
   white syndicate chief. While a mistress of the gangland
   boss, Melinda had taped several conversations he had with
   other mobsters.   In helping Frankie find out the
   particulars of the murder, an ex-girlfriend (Rosalind
   Cash) gets kidnapped.

MELODIES OLD AND NEW
Series: Our Gang
Nar/Cast: Our Gang + Billie Thomas*
Producer: MGM   Director: Edward Cahn
Studio/Company: MGM
Tech Info: bw/sound/1 reel

Date/Country: 1942 + USA   Type: Comedy Short
Annotation: To raise money for new football uniforms the
    gang puts on a show. But Mickey lets most of the audience
    in free. Froggy's uncle Walt comes through, anyway, with
    new uniforms as a reward for Mickey's good deed.   Billie
    Thomas stars as Buckwheat.

MELODY_FOR_TWO
Nar/Cast: James Metton + Patricia Ellis + Eddie Anderson*
Screenplay: George Bricker + Luci Ward   Story: Richard Ma-
    cauley   Director: Louis King
Studio/Company: Warner Brothers
Tech Info: 16 mm/sound/bw/60 min.
Date/Country: 1939 + USA
Distr/Arch: uas
Annotation: Musical about singers for rival bands and their
    romance with Eddie "Rochester" Anderson supplying comedic
    relief.

MELODY_MAKERS_SERIES
Nar/Cast: Frank Wilson*
Studio/Company: Wardour Films
Date/Country: 1932   Type: Short
Annotation: Stephen Foster's songs are background for
    familiar shots of Blacks "in the quarter." Wilson is the
    only one of the black company to get a credit line.

MELODY_PARADE
Nar/Cast: Mary Beth Hughes + Irene Ryan + Mantan Moreland*
    Director: Arthur Dreifuss
Studio/Company: Monogram
Tech Info: 16 mm/sound/bw/70 min.
Date/Country: 1943 + USA   Type: Feature
Distr/Arch: mog

MEMBER_OF_THE_WEDDING
Nar/Cast: Ethel Waters* + Julie Harris + James Edwards*
Screenplay: Edna Anhalt + Edward Anhalt   Story: Carson Mc-
    Cullers (Play)
Producer: Stanley Kramer   Director: Fred Zinnemann
Studio/Company: Paramount
Tech Info: 16mm/ bw/ sound/ 3 reels/ 91 min.
Date/Country: 1952 + USA   Type: Feature
Distr/Arch: buc + mac + swa
Annotation: In this film, Ethel Waters portrays Berenice
    Brown, a cook who befriends a troubled young girl (Harris)
    with warmth and compassion. She also has some life of her
    own, which she talks about, and a restless, unhappy
    nephew, Honey Brown, played by James Edwards, whom she
    tries to help.

MEMORIAL_SERVICES_AT_THE_TOMB_OF_"PRINCE_HALL"
Studio/Company: Peacock Photoplay Company
Date/Country: 1922 + USA   Type: Newsreel

MEMORY_FOR_TWO
Nar/Cast: Phil Harris + Eddie Anderson* + Leslie Brooke +
    Walter Catlett + Frank Sully + Louise Franklin*   Story:

John Gray   Director: Del Lord
Studio/Company: Columbia
Date/Country: 1946 + USA   Type: Feature

MEMPHIS SLIM
Nar/Cast: Memphis Slim*   Director: Yannick Bruynoghe
Tech Info: 35 min.
Date/Country: 1960 + Belgium   Type: Musical Short
Annotation: Impressionistic film view of blues singer, Mem-
   phis Slim.

MEN IN FRIGHT
Series: Our Gang
Nar/Cast: Our Gang + Billie Thomas*
Screenplay: Carl Dudley + Marty Schwartz
Producer: Jack Chertok   Director: George Sidney
Studio/Company: MGM
Tech Info: bw/sound/1 reel
Date/Country: 1938 + USA   Type: Comedy Short
Annotation: The gang visits Darla who is in the hospital
   recovering from a tonsillectomy. They've brought
   mountains of food for her though they know she can't eat
   anything.   Their resultant stomach aches land them in the
   hospital.   Billie Thomas stars as Buckwheat.

MEN OF AFRICA
Nar/Cast: Leslie Mitchell
Producer: Basil Wright   Director: Alexander Sahw
Studio/Company: Colonical Marketing Board
Tech Info: 35 mm/bw/sound/1686 ft./19 min.
Date/Country: 1939 + Britain   Type: Documentary
Distr/Arch: iwm
Annotation: This is a documentary illustrating the
   principles of British administration in the health, educa-
   tion and agricultural services of East Africa.

MEN OF BRONZE   Director: William Miles*
Tech Info: 58 min.
Date/Country: 1976 + USA   Type: Documentary
Distr/Arch: fnc
Annotation: Miles's first documentary film depicts the con-
   tributions of Blacks to the Military during WWI.

MERRIE HOWE CARFE
Nar/Cast: Freddie Jackson* + Jeni LeGon* + Monte Hawley*
Studio/Company: Argus Production

MERRILY WE LIVE
Nar/Cast: Willie Best* + Constance Bennett + Brian Aherne
Screenplay: Eddie Moran + Jack Jevne
Producer: Milton H.Bren   Director: Norman Z. McLeod
Studio/Company: Hal Roach
Tech Info: sound/bw/95 min.
Date/Country: 1938
Annotation: One of Best's usual roles as George, in a comedy
   modeled on My Man Godfrey.

MERRY WIDOW, THE

Nar/Cast: Mae Murray + John Gilbert + Roy D'Arey + Carolynne
   Snowden* + Zack Williams*   Director: Erich Von Stroheim
Studio/Company: MGM
Tech Info: 35 mm/silent/bw/10 reels
Date/Country: 1925 + USA   Type: Feature
Annotation: Zack Williams plays a small dandified role in
   this adaptation of the musical comedy with Mae Murray as
   the merry widow.

MESSENGER FROM VIOLET DRIVE, THE
Producer: NET
Tech Info: 16 mm/sound/bw/1 reel/29 min.
Date/Country: 1964   Type: Documentary
Distr/Arch: iu
Annotation: Presents an interview with Elijah Muhammad,
   leader cf the Black Muslims, who discusses the philosophy
   of total separation of Negroes and whites in America.
   Discusses Muhammad's beliefs concerning the origins of the
   Negro and Caucasian races, his prophesied destruction of
   America, and his mission as the 'last messenger from Allah
   to the American Negro.'

MEXICAN SPITFIRE SEES A GHOST
Nar/Cast: Leon Errol + Lupe Velez + Mantan Moreland*
Screenplay: Charles E. Roberts + Monte Brice
Producer: Cliff Reid   Director: Leslie Goodwins
Studio/Company: RKO Radio
Date/Country: 1942 + USA   Type: Feature
Annotation: Mantan Moreland is Lightnin' in this sixth in
   the Mexican Spitfire series which has Lupe Velez playing
   Leon Errol's niece. Uncle Matt is one of his three roles.

MEXICAN SUITE, THE
Nar/Cast: Duke Ellington and His Orchestra*   Director: Gary
   Keys
Date/Country: 1972 + USA
Annotation: Views Duke Ellington and his orchestra through
   their concerts in Mexico.

MIDNIGHT ACE, THE
Nar/Cast: A.B. Comathiere* + Mabel Kelly* + Susie Sutton* +
   William Edmondson* + Walter Cormick*
Producer: Swan Micheaux*
Studio/Company: Dunbar Film Corporation
Date/Country: 1928 + USA   Type: Feature
Annotation: Melodrama about a young woman who is torn
   between the bad (a master criminal) and the good (young
   detective who tracks down the criminal). Numerous com-
   plications arise before the happy ending. Shot at the old
   Vitagraph studio in Brooklyn.

MIDNIGHT COWBOY
Nar/Cast: Dustin Hoffman + Jon Voight   Director: John Sch-
   lesinger
Studio/Company: United Artists
Tech Info: 16 mm/sound/color/111 min.
Date/Country: 1969 + USA   Type: Feature
Distr/Arch: uas

Annotation: Black director Hugh Robertson was a film editor
   on this highly successful film about two losers who
   survive in New York for a time by establishing a most unlikely friendship.

MIDNIGHT_FACES
Alt Title(s): Midnight Fires
Nar/Cast: Martin Turner* + Francis X. Bushman, Jr. + Kathryn
   McGuire
Screenplay: Bennett Cohn   Director: Bennett Cohn
Studio/Company: Otto K. Schreier Productions
Tech Info: 16 mm/silent/bw/60 min.
Date/Country: 1926 + USA   Type: Feature
Distr/Arch: sel + wil
Annotation: Martin Turner is Trohelius Snapp, valet to
   Richard Mason in this "melodrama" about inheritance and
   swindling which takes place in a deserted house in the
   Florida Everglades.   (May have been released as Midnight
   Fires.)

MIDNIGHT_LODGE
Nar/Cast: Aubrey Lyles* + Flournoy E. Miller*
Studio/Company: Vitagraph
Date/Country: 1930 + USA
Annotation: The treasurer of a black lodge is confronted by
   members about missing lodge funds amid familiar renditions
   of songs by the lodge members.

MIDNIGHT_MENACE
Nar/Cast: Sybil Lewis* + George Wiltshire* + James Dunsmore*
   + Harold Coke* + Leon Poke* + Amust Austin* + Jimmy
   Walker* + Black Diamond Dollies*
Studio/Company: All American News
Date/Country: 194- + USA

MIDNIGHT_SHADOW
Nar/Cast: Frances Redd* + Buck Woods* + Richard Bates* +
   Ollie Ann Robinson* + Clinton Rosemond* + Ruby Dandridge*
Producer: George Randol*   Director: George Randol*
Studio/Company: Randol Productions + Sack Amusement Enter-
   prises
Tech Info: 35 mm/bw/sound/6 reels
Date/Country: 1939 + USA   Type: Feature

MIDSHIPMAN_EASY
Nar/Cast: Margaret Lockwood + Hugh Green + Robert Adams*
   Story: Captain Marryat   Director: Carol Reed
Studio/Company: British Lion
Tech Info: 16 mm/sound/bw/70 min.
Date/Country: 1935 + Britain
Distr/Arch: jan + mog
Annotation: In this film version of the story of Captain
   Marryat, Robert Adams plays a cabin boy on H.M.S. Harpy
   who, among his other exploits, rescues Midshipman Easy,
   played by Hugh Green.

MIGHTY_LAK_A_GOAT
Series: Our Gang

Nar/Cast: Our Gang + Billie Thomas*
Screenplay: Hal Law + Robert A. McGowan
Producer: MGM   Director: Herbert Glazer
Studio/Company: MGM
Tech Info: bw/sound/1 reel
Date/Country: 1942 + USA   Type: Comedy Short
Annotation: A cleaning fluid Froggy cooks up for the gang
   after they've been splashed with mud has classmates,
   buses, theater audiences and even on screen actors fleeing
   from the smell. Billie Thomas stars as Buckwheat.

MIKE_FRIGHT
Series: Our Gang
Nar/Cast: Our Gang + Matthew Beard*
Screenplay: Hal E. Roach
Producer: Hal Roach   Director: Gus Meins
Studio/Company: MGM + Roach
Tech Info: super 8 mm/16 mm/bw/sound/1 reel/18 min.
Date/Country: 1934 + USA   Type: Comedy Short
Distr/Arch: roa + bla
Annotation: The gang wins a radio audition contest. Matthew
   Beard stars as Stymie.

MILDRED_PIERCE
Nar/Cast: Joan Crawford + Jack Carson + Zachary Scott + Eve
   Arden + Bruce Bennett + Ann Blyth + Lee Patrick + Butter-
   fly McQueen*
Screenplay: Ronald MacDougall + Catherine Turney   Story:
   James M.Cain
Producer: Jerry Wald   Director: Michael Curtiz
Studio/Company: Warners
Tech Info: 16 mm/sound/bw/3 reels/111 min.
Date/Country: 1945 + USA
Distr/Arch: uas + eas
Annotation: Joan Crawford plays a self made business woman
   who has to put up with a very spoiled daughter. Butterfly
   McQueen is featured as a maid who helps Mildred in her
   pie/restaurant business.

MILK-FED_HERO
Nar/Cast: Ebony Players*
Studio/Company: Ebony Film Corporation
Date/Country: 1918 + USA

MILLIONAIRE_PLAYBOY
Nar/Cast: Mantan Moreland*   Director: David Howard
Date/Country: 1937 + USA   Type: Feature

MILLIONAIRE,_THE
Nar/Cast: Grace Smith* + Lawrence Criner* + Cleo Desmond* +
   Lionel Monagas* + William Edmonson* + Vera Brocker* + S.T.
   Jacks* + E.G. Tatum* + Robert S. Abbott*   Story: Oscar
   Micheaux*   Director: Oscar Micheaux*
Studio/Company: Micheaux Film Corporation
Date/Country: 1927 + USA   Type: Feature
Annotation: The story of a young black man who makes his
   fortune in South America, returns to Harlem where a
   beautiful but corrupt woman connected with gangsters tries

to trap him into marriage.

MIND READER, THE
Nar/Cast: Warren Williams + Constance Cummings + Clarence
    Muse*
Screenplay: Vivian Cosby   Director: Roy Del Ruth
Studio/Company: Warners
Tech Info: 16 mm/sound/bw/70 min.
Date/Country: 1933 + USA   Type: Feature
Distr/Arch: uas
Annotation: A seller of patent medicine decides to hit the
    carnival trail as a clairvoyant. Film shows the various
    ways a clairvoyant deceives the public. Muse has a small
    role.

MINGUS
Nar/Cast: Charles Mingus* + Carolyn Mingus*
Producer: Tom Reichman   Director: Tom Reichman
Studio/Company: Filmmakers' Distribution Center + Inlet
Tech Info: 16 mm/bw/sound/2 reels/60 min.
Date/Country: 1966 + USA   Type: Documentary
Distr/Arch: gro + imp + fnc
Annotation: Mingus is a close-up of bassplayer and composer
    Charlie Mingus as he and his five-year old daughter await
    eviction by the City of New York. The film is intercut
    with Mingus and performing groups. Poetry and much of the
    music by Mingus*.

MINISTER'S TEMPTATION, A
Studio/Company: Democracy Film Corporation
Date/Country: 1919 + USA

MINNIE THE MOOCHER
Series: Betty Boop cartoon
Producer: Max Fleischer   Director: Dave Fleischer
Studio/Company: Warners
Tech Info: 16 mm/sound/1 reel/6-8 min.
Date/Country: 1932 + USA   Type: Animated Short
Distr/Arch: emg + kpf
Annotation: Opens with Cab Calloway and his special "truck-
    in'" act. Betty is very distressed at having to listen to
    her parents' admonitions all the time and runs away with
    Bimbo. Spooks and goblins send her flying back home.

MINORITIES: PATTERNS OF CHANGE
Series: Minorities
Producer: Coronet Films
Tech Info: 16 mm/sound/color/1 reel/13 min.
Date/Country: 1972 + USA   Type: Documentary
Distr/Arch: iu + corf
Annotation: Discusses from several different viewpoints
    whether there are more minority problems in the United
    States today than in the past. Examines whether educa-
    tion, employment, and political action are improving the
    condition of minority groups.

MINORITIES: WHAT'S A MINORITY
Series: Minorities

Producer: Coronet Films
Tech Info: 16 mm/sound/color/1 reel/13 min.
Date/Country: 1972 + USA   Type: Documentary
Distr/Arch: iu + corf
Annotation: Introduces the concept of 'minority' and
    provides various academic and popular approaches to its
    definition. Concludes, through interviews with both ex-
    perts and non-experts, that in the United States 'minority
    group' refers to people who can be distinguished by
    physical characteristics, religious beliefs, and national
    origins which differ from white, Anglo-Saxon, Protestant
    model thought to make up the majority of the population.

MINORITY YOUTH: FELICIA
Producer: Stuart Roe
Tech Info: 16 mm/sound/bw/1 reel/12 min.
Date/Country: 1971 + USA   Type: Documentary
Distr/Arch: iu + bfa
Annotation: Presents the reflections of Felicia, a black
    high school junior from the Watts area of Los Angeles, on
    herself, her family, her school friends, her race, and her
    community. Relates her feelings on discrimination and
    prejudice and expresses hope that the next generation's
    efforts will result in change.

MINSTREL MAN
Nar/Cast: Art Evans* + Gene Bell* + Glynn Turman* + Stanley
    Clay*
Screenplay: Richard Shapiro + Esther Shapiro
Producer: Michael Levenheim + Richard Brower   Director:
    William Sraham
Studio/Company: Roger Gimble Tomorrow Enterprises
Tech Info: cclor/sound/90 min.
Date/Country: 1977 + USA   Type: TV Feature
Annotation: The story of black minstrels minstrelry told
    through the fictional experience of two brothers who begin
    their stage career with their father. Rennie (Stanley
    Clay), the sensitive and creative pianist- composer,
    resents and rejects the racist strictures of the minstrel
    show. Through his posthumous influence, Harry, the older
    brother (song/dance man) played by Glynn Turman, changes
    the face and format of the show, adding dignity to the
    black man's performance.

MIRACLE IN HARLEM
Nar/Cast: Sheila Guyse* + Stepin Fetchit* + Hilda Offley* +
    Creighton Thompson* + Kenneth Freeman* + Savannah
    Churchill* + William Greaves* + Juanita Hall Choir* +
    Lawrence Criner* + Jack Carter*
Screenplay: Vincent Valentini   Story: Vincent Valentini
Producer: Jack Goldberg   Director: Jack Kemp
Studio/Company: Jack Goldberg-Herald Pictures, Inc. + Screen
    Guild Productions
Tech Info: 16 mm/bw/sound/3 reels (spliced from original 8)
Date/Country: 1948 + USA   Type: Feature
Distr/Arch: lc
Annotation: Aunt Hattie, a kind old woman (Offley) and her
    niece Julie (Sheila Guyse) are swindled out of their candy

store by the son of the owner of a chain of candy stores.
The owner of the chain is killed and many are suspected,
including Julie. Fetchit plays Swifty who works for Aunt
Hattie and Julie, but not too assiduously.

MIRACLE OF OUR LADY FATIMA, THE
Nar/Cast: Frank Silvera* + Susan Whitney
Screenplay: Crane Wilbur + James O'Hanlon
Producer: Bryan Foy   Director: John Brahm
Studio/Company: Warner Brothers
Date/Country: 1952 + USA   Type: Feature
Annotation: Film version of the mysterious events of 1917 in
    Portugal in which three children claimed to have seen a
    vision of a lady near the village of Fatima. Frank
    Silvera plays a provincial administrator whose job is to
    ask the tough questions, not an easy matter when one is
    dealing with miracles.

MIRACLE WORKER, THE
Nar/Cast: Anne Bancroft + Patty Duke + Beah Richards* + An-
    drew Prine
Screenplay: William Gibson   Story: William Gibson
Producer: Fred Coe   Director: Arthur Penn
Studio/Company: United Artists
Tech Info: 16 mm/sound/bw/107 min.
Date/Country: 1962 + USA   Type: Feature
Distr/Arch: nef + uas
Annotation: Film adaptation of William Gibson's play of how
    Anne Sullivan changed the course of Helen Keller's life,
    with Beah Richards playing the part of Vinny.

MIRAGE
Nar/Cast: Hari Rhodes* + Gregory Peck + Diane Baker
Screenplay: Peter Stone
Producer: Harry Keller   Director: Edward Dmytryk
Studio/Company: Universal
Tech Info: 16 mm/sound/bw/109 min.
Date/Country: 1965 + USA   Type: Feature
Distr/Arch: ccc + cou + swa + tmc + uni
Annotation: A thriller with music scores by Quincy Jones*.

MISSIN ACHIEVEMENTS
Series: National Archives Gift Collection
Tech Info: 16 mm/silent/3 reels/bw
Annotation: Activities of Protestant denominations in Afri-
    ca. (Part of Record Group 200 HF series, Harmon Founda-
    tion Collection).

MISSING LINK, THE
Nar/Cast: Syd Chaplin + Ruth Hiatt + Tom McGuire + Crawford
    Kent + Sam Baker*
Screenplay: Darryl Francis Zanuck   Director: Charles
    F. Reisner
Studio/Company: Warner Brothers Pictures
Tech Info: 35 mm/silent/bw/7 reels
Date/Country: 1927 Type: Feature
Annotation: A hunt in Africa for "the missing link" played
    by Sam Baker is the backdrop for romance. The young male

subdues "the missing link," becomes the hero and wins his
lady's love.

MISSING_PAGES
Producer: Fisk University
Tech Info: 16 mm/sound/color/13 min.   Type: Dramatized
    Documentary
Distr/Arch: per
Annotation: An account of the underground railroad told with
    drawings by Charles White*, reenactments and mime.
    Provided by Center for Southern Folklore.

MISSION_TO_MOSCOW
Nar/Cast: Walter Huston + Ann Harding + Leigh Whipper*
Screenplay: Howard Koch   Story: Joseph E. Davies
Producer: Robert Buckner   Director: Michael Curtiz
Studio/Company: Warner Brothers
Tech Info: 16 mm/sound/bw/124 min.
Date/Country: 1943 + USA   Type: Feature
Distr/Arch: uas
Annotation: Based on a book by former ambassador to Russia
    Joseph Davies, the film depicts the beginnings of WWII.
    Leig Whipper plays Haile Selassie.

MISSIONARIES_IN_DARKEST_AFRICA   Director: Gene Gauntier
Date/Country: 1912 + USA   Type: Dramatic Short
Annotation: The film treats a kidnapping theme, and relates
    miscegination to the suicide of a missionary's daughter.

MISSISSIPPI_DELTA_BLUES
Producer: Bill Ferris + Josette Rossi + Judy Peiser + Center
    for Southern Folklore
Tech Info: 16 mm/sound/bw/18 min.
Date/Country: 1974 + USA   Type: Documentary
Distr/Arch: csf
Annotation: A collection of filmed field research (1968-
    1970) which shows the richness of Delta Blues.   Includes
    Louis Dotson*, James "Sonny Ford" Thomas, "Little Son"
    Jefferson*, others.   Provided by Center for Southern
    Folklore.

MISSISSIPPI_SUMMER
Nar/Cast: J.A. Preston + Lisle Wilson + Jared Martin +
    Robert Earl Jones*
Screenplay: William Bayer
Producer: William Bayer + Eric Peniston   Director: William
    Bayer
Studio/Company: New Line Cinema
Tech Info: 16 mm/35 mm/color/sound/2 reels/88 min.
Date/Country: 1970 + USA   Type: Feature Documentary
Distr/Arch: nlc
Annotation: The film shows the attitudinal changes that oc-
    cur in an integrated acting company as it tours the South
    during the Civil Rights struggles of the sixties.

MISSISSIPPI
Nar/Cast: Bing Crosby + W.C. Fields + Libby Taylor*
Screenplay: Francis Martin + Jack Cunningham   Story: Booth

Tarkington
Producer: Arthur Hornblow, Jr.   Director: Ed Sutherland
Studio/Company: Paramount
Tech Info: 16 mm/sound/bw/54 min.
Date/Country: 1935 + USA   Type: Feature
Distr/Arch: swa + uni
Annotation: Libby Taylor plays Lavinia, a bit part, in this
   W.C.   Fields vehicle in which he makes the famous remark
   "get along, you Senegambian" to a black coachman.

MISTER BUDDWING
Nar/Cast: Raymond St. Jacques* + James Garner + Suzanne
   Pleshette
Screenplay: Dale Wasserman
Producer: Douglas Laurence + Delbert Mann   Director: Del-
   bert Mann
Studio/Company: MGM
Tech Info: 16 mm/sound/bw/100 min.
Date/Country: 1966 + USA   Type: Feature
Distr/Arch: fnc
Annotation: St. Jacques is a Harlem dice-shooter gambler
   (Hank), one of a number of characters whom Garner (Mr.
   Buddwing) encounters while he is suffering from amnesia.

MISTER ROCK AND ROLL
Nar/Cast: Alan Freed + Rocky Graziano
Screenplay: James Blumgarten
Producer: Ralph Serpe + Howard Kreitek   Director: Charles
   Dubin
Studio/Company: Paramount
Tech Info: 74 min.
Date/Country: 1957 + USA   Type: Feature
Annotation: Lionel Hampton, Little Richard and Chuck Berry
   add to the series of musical numbers that make up this
   relatively plotless film.

MIXED COLORS
Studio/Company: Pathe   Type: Comedy Short
Annotation: Humor in this film constructed on the basis of a
   black baby being painted white and a white black by a boy
   prankster, and then placed in the other's carriage.

MOAN AND GROAN, INC.
Series: Our Gang
Nar/Cast: Our Gang + Allen Hoskins*
Screenplay: Robert F. McGowan
Producer: Robert F. McGowan + Hal Roach   Director: Robert
   F. McGowan
Studio/Company: MGM + Roach
Tech Info: super 8 mm/16 mm/bw/sound/1 reel/20 min.
Date/Country: 1929 + USA   Type: Comedy Short
Distr/Arch: bla + roa
Annotation: Officer Kennedy captures a madman who delights
   in scaring the gang while they play in his old, apparently
   deserted, spooky mansion. Allen Hoskins stars as Farina.

MODERN CAIN, A
Nar/Cast: Norman Ward* + Vivian Quarles* + Theodore Willi-

ams* + Harriet Harris* + Fred Williams*
Studio/Company: J.W. Fife Productions
Date/Country: 1921 + USA

MOGAMBO
Nar/Cast: Clark Gable + Ava Gardner + Grace Kelly
   Director: John Ford
Studio/Company: MGM
Tech Info: 16 mm/sound/color/116 min.
Date/Country: 1953   Type: Feature
Annotation: Clark Gable plays a plantation overseer in Kenya
   who is tough with his Kenyan bearers but less than able to
   handle both Ava Gardner and Grace Kelly. Remake of Red
   Dust (1932).

MOI UN NOIR
Alt Title(s): Treichville
Nar/Cast: Oumarou Ganda* + Petit Toure* + Alassane Maiga* +
   Amadou Demba* + Seydou Gude* + Karidyo Faoudou* + Mlle
   Gambi*
Producer: Roger Fleytoux   Director: Jean Rouch
Studio/Company: Films de la Pleiade
Tech Info: color
Date/Country: 1959 + France
Distr/Arch: saf
Annotation: Views the life of three young Nigerians in the
   poor quarter of Abidjan, Frenchville who have left their
   ancestral home for the big city where they dream of money
   and girls. Winner of Louis Delluc Prize, 1959. (Archived
   only).

MOJO   Director: Ed Guerrero
Tech Info: 16 mm/3.5 min./bw/sound   Type: Animated Short
Distr/Arch: can
Annotation: A cartoon using African and Far Eastern images.

MOL
Nar/Cast: Med Hondo* + Ousmane Gadiaga* + Alice Bengeloun* +
   Etienne William* + Francois Anchouet* + Nicolas N'Diaye* +
   Awa Gadiaga*
Screenplay: Renee Clarke
Producer: Groupe Africain Production   Director: Paulin
   Soumanou Vieyra*
Tech Info: color/sound/25 min./French commentary by Med
   Hondo*
Date/Country: 1966 + Senegal
Annotation: Young Ousmane is a fisherman who decides to
   break tradition and motorize his boat. Before he buys the
   motor he must get the elder's permission and travel to
   another city to work and establish credit for a loan. The
   motor is obtained and upon Ousmane's return the village
   celebrates.

MOMENT OF DANGER
Nar/Cast: Dorothy Dandridge*   Director: Laslo Benedek
Date/Country: 1959 + USA   Type: Feature

MONEY ORDER, THE

Alt Title(s): see Mandari

MONEYCHANGERS, THE
Nar/Cast: Kirk   Douglas + Christopher Plummer + Percy
   Rodrigues* + Lincoln Kilpatrick* + Helen Hayes + Jean
   Peters + Susan Flannery + Lorne Greene   Story: Arthur
   Hailey
Producer: Ross Hunter   Director: Boris Segall
Studio/Company: Paramount TV
Tech Info: sound/color/180 min.
Date/Country: 1977 + USA   Type: TV Feature
Annotation: The ways that bankers make and manipulate the
   money of depositors, large and small. Sex is one of those
   ways. Some social consciousness is demonstrated by the
   good banker (Douglas). Rodrigues plays the bank's chief
   of security. Kilpatrick is the leader of the Forum East
   minority group which bears the brunt of the manipulative
   tactics of the bad banker (Greene).

MONKEY BUSINESS
Series: Our Gang
Nar/Cast: Our Gang + Allen Hoskins* + Jannie Hoskins*
Screenplay: Hal Roach
Producer: Hal Roach   Director: Robert McGowan
Studio/Company: Pathe
Tech Info: silent/bw/2 reels
Date/Country: 1926 + USA   Type: Comedy Short
Annotation: With the gang always picking on Farina, he be-
   comes allies with a monkey that has escaped from a
   sideshow. The ape has a unique talent: it can fight bet-
   ter than anyone. Between the gang and the monkey, they
   wreak havoc in a quiet town.   Allen Hoskins stars as
   Farina.

MONSIEUR ALBERT, PROPHETE   Director: Jean Rouch + Jean
   Ravel
Studio/Company: Argos Films
Tech Info: 35 mm/900 m./color
Date/Country: 1963 + France
Distr/Arch: saf
Annotation: This film is a true story of the most recent of
   the African religions of Christian influence: le harisme,
   and in particular of the life of a hospital village, Breg-
   bo, organized spontaneously by the disciples of this
   religion. Over the past twelve years it has received
   about 5,000 mentally ill patients who have received treatment for both the body and the mind.

MONSTER WALKS, THE
Nar/Cast: Willie Best* + Mischa Auer
Studio/Company: Mayfair
Tech Info: 16 mm/sound/bw/60 min.
Date/Country: 1932 + USA   Type: Feature
Distr/Arch: mog + bla
Annotation: Willie Best was listed in the credits as "Sleep
   'n' Eat" in this humor-horror film.

MOO COW BOOGIE

Nar/Cast: Dorothy Dandridge* + Stepin Fetchit*
Date/Country: 1943 + USA

MOON_OVER_HARLEM
Nar/Cast: Bud Harris* + Cora Green* + Izinetta Wilcois* +
  Carl Gough* + Marieluise Behet* + Slim Thompson* + Alec
  Lovejoy* + Sidney Bechet*
Screenplay: Sherle Castle   Story: Frank Wilson*
Producer: Edgar G. Ulmer   Director: Edgar G. Ulmer
Studio/Company: Meteor Productions
Tech Info: 16 mm/bw/sound/8 reels/67 min.
Date/Country: 1939 + USA   Type: Feature
Annotation: A Harlem widow unwittingly marries a double-
  talking gangster who is involved in the numbers racket.
  Some complexities of black life in Harlem are shown in the
  context of a musical melodrama. Music by Donald Heywood*.

MOONFIRE
Nar/Cast: Richard Egan + Charles Napier + Sonny Liston*
Producer: Michael Parkhurst   Director: Michael Parkhurst
Studio/Company: Hollywood Continental Inc.
Tech Info: sound/color
Date/Country: 1970 + USA   Type: Feature
Annotation: Sonny Liston, "the farmer," is hired for his
  brawn to protect 2 million dollars and the two truckers
  who drive the money to Mexico where an ex-Nazi is holding
  hostage a pilot (the head of an airline company) whose
  experimental capsule "Moonfire" has been downed on the
  Nazi's ranch.

MOONRISE
Nar/Cast: Rex Ingram* + Dave Clark + Gail Russell
Screenplay: Charles Haas   Story: Theodore Strauss
Studio/Company: Republic
Tech Info: 16 mm/sound/bw
Date/Country: 1948 + USA   Type: Feature
Annotation: Young white--a restless community outcast--Danny
  (Clark) meets Mose (Ingram) in the woods. They hunt, fish
  together. Mose discovers Danny has killed a rich banker's
  son and persuades him to go back, to fight the outcast
  role, attempts to give him back his manhood.

MORT_DU_CYGNE,_LA   Director: Jean Benoit-Levy + Marie Epstein
Date/Country: 1937 + France   Type: Feature
Annotation: Ballet film in which a black child (female) is a
  member of the school attached to the Paris Opera and func-
  tions with no apparent discrimination.

MOST_DANGEROUS_GAME,_THE
Alt Title(s): The Hounds of Zaroff
Nar/Cast: Joel McCrea + Leslie Banks* + Fay Wray + Noble
  Johnson*   Story: Richard Connell
Producer: David Selznick + Merian Cooper   Director: Ernest
  B. Schoedsack + Irving Pichel
Studio/Company: RKO Radio
Tech Info: 16 mm/sound/bw/65 min.
Date/Country: 1932 + USA   Type: Feature

Distr/Arch: bud + cfm + amg + ima + jan + kpf + cie
Annotation: Concerns a once famous explorer who lives on a
remote island and who re-lives the thrill of hunting by
using humans as his victims. Produced at the same time
and on the same set using the same technicians as King
Kong. Noble Johnson appears as a "Tartar" servant,
strong, silent, and head-wrapped.

MOTHER GOOSE A GO-GO
Nar/Cast: Barbara McNair* + Tommy Kirk + Anne Helm
Screenplay: Jack H. Harris
Producer: Jack H. Harris   Director: Jack H. Harris
Tech Info: 16 mm/sound/color/90 min.
Date/Country: 1960 + USA   Type: Feature
Distr/Arch: mac
Annotation: Barbara McNair sings in this comedy about newly-
weds, hallucinations and psychiatric solutions to a
"Mother Goose" complex.

MOTHER, JUGS AND SPEED
Nar/Cast: Raquel Welch + Bill Cosby* + Harvey Keitel + Larry
Hagman + L.Q. Jones
Screenplay: Tom Mankiewicz
Producer: Peter Yates   Director: Peter Yates + Tom Mank-
iewicz
Studio/Company: Twentieth Century Fox
Tech Info: 16 mm/color/sound/3 reels/98 min.
Date/Country: 1976 + USA   Type: Feature
Distr/Arch: fnc
Annotation: A comedy about the trials and tribulations of a
private ambulance service. Cosby plays "Mother," one of
the drivers who is particularly fond of beer which he al-
ways drinks while driving. Racquel Welch is "Jugs."

MOTHER
Studio/Company: Foster Photoplay Company
Date/Country: 191- + USA

MOUNTAIN ROAD, THE
Nar/Cast: James Stewart + Lisa Lu + Frank Silvera*
Screenplay: Alfred Hayes   Story: Theodore White
Producer: William Goetz   Director: Daniel Mann
Studio/Company: Columbia
Tech Info: sound/102 min.
Date/Country: 1960 + USA   Type: Feature
Annotation: Frank Silvera is Kevan in this drama about an
American demolition team commanded by Major Baldwin
(Stewart) in Chinese back country trying to stop the ad-
vance of Japanese troops toward the end of World War II.

MOVE
Nar/Cast: Elliot Gould + Paula Prentiss + Ron O'Neal*
Screenplay: Joel Leiber + Stanley Lieber
Producer: Pandro S. Berman   Director: Stuart Rosenberg
Studio/Company: 20th Century Fox
Tech Info: 16 mm/sound/color/90 min.
Date/Country: 1970 + USA   Type: Feature
Distr/Arch: fnc

Annotation: Story of an impoverished New York playwright who walks dogs and writes porno to eke out a living. Ron O'Neal is Peter.

MR. ADAM'S BOMB
Nar/Cast: Gene Ware* + Eddie Green*   Director: Eddie Green*
Studio/Company: Sepia Productions
Tech Info: 35 mm/sound/bw/2 reels
Date/Country: 1949 + USA   Type: Comedy Short
Distr/Arch: lc

MR. BLANDINGS BUILDS HIS DREAMHOUSE
Nar/Cast: Melvin Douglas + Cary Grant + Myrna Loy + Louise Beavers*
Screenplay: Norman Panama + Melvin Frank   Story: Eric Hodgins
Producer: Norman Panama + Melvin Frank   Director: H.C. Potter
Studio/Company: RKO Radio Pictures
Tech Info: 16 mm/bw/sound/3 reels/94 min.
Date/Country: 1948 + USA   Type: Feature
Distr/Arch: fnc
Annotation: A young advertising executive on the verge of losing his job and new house is saved when his black maid comes up with a sure-fire slogan for his most important account: "If you ain't eatin' Wham you ain't eatin' ham." Beavers is Gussie the maid.

MR. CREEPS
Nar/Cast: Mantan Moreland* + Flournoy E. Miller*
Studio/Company: Toddy Pictures
Date/Country: 1938

MR. MILLER'S ECONOMICS
Studio/Company: Triangle
Date/Country: 1916 + USA
Annotation: A black washerwoman steals clothes from "the big house" for her husband's appearance at an "Afro-Aryon Ball."

MR. MOSES
Nar/Cast: Robert Mitchum + Carroll Baker + Raymond St. Jacques* + Orlando Martins*
Screenplay: Charles Beaumont + Manja Danischewsky
Producer: Frank Ross   Director: Ronald Neame
Studio/Company: United Artist
Tech Info: 16 mm/sound/color/114 min.
Date/Country: 1965 + USA
Distr/Arch: uas
Annotation: Robert Mitchum (Joe Moses) helps a tribe of Masai move to a new area after their old tribal land is to be flooded with waters from a new dam.   St. Jacques is the U.S. educated son of a witch doctor, who resents Moses' interference; Martins is the chief.

MR. SMITH GOES GHOST
Nar/Cast: Dewey "Pigment" Markham* + Hawley Monte* + Randolf Lilian* + Lawrence Criner* + Vernon McCalla* + Millie Mon-

roe*
Screenplay: Ralph Cooper*
Producer: Dewey "Pigment" Markham*
Date/Country: 1940 + USA

MR. WASHINGTON GOES TO TOWN
Nar/Cast: Mantan Moreland* + Flourney Miller*
Producer: Jed Buell   Director: Jed Buell
Studio/Company: Dixie National Pictures
Tech Info: sound/bw/62 min.
Date/Country: 1940 + USA   Type: Feature
Annotation: Slapstick routines by Moreland and Miller in
   this comedy written by whites, among them Walter Weems,
   produced by a white company made up of Jed Buell, James
   Frederick, Ted Toddy.

MR. WELLS
Producer: Adrian O. Natalini
Tech Info: 16 mm/sound/bw/10 min.
Date/Country: 1973 + USA   Type: Documentary
Distr/Arch: nat
Annotation: Story of a man caught between two cultures:
   Afro-American and American Indian. Describes Chicagoan
   Bill Chambers' view of the world and his hostile environ-
   ment. Provided by Center for Southern Folklore.

MR. WISE GUY
Nar/Cast: Ernie Morrison* + Leo Garcy + Huntz Hall +   Bobby
   Jordan
Screenplay: Sam Robins + Harvey Gates + Jack Henley
Producer: Sam Katzman   Director: William Nigh
Studio/Company: Monogram
Tech Info: 16 mm/sound/bw/60 min.
Date/Country: 1941 + USA   Type: Feature
Distr/Arch: bud + mog + cie + thu
Annotation: "Sunshine" Sammy (Ernie Morrison), the first
   black to appear in Our Gang silents, (listed in the
   credits as Sunshine Morrison) as "Scruno," cavorts with
   the East Side kids in another of their romps and clashes
   with the law.

MUHAMMAD ALI -- SKILL, BRAINS AND GUTS
Nar/Cast: Muhammad Ali* + Angelo Dundee
Studio/Company: Macmillan
Tech Info: 16 mm/sound/color/90 min.
Date/Country: 1975 + USA   Type: Documentary
Distr/Arch: mac
Annotation: Film follows Muhammad Ali from his teens to his
   status as heavyweight champion of the world.

MULE FOR THE MARQUESA, A
Alt Title(s): see Professionals, The

MUMMY LOVE
Studio/Company: F.B.O.
Date/Country: 1926 + USA   Type: Comedy Short
Annotation: A black porter wins the keys to the tomb in
   which the heroine (white) is held by cheating at craps

with the black guards to the mummy vault. It is through
his help that the white protagonist wrests the girl he
loves from a lecherous sheik.

MURDER AT THE VANITIES
Nar/Cast: Carl Brisson + Jack Oakie + Kitty Carlisle +
    Victor McLaglen + Duke Ellington* Director: Mitchell
    Leisen
Studio/Company: Paramount
Tech Info: 87 min.
Date/Country: 1934 + USA   Type: Feature
Annotation: Comedy-mystery set behind the scenes at the fic-
    tional-film version of Earl Carroll's Vanities includes a
    production number by Duke Ellington and his orchestra.

MURDER AT THE WORLD SERIES
Nar/Cast: Lynda Day George + Karen Valentine + Gerald S.
    O'Loughlin + Michael Parks + Tamara Dobson*
Screenplay: Cy Chermak
Producer: Cy Chermak   Director: Andrew V. McLaglen
Studio/Company: ABC Circle Films
Date/Country: 1977 + USA   Type: TV Feature
Annotation: Tamara Dobson plays one of five women threatened
    by a rejected and angry young man who intends to kidnap,
    or even murder, one of them at the final two games of the
    World Series in Houston.

MURDER IN SOHO
Nar/Cast: Jack LaRue + Sandra Storme + Bernard Lee + Martin
    Walker + James Hayter + Orlando Martins*
Screenplay: McGrew Willis   Director: Norman Lee
Studio/Company: Associated British
Date/Country: 1939 + Britain   Type: Feature
Annotation: Martins plays a bit role in this British
    mystery.

MURDER IN SWINGTIME
Nar/Cast: Les Hite and His Orchestra* + June Richmond*
Studio/Company: RKO Radio
Tech Info: 10 min.
Date/Country: 1937 + USA   Type: Musical Short
Annotation: This musical short features Les Hite and his
    orchestra with June Richmond performing the vocals.

MURDER IN TRINIDAD
Nar/Cast: Nigel Bruce + Heather Angel + Noble Johnson* +
    Victor Jory   Story: John W. Vandercock   Director: Louis
    King
Studio/Company: Fox
Tech Info: sound/bw
Date/Country: 1934 + USA   Type: Feature
Annotation: Stepping out from Sherlock Holmes' shadow, Nigel
    Bruce plays a British sleuth who goes to Trinidad to break
    a diamond smuggling ring and solve the stabbing murder of
    his assistant. He is guided to safety through the Caroni
    swamps by Queochie, played by Noble Johnson.

MURDER OF FRED HAMPTON, THE

Producer: Mike Fay Associates
Studio/Company: National Talent Service
Tech Info: 16 mm/sound/bw/88 min.
Date/Country: 1971 + USA   Type: Documentary
Distr/Arch: tri + utn
Annotation: This film began as a documentary on the Chicago
  Black Panther Party and its chairman Fred Hampton*.
  Midway through the film Fred Hampton and fellow panther
  Mark Clark* were killed. The film then became an in-
  vestigation of their murder.

MURDER ON A BRIDLE PATH
Nar/Cast: James Gleason + Helen Boderick + Willie Best*
Screenplay: Dorothy Yost   Story: Stuart Palmer
Producer: William Sistron   Director: Ed Kelley
Studio/Company: RKO Radio
Date/Country: 1936
Annotation: Murder mystery with Willie Best featured for
  light comedy.

MURDER ON A HONEYMOON
Nar/Cast: Willie Best* + Edna May Oliver + James Gleason
Screenplay: Stan Miller + Robert Benchley
Producer: Kenneth Macgowan   Director: Lloyd Corrigan
Studio/Company: RKO Radio
Date/Country: 1935   Type: Feature
Annotation: Robert Benchley coscripted this murder mystery
  which features Willie Best in the role of a porter.

MURDER ON LENOX AVENUE
Nar/Cast: Mamie Smith* + Alec Lovejoy* + Edna Mae Harris* +
  Dene Larry* + Norman Astwood* + Guy Smith* + Alberta Perk-
  ins* + George Williams* + Sidney Easton + Frank Wilson*
Screenplay: Robert Crandall   Story: Frank Wilson*
Producer: Colonnade Pictures   Director: Arthur Dreifuss
Studio/Company: Goldberg
Tech Info: 16 mm/bw/sound/2 reels/65 min.
Date/Country: 1941 + USA   Type: Feature
Distr/Arch: bud + emg + kpf
Annotation: Murder on Lenox Avenue is a black gangster film
  with a modern "Othello-like" story line. Scored by Donald
  Heywood*; Mamie Smith sings one song.

MURDER TRAP
Alt Title(s): see Take My Life

MURDER WITH MUSIC
Nar/Cast: Bob Howard* + Nellie Hill* + Milton Williams* +
  Ken Renard* + Noble Sissle* and his Orchestra + George
  Oliver* + Bill Dillard*   Director: George P. Quigley
Studio/Company: Century Productions
Tech Info: 16 mm/sound/bw/2 reels/59 min.
Date/Country: 1941 + USA   Type: Feature
Distr/Arch: kpf + thu
Annotation: Music and dance numbers embellished by a murder
  mystery which involves a young woman who works at a
  cabaret as a performer and her former boy friend who
  escapes from prison.

MUSH AND MILK
Series: Our Gang
Nar/Cast: Our Gang + Matthew Beard*
Producer: Robert F. McGowan   Director: Robert F. McGowan
Studio/Company: MGM + Roach
Tech Info: super 8 mm/16 mm/bw/sound/1 reel/20 min.
Date/Country: 1933 + USA   Type: Comedy Short
Distr/Arch: kpf + bla
Annotation: The gang gets mush at the boarding school every
    morning although Old Cap, the teacher, promises big things
    as socn as his back pension comes through. One   classroom
    sequence has Stymie supposedly playing Brahms's 'Hungarian
    Dance *5' - on harmonica.

MUSIC BOX, THE
Alt Title(s): see Sing As You Swing

MUSIC GOES 'ROUND, THE
Nar/Cast: Eddie Anderson* + Harry Richman + Rochelle Hudson
Screenplay: Jo Swerling   Story: Sidney Buchman   Director:
    Victor Schertzinger
Studio/Company: Columbia
Date/Country: 1936 + USA   Type: Feature
Annotation: Eddie Anderson appears in this musical which
    includes a show boat troupe so bad, it is brought to
    Broadway by the musical comedy star to make his revue a
    hit.

MUSIC HATH CHARMS
Series: Christie Comedy
Nar/Cast: Evelyn Preer* + Edward Thompson* + Spencer Willi-
    ams* + Florian Slappey* + Zenia Sprawl* + Sam Ginn* +
    Lawyer Cheev* + Roscoe Griggers*
Screenplay: Octavus Roy Cohn + Spencer Williams*
Producer: Al Christie
Studio/Company: Paramount
Tech Info: sound/bw/2 reels
Date/Country: 1929 + USA   Type: Comedy Short
Annotation: Rivalry over who will lead the band in a
    Birmingham nightclub is the basis of the conflict in this
    "Negro dialect" comedy.

MUSIC IS MAGIC
Nar/Cast: Hattie McDaniel*
Date/Country: 1935 + USA   Type: Feature
Annotation: McDaniel plays a spirited maid in this musical.

MUSIC OF AFRICA
Producer: NET
Tech Info: 16 mm/sound/bw/1 reel/30 min.
Date/Country: 1963   Type: Documentary
Distr/Arch: iu
Annotation: Features Fela Sowande of Nigeria, a leading
    African musicologist, composer, and organist, with a group
    of Nigerian musicians demonstrating how contemporary
    African music has mingled traditional African and Western
    idioms to create new forms.

MUSS 'EM UP
Nar/Cast: Preston Foster + Margaret Callahan + Clarence
    Muse* + Ward Bond
Screenplay: Erwin Gelsey
Producer: Pandro S. Berman   Director: Charles Vidor
Studio/Company: RKO Radio
Tech Info: sound/bw
Date/Country: 1936 + USA   Type: Feature
Annotation: Preston Foster   plays   a hard-boiled detective
    brought cross-country by an eccentric millionare to   solve
    the murder of the millionare's dog.   Clarence Muse plays
    William, a bit part, in this mystery   entertainment   which
    becomes complicated by a kidnap, a ransom and a murder.

MUTINY ON THE BOUNTY
Nar/Cast: Frank Silvera* + Marlon Brando + Trevor Howard
Screenplay: Charles Lederer
Producer: Aaron Rosenberg   Director: Lewis Milestone
Studio/Company: MGM
Tech Info: 16 mm/sound/color/179 min.
Date/Country: 1962 + USA   Type: Feature
Distr/Arch: fnc
Annotation: Silvera is Minarii in this remake of the 1935
    MGM film about mutineers on the H.M.S. Bounty in 1787.

MY BABY IS BLACK
Alt Title(s): see Les Laches Vivant d'Espoir

MY BLUE HEAVEN
Nar/Cast: Louise Beavers* + Betty Grable + Dan Dailey
Screenplay: Lamar Trotti + Claude Binyon
Producer: Sol C. Siegel   Director: Henry Koster
Studio/Company: 20th Century Fox
Tech Info: 16 mm/sound/bw/96 min.
Date/Country: 1950 + USA   Type: Feature
Distr/Arch: fnc
Annotation: Film about TV's top husband and wife team who
    finally get their wish, a child. Louise Beavers plays the
    maid.

MY BROTHER TALKS TO HORSES
Nar/Cast: Ernest Whitman* + Butch Jenkins + Peter Lawford +
    Lillian Yarbo*
Screenplay: Morton Thompson
Producer: Samuel Marx   Director: Fred Zinnemann
Studio/Company: MGM
Tech Info: 16 mm/sound/bw/93 min.
Date/Country: 1946 + USA   Type: Feature
Distr/Arch: fnc
Annotation: Ernest Whitman is Mr. Mordecai and Lillian Yarbo
    Psyche in this film adaptation of Mort Thompson's story
    about a little boy, "Butch" Jenkins, who has a way with
    horses.

MY CHILDHOOD: JAMES BALDWIN'S HARLEM
Nar/Cast: James Baldwin*
Producer: Metropolitan, Inc.

Tech Info: 16 mm/sound/bw/1 reel/25 min.
Date/Country: 1964 + USA   Type: Dramatized Documentary
Distr/Arch: iu
Annotation: Uses narration by James Baldwin to present the
    poverty and despair of his childhood days in Harlem.
    Depicts the decaying buildings, people without work, and a
    bitter father. Recounts that school and literature
    provided Baldwin with a means of escape from a despairing
    world.

MY SONG GOES FORTH
Nar/Cast: Paul Robeson*
Producer: Gilbert Church
Studio/Company: Ambassador Films
Date/Country: c. 1947 + USA   Type: Documentary

MY SWEET CHARLIE
Nar/Cast: Patty Duke + Al Freeman, Jr.* + Ford Rainey + Wil-
    liam Hardy
Screenplay: Richard Levinson
Producer: Richard Levinson   Director: Lamont Johnson
Studio/Company: Universal
Tech Info: 16 mm/color/sound/3 reels/97 min.
Date/Country: 1970 + USA   Type: Feature
Distr/Arch: ccc + roa + twy + uni
Annotation: Two refugees from society--an unmarried
    pregnant, bigoted girl (Duke) and a black lawyer (Freeman)
    who killed a white man in self-defense--are thrown
    together by chance in an abandoned house on the Gulf Coast
    of Texas: a drama about the uselessness of racial
    antagonism.

MYRA BRECKINRIDGE
Nar/Cast: Mae West + Calvin Lockhart* + Farrah Fawcett +
    Raquel Welch
Screenplay: Michael Sarne + David Giler   Story: Gore Vidal
Producer: Robert Fryer   Director: Michael Sarne
Studio/Company: 20th Century Fox
Tech Info: 16 mm/sound/color/94 min.
Date/Country: 1970 + USA   Type: Feature
Distr/Arch: fnc
Annotation: Gore Vidal's novel (about a New York film critic
    who undergoes a sex-change operation) brought to the
    screen, with Mae West in her first role in many years.
    Calvin Lockhart is Irving Amadeus.

MYSTERIOUS MYSTERY!, THE
Series: Our Gang
Nar/Cast: Our Gang + Allen Hoskins* + Eugene Jackson*
Screenplay: Hal Roach
Producer: Hal Roach   Director: Robert McGowan
Studio/Company: Pathe
Tech Info: silent/bw/2 reels
Date/Country: 1924 + USA   Type: Comedy Short
Annotation: When little rich boy Adelbert Wallingford is
    kidnapped, the gang tries to solve the mystery. Their
    misadventures include capturing the detective on the case,
    unknowingly delivering the ransom note, and finally

crashing a plane into the hideout. Allen Hoskins stars as Farina.

MYSTERY_IN_SWING
Nar/Cast: Monte Hawley* + Marguerite Whittier* + Bob Webb* + Sybil Lewis* + Josephine Edwards* + F.E. Miller* + Halley Harding* + Jesse Lee Brooks* + Cee Pee Johnson* and Orchestra + Tommy Moore* + Edward Thompson* + Buck Woods* + The Four Toppers*
Producer: Arthur Dreifuss   Director: Arthur Dreifuss
Studio/Company: International Road Show + Bert and Jack Goldberg
Tech Info: 16 mm/sound/bw/8 reels
Date/Country: 1938 + USA   Type: Feature
Annotation: Monte Hawley is a journalist press agent to a female singer who fires him when she gets a Hollywood con- tract. The film includes murder, music and vaudeville comedy.

MYSTERY_RANCH
Nar/Cast: George O'Brian + Cecilia Parker + Noble Johnson* Story: Stewart Edward White   Director: David Howard
Studio/Company: Fox Film Corp.
Tech Info: sound/bw
Date/Country: 1932 + USA   Type: Feature
Annotation: Classic thirties western that has the villain trying to take the ranch that rightfully belongs to the heroine and also force the unwilling lady into marriage. Noble Johnson has a small part as Mudo.

NAGANA
Nar/Cast: Tala Birell + Melvyn Douglas + M. Morita + Dr. Billie McClain* + Everett Brown* + Noble Johnson*   Story: Lester Cohen   Director: Ernest L. Frank
Studio/Company: Universal
Date/Country: 1933 + USA
Annotation: Filmed mostly at Universal City with several scenes photographed in Africa, **Nagana**, meaning sleeping sickness caused by the tse-tse fly, is replete with vicious natives (and a few good ones), doctor scientists and the inevitable female (white). Science wins over sex however and Dr. Radnor (Douglas), and Noger (Brown) respond favorably to Radnor's antidote to the poisonous infection of serum from the tse-tse fly. Johnson is the head boatman, McClain the native King.

NAKED_PREY,_THE
Nar/Cast: Cornel Wilde + Gert Van Der Berg + Ken Gamper*
Screenplay: Clint Johnston + Don Peters
Producer: Sven Persson + Cornel Wilde   Director: Cornel Wilde
Studio/Company: Paramount
Tech Info: 16 mm/sound/color/93 min.
Date/Country: 1966   Type: Feature
Distr/Arch: rbc
Annotation: Cornel Wilde is the leader of a safari ready to dispense trinkets to the African tribesmen but is prevented from doing so by Gert Van Der Berg, a villainous

sort who only cares about hunting and killing elephants. The disappointed tribesmen turn on the outsiders and do a bit of killing of their own, with Cornel Wilde as the "prey" of the title, Ken Gamper is the leader of the tribal warriors.

NANCY DREW, TROUBLE SHOOTER
Nar/Cast: Bonita Granville + Frankie Thomas + Willie Best*
  Director: William Clemens
Studio/Company: Warner
Tech Info: 16 mm/bw/sound/69 min.
Date/Country: 1939 + USA   Type: Feature
Distr/Arch: uas
Annotation: Willie Best has a small role in this mystery for
  the young audience with Bonita Granville playing the
  teen-age sleuth.

NARROW STREET
Nar/Cast: Matt Moore + Dorothy Devore + Madame Sul-te-Wan*
Producer: Edward Bateman Morris   Director: William Beaudine
Tech Info: bw/silent
Date/Country: 1925 + USA   Type: Feature
Annotation: Amusing romantic farce with Madame Sul-te-Wan as
  the house keeper whose presence makes it all right for the
  fairly ingenious romantic farce to take place in Moore's
  domicile.

NASHVILLE
Nar/Cast: Henry Gibson + Shirley Duvall + Robert DoQui* +
  Geraldine Chaplin + Lily Tomlin
Producer: Robert Altman + Jerry Weintraub Production
  Director: Robert Altman
Studio/Company: Paramount Pictures
Tech Info: sound/color/120 min.
Date/Country: 1975 + USA   Type: Feature
Annotation: The inside and outside story of country music
  performers.   High drama when politics and the music scene
  converge. Robert DoQui is Wade, the "Charlie Pride type."

NAT "KING" COLE AND JOE ADAMS' ORCHESTRA   Director: Will
  Cowan
Studio/Company: Universal-International
Tech Info: 15 min.
Date/Country: 1951 + USA   Type: Musical Short
Annotation: Music short of Joe Adams* orchestra. Nat "King"
  Cole sings three numbers including the popular "Too
  Young."

NAT "KING" COLE AND RUSS MORGAN'S ORCHESTRA   Director: Will
  Cowan
Studio/Company: Universal
Tech Info: 18 min.
Date/Country: 1953 + USA   Type: Musical Short
Annotation: Nat "King" Cole plays and sings.

NAT "KING" COLE MUSICAL STORY, THE
Nar/Cast: Nat "King" Cole*   Director: Will Cowan
Tech Info: cclor/18 min.

Date/Country: 1955 + USA   Type: Musical Short
Annotation: Details Cole's discovery and rise to fame. Includes "Sweet Lorraine," "Route 66," and "Straighten Up
   and Fly Right." Commentary by Jeff Chandler.

NATION AFLAME, A
Nar/Cast: Noel Madison + Lila Lee + Douglas Walton + Harry
   Holman   Story: Thomas Dixon   Director: Victor Halperin
Studio/Company: Halperin
Tech Info: 16 mm/sound
Date/Country: 1938 + USA   Type: Feature
Annotation: Adapted from a book by Thomas Dixon, this is the
   story about a secret society, organized like the KKK, and
   of a reporter who tries to expose those who have taken
   over the group in order to use it for their own purposes.

NATIONAL FOLK FESTIVAL PART 2
Producer: U.S. Army
Tech Info: 16 mm/sound/bw/10 min.
Date/Country: 1950   Type: Documentary
Distr/Arch: nac
Annotation: Includes folk songs of Black Americans, as well
   as those of other ethnic groups. Provided by Center for
   Southern Folklore.

NATIVE LAND
Nar/Cast: Paul Robeson* + Howard Da Silva + Bert Conway +
   Mary George
Screenplay: Paul Strand   Story: David Wolff   Director: Leo
   Hurwitz + Paul Strand
Studio/Company: Frontier Films
Tech Info: 16 mm/35 mm/bw/sound/3 reels/85 min.
Date/Country: 1942 + USA   Type: Documentary
Distr/Arch: rad + imp
Annotation: Taken from testimony before the Senate Civil
   Liberties Committee in 1938, this film re-enacts viola-
   tions of the Bill of Rights. The various incidents are
   linked together by Paul Robeson's narration, commentary
   and songs. Score composed by Marc Blitzstein.

NATIVE SON
Nar/Cast: Richard Wright* + Jean Wallace + Gloria Madison* +
   Willa Pearl Curtiss*   Story: Richard Wright*   Director:
   Pierre Chenel
Studio/Company: Independent, Argentina Sono Film + Classic
   Pictures
Tech Info: 35 mm/bw/sound/10 reels
Date/Country: 1951 + Argentina   Type: Feature
Distr/Arch: lc
Annotation: Based on the classic novel by Richard Wright,
   the film concerns a young black man, Bigger Thomas, who is
   hardened by life in the slums of Chicago and whose efforts
   to free himself prove hopeless. Richard Wright plays the
   role of Bigger, Gloria Madison is Bessie Mears. Footage
   of Chicago's south side, locale of the novel, is intercut
   with scenes shot in Argentina.

NATURAL BORN GAMBLER, A

Nar/Cast: Bert Williams*   Director: G.W. Bitzer
Studio/Company: Biograph
Tech Info: 16 mm/bw/sound added/1 reel/12 min.
Date/Country: 1916 + USA   Type: Comedy Short
Distr/Arch: kpf
Annotation: Features Bert Williams in a comedy, with music
   and narration added, in which he does his inimitable,
   mimed card playing act.

NAVIGATOR, THE
Nar/Cast: Buster Keaton + Kathryn McGuire + Noble Johnson*
Producer: Joseph Schenck   Director: Donald Crisp + Buster
   Keaton
Studio/Company: MGM
Tech Info: 16 mm/silent/bw/70 min.
Date/Country: 1924 + USA   Type: Feature
Distr/Arch: mac
Annotation: Buster Keaton and Kathryn McGuire get stranded
   on a deserted isle, where he saves her from cannibals.
   Noble Johnson has a bit role.

NAVY STEWARD, THE
Producer: U.S. Navy
Studio/Company: U.S. Navy
Tech Info: 16 mm/bw/sound/1 reel/13 min.
Date/Country: 1953 + USA   Type: Documentary
Distr/Arch: kpf
Annotation: Blacks in the Navy are shown being taught how to
   serve in the white officers' mess.

NE'ER DO WELL, THE
Nar/Cast: Jules Cowles + Thomas Meighan + Lila Lee +
   Gertrude Astor + John Miltern + Gus Weinberg   Director:
   Alfred E. Green
Studio/Company: Famous Players-Lasky Corp.
Tech Info: 35 mm/silent/bw/8 reels
Date/Country: 1923 + USA   Type: Feature
Annotation: Jules Cowles (in blackface) plays a black
   soldier of fortune in Panama who aids a young man seeking
   success   and fortune with the railroad and the daughter of
   a Panamanian general.

NEGRO AMERICAN, THE
Producer: Solis-Jones Productions
Tech Info: 16 mm/color/sound/1 reel/14 min.
Date/Country: 1966 + USA   Type: Documentary
Distr/Arch: iu + bfa + iws
Annotation: Discusses the contributions of the Negro to
   American civilization.   Traces the history of the Aboli-
   tionist movement to free the slaves with   Frederick
   Douglass as the main leader of the movement.   s

NEGRO AND ART, THE
Series: National Archives Gift Collection
Tech Info: 16 mm/silent/1 reel/bw
Annotation: Based on the Harmon Foundation's 1931 Exhibit of
   Work of Negro Artists, shows work and some of the artists.
   (Part of Record Group 200 HF series, Harmon Foundation

Collection).

NEGRO AND THE AMERICAN PROMISE, THE
Producer: NET
Tech Info: 16 mm/sound/bw/2 reels/59 min.
Date/Country: 1962 + USA   Type: Documentary
Distr/Arch: iu
Annotation: Brings together four prominent Afro-American
    leaders who discuss the American Negro's movement for
    racial and social equality, and their own motivations,
    doctrines, methods and goals. Features James Baldwin*,
    Malcolm X*, Martin Luther King*, and Dr. Kenneth Clark* as
    host.

NEGRO AND THE SOUTH, THE
Series: History of the Negro People
Producer: NET
Tech Info: 16 mm/sound/bw/1 reel/30 min.
Date/Country: 1965   Type: Documentary
Distr/Arch: iu
Annotation: Interviews both Negroes and whites of Mississip-
    pi to depict 'the Southern way of life': whites inter-
    viewed include a mayor, a sheriff, and a judge; Blacks
    interviewed include a teacher, a mechanic, and a minister.

NEGRO COLLEGE IN WARTIME, THE
Producer: Office of War Information
Date/Country: 1945 + USA   Type: Documentary
Annotation: Documents plack participation in World War II.

NEGRO EDUCATION AND ART IN THE UNITED STATES
Series: National Archives Gift Collection
Annotation: Several films are sublisted under this title.
    Among those included are: Art and Sculpture and Negro
    Notables. (Part of Record Group 200 HF series, Harmon
    Foundation Collection).

NEGRO HEROES FROM AMERICAN HISTORY
Producer: Atlantis
Tech Info: 16 mm/sound/color/11 min.
Date/Country: 1966 + USA   Type: Documentary
Distr/Arch: atl + nyu + usc
Annotation: A historical view of little known black heroes
    from the Revolutionary War to the present.

NEGRO IN ENTERTAINMENT, THE
Nar/Cast: W.C. Handy* + Ethel Waters* + Louis Armstrong* +
    Bill Robinson* + Duke Ellington* + Fats Waller*
Producer: E.M. Glucksman   Director: William Trent, Jr.
Tech Info: 16 mm/bw/sound/1 reel/10 min.
Date/Country: 1950 + USA   Type: Musical Short
Distr/Arch: kpf + bud + emg
Annotation: The Negro in Entertainment is a short featuring
    many black stars; hosted by Bill Lund and Etta Moten,
    smoking cigarettes. Presented by Chesterfield cigarettes.

NEGRO IN PENNSYLVANIA HISTORY, THE
Producer: Pennsylvania Dept. of Public Instruction

Tech Info: 16 mm/bw/24 min.
Date/Country: 1968 + USA   Type: Documentary
Distr/Arch: psu
Annotation: Traces movement of Blacks from the South to Pennsylvania through the use of film clips and photographs. Provided by Center for Southern Folklore.

NEGRO IN SPORTS, THE
Nar/Cast: Jesse Owens*
Producer: E.M. Glucksman   Director: William Trent, Jr.
Tech Info: 16 mm/bw/sound/1 reel/10 min.
Date/Country: 1950 + USA   Type: Documentary
Distr/Arch: kpf + emg
Annotation: A Chesterfield Cigarette produced short featuring many black athletes of the period. Narrated by Jesse Owens; Bill Lund acts as host.

NEGRO KINGDOMS OF AFRICA'S GOLDEN AGE
Nar/Cast: Guy Runnios
Producer: Atlantis, J. Simmons
Tech Info: 16 mm/color/sound/1 reel/16 min.
Date/Country: 1968 + West Africa   Type: Documentary
Distr/Arch: uill + iuasp + ucemc + suf + atlap
Annotation: Emphasis of the film is on the important contributions made by some of the West African Kingdoms.

NEGRO LIFE
Series: National Archives Gift Collection
Annotation: Part of Record Group 200 HF series, Harmon Foundation Collection.

NEGRO MARCHES ON, THE
Nar/Cast: Elder Soloman Lightfoot Micheaux*
Producer: Jack Goldberg   Type: Documentary
Annotation: Evangelist Micheaux figures prominently in this documentary about the "progress" of the Negro.

NEGRO NEWS REEL
Producer: Will Herman
Date/Country: 1923 + USA   Type: Newsreel
Annotation: Contains segments of a Baptist convention, U.N.I.A. and Marcus Garvey.

NEGRO SAILOR, THE
Nar/Cast: Leigh Whipper* + Joel Fluellen*
Producer: All American News   Director: Henry Lieven
Studio/Company: U.S. War Department
Tech Info: 16 mm/bw/sound/1 reel/29 min.
Date/Country: 1944 + USA   Type: Documentary
Distr/Arch: kpf
Annotation: The role of the black sailor from the U.S. Navy's standpoint in 1944 is portrayed in this film.

NEGRO SLAVERY
Series: American History
Producer: McGraw Hill
Tech Info: 16 mm/sound/color/1 reel/25 min.
Date/Country: 1968 + USA   Type: Documentary

Distr/Arch: iu + con
Annotation: Shows the beginning and development of slavery
    as an institution in the United States and records the
    life of the slave.

NEGRO SOLDIER, THE
Nar/Cast: Carlton Moss* + Bertha Wolford* + Lt. Norman Ford*
    + Clarence Brooks* + William Broadus* + Sgt. Clyde Turner*
Screenplay: Carlton Moss*
Producer: Special Coverage Section, U.S. Army Signal Corps,
    presented by U.S. War Department   Director: Stuart
    Heisler
Tech Info: 16 mm/bw/sound/1 reel/45 min.
Date/Country: 1943 + USA   Type: Dramatized Documentary
Distr/Arch: mac + lc
Annotation: A Frank Capra supervised film about life for
    black soldiers in the U.S. Army, World War II. Moss nar-
    rates and plays the minister, Bertha Wolford the mother,
    lt. Ford the son. Sequences show participation of Afro-
    Americans in past wars from the Revolutionary war to World
    War I. Premiered in London, October, 1943; shown in the
    Pentagon, Jan. 1944. Print on sale at National AV Center.

NEW CENTURIONS, THE
Nar/Cast: George C. Scott + Stacy Keach + Rosalind Cash*
    Story: Joseph Wambaugh   Director: Richard Fleischer
Tech Info: 16 mm/color/sound/103 min.
Date/Country: 1972 + USA   Type: Feature
Distr/Arch: swa
Annotation: The film telescopes several years in the lives
    of several Los Angeles policemen--their ambitions, their
    fears, how they learn to cope with the limitations of
    their job and the strain it places on their personalities
    and their home lives. Rosalind Cash is the extra-cur-
    ricular love interest. Music score by Quincy Jones*.

NEW FACES IN HELL
Alt Title(s): see P.J.

NEW FACES
Nar/Cast: Eartha Kitt* + June Carroll + Ronny Graham + Alice
    Ghostly + Paul Lynde
Producer: Ed Alperson   Director: Harry Horner
Studio/Company: 20th Century Fox
Tech Info: 16 mm/sound/color/98 min.
Date/Country: 1954   Type: Feature
Distr/Arch: fnc + sel + wil
Annotation: Film version of the popular stage revue that
    featured Eartha Kitt.

NEW INTERNS, THE
Nar/Cast: Ena Hartman* + Michael Callan + George Segal +
    Dean Jones + Greg Morris*
Screenplay: William Schiller
Producer: Robert Cohn   Director: John Rich
Studio/Company: Columbia
Tech Info: 16 mm/sound/bw/123 min.
Date/Country: 1964 + USA

Distr/Arch: arg + mod
Annotation: The hectic lives of interns is shown, with Ena
  Hartman playing a black nurse. Greg Morris is Clark.

NEW MOOD
Series: History of the Negro People
Producer: NET
Tech Info: 16 mm/sound/bw/1 reel/30 min.
Date/Country: 1965   Type: Documentary
Distr/Arch: iu
Annotation: Reviews the civil rights struggle of the past
  decade and traces the impact of the new Negro militancy on
  both white and black Americans. Reviews the implications
  of   the   1956 Supreme Court decision repudiating the
  doctrine of 'separate but equal' facilities in public
  schools and elsewhere.

NEW ORLEANS
Nar/Cast: Arturo de Cordova + Dorothy Patrick + Marjorie
  Lord + Irene Rich + Richard Hageman + Louis Armstrong* +
  Billie Holiday*
Producer: Jules Levey   Director: Arthur Lubin
Studio/Company: Majestic-United Artists
Tech Info: 16 mm/sound/bw/89 min.
Date/Country: 1947 + USA   Type: Feature
Distr/Arch: bud + sel + wil
Annotation: "Long-hair" music and jazz collide in this story
  of the birth and evolution of the Basin street sound.
  Film features jazz greats like Louis Armstrong*, Woody
  Herman, and Billie Holiday*.

NEW PUPIL, THE
Series: Our Gang
Nar/Cast: Our Gang + Billie Thomas*
Screenplay: Hal Law + Robert A. McGowan
Producer: Jack Chertok + Richard Goldstone   Director:
  Edward Cahn
Studio/Company: MGM
Tech Info: bw/sound/1 reel
Date/Country: 1940 + USA   Type: Comedy Short
Annotation: New girl in town, Sally, conspires with Darla to
  embarrass Spanky and Alfalfa for snubbing Darla at lunch.
  The two are made to dress up in women's clothes and play
  tea time with Sally while the gang looks on.   Billie
  Thomas stars as Buckwheat.

NEW SOUTH
Producer: NET
Tech Info: 16 mm/bwsound/2 reels/58 min.
Date/Country: 1970 + USA   Type: Documentary
Distr/Arch: iu
Annotation: Author Pat Watters gathers opinions of black and
  white Georgia citizens in this documentary examining
  changing social and economic conditins in the South.
  Students explain their opinions about school integration,
  and John Lewis*, a founder of SNCC, addresses the issues
  and explains the goals of voter registration.

NEWEST NEGRO, THE
Series: Epitaph for Jim Crow
Producer: NET
Tech Info: 16 mm/bw/sound/30 min.
Date/Country: 1961 + USA   Type: Documentary
Distr/Arch: adl
Annotation: Whitney Young*, Director of the National Urban
    League, discusses the meaning and value of direct action
    protest against segregation with Thomas Pettigrew.

NEWMAN'S LAW
Nar/Cast: George Peppard + Shirley Jo Finney*

NEWS REEL /1
Nar/Cast: Chappie Gardner*
Studio/Company: Bilmore Film Company
Date/Country: 1930 + USA
Annotation: Parachute jump by Mary Doughtry, only black
    parachute jumper of the American Aviation School; Charles
    James' flight at Curtis field. Narrated by Chappie Gard-
    ner.

NEWS REEL /2
Studio/Company: Peacock Photoplay Company
Date/Country: 1922 + USA   Type: Newsreel
Annotation: Newsreel contains: Ned Gourdin, Harvard athlete,
    winning the 100 yard dash over Abraham of England, and
    breaking the world's record in the running broad jump;
    Florence Parlam, the child actress; a review of Tuskegee
    Institute, a 10 year perspective.

NEXT TIME I MARRY
Nar/Cast: Lucille Ball + James Ellison + Mantan Moreland*
Screenplay: John Twist + Helen Meinardi
Producer: Cliff Reid   Director: Garson Kanin
Studio/Company: RKO Radio
Date/Country: 1938 + USA
Annotation: Comedy which has rich girl (Ball) falling in
    love with James Ellison on a cross-country trip. Mantan
    Moreland plays Tilby.

NGONO AND HER PEOPLE
Series: National Archives Gift Collection
Tech Info: 16 mm/silent/3 reels/bw
Annotation: Dramatic story. A child wife reared in a mis-
    sion school marries a native teacher and they become
    Christian leaders. (Part of Record Group 200 HF series,
    Harmon Foundation Collection).

NIEMANDSLAND
Alt Title(s): War is Hell + Hell on Earth + No Man's Land
Nar/Cast: Louis Douglas* + Vladimir Sokoloff
Producer: Victor Trivas   Director: Victor Trivas
Tech Info: bw/93 min.
Date/Country: 1932 + Germany   Type: Feature
Annotation: The film shows various nationality types and
    their reactions to being trapped in "No Man's Land." The
    black soldier (Douglas) is a rather "typical", happy

dancer but he rescues a British soldier and is the first
to shed his uniform, demonstrating his opposition to the
war.

NIGERIA: A CULTURE IN TRANSITION
Producer: New Mark Internationals
Tech Info: 16 mm/soundbw/54 min.
Date/Country: 1973 + Nigeria   Type: Documentary
Distr/Arch: mtp + mom
Annotation: Poetry, dance, a selection from Amos Tutuala's*
   The Palm Wine Drinkard and a folk opera appear in the
   first half of the film. A performance of Wole Soyinka's*
   play with a commentary by the author makes up the second
   half.

NIGERIA: GIANT IN AFRICA
Producer: National Film Board of Canada
Tech Info: 16 mm/sound/bw/52 min.
Date/Country: 1961 + Nigeria   Type: Documentary
Distr/Arch: iu + mghf + psu + fsu + suf + mhf + nfb
Annotation: The history and development of Nigeria as a na-
   tion, covering the period up to 1960.

NIGERIA--A SCHOOL FOR JACOB
Producer: NET
Tech Info: bw/30 min.
Distr/Arch: iu
Annotation: Jacob Ajibola is an eleven-year-old Nigerian boy
   typical of the young Africa today who has ambition yet
   lacks the education necessary to find his own place in the
   world. Contrasting Jacob with a boy in Appalachia with
   similar aspirations, this film raises the question: can
   U.S. taxpayers afford to educate both Americans and those
   abroad who are in need?

NIGGER IN THE WOODPILE, A
Date/Country: 1904 + USA   Type: Comedy Short
Annotation: Theft in the woodpile by a "Negro Deacon"--white
   in blackface--is discovered when the loaded stick (of
   dynamite) placed there by the farmer explodes.

NIGGER, THE
Alt Title(s): The Governor
Nar/Cast: William Farnum   Story: Edward Sheldon
Studio/Company: Fox
Date/Country: 1915 + USA
Annotation: A Southern governor finds out he has black blood
   and feels obligated to give up his offce and the woman he
   loves. Farnum plays Phillip Morrow, the Mulatto governor.
   Title changed by some exhibitors in order to obviate
   criticism of both the title and the subject matter: in-
   cludes a rape by a black drunk and a lynchng.

NIGHT 'N' GALES
Series: Our Gang
Nar/Cast: Our Gang + Billie Thomas*
Producer: Hal Roach   Director: Gordon Douglas
Studio/Company: MGM + Roach

Tech Info: super 8 mm/16 mm/bw/sound/1 reel/10 min.
Date/Country: 1937 + USA   Type: Comedy Short
Distr/Arch: roa + bla
Annotation: The gang gets invited to stay the night at
    Darla's when a storm prevents their return home. But Mr.
    Hood can't stand them. The boys bunk with Mr. Hood and
    before long the feeling is mutual. Billie Thomas stars as
    Buckwheat.

NIGHT_AFFAIR
Alt Title(s): see Le Desordre et la Nuit

NIGHT_AND_DAY
Nar/Cast: Cary Grant + Alexis Smith + Monty Wooley +
    Clarence Muse* + Hazel Scott*
Screenplay: Charles Hoffman + Leo Townsend + William Bowers
Producer: LeRoy Prinz   Director: Michael Curtiz
Studio/Company: Warner Brothers
Tech Info: 16 mm/sound/color/128 min.
Date/Country: 1946 + USA   Type: Feature
Distr/Arch: uas
Annotation: Romanticized "biography" of songwriter Cole
    Porter. Blacks appear as servants, first liveried table
    waiters in posh home of Cole's parents; then a couple of
    tapdancers in spangles; finally waiters on the train with
    speaking lines.   Hazel Scott appears (and entertains) as
    herself.

NIGHT_CLUB_GIRL
Alt Title(s): One Dark Night
Nar/Cast: Mantan Moreland*
Studio/Company: Toddy Films + Million Dollar Studios
Date/Country: 1942 + USA

NIGHT_I_FOUGHT_JACK_JOHNSON,_THE
Studio/Company: Vitagraph
Date/Country: 1913 + USA
Annotation: White opponent of a black boxer fights the re-
    feree to avoid fighting his black competitor. (Whites
    made up as blacks to play black roles).

NIGHT_IN_HARLEM
Tech Info: 10 min.
Date/Country: 1947 + USA   Type: Musical Short
Annotation: Musical short features Dizzy Gillespie and His
    Bebop Orchestra.

NIGHT_IN_THE_JUNGLE,_A
Studio/Company: Selig
Tech Info: silent/bw
Date/Country: 1915 + USA
Annotation: The one assertive black in the picture is killed
    by a tame leopard trained to fight off black aggressors.

NIGHT_OF_THE_LIVING_DEAD,_THE
Nar/Cast: Duane Jones* + Judith O'Den + Karl Hurdman
Screenplay: John A. Russo
Producer: Russell Streiner   Director: George A. Romero

Studio/Company: Image Ten + Continental Dist.
Tech Info: 16 mm/sound/bw/90 min.
Date/Country: 1968 + USA
Distr/Arch: kpf + cwf + roa + twy + wrs
Annotation: A horror film about the unburied dead returning
   to life to devour the living, Night_of_the_Living_Dead is
   perhaps the only film in this genre to have a black
   hero--Ben (played by Jones) a young salesman who takes
   charge of the survivors and desperately attempts to sup-
   press the dead.

NIGHT_OF_THE_QUARTER_MOON,_THE
Alt Title(s): Flesh and Flame
Nar/Cast: Nat Cole* + James Edwards* + Marguerite Belafonte*
   + Billy Daniels* + Julie London + John Drew Barrymore
Screenplay: Frank Davis + Franklin Coen
Producer: Albert Zugsmith   Director: Hugo Haas
Studio/Company: MGM
Date/Country: 1959   Type: Feature
Annotation: When it is discovered that rich boy Barrymore
   has married a quadroon, the press, family and supposed
   friend move in to wreck the marriage. Julie London plays
   the "passing" role; James Edwards is her lawyer and Nat
   (King) Cole, who sings one number, a night-club friend.

NIGHT__THE_SUN_CAME_OUT,_THE   Director: Melvin Van Peebles*

NIGHT_TRAIN_TO_MEMPHIS
Nar/Cast: Nina Mae McKinney* + Roy Acuff + Adele Mara
   Director: Lesley Selander
Studio/Company: Republic
Tech Info: 16 mm/sound/bw/67 min.
Date/Country: 1946 + USA   Type: Feature
Distr/Arch: ivy
Annotation: Nina Mae McKinney has a minor role in this ad-
   venture with songs.

NIGHT_WITH_THE_DEVIL,_A   Story: Wilson and Grant
Studio/Company: Toddy Pictures
Tech Info: 71 min.
Date/Country: pre-1946

NIGHT_WITHOUT_SLEEP
Nar/Cast: Linda Darnell + Gary Merrill + Hildegarde Neff +
   Ben Carter* + Mae Marsh + Bill Walker*
Screenplay: Frank Partos + Elick Moll
Producer: Robert Bassler   Director: Roy Baker
Studio/Company: 20th Century Fox
Tech Info: 16 mm/sound/bw/77 min.
Date/Country: 1952 + USA   Type: Feature
Distr/Arch: fnc
Annotation: The story of a man who has squandered his life
   and his career waking up one night to discover he has
   killed his wife. Walker is Henry; Carter, Benny.

NIGHTMARE_IN_THE_SUN
Nar/Cast: Sammy Davis, Jr.* + Ursula Andress
Screenplay: Ted Thomas + Fanya Lawrence

Producer: Marc Lawrence + John Derek   Director: Marc
   Lawrence
Studio/Company: Zodiac
Tech Info: 16 mm/sound/color/81 min.
Date/Country: 1964 + USA   Type: Feature
Distr/Arch: sel + wil
Annotation: Davis is a truck driver in this melodrama about
   a jealous, wealthy rancher who murders his wife during a
   drunken rage.

NINE LIVES OF FRITZ THE CAT, THE   Director: Robert Taylor
Studio/Company: American International
Tech Info: color/76 min.   Type: Feature
Annotation: This feature-length cartoon is the sequel to
   Fritz the Cat. Fritz leaves a nagging wife to investigate
   his other lives, including rocketing to Mars, working for
   the CIA and becoming involved with pornography. Sound-
   track music provided by Tom Scott and the L.A. Express.
   Blacks figure prominently in Fritz's experiences.

NINE LIVES
Nar/Cast: Butterbeans* and Susie* (Joe and Susie Edwards)
Studio/Company: Colored Motion Picture Producers of America
Date/Country: 1926 + USA
Annotation: The husband and wife team of Butterbeans and
   Susie perform.

NJANGAAN
Nar/Cast: Fatim Diagne* + Mame N'Diaye* + Mody Gueye* + Abou
   Camera*
Screenplay: Fraore Seck* + Sherif Adrame Seck*
Producer: Sunu Film   Director: Mahama Traore*
Tech Info: sound/color/90 min./Wolof and French with English
   subtitles
Date/Country: 1974   Type: Feature
Distr/Arch: nyf
Annotation: The story of a young boy who is sent to the
   Koranic school by his father to be educated, but he, like
   all the children (Njangaan) attending the "Dara" or
   "Koteb" is exploited by the Marabout (religious teacher)
   in the name of religion, and turned into a professional
   beggar.

NO HIDING PLACE: MINORITY CONFLICTS IN THE SUBURBS
Producer: NET
Tech Info: 16 mm/bw/sound/2 reels/59 min.
Date/Country: 1968 + USA   Type: Documentary
Distr/Arch: iu + adl
Annotation: This film studies tensions which divide black
   and white communities in a typical American suburb. It
   interviews representative citizens including ghetto
   youths, housewives, the local NAACP president, an al-
   derman, and others to reveal their opinions concerning
   racial problems in the town

NO LEAVE, NO LOVE
Nar/Cast: Van Johnson + Keenan Wynn + "Sugar Chile" Robinson*

Screenplay: Charles Martin + Leslie Kordos
Producer: Joe Pasternak   Director: Charles Martin
Studio/Company: MGM
Tech Info: 118 min.
Date/Country: 1946 + USA   Type: Feature
Annotation: "Sugar Chile" Robinson, listed as Boy Pianist
    makes an early appearance in this Marine musical, playing
    "junior boogie-woogie" piano.

NO NOISE
Series: Our Gang
Nar/Cast: Our Gang + Ernie Morrison* + Allen Hoskins*
Screenplay: Hal Roach
Producer: Hal Roach   Director: Robert McGowan
Studio/Company: Pathe
Tech Info: silent/bw/2 reels
Date/Country: 1923 + USA   Type: Comedy Short
Annotation: Mickey is in the hospital getting his tonsils
    removed, so the gang forsakes football practice to see
    him, resulting in utter chaos at the hospital.   Allen
    Hoskins stars as Farina.

NO TIME FOR COMEDY
Nar/Cast: James Stewart + Rosalind Russell + Charles Ruggles
    + Louise Beavers*
Screenplay: Julius Phillip Epstein   Director: William
    Keighley
Studio/Company: Warners
Tech Info: 16 mm/sound/bw/93 min.
Date/Country: 1941 + USA   Type: Feature
Distr/Arch: uas
Annotation: James Stewart plays a shy playwright from the
    West in New York to see the production of his first play.
    There he falls in love and marries - all the while being
    chased by another woman. Louise Beavers plays Clementine
    in this comedy adapted from a successful Broadway play.

NO TIME FOR ROMANCE
Nar/Cast: Eunice Wilson* + Austin McCoy* + Joel Fluellen* +
    Bill Walker* + Shirley Haven* + Ray Martin* + Jay Brooks*
    + Mildred Boyd* + DeForrest Covan* + Austin McCoy's Band*
Studio/Company: Norwanda Pictures
Date/Country: 1948 + USA

NO VIETNAMESE EVER CALLED ME NIGGER
Producer: David Loeb Weiss   Director: David Loeb Weiss
Studio/Company: Paradigm Films
Tech Info: 16 mm/bw/sound/2 reels/75 min.
Date/Country: 1968 + USA   Type: Documentary
Distr/Arch: imp + adf
Annotation: In this film, three black veterans discuss their
    experiences in the Vietnam war, the racism that exists in
    the armed forces, and their dissatisfaction with life in
    the U.S. upon their return.

NO WAY OUT
Nar/Cast: Sidney Poitier* + Richard Widmark + Linda Darnell
    + Stephen McNally + Ruby Dee* + Bobby Darin + Mildred

Joanne Smith* + Frederick O'Neal* + Dotts Johnson* + Maude
  Simmons* + Ossie Davis* + J. Louis Johnson*
Screenplay: Joseph Manckiewicz + Lester Samuels
Producer: D.F. Zanuck   Director: Joseph Manckiewicz
Studio/Company: Twentieth Century Fox
Tech Info: 16 mm/bw/sound/3 reels/106 min.
Date/Country: 1950 + USA   Type: Feature
Distr/Arch: fnc
Annotation: In this film, a bigoted psychotic white man
  blames a black doctor (played by Sidney Poitier) for his
  brother's death. When the doctor refuses to allow an
  autopsy, the brother organizes his equally prejudiced
  friends into a mob to attack the black area of town. Even
  though a subsequent autopsy proves the doctor's innocence,
  he is still the object of hatred and scorn.

NOBLE SISSLE AND EUBIE BLAKE
Nar/Cast: Noble Sissle + Eubie Blake*
Studio/Company: Vitaphone
Tech Info: 9 min
Date/Country: 1927 + USA   Type: Musical Short
Annotation: Sissle and Blake perform numbers which include
  "I Wonder Where My Sweetie Can Be."

NOBODY'S CHILDREN
Nar/Cast: Richard Maurice* + Jacque Farmer* + Alex Griffin*
  + Joe Green* + Vivian Maurice* + Howard Nelson*
Studio/Company: Maurice Film Company
Tech Info: bw/silent
Date/Country: 1920 + USA   Type: Feature
Annotation: Melodrama about the kidnapping of a young girl
  by her stepfather, her rescue by her brother who kills the
  stepfather and his gangland crony, the brother's arrest
  and ultimate exoneration.

NOISY NOISES
Series: Our Gang
Nar/Cast: Our Gang + Allen Hoskins*
Producer: Robert F. McGowan + Hal Roach   Director: Robert
  F. McGowan
Studio/Company: MGM + Roach
Tech Info: super 8 mm/16 mm/bw/silent/1 reel
Date/Country: 1924 + USA   Type: Comedy Short
Distr/Arch: roa + bla
Annotation: Farina convinces Joe that the gang can take care
  of his toothache without a dentist, which aided by Pete
  the dog, they do. Allen Hoskins stars as Farina.

NON VOGLIAMO MORIRE
Nar/Cast: John Kitzmiller*
Date/Country: 1954 + Italy   Type: Feature

NONE BUT THE BRAVE
Nar/Cast: Rafer Johnson* + Frank Sinatra + Tommy Sands +
  Tatsuya Mihashi + Tukeshi Kuto
Screenplay: John Twist + Katsuya Susaka
Producer: Frank Sinatra   Director: Frank Sinatra
Studio/Company: Warner Brothers

Tech Info: 16 mm/sound/color/105 min.
Date/Country: 1965   Type: Feature
Distr/Arch: arg + bud + ccc + ker + mac + mod + mot + roa +
   sel + swa + tfc + unf + wcf + wil
Annotation: Johnson plays an Army officer on patrol in the
   South Pacific, on an island where two groups of soldiers
   -- one American, one Japanese -- are stranded. First they
   fight, then they settle on an uneasy truce. Fighting
   resumes when an American warship arrives; only a few
   survive.

NONE CAN DO MORE
Date/Country: 191- + USA
Annotation: Loyal Uncle Mose dies in the process of freeing
   his master from a Yankee prison.

NORMAN...IS THAT YOU?
Nar/Cast: Redd Foxx* + Pearl Bailey* + Michael Warren* +
   Dennis Dugan + Tamara Dobson* + Vernee Watson*
Screenplay: Ron Clark + Sam Bobrick
Producer: George Schlatter   Director: George Schlatter
Studio/Company: MGM + United Artists
Tech Info: 16 mm/color/sound/3 reels/91 min.
Date/Country: 1976 + USA   Type: Feature
Distr/Arch: fnc
Annotation: A Redd Foxx-Pearl Bailey feature that tries to
   deal humorously with the subject of interracial
   homosexuality. The film also features Motown music and
   the singing of Smokey Robinson* and Thelma Houston*.
   Michael Warren, former UCLA basketball star is the un-
   likely homosexual Norman; Fox and Bailey, his estranged
   parents.

NOTHING BUT A MAN
Nar/Cast: Ivan Dixon* + Abbey Lincoln* + Gloria Foster* +
   Julius Harris* + Stanley Greene* + Helene Arrindell* +
   Leonard Parker* + Yaphet Kotto* + Helen Lounck + Walter
   Wilson + Gertrude Jeanette* + Richard Ward* + Moses Gunn*
   + Esther Rolle* + Martin Priest* + Melvin Stewart*
Screenplay: Michael Roemer + Robert Young
Producer: Michael Roemer + Robert Young + Robert Rubin
   Director: Michael Roemer
Tech Info: 16 mm/bw/sound/3 reels/92 min.
Date/Country: 1963 + USA   Type: Feature
Distr/Arch: aim + cal + imp + mac
Annotation: Drama about a Southern black man and his wife in
   a hostile society. Ivan Dixon is Duff, Julius Harris his
   father, Abbey Lincoln, the schoolteacher he quits his
   railroad job to marry.

NOTHING BUT THE TRUTH
Nar/Cast: Bob Hope + Paulette Goddard + Willie Best*
Screenplay: Don Hartman + Ken Englund
Producer: Arthur Hornblow, Jr.   Director: Elliott Nugent
Studio/Company: Paramount
Date/Country: 1941 + USA   Type: Feature
Annotation: Willie Best has a bit part as Samuel in this Bob
   Hope comedy farce.

NOTHING SACRED
Nar/Cast: Fredric March + Carole Lombard + Charles Winninger
    + Walter Connolly + Frank Fay + Monty Woolley + Troy Brown
    + Hattie McDaniel*
Screenplay: Ben Hecht
Producer: David O. Selznick   Director: William Wellman
Studio/Company: United Artists
Tech Info: 16 mm/sound/bw/3 reels/85 min.
Date/Country: 1937 + USA   Type: Feature
Distr/Arch: cie + mog
Annotation: Nothing Sacred parodies the lifestyle   and
    professionalism of big city newspaper men. Hattie Mc-
    Daniel plays Mrs. Walker.

NOTORIOUS ELINOR LEE, THE
Nar/Cast: Edna Mae Harris* + Gladys Williams* + Carmen   New-
    some* + Robert Earl Jones* + Vera Burelle* + Laura Bowman*
    + Amanda Randolph* + Juano Hernandez*
Producer: Hubert Julian* + Oscar Micheaux*   Director: Oscar
    Micheaux*
Studio/Company: Micheaux Film Corporation
Tech Info: sound/bw
Date/Country: 1940 + USA   Type: Feature
Annotation: Robert Earl Jones plays a fighter on the rise
    and Edna Mae Harris, the woman who tries to stop him by
    using her wiles and getting him to "throw" the fight.
    Hernandez plays a fight trainer.

NOW IS THE TIME
Nar/Cast: Ruby Dee* + Ossie Davis*
Producer: WCAU-TV
Studio/Company: Carousel Films
Tech Info: 16 mm/bw/sound/1 reel/36 min.
Date/Country: 1967 + USA   Type: TV Dramatic Short
Distr/Arch: roa + adl + psu + carouf
Annotation: The film recreates through the words of black
    poets and writers the struggle from slavery to equal
    rights. Included are works by James Baldwin*, Countee
    Cullen*, Langston Hughes*; statements of black civil
    rights leaders; and music--spirituals, blues, jazz-set
    against photographs and film.

NUER, THE
Producer: Peabody Museum Film Study Center
Tech Info: 16 mm/sound/color/2 reels/74 min.
Date/Country: 1970   Type: Documentary
Distr/Arch: iu + mghf
Annotation: Documents the lives of the villagers of Lara in
    the Gaajak Jikany section of the Nuer Lands in South-
    western Ethiopia, showing life style, religious rites, and
    manhood ('Gar') ceremony. Illustrates daily tasks of the
    men.

NUMBER ONE
Nar/Cast: Charlton Heston + Jessica Walter + Bruce Dern +
    Ernie Barnes* + Mike Henry
Screenplay: David Moessinger

Producer: Walter Seltzer   Director: Tom Gries
Studio/Company: United Artist
Tech Info: 16 mm/sound/color/105 min.
Date/Country: 1964 + USA   Type: Feature
Distr/Arch: uas
Annotation: Heston as an aging pro quarterback who has held
    on longer than he should have.   Ernie Barnes is Deke
    Coleman; the New Orleans Saints are themselves.

NUN AND THE SERGEANT, THE
Nar/Cast: Hari Rhodes* + Anna Sten + Robert Webber
Screenplay: Don Cerveris
Producer: Eugene Frenke   Director: Franklin Adreon
Studio/Company: United Artists
Tech Info: sound/bw/73 min.
Date/Country: 1962 + USA   Type: Feature
Annotation: Rhodes is Hall, one of the motley group of
    marines from the brig that Sgt. McGrath (Webber) takes on
    a critical mission behind enemy lines in Korea.

O DEM WATERMELONS   Director: Ralph Nelson
Tech Info: 16 mm/sound/color/8 min.   Type: Comedy Short
Annotation: An animated watermelon shown in various environ-
    ments, including the stereotypical ones.

O POVO ORGANIZADO
Alt Title(s): People Organized, The
Nar/Cast: Robert Von Lierop*
Screenplay: Robert Von Lierop*
Producer: Robert Von Lierop*   Director: Robert Von Lierop*
Tech Info: 16 mm/sound/color/2 reels/67 min.
Date/Country: Mozambique   Type: Documentary
Distr/Arch: tri
Annotation: Documentary of Machell's reorganization of
    Mozambique after independence from Portugal. Second film
    in Van Lierop's trilogy; sequel to A Luta Continua.

O'SHAUGHNESSY'S BOY
Nar/Cast: Wallace Beery + Jackie Cooper + Sara Haden +
    Spanky McFarland + Clarence Muse*
Screenplay: Leonard Praskins
Producer: Phillip Goldstone   Director: Richard Boleslawski
Studio/Company: MGM
Date/Country: 1935 + USA   Type: Feature
Annotation: Circus tale about the downfall of an animal
    trainer when his son is taken from him. Clarence Muse
    plays Jeff in something slightly more significant than the
    usual bit role.

OCEAN'S ELEVEN
Nar/Cast: Frank Sinatra + Sammy Davis, Jr.* + Dean Martin +
    Peter Lawford
Screenplay: Harry Brown + Charles Ledner
Producer: Frank Sinatra   Director: Lewis Milestone
Studio/Company: Warner Brothers
Tech Info: 16 mm/sound/color/127 min.
Date/Country: 1960 + USA   Type: Feature
Distr/Arch: arg + bud + ccc + cha + ics + mac + mod + mot +

roa + sel + swa + tfc + tmc + twf + unf + wel + wil
Annotation: The famous "clan" with Davis in a prominent role
   as a member of a daring gang that plans to   hold   up   Las
   Vegas nightspots.

OCTOROON, THE
Nar/Cast: Guy Coombes + Marguerite Courtot   Story: Dion
   Boucicault
Date/Country: 1913 + USA
Annotation: The classic "tragic Mulatto" theme in   an   early
   film treatment of Boucicault's melodrama.

ODDS AGAINST TOMORROW
Nar/Cast: Harry Belafonte* + Carmen de Lavallade* + Robert
   Ryan + Shelley Winters + Ed Begley
Screenplay: John O. Killens*
Producer: Robert Wise   Director: Robert Wise
Studio/Company: United Artists
Tech Info: 16 mm/bw/sound/3 reels/95 min.
Date/Country: 1959 + USA   Type: Feature
Distr/Arch: uas
Annotation: Robert Ryan plays a bigot who distrusts Harry
   Belafonte, and Ed Begley plays the mastermind who tries to
   hold things together as the three attempt a stick-up in a
   Hudson valley town.

OF MICE AND MEN
Nar/Cast: Lon Chaney, Jr. + Burgess Meredith + Betty Field +
   Charles Bickford + Noah Berry, Jr. + Leigh Whipper*
   Story: John Steinbeck
Producer: Hal Roach   Director: Lewis Milestone
Studio/Company: United Artists
Tech Info: 16 mm/bw/sound/3 reels/108 min.
Date/Country: 1939 + USA   Type: Feature
Distr/Arch: kpf + usf
Annotation: This film version of the classic Steinbeck novel
   of George and his retarded friend, Lenny who find cruelty
   and hate instead of a ranch in California's Salinas Val-
   ley; also has a dignified portrayal of a black ranch hand,
   played by Leigh Whipper.

OF ONE BLOOD
Nar/Cast: Spencer Williams* + Geraldine Maynard*   Director:
   Spencer Williams*
Studio/Company: Sack Attractions
Tech Info: 35 mm/silent/bw/7 reels/5,498 ft.
Date/Country: USA   Type: Feature
Distr/Arch: lc
Annotation: Williams plays a deaf mute who is actually an
   undercover FBI agent in this film which contains some of
   his religious/moral symbols.

OFF TO BLOOMINGDALE ASYLUM
Producer: George Melies
Studio/Company: Independent
Date/Country: 1902 + France

OFFICIAL OFFICERS

Series: Our Gang
Nar/Cast: Our Gang + Allen Hoskins*
Screenplay: Hal Roach
Producer: Hal Roach   Director: Robert McGowan
Studio/Company: Pathe
Tech Info: silent/bw/2 reels
Date/Country: 1925 + USA   Type: Comedy Short
Annotation: With the help of kindly Inspector Malone, the
  gang becomes junior police members, setting up their own
  paddy wagon and jail - they also help in capturing their
  old nemesis who has assaulted Malone. Allen Hoskins stars
  as Farina.

OFT_IN_THE_SILLY_NIGHT
Series: Christie Comedy
Nar/Cast: Spencer Williams* + Evelyn Preer* + Edward Thomp-
  son*
Screenplay: Octavius Roy Cohen + Spencer Williams*
Producer: Al Christie
Studio/Company: Paramount
Tech Info: sound/bw/2 reels
Date/Country: 1929 + USA   Type: Comedy Short
Annotation: Romance blossoms between a black chauffeur and
  the boss's daughter.

OH,_FREEDOM
Series: On Black America
Producer: Rediscovery Productions, Inc.
Tech Info: 16 mm/sound/color/28 min.
Date/Country: 1971 + USA
Distr/Arch: red
Annotation: The history of the civil rights movement is
  traced. Provided by Center for Southern Folklore.

OLD_AGE
Series: Family of Man
Producer: BBC-TV
Tech Info: 16 mm/sound/color/2 reels/45 min.
Date/Country: 1971 + Botswana   Type: TV Documentary
Distr/Arch: tim
Annotation: How people in different countries handle old
  age. Grandchildren and continued activity seem to be the
  answer in all cultures.

OLD_BONES_OF_THE_RIVER
Nar/Cast: Will Hay + Robert Adams* + Moore Marriott + Graham
  Moffatt + Wyndham Goldie + Jack Livesey   Director: Marcel
  Varnel
Studio/Company: Gainsborough
Date/Country: 1939 + Britain   Type: Feature
Annotation: A take-off on Sanders of the River with Robert
  Adams in a parody of the Bosambo role.

OLD_GRAY_HOSS,_THE
Series: Our Gang
Nar/Cast: Our Gang + Allen Hoskins
Screenplay: Robert F. McGowan
Producer: Hal Roach + Robert F. McGowan   Director: Anthony

Mack
Studio/Company: MGM + Roach
Tech Info: super 8 mm/16 mm/bw/silent
Date/Country: 1928 + USA   Type: Comedy Short
Distr/Arch: bla
Annotation: The gang sabotages a new cab company's taxi, to
    save the horse cab of old Mr. Cummings. Alan Hoskins
    stars as Farina.

OLD_IRONSIDES
Nar/Cast: Esther Ralston + Wallace Beery + George Bancroft +
    Charles Farrell + Johnny Walker + George Godfrey* + Boris
    Karloff + Tetsu Komai   Director: James Cruze
Studio/Company: Paramount Famous Lasky Corp.
Tech Info: 35 mm/silent/bw/12 reels
Date/Country: 1926 + USA   Type: Feature
Distr/Arch: lc
Annotation: Piracy, desertion, and a little romance take
    place amid battles at sea in this film that includes the
    Battle of Tripoli. George Godfrey plays a ship's cook
    aboard the Constitution. He is part of a dangerous
    landing party mission that helps to bring about victory
    for the Americans.

OLD_MAMMY'S_CHARGE
Annotation: Mammy goes north to serve her married mistress.
    Later when both parents die Mammy struggles for custody
    rather than give their new orphaned child to the courts.
    The baby's grandfather rescues Mammy and child and takes
    them back to the safety of the South.

OLD_MAMMY'S_SECRET_CODE
Date/Country: 191- + USA
Annotation: Loyal old Mammy (white in blackface) is executed
    as a spy, having used her clothesline - inside Grant's
    headquarters - to send coded messages to the rebels.

OLD_OAK'S_SECRET,_THE
Annotation: Old Mose, finding freedom difficult, hides the
    Master's will, freeing all his slaves, in an old oak tree.

OLD_WALLOP,_THE
Series: Our Gang
Nar/Cast: Our Gang + Allen Hoskins*
Producer: Robert F. McGowan + Hal Roach   Director: Robert
    F. McGowan
Studio/Company: MGM
Tech Info: bw/silent/2 reels
Date/Country: 1927 + USA   Type: Comedy Short
Annotation: Wheezer is a baby who likes to punch people -
    his brother, policemen, Farina, passersby.   Somehow the
    gang gets to a construction site where Farina gets en-
    tangled in some building materials and is carried aloft.
    The gang finally rescues him.   Allen Hoskins stars as
    Farina.

OLD,_BLACK_AND_ALIVE
Producer: National Caucaus on the Black Aged

Tech Info: 16 mm/sound/color/28 mn.
Date/Country: 1975 + USA   Type: Documentary
Distr/Arch: cal + umic + nef
Annotation: Filmed in Macon County, Georgia, seven elderly
    black men and women share their thoughts on old age,
    aging, life and death.

OLE_MAN_OF_THE_MOUNTAIN
Series: Betty Boop cartoons
Nar/Cast: Cab Calloway* and his orchestra
Producer: Max Fleischer   Director: Max Fleischer
Studio/Company: Paramount
Tech Info: 16 mm/sound/1 reel/6-8 min.
Date/Country: 1933 + USA   Type: Animated Short
Distr/Arch: emg + kpf
Annotation: Cab Calloway and his orchestra do the singing
    and talking for this Betty Boop cartoon, a short, comic
    operetta with a funky flavor.

OLYMPIC_GAMES
Series: Our Gang
Nar/Cast: Our Gang + Allen Hoskins* + Jannie Hoskins*
Screenplay: Hal Roach
Producer: Hal Roach   Director: Anthony Mack
Studio/Company: Pathe
Tech Info: silent/bw/2 reel
Date/Country: 1927 + USA   Type: Comedy Short
Annotation: The gang's misadventures as they try a backyard
    Olympic are highlighted. Allen Hoskins stars as Farina
    and Jannie Hoskins stars as Mango.

OMEGA_MAN,_THE
Nar/Cast: Charlton Heston + Rosalind Cash* + Paul Koslo
Screenplay: John William + Joyce Corrington
Producer: Walter Seltzer   Director: Boris Sagal
Studio/Company: Warner Brothers
Tech Info: 16 mm/color/sound/3 reels/98 min.
Date/Country: 1971 + USA   Type: Feature
Distr/Arch: buc + cwf + tfc + who + roa
Annotation: A scientist-survivor (Heston) of nuclear holo-
    caust is hunted by plague stricken mutants who believe he
    represents the technology that destroyed them.   The
    mutants prepare to execute him, but he is saved by Lisa
    (Rosalind Cash) and Dutch (Koslo).

OMOWALE--THE_CHILD_RETURNS_HOME
Series: History of the Negro People
Producer: NET
Tech Info: 16 mm/sound/bw/1 reel/30 min.
Date/Country: 1965   Type: Documentary
Distr/Arch: iu
Annotation: Pictures John Williams, Mississippi-born black
    writer, on an odyssey to Africa to explore his ancestral
    roots. Williams explores the relationship of the American
    Negro to Africa and the Africans. Emphasizes that the
    Afro- American is several generations removed from the
    African, both culturally and economically.

ON JAZZ
Series: Inside Music
Producer: Univ. of Michigan Television Center
Tech Info: 16 mm/sound/bw/29 min. (also available on vide-
    otape)
Date/Country: 1972 + USA   Type: Documentary
Distr/Arch: umic
Annotation: Traces the story of jazz from its New Orleans
    beginnings. Provided by Center for Southern Folklore.

ON MERIT
Screenplay: William Greaves*
Producer: William Greaves*   Director: William Greaves*
Studio/Company: PBS
Tech Info: 16 mm/color/sound/1 reel/23 min.
Date/Country: 1970   Type: TV Documentary
Annotation: On Merit is adressed to the high school or
    junior college student facing that crucial decision, "What
    do I do when I leave school?"

ON SOUL MUSIC
Series: Inside Music
Producer: Univ. of Michigan Television Center
Tech Info: 16 mm/sound/bw/29 min. (also available on vide-
    otape)
Date/Country: 1972 + USA   Type: Documentary
Distr/Arch: umic
Annotation: Explains why soul music must be distinctly black
    and why some musicians won't play soul music not composed
    by Blacks. Provided by Center for Southern Folklore.

ON SUCH A NIGHT
Nar/Cast: Karen Morzley + Grant Richards + Eddie Anderson*
Screenplay: Doris Malloy + Bill Lipman   Story: Morley Cas-
    sidy + S.S. Field
Producer: Emanuel Cohen   Director: E.A.DuPont
Studio/Company: Paramount
Date/Country: 1937 + USA   Type: Feature
Annotation: Trapped in an ante-bellum mansion as the Missis-
    sippi rises, a convicted murderer looks for the true
    murderer. Eddie Anderson has a bit part.

ON THE AVENUE
Nar/Cast: Dick Powell + Alice Faye + Stepin Fetchit*
    Director: Roy del Ruth
Studio/Company: Fox
Tech Info: 16 mm/sound/bw/90 min.
Date/Country: 1937 + USA   Type: Feature
Distr/Arch: sel + wil
Annotation: Stepin Fetchit in one of his usual roles in this
    Fox musical.

ON THE BATTLEFIELD
Nar/Cast: Rev. Charles Koen + Bob Williams   Director: Peter
    Biskind
Studio/Company: Tri-Continental
Tech Info: 16 mm/bw/sound/82 min./20 min. (short version)
Date/Country: 1972 + USA   Type: Documentary

Distr/Arch: tri
Annotation: On the Battlefield is a documentary account of
   racial hatred and violence in America. The film explores
   the small midwestern community of Cairo, Illinois, where
   the racial situation is one that a U.S. Commission on
   Civil Rights report has described as "racism at flood-
   tide."

ON THE BOWERY
Producer: Lionel Rogosin   Director: Lionel Rogosin
Tech Info: 16 mm/bw/sound/65 min.
Date/Country: 1955   Type: Documentary
Distr/Arch: gro + imp
Annotation: This film goes into dark streets and flophouses
   to tell this story of an ex-lawyer who has drifted into
   its life-stream, as seen through his eyes.

ON THE ROAD WITH DUKE ELLINGTON
Producer: Drew Associates
Tech Info: 58 min./color
Date/Country: 1974 + USA   Type: Documentary
Annotation: Originally produced in 1967 when Ellington was
   68, this documentary was updated after his death. Includes performances at the piano of several numbers; shows
   him composing, talking about his family, receiving honary
   doctorates at Morgan State and Yale.

ON THE STROKE OF TWELVE
Nar/Cast: Martin Turner* + David Torrence + June Marlowe
   Director: Charles J. Hunt
Studio/Company: Trem Carr Productions
Tech Info: 35 mm/silent/bw/6 reels/5,842 ft.
Date/Country: 1927 + USA   Type: Feature
Annotation: Martin Turner plays George in this "society
   drama" originally distributed by Rayart Pictures.

ON VELVET
Nar/Cast: Nina Mae McKinney* + Wally Patch + Leslie Bradley
   + Vi Kaley + Garland Wilson   Director: Widgey Newman
Studio/Company: Columbia
Date/Country: 1938 + Britain   Type: Feature
Annotation: Nina Mae McKinney is featured in this musical
   about a TV station.

ON WITH THE SHOW
Nar/Cast: Ethel Waters* + Joe E. Brown + Betty Compson
   Director: Alan Crosland
Studio/Company: Warner Brothers
Tech Info: 16 mm/sound/"natural color"/108 min.
Date/Country: 1929 + USA   Type: Feature
Distr/Arch: uas
Annotation: First dialogue film in "natural color," an early
   techniccdor process. Ethel Waters, along with a number of
   other musical performers is featured; she sings "Am I
   Blue?"

ONCE UPON A TIME IN THE WEST
Nar/Cast: Henry Fonda + Claudia Cardinale + Woody Strode* +

Jason Rcbards
Screenplay: Sergio Leone + Sergio Donati   Story: Dario
   Argento + Bernard Bertolucci + Sergio Leone
Producer: Fulvio Morselle   Director: Sergio Leone
Studio/Company: Paramount
Tech Info: 16 mm/sound/color/165 min.
Date/Country: 1969 + USA + Italy   Type: Feature
Distr/Arch: fnc
Annotation: Various interest groups vie for a valuable plot
   of land important in the westward movement of the railroad
   resulting in the classic Western confrontation. Woody
   Strode plays Stony.

ONE_BIG_MISTAKE
Nar/Cast: Dewey "Pigmeat" Markham*
Screenplay: Dewey Markham*
Producer: Markham* and Heckle*
Date/Country: 1940 + USA

ONE_DARK_NIGHT
Nar/Cast: Mantan Moreland* + Bettie Treadville* + Josephine
   Pearson* + Bobby Simmon* + Lawrence Criner* + Arthur Ray*
   + Monte Hawley* + Ruby Logan* + Alfred Grant* + Herbert
   Skinner* + The Four Tones*   Story: Billy Meyers
   Director: Leo C. Popkin
Studio/Company: Million Dollar Productions
Date/Country: 1939 + USA   Type: Feature
Annotation: Mantan becomes an absentee father who leaves his
   wife tc support the family alone; they are the parents of
   two children. Eventually he returns after having acquired
   a radium mine, re-instates himself with his wife--
   eliminating a prospective suitor--buys a nightclub and
   ingratiates himself with his children for a happy ending.

ONE_DARK_NIGHT
Alt Title(s): see Night Club Girl

ONE_EXCITING_NIGHT
Nar/Cast: Porter Strong + Lillian Gish + Dorothy Gish +
   Joseph Schildkraut + Creighton Hale + Louis Wolheim + Irma
   Harrison + Percy Carr
Screenplay: Irene Sinclair (pseudonum D.W. Griffith)
Producer: D.W. Griffith   Director: D.W. Griffith
Studio/Company: United Artists
Tech Info: 16 mm/silent/11 reels
Date/Country: 1922 + USA   Type: Feature
Distr/Arch: moma
Annotation: The story of Agnes, a young American girl born
   in Africa, who is brought to live in Kentucky. After
   several murders and a violent storm, the mystery of the
   girl's parentage is unraveled in part by the coincidental
   appearance of a former servant of Agnes' mother (in blackface). Porter Strong (as Romeo Washington) and Irma Harrison as his maid girlfriend are both in blackface and
   predictably terrified of both storm and murderings.

ONE_MAN'S_WAY
Nar/Cast: Charles Lampkin* + Don Murray + Diana Hyland

Screenplay: Eleanore Griffin + John BlOck
Producer: Frank Ross   Director: Denis Sanders
Studio/Company: United Artists
Tech Info: 16 mm/sound/bw/105 min.
Date/Country: 1964 + USA   Type: Feature
Distr/Arch: uas
Annotation: Charles Lampkin is Rafe in this biographical
   drama of the life of Norman Vincent Peale (Murray).

ONE MILE FROM HEAVEN
Nar/Cast: Claire Trevor + Sally Blaine + Fredi Washington* +
   Bill Robinson* + Eddie Anderson*
Screenplay: Lou Brestow + John Patrick   Story: Judge Ben D.
   Lindsey   Director: Allan Dwan
Studio/Company: Twentieth-Century Fox
Date/Country: 1937 + USA   Type: Feature
Annotation: In this film Fredi Washington appers opposite
   Bill Rcbinson (in serious role) as the radiant beauty who
   discovers a white foundling and wants to raise the child
   as her cwn.

ONE MORE SPRING
Nar/Cast: Janet Gaynor + Warner Baxter + Stepin Fetchit*
Screenplay: Edwin Burke   Story: Robert Nathan
Producer: Winfield Sheehan   Director: Henry King
Studio/Company: Fox Productions
Date/Country: 1935 + USA   Type: Feature
Annotation: Depression comedy as three misfits try to
   survive a winter in a Central Park tool shed. Fetchit
   plays one of his bit roles (uncredited).

ONE MORE TIME
Nar/Cast: Sammy Davis, Jr.* + Peter Lawford
Screenplay: Michael Pertwee
Producer: Milton Ebins   Director: Jerry Lewis
Studio/Company: United Artists
Tech Info: 16 mm/color/sound/3 reels/93 min.
Date/Country: 1970 + USA   Type: Feature
Distr/Arch: uas
Annotation: Sammy Davis, Jr. and Peter Lawford continue
   their antics in this Jerry Lewis directed sequel to Salt
   and Pepper, about the misadventures of two London club
   owners.

ONE POTATO, TWO POTATO
Nar/Cast: Barbara Barrie + Bernie Hamilton* + Robert Earle
   Jones* + Vinette Carroll*
Screenplay: Raphael Hayes + Orville H. Hampton   Story:
   Orville H. Hampton
Producer: Sam Weston   Director: Larry Peerce
Studio/Company: Bawalco Picture Company
Tech Info: 16 mm/bw/sound/3 reels/92 min.
Date/Country: 1964 + USA   Type: Feature
Distr/Arch: arg + bud + cal + ccc + cha + con + mod + swa +
   twf + twy
Annotation: A white divorcee in a midwestern town marries a
   black cc-worker and they move in with his parents who run
   a small farm. Her white ex-husband returns and fights for

legal custody of their daughter on the grounds that he
does not want her raised with her half-brother.

ONE ROUND JONES
Nar/Cast: Eddie Green* + Lorenzo Tucker*
Studio/Company: Sepia Arts
Date/Country: 1946 + USA
Annotation: Comedy about a prize fighter, played by Eddie
    Green.

ONE TENTH OF OUR NATION   Director: Henwar Rodakiewiecz
Studio/Company: American Film Centre
Date/Country: 1940 + USA   Type: Documentary
Annotation: Documentary for Blacks showing inadequate condi-
    tions of education in the South.

ONE TERRIBLE DAY
Series: Our Gang
Nar/Cast: Our Gang + Ernie Morrison* + Allen Hoskins*
Screenplay: Hal Roach + Tom McNamera
Producer: Hal Roach   Director: Robert McGowan + Tom Mc-
    Namera
Studio/Company: Pathe
Tech Info: silent/bw/2 reels
Date/Country: 1922 + USA   Type: Comedy Short
Annotation: A society matron decides to treat the gang
    members to a day out at her country estate, much to her
    later dismay. Allen Hoskins stars as Farina.

ONE WILD RIDE
Series: Our Gang
Nar/Cast: Our Gang + Allen Hoskins*
Screenplay: Hal Roach
Producer: Hal Roach   Director: Robert McGowan
Studio/Company: Pathe
Tech Info: silent/bw/2 reels
Date/Country: 1925 + USA   Type: Comedy Short
Annotation: The gang modifies a junked car into a horse-
    propelled sight seeing taxi and the fun lasts until the
    horse is repossessed. Then a kind moterist gives them a
    tow.   Farina manages to go for a solo ride out of control
    and ends by crashing into a watermelon cart.   Allen
    Hoskins stars as Farina.

ONKEL TOM'S HUTTE
Alt Title(s): Uncle Tom's Cabin
Nar/Cast: John Kitzmiller* + Herbert Tom + Eartha Kitt* +
    Dorothee Gelison*
Producer: Aldo von Pinelli   Director: Gera Radvanyi
Studio/Company: Melodie-Film + filmkunst-Avaln Films
Tech Info: 35 mm/sound/color/cinemascope/170 min./70 mm
    (original)
Date/Country: 1965 + Yugoslav/German   Type: Feature
Annotation: Released in 1965 in West Germany, U.S. opening
    1969. Another version of Uncle Tom's Cabin with Kitzmil-
    ler in the title role. This one ends with a slave revolt
    and escape to safety.

ONLY THE BRAVE
Nar/Cast: Gary Cooper + Mary Brian
Screenplay: Agnes Brand Leaty   Story: Keene Thompson
   Director: Frank Tuttle
Studio/Company: Paramount
Tech Info: 16 mm/sound/bw/71 min.
Date/Country: 1930 + USA   Type: Feature
Distr/Arch: uni
Annotation: Civil war spy film with Blacks as background and
   the Yankee spy (Cooper) the hero.

ONLY WHEN I LARF
Nar/Cast: Calvin Lockhart* + Richard Attenborough + David
   Hemmings   Director: Basil Dearden
Studio/Company: Paramount
Tech Info: 16 mm/sound/color/104 min.
Date/Country: 1968 + Britain   Type: Feature
Distr/Arch: rbc
Annotation: Crime comedy about con men and con women with
   the female having the last laugh. In one incident the
   confidence-tricksters set up a scheme to sell arms to a
   militant African diplomat-revolutionary (Lockhart).   They
   don't plan to follow through but that scheme backfires.

OOP BOOP SH'BAM
Nar/Cast: Dizzy Gillespie and his Bebop Orchestra* + Taylor
   and Burley* + The Hubba Hubba Girls* + Ray Smith*
Tech Info: 10 min.
Date/Country: 1947 + USA   Type: Musical Short

OPERATION BOOTSTRAP
Producer: Educational Communications and Operation Bootstrap
Tech Info: 16 mm/sound/bw/58 min.
Date/Country: 1968 + USA   Type: Documentary
Distr/Arch: ebec
Annotation: The redevelopment of Watts, California.

OPERATOR 13
Alt Title(s): Spy 13
Nar/Cast: Marion Davies + Gary Cooper + Hattie McDaniel* +
   The Mills Brothers*   Story: Robert W. Chambers
   Director: Richard Boleslawski
Studio/Company: MGM
Date/Country: 1934 + USA   Type: Feature
Annotation: Musical civil war spy movie that features Marion
   Davies (in a black wig and dark makeup) playing a mulatto
   to gather information about confederate troop movements.
   Features the Mills Brothers* singing several numbers.

ORCHESTRA WIVES
Nar/Cast: George Montgomery + Ann Rutherford + Nicholas
   Brothers*
Screenplay: Karl Tunberg + Darrell Ware   Story: James
   Prindle
Producer: William Le Baron   Director: Archie Mayo
Studio/Company: 20th Century Fox
Date/Country: 1942 + USA   Type: Feature
Annotation: The Nicholas Brothers are featured in this tale

of behind-the- scenes discord of a traveling band.

ORGANIZATION, THE
War/Cast: Sidney Poitier* + Barbara McNair* + Gerald S.
   O'Loughlin + Sheree North + Bernie Hamilton*   Director:
   Don Medfor
Studio/Company: United Artists
Tech Info: 16 mm/sound/color/3 reels/107 min.
Date/Country: 1971 + USA   Type: Feature
Distr/Arch: uas
Annotation: A sequel to Mr. Tibbs, this film deals with
   hoodlums, heroin and rivalry between an amitious policeman
   (Hamilton) and detective Tibbs (Poitier).

OS DEUSES E OS MORTOS
Alt Title(s): The Gods and the Dead
Producer: Freddy Rozenburg   Director: Ray Guerra
Tech Info: 16 mm/sound/color/3 reels/97 min./Portugese with
   English subtitles
Date/Country: 1971 + Brazil   Type: Feature
Distr/Arch: nyf
Annotation: The fight for power by two plantation owners.
   Includes folk-based musical score.

OS FUZIS
Alt Title(s): The Guns   Director: Ruy Guerra
Tech Info: 16 mm/sound/3 reels/109 min./Portugese with En-
   glish subtitles
Date/Country: 1963 + Brazil   Type: Documentary
Distr/Arch: nyf
Annotation: The setting is a small village in barren
   northeast Brazil. Gathered there are starving peasants
   awaiting government relief, and a band of pilgrims with
   their beato (holy man), who expect a miracle to occur.

OTHELLO   Director: Jack Goldberg
Date/Country: 194-

OTHER AMERICANS, THE
Producer: Westinghouse + WJZ-TV
Tech Info: 16 mm/sound/color/52 min.
Date/Country: 1969 + USA   Type: TV Documentary
Distr/Arch: wjz
Annotation: Effects of extreme poverty, particularly on
   children, are examined. Interviewed are individuals who,
   in spite of poverty, have achieved success.

OTHER FACE OF DIXIE, THE
Producer: CBS
Tech Info: 16 mm/sound/bw/54 min.
Date/Country: 1962   Type: Documentary
Distr/Arch: car
Annotation: Contrasts the 'segregation wars' of the past
   with current attitudes in the South.

OTHER FRANCISCO, THE
Alt Title(s): see Otro Francisco, El

OTRO_FRANCISCO,_EL
Nar/Cast: Miguel Benavides + Alina Sanchez + Ramon Veloz +
   Margarita Balboa + Adolfo Llaurado
Screenplay: Sergio Giral   Story: Anselmo Suarez Romero
Producer: Instituto Cubano del Arte e Industria Cinemato-
   graphics (ICIAC)   Director: Sergio Giral
Tech Info: 16 mm/bw/sound/3 reels/100 min./Spanish with En-
   glish subtitles
Date/Country: 1975 + Cuba   Type: Feature
Distr/Arch: tri
Annotation: Based on the first anti-slavery novel in Latin
   America, The_Other_Francisco treats the institution of
   slavery as it existed in Cuba. Second part of the film is
   a critique of the novel.

OUANGA
Alt Title(s): see Drums of the Jungle

OUR_COLORED_FIGHTERS
Date/Country: 1918 + USA
Annotation: Emphasizes the labor role of the black soldier;
   shown to black soldiers only; made late in war.

OUR_COUNTRY_TOO
Series: History of the Negro People
Producer: NET
Tech Info: 16 mm/sound/bw/1 reel/30 min.
Date/Country: 1965 + USA   Type: Documentary
Distr/Arch: iu
Annotation: Explores the inner world of the Afro-American--
   his views, attitudes and impressions of life.   Interviews
   at various places, including an African rite in Harlem,
   debutante ball, the office of a black newspaper, and a
   Negro owned radio station.

OUR_GANG_FOLLIES_OF_1936
Series: Our Gang
Nar/Cast: Our Gang + Billie Thomas*
Producer: Hal Roach   Director: Gus Meins
Studio/Company: MGM + Roach
Tech Info: super 8 mm/16 mm/bw/1 reel/10 min.
Date/Country: 1935 + USA   Type: Comedy Short
Distr/Arch: roa + bla
Annotation: The gang stages a neighborhood musical revue.
   Billie Thomas stars as Buckwheat.

OUR_GANG_FOLLIES_OF_1938
Series: Our Gang
Nar/Cast: Our Gang + Billie Thomas*
Producer: Hal Roach   Director: Gordon Douglas
Studio/Company: MGM
Tech Info: super 8 mm/16 mm/bw/sound/1 reel/21 min.
Date/Country: 1937 + USA   Type: Comedy Short
Distr/Arch: bla
Annotation: The gang stages a musical show in its kid-rigged
   cellar theatre. Alfalfa dreams of an opera singing future
   but comes back from his nightmare to sing Bing Crosby
   style for the gang's show . Buckwheat has the role of a

Stokowski-like conductor. Billie Thomas stars as Buckwheat.

OUR GANG
Series: Our Gang
Nar/Cast: Our Gang + Ernie Morrison*
Screenplay: Hal E. Roach
Producer: Hal Roach   Director: Robert F. McGowan
Studio/Company: Pathe
Tech Info: silent/bw/2 reels
Date/Country: 1922 + USA   Type: Comedy Short
Annotation: First of Our Gang series; story line has the
   gang helping the widowed mother of one of the gang members
   who runs the village store recapture business lost to an
   unscrupulous new merchant. Ernie Morrison stars as Sun-
   shine Sammy.

OUR HELL FIGHTERS
Tech Info: 1 reel
Date/Country: 1918 + USA   Type: Documentary
Annotation: This film is on the 369th all-Negro Regiment and
   its contribution to the war effort (World War I).

OUR MAN FLINT
Nar/Cast: James Coburn + Ena Hartman* + Lee J. Cobb + Gila
   Golar + Edward Mulhare
Screenplay: Hal Fimberg + Ben Starr
Producer: Saul David   Director: Daniel Mann
Studio/Company: 20th Century Fox
Tech Info: 16 mm/sound/color/107 min.
Date/Country: 1966 + USA   Type: Feature
Distr/Arch: fnc
Annotation: James Coburn plays Flint in a parody of 007
   movies. In this film Flint tries to thwart a group of
   scientists and keep them from taking over the world. Ena
   Hartman is WAC one of the many females who dote on Flint.

OUT OF SLAVERY 1619-1860
Series: History of the Negro in America
Producer: Niagara Films
Tech Info: 16 mm/bw/sound/1 reel/21 min.
Date/Country: 1965 + USA   Type: Documentary
Distr/Arch: iu + mghf
Annotation: This film traces the history of Blacks in
   America from first arrival to the outbreak of the Civil
   War.   Pictures slavery in the ancient world and outlines
   the development of the slave trade in America.   While
   depicting the life of the Afro-American as a slave in the
   South and a free man in the North, the film also shows his
   role in the American Revolution and discusses slave labor
   as the foundation of Southern wealth.

OUT-OF-TOWNERS, THE
Nar/Cast: Jack Lemmon + Sandy Dennis
Screenplay: Neil Simon
Producer: Paul Nathan   Director: Arthur Hellis
Studio/Company: MGM
Tech Info: 16 mm/sound/color/97 min.

Date/Country: 1969 + USA   Type: Feature
Distr/Arch: fnc
Annotation: A day in the life of an Ohio couple contem-
    plating a move to New York City which for sundry reasons
    will not happen. Musical score by Quincy Jones*.

OUTRAGE
Nar/Cast: Robert Culp + Marlyn Mason + Beah Richards*
Studio/Company: ABC-TV
Date/Country: 1973 + USA   Type: TV Feature
Annotation: Young teenagers taunt and terrorize a man (Culp)
    to the point where he takes the law into his own hands to
    stop them. Marlyn Mason is his wife, Beah Richards their
    maid.

OVOUTIE O'ROONEY
Nar/Cast: Slim Gaillard*
Studio/Company: Astor Pictures Corporation
Date/Country: 1947   Type: Feature
Annotation: An all black musical.

OX-BOW INCIDENT
Alt Title(s): Strange Incident
Nar/Cast: Leigh Whipper* + Henry Fonda + Anthony Quinn +
    Henry Morgan + Dana Andrews
Screenplay: Lamar Trotti   Story: Walter Van Tillberg Clark
Producer: Lamar Trotti   Director: William Wellman
Studio/Company: Twentieth Century Fox
Tech Info: 16 mm/bw/sound/2 reels/76 min.
Date/Country: 1943 + USA   Type: Feature
Distr/Arch: fnc
Annotation: A psychological drama set in the old West about
    three men wrongly accused of cattle rustling and murder.
    They are lynched by a mob of vigilantes. Leigh Whipper
    plays Sparks, a black preacher who stands up to the mob,
    asking for time for the men to prove their innocence, but
    to no avail.

P.J.
Alt Title(s): New Faces in Hell
Nar/Cast: Brock Peters* + George Peppard + Raymond Burr
Screenplay: Phillip Reisman
Producer: Edward Montagne   Director: John Guillermin
Studio/Company: Universal
Tech Info: 16 mm/sound/bw/109 min.
Date/Country: 1968 + USA   Type: Feature
Distr/Arch: cwf + uni
Annotation: Peppard is hired as bodyguard for a rich man's
    mistress in this crime melodrama. Peters plays a police
    chief, Waterpark, who has an uneasy truce with Peppard.

PA'S FAMILY TREE
Studio/Company: E.   R. Jungle Film Co.
Date/Country: 1916 + USA
Annotation: A parody of jungle movies in which a white man
    dreams of being over-powered by jungle Blacks only to have
    his white wife, as queen of the jungle, save him.

PAISAN
Nar/Cast: Dots M. Johnson* + Carmella Salzo + Robert Von
    Loon
Screenplay: Sergio Amidei + Klaus Mann + Alfred Hayes +
    Marcello Paglieri + Federico Fellini + Roberto Rossellini
Producer: Roberto Rossellini   Director: Roberto Rossellini
Studio/Company: Mayer-Burstyn Inc.
Tech Info: 16 mm/sound/bw/115 min.
Date/Country: 1946 + Italy   Type: Feature
Distr/Arch: kpf + ree
Annotation: There are six vignettes in this film about   how
    war affects the lives of ordinary human beings. In one,
    Dots Johnson plays an American MP in Naples whose shoes
    are stolen by a street urchin. When he tries to recover
    them, he discovers the incredible squalor in which the
    child lives. Released in the U.S. in 1948.

PALMOUR STREET
Screenplay: George Stoney
Producer: Department of Public Health, Georgia
Tech Info: 16 mm/sound/bw/27 min.
Date/Country: 1956 + USA   Type: Documentary
Distr/Arch: uca
Annotation: The problems of black people on a typical street
    in Georgia.

PANAMA HATTIE
Nar/Cast: Ann Southern + Red Skelton + Rags Ragland + Ben
    Blue + Marsha Hunt + Virginia O'Brian + Carl Esmond + The
    Berry Brothers* (Nyas, James and Warren) + Lena Horne*
Screenplay: Jack McGowan + Willkie Mahoney   Story: Herbert
    Fields + B.G. de Sylva
Producer: Arthur Freed   Director: Norman Z. McLeod
Studio/Company: MGM
Date/Country: 1943 + USA   Type: Feature
Annotation: Cole Porter musical comedy starring Red Skelton
    and Ann Southern. Featuring Lena Horne in her first major
    film appearance, singing "Just One of Those Things."

PANIC ON THE 5:22
Nar/Cast: Lynda Day George + Ina Balin + Bernie Casey* +
    Lawrence Luckinbill + Charles Lampkin*
Screenplay: Eugene Price
Producer: Anthony Spinner   Director: Harry Hart
Studio/Company: Quinn Martinn
Tech Info: 16 mm/color/sound/90 min.
Date/Country: 1974 + USA   Type: TV Feature
Annotation: Three armed men gain control of a luxury rail-
    road club car, determined to rob and kill their hostages
    while the unarmed passengers try to outwit them.   Casey
    plays Wendell Weaver; Lampkin is George Lincoln.

PANTHERS, THE
Producer: ABC
Tech Info: 16 mm/sound/color/25 min.
Date/Country: 1971 + USA   Type: TV Documentary
Distr/Arch: xer
Annotation: Shows scenes of the Panthers at work in the com-

munity and white and black attitudes toward them. Includes comments by Julian Bond*, David Hilliard and Andrew
Young*.

PAPER_LION
Nar/Cast: Alan Alda + Lauren Hutton + Sugar Ray Robinson* +
   Frank Gifford + Roger Brown* + Lem Barney* + Alex Karras
Screenplay: Lawrence Roman   Story: George Plimpton
Producer: Stuart Miller   Director: Alex March
Studio/Company: United Artists
Tech Info: 16 mm/sound/color/3 reels/105 min.
Date/Country: 1968 + USA   Type: Feature
Distr/Arch: cwf + uas
Annotation: Story of a reporter who tries out as a pro foot-
   ball quarterback and his experiences with the Detroit
   Lions, like Brown, Barney, and Karras.

PAPER_MOON
Alt Title(s): Addie Pray (novel)
Nar/Cast: Ryan O'Neal + Tatum O'Neal + Madeline Kahn + PJ
   Johnson*
Screenplay: Alvin Sargent   Story: Joe David Brown
   Director: Peter Bogdanavich
Studio/Company: Paramount
Tech Info: 16 mm/sound/bw/102 min.
Date/Country: 1973 + USA   Type: Feature
Distr/Arch: fnc
Annotation: A con man (Ryan O'Neal) meets up with a young
   girl (Tatum O'Neal) who is even better at the game than he
   is.   The film is a story of their misadventures as they
   team up to con everyone across the Midwest. P.J. Johnson*
   plays Imogene, a good friend of Tatum O'Neal's and maid of
   sorts to Madeline Kahn.

PARADISE_IN_HARLEM
Nar/Cast: Frank Wilson* + Mamie Smith* + Juanita Hall* + Joe
   Joe Thomas* + Perry Bradford* + Alphabetical Four* + Edna
   Mae Harris* + Norma Atwood* + Merritt Smith* + Francine
   Everett* + Lucky Millinder* and his orchestra
Screenplay: Vincent Valentini   Story: Frank Wilson*
Producer: Jack Goldberg + Dave Goldberg   Director: Joseph
   Seiden
Studio/Company: Goldberg Productions + Negro Marches On
Tech Info: 16 mm/bw/sound/2 reels/85 min.
Date/Country: 1939 + USA   Type: feature
Distr/Arch: ncs + kpf + emg
Annotation: Gangster plot set against a backdrop of late
   thirties jazz, with Lucky Millendar and his orchestra.

PARADISO_NERO
Nar/Cast: John Kitzmiller*
Date/Country: 1947 + Italy   Type: Feature

PARIS_BLUES
Nar/Cast: Sidney Poitier* + Paul Newman + Diahann Carroll* +
   Joanne Woodward + Louis Armstrong*
Screenplay: Jack Sher + Irene Kamp + Walter Bernstein
Producer: Sam Shaw + George Glass + Walter Seitzer

Director: Martin Ritt
Studio/Company: United Artists
Tech Info: 16 mm/bw/sound/3 reels/98 min.
Date/Country: 1960 + USA   Type: Feature
Distr/Arch: uas
Annotation: The story concerns two American expatriate jazz-
    men (Poitier and Newman) who have a romance with two
    American girls on the loose (Carroll and Woodward) in
    Paris. Music score by Duke Ellington*; jazz sequences
    feature Louis Armstrong*.

PART 2, SOUNDER
Alt Title(s): Sounder, Part 2
Nar/Cast: Taj Mahal*   Director: Graham William
Tech Info: 16 mm/sound/color/98 min.
Date/Country: 1976 + USA   Type: Feature
Annotation: Sequel to Sounder. Taj Majal scored the film,
    also appears in it as a folk singer.

PARTY FEVER
Series: Our Gang
Nar/Cast: Our Gang + Billie Thomas*
Screenplay: Howard Dimsdale
Producer: Jack Chertok   Director: George Sidney
Studio/Company: MGM
Tech Info: bw/sound/1 reel
Date/Country: 1938 + USA   Type: Comedy Short
Annotation: Waldo, Butch, and Alfalfa all vie to be Darla's
    escort to the Strawberry Festival. It is determined that
    the winner of junior mayor for Boy's Week election will
    escort her.   Just as it appears Alfalfa has won, Waldo's
    uncle, the mayor appoints Waldo. Billie Thomas stars as
    Buckwheat.

PASSION SONG
Nar/Cast: Gertrude Olmsted + Noah Beery + Gordon Elliott +
    Edgar Washington*   Director: Harry O. Hoyt
Studio/Company: Excellent Pictures
Tech Info: 35 mm/silent/bw/6 reels
Date/Country: 1928
Annotation: Ulamba (Washington) is a tribal chief leading a
    rebellion in Africa which kills Ulamba's enemy, a Boer who
    made his fortune in South Africa.

PATCH OF BLUE, A
Nar/Cast: Sidney Poitier* + Elizabeth Hartman + Shelley
    Winters + Ivan Dixon* + Wallace Ford + Diahann Carroll*
Screenplay: Guy Green   Story: Elizabeth Kada
Producer: Pandro S. Berman   Director: Guy Green
Studio/Company: MGM
Tech Info: 16 mm/bw/sound/3 reels/105 min.
Date/Country: 1965 + USA   Type: Feature
Distr/Arch: fnc
Annotation: Remembering only the sky as "a patch of blue," a
    blind white girl of 18, abused by her drunken grandfather
    and prostitute mother, falls in love with a black man
    (Poitier), much to her family's horror. Poitier is Gordon
    Ralfe, Dixon is his brother Mark.

PATTON: A SALUTE TO A REBEL
Nar/Cast: George C. Scott + Karl Malden + James Edwards*
Screenplay: Francis Ford Coppela + Edmund North
Producer: Frank McCarthy   Director: Franklin Schaffner
Studio/Company: 20th Century Fox
Tech Info: 16 mm/sound/color/171 min.
Date/Country: 1970 + USA   Type: Feature
Distr/Arch: fnc
Annotation: The film covers General George S. Patton through
    the war years. George C. Scott won the oscar for his per-
    formance as Patton. James Edwards' last film.

PAUL LAURENCE DUNBAR: AMERICA'S FIRST BLACK POET
Nar/Cast: Davis Roberts* + Will Geer + Leon Bailey* +
    Michael Moore* + Edward Neal, Jr.*
Screenplay: Carlton Moss*
Producer: Carlton Moss* + Fisk University   Director:
    Carlton Moss*
Studio/Company: Pyramid
Tech Info: 16 mm/sound/bw/1 reel/23 min.
Date/Country: 1972 + USA   Type: Dramatized Documentary
Distr/Arch: roa + pyr
Annotation: Produced in 1972 on the hunredth anniversary of
    Paul Laurence Dunbar's birth, this tribute to the life and
    work of the man known as the 'Negro Poet Laureate' is a
    collage of still pictures, paintings, art, and film
    dramatizations including poetry and biography. Additional
    participating faculty, Fisk Art Department: David
    Driskell*, Earl Hooks*, Robert Sengstacke*, Jai-B. Bond*;
    music, Robert Holmes*.

PAUL LAURENCE DUNBAR: AMERICAN POET
Producer: Vignette
Tech Info: 16 mm/sound/color/14 min.
Date/Country: 1966 + USA   Type: Documentary
Distr/Arch: bfa
Annotation: Portrait of the son of an escaped slave who be-
    came an eminent black writer, sometimes referred to as the
    "Negro Poet Laureate."

PAWNBROKER, THE
Nar/Cast: Rod Steiger + Geraldine Fitzgerald + Brock Peters*
    + Jaime Sanchez* + Juano Hernandez* + Thelma Oliver* +
    Roscoe Lee Brown*
Screenplay: Morton Fine + David Friedkin   Story: Edward
    Lewis Wallant
Producer: Worthington Miner   Director: Sidney Lumet
Studio/Company: Landau
Tech Info: 16 mm/color/sound/4 reels/114 min.
Date/Country: 1965 + USA   Type: Feature
Distr/Arch: mac
Annotation: A film about Sol Nazeman, a Jewish pawnbroker
    (Rod Steiger) who has survived the horrors of a concentra-
    tion camp leaving him emotionally and intellectually dead.
    Various people including his black Puerto Rican assistant
    try to break down the wall he has built but to no avail,
    until a dramatic moment when his assistant is killed

protecting him.   Music score by Quincy Jones*, his first
for an American film.

PAY AS YOU EXIT
Series: Our Gang
Nar/Cast: Our Gang + Billie Thomas*
Producer: Hal Roach   Director: Gordon Douglas
Studio/Company: MGM
Tech Info: super 8 mm/16 mm/bw/sound/1 reel/11 min.
Date/Country: 1936 + USA   Type: Comedy Short
Distr/Arch: bla
Annotation: The gang produces a "Romeo and Juliet" with a
    pay as you exit promotion scheme, but leading man Alfalfa
    has been eating onions and drives off leading lady Darla.
    Buckwheat, cast as a Nubian slave, is brought in as a sub-
    stitute Juliet.

PAYSANS (LES) NOIRS
Alt Title(s): Famoro le Tyran
Nar/Cast: Louis Arbessier + Antoine Balpetre + Georges
    Hubert
Screenplay: Rene Barjavel + Georges Regnier   Story: Robert
    Delavignette   Director: Georges Regnier
Studio/Company: S.D.A.C.-U. G. C.
Tech Info: sound/99 min.
Date/Country: 1948 + France   Type: Feature
Distr/Arch: saf
Annotation: In this African drama, a young administrator is
    assigned to replace one of his assassinated colleagues.
    Soon after his arrival, he comes up against a caste which
    is oppressing the peasants and, aided by the doctor and by
    an engineer, he is able to restore their confidence.   The
    oppressors start a reign of terror, but the young ad-
    ministrator is able to renden justice by the grace of his
    Will and the help of the black peasants. (This film may
    be consulted at the Archive.)

PEANUT MAN
Nar/Cast: Clarence Muse* + Ernest Anderson* + Maidie Norman*
Studio/Company: Consolidated Pictures
Tech Info: sound/color
Date/Country: 1947 + USA
Annotation: Clarence Muse plays Dr. George Washington
    Carver.

PEARLS OF THE CROWN, THE
Alt Title(s): see Les Perles de la Couronne

PECK'S BAD BOY WITH THE CIRCUS
Nar/Cast: Tommy Kelly + Ann Gillis + Louise Beavers* +
    Benita Hume
Screenplay: Al Martin + Dave Boehm + Robert Neville
Producer: Sol Lessor   Director: Edward F. Cline
Studio/Company: RKO Radio Pictures
Tech Info: 16 mm/sound/bw/75 min.
Date/Country: 1938 + USA   Type: Feature
Distr/Arch: bud + cha + cwf + ics + mog + roa + who + nil
Annotation: Movie for the younger set complete with Tom

Sawyerish pranks, circus acts and a young hero winning the
big race. Louise Beavers plays her usual maid's role.

PENDULUM
Nar/Cast: Isabell Sanford* + George Peppard + Jean Seberg
Screenplay: Stanley Niss
Producer: Stanley Niss   Director: George Schaefer
Studio/Company: Columbia
Tech Info: 16 mm/sound/color/105 min.
Date/Country: 1969 + USA   Type: Feature
Distr/Arch: cwf + ics + mac + roa + swa + twy + who
Annotation: Isabell Sanford is Effie, a small role, in this
   crime melodrama about a police captain accused of
   murdering his wife and her lover.

PENNIES FROM HEAVEN
Nar/Cast: Bing Crosby + Madge Evans + Edith Fellowes +
   Donald Meek + Louis Armstrong* + Lionel Hampton*
Screenplay: Jo Swerling   Story: Katherine L. Moore (Book)
Producer: Emanuel Cohen   Director: Norman McLeod
Studio/Company: Columbia
Tech Info: 16mm/ bw/ sound/ 81 min.
Date/Country: 1937 + USA   Type: Feature
Distr/Arch: cwf + tfc
Annotation: Bing Crosby as a wanderer who has a family in-
   formally adopt him after he deliers a message to them from
   a dying man. Louis Armstrong and his orchestra are
   featured in a nightclub sequence; Lionel Hampton also ap-
   pears in one number, "Skeleton in the Closet."

PENROD AND SAM
Nar/Cast: Frank Craven + Billy Mauch + Craig Reynolds +
   Spring Byington + Philip Hurlic*
Studio/Company: Warners
Tech Info: 16 mm/sound/bw/64 min.
Date/Country: 1937 + USA   Type: Feature
Distr/Arch: uas
Annotation: This film was one of a series, an extension of
   the "Our Gang" type of movie, in which Penrod's gang was
   composed of several white boys and one black child, played
   by Philip Hurlic.

PENROD
Nar/Cast: Wesley Barry + Tully Marshall + Claire McDowell +
   Ernie Morrison* + Florence Morrison*
Studio/Company: Marshall Neilan Productions
Tech Info: 35 mm/silent/bw/8 reels
Date/Country: 1922 + USA   Type: Feature
Annotation: Sunshine (Ernie Morrison) and Florence Morrison
   play 2 members of a boy's club who get rid of the rival
   bully and help make a hero out of young Penrod and the
   gang so that Penrod can impress his girl.

PENSIONE EDELWEISS
Nar/Cast: John Kitzmiller*
Date/Country: 1959 + Italy   Type: Feature

PEOPLE ORGANIZED, THE

Alt Title(s): see Povo Organizado, O

PEOPLE, POWER, CHANGE
Producer: Univ. of Minnesota
Tech Info: 16 mm/color/29 min.
Date/Country: 1968 + USA   Type: Documentary
Distr/Arch: umn
Annotation: Black Power and Protestant Pentecostal, two
   social movements, are analyzed and compared. Provided by
   Center for Southern Folklore.

PERFECT DREAMER, THE
Studio/Company: Young Producers Filming Company
Tech Info: 35 mm/silent/bw
Date/Country: 1922 + USA   Type: Feature
Annotation: A story of "Negro" life.

PETE KELLY'S BLUES
Nar/Cast: Ella Fitzgerald* + Andy Devine + Lee Marvin + Jack
   Webb + Edmond O'Brien   Director: Jack Webb
Studio/Company: Warner Brothers
Tech Info: 16 mm/color/sound/3 reels/95 min.
Date/Country: 1955 + USA   Type: Feature
Distr/Arch: wsa
Annotation: In this saga of Pete Kelley, Jack Webb stars as
   a Kansas City Jazzman who blew a cornet because he loved
   to play and they paid him for it. Ella Fitzgerald adds
   her voice to the speakeasy sounds. Opening sequence is a
   black cornetist's funeral.

PETRIFIED FOREST, THE
Nar/Cast: Leslie Howard + Bette Davis + Genivieve Tobin +
   Humphrey Bogart + Porter Hall + Edward Thompson* + John
   Alexander*
Screenplay: Delmer Daves + Charles Kenyon   Story: Robert E.
   Sherwood   Director: Archie Mayo
Studio/Company: Warners
Tech Info: 16 mm/sound bw/83 min.
Date/Country: 1936 + USA   Type: Feature
Distr/Arch: uas
Annotation: Film adaptation of Robert Sherwood's hit play
   with Leslie Howard and Humphrey Bogart recreating their
   roles. There is an interesting scene between Edward
   Thompson as Slim Johnson, the black gangster, and John
   Alexander as the obsequious "colored" chauffeur.

PHANTOM KILLER, THE
Nar/Cast: Dick Purcell + Mantan Moreland*   Director: Willi-
   am Beaudine
Date/Country: 1943 + USA   Type: Feature
Annotation: Mantan Moreland co-stars with Dick Purcell as
   his "side-kick" in this follow up to King of the Zombies.

PHANTOM OF KENWOOD   Director: Oscar Micheaux*
Studio/Company: Micheaux Film Corporation
Date/Country: 1933 + USA

PHANTOM PRESIDENT, THE

Nar/Cast: George M. Cohan + Claudette Colbert + Jimmy
   Durante
Screenplay: Walter Deleon + Harlan Thompson   Story: George
   F. Worts   Director: Norman Taurog
Studio/Company: Paramount
Tech Info: 16 mm/sound/bw/81 min.
Date/Country: 1932 + USA   Type: Feature
Distr/Arch: uni
Annotation: George M. Cohan does a blackface minstrel
   routine along with his dual role of poliician-banker.

PHELA_NDABA:_END_OF_THE_DIALOGUE
Alt Title(s): see End of the Dialogue

PHENIX_CITY_STORY,_THE
Nar/Cast: John McIntire + Richard Kiley + James Edwards*
Screenplay: Crane Wilber + Dan Mainwaring
Producer: Sam Bischoff   Director: Phil Karlson
Studio/Company: Allied Artists
Tech Info: 16 mm/sound/bw/100 min.
Date/Country: 1955 + USA   Type: Feature
Distr/Arch: cin
Annotation: Chronicles the activities which lead to the
   murder of anti-vice crusader Albert Patterson (McIntire)
   in Phenix City, Alabama. James Edwards plays Zeke Ward.

PHYLLIS_AND_TERRY
Producer: Mamer Films
Tech Info: 16 mm/sound/bw/36 min.
Date/Country: 1965 + USA   Type: Dramatized Documentary
Distr/Arch: cal + cemc
Annotation: Two ghetto black teenagers, Phyllis and Terry,
   express their feelings about life and their prospects for
   the future in this improvised film of a day in their
   lives.

PHYNX,_THE
Nar/Cast: Richard Pryor* + Joe Lewis* + Butterfly McQueen*
Screenplay: Stan Cornyn
Producer: Bob Booker   Director: Lee H.Katzin
Studio/Company: Cinema Organization + Warner Brothers
Tech Info: sound/color/91 min.
Date/Country: 1970 + USA   Type: Feature
Annotation: A farce about the kidnapping of American show
   business people by Communist Albania and a scheme to
   combat the kidnappings. Pryor, Louis, McQueen join a raft
   of guest stars.

PICKANINNY_BLUES
Alt Title(s): see Uncle Tom and Little Eva

PIE,_PIE_BLACKBIRD
Nar/Cast: Nina Mae McKinney* + Eubie Blake and his Band* +
   Nicholas Brothers*
Producer: Warner Brothers   Director: Roy Mack
Tech Info: 1 reel/10 min./bw/sound
Date/Country: 1932 + USA   Type: Musical Short
Distr/Arch: emg

Annotation: A vitaphone short featuring instrumental, vocal
  and dance numbers, among them: "Blackbird Pie" and "You
  Rascal You."

PIECE OF THE ACTION, A
Nar/Cast: Sidney Poitier* + Bill Cosby* + Sheryl Lee Ralph*
  + James Earl Jones*
Producer: Sidney Poitier*   Director: Sidney Poitier*
Studio/Company: Warner Brothers
Tech Info: 16 mm/sound/color/133 min.
Date/Country: 1977 + USA   Type: Feature
Distr/Arch: swa
Annotation: Cosby, a safe cracker, and Poitier, a con man,
  are blackmailed by Jones, an ex-policeman who knows their
  history, into doing altruistic work for the community and
  the young folk.

PIGMEAT MARKHAM'S LAUGH HEPCATS
Nar/Cast: Dewey "Pigmeat" Markham*
Studio/Company: Toddy Productions
Tech Info: 36 min.
Date/Country: 194-

PIGSKIN PALOOKA, THE
Series: Our Gang
Nar/Cast: Our Gang + Billie Thomas*
Producer: Hal Roach   Director: Gordon Douglas
Studio/Company: MGM + Roach
Tech Info: super 8 mm/16 mm/bw/sound/1 reel/10 min.
Date/Country: 1937 + USA   Type: Comedy Short
Distr/Arch: kpf + bla
Annotation: Alfalfa tries to impress Darla with stories that
  he's a big football star at military school, but comes
  home to find himself recruited for Spanky's all stars.
  Assisted by Buckwheat and Spanky, Alfalfa inadvertently
  wins the game. Billie Thomas stars as Buckwheat.

PILGRIMAGE TO TOUBA
Alt Title(s): see Grand Magal a Touba

PILLOW TO POST
Nar/Cast: Ida Lupino + Sidney Greenstreet + Willie Best*
  Story: Rose Simon Kohn (Play)
Studio/Company: Warner Brothers
Tech Info: 16mm/ sound/ bw/ 96 min.
Date/Country: 1945 + USA   Type: Feature
Annotation: A comic farce about an unmarried couple mistaken
  for a married one, and the charade they're forced to act
  out. Willie Best has a bit role.

PINCH SINGER, THE
Series: Our Gang
Nar/Cast: Our Gang + Billie Thomas*
Producer: Hal Roach   Director: Fred Newmeyer
Studio/Company: MGM + Roach
Tech Info: super 8 mm/16 mm/sound/bw/2 reels/17 min.
Date/Country: 1936 + USA   Type: Comedy Short
Distr/Arch: roa + bla

Annotation: The gang holds auditions to choose a contestant
   to try for a radio contest's $50 prize.   Alfalfa finally
   wins through another ingenious ruse by the gang, Buckwheat
   (Billie Thomas) among them.

PINKY
Nar/Cast: Ethel Waters* + Jeanne Crain + Ethel Barrymore +
   Frederick O'Neal* + Nina Mae McKinney* + Kenny Washington*
Screenplay: Phillip Dunne   Story: Cid R. Sumner
Producer: Darryl Zanuck   Director: Elia Kazan
Studio/Company: Twentieth Century Fox
Tech Info: 16 mm/bw/sound/3 reels/100 min.
Date/Country: 1949 + USA   Type: Feature
Distr/Arch: fnc
Annotation: A young nurse (Jeanne Crain) who has been pas-
   sing fcr white returns to her home in the south where she
   faces decisions about herself, love and her purpose in
   life.   She's helped by her grandmother (Waters) and her
   grandmother's former employer (Barrymore). Nina Mae McK-
   inney has a brief role as an unsavory companion of
   Frederick O'Neal's.

PIPE DREAMS
Nar/Cast: Gladys Knight* + Barry Hankerson*
Screenplay: Stephen F. Vervona   Director: Stephen F. Verona
Studio/Company: Embassy + 16 + 16 mm/color/sound/91 min. +
   17 + 1976 + USA   Type: Feature
Distr/Arch: swa
Annotation: Romantic adventure about an Atlanta
   schoolteacher (Gladys Knight) who leaves her job and goes
   to join her husband (Barry Hankerson), who works on the
   Alaskan pipeline. She also sings.

PIRATE, THE
Nar/Cast: Judy Garland + Gene Kelly + Nicholas Brothers*
Screenplay: Albert Hackett + Francis Goodrich   Story: S.N.
   Behrman
Producer: Arthur Freed   Director: Vincente Minnelli
Studio/Company: MGM
Tech Info: 16 mm/sound/color/102 min.
Date/Country: 1948 + USA   Type: Feature
Distr/Arch: fnc
Annotation: Musical showcasing the talents of Judy Garland,
   Gene Kelly, and the Nicholas Brothers, as Gene Kelly tries
   to thwart the upcoming marriage of Ms. Garland to a stuffy
   nobility type.

PIRATES OF TORTUGA, THE
Nar/Cast: Rafer Johnson* + Leticia Roman
Screenplay: Melvin Levy + Jesse Lasky, Jr.
Producer: Sam Katzman   Director: Robert Webb
Studio/Company: Fox
Tech Info: 16 mm/sound/color/97 min.
Date/Country: 1961 + USA   Type: Feature
Distr/Arch: mod + wsa
Annotation: Rafer Johnson is John Gamel in this 17th century
   adventure melodrama about privateers on the high seas.

PITTSBURGH KID, THE
Nar/Cast: Jean Parker + Billy Conn + Ernest Whitman* + Etta
   McDaniel* + Henry Armstrong*
Screenplay: Eal Felton + Houston Branch   Story: Octavius
   Roy Cohen   Director: Jack Townley
Studio/Company: Republic
Tech Info: 16 mm/sound/bw/76 min.
Date/Country: 1942 + USA   Type: Feature
Distr/Arch: ivy
Annotation: Boxer Billy Conn tries his hand at acting in
   this tale about a boxer who tries to decide between 2
   managers, one honest, one not so, while also trying to
   keep his girlfriend.   Henry Armstrong plays one of his
   sparring partners; Ernest Whitman is Feets Johnson and
   Etta McDaniel is Magenta.

PIZZA PIZZA DADDY-O
Producer: Bess Lomax Hawes + Robert Eberlein
Tech Info: 16 mm/sound/bw/18 min.
Date/Country: 1969 + USA   Type: Documentary
Distr/Arch: ucemc
Annotation: "Pizza Pizza Daddy-O" is one light game song
   played/sung by fourth-grade Afro-American girls on a Los
   Angeles playground.   Call-and-response is a salient
   stylistic feature of the game/play.

PLACE CALLED TODAY, A
Nar/Cast: J. Herbert Kerr, Jr.* + Lana Wood + Cheri Caffaro
Screenplay: Don Schain
Producer: Ralph J. Desiderio   Director: Don Schain
Studio/Company: AVCO Embassy
Tech Info: 16 mm/sound/color/99 min.
Date/Country: 1972 + USA   Type: Feature
Distr/Arch: mac
Annotation: A black mayoral candidate's complicated private
   life and corrupt political campaign.

PLACE TO LIVE, A   Director: Irving Lerner
Studio/Company: Philadelphia Housing Association
Date/Country: 1941 + USA   Type: Documentary
Annotation: Documentary on housing conditions among Negroes
   and whites in Philadelphia.

PLAINSMAN, THE
Nar/Cast: Percy Rodrigues* + Don Murray + Guy Stockwell
Screenplay: Michael Blankfort
Producer: Richard Lyons   Director: David Lowell Rick
Studio/Company: Universal
Tech Info: 16 mm/sound/bw/113 min.
Date/Country: 1966 + USA   Type: Feature
Distr/Arch: ccc + cou + cwf + tmc + uni
Annotation: Percy Rodrigues is Brother John in this western
   melodrama about Cheyenne Indians, the two famous Bills
   Hickock and Cody, Calamity Jane and General Custer.

PLAY MISTY FOR ME
Nar/Cast: James McEachin* + Clint Eastwood + Jessica Walter
   + Cannonball Adderley*

Screenplay: Jo Helms + Dean Riesner   Story: Jo Helms
Producer: Robert Doley   Director: Clint Eastwood
Studio/Company: Universal
Tech Info: 16 mm/sound/color/102 min.
Date/Country: 1971 + USA   Type: Feature
Distr/Arch: swa + twy + uni
Annotation: Disc Jockey with two women - one he loves, the
    other loves him despite his attempts to brush her off.
    James McEachin plays a fellow DJ.   The rejected woman
    plays a homicidal game to get Eastwood. Adderley is seen
    and heard briefly.

PLAYIN' HOOKEY
Series: Our Gang
Nar/Cast: Our Gang + Allen Hoskins* + Jannie Hoskins*
Screenplay: Hal Roach
Producer: Hal Roach   Director: Anthony Mack
Studio/Company: Pathe
Tech Info: bw/silent/2 reels
Date/Country: 1928 + USA   Type: Comedy Short
Annotation: Pete 'Pansy' the Pup gets a movie tryout but
    fails to do his stuff. When the studio employees try to
    eject him, the gang responds by destroying scenes and
    sets.   Allen Hoskins stars as Farina and Jannie Hoskins
    stars as Mango.

PLEASANT JOURNEY, A
Series: Our Gang
Nar/Cast: Our Gang + Ernie Morrison* + Allen Hoskins* +
    Ernie Morrison, Sr.*
Screenplay: Hal Roach
Producer: Hal Roach   Director: Robert McGowan
Studio/Company: Pathe
Tech Info: silent/bw/2 reels
Date/Country: 1923 + USA   Type: Comedy Short
Annotation: The gang trades places with a group of runaways
    being returned to San Francisco by train. On the train,
    they get ahold of a traveling salesman's kit full of magic
    tricks and practical jokes with which they throughly dis-
    rupt the train. Allen Hoskins stars as Farina.

POCOMANIA: A LITTLE MADNESS
Studio/Company: BBC
Tech Info: bw/22 min.
Date/Country: 1968
Annotation: A Jamaican Pocomania cult is observed during
    their secret ritual of "speaking in tongues."

POJKEN I TRADET
Alt Title(s): Boy in the Tree   Director: Arne Sucksdorff
Tech Info: 86 min.
Date/Country: 1961 + Sweden   Type: Feature
Annotation: Quincy Jones* wrote the music, his first feature
    film score, for this tale of a teenager who has problems
    communicating and feels he is misunderstood.

POLICY MAN, THE
Nar/Cast: James Baskette*

POLITICS OF RESISTANCE, THE
Series: The Black Experience
Producer: Univ. of Michigan Television Center
Tech Info: 16 mm/bw/29 min. (also available on videotape)
Date/Country: 1970 + USA   Type: Documentary
Distr/Arch: umic
Annotation: Explores black insurrections of the eighteenth
   century and conflicts within the slave system. Provided
   by Center for Southern Folklore.

PONCONMANIA
Studio/Company: Inwall Productions
Date/Country: 1939

POOCH, THE
Series: Our Gang
Nar/Cast: Our Gang + Matthew Beard*
Screenplay: Hal E. Roach + H.M. Walker
Producer: Hal Roach + Robert F. McGow F.   Director: Robert
   McGowan
Studio/Company: MGM + Roach
Tech Info: super 8 mm/16 mm/sound/bw/1 reel/20 min.
Date/Country: 1932 + USA   Type: Comedy Short
Distr/Arch: roa + bla
Annotation: Stymie, hungry and looking for food, gets in
   trouble with the gang for stealing a pie, but wins back
   friendship by saving their dogs from the dog catcher.
   Stymie (Matthew Beard) has a major role in this one.

PORGY AND BESS
Nar/Cast: Sidney Poitier* + Dorothy Dandridge* + Sammy
   Davis, Jr.* + Pearl Bailey* + Brock Peters* + Diahann Car-
   roll* + Clarence Muse* + Joel Fluellen*
Screenplay: N. Richard Nash   Story: DuBose Heyward +
   Dorothy Heyward (Opera)
Producer: Samuel Goldwyn   Director: Otto Preminger
Studio/Company: Columbia
Tech Info: 16mm/ color/ sound/ 4 reels/ 138 min.
Date/Country: 1959 + USA   Type: Feature
Distr/Arch: aim + mac
Annotation: A poignant love story set against the backdrop
   of Catfish Row in post-Civil War South. The film show-
   cases many black stars: Poitier plays Porgy, Dandridge is
   Bess, Peters is Crown, Davis is Sportin' Life. George
   Gershwin's score won an oscar.

PORK CHOP HILL
Nar/Cast: Gregory Peck + Harry Guardino + James Edwards* +
   Woody Strode*
Screenplay: James R. Webb
Producer: Sy Bartlett   Director: Lewis Milestone
Studio/Company: United Artist
Tech Info: 16 mm/sound/bw/97 min.
Date/Country: 1959 + USA   Type: Feature
Distr/Arch: uas
Annotation: Grim war movie which has Blacks in realistic
   roles and tacitly points to the obsolescence of ground

warfare.

POBTERS, THE
Nar/Cast: Ebony Players*
Studio/Company: Ebony Film Corporation
Date/Country: 1918 + USA

PORTRAIT IN BLACK AND WHITE
Series: Of Black America
Producer: CBS
Tech Info: 16 mm/sound/bw/54 min.
Date/Country: 1968 + USA   Type: TV Documentary
Distr/Arch: bfa + uca + uco
Annotation: TV survey of opinions Blacks and whites have
  about each other.

PORTRAIT IN BLACK: A. PHILIP RANDOLPH
Producer: Sterling Education Films, Inc.
Tech Info: 16 mm/sound/color/1 reel/11 min.
Date/Country: USA   Type: Documentary
Distr/Arch: iu + ste
Annotation: Discusses the renowned civil rights leader A.
  Philip Randolph, his struggle to get equal jobs with equal
  pay for black people. Stresses Randolph's support of the
  refusal by Blacks to join a segregated army. Shows the
  civil rights march on Washington, D.C., during Kennedy's
  administration.

PORTRAIT OF A DEAF CITY
Producer: Sterling
Tech Info: 16 mm/sound/color/15 min.
Date/Country: 1972 + USA   Type: Documentary
Distr/Arch: sef
Annotation: How people from various levels of life view
  their city and their relative power within the structure.

PORTRAIT OF JASON
Nar/Cast: Jason Holliday*
Producer: Shirley Clarke   Director: Shirley Clarke
Studio/Company: Filmmakers
Tech Info: 16 mm/bw/sound/3 reels/105 min.
Date/Country: 1967 + USA   Type: Documentary
Distr/Arch: nyf
Annotation: Jason Holliday, a 33-year old black male
  prostitute, spent 12 hours before Shirley Clarke's camera
  one night; the film is edited down to less than two hours.
  It reveals what society can do to a man it doubly rejects,
  as a black and as a homosexual.

POSTAL INSPECTOR
Nar/Cast: Hattie McDaniel*
Date/Country: 1936 + USA   Type: Feature
Annotation: Hattie McDaniel plays a maid/servant role.

POUND
Nar/Cast: Carl Lee* + Joe Madden
Screenplay: Robert Downey
Producer: Floyd Peterson   Director: Robert Downey

Studio/Company: United Artists
Tech Info: 16 mm/sound/color/92 min.
Date/Country: 1970 + USA   Type: Feature
Distr/Arch: uas
Annotation: Carl Lee is "thief" in this allegorical tale
    about assorted canines awaiting execution at the city dog
    pound while a mass murderer, "Honky Killer" terrifies New
    York.

POWER VERSUS THE PEOPLE
Screenplay: William Greaves*
Producer: William Greaves*   Director: William Greaves*
Studio/Company: PBS
Tech Info: 16 mm/color/sound/1 reel/36 min.
Date/Country: 1970 + USA   Type: TV Documentary
Annotation: A filmed record of the hearings conducted by the
    Equal Employment Opportunity Commission in Houson, Texas.

PRACTICAL JOKERS
Series: Our Gang
Nar/Cast: Our Gang + Billie Thomas*
Screenplay: Hal Law + Robert A. McGowan
Producer: Jack Chertok   Director: George Sidney
Studio/Company: MGM
Tech Info: bw/sound/1 reel
Date/Country: 1938 + USA   Type: Comedy Short
Annotation: Tired of Butch's practical jokers, the gang
    plants a firecracker on Butch's birthday cake. But the
    joke backfires when the cake blows up in Alfalfa's face.
    Billie Thomas stars as Buckwheat.

PRAIRIE COMES TO HARLEM
Studio/Company: Toddy Pictures
Tech Info: sound/bw/61 min.
Date/Country: 194- + USA
Annotation: A sequel to Harlem on the Prairie.

PRELUDE TO REVOLUTION
Producer: John Evans + Stephen Lighthill + Jerry Stoll
Tech Info: 16 mm/sound/color/36 min.
Date/Country: 1967 + USA   Type: Documentary
Distr/Arch: imp
Annotation: Heuey Newton* gives his views of the Black
    Panther Party and its role in the movement for black
    liberation.

PRESIDENT'S ANALYST, THE
Nar/Cast: Godfrey Cambridge* + James Coburn
Screenplay: Theodore J. Flicker
Producer: Stanley Rubin   Director: Theodore J. Flicker
Studio/Company: Paramount
Tech Info: 16 mm/sound/color/103 min.
Date/Country: 1967   Type: Feature
Distr/Arch: rbc
Annotation: A take-off on governmental security, automation,
    and international intrigue involving U.S. and foreign
    agents. Cambridge is Don Masters, one of the analyst's
    (Coburn) patients, along with the President of the U.S.

PRESSURE POINT
Nar/Cast: Sidney Poitier* + Bobby Darin + Carl Benton Reid +
    Peter Falk
Screenplay: Herbert Carfield + S. Lee Pogostin   Story:
    Robert Lidner
Producer: Stanley Kramer   Director: Hubert Cornfield + S.
    Lee Pogostin
Studio/Company: United Artists
Tech Info: 16 mm/bw/sound/3 reels/89 min.
Date/Country: 1962 + USA   Type: Feature
Distr/Arch: uas
Annotation: Poitier plays a psychiatrist who attempts to
    rehabilitate Nazi patient (Darin), an inmate at a federal
    prison during World War II.

PRESTIGE
Nar/Cast: Adolphe Menjou + Melvyn Douglas + Ann Harding +
    Clarence Muse*   Story: Harry Harvey   Director: Tay
    Garnett
Studio/Company: RKO Radio
Date/Country: 1932 + USA   Type: Feature
Annotation: Melodramatic story of life in a small French
    penal colony in the backwaters of Indochina. Muse is the
    faithful friend and servant of Douglas who plays a French
    officer often in his cups.

PRIDE OF THE BLUE GRASS
Nar/Cast: Sam McDaniel* + Edith Fellows   Director: William
    McGann
Studio/Company: Warners
Tech Info: 16 mm/sound/bw/65 min.
Date/Country: 1937 + USA   Type: Feature
Annotation: Sam McDaniel plays a fast talking groom in this
    horseracing tale.

PRINCE OF HIS RACE, A
Nar/Cast: Shingzie Howard* + Harry Henderson* + Lawrence
    Chenault* + William Clayton* + Ethel Smith* + William
    Smith*   Director: Roy Calnek
Studio/Company: Colored Players Film Corporation
Date/Country: 1926 + USA
Annotation: Henderson is Tom Beuford, the wronged hero, in
    this melodrama about a young man whose false friend is
    instrumental in sending him to prison and who also tries
    to appropriate the woman Beuford loves.

PRINCESS TAM TAM
Nar/Cast: Josephine Baker*

PRISON BAIT
Alt Title(s): see Reform School

PRISON
Producer: NET
Tech Info: 16 mm/sound/bw/2 reels/59 min.
Date/Country: 1971 + USA   Type: Documentary
Distr/Arch: iu

Annotation: Visits Bucks County Prison in Doylestown, Pa.
and provides interviews with prisoners who complain of
racism, prejudice, a lack of respect for human dignity,
and the prevalence of homosexual activity. Suggests that
separating most prisoners from society only makes them
more bitter and provides many with refined illegal trades.

PRISONER OF SHARK ISLAND, THE
Nar/Cast: Warner Baxter + Gloria Stuart + Arthur Byron +
Harry Carey + John Carradine + Ernest Whitman* + Hattie
McDaniel*
Screenplay: Nunnally Johnson
Producer: Darryl F. Zanuck   Director: John Ford
Studio/Company: Twentieth Century Fox
Tech Info: 16 mm/bw/sound/3 reels/95 min.
Date/Country: 1936 + USA   Type: Feature
Annotation: Based on the actual story of the imprisonment of
Dr. Mudd, the southern physician, who unwittingly at-
tended the wounds of John Wilkes Booth, the assassin of
Abraham Lincoln.   During his imprisonment he faces down
rioting black troops in intrepid "Southern style" Ernest
Whitmann plays Buck, faithful servant type who joins the
army and follows Mudd to Florida.

PROFESSIONALS, THE
Alt Title(s): A Mule for the Marquesa
Nar/Cast: Burt Lancaster + Lee Marvin + Woody Strode* +
Claudia Cardinale
Screenplay: Richard Brooks   Story: Frank O'Rourke
Producer: Pax Enterprises   Director: Richard Brooks
Studio/Company: Columbia Pictures
Tech Info: 16 mm/sound/color/117 min.
Date/Country: 1966 + USA   Type: Feature
Distr/Arch: arg + buc + bud + ccc + con + cwf + ics + ker +
mac + mod + mot + roa + sel + swa + tfc + twy + unf + wcf
+ who + wil
Annotation: Four professional fighters are hired by a rich
American to go into Mexico to bring back his kidnapped
wife.   Woody Strode is one of the gun-toting mercenaries.

PROFESSOR CREEPS
Nar/Cast: Mantan Moreland* + Flourney E. Miller* + Arthur
Ray* + Zack Williams* + John Lester Johnson* + Florence
O'Brien* + Margaretta Whitten* + Billy Mitchell*
Studio/Company: Dixie National Pictures
Tech Info: sound/bw/63 min.
Date/Country: 1961 + USA   Type: Feature
Annotation: Jefferson (Miller) and Washington (Moreland)
operate a not too successful detective agency.   While Jef-
ferson is trying to raise money, Washington day dreams a
series of comically horrifying experiences.

PROGRAM OF SONGS BY "LIGHTNIN'" SAM HOPKINS, A
Producer: University of Washington Archives of Ethnic Music/
Dance
Tech Info: 16 mm/sound/bw/8 min.
Date/Country: 1971 + USA   Type: Documentary
Distr/Arch: uwap

Annotation: Informal performance of Lightnin' Hopkins of
  three numbes including "Baby, Please Don't Go."

PROTEST: BLACK POWER
Producer: Reaction Films
Tech Info: 16 mm/sound/color/1 reel/15 min.
Date/Country: 1969 + USA   Type: Documentary
Distr/Arch: iu
Annotation: Utilizes excerpts from speeches and interviews
  of many leading black activists to exemplify the various
  components of 'Black Power.' Ranges from discussion of
  black separation and violence to non-violent intergration.
  Interviews Adam Clayton Powell*, Stokely Carmichael*,
  Muhammad Ali*, Floyd McKissick*, Malcolm X*, Martin Luther
  King, Jr.*, Whitney Young*, H. Rap Brown*, Dick Gregory*,
  Eldridge Cleaver*.

PROUD VALLEY, THE
Alt Title(s): The Tunnel
Nar/Cast: Paul Robeson* + Edward Chapman + Simon Lach +
  Rachel Thomas + Edward Rigby + Janet Johnson
Screenplay: Jack Jones + Louis Golding + Roland Pertwee
  Story: Herbert Marshall + Fredda Brilliant
Producer: Sir Michael Bacon   Director: Pen Tennyson
Studio/Company: Ealing
Tech Info: 16 mm/bw/sound/2 reels/77 min.
Date/Country: 1940 + Britain   Type: Feature
Distr/Arch: jan + moma
Annotation: David Goliath (Paul Robeson), a black stoker,
  finds work in the coal mines in the Blaendy district of
  Wales. When the mines are closed because of an explosion,
  the entire village is thrown out of work. They do not
  reopen again until a successful march of 200 miles, led by
  Goliath, catches the attention of the mine owners in
  London. Opportunities are created to present the powerful
  singing voice of Paul Robeson.

PSYCH-OUT
Nar/Cast: Max Julien* + Susan Strasberg + Jack Nicholson
Screenplay: Betty Tasher + Betty Glius
Producer: Dick Clark   Director: Richard Rush
Studio/Company: American International
Tech Info: 16 mm/sound/color/101 min.
Date/Country: 1968 + USA   Type: Feature
Distr/Arch: mod + upa
Annotation: Max Julien plays Edward who, although high on
  pot, manages to save Jennie (Strasberg) a deaf teenage
  runaway--to Haight/Asbury -- from a gang rape.

PUBLIC HERO NUMBER ONE
Nar/Cast: Chester Morris + Lionel Barrymore + Jean Arthur +
  Joseph Calleia + Lewis Stone + Paul Kelly + Sam Baker*
Screenplay: Wells Root
Producer: Lucien Hubbard   Director: J. Walter Ruben
Studio/Company: MGM
Date/Country: 1935 + USA   Type: Feature
Annotation: Romanticized gangster melodrama loosely-based on
  John Dillinger's last days. Sam Baker plays "Mose."

PULLMAN PORTER, THE
Nar/Cast: Lottie Grady* + Jerry Mills*
Studio/Company: Foster Photoplay Company
Date/Country: 1910 + USA

PUPS IS PUPS
Series: Our Gang
Nar/Cast: Our Gang + Allen Hoskins*
Screenplay: Robert F. McGowan
Producer: Robert F. McGowan + Hal Roach   Director: Robert
  F. McGowan
Studio/Company: MGM Roach
Tech Info: super 8 mm/16 mm/bw/sound/1 reel/20 min.
Date/Country: 1930 + USA   Type: Comedy Short
Distr/Arch: roa + bla
Annotation: Farina gets a job as a page in a pet show (Jack
  wants to apply, but Chubby explains the ad is for 'colored
  boys...to act as pages' with, 'They want boys like
  Farina.') When the gang decides to sneak their animals
  inside, they cause havoc and get Farina fired, so all
  return to the clubhouse.

PUTNEY SWOPE
Nar/Cast: Arnold Johnson* + Laura Greene* + Antonio Fargas*
  + Mel Brooks
Screenplay: Robert Downey
Producer: Ron Sullivan   Director: Robert Downey
Studio/Company: Cinema V
Tech Info: 16 mm/bw/color/sound/84 min.
Date/Country: 1969 + USA   Type: Feature
Distr/Arch: civ
Annotation: Story of what happens when Blacks take over a
  Madison Avenue ad firm. Arnold Johnson is Putney Swope.

PYGMIES OF AFRICA
Producer: Encyclopedia Britannica Films + H.C. Haven
Tech Info: 16 mm/sound/bw/1 reel/20 min.
Date/Country: 1938 + Central Africa   Type: Documentary
Distr/Arch: kent + iowa + umnav + ebec + psu + uill + ueuwis
  + iu + msu + ucemc + fsu + suf + mp + wasu + bu + byu
Annotation: This film shows the pygmies' unending search for
  food, stalking techniques used, various handicrafts and
  sacrificial ceremonies.

QUEEN BEE
Nar/Cast: Joan Crawford + Barry Sullivan + Bill Walker* +
  Willa Pearl Curtis* + Betsy Palmer + Fay Wray
Screenplay: Ronald McDougall
Producer: Jerry Wald   Director: Ronald McDougall
Studio/Company: Columbia
Date/Country: 1955 + USA   Type: Feature
Annotation: Joan Crawford plays a bitter, hard drinking wife
  of a Southern mill owner whose ruthless behavior and
  poisonous tongue wreaks havoc on everyone she knows. Bit
  roles are played by Bill Walker as Sam, and Willa Pearl
  Curtis as Miss George.

QUEEN FOR A DAY
Annotation: The black maid of a missionary and his daughter
   saves their lives by taking over the Zulu throne and
   helping them escape.

QUEEN OF APOLLO
Producer: Richard Leacock
Tech Info: 16 mm/color/12 min.
Date/Country: 1970 + USA   Type: Documentary
Distr/Arch: pen
Annotation: The Mardi Gras ball on debutante night: with the
   1970 debutante queen.   Provided by Center for Southern
   Folklore.

QUEEN OF THE BOOGIE
Nar/Cast: Hadda Brooks*
Studio/Company: All American Pictures
Tech Info: 35 mm/sound/bw/1 reel
Date/Country: 1947 + USA   Type: Musical Short
Distr/Arch: lc
Annotation: Hadda Brooks is at the piano in this musical
   short.

QUEMAD" QUEIMADA
Alt Title(s): see Burn!

QUICK, BEFORE IT MELTS
Nar/Cast: Davis Roberts* + Robert Morse + George Maharis
Producer: Douglas Laurence   Director: Delbert Mann
Studio/Company: MGM
Tech Info: 16 mm/sound/color/98 min.
Date/Country: 1965 + USA   Type: Feature
Distr/Arch: fnc
Annotation: Roberts is one of the military men in this
   comedy about a magazine reporter assigned to cover a naval
   expedition to the Antarctic.

QUIET ONE, THE
Nar/Cast: Gary Merrill + Estelle Evans* + Sadie Stockton* +
   Donald Thompson* + Clarence Cooper + Paul Bawam + Staff of
   the Wiltwyck School
Screenplay: James Agee + Helen Levitt + Sidney Meyers +
   Janet Loeb
Producer: Sidney Meyers + Janet Loeb   Director: Sidney Mey-
   ers
Studio/Company: Independent
Tech Info: 16 mm/bw/sound/2 reels/67 min.
Date/Country: 1958 + USA   Type: Dramatized Documentary
Distr/Arch: mac + cal + con + ill + imp + kpf + mac + mmm +
   mog + rca
Annotation: A documentary-drama that tells the story of a
   Harlem youth who grows up feeling rejected and withdrawn,
   eventually drifting into delinquency.   At the Wiltwyck
   School for Boys, he becomes a "quiet one," building a wall
   of silence around himself to hide the bitterness.   The
   film won awards at the Venice and Edinburgh Film
   Festivals.

QUIET_STREET,_A
Series: Our Gang
Nar/Cast: Our Gang + Ernie Morrison* + Ernie Morrison, Sr.*
Screenplay: Hal Roach
Producer: Hal Roach   Director: Robert McGowan + Tom Mc-
   Namera
Studio/Company: Pathe
Tech Info: silent/bw/2 reels
Date/Country: 1922 + USA   Type: Comedy Short
Annotation: While administering a beating to the new kid on
   the block, the gang gets interupted by the police. In
   their attempts to elude the police, they capture the
   criminal the police are really looking for. Ernie Mor-
   rison stars as Sunshine Sammy.

RACING_LADY
Nar/Cast: Willie Best*
Date/Country: 1937 + USA   Type: Feature
Annotation: Willie Best has a bit part in this race track
   film.

RACKET_DOCTOR
Alt Title(s): see Am I Guilty?

RADIO_BUGS
Series: Our Gang
Nar/Cast: Our Gang + Billie Thomas*
Screenplay: Hal Law + Robert A. McGowan
Producer: MGM   Director: Cyril Endfield
Studio/Company: MGM
Tech Info: bw/sound/1 reel
Date/Country: 1944 + USA   Type: Comedy Short
Annotation: The gang tries comedy and Shakespeare but can't
   get a sponsor to help them break into radio.   Billie
   Thomas stars as Buckwheat.

RAFER_JOHNSON_STORY,_THE
Producer: Sterling
Tech Info: 16 mm/sound/bw/55 min.
Date/Country: 1961 + USA   Type: Documentary
Distr/Arch: sef
Annotation: The story of Rafer Johnson, famous black ath-
   lete.

RAID_ON_ENTEBBE
Nar/Cast: Yaphet Kotto* + Martin Balsam + Peter Finch +
   Charles Bronson + Horst Bucholz + Sylvia Sidney + Dora
   Bloch
Producer: NBC
Tech Info: 120 min.
Date/Country: 1976 + USA   Type: TV Feature
Annotation: Air Force flight from Tel Aviv to Paris with
   stop at Athens is highjacked by PLO terrorists (2 men, 1
   woman) and rerouted to Entebbe. Yaphet Kotto plays Idi
   Amin. Operation "Thunderbolt" planned and executed by the
   Israelis frees the hostages.

RAILROAD_PORTER,_THE

Nar/Cast: Lettie Grady* + Jerry Mills*
Producer: William Foster*
Studio/Company: Foster Photoplay Company
Date/Country: 1912 + USA   Type: Comedy Short
Annotation: Perhaps the first black movie, The Railroad
    Porter is a comedy in the keystone cop genre.

RAILROADIN'
Series: Our Gang
Nar/Cast: Our Gang + Allan Hoskins*
Screenplay: Robert F. McGowan
Producer: Robert F. McGowan + Hal Roach   Director: Robert
    F. McGowan
Studio/Company: MGM
Tech Info: super 8 mm/16 mm/bw/sound on disc/1 reel/16 min.
Date/Country: 1929 + USA   Type: Comedy Short
Distr/Arch: bla
Annotation: The central action involves the gang at the con-
    trols of a runaway train which after much adventure they
    manage to bring to a halt. At the end of the film all is
    revealed to have been Farina's dream.   Farina (Allen
    Hoskins) plays a central role; he is seen praying for
    deliverance, being repeatedly 'run-over' by the engine and
    twice hit in the face by an egg.

RAIN OR SHINE
Nar/Cast: Joe Cook + Joan Peers + Clarence Muse*   Director:
    Frank Capra
Tech Info: sound/bw
Date/Country: 1930 + USA   Type: Feature
Annotation: A Broadway musical comedy adapted for new sound
    films (sans the music) is a humorous circus yarn with
    Clarence Muse in a bit role.

RAINBOW BLACK: POET SARAH W. FABIO
Producer: Cheryl Fabio*   Director: Cheryl Fabio*
Tech Info: 16 mm/sound/color/1 reel/31 min.
Date/Country: 1975 + USA   Type: Documentary
Distr/Arch: ucemc
Annotation: A portrait of poet Sarah Fabio whose work is a
    study of the black female experience. She reads,
    lectures, and is interviewed. She discusses the use of
    color imagery and jazz impulse as the rudimentary tools of
    her expression.

RAINBOW ON THE RIVER
Nar/Cast: Louise Beavers* + Bobby Breen + Clarence Muse* +
    May Robson + Lillian Yarbo* + Matthew Beard* + Hall John-
    son Choir* + Matthew Beard*
Screenplay: Earl Snell + Will Hurlbert
Producer: Sol Lesser   Director: Kurt Newmann
Studio/Company: RKO
Date/Country: 1936 + USA   Type: Feature
Distr/Arch: roa
Annotation: Story of a Mammy (Beavers) who fights for
    custody of the orphaned white boy, Phillip (Breen), she
    cared for throughout the Civil War.   Beavers' Mammy is
    called Toinette; Lillian Yarbo is Seline; Matthew (Stymie)

Beard is "Lilybell"; the Hall Johnson choir contributes
the songs along with precocious Phillip.

RAINBOW RANGERS
Nar/Cast: Martin Turner* + Pete Morrison + Peggy Montgomery
Screenplay: Forrest Sheldon   Director: Forrest Sheldon
Studio/Company: William Steiner Productions
Tech Info: 35 mm/silent/bw/5 reels/4,982 ft.
Date/Country: 1924 + USA   Type: Feature
Annotation: Martin Turner plays Barbecue Sam, the cook, in
    this "Western comedy melodrama" with Pete Morrison as
    Buck. They, along with other "comic rangers," rescue Rose
    Warner (Peggy Montgomery) and her father from desperadoes.
    Buck does, in addition, get the girl.

RAINTREE COUNTY
Nar/Cast: Montgomery Clift + Elizabeth Taylor
Screenplay: Millard Kaufman   Story: Ross Lockridge
Producer: David Lewis   Director: Edward Dmytryk
Studio/Company: MGM
Tech Info: 16 mm/sound/color/97 min.
Date/Country: 1957 + USA   Type: Feature
Distr/Arch: fnc
Annotation: Fashioned from Ross Lockridge's novel about a
    young man (Clift) who wants to find the raintree--mythical
    source of life--this film stars Elizabeth Taylor as a
    Southern belle who goes slowly insane because she thinks
    she may be part black. First she is taken to a mental
    institution and later she is found dead, under the
    raintree.

RAINY DAYS
Series: Our Gang
Nar/Cast: Our Gang + Allen Hoskins*
Screenplay: Robert F. McGowan
Producer: Robert F. McGowan + Hal Roach   Director: Anthony
    Mack
Studio/Company: MGM
Tech Info: super 8 mm/bw/silent/2 reels
Date/Country: 1928 + USA   Type: Comedy Short
Distr/Arch: bla
Annotation: Jay is left to babysit Wheezer and Jean on a
    rainy day. The two kids manage to chalk up the walls and
    Jay is forced to call on the gang to help repair the
    damage. Their solution is to wallpaper the entire house,
    which job provides most of the comedy. Allen Hoskins
    stars as Farina.

RAISIN IN THE SUN, A
Nar/Cast: Sidney Poitier* + Claudia McNeil* + Ruby Dee* +
    Diana Sands* + Ivan Dixon* + John Fiedler + Joel Fluellen*
    + Roy Glenn* + Louis Gossett*
Screenplay: Lorraine Hansberry*   Story: Lorraine Hansberry*
Producer: David Susskind + Phillip Rose   Director: Daniel
    Petrie
Studio/Company: Columbia + 16 + 16 mm/bw/sound/3 reels/128
    min. + 17 + 1961 + USA   Type: Feature
Distr/Arch: bud + arg + ccc + cha + cwf + imp + mac + mod +

mot + new + roa + sel + swa + twy + wcf + wel + who +   wil
Annotation: This adaptation of the late Lorraine Hansberry's
   award-winning play treats the ambitions, dreams and
   frustrations of a black family living in three crowded
   rooms on Chicago's South Side.   The squalid routine of
   their lives is suddenly disrupted when Lena (Claudia Mc-
   Neil) receives a $10,000 check from the company that in-
   sured her late husband.

RALPH ELLISON, ON WORKS IN PROGRESS
Series: The Novel
Tech Info: 16 mm/sound/bw/1 reel/30 min.
Date/Country: 1966 + USA   Type: Documentary
Distr/Arch: iu
Annotation: An interview with Ralph Ellison* during which he
   discusses his philosophy as to writers, American novels,
   the unity of the American spirit, and the genesis of his
   first novel, The Invisible Man. Further insight into the
   personality of Mr. Ellison is provided by a brief synopsis
   of his life and views of the interior of his apartment.
   He discusses and reads from his work in progress.

RANK AND FILE
Series: Black Journal
Producer: NET
Tech Info: 16 mm/sound/bw/15 min.
Date/Country: 1970 + USA   Type: Documentary
Distr/Arch: iu
Annotation: In the New York local of the Transport Worker
   Union, Blacks and Puerto Ricans are fighting to form their
   own union in order to counter the discrimination they find
   in the present union. Although the TWU organizes on Tran-
   sit Authorit property, Blacks are not allowed this
   privilege, and they are threatened with arrest for attem-
   pting to claim the same rights as the white dominated TWU.

RAPPING (Rev. Jesse Jackson)
Producer: Nat King + Tom McCarthy
Studio/Company: Frith Films
Tech Info: 16 mm/bw/sound/1 reel/14 min.
Date/Country: 1969 + USA   Type: Documentary
Distr/Arch: kpf
Annotation: Reverend Jesse Jackson* talks informally about
   some of the problems facing the black community and about
   those of his own background.

RAPPING
Producer: Frith
Tech Info: 16 mm/sound/bw/14 min.
Date/Country: 1969 + USA   Type: Documentary
Distr/Arch: par + uca
Annotation: San Francisco's Mission Rebels leader tells the
   story of his life from correctional institution inmate to
   leader and counselor of young people.

RASSLIN' MATCH
Studio/Company: RKO Radio
Tech Info: 16 mm/bw/sound/1 reel/10 min.

Date/Country: 1934 + USA   Type: Animated Short
Distr/Arch: kpf
Annotation: An Amos 'n Andy animated cartoon with the
    original radio voices of Gosden and Carrell. The title
    characters are depicted in blackface with thick white
    lips.

RASTUS SERIES
Producer: Sigmund Lubin
Studio/Company: Pathe
Tech Info: bw/ 1 reel
Date/Country: 1910-11 + USA   Type: Comedy Shorts
Annotation: How Rastus Got His Turkey was the first of the
    series which included: How Rastus Got His Pork Chop,
    Rastus and Chicken, Chicken Thief, Pickaninnies and
    Watermelon, Rastus' Riotous Ride, Rastus in Zululand. The
    latter is a comic version of Biograph's The Zulu's Heart
    (1908). Rastus is a pre-Fetchit character whose antics
    are for the most part obvious from the title of the short.

READIN' AND WRITIN'
Series: Our Gang
Nar/Cast: Our Gang + Matthew Beard* + Carlena Beard*
Screenplay: H. W. Walker
Producer: Robert F. McGowan + Hal Roach   Director: Robert
    F. McGowan
Studio/Company: MGM + Roach
Tech Info: super 8 mm/16 mm/bw/sound/1 reel/21 min.
Date/Country: 1932 + USA   Type: Comedy Short
Distr/Arch: roa + bla
Annotation: Breezy hopes to get kicked out of school for
    playing pranks. He succeeds, but once freed can find no
    one to play with and nothing to do. He returns sheepishly
    to school and endures the punishment of having to read a
    sappy poem in front of the class. Matthew Beard stars as
    Stymie and Carlena Beard stars as Marmalade.

REAL SELF
Producer: NEA + Guggenheim Prod., Inc.
Tech Info: 16 mm/sound/bw/1 reel/14 min.
Date/Country: 1970 + USA   Type: Documentary
Distr/Arch: iu
Annotation: Presents, from the perspective of Blacks and
    Chicanos, some of the cultural uniqueness which they feel
    is being ignored or minimized by the white culture.
    Argues that schools and teachers need to recognize, under-
    stand, and inspire a pride of culture.

REALIZATION OF A NEGRO'S AMBITION, THE
Nar/Cast: Noble Johnson* + Clarence Brooks* + Beulah Hall* +
    Lottie Boles*
Studio/Company: Lincoln Motion Picture Company
Tech Info: silent/bw/2 reels
Date/Country: 1916 + USA   Type: Feature
Annotation: Lincoln's first film is the story of a young
    black civil engineer (graduate of Tuskegee) who goes West
    "to make his fortune" in oil. After a number of
    frustrating experiences, including racial prejudice, he

does realize his ambition much closer to home.   He
achieves success in discovering oil, acquiring independent
income and marrying the girl of his choice--all through
persistence, decency and integrity.

REAP THE WILD WIND
Nar/Cast: Ray Milland + John Wayne + Paulette Goddard +
   Louise Beavers*
Screenplay: Alan Le May + Charles Bennett   Story: Thelma
   Strabel
Producer: Cecil B. DeMille   Director: Cecil B. DeMille
Studio/Company: Paramount
Tech Info: 16 mm/sound/color
Date/Country: 1942 + USA   Type: Feature
Distr/Arch: uni
Annotation: John Wayne and Ray Milland battle each other for
   Paulette Goddard, but join forces to fight ship wreckers
   off the Florida Keys. Louise Beavers plays "Maum Maria."

REBECCA OF SUNNYBROOK FARM
Nar/Cast: Bill Robinson* + Shirley Temple + Randolph Scott +
   Jack Haley + Gloria Stuart
Screenplay: Karl Tunberg + Don Ettlinger   Story: Kate D.
   Wiggin
Producer: Raymond Griffith   Director: Allan Dwan
Studio/Company: 20th Century Fox
Tech Info: 16 mm/sound/bw/80 min.
Date/Country: 1938 + USA   Type: Feature
Distr/Arch: fnc
Annotation: Shirley Temple stars as a relative unknown
   selected to do a nationwide corn flake program against her
   aunt's wishes. Movie co-stars Bill Robinson.

RECKLESS LIVING
Nar/Cast: Louise Beavers*   Director: Frank McDonald
Date/Country: 1938 + USA   Type: Feature

RECKLESS MONEY
Nar/Cast: Sherman H. Dudley, Jr.* + John La Rue*
Producer: Sherman H. Dudley, Jr.*
Date/Country: 1926 + USA

RECKLESS SEX, THE
Date/Country: 1925 + USA   Type: Feature
Annotation: The story of an actress stranded in the South-
   west has the company playing Uncle Tom's Cabin.

RECKLESS
Nar/Cast: Jean Harlow + William Powell + Nina Mae McKinney*
   + Allen Hoskins*
Screenplay: P.J. Wolfson   Story: Oliver Jeffries
Producer: David O. Selznick   Director: Victor Fleming
Studio/Company: MGM
Tech Info: 16 mm/sound/bw/96 min.
Date/Country: 1935   Type: Feature
Distr/Arch: fnc
Annotation: Jean Harlow plays a musical comedy star who mar-
   ries a millionaire playboy. When he kills himself, the

family and public blame her and she struggles to win back her career. Nina Mae McKinney dubbed Ms. Harlow's voice in the singing scenes.

RED ACE
Nar/Cast: Noble Johnson*
Studio/Company: Universal
Annotation: A universal B movie with a bit role for Noble Johnson.

RED BALL EXPRESS
Nar/Cast: Sidney Poitier* + Jeff Chandler + Alex Nicol
Screenplay: J. Michael Hayes   Story: Marcel Klauber + Bill Grady, Jr.
Producer: Aaron Rosenberg   Director: Budd Boetticher
Studio/Company: Universal-International
Tech Info: 16 mm/sound/bw/83 min.
Date/Country: 1952 + USA   Type: Feature
Distr/Arch: cwf + uni
Annotation: In this version of the Red Ball Express, the Black Quartermaster troops are mostly white, with Sidney Poitier the notable exception. Jeff Chandler plays the lieutenant hated by his men until the end, when, with an act of bravery he wins their respect.

RED DRAGON, THE
Series: Charlie Chan
Nar/Cast: Willie Best* + Sidney Toler + Benson Fong + Bonanova
Screenplay: George Callahan   Story: Earl Derr Biggers
Producer: James S. Burkett   Director: Phil Rosen
Studio/Company: Monogram
Tech Info: 16 mm/sound/bw/2 reels/64 min.
Date/Country: 1946 + USA   Type: Feature
Annotation: This is Willie Best's only appearance in the Chan series.

RED FEATHER SPECIALS
Nar/Cast: Noble Johnson*
Studio/Company: Universal   Type: Feature
Annotation: One of Universal's specials with Noble Johnson in a small role.

RED LIGHTS
Nar/Cast: George Reed* + Marie Prevost + Alice Lake + Johnny Walker + Jean Hersholt   Director: Clarence Badger
Date/Country: 1923 + USA   Type: Feature
Annotation: George Reed plays a black porter in this mystery drama about the daughter of a railroad magnate and the strange threats on her life.

RED STALLION
Nar/Cast: Robert Paige + Noreen Nash + Willie Best*
Screenplay: Robert Kent + Wilbur Crane
Producer: Ben Stoloff   Director: Lesley Selander
Studio/Company: Eagle-Lion Films
Tech Info: 16 mm/sound/color/82 min.
Date/Country: 1947 + USA

Distr/Arch: ivy
Annotation: Tale of a boy's love for his horse, but is wil-
    ling to part with it to save his grandmother's ranch.
    Willie Best is featured as the groom.

RED_WHITE_AND_BLACK,_THE
Alt Title(s): See Soul Soldier

REET,_PETITE_AND_GONE
Nar/Cast: Louis Jordan and His Tympany Five* + June Rich-
    mond* + Lorenzo Tucker* + Milton Woods*
Screenplay: Irwin Winehouse   Story: William Forrest
Producer: Savini and Adams   Director: William Forrest Crouch
Studio/Company: Astor Productions
Tech Info: 16 mm/bw/sound/2 reels/65 min.
Date/Country: 1947 + USA   Type: Feature
Distr/Arch: bud + kpf + emg
Annotation: The search is on to find the girl whose measure-
    ments fit those prescribed in the will of the hero's un-
    cle.   Locus Jordan's orchestra and the musical talents of
    Blacks are showcased to support the thin plot.

REFORMATION
Studio/Company: Democracy Film Corporation
Date/Country: 1919 + USA

REGARD_SUR_L'AFRIQUE_NOIRE
Producer: Les Actualites Francaises + A. Mahuzier
Tech Info: 16 mm/sound/bw/1 reel/20 min.
Date/Country: 1947 + Chad   Type: Documentary
Distr/Arch: moma + fi
Annotation: The 20th century influences on French Equatorial
    African life are recorded in this film.

REGENERATION
Nar/Cast: Carey Brooks* + Stella Mayo* + Alfred Norcom* +
    Clarence Rucker* + Charles Gains* + Dr. R.L. Brown* +
    Steve Reynolds* + M.C. Maxwell*
Studio/Company: Norman Film Manufacturing Company
Tech Info: bw/silent
Date/Country: 1923 + USA   Type: Feature
Annotation: Melodrama about buried treasure, villainy,
    shipwreck and romance.   "Regeneration" is the island the
    lovers are cast upon and which "coincidentally" is where
    the treasure is buried.

REGGAE
Nar/Cast: King Kong* + Enoch Powell* + The Pyramids* + Count
    Prince Miller*   Director: Horace Ove
Studio/Company: Impact
Tech Info: 15 mm/sound/color/70 min.
Date/Country: 1970 + Britain   Type: Documentary
Distr/Arch: imp
Annotation: Documents, via the Caribbean Music Festival held
    in England in 1970, with some of the outstanding per-
    formers of Reggae, the impact of this Jamaican music on
    the English working class.   A social documentary on one
    aspect of the black experience.

REGGIE
Tech Info: 16 mm/sound/color/10 min.
Date/Country: 1971 + USA   Type: Documentary
Distr/Arch: aci
Annotation: The works of young black artist Reginald Gammon
  express his personal frustration and alienation.

REIVERS, THE
Nar/Cast: Steve McQueen + Rupert Crosse* + Sharon Farrell   +
  Will Geer + Juano Hernandez*
Screenplay: Irving Ravetch + Harriet Frank, Jr.   Story:
  William Faulkner
Producer: Irving Ravetch   Director: Mark Rydell
Studio/Company: Cinema Center Film Presentation +   National
  General
Tech Info: 16 mm/color/sound/3 reels/107 min.
Date/Country: 1969 + USA   Type: Feature
Distr/Arch: swa
Annotation: A story about turn-of-the-century South which
  focuses on the education of young men by adventures in the
  big city.   Rupert Crosse plays Ned McCaslin, a liberated
  philosopher-type; Hernandez is Uncle Possum.

REMAINS TO BE SEEN
Nar/Cast: Dorothy Dandridge* + Van Johnson + June Allyson
  Story: Howard Lindsay + Russel Crouse   Director: Don Weis
Studio/Company: MGM
Tech Info: 16 mm/sound/bw/89 min.
Date/Country: 1953 + USA   Type: Feature
Distr/Arch: fnc
Annotation: Dorothy Dandridge plays herself and sings in
  this murder mystery with Van Johnson as an apartment
  manager and June Allyson as his girlfriend.   One   other
  black actor (uncredited) appears as Ben the janitor.

REMEDY FOR RIOT
Producer: CBS
Tech Info: 16 mm/sound/bw/1 reel/36 min.
Date/Country: 1968 + USA   Type: Documentary
Distr/Arch: iu + carouf + adl
Annotation: Traces and analyzes the rise in civil disorders
  in the United States and discusses the problem of racism
  and its possible outcome. Presents the findings and re-
  commendations of the President's Advisory Commission on
  Civil Disorders, giving the "hows" and "whys" of racial
  disorders in the cities. Illustrates effective controls
  and ideas on community development activities as possible
  answers to the black and white communities.

REOUH-TAKH
Alt Title(s): Big City
Nar/Cast: Alain Christian Plennet* + N'Dack Gueye* + Medoune
  Faye* + Khady Fall* + Dodo Diop* + Diobaye*
Producer: Suner Film (Dakar)   Director: Mahama Traore*
Tech Info: 16 mm/color/sound/2 reels/60 min./French and En-
  glish with English subtitles
Date/Country: 1971 + Senegal   Type: Feature

Distr/Arch: tri
Annotation: Depicts a young Afro-American's visit to Senegal
in search of his origins and cultural identity.

REPORT OF THE NATIONAL ADVISORY COMMISSION ON CIVIL DIS-
ORDERS: A CONVERSATION BETWEEN DORE SCHARY AND FATHER THE-
ODORE HESBURGH, THE
Nar/Cast: Father Theodore Hesburgh
Screenplay: Dore Schary
Producer: Dore Schary   Director: Dore Schary
Tech Info: 16 mm/bw/sound/1 reel/29 min.
Date/Country: 1968 + USA   Type: Documentary
Distr/Arch: adl
Annotation: Dore Schary expresses the mood of concerned
America as he talks with Father Theodore Hesburgh of Notre
Dame and member of the U.S. Commission on Civil Rights.
They discuss the Advisory Commission's findings that white
attitudes create ghettoes, perpetuate inferior schooling,
and keep Blacks from competing equally for jobs.

REPRIEVE
Alt Title(s): Convicts 4

REPUBLIC OF CHAD, THE
Series: Peoples of Africa
Producer: Potter, Orchard, Petric, Inc. +   Universal Educa-
tion and Visual Arts
Tech Info: 16 mm/sound/bw/1 reel/20 min.
Date/Country: 1967 + Chad   Type: Documentary
Distr/Arch: iu + umavec + suf + ueva
Annotation: The film depicts the people of Chad working to
develop their resources, such as their cotton industry.
Emphasis is placed on the ingenuity and intelligence of
Chadians.

REPUBLIC OF NIGER
Producer: Potter
Tech Info: 16 mm/sound/bw/1 reel/20 min.
Date/Country: 1967   Type: Documentary
Distr/Arch: iu + ueva
Annotation: Introduces the way of life of the Nomad which is
governed by the climate.   Illustrates the method of
survival as it revolves around the search for and use of
water. Shows the efforts being made to modernize and in-
dustrialize their land.

REQUIEM FOR A SLAVE
Producer: WTTW-TV, Chicago
Tech Info: 16 mm/bw/27 min.
Date/Country: 1968 + USA   Type: Dramatic Short
Distr/Arch: ore
Annotation: Operatic dance drama in modern jazz based on the
life and death of a black slave. Provided by Center for
Southern Folklore.

RESPECTFUL PROSTITUTE, THE
Nar/Cast: Barbara Laage + Walter Bryant* + Ivan Desny
  Story: Jean Paul Sartre   Director: Marcel Pagliero +

Charles Brobant
Date/Country: 1952 + France   Type: Feature
Annotation: Barbara Laage is the prostitute who is first
molested by the worthless, liquor sodden nephew of a
Southern senator. Then he, along with his son and others,
tries to force her to testify that this same nephew who
has killed a black man (Bryant) did so to protect her from
rape. She does not however succumb to their coercive
tactics. The lynching of an innocent black man has an
effect on her decision.

RETURN_OF_FRANK_JAMES
Nar/Cast: Henry Fonda + Gene Tierney + Jackie Cooper + Mat-
thew Beard* + Ernest Whitman*
Screenplay: Sam Hellman
Producer: Darryl F. Zanuck   Director: Fritz Lang
Studio/Company: 20th Century Fox
Tech Info: 16 mm/sound/bw/92 min.
Date/Country: 1940 + USA   Type: Feature
Distr/Arch: bud + sel + unf + wcf + wil
Annotation: Henry Fonda plays Frank James out to revenge the
murder of his brother, Jesse. Whitman is "Pinky" and
Beard plays "Mose."

RETURN_OF_MANDY'S_HUSBAND
Nar/Cast: Mantan Moreland* + Flournoy E. Miller* + Johnny
Lee*
Studio/Company: Lucky Star Productions
Date/Country: 1948 + USA

RETURN_TO_PEYTON_PLACE
Nar/Cast: Hari Rhodes* + Carol Lynley + Eleanor Parker
Screenplay: Ronald Alexander
Producer: Jerry Wald   Director: Jose Ferrer
Studio/Company: Fox
Tech Info: 16 mm/sound/color/122 min.
Date/Country: 1961 + USA   Type: Feature
Distr/Arch: fnc
Annotation: Hari Rhodes is Arthur, a bit role in this sequel
to Peyton Place which has Allison MacKenzie (Lynley)
reaping what she has sown in her novel about the residents
of her home town.

REUNION_IN_RHYTHM
Series: Our Gang
Nar/Cast: Our Gang + Matthew Beard* + Billie Thomas*
Producer: Hal Roach
Studio/Company: MGM + Roach
Tech Info: super 8 mm/16 mm/bw/sound/1 reel/10 min.   Type:
Comedy Short
Distr/Arch: roa + bla
Annotation: As part of a class reunion the gang stages a
musical show. Matthew Beard stars as Stymie and Billie
Thomas stars as Buckwheat.

REUNION
Nar/Cast: Dionne Quintuplets + Jean Hersholt + Hattie Mc-
Daniel* + George Ernest

Screenplay: Sonya Levian + Sam Hellman +   Gladys Lehman
   Director: Norman Taurog
Studio/Company: 20th Century Fox
Date/Country: 1936 + USA   Type: Feature
Annotation: Story of an obstetrician and the 3000 odd people
   he brought into the world as they gather   for   a   reunion.
   Hattie McDaniel has a small role.

REVEILLE_WITH_BEVERLY
Nar/Cast: Ann Miller + Will Wright + Mills Brothers* + Duke
   Ellington* + Count Basie*
Screenplay: Howard Green + Jack Henley + Albert Duffy
Producer: Sam White   Director: Charles Barton
Studio/Company: Columbia
Tech Info: 16 mm/sound/bw/78 min.
Date/Country: 1943 + USA   Type: Feature
Distr/Arch: bud
Annotation: A series of musical numbers strung together with
   Ann Miller providing what little story line there is.

REVENGE_OF_THE_ZOMBIES
Nar/Cast: John Carradine + Gale Storm + Mantan Moreland*
   Director: Steve Sekely
Studio/Company: Monogram
Tech Info: 16 mm/sound/color/70 min.
Date/Country: 1943 + USA   Type: Feature
Distr/Arch: mog + wcf

REVENGERS, THE
Nar/Cast: Woody Strode* + William Holden + Ernest Borgnine
Screenplay: Wendell Mayes   Director: Daniel Mann
Studio/Company: National General
Tech Info: 16 mm/sound/color/107 min.
Date/Country: 1972 + USA   Type: Feature
Distr/Arch: swa
Annotation: A man seeks revenge for the death of his wife
   and children by the Indians. He is helped by 6 members of
   a chain gang.

REVOLUTIONARY, THE
Nar/Cast: Earl Cameron* + Jon Voigt
Screenplay: Hans Koningsberger
Producer: Edward Pressman   Director: Paul Williams
Studio/Company: United Artists
Tech Info: 16mm/ sound/ color/ 101 min.
Date/Country: 1970 + USA   Type: Feature
Distr/Arch: uas
Annotation: Earl Cameron is "Speaker" in this drama about a
   radical student which takes place in an unspecified
   country. It depicts him in his various developmental
   stages until he reaches the far left and is left holding a
   bomb and facing the judge whom he is supposed to assas-
   sinate.

RHAPSODY_IN_BLACK_AND_BLUE
Nar/Cast: Louis Armstrong* + Sidney Easton* + Victoria
   Spivey*   Director: Aubrey Scott
Studio/Company: Paramount

Tech Info: 16 mm/bw/sound/1 reel/10 min.
Date/Country: 1932 + USA   Type: Musical Short
Distr/Arch: kpf
Annotation: A jazz buff, Sidney Easton, finds himself in a
    fantasied Jazzylvania, where King Louis performs several
    of his big hits, on trumpet and vocally, after his ex-
    asperated wife, played by Victoria Spivey, crowns him with
    a mophandle.

RHAPSODY IN BLACK   Director: Neil McGuire
Studio/Company: Organlogue
Tech Info: 16 mm/bw/sound/1 reel/10 min.
Date/Country: 1933 + USA   Type: Dramatic Short
Distr/Arch: kpf
Annotation: A sing-a-long with Negro spirituals. A typical
    sequence shows a black man climbing a literal stairway to
    heaven with giant dice in the sky.

RHAPSODY IN BLUE
Nar/Cast: Robert Alda + Joan Leslie + Hazel Scott* + Alexis
    Smith
Screenplay: Howard Koeh + Elliot Paul   Story: Sonya Levian
Producer: Jesse H. Lasky   Director: Irving Rapper
Studio/Company: Warner Brothers
Tech Info: 16 mm/sound/bw/93 min.
Date/Country: 1945 + USA   Type: Feature
Distr/Arch: uas
Annotation: Episodic adaptation of George Gershwin's life
    that features Hazel Scott on piano.

RHODESIAN COUNTDOWN
Producer: Michael Raeburn
Tech Info: sound/bw/30 min.
Date/Country: 196- + Zimbabwe   Type: Documentary
Distr/Arch: grove
Annotation: Produced before 1969, this film records the in-
    dignities Blacks endure under the Rhodesian system of
    separation and discrimination and their developing at-
    titude of defiance against the system which results in
    acts of hostility.

RHYTHM AND BLUES REVUE
Nar/Cast: Lionel Hampton* + Count Basie* + Cab Calloway* +
    Nat "King" Cole* + Joe Turner* + Sara Vaughn* + Little
    Buck* + Delta Rhythm Boys + The Larks* + Herb Jeffries* +
    Freddy and Flo* + Martha Davis* + Amos Milburn* + Faye
    Adams* + bill Bailey* + Mantan Moreland* + Nipsy Russell*
    + Ruth Brown*
Producer: Ben Frye   Director: Joseph Kohn
Studio/Company: Studio Films, Inc.
Tech Info: 16 mm/bw/sound/2 reels/70 min.
Date/Country: 1955 + USA   Type: Feature
Distr/Arch: kpf + emg
Annotation: Filmed on stage at Harlem theatres, this variety
    musical was produced for all black audiences.

RHYTHM IN A RIFF
Nar/Cast: Billy   Ekstine*   +   Emmett   "Babe" Wallace* + Ray

Moore* + Sarah Harris* + Ann Baker* + Garfield Love* + Hortense Allen*
Studio/Company: Associated Producers of Negro Motion Pictures
Tech Info: 45 min.
Date/Country: 1947 + USA   Type: Feature

RHYTHM_OF_AFRICA
Nar/Cast: Kenneth Spencer*
Screenplay: Langston Hughes*
Producer: Jean Cocteau + Francois Villiers
Tech Info: 16 mm/sound/bw/1 reel/17 min.
Date/Country: 1947 + Chad   Type: Documentary
Distr/Arch: psu + umnav + radim + iuasp + fsu + mab + iuasp + ccunesco
Annotation: This film shows the people of Chad working at various jobs and at the market. Also shows village life and a ceremonial dance of atonement.

RHYTHM_OF_THE_ISLANDS
Nar/Cast: Step Brothers* + Lester Horton Dancers*
Studio/Company: Universal
Date/Country: 1943 + USA   Type: Feature

RHYTHM_ON_THE_RUN
Nar/Cast: Lucky Millinder* + Edna Mae Harris*
Date/Country: 1942 + USA

RHYTHM_PARADE
Nar/Cast: Ted Fiorito and His Orchestra + The Mills Brothers*   Director: Howard Bretherton
Studio/Company: Monogram
Tech Info: 70 min.
Date/Country: 1942 + USA
Annotation: Musical revue including performances by the Mills Brothers.

RHYTHM_RODEO
Nar/Cast: Troy Brown* + Jackson Brothers* + Rosalie Lincoln* + Jim Davis*
Screenplay: George Randol*   Director: George Randol*
Tech Info: 16 mm/bw/sound/1 reel/20 min.
Date/Country: 1938 + USA   Type: Musical Short
Distr/Arch: kpf
Annotation: A musical western, produced for all black theatres, employs an all black cast.

RHYTHMETRON:___THE__DANCE__THEATRE__OF__HARLEM__WITH__ARTHUR MITCHELL
Producer: Milton Fruchtman
Tech Info: 16 mm/sound/color/40 min.
Date/Country: 1973 + USA   Type: Documentary
Distr/Arch: mgh
Annotation: Arthur Mitchell* discusses the dance styles and the exercises of the dancers.

RHYTHMS_FROM_AFRICA
Series: Ripples

Producer: National Instructional Television
Tech Info: 16 mm/color/15 min. (also available on videotape)
Date/Country: 1971 + USA   Type: Documentary
Distr/Arch: ait
Annotation: Depicts Americans of African descent actively in
    search of their historical past. Provided by Center for
    Southern Folklore.

RIDE'EM COWBOY
Nar/Cast: Abbott and Costello + Dick Foran + Anne Gwynne +
    Ella Fitzgerald*
Screenplay: True Boardman + John Grant   Director: Arthur
    Lubin
Studio/Company: Universal Pictures
Tech Info: 85 min.
Date/Country: 1941 + USA   Type: Feature
Annotation: An Abbott and Costello dude ranch burlesque with
    Ella Fitzgerald as Ruby, and a performance by a group of
    black jitterbug dancers.

RIDER ON A DEAD HORSE
Nar/Cast: Charles Lampkin* + John Vivijan + Bruce Gordon
Screenplay: Stephen Longstreet
Producer: Kenneth Altose   Director: Herbert Strock
Studio/Company: Allied Artists
Tech Info: sound/ bw/ 72 min.
Date/Country: 1962 + USA   Type: Feature
Annotation: Lampkin is Taylor, one of a triumvirate of gold
    prospectors, but he is the first to be expendable. Senn
    (Gordon) guns him down after they have buried the gold to
    keep it safe from the bellicose Apaches. In the rest of
    the film, Senn and Hayden (Vivijan) fight it out for pos-
    session of the gold.

RIDERS OF THE WHISTLING SKULL
Nar/Cast: Robert Livingston   Director: Mack V. Wright
Studio/Company: Republic
Tech Info: 16 mm/sound/bw/54 min.
Date/Country: 1937 + USA   Type: Feature
Distr/Arch: ivy

RIDING HIGH
Nar/Cast: Clarence Muse* + Bing Crosby + Coleen Gray
Screenplay: Robert Riskin   Story: Mark Hellinger
Producer: Frank Capra   Director: Frank Capra
Studio/Company: Paramount
Date/Country: 1950 + USA   Type: Feature
Annotation: Bing Crosby stars in a remake of Broadway Bill
    about a happy-go-lucky horse trainer and his groom
    pursuing their fortunes with their one-horse stable.
    Clarence Muse plays Crosby's groom.

RIGHT CROSS
Nar/Cast: June Allyson + Dick Powell + Ricardo Montalban +
    Robert "Smoke" Whitfield*
Screenplay: Charles Schnee
Producer: John Sturges   Director: Armand Deutsch
Studio/Company: MGM

Tech Info: 16 mm/sound/bw/90 min.
Date/Country: 1950 + USA   Type: Feature
Distr/Arch: fnc
Annotation: Ricardo Montalban as a Chicano boxing champion
   who feels people put up with him only because he's cham-
   pion. Whitfield plays small role.

RIGHT_ON
Nar/Cast: Last Poets* + Gylan Kain* + Felipe Luciano* +
   David Nelson*
Producer: Woodie King*   Director: Herb Danska*
Studio/Company: Concept East Ltd.
Tech Info: 16 mm/color/sound/3 reels/85 min.
Date/Country: 1971 + USA   Type: Feature
Distr/Arch: nlc
Annotation: A serious film about black revolution in Ameri-
   ca, Right_On was seen at the Cannes Film Festival, the Pan
   American, Carthage and San Francisco Film Festivals. The
   Last Poets perform their poetry from the rooftops of New
   York.

RIGHT_TO_BE_DIFFERENT:_CULTURE_CLASHES
Producer: ABC
Tech Info: 16 mm/color/29 min.
Date/Country: 1972 + USA   Type: Documentary
Distr/Arch: xex
Annotation: Explores groups of people in the U.S., set apart
   from the larger society by their way of life, language or
   color. Provided by Center for Southern Folklore.

RIO_CONCHOS
Nar/Cast: Jim Brown* + Richard Boone + Stuart Whitman
Screenplay: Joseph Landon
Producer: David Weisbart   Director: Gordon Douglas
Studio/Company: 20th Century Fox
Tech Info: 16mm/ color/ sound/ 3 reels/ 107 min.
Date/Country: 1964 + USA   Type: Feature
Distr/Arch: fnc
Annotation: Brown plays U.S. Cavalry Sergeant Ben Franklyn,
   one of four men to recover rifles stolen from a U.S.
   Cavalry command. Franklyn and Lassitec (Boone) sacrifice
   their lives to destroy the Apache camp and keep the
   Apaches from using the guns.

RIOT
Nar/Cast: Jim Brown* + Gene Hackman + Ben Carruthers* + Bill
   Walker
Screenplay: James Poe
Producer: William Castle   Director: Buzz Kulik
Studio/Company: Paramount
Tech Info: 16 mm/color/sound/3 reels/97 min.
Date/Country: 1968 + USA   Type: Feature
Distr/Arch: rbc
Annotation: While going through a period of politicization a
   group of prison inmates organizes an escape. Cully (Jim
   Brown) emerges as leader of the group. Filmed on location
   at the Arizona State Prison.

RIVER NIGER, THE
Nar/Cast: Cicely Tyson* + James Earl Jones* + Lou Gossett* +
    Ralph Wilcox* + Glynn Turman* + Shirley Jo Finney*
    Story: Joseph A. Walker*   Director: Krishna Shah*
Studio/Company: Cine Arts + Columbia
Tech Info: 16 mm/color/sound/3 reels/105 min.
Date/Country: 1976 + USA   Type: Feature
Distr/Arch: swa
Annotation: The River Niger is a realistic yet poetic
    portrayal of survival in the ghetto of Watts, Los Angeles.

ROAD DEMON
Nar/Cast: Bill Robinson*
Date/Country: 1938 + USA   Type: Feature
Annotation: Bill Robinson has a small role in this, one of
    the four films he made in 1938.

ROAD TO MANDALAY
Nar/Cast: Clarence Muse* + Sam Baker* + Lon Chaney + Lois
    Moran
Screenplay: Elliott Clauson   Story: Tod Browning + Herman
    Mankiewicz   Director: Tod Browning
Studio/Company: MGM
Tech Info: bw/silent
Date/Country: 1926 + USA   Type: Feature
Annotation: A melodrama set in Singapore with Lon Chaney as
    "One-Eyed Joe," father of the heroine (Moran).   Muse and
    Baker have bit roles diversifying the Singapore scene.

ROAD TO ZANZIBAR   Director: Victor Schertzinger
Tech Info: 92 min.
Date/Country: 1945 + USA   Type: Feature
Annotation: Comedy vehicle for Hope, Crosby and Lamour set
    in Paramount's idea of the African interior.

ROAMIN' HOLIDAY
Series: Our Gang
Nar/Cast: Our Gang + Billie Thomas*
Producer: Hal Roach   Director: Gordon Douglas
Studio/Company: MGM
Tech Info: super 8 mm/16 mm/bw/sound/1 reel/11 min.
Date/Country: 1937 + USA   Type: Comedy Short
Distr/Arch: bla
Annotation: Spanky, Alfalfa, Porky and Buckwheat run away
    from home until taught a lesson by adults, and finally
    chased by bees, they hurry back home.   Billie Thomas stars
    as Buckwheat.

ROBERTA FLACK
Series: Artists in America
Producer: Film Fair Communications
Tech Info: 16 mm/sound/color/1 reel/11 min.
Date/Country: 1971 + USA   Type: Documentary
Distr/Arch: iu + pyr
Annotation: Provides a close look at the works and creative
    philosophy of black singer and pianist Roberta Flack.
    Shows Miss Flack and her husband, bassist Steve Novosel,
    discussing the problems of a mixed marriage and dual

careers.   Includes her singing appearances at the Newport
Jazz Festival and at Mr. Henry's in Washington, D.C.

ROBIN AND THE 7 HOODS
Nar/Cast: Sammy Davis, Jr.* + Frank Sinatra + Dean Martin
Screenplay: David R. Schwartz
Producer: Frank Sinatra   Director: Gordon Douglas
Studio/Company: Warner Brothers
Tech Info: 16 mm/sound/color/4 reels/120 min.
Date/Country: 1964 + USA + 18 + Feature + 19 + roa + arg +
   bud + ccc + cha + cwf + ics + ker + mac + mud + nat + tfc
   + tmc + unf + wcf + wel +
Annotation: Tale of musical whimsey set in prohibition era
   Chicago; has a mob trying to enhance its public image by
   giving money to charities. Davis is Will, one of the
   hoods who sings.

ROBINSON CRUSOE
Nar/Cast: Noble Johnson*
Tech Info: bw/silent
Date/Country: 1922 + USA   Type: Feature
Annotation: Noble Johnson plays Friday in this silent
   version of the DeFoe novel.

ROBOT WRECKS
Series: Our Gang
Nar/Cast: Our Gang + Billie Thomas*
Screenplay: Hal Law + Robert A. McGowan
Producer: MGM   Director: Edward Cahn
Studio/Company: MGM
Tech Info: bw/sound/1 reel
Date/Country: 1941 + USA   Type: Comedy Short
Annotation: The gang decides to build a robot to help with
   their chores.   Slicker cons them into believing they've
   bought 'invisible rays' while he fits Boxcar into the
   robot suit. After the inevitable destruction of Froggy's
   lawn, his father appears and forces Slicker and Boxcar to
   set things right.   Billie Thomas stars as Buckwheat.

ROCK 'N' ROLL REVUE
Nar/Cast: Duke Ellington* + Larry Darnell + Honi Coles and
   Cholley Atkins* + The Clovers* + Dinah Washington* + Nat
   "King" Cole* + Lionel Hampton* + Conrad "Little Buck"
   Buckner* + Delta Rhythm Boys* + Mantan Moreland* + Nipsy
   Russell* + Ruth Brown*
Producer: Ben Frye   Director: Joseph Kohn
Studio/Company: Studio Films, Inc.
Tech Info: 16 mm/tinted/sound/70 min.
Date/Country: 1955 + USA   Type: Feature
Distr/Arch: kpf
Annotation: Produced for all black theatres, this "harlem
   Variety Parade" feature was filmed at various theatres in
   Harlem.

ROCKIN' THE BLUES
Nar/Cast: Mantan Moreland* + F.E. Miller* + Connie Carroll*
   + Harpstones* + Linda Hopkins* + Wanderers* + Pearl Woods*
   + Hurricanes* + Miller Sisters* + Reese La Rue* + Marilyn

Bennett* + Elyce Roberts* + Lee Lynn* + Cuban Dancers*
Studio/Company: Fritz Pollard Associates + Austin Productions
Tech Info: 35 mm/7 reels/sound/bw
Date/Country: 195- + USA
Distr/Arch: lc

ROCKY
Nar/Cast: Sylvester Stallone + Carl Weathers* + Talia Shire
Screenplay: Sylvester Stallone
Studio/Company: United Artists
Date/Country: 1976 + USA   Type: Feature
Annotation: An unlikely fighter tools up to battle the champion played by Carl Weathers.

ROLLERBALL
Nar/Cast: James Caan + John Houseman + Moses Gunn*
   Director: Norman Jewison
Studio/Company: United Artists
Tech Info: 16 mm/sound/color/128 min
Date/Country: 1975 + USA   Type: Feature
Distr/Arch: uas
Annotation: In the 21st century, the only aggression allowed
   is a brutal game called "Rollerball" which is staged for
   the benefit of a tranquil mega society. Rollerball hero,
   Jonathan E., is the only one who can't be controlled by
   corporate society. Once he steps out of line and refuses
   to quit playing Rollerball, there are very few people to
   help him. Moses Gunn is one who tries.

ROMANCE OF HAPPY VALLEY
Nar/Cast: Porter Strong + Lillian Gish + Robert Harron
Screenplay: D. W. Griffith   Story: Mary Castelman
Producer: Paramount + Art Craft   Director: D. W. Griffith
Studio/Company: Art Craft
Tech Info: 35 mm/silent/bw/5,905 ft./6 reels
Date/Country: 1919 + USA   Type: Feature
Distr/Arch: moma
Annotation: "Blacks" are part of the shantytown atmosphere
   in this film. Porter Strong in black face plays a happy-
   go-lucky farm hand.

ROMANCE ON THE BEAT
Nar/Cast: Lord Randall* + Lionel Monagas* + Tiny Dickerson*
   + Hughie Walker* + The Four Master Keys* and Doc Rhythm* +
   Ida James* + Dotty Rhodes*   Director: Bud Pollard
Studio/Company: All American Studio
Tech Info: 16 mm/bw/sound/1 reel/30 min.
Date/Country: 1945 + USA   Type: Musical Short
Distr/Arch: kpf + lc

ROMANCE ON THE HIGH SEAS
Nar/Cast: Jack Carson + Doris Day + Avon Long*   Director:
   Michael Curtiz
Studio/Company: Warners
Tech Info: 16 mm/sound/bw/3 reels/99 min
Date/Country: 1948 + USA   Type: Feature
Distr/Arch: uas

Annotation: Black Broadway star Avon Long dances in this
    film.

ROOSEVELT CITY
Producer: NET
Tech Info: 16 mm/sound/bw/9 min.
Date/Country: 1968 + USA   Type: Documentary
Distr/Arch: iu
Annotation: Roosevelt City is about the program of self-
    determination in this newly incorporated all-black city in
    Alabama.

ROOSEVELT SYKES   Director: Buba D. Nelson
Tech Info: 30 min.
Date/Country: 1972 + USA   Type: Documentary
Annotation: An impression of the life and work of Roosevelt
    Sykes*, with piano and vocal numbers.

ROOTS OF AMERICAN MUSIC: COUNTRY AND URBAN MUSIC, PART 1
Producer: Univ. of Washington School of Music
Tech Info: 16 mm/color/40 min.
Date/Country: 1971 + USA   Type: Documentary
Distr/Arch: uwap
Annotation: Black musician Jesse Fuller, Son House, Mance
    Lipscomb, Furry Lewis, Robert Pete Williams, and John Lee
    Hooker perform. Provided by Center for Southern Folklore.

ROOTS OF AMERICAN MUSIC: COUNTRY AND URBAN MUSIC, PART 2
Producer: Univ. of Washington School of Music
Tech Info: 16 mm/color/33 min.
Date/Country: 1971 + USA   Type: Documentary
Distr/Arch: uwap
Annotation: Sonny Terry* and Brownie McGhee* (duet), Johnny
    Shines*, The Georgia Sea Island Singers* and Jesse Fuller*
    perform. Provided by Center for Southern Folklore.

ROOTS OF AMERICAN MUSIC: COUNTRY AND URBAN MUSIC, PART 3
Producer: Univ. of Washington School of Music
Tech Info: 16 mm/color/23 min.
Date/Country: 1971 + USA   Type: Documentary
Distr/Arch: uwap
Annotation: Fred McDowell* performs. Provided by Center for
    Southern Folklore.

ROOTS OF HEAVEN, THE
Nar/Cast: Errol Flynn + Orson Wells + Dan Jackson* + Habib
    Benglia* + Juliette Greco + Trevor Howard + Edric Connor*
Screenplay: Romain Gary + Pat Leigh-Fremer
Producer: Darryl F. Zanuk   Director: John Huston
Studio/Company: 20th Century Fox
Tech Info: 16 mm/sound/color/131 min.
Date/Country: 1958 + USA   Type: Feature
Distr/Arch: fnc
Annotation: Trevor Howard gathers an odd collection of human
    flotsam to aid in his crusade against the poaching of
    elephants. Connor is Spokesmn for black nationalism.

ROOTS

Nar/Cast: Cicely Tyson* + Maya Angelou* + Le Var Burton* +
   Ben Vereen* + Moses Gunn* + Thalmus Rasulala* + Madge
   Sinclair* + Leslie Uggams* + Louis Gossett, Jr.* + Georg
   Stanford Brown* + Ed Asner + Lorne Greene + Harry Rhodes*
   + Ji-Tu Cumbuka* + O.J. Simpson* + Richard Roundtree* +
   Olivia Cole* + Lynn Moody* + Lawrence-Hilton Jacobs
   Story: Alex Haley*
Producer: David Wolper   Director: Marvin Chomsky + David
   Greene + Gilbert Moses* + John Erman
Studio/Company: ABC-TV
Tech Info: 16 mm/sound/color/720 min./in 12 parts
Date/Country: 1977 + USA   Type: TV Feature
Distr/Arch: fnc
Annotation: The serialized TV extravaganza adapted from
   Haley's book of "faction" as he calls it; tracing the fam-
   ily history from Mandika antecedents in the Gambia of the
   1750's through the abduction and enslavement of his for-
   bear Kunta Kinte, down to his parents' generation demon-
   strating their heroic survival in America.

ROSEDALE: THE WAY IT WAS
Producer: NET
Tech Info: 16 mm/sound/color/2 reels/57 min.
Date/Country: 1976 + USA   Type: Documentary
Distr/Arch: iu
Annotation: Documents the racial tensions stemming from one
   incident in the Rosedale section of Queens, New York, and
   records the bitterness and hostility of white adults and
   children toward the presence of Blacks in Rosedale.

ROSIE
Nar/Cast: Rosalind Russell + Sandra Dee + James Farentino +
   Juanita Moore*
Screenplay: Samuel Taylor   Story: Phillippe Heriat
Producer: Jacques Mapes   Director: David Lowell Rich
Studio/Company: Universal
Tech Info: 16 mm/sound/color/97 min.
Date/Country: 1967 + USA + 18 + Feature + 19 + uni
Annotation: Rosalind Russell portrays a madcap widow whose
   relatives try to do away with her to get their hands on
   her money. Juanita Moore plays the nurse.

ROUSTABOUT
Nar/Cast: Joel Fluellen* + Elvis Presley + Barbara Stanwyck
Screenplay: Anthony Lawrence
Producer: Hal Wallis   Director: John Rich
Studio/Company: Paramount
Tech Info: sound/color/101 min.
Date/Country: 1964 + USA   Type: Feature
Annotation: Fluellen is Cody Marsh in this melodrama with
   music about a carnival that is saved from bankruptcy by a
   singer-guitarist (Presley), who falls in love with the
   daughter of the carnival owner (Stanwyck).

ROVER'S BIG CHANCE
Series: Our Gang
Nar/Cast: Our Gang + Billie Thomas*
Screenplay: Hal Law + Robert A. McGowan

Producer: MGM   Director: Herbert Glazer
Studio/Company: MGM
Tech Info: bw/sound/1 reel
Date/Country: 1942 + USA   Type: Comedy Short
Annotation: Rover is given a chance in pictures, but the
    screen test flops when the gang can't persuade him to bark
    on cue. Billie Thomas stars as Buckwheat.

ROXBURY EXPERIMENT, THE
Producer: Afram
Tech Info: 16 mm/sound/bw/30 min.
Date/Country: USA   Type: Documentary
Distr/Arch: afr
Annotation: Shows how Highland Park Free School in Roxbury,
    Mass. developed into a parent-controlled school.

ROYAL AMERICAN, THE
Nar/Cast: Martin Turner*
Screenplay: George W. Pyper   Director: Harry J. Brown
Studio/Company: Harry J. Brown Productions
Tech Info: 35 mm/silent/bw/5 reels/5,100 ft.
Date/Country: 1927 + USA   Type: Feature
Annotation: No information available about Martin Turner's
    role in this "adventure melodrama" of the sea.

ROYAL ROMANCE, A
Nar/Cast: Clarence Muse* + William Collier, Jr. + Pauline
    Starke   Director: Erle C.Kenton
Studio/Company: Columbia
Date/Country: 1930 + USA   Type: Feature
Annotation: Clarence Muse plays valet to William Collier, a
    writer who inherits a castle and wealth in Latvia. Once
    there, the writer falls for a countess, and in saving her
    from an evil count, has his fortune confiscated. But all
    ends happily.

RPM
Nar/Cast: Anthony Quinn + Ann-Margret + Paul Winfield*
Screenplay: Erich Segal
Producer: Stanley Kramer   Director: Stanley Kramer
Studio/Company: Columbia
Tech Info: 16 mm/sound/color/97 min.
Date/Country: 1970 + USA   Type: Feature
Distr/Arch: ccc + mod + roa + wel
Annotation: Puerto Rican sociology professor Quinn becomes
    acting college president and is faced with a coalition of
    black and white students who have taken over the ad-
    ministration building. While his feelings may be with the
    students, his responsibilities lie with his job. Winfield
    is the leader of the black students.

RUANDA ET BURUNDI
Producer: Central African Productions
Tech Info: 16 mm/sound/2 reels/50 min.
Date/Country: 1962 + Ruanda + Burundi   Type: Documentary
Distr/Arch: colsc
Annotation: Delineates the problems present with rapid
    development.

RUBY_GENTRY
Nar/Cast: Jennifer Jones + Charlton Heston + Karl Malden
Screenplay: Sylvia Richards   Story: Arthur Fitz-Richard
Producer: King Vidor   Director: King Vidor
Studio/Company: Twentieth Century Fox
Tech Info: 16 mm/sound/bw/82 min.
Date/Country: 1952 + USA   Type: Feature
Distr/Arch: mac
Annotation: Jennifer Jones is Ruby Gentry, a girl from the
   wrong side of the tracks, in this romantic drama set in
   North Carolina. Blacks are background as country club
   waiters and bartenders (uncredited).

RUFUS_GREEN_IN_HARLEM
Studio/Company: Toddy Pictures
Date/Country: 194- + USA

RUFUS_JONES_FOR_PRESIDENT
Nar/Cast: Ethel Waters* + Sammy Davis, Jr.*   Director: Roy
   Mack
Studio/Company: Warners + Vitaphone
Tech Info: 16 mm/16 min.
Date/Country: 1933   Type: Comedy Short
Distr/Arch: emg
Annotation: Burlesque on politics. A very young Sammy
   Davis, Jr. appears.

RUN_FROM_RACE,_THE
Series: Metropolis: Creator of Destroyer?
Producer: NET
Tech Info: 16 mm/bw/sound/1 reel/30 min.
Date/Country: 1964 + USA   Type: Documentary
Distr/Arch: iu
Annotation: Filmed in Philadelphia, where Blacks--a
   minister, a university professor, a real estate salesman,
   and a housewife--tell of life and problems in a Negro community. Shows a city-planner defending Philadelphia's
   redevelopment plans and the criticism of a white
   sociologist. Asks the critical questions--why do some
   stay when a neighborhood begins to integrate?...why do
   some run from the problem?

RUSHIN'_BALLET
Series: Our Gang
Nar/Cast: Our Gang + Billie Thomas*
Producer: Hal Roach   Director: Gordon Douglas
Studio/Company: MGM
Tech Info: super 8 mm/16 mm/sound/bw/1 reel/11 min.
Date/Country: 1937 + USA   Type: Comedy Short
Distr/Arch: bla
Annotation: Butch picks on the two youngsters, Porky and
   Buckwheat (Billie Thomas) breaking up their game and
   smearing their faces with tomatoes. Alfalfa and Spanky
   decide to defend the two and a running battle ensues.
   Finally, Porky and Buckwheat take their own revenge -
   again with tomatoes.

RUY BLAS
Nar/Cast: Danielle Darrcieux + Jean Marais
Screenplay: Jean Cocteau   Story: Victor Hugo
Producer: Andre Paulve + Georges Legrand   Director: Pierre
    Billon
Studio/Company: Discina International Films
Date/Country: 1948 + France   Type: Feature
Annotation: Innocuous black servants appear in this Cocteau
    adaptation about a young student, Ruy Blas (Marais) who
    becomes involved unwittingly in a plot against the queen
    of Spain (Darrieux).

SABU AND THE MAGIC RING
Nar/Cast: Sabu + William Marshall* + Daria Massey
    Director: George Blair
Studio/Company: Allied Artists
Tech Info: 16 mm/color/sound/2 reels/62 min.
Date/Country: 1957   Type: Feature
Distr/Arch: cin
Annotation: Sabu, the caliph's elephant boy, finds a ring
    which he need only rub to summon a huge genie ready to
    answer his every wish. William Marshall handles the
    magic.

SADDLE DAZE
Nar/Cast: Wild West Rodeo*

SAFARI
Nar/Cast: Earl Cameron* + Orlando Martins* + Cy Grant* +
    Victor Mature + Janet Leigh + Juma* + Lionel Ngakane*
Screenplay: Anthony Veiller
Producer: Adrian D. Worker   Director: Terrence Young
Studio/Company: Columbia
Tech Info: 16 mm/sound/color/91 min.
Date/Country: 1956   Type: Feature
Distr/Arch: bud + cha + ics + mod + new + roa
Annotation: While on safari, white hunter Victor Mature goes
    ater the Mau-Mau leader who killed his sister and son.
    Film features African actors.

SAFARI
Nar/Cast: Douglas Fairbanks, Jr. + Madeleine Carroll +
    Clinton Rosemond* + Ben Carter*
Screenplay: Delmer Daves   Story: Paul Hervey Fox
    Director: Edward H. Griffith
Studio/Company: Paramount
Tech Info: 16 mm/sound/bw/81 min.
Date/Country: 1940 + USA   Type: Feature
Distr/Arch: uni
Annotation: Love story set on an African safari just before
    the outbreak of WW2. Clinton Rosemond plays Mike.

SAFE IN HELL
Alt Title(s): The Lost Lady
Nar/Cast: Dorothy Mackaill + Clarence Muse* + Don Cook +
    Ivan Simpson + Nina Mae McKinney* + Noble Johnson*
    Story: Branch Houston   Director: William Wellman
Studio/Company: First National

Tech Info: 16 mm/sound/bw/74 min.
Date/Country: 1931 + USA   Type: Feature
Distr/Arch: uas
Annotation: A melodrama about a New Orleans hooker who kills
    an old boy friend, escapes to a Caribbean Island, is
    befriended by Leonie, a black waitress (Nina Mae McKinney)
    and eventually confesses and kills herself. Noble Johnson
    plays Bobo Bruno, the Captain's sergeant; Clarence Muse is
    Newcastle. McKinney also sings one number.

SAHARA
Nar/Cast: Humphrey Bogart + Rex Ingram* + Lloyd Bridges +
    Dan Duryea + J. Carroll Naish
Screenplay: John Howard Lawson + Zoltan Korda   Director:
    Zoltan Korda
Studio/Company: Columbia
Tech Info: 16 mm/bw/sound/3 reels/97 min.
Date/Country: 1943 + Libya   Type: Feature
Distr/Arch: mac + transw + buc + bud + cha + cwf + mod + sel
    + twy + unf + wcf + wel + who + wil
Annotation: Tale of a handful of men cut off from their
    lines in the desert forced to fend for themselves against
    the heat, thirst, sand and Nazis. Rex Ingram recieved a
    special award from the Motion Picture Committe for Unity,
    as the "most outstanding" black actor of the year for his
    portrayal of a Sudanese corporal, Tambul.

SAILOR TAKES A WIFE, THE
Nar/Cast: Robert Walker + June Allyson + Eddie Anderson*
    Story: Chester Erskine   Director: Richard Whorf
Studio/Company: MGM
Tech Info: 16 mm/sound/bw/92 min.
Date/Country: 1946 + USA   Type: Feature
Distr/Arch: fnc
Annotation: The trials of a newly married couple moving into
    an apartment where almost nothing works, and beautiful
    next door neighbor, all this before the honeymoon. Film
    was censored by Memphis Board because star Robert Walker
    tipped his hat to a Black.

SAL OF SINGAPORE
Nar/Cast: Noble Johnson* + Phyllis Haver + Alan Hale
    Director: Howard Higgins
Date/Country: 1928 + USA   Type: Feature
Annotation: A seafaring melodrama which includes several sea
    captains, Sunday and Erickson (Hale), a helpless infant,
    and a Singapore dance hall girl (Haver). Noble Johnson is
    cast in a bit role.

SALAMBO
Tech Info: 16 mm/bw/tinted sequences/silent/5 reels/75 min.
Date/Country: 1915 + Italy   Type: Feature
Distr/Arch: emg
Annotation: An Italian spectacle, in which a black man
    (uncredited) plays a major role as the sidekick of the
    hero.

SALT AND PEPPER

Nar/Cast: Peter Lawford + Sammy Davis, Jr.* + Michael Bates
   + Calvin Lockhart*
Screenplay: Michael Pertwee
Producer: Milton Ebbins   Director: Richard Donner
Studio/Company: United Artists
Tech Info: 16 mm/sound/color/3 reels/110 min.
Date/Country: 1968 + USA + Britain   Type: Feature
Annotation: Comedy-drama about the owners of a London
   gambling club caught in a plot by a madman to overthrow
   the British government. Lawford is Pepper, Davis is Salt.

SALUTE TO DUKE ELLINGTON*   Director: Will Cowan
Studio/Company: Universal-International
Tech Info: 15 min./bw
Date/Country: 1950 + USA   Type: Musical Short
Annotation: Features band performances by Duke Ellington*
   and his orchestra.

SALUTE
Nar/Cast: George O'Brian + Stepin Fetchit* + Joyce Compton +
   Frank Albertson
Screenplay: James K. McGuinness   Director: John Ford
Studio/Company: Fox
Tech Info: sound/bw
Date/Country: 1929 + USA
Annotation: Story of two brothers, one who goes to West
   Point, and the other who has just started at Annapolis and
   how they get on at school. Fetchit has a small comedy
   role.

SAM "LIGHTNIN'" HOPKINS
Producer: KUHT-TV + Public Television Library
Tech Info: 16 mm/color/sound/1 reel
Date/Country: 1971 + USA   Type: Documentary
Distr/Arch: iu
Annotation: For over fifty years "Lightnin" Hopkins has been
   singing and playing the blues in what has been termed
   "gutsy, funky, Southwestern" style. In this film he sings
   from more than ten of his songs. As he sings about
   slavery, death, rats, and loneliness, his music reflects
   his life and the lives of many black Americans.

SAM WHISKEY
Nar/Cast: Burt Reynolds + Ossie Davis* + Angie Dickinson
Screenplay: William Norton
Producer: Jules Levy + Arthur Gardner + Arnold Lavin
   Director: Arnold Laver
Studio/Company: United Artists
Tech Info: 16 mm/sound/color/96 min.
Date/Country: 1969 + USA   Type: Feature
Distr/Arch: uas
Annotation: Eccentric widow Angie Dickinson leaves Burt
   Reynolds (Sam Whiskey) to salvage $250,000 in gold from a
   sunken river boat and smuggle it back into the U.S. Mint
   in Denver, where it was stolen from. The widow wants to
   return it to clear the family name. Davis is Jedidiah
   Hooker, a blacksmith, who recasts the recovered gold into
   a bust of George Washington.

SAMBA TALI
Nar/Cast: Malick Cisse* + Madame Mane* + Christophe Colomb*
    + Isseu Niang* + Langouste* + Sala Nder*
Producer: Societe Nationale de Cinematographie   Director:
    Ben Diogaye Beye*
Tech Info: sound/color/some Wolof/French subtitles
Date/Country: 1975 + Senegal
Annotation: Episodic film of Samba, a shoeshine boy in
    Dakar, who works in the city and sends money and letters
    home to his mother in a nearby village. Shows a day in
    his life and the people with whom he meets and talks.

SAMBA   Director: August Bruckner
Studio/Company: Munchener Lichtspielkunst Emelka + Compagnie
    Coloniale du Film
Tech Info: 35 mm/bw and tint/1685 meters/silent
Date/Country: 1928 + Germany   Type: Feature
Distr/Arch: saf
Annotation: The first Negro film conceived and realized by
    French blacks; it is a faithful rendering of the life of
    Samba and Fatou made with nonprofessional actors.

SAMBIZANGA
Nar/Cast: Domingas Oliviera* + Elisa Andrade*
Screenplay: Mario de Andrade* + Maurice Pons + Sarah
    Maldoror*   Story: Luandino Viera* (novel)   Director:
    Sarah Maldorov*
Tech Info: 16 mm/sound/color/4 reels/102 min./Portugese with
    English subtitles
Date/Country: 1972 + Angola   Type: Feature
Distr/Arch: nyf
Annotation: Sambizanga portrays the Angolan struggle against
    colonial repression to gain national liberation, in the
    context of a story about a woman's search for her missing
    husband.   The film was shot on location in the Congolese
    republic of Brazzaville by Maldoror, an assistant to Gillo
    Pontecarvo on The Battle of Algiers. Sambizanga won
    Golden Palm Award, Carthage Film Festival, 1972.

SAMMY GOING SOUTH
Alt Title(s): see A Boy Ten Feet Tall

SANCTUARY
Nar/Cast: Odetta* + Lee Remick + Yves Montand
Screenplay: James Poe
Producer: Richard Zanuck   Director: Tony Richardson
Studio/Company: Fox
Tech Info: 16 mm/sound/bw/90 min.   Type: Feature
Distr/Arch: ics + mac + mod
Annotation: Adaptation of William Faulkner's Sanctuary and
    Requiem for a Nun. Odetta plays Mannigoc, Temple Drake's
    (Lee Remick) maid who smothers Temple's infant son (and
    thereby sacrifices herself) to keep Temple from ruining
    her life.

SANDERS OF THE RIVER
Nar/Cast: Paul Robeson* + Leslie Banks* + Nina Mae McKinney*

+ Robert Cochran + Robert Walker + Toto Ware*
Screenplay: Edgar Wallace + Lajos Biro + Jeffrey Dell
Producer: Alexander Korda   Director: Zoltan Korda
Studio/Company: Alexander Korda London Films
Tech Info: 16 mm/bw/sound/2 reels/88 min.
Date/Country: 1935 + Britain   Type: Feature
Distr/Arch: bud + cie + emg
Annotation: Sanders was shot in Africa and England. Robeson
    in loincloth plays Bosambo, a self-appointed leader of the
    river people who respects "Sandi," the representative of
    the English crown in this part of West Africa.   Complica-
    tions arise when a bellicose tribal chief foments bloody
    rebellion by attacking Bosambo's people, and kidnaping
    Lilongo (McKinney), Bosambo's beautiful wife. Sanders
    rescues Lilongo and re-establishes Bosambo as King.

SANDPIPER, THE
Nar/Cast: Elizabeth Taylor + Richard Burton + James Edwards*
Screenplay: Dalton Trumbo + Michael Wilson
Producer: Martin Ransoff   Director: Vincente Minnelli
Studio/Company: MGM
Tech Info: 16 mm/sound/color/116 min.
Date/Country: 1965 + USA   Type: 1 Feature
Distr/Arch: fnc
Annotation: An affair between artist Elizabeth Taylor and a
    school teacher/ clergyman set against the back of Cali-
    fornia's Big Sur coastline. Edwards is Larry Brant.

SANTA FE TRAIL
Nar/Cast: Errol Flynn + Olivia de Havilland + Raymond Massey
    + Ronald Williams + Alan Baxter + John Litel + David Bruce
    + Ward Bond + Erville Alderson
Screenplay: Robert Buckner   Director: Michael Curtiz
Studio/Company: Warners
Tech Info: 16 mm/sound/bw/110 min.
Date/Country: 1940 + USA   Type: Feature
Distr/Arch: bud + uas + cie + thu
Annotation: Massey as John Brown, and his abolitionist fol-
    lowers are depicted as wrong-headed zealots polarizing the
    country.   Brown is violently and inhumanely fanatical
    while   Stewart   (Flynn)   and   Custer   (Reagan)   are
    characterized as gentleman-adversaries.

SAPPHIRE
Nar/Cast: Nigel Patrick + Michael Craig + Paul Massie + Earl
    Cameron* + Gordon Heath* + Harry Baird* + Yvonne Mitchell
    + Robert Adams* + Bernard Miles
Producer: Michael Relph   Director: Basil Dearden
Studio/Company: J. Arthur Rank
Tech Info: 16 mm/sound/bw/92 min.
Date/Country: 1959 + Britain   Type: Feature
Distr/Arch: ast
Annotation: The so-called Notting Hill race riots in 1958
    created a racial millieuu in Britain from which a number
    of "immigrant problem" films like Sapphire were produced.
    The story is basically a mystery with the police searching
    for the murderer of a girl passing for white and the con-
    flicts their search arouses.

SARAH_VAUGHN*_AND_HERB_JEFFRIES*/KID_ORY_AND_HIS_CREOLE_JAZZ
   BAND   Director: Will Cowan
Studio/Company: Universal-International
Tech Info: 15 min.
Date/Country: 1950 + USA   Type: Musical Short
Annotation: Features songs by Sarah Vaughn

SARATOGA_TRUNK
Nar/Cast: Ingrid Bergman + Gary Cooper + Flora Robson + Jery
   Austin + Jon Warburton + Florence Bates
Screenplay: Casey Robinson   Story: Edna Ferber   Director:
   Sam Wood
Studio/Company: Warners
Date/Country: 1946 + USA   Type: Feature
Annotation: An important black role, Angelique Pluton, was
   played by white actress Flora Robson in blackface in this
   film about a money mad creole lady and a Texas gambler.

SARATOGA
Nar/Cast: Jean Harlow + Clark Gable + Hattie McDaniel*
Screenplay: Anita Loos + Robert Hopkins
Producer: Bernard H. Hyman   Director: Jack Conway
Studio/Company: MGM
Tech Info: 16 mm/sound/bw/94 min.
Date/Country: 1937 + USA   Type: Feature
Distr/Arch: fnc
Annotation: Hattie McDaniel is Rosetta, Jean Harlow's maid,
   in this race track comedy in which Harlow is pursued by
   Walter Pidgeon and Clark Gable. This was Harlow's last
   film. McDaniel also does some singing; along with ad-
   vising and protecting her mistress

SARONG_GIRL
Nar/Cast: Ann Corio + Tim Ryan + Mantan Moreland*
Screenplay: Charles R. Marion + Arthur Hoerl
Producer: Phillip N. Krasne   Director: Arthur Dreifus
Studio/Company: Monogram
Date/Country: 1943 + USA
Annotation: After the star of a burlesque show is raided by
   a bluencse, she sets out to trap the bluenose's son into
   marriage. Mantan Moreland plays Maxwell.

SARZAN   Story: Berago Diop*   Director: Momar Thiam*
Tech Info: 16 mm/35 mm/32 min./in French
Date/Country: 1963 + Senegal   Type: Dramatic Short
Annotation: A proud soldier, a "Sarzan" (pidgin for
   Sergeant), returns to his native village after a European
   tour of duty. He tries to change, to "civilize" the village, but offends the dignity of the villagers who then
   turn against him.   After he unwittingly commits a
   sacrilege against the ancestors, his family disavows him
   and he finally goes mad.

SATAN_BUG,_THE
Nar/Cast: Hari Rhodes* + George Maharis + Richard Basehart
Screenplay: James Clovell + Edward Anhalt
Producer: John Sturges   Director: John Sturges

Studio/Company: United Artists
Tech Info: 16 mm/sound/color/114 min.
Date/Country: 1965 + USA   Type: Feature
Distr/Arch: uas
Annotation: Hari Rhodes is Johnson in this science fiction
    melodrama about a special government investigator and a
    stolen, potentially lethal virus, the "Satan bug."

SATCHMO THE GREAT
Nar/Cast: Louis Armstrong*
Producer: Edward R. Murrow + Fred W. Friendly
Tech Info: 64 min.
Date/Country: 1956 + USA
Annotation: Louis Armstrong and his all star's tour of
    Africa and Europe is recorded on this footage originally
    shot for an Ed Murrow show.

SATURDAY MORNING
Series: Our Gang
Nar/Cast: Our Gang + Ernie Morrison* + Ernie Morrison, Sr.*
    + Allen Hoskins* + Aunty Jackson*
Screenplay: Hal Roach
Producer: Hal Roach   Director: Robert McGowan + Tom Mc-
    Namera
Studio/Company: Pathe
Tech Info: silent/bw/2 reels
Date/Country: 1922 + USA   Type: Comedy Short
Annotation: The gang members break from their chores to play
    pirate, which goes well until their parents find out where
    they are and what they're up to. Ernie Morrison and Ernie
    Morrison, Sr. appear, along with Allen Hoskins as Farina.

SATURDAY'S LESSON
Series: Our Gang
Nar/Cast: Our Gang + Allen Hoskins*
Screenplay: Robert F. McGowan
Producer: Robert F. McGowan + Hal Roach   Director: Robert
    McGowan
Studio/Company: MGM + Roach
Tech Info: super 8 mm/16 mm/bw/silent w/synchronized music
    track and sound effects/1 reel
Date/Country: 1929 + USA   Type: Comedy Short
Distr/Arch: bla
Annotation: The kids' Saturday dreams are interrupted by
    their mothers who want them to do chores and warn that the
    devil will get them if they don't obey. Farina's (Allen
    Hoskins) Saturday dream involves a table piled with food,
    served to him by a butler.

SAVAGE SEVEN, THE
Nar/Cast: Robert Walker + Adam Roarke + Max Julien* + Joanna
    Frank
Screenplay: Michael Fisher
Producer: Dick Clark   Director: Richard Rush
Studio/Company: American International
Tech Info: 16 mm/sound/color/97 min.
Date/Country: 1968 + USA   Type: Feature
Distr/Arch: unf

Annotation: Motorcyclists and Indians in a California desert
    town fight in this movie confrontation between these two
    subcultures. Max Julien plays Grey Wolf, one of the Indi-
    ans involved in the final battle with the motorcycle gang.

SAVAGE SISTERS
Nar/Cast: Gloria Hendry* + Cheri Caffard + Rosanna Ortiz +
    Sid Haig
Screenplay: H. Franco Moon + Harry Corner
Producer: David J. Cohen + John Ashley + Eddie Romero
    Director: Eddie Romero
Studio/Company: American International
Tech Info: 16 mm/sound/color/89 min.
Date/Country: 1974 + USA   Type: Feature
Distr/Arch: swa
Annotation: Three adventurous young women get together in an
    effort to rid an island of its ruthless dictator and re-
    cover a million dollars. Gloria Hendry plays Lynn Jack-
    son, one of the three.

SAVAGE
Studio/Company: New World
Date/Country: 1973 + USA   Type: Feature

SAVE THE CHILDREN
Alt Title(s): see Brothers and Sisters in Concert

SAY GOODBYE, MAGGIE COLE
Nar/Cast: Michael Constantine + Dane Clark + Maidie Norman*
    + Susan Hayward
Screenplay: Sandor Stern   Director: Jud Taylor
Studio/Company: Spelling/Goldberg Production
Date/Country: 1972 + USA   Type: TV Feature
Annotation: A doctor, widowed (Hayward) recently, goes to
    work in a slum section of Chicago and must come to grips
    with the decision to remain at work there or to find a
    safer place for herself away from personal involvements
    with her patients. Maidie Norman plays Fergie.

SCALPHUNTERS, THE
Nar/Cast: Burt Lancaster + Ossie Davis* + Shelley Winters
Screenplay: William Norton
Producer: Jules Levy + Arthur Gardner + Arnold Laven
    Director: Sydney Pollack
Studio/Company: United Artists
Tech Info: 16 mm/color/sound/3 reels/102 min.
Date/Country: 1968 + USA   Type: Feature
Distr/Arch: uas
Annotation: Western drama involving a furtrapper (Lancaster)
    with a captured runaway slave (Davis as Joseph Lee)
    stalking a scalphunting gang to retrieve stolen furs.
    Lee, trying to gain his freedom by outwitting whites,
    proves that white is not omnipotent.

SCANDAL STREET
Nar/Cast: Louise Beavers*   Director: James Hogan
Date/Country: 1938 + USA   Type: Feature
Annotation: Another Beavers maid role.

SCAPEGOAT, THE
Nar/Cast: Abbie Mitchell* + Walker Thompson* + Maud Jones* +
    Sidney Kirkpatrick* + Leon Williams* + Mabel Young* + Lit-
    tle Jeff* + Jack Thornton* + Lorrine Harris*   Story: Paul
    Laurence Dunbar*
Studio/Company: Frederick Douglass Film Company
Date/Country: 1920 + USA

SCAR OF SHAME
Nar/Cast: Harry Henderson* + lucia Lynn Moses* + Norman John
    Stone* + Ann Kennedy* + William E. pettus* + Pearl Mac-
    Cormick* + lawrence Chenault*   Story: David Starkman
Producer: Sherman Dudley*   Director: Frank Peregini
Studio/Company: Colored Players Film Corp. of Philadelphia
Tech Info: 16 mm/silent/bw/3 reels/90 min.
Date/Country: 1927 + USA   Type: Feature
Distr/Arch: emg + sta + kpf + lc + eas
Annotation: A story about an ill-matched marriage between a
    black concert pianist and a poor, lower class young black
    woman. The color caste system and the divisions that ex-
    ist among Afro-Americans are explored, as well as class
    and its relationship to ambition in the black community.

SCARLET CLAW
Alt Title(s): see The Crimson Skull

SCARLET CLUE, THE
Series: Charlie Chan
Nar/Cast: Sydney Toler   + Mantan Moreland* + Ben Carter* +
    Benson Fong + Virginia Brissac   Story: Earl Derr Biggers
      Director: Phil Rosen
Studio/Company: Monogram
Tech Info: 16 mm/sound/bw/65 min.
Date/Country: 1945 + USA   Type: Feature
Distr/Arch: uas
Annotation: Mantan Moreland is Birmingham Brown, Charlie
    Chan's chauffeur and comic foil.

SCARLET HOUR, THE
Nar/Cast: Nat King Cole*   Director: Michael Curtiz
Tech Info: 94 min.
Date/Country: 1955 + USA
Annotation: Nat King Cole sings "Never Let Me Go" in a guest
    appearance in this conventional melodrama.

SCATTERGOOD BAINES
Nar/Cast: Guy Kibbee + Benny Carter   Director: Christy
    Cabanne
Studio/Company: RKO
Tech Info: 16 mm/sound/bw/68 min.
Date/Country: 1941 + USA   Type: Feature
Distr/Arch: roa
Annotation: Ben Carter is Scattergood's "colored assistant"
    in a comedy bit.

SCHEMERS, THE
Nar/Cast: Edna Morton* + Lawrence Chenault* + Edward Brown*

Studio/Company: Reol Productions
Tech Info: silent/bw
Date/Country: 1922 + USA   Type: Feature
Annotation: Melodrama about a young chemist who develops a
    formula for gasoline and finds himself in danger of having
    it stolen from him by big time swindlers.

SCHOOL_BEGINS
Series: Our Gang
Nar/Cast: Our Gang + Allen Hoskins*
Screenplay: Robert F. McGowan
Producer: Robert F. McGowan + Hal Roach   Director: Anthony
    Mack
Studio/Company: MGM
Tech Info: bw/silent/2 reels
Date/Country: 1928 + USA   Type: Comedy Short
Annotation: Farina is conned into carrying a forged excuse
    to school which backfires when its supposed author shows
    up at the school.

SCHOOL'S_OUT
Series: Our Gang
Nar/Cast: Our Gang + Allen Hoskins* + Matthew Beard*
Screenplay: H.M. Walker (dialogue)
Producer: Hal Roach   Director: Robert F. McGowan
Studio/Company: MGM + Roach
Tech Info: super 8 mm/16 mm/sound/bw/1 reel/20 min.
Date/Country: 1930 + USA   Type: Comedy Short
Distr/Arch: bla + kpf
Annotation: Jackie's so in love with Miss Crabtree he wants
    to keep school open all summer and when a man comes to
    school looking for her, Jackie's convinced he's a suitor
    and tries to discourage him with outrageous lies about
    Miss Crabtree.   (The one liners the kids use in the class-
    room are discovered by Miss Crabtree to come from a book
    called 'The Minstrel and Blackface Joke Book.')

SCORE,_THE
Producer: BMI
Tech Info: 59 min.
Date/Country: c. 1971 + USA   Type: Documentary
Annotation: Explores the process of writing music for the
    movies and for TV. Includes, among others, Quincy Jones*
    working on his score for In_Cold_Blood.

SCOTT_JOPLIN,_KING_OF_RAGTIME_COMPOSERS
Nar/Cast: Eartha Kitt*
Screenplay: Amelia Anderson   Director: Amelia Anderson
Tech Info: 16 mm/sound/color/1 reel/15 min.
Date/Country: 1977 + USA   Type: Documentary
Distr/Arch: pyr
Annotation: Story of Joplin's life from his discovery at the
    Maple Leaf Club, through his great initial success at rag-
    time, his turning to serious composition, the failure of
    his opera Treemonisha and his early death in poverty and
    obscurity.   Film includes many Joplin pieces and excerpts
    from the opera. Appearances by Eubie Blake*, and Taj
    Mahal*.

SCOTT JOPLIN
Nar/Cast: Billy Dee Williams* + Margaret Avery* + Art Carney
   + Clifton Davis* + Eubie Blake* + Godfrey Cambridge* + Taj
   Mahal* + Mabel King* + DeWayne Jessie* + Spoe-De-Odee* +
   Marcus Grapes* + The Commodores*   Director: Jeremy Paul
   Kagan
Studio/Company: Universal
Tech Info: 16 mm/sound/color/92 min.
Date/Country: 1977 + USA   Type: Feature
Distr/Arch: swa
Annotation: Billy Dee Williams plays Scott Joplin, the great
   composer of ragtime and of the opera Treemonisha in this
   fictional biography of the tragic struggle of a black
   musician for success against insurmountable odds.

SCRAP IN BLACK AND WHITE, A
Studio/Company: Edison
Date/Country: 1903 + USA
Annotation: A fight between two boys - one black and one
   white - ends without a clear cut winner. The implication
   is that the black boy wins.

SCREAM BLACULA SCREAM
Nar/Cast: William Marshall* + Pam Grier* + Don Mitchell*
Screenplay: Leon Capetanos + Joan Torres + Raymond Koenig
Producer: Joseph T. Naar   Director: Bob Kelljan
Studio/Company: American International
Date/Country: 1973 + USA   Type: Feature
Annotation: In this sequel to Blacula, William Marshall
   stars as Count Mamuwalde/Blacula and travels among a group
   of young swingers, moving about at night in a bloodsucking
   rampage.   Pam Grier and Don Marshall are among those who
   ultimately drive the vampire out of town.

SEA BEAST, THE
Nar/Cast: Sam Baker* + John Barrymore + Dolores Costello +
   George O'Hara   Director: Millard Webb
Studio/Company: Warner Brothers Pictures
Date/Country: 1926 + USA   Type: Feature
Annotation: Sam Baker plays Queequeg in this rather far-
   fetched adaptation of Moby Dick.

SEA WIFE, THE
Nar/Cast: Cy Grant* + Joan Collins + Richard Burton   Story:
   J. M. Scott
Producer: Andre Hakim   Director: Bob McNaught
Studio/Company: Twentieth Century Fox
Tech Info: 16 mm/sound/color/82 min.
Date/Country: 1957 + USA   Type: Feature
Distr/Arch: fnc
Annotation: Story of revenge of the grave as 3 survivors of
   a shipwreck wonder what retribution will be theirs after
   they leave the fourth (Cy Grant) swimming after them in
   shark-infested water.

SECOND CHILDHOOD
Series: Our Gang

Nar/Cast: Our Gang + Billie Thomas*
Producer: Hal Roach   Director: Gus Meins
Studio/Company: MGM + Roach
Tech Info: super 8 mm/16 mm/bw/sound/1 reel/19 min.
Date/Country: 1936 + USA   Type: Comedy Short
Distr/Arch: roa + bla
Annotation: A lonely, crotchety woman discovers her second
  childhood when she finds herself involved with the gang.
  Billie Thomas stars as Buckwheat.

SECOND NEWS REEL
Studio/Company: All American News
Date/Country: 1942 + USA
Annotation: Victory Parade; football game between New York
  Bombers and Washington Lions; black cavalry troops at Ft.
  Myers, Virginia; training of black doctors and nurses at
  Meharry Medical College, Nashville, Tennessee; Fisk
  University Choir.

SECOND WAR OF LIBERATION
Alt Title(s): see Angola: The People Have Chosen

SECOND WOMAN, THE
Nar/Cast: Robert Young + Betsy Drake + Robert "Smokey" Whit-
  field*
Screenplay: Robert Smith
Producer: Robert Smith   Director: James V. Kern
Studio/Company: United Artists
Tech Info: 16 mm/sound/bw/91 min.
Date/Country: 1951 + USA   Type: Feature
Distr/Arch: bud + unf
Annotation: A young woman helps prove that the man she loves
  is not going insane. Whitfield plays a porter.

SECRET SERVICE
Nar/Cast: Richard Dix + Shirley Grey + Gavin Gordon + Willi-
  am Post, Jr.   Story: William Gillette   Director: J.
  Walter Ruben
Studio/Company: RKO Radio
Tech Info: sound/bw
Date/Country: 1931 + USA   Type: Feature
Annotation: Another of the Civil War genre in which the vil-
  lains are inevitably Northern and Yankee, the good folk
  gallant, confederate and gentlemanly (Dix), almost in-
  evitably surrounded by faithful retainers (black).

SECRET SORROW
Studio/Company: Reol Motion Picture Corp.

SECRET WITNESS
Alt Title(s): Secret Wilderness
Nar/Cast: Una Merkel + William Collier Jr. + Zazu pitts +
  Clarence Muse*   Story: Samuel Spewacks   Director:
  Thornton Freeland
Studio/Company: Columbia
Date/Country: 1931 + USA   Type: Feature
Annotation: Murder mystery which features Clarence Muse.

SECRETS OF A NURSE
Nar/Cast: Edmund Lowe + Helen Mack + Dick Foran + Clarence
    Muse*
Screenplay: Tom Lennon + Lester Cole   Story: Quentin
    Reynolds   Director: Arthur Lubin
Studio/Company: Universal
Date/Country: 1938 + USA   Type: Feature
Annotation: Prizefighting, murder and corruption all are a
    part of this melodrama. Helen Mack is the nurse with the
    secrets, Dick Foran the unfortunate fighter and Edmund
    Lowe, a criminal lawyer. Clarence Muse has a small role as
    Tiger.

SEDUTO ALLA SUA DESTRA
Alt Title(s): Black Jesus
Nar/Cast: Woody Strode* + Jean Servais + Franco Citti
Screenplay: Franco Brusati
Producer: Carlo Lizzani   Director: Valerio Zurlin
Studio/Company: Plaza Pictures
Tech Info: mixture of English and dubbed English
Date/Country: 1971 + Italian   Type: Feature
Annotation: Strode plays a   nonviolent African leader im-
    prisoned and tortured by brutal whites who run the prison.

SEE HOW THEY RUN
Alt Title(s): see Bright Road

SEE MY LAWYER
Nar/Cast: Olsen and Johnson + Nat "King" Cole*
Screenplay: Edmund Hartman + Stanley Davis
Producer: Edmund Hartman   Director: Eddie Cline
Studio/Company: Universal
Tech Info: 59 min.
Date/Country: 1945 + USA   Type: Feature
Annotation: The King Cole trio is featured in this Olsen and
    Johnson farce.

SEEIN' THINGS
Series: Our Gang
Nar/Cast: Our Gang + Allen Hoskins* + Ernie Morrison*
Screenplay: Hal Roach
Producer: Hal Roach   Director: Robert McGowan
Studio/Company: Pathe
Tech Info: silent/bw/2 reels
Date/Country: 1924 + USA   Type: Comedy Short
Annotation: Surreal comedy about what happens to Farina when
    he over-eats, especially meat. Included in this short are
    some interesting technical shots. Allen Hoskins stars as
    Farina.

SEEING THE WORLD
Series: Our Gang
Nar/Cast: Our Gang + Allen Hoskins*
Screenplay: Hal Roach
Producer: HalRoach   Director: Robert McGowan
Studio/Company: Pathe
Tech Info: silent/bw/2 reels
Date/Country: 1926 + USA   Type: Comedy Short

Annotation: The gang accompanies school teacher Finlayson
when he wins a trip to Europe, where they wreak their
usual havoc up to and including having Farina and the
teacher fall off the Eiffel Tower. Finlayson is thus
shocked out of his prank induced daydream. Allen Hoskins
stars as Farina.

SEGREGATION_IN_SCHOOLS
Nar/Cast: Edward R. Murrow
Producer: CBS
Tech Info: 16 mm/sound/bw/1 reel/28 min.
Date/Country: 1955 + USA   Type: Documentary
Distr/Arch: iu + mghf
Annotation: Relates the varied reactions of citizens of two
southern cities, Gastonia, N.C., and Natchitoches, Louisi-
ana, to the Supreme Court ruling against segregation in
public schools. Shows several interviews of prominent
persons in the communities regarding this issue.

SEGREGATION_NORTHERN_STYLE
Tech Info: 16 mm/sound/bw/30 min.
Date/Country: 1965 + USA   Type: Documentary
Annotation: The problems faced by a black couple trying to
buy a home in a middle-income northern suburb. Though
they have all the social and economic qualifications, they
meet with direct opposition.

SELECTED_NEGRO_WORK_SONGS
Tech Info: 16 mm/bw/9 min.
Date/Country: 1952 + USA   Type: Documentary
Distr/Arch: uill
Annotation: Two black laborers' songs, "Let the Church Roll
On" and "Dis Old Hammer," sung by a mixed chorus.
Provided by Center for Southern Folklore.

SELL_'EM_COWBOY
Nar/Cast: Martin Turner* + Ed lytell + Dick Hatton
Screenplay: Bennett Cohen   Director: Ward Hayes
Studio/Company: Ben Wilson Productions
Tech Info: 35 mm/silent/bw/5 reels/4,821 ft.
Date/Country: 1924 + USA   Type: Feature
Annotation: Martin Turner plays Romeo in this "Western
comedy- melodrama" about nefarious business practices in
Arizona. Dick Hatton as "Young" Mattewson solves the pro-
blems and romances the daughter of his father's client.

SENEGAL
Series: Peoples of Africa
Producer: Universal Education and Visual Arts
Tech Info: 16 mm/sound/bw/1 reel/20 min.
Date/Country: 1967 + USA   Type: Documentary
Distr/Arch: iu + ueva
Annotation: Contrasts the political independence and the
economic dependence of Senegal. Illustrates how deep
seated tradition has retarded the development of a new
economy. Reveals difference between city and rural life
in Senegal.

SENSATIONS OF 1945
Nar/Cast: Eleanor Powell + Dennis O'Keefe + Cab Calloway*
Screenplay: Dorothy Bennett + Andrew Stone
Producer: Andrew Stone   Director: Andrew Stone
Studio/Company: United Artists
Tech Info: 16 mm/sound/bw/85 min.
Date/Country: 1945 + USA   Type: Feature
Distr/Arch: bud + ivy + mog + roa + tmc + unf
Annotation: The movie is a series of vaudeville acts and
  orchestra productions strung together with a loose story.
  Features Cab Calloway.

SENZA PIETA
Alt Title(s): Without Pity
Nar/Cast: John Kitzmiller* + Carla del Poggio + Giuletta
  Masina   Story: Frederico Fellini + Perelli
Producer: Carlo Ponti   Director: Alberto Lattuada
Date/Country: 1948 + Italy   Type: Feature
Annotation: Jerry, an American G.I. in Italy, is played by
  Katzmiller. He gets involved in black marketeering, flls
  in love with an Italian girl, but is killed before the
  romance develops.

SEPARATE BUT EQUAL
Producer: Encyclopedia Britannica Educational Corp.
Tech Info: 16 mm/sound/color/1 reel/8 min.
Date/Country: 1971 + USA   Type: Documentary
Distr/Arch: iu + ebec
Annotation: Outlines the political, economic, and social
  position of Blacks in the South from the time of the Civil
  War. Emphasizes the effect of the 'separate but equal'
  policy derived from the Supreme Court decision in Plessy
  vs. Ferguson and questioned in Brown vs. Board of Educa-
  tion, Topeka, Kansas.

SEPIA CINDERELLA
Nar/Cast: Billy Daniels* + Sheila Guyse* + Ruby Blake* +
  Walter Fuller* + John Kirby* + Fred Gordon + Freddie
  Bartholomew + Tondaleyo*
Screenplay: Vincent Valentini
Producer: Jack Goldberg   Director: Arthur Leonard
Studio/Company: Herald Pictures
Tech Info: 16 mm/sound/bw/67 min.
Date/Country: 1947 + USA   Type: Herald Pictures
Distr/Arch: emg
Annotation: A musical romance of a songwriter and a singer
  who, after trials and tribulations, get back together to
  the tune of his "Cinderella Song." Bartholomew makes a
  cameo appearance.

SERGEANT JOE LOUIS ON TOUR
Studio/Company: Toddy Pictures
Date/Country: 1943   Type: Documentary
Annotation: Follows the great boxer's tours for the Army
  during World War II.

SERGEANT RUTLEDGE
Nar/Cast: Woody Strode* + Jeffrey Hunter + Billie Burke +

Juano Hernandez*
Screenplay: James Bellah + Willis Goldbeck
Producer: Patrick Ford + Willis Goldbeck   Director: John
   Ford
Studio/Company: Warner Brothers
Date/Country: 1960 + USA   Type: Feature
Annotation: Woody Strode stars as a cavalry man accused of
   double murder and rape. In the face of a biased tribunal
   he and his friends try to prove his innocence.

SERGEANT, THE
Nar/Cast: Rod Steiger + John Phillip Law + Memphis Slim*
Screenplay: Dennis Murphy
Producer: Richard Goldstone   Director: John Flynn
Studio/Company: Warner Brothers-Seven Arts
Tech Info: 108 min.
Date/Country: 1968 + USA   Type: Feature
Annotation: Memphis Slim appears briefly as a nightclub
   singer in this melodrama about an army sergeant (Steiger)
   and his homosexual attraction to a young private (Law)
   both on duty in post war France.

SERGEANTS 3
Nar/Cast: Frank Sinatra + Peter Lawford + Sammy Davis, Jr.*
   + Dean Martin
Screenplay: W.R. Burnerr
Producer: Frank Sinatra   Director: John Sturges
Studio/Company: United Artists
Date/Country: 1962 + USA   Type: Feature
Annotation: Martin and Lawford play U.S cavalrymen holding
   out at a fort in the wild west of 1870's. This is meant
   to be an adaptation of Kipling's Gunga Din with Davis as a
   freed slave who attaches himself to the three sergeants.

SERIE NOIRE
Nar/Cast: Sidney Bechet* + Erich von Stroheim   Director:
   Pierre Foucard
Tech Info: 88 min.
Date/Country: France + 1955   Type: Feature
Annotation: A gangster movie which features Sidney Bechet.

SET MY PEOPLE FREE
Date/Country: 1948

SET-UP, THE
Nar/Cast: James Edwards* + Audrey Totter + Robert Ryan
   Director: Robert Wise
Studio/Company: RKO
Tech Info: 16 mm/sound/bw/72 min.
Date/Country: 1949 + USA   Type: Feature
Distr/Arch: fnc
Annotation: James Edwards plays a confident young boxer in a
   film which stars Robert Ryan as an aging fighter nearing
   the end of his career.

SEVEN CHANCES
Nar/Cast: Buster Keaton + Roy Barnes + Ruth Dwyer
   Director: Buster Keaton

Studio/Company: Metro
Tech Info: 16 mm/silent/bw/70 min.
Date/Country: 1925 + USA   Type: Feature
Distr/Arch: mac
Annotation: Buster Keaton's comic farce about a young man
  who will inherit millions from an uncle with the proviso
  that he must be married. Includes two black characters,
  both played by whites in blackface: a witless lethargic
  messenger who adds to the comic-suspense and one of the
  aspiring brides-to-be who answers the frantic hero's ad.

SEVEN_MINUTES,_THE
Nar/Cast: Lynn Hamilton* + Yvonne de Carlo + Wayne Mounder
Screenplay: Richard Warren Lewis   Story: Irving Wallace
Producer: Russ Meyer   Director: Russ Meyer
Studio/Company: Fox
Tech Info: 16 mm/sound/color/116 min.
Date/Country: 1971 + USA   Type: Feature
Distr/Arch: fnc
Annotation: Courtroom drama centered around a novel called
  "The Seven Minutes" and the author's battle against ob-
  scenity laws.

SEVEN_SWEETHEARTS
Nar/Cast: Kathryn Grayson + Van Heflin + Louise Beavers*
Screenplay: Walter Reisch + Leo Townsend
Producer: Joe Pasternak   Director: Frank Borzage
Studio/Company: MGM
Date/Country: 1942 + USA   Type: Feature
Annotation: Louise Beavers is Petunia in this musical about
  seven sisters who by tradition must be married off in
  proper chronological order.

SEVEN_WOMEN
Nar/Cast: Woody Strode* + Anne Bancroft + Margaret Leighton
  + Mildred Dunnock
Screenplay: Janet Green + John McCormick   Director: John
  Ford
Studio/Company: MGM
Tech Info: 16 mm/sound/color/93 min.
Date/Country: 1966 + USA   Type: Feature
Distr/Arch: fnc
Annotation: Woody Strode is a Mongol warrior in this drama
  about an American mission on the Chinese border invaded by
  Mongol Tanga Khan and his men in the 1930's.

SEX_AND_THE_SINGLE_GIRL
Nar/Cast: Natalie Wood + Tony Curtis + Count Basie and his
  Orchestra*
Screenplay: Joseph Heller + David Schwartz   Story: Helen
  Gurley Brown
Producer: William Orr   Director: Richard Quine
Studio/Company: Warners
Tech Info: 16 mm/sound/color/110 min.
Date/Country: 1964 + USA   Type: Feature
Distr/Arch: ccc + mac + sel + twy + wil
Annotation: Count Basie and Orchestra appear in a nightclub
  sequence, also play "What Is This They Called Love" in

this comedy adaptation of the book by Helen Gurley Brown.

SHADOW OF A DOUBT
Nar/Cast: Teresa Wright + Joseph Cotten + MacDonald Carey +
   Clarence Muse*
Screenplay: Thornton Wilder + Sally Benson + Alma Reville
Producer: Jack H. Skirball   Director: Alfred Hitchcock
Studio/Company: Universal
Tech Info: 16 mm/sound/bw
Date/Country: 1943 + USA   Type: Feature
Distr/Arch: twy + uni
Annotation: Hitchcock thriller that has Joseph Cotten as a
   murderer of rich old widows. Clarence Muse plays a pul-
   lman porter.

SHADOW OF THE THIN MAN
Nar/Cast: Louise Beavers* + William Powell + Myrna Loy +
   Barry Nelson + Donna Reed
Screenplay: Irving Brecher + Harry Kurnitz   Story: Harry
   Kurnitz
Producer: Hunt Stromberg   Director: Major W.S. Van Dyke
Studio/Company: MGM
Tech Info: 16 mm/sound/bw/97 min.
Date/Country: 1941 + USA   Type: Feature
Distr/Arch: fnc
Annotation: Another in the Thin Man series, with Nick and
   Nora out to clear a friend of a murder charge. Louise
   Beavers plays Stella.

SHADOW OVER CHINATOWN
Series: Charlie Chan
Nar/Cast: Mantan Moreland* + Victor Sen Young + Sidney Toler
Screenplay: Raymond Schrock   Story: Earl Derr Biggers
Producer: James S.Burkett   Director: Terry Morse
Studio/Company: Monogram
Tech Info: 16 mm/bw/sound/2 reels/80 min.
Date/Country: 1946 + USA   Type: Feature
Distr/Arch: cin
Annotation: Birmingham, Chan's chauffeur (Mantan Moreland),
   provides comic relief from the tension of the torso murder
   mystery which Charlie solves in San Francisco, despite the
   "assistance" of his number two son and Birmingham. The
   film ends with another Birmingham malapropism - "Confusion
   says..."

SHADOWED BY THE DEVIL
Studio/Company: Unique Film Company
Date/Country: 1916 + USA

SHADOWS
Nar/Cast: Lelia Goldoni + Ben Carruthers* + Hugh Hurd* +
   Anthony Ray + Rupert Crosse* + Lynn Hamilton*
Producer: Maurice McEndree   Director: John Cassavetes
Studio/Company: Lion International
Tech Info: 16 mm/bw/sound/3 reels/81 min.
Date/Country: 1959 + USA   Type: Feature
Distr/Arch: fif + mac + mod + roa + twy
Annotation: Shadows grew out of a series of improvisations

at the Variety Arts Studio in New York. The story concerns a young would-be writer who falls in love with a girl (Goldoni) he thinks is white. Her experiences and those of her two darker brothers (Carruthers and Hurd) are the basis of the film. Cassavetes took his actors to various New York City locations and allowed them to improvise their basic characterizations. Music by Charles Mingus*.

SHAFT IN AFRICA
Nar/Cast: Richard Roundtree* + Vonetta McGee* + Frank Finlay + Neda Arneric
Screenplay: Stirling Silliphant
Producer: Roger Lewis   Director: John Guillermin
Studio/Company: MGM
Tech Info: 16 mm/color/sound/3 reels/112 min.
Date/Country: 1973 + USA   Type: Feature
Distr/Arch: fnc
Annotation: This third adventure takes Shaft (Richard Roundtree) into Africa to infiltrate and break up a ring smuggling cheap labor into Europe.

SHAFT'S BIG SCORE
Nar/Cast: Richard Roundtree* + Moses Gunn* + Drew Brown + Rosalind Miles + Julius Harris*
Screenplay: Ernest Tidyman
Producer: R. lewis + Ernest Tidyman   Director: Gordon Parks*
Studio/Company: MGM
Tech Info: 16 mm/color/sound/3 reels/105 min.
Date/Country: 1972 + USA   Type: Feature
Distr/Arch: fnc
Annotation: In this sequel John Shaft finds himself in the middle of a black/white gangland feud over control of the numbers rackett in Queens.

SHAFT
Nar/Cast: Richard Roundtree* + Moses Gunn* + Charles Cioffi + Christopher St. John* + Gwen Mitchell*
Screenplay: Ernest Tidyman
Producer: Joel Freeman   Director: Gordon parks*
Studio/Company: MGM
Tech Info: 16 mm/color/sound/3 reels/98 min.
Date/Country: 1971   Type: Feature
Distr/Arch: fnc
Annotation: Black private eye Shaft (Roundtree) is hired to find the daughter of a black underworld leader (Gunn) kidnapped in a power struggle to control the drug, prostitution and numbers rackets in Harlem. Shaft locates the girl and effects her release with the aid of a black revolutionary and his buddies. Oscar winning music by Isaac Hayes*; orchestration by J.J. Johnson*.

SHAKE, RATTLE AND ROCK
Nar/Cast: Fats Domino* + Dick Clark   Director: EdwardL. Clark
Studio/Company: American International
Tech Info: 16 mm/sound/bw/77 min.

Date/Country: 1956 + USA   Type: Feature
Distr/Arch: unf
Annotation: Fats Domino and his band are able to persuade
   the worried adults in this film that rock and roll will
   not ruin their teenage children.

SHALAKO
Nar/Cast: Sean Connery + Brigitte Bardot + Woody Strode*
Screenplay: J.J. Griffith + Hal Hopper + Scot Finch   Story:
   Louis L'Amour
Producer: Evan Lloyd   Director: Edward Dmytryk
Studio/Company: Cinerama
Tech Info: 16 mm/sound/color/113 min.
Date/Country: 1968 + Britain   Type: Feature
Distr/Arch: fnc
Annotation: Western that has European aristocrats on an
   1880's safari when confronted with the various dangers of
   the old American west. Strode is Chato, son of the Apache
   chief, who launches an attack on the intruders and later
   challenges Shalako (Connery), a former cavalry officer, to
   single combat with spears.

SHANGHAI CHEST, THE
Series: Charlie Chan
Nar/Cast: Roland Winters + Mantan Moreland* + Deannie Best*
Screenplay: Sam Newman   Story: W. Scott Darling
Producer: James S. Burkeet   Director: William Beaudine
Studio/Company: Monogram
Tech Info: 16 mm/sound/bw/65 min.
Date/Country: 1948 + USA   Type: Feature
Distr/Arch: cin
Annotation: Moreland is Birmingham, Chan's driver and all-
   around man-servant who helps number 2 son get in Charlie's
   way and helps Chan dig up bodies that aren't in their
   cemetery plots.   His feet won't move again when he's ter-
   rified, but he does accidentally stop the murderer from
   escaping when he happens to be in the way.

SHANGO
Nar/Cast: Geoffrey Holder*   Director: Fritz Henle
Tech Info: color/10 min.
Date/Country: 1953
Distr/Arch: mac
Annotation: Trinidad's musical heritage is illustrated
   through the authentic tribal dances performed by Geoffrey
   Holder and his troupe.   One of the dances is a ritual
   dance in which a chicken is sacrificed.

SHE DEVIL
Alt Title(s): Louisiana
Nar/Cast: Laura Bowman*
Studio/Company: Louis Weiss Production
Tech Info: sound/bw/62 min.
Date/Country: 1940 + USA   Type: Feature
Distr/Arch: kpf
Annotation: This film has also been listed as Louisiana

SHE DONE HIM WRONG

Nar/Cast: Mae West + Cary Grant + Louise Beavers*
Screenplay: Harvey Thew + John Bright   Director: Lowell
  Sherman
Studio/Company: Paramount
Tech Info: 16 mm/sound/bw/2 reels/65 min.
Date/Country: 1933 + USA   Type: Feature
Distr/Arch: uni
Annotation: Louise Beavers is featured as Mae West's maid,
  Pearl in this Gay Nineties tale of Lady Lou (West) the hit
  of the Bowery clubs who does her men wrong until she falls
  in love with "Hawk" (Cary Grant).

SHE'S TOO MEAN TO ME
Nar/Cast: Mantan Moreland* + Johnny Lee* + Flournoy E. Mil-
  ler*
Studio/Company: Goldmax
Date/Country: 1948 + USA

SHE'S WORKING HER WAY THROUGH COLLEGE
Nar/Cast: Virginia Mayo + Ronald Reagan + Gene Nelson +
  Amanda Randolph*
Screenplay: Peter Milne   Story: James Thurber
Studio/Company: Warner Brothers
Tech Info: 16 mm/color/sound
Date/Country: 1952 + USA   Type: Feature
Annotation: Musical reworking of Thurber's "The Male Animal"
  about a burlesque queen working her way through college.
  Amanda Randolph plays Virginia Mayo's maid.

SHE
Nar/Cast: Helen Gahagan + Randolph Scott + Noble Johnson*
Screenplay: Ruth Rose + Dudley Nichols
Producer: Marian C. Cooper   Director: Irving Pichel + Lan-
  sing G. Holden
Studio/Company: RKO Radio Pictures
Tech Info: sound/bw
Date/Country: 1935 + USA   Type: Feature
Annotation: Based on Sir Rider Haggard's novel, the film is
  about a lost kingdom ruled by a woman who has gained im-
  mortality, and her love for the English scientist who
  stumbles upon her kingdom.   Noble Johnson plays the
  Amahagger chief.

SHERIFF, THE
Nar/Cast: Ossie Davis* + Ruby Dee* + Moses Gunn* + Brenda
  Sykes* + Joel Fluellen* + Kyle Johnson* + Ross Martin
Tech Info: sound/color/90 min.
Date/Country: 1971 + USA   Type: TV Feature
Annotation: Ossie Davis plays a sheriff in loma County, a
  small West coast town. The daughter of his friend, played
  by Moses Gunn, is raped by Ross Martin, a white insurance
  salesman and is shot by Gunn. The sheriff is then forced
  to jail his friend. Further complicatons arise because
  the rape victim is a girlfriend of the sheriff's stepson.

SHIRLEY CHISHOLM: PURSUING THE DREAM
Nar/Cast: Shirley Chisholm*
Studio/Company: New Line Cinema

Tech Info: 16 mm/color/sound/1 reel/42 min.
Date/Country: 1972   Type: Documentary
Distr/Arch: new
Annotation: A documentary film of Congresswoman Shirley
    Chisholm's 1972 Presidential campaign.

SHIVER MY TIMBERS
Series: Our Gang
Nar/Cast: Our Gang + Matthew Beard*
Screenplay: H.M. Walker
Producer: Robert F. McGowan + Hal Roach   Director: Robert
    McGowan
Studio/Company: MGM + Roach
Tech Info: super 8 mm/16 mm/bw/sound/2 reels
Date/Country: 1931 + USA   Type: Comedy Short
Distr/Arch: roa + bla
Annotation: The gang turns the table on a storytelling sea
    captain and his crew who scheme to scare them out of their
    fondness for sea stories.

SHIVERING SHAKESPEARE
Series: Our Gang
Nar/Cast: Our Gang + Allen Hoskins*
Screenplay: Robert F. McGowan
Producer: Hal Roach + Robert F. McGowan   Director: Anthony
    Mack
Studio/Company: MGM + Roach
Tech Info: super 8 mm/16 mm/bw/sound/1 reel/18 min.
Date/Country: 1930 + USA   Type: Comedy Short
Distr/Arch: bla + roa + kpf
Annotation: A 'cultured' dramatic evening with child actors
    is interrupted by egg throwing kids who were hept out of
    the show.   The whole theater eventually erupts in a pie
    throwing melee. Allen Hoskins stars as Farina.

SHIVERING SPOOKS
Series: Our Gang
Nar/Cast: Our Gang + Allen Hoskins*
Screenplay: Hal Roach
Producer: Hal Roach   Director: Robert McGowan
Studio/Company: Pathe
Tech Info: silent/bw/2 reels
Date/Country: 1926 + USA   Type: Comedy Short
Annotation: When Prof. Fleece, a fake spiritualist, disrupts
    the gang's baseball game, the gang tunnels under his house
    and discovers the prof.'s con. Now it's their turn to do
    the disrupting. Allen Hoskins stars as Farina.

SHOCK CORRIDER
Nar/Cast: Peter Breck + Constance Towers + Hari Rhodes*
Screenplay: Sam Fuller
Producer: Sam Fuller   Director: Sam Fuller
Studio/Company: Allied Artists
Tech Info: 16 mm/bw with color sequences/sound/3 reels/101
    min.
Date/Country: 1963 + USA   Type: Feature
Distr/Arch: cin
Annotation: An ambitious reporter has himself committed to a

mental institution to uncover the unsolved murder of a patient. Rhodes is Treat, one of the three patients who supposedly witnessed the murder. The reporter eventually gets a confession, writes his expose for which he recieves the Pulitzer Prize, but is so broken by the experience he has to be returned to the institution.

SHOCK TREATMENT
Nar/Cast: Stuart Whitman + Lauren Bacall + Ossie Davis* + Carol Lynley + Roddy McDowell
Screenplay: Sydney Boehm
Producer: Aaron Rosenberg   Director: Denis Sanders
Studio/Company: 20th Century Fox
Tech Info: 16 mm/sound/bw/94 min.
Date/Country: 1964 + USA   Type: Feature
Distr/Arch: fnc
Annotation: Stuart Whitman is hired to impersonate his way into an insane asylum and befriend killer/patient Roddy McDowell to find where McDowell hid a cache of money. Ossie Davis is Capshaw, a small role in this mystery drama.

SHOE SHINE BOY
Studio/Company: MGM
Date/Country: 1943 + USA   Type: Dramatic Short
Annotation: A World War II short tale about a black shoeshine boy who buys a pawnshop trumpet and impresses a couple of impressarios who put him in a show. However, he really wants only to blow his horn for Uncle Sam.

SHOOT 'EM UP, SAM
Studio/Company: Black Western Film Company
Date/Country: 1922 + USA

SHOOTIN' INJUNS
Series: Our Gang
Nar/Cast: Our Gang + Allen Hoskins* + Eugene Jackson*
Screenplay: Hal Roach
Producer: Hal Roach   Director: Robert McGowan
Studio/Company: Pathe
Tech Info: silent/bw/2 reels
Date/Country: 1925 + USA   Type: Comedy Short
Annotation: Planning to run away to the West to fight Indians, the gang plans to meet late at night to start their trek. When it starts to rain, they retire to a house that's about to be sold to an amusement park and there they get a full dose of the frights.

SHOPWORN ANGEL, THE
Alt Title(s): Private Pettigrew's Girl (book)
Nar/Cast: Margaret Sullavan + James Stewart + Walter Pidgeon + Hattie McDaniel* + Nat Pendleton + Alan Curtis
Screenplay: Walter Salt   Story: Dana Burnet
Producer: Joseph L. Mankiewicz   Director: H.C. Potter
Studio/Company: MGM
Tech Info: 16 mm/sound/bw85 min.
Date/Country: 1938 + USA   Type: Feature
Distr/Arch: fnc

Annotation: The romance between a private and a showgirl
    leads to marriage for sentimental reasons. Hattie Mc-
    Daniel plays Martha.

SHORT EYES
Nar/Cast: Nathan George* + Don Blakely* + Curtis Mayfield* +
    Bruce Davison + Jose Perez + Miguel Pinero + Freddie
    Fender
Screenplay: Miguel Pinero   Story: Miguel Pinero
Producer: Lewis Harris   Director: Robert M. Young
Studio/Company: Film League Presentation
Tech Info: 16 mm/sound/color/104 min.
Date/Country: 1977 + USA   Type: Feature
Distr/Arch: crnf
Annotation: Adaptation of Pinero's prizewinning play about a
    white man, imprisoned for the first time, who is accused
    of being a child molester, a "short eyes" in prison argot.
    The prison hierarchy-black/Puerto Rican/white--as a
    microcosm of the society is examined as Short Eyes becomes
    the object of intense hatred and abuse. Curtis Mayfield
    scored and composed the music.

SHOT IN THE DARK, A
Nar/Cast: Tracy Reed* + Peter Sellers + Elke Sommer
Screenplay: Blake Edwards + William Peter Blatty
Producer: Blake Edwards   Director: Blake Edwards
Studio/Company: United Artists
Tech Info: 16 mm/sound/color/101 min.
Date/Country: 1964 + USA   Type: Feature
Distr/Arch: uas
Annotation: Tracy Reed is Dominique Ballon whose maid is
    among the numerous victims of a mysterious murderer for
    whom Inspector Clouseau (Sellers) blunderingly seeks.

SHOT IN THE NIGHT, A
Nar/Cast: Bobby Smart* + Walter Holeby* + Walter Long* +
    Ruth Freeman* + Tom Amos* + Tolliver Brothers*
Producer: Ben Strasser
Studio/Company: North State Film Corporation
Tech Info: silent/bw
Date/Country: 1922 + USA   Type: Feature
Annotation: A young boy (Bobby Smart) is responsible for
    solving the mystery which includes murder, robbery and an
    elusive criminal, "The Masked Terror."

SHOUTIN' THE BLUES
Producer: Jack Agins
Tech Info: 16 mm/color/6 min.
Date/Country: 1974 + USA   Type: Documentary
Distr/Arch: serb
Annotation: The "world's greatest harmonica player." Sonny
    Terry*, improvises a composition on the harmonica.
    Provided by Center for Southern Folklore.

SHOW BOAT
Nar/Cast: Stepin Fetchit* + Gertrude Howard* + Jules Bled-
    sor* + Tess Gardella and the Jubilee Singers* + Joseph
    Shildkraut + Richard Coleman* + Laura La Plante   Story:

Edna Ferber
Producer: Carl Laemmle   Director: Harry A. Polland
Studio/Company: Universal
Tech Info: 35 mm/bw/silent with sound sequences/126 min. and
    18 min prologue
Date/Country: 1929 + USA   Type: Feature
Annotation: First film adaptation of the Ferber romantic
    novel about life on a Mississippi riverboat with Fetchit
    and Howard as Joe and Queenie. Begun as a silent, addi-
    tion of "goat glands" (sound sequence) necessary with ad-
    vent of sound. Numbers from the stage production in-
    cluded. Blidsoe sings "Ol' Man River" but miscegenation
    theme omitted.

SHOW BOAT
Nar/Cast: Irene Dunne + Paul Robeson* + Allan Jones +
    Charles Winninger + Helen Morgan + Hattie McDaniel* +
    Clarence Muse* + George Reed* + Eddie Anderson*
Screenplay: Oscar Hammerstein   Story: Edna Ferber + Jerome
    Kern
Producer: Carl Laemmle, Jr.   Director: James Whale
Studio/Company: Universal
Tech Info: 16 mm/sound/bw/4 reels/113 min.
Date/Country: 1936 + USA   Type: Feature
Distr/Arch: fnc
Annotation: Life and love on a Mississippi riverboat are the
    themes in this 1936 remake of Edna Ferber's novel,
    featuring paul Robeson as Joe, Hattie McDaniel as Queenie.
    The miscegenation theme reappears with Helen Morgan as the
    mulatto Julie. Irene Dunne as Magnolia does a black face
    routine; Clarence Muse is Sam the Doorman at the Tro-
    cadero; George Reed and Eddie Anderson are cast listed as
    "Old Negro" and "Young Negro."

SHOW BOAT
Nar/Cast: William Warfield* + Kathryn Grayson + Ava Gardner
    + Howard Keel + Joe E. Brown + Frances Williams*
Screenplay: John lee Makin   Story: Edna Ferber
Producer: Arthur Freed   Director: George Sidney
Studio/Company: MGM
Tech Info: 16 mm/sound/color/3 reels/108 min.
Date/Country: 1951   Type: Feature
Distr/Arch: bud
Annotation: Technicolor version of Edna Ferber's classic
    tale of romance on the Mississippi. William Warfield
    plays Joe in this version. The miscegenation theme is
    retained, Ava Gardner playing Julie the "Mulatto." Frances
    Williams plays the truncated role of Queenie. Joe's role
    is almost entirely limited to "Ol Man River" and reprise.

SHOW-OFF, THE
Nar/Cast: Red Skelton + Marilyn Maxwell + Eddie Anderson*
Screenplay: George Wells
Producer: Albert Lewis   Director: Harry Beaumont
Studio/Company: MGM
Tech Info: 16 mm/sound/bw/83 min.
Date/Country: 1946 + USA   Type: Feature
Distr/Arch: fnc

Annotation: Eddie Anderson has a small part in this adaptation of George Kelly's play in which Red Skelton plays a well-meaning braggart whose blunders are covered by his family.

SHRIMPS FOR A DAY
Series: Our Gang
Nar/Cast: Our Gang + Matthew Beard* + Billie Thomas*
Producer: Hal Roach   Director: Gus Meins
Studio/Company: MGM + Roach
Tech Info: super 8 mm/16 mm/sound/bw/1 reel/19 min.
Date/Country: 1934 + USA   Type: Comedy Short
Distr/Arch: bla + roa
Annotation: A magic lamp shrinks the daughter of an orphanage sponsor and her boyfriend with the result that they are taken back to the orphanage. There they discover the cruel treatment afforded the kids by Mr. Crutch.

SHUFFLING JANE
Studio/Company: Tropical Photoplay Company
Date/Country: 1921 + USA

SHUT MY BIG MOUTH
Nar/Cast: Dewey "Pigmeat" Markham* + John Murray
Studio/Company: Toddy Pictures
Tech Info: sound/bw/63 min.
Date/Country: 194- + USA

SIGN OF THE CROSS, THE
Nar/Cast: Rex Ingram* + Fredric March + Elissa Landi + Charles Laughton   Story: Wilson Barrett   Director: Cecil B. DeMille
Tech Info: 16 mm/sound/bw/120 min.
Date/Country: 1932 + USA   Type: Feature
Distr/Arch: uni
Annotation: Rex Ingram has a bit part in this DeMille extravaganza of religion, sensuality and violence with Laughton as Nero, casually sending Christians by the hundreds to their death.

SILENT SHELDON
Nar/Cast: Martin Turner* + Jack Perrin + Josephine Hill
   Story: Pierre Couderc   Director: Harry Webb
Studio/Company: Harry Webb Productions
Tech Info: 35 mm/silent/bw/5 reels/4,800 ft.
Date/Country: 1925 + USA   Type: Feature
Annotation: Martin Turner plays Ivory, valet to Jack Sheldon (Perrin). No further information available.

SILVER DEVIL
Studio/Company: Aston Pictures
Date/Country: 1947 + USA

SILVER STREAK
Nar/Cast: Scatman Crothers* + Gene Wilder + Richard Pryor* + Jill Clayburh + Patrick McGoohan   Director: Arthur Hiller
Studio/Company: 20th Century Fox
Tech Info: 16 mm/sound/color

Date/Country: 1976 + USA   Type: Feature
Annotation: George Coldivell a young editor takes the Silver
    Streak, a cross country passenger train, from los Angeles
    to Chicago "just to be   bored." George's troubles begin
    after he witnesses the body of a man being thrown off the
    train.   His attempts to investigate the matter include
    encounters with Richard Pryor who helps him in one se-
    quence disguise himself as a "brother."

SIMBA
Nar/Cast: Dirk Bogarde + Earl Cameron* + Orlando Martins* +
    Ben Johnson* + Virginia McKenna + Joseph Tomelty*
Screenplay: John Baines + Robin Estridge
Producer: Peter de Sarigny   Director: Brian D. Hurst
Studio/Company: Arthur Rank Production
Date/Country: 1955 + Britain   Type: Feature
Annotation: Story of terrorism and revenge, a semi-docu-
    mentary of the Mau-Mau movement in Kenya. Earl Cameron is
    Karanja; Ben Johnson, Kimani; Orlando Martins, a Headman;
    and Joseph Tomelty, Dr. Hughes, the martyred physician.

SIMP, THE
Nar/Cast: S.H. Dudley, Jr.* + Inez Clough* + Edna Morton* +
    Alex K. Shannon* + Percy Verwayen*
Studio/Company: Reol Productions
Tech Info: 35 mm/silent/bw
Date/Country: 1921 + USA

SINCE YOU WENT AWAY
Nar/Cast: Hattie McDaniel* + Claudette Colbert + Jennifer
    Jones + Joseph Cotten
Screenplay: David O. Selznick
Producer: David Selznick   Director: John Cromwell
Studio/Company: United Artists
Tech Info: 16 mm/sound/bw/4 reels/140 min.
Date/Country: 1944 + USA   Type: Feature
Distr/Arch: mac
Annotation: Chronicles the hardships of one midwestern fam-
    ily whose men are off to war. Hattie McDaniel plays
    Fidelia the maid who refuses to leave her "white folk" and
    sticks around on reduced pay.

SING AS YOU SWING
Alt Title(s): Swing Tease + The Music Box
Nar/Cast: Mills Brothers* + Nat Gonella and His Georgians
    Director: Redd Davis
Tech Info: 82 min.
Date/Country: 1937 + Britain
Annotation: Two radio stations compete in this feature which
    includes performances by the Mills Brothers and Nat Gonel-
    la and His Georgians.

SING SINNER SING
Nar/Cast: Lionel Hampton* + Paul Lukas + Leila Hyams
    Story: Wilson Collison   Director: Howard Christy
Studio/Company: Majestic
Tech Info: sound/74 min.
Date/Country: 1933 + USA   Type: Feature

Annotation: Parallels the Smith Reynolds/Libby Holman case;
   the story is about a singer who marries a wealthy playboy
   and is later tried for his murder.   Lionel Hampton
   furnishes the music.

SING-SING THANKSGIVING
Nar/Cast: B.B. King* + Joan Baez + Voices of East Harlem* +
   Mimi Farina and the inmates of Sing-Sing prison.
Producer: David Hoffman + Harry Wiland   Director: David
   Hoffman + Harry Wiland
Tech Info: 16 mm/color/sound/2 reels/78 min.
Date/Country: 1974 + USA   Type: Documentary
Distr/Arch: new
Annotation: A documentary interpretation of the reality of
   prison life and those who live it is transmitted through
   this Red Ribbon winner at the American Film Festivl in
   1974.

SINGING KID, THE
Nar/Cast: Al Jolson + Sybil Jason + Edward Everett Horton +
   Cab Calloway* + Avenelle Harris*
Screenplay: Warren Duff + Patsy Flick   Director: William
   Keighley
Studio/Company: Warners
Tech Info: 16 mm/sound/bw/84 min.
Date/Country: 1936 + USA   Type: Feature
Distr/Arch: uas
Annotation: Jolson as a Broadway star who loses his fortune
   and voice but finally regains both and a girl.   In this a
   black is shown in a friendly relationship with a white.
   Harris appears with a group in one of the scenes with
   Jolson in black face.

SINGING NUN, THE
Nar/Cast: Debbie Reynolds + Ricardo Montalban + Juanita
   Moore*
Screenplay: Sally Benson + John Furia   Story: John Furia
Producer: John Beck   Director: Henry Koster
Studio/Company: MGM
Tech Info: 16 mm/sound/color/98 min.
Date/Country: 1966 + USA   Type: Feature
Distr/Arch: fnc
Annotation: Juanita Moore is Sister Mary who has very little
   to do with plot or action in this fictional treatment of
   the life of Soeur Sourire, a Belgian Dominican nun (Debbie
   Reynolds as Sister Ann in the film), whose songs won world
   wide acclaim.   Conflict between the secular and the
   spiritual is resolved when Sister Ann gives away her
   guitar and heads for an African village, there to spread
   the gospel.

SINS OF RACHEL CADE, THE
Nar/Cast: Angie Dickinson + Woody Strode* + Juano Hernandez*
   + Errol John* + Rafer Johnson* + Scatman Crothers*
Screenplay: Edward Anhalt
Producer: Henry Blanke   Director: Gordon Douglas
Studio/Company: Warner Brothers
Date/Country: 1961 + USA   Type: Feature

Annotation: Angie Dickinson as a missionary nurse raising
her illegitimate son in the Belgian Congo finds she has
suitors to contend with as well as various medical
emergencies. Among the Congolese natives are: Strode as
Muwango; Errol John, Kalu; Hernandez as Kalanumu; O'Neal
as Buderga; Crothers as Musinga; and Johnson as Kosongo.

SIREN OF THE TROPICS
Alt Title(s): see La Sirene des Tropiques

SIRENE DES TROPIQUES, LA
Alt Title(s): Siren of the Tropics
Nar/Cast: Josephine Baker* + Signor Albertini + Count Pepito
Di Abatino + Pierre Batcheff
Screenplay: Maurice De Kobra   Director: Mario Nalpas + Hen-
ri Etierant
Studio/Company: Gold Talking Picture Company
Date/Country: 1927 + France   Type: Feature
Distr/Arch: imp
Annotation: Josephine Baker as Papitou, beautiful West Indi-
an mulatto daughter of a white man and a black woman,
falls in love with Berval, a visiting Frenchman; a number
of complicated circumstances bring her to Paris where she
performs in a music hall, shoots a villainous marquis (for
the sake of her lover) and manages to survive a disap-
pointing denouement to her love affair.

SISSLE AND BLAKE
Nar/Cast: Noble Sissle* + Eubie Blake*
Producer: Phonofilms
Studio/Company: Lee De Forest + Phonofilms
Tech Info: 35 mm/sound/bw/1 reel
Date/Country: 1925 + USA   Type: Musical Short
Distr/Arch: lc
Annotation: The famous team performs "I'll Never Roam From
My Swanee Home," "Affectionate Doll," and "All God's
Children."

SIT-IN
Studio/Company: NBC
Tech Info: 16 mm/sound/bw/54 min.
Date/Country: 1961 + USA   Type: Documentary
Distr/Arch: uca
Annotation: The first lunch counter 'sit-ins' in Nashville,
Tennessee, 1960.

SITTING BULL
Nar/Cast: Dale Robertson + J. Carroll Naish + John Hamilton
+ Joel Fluellen*
Screenplay: Jack DeWitt + Sidney Salkow
Producer: W.R. Frank Production   Director: Sidney Salkow
Studio/Company: United Artists
Tech Info: sound/color
Date/Country: 1954 + USA   Type: Feature
Annotation: Joel Fluellen is Sam, a small role, in this
rewrite of history and the creation of a meeting between
Sitting Bull (Naish) and President Grant (Hamilton).

SKEZAG
Producer: Joel L. Freedman + Philip F. Messina
Tech Info: 16 mm/sound/color/73 min.
Date/Country: 1970 + USA   Type: Documentary
Distr/Arch: soh
Annotation: Award-winning film depicts an encounter with a
   hustler-dope pusher-veteran who later becomes an addict,
   after having bragged that he was above addiction. Ghetto
   life and race relations are also delineated.

SKIN GAME
Nar/Cast: James Garner + Lou Gossett* + Susan Clark + Brenda
   Sykes* + Edward Asner
Screenplay: Pierre Morton
Producer: Harry Keller + Meta Rosenberg   Director: Paul
   Bogart
Studio/Company: Warner Brothers
Tech Info: 16 mm/color/sound/ 102 min.
Date/Country: 1971   Type: Feature
Distr/Arch: mac + mod + tfc + who
Annotation: James Garner and lou Gossett as a pair of con
   artists. Their game is: Garner sells Gossett as a slave;
   Gossett later escapes; the pair split the profits.

SKULLDUGGERY
Nar/Cast: William Marshall* + Susan Clark + Burt Reynolds
Screenplay: Nelson Gidding
Producer: Saul David   Director: Gordon Douglas
Studio/Company: Universal
Tech Info: 16 mm/sound/color/100 min.
Date/Country: 1970 + USA   Type: Feature
Distr/Arch: tmc + uni
Annotation: William Marshall is the attorney general in-
   volved in the trial of Douglas (Reynolds), a young ad-
   venturer searching for phosphorus deposits in New Guinea,
   who gets involved in a controversy over a newly discovered
   species of Ape-Man about to be bred and enslaved by
   American scientists. The film raises the ubiquitous
   "master" race/white supremacy issue.

SKY DRAGON, THE
Series: Charlie Chan
Nar/Cast: Roland Winters + Mantan Moreland* + Keye Luke +
   Tim Ryan
Screenplay: Oliver Drake   Story: Clint Johnstone
Producer: James S. Burkett   Director: Lesley Selander
Studio/Company: Monogram
Tech Info: 16 mm/sound/bw
Date/Country: 1949 + USA   Type: Feature
Annotation: Mantan Moreland is Birmingham Brown, Charlie
   Chan's chauffeur and comic foil.

SKYJACKED
Nar/Cast: Charlton Heston + Roosevelt Grier* + Leslie Ug-
   gams* + Yvette Mimieux
Screenplay: Stanley R. Greenberg   Story: David Harper
Producer: Walter Seltzer   Director: John Guillermin
Studio/Company: MGM

Tech Info: 100 min.
Date/Country: 1972 + USA   Type: Feature
Distr/Arch: fnc
Annotation: Rosie Grier plays a jazz cellist in this air
    flight adventure.

SLAMS, THE
Nar/Cast: Jim Brown* + Judy Pace* + Roland Harris
    Director: Jonathan Kaplan
Studio/Company: MGM
Tech Info: 16 mm/sound/color/3 reels/97 min.
Date/Country: 1973 + USA   Type: Feature
Distr/Arch: fnc
Annotation: In "the slams" for stealing a million in Mafia
    drug money, Brown meets a lot of "friendly" folk who would
    like to have the money. But he remains invincible against
    the white mobs, black militants, corrupt prison officials.

SLAUGHTER'S BIG RIP-OFF
Nar/Cast: Jim Brown* + Brock Peters* + Don Stroud
Screenplay: Charles Johnson
Producer: Monroe Sachson   Director: Gordon Douglas
Studio/Company: American International
Tech Info: 16 mm/sound/color/94 min.
Date/Country: 1973 + USA   Type: Feature
Distr/Arch: swa
Annotation: Slaughter (Jim Brown) seeks revenge on a mob
    boss who tried to kill him and in so doing killed some of
    his friends.

SLAUGHTER
Nar/Cast: Jim Brown* + Stella Stevens + Rip Torn
Screenplay: M. Hanna + D. Williams
Producer: Monroe Sachson   Director: Jack Starrett
Studio/Company: Universal International
Tech Info: 16 mm/sound/color/3 reels/92 min.
Date/Country: 1972 + USA
Annotation: Brown is an ex-Green Beret whose life is tem-
    porarily shattered by a gangster planted bomb which kills
    his mother and father. He searches for the killer seeking
    revenge. In his rampage, he encounters Mafia henchmen,
    government agents and beautiful ladies.

SLAVE EXPERIENCE, THE
Producer: Doubleday
Tech Info: 16 mm/color/9 min.
Date/Country: 1970 + USA   Type: Dramatized Documentary
Distr/Arch: dc
Annotation: The story of slavery in North Carolina seen
    through the eyes of the slaves. Uses graphics, en-
    gravings, etchings and music. Provided by Center for
    Southern Folklore.

SLAVE REVOLT
Producer: WCBS-TV + Columbia University
Tech Info: 16 mm/bw/30 min.
Date/Country: 1968 + USA   Type: Documentary
Distr/Arch: umic

Annotation: The history of slave rebellions discussed by
Lerone Bennett*. Provided by Center for Southern
Folklore.

SLAVE SHIP
Nar/Cast: Warner Baxter + Wallace Beery + Elizabeth Allen +
Mickey Rocney + Hall Johnson Choir*
Producer: Nunnally Johnson   Director: Tay Garnett
Studio/Company: Twentieth Century-Fox
Tech Info: 16 mm/sound/bw/92 min.
Date/Country: 1937 + USA   Type: Feature
Distr/Arch: fnc
Annotation: Warner Baxter plays a captain of a slave ship.
He falls in love with Elizabeth Allen who talks him out of
slaving, thereby precipitating a mutiny. The Hall Johnson
Choir occupy the hold of the ship and later leap into the
sea coffled together and chained to an anchor.

SLAVE'S DEVOTION, A
Date/Country: 191- + USA
Annotation: Loyal slave Jim flees a cruel overseer, becomes
a Confederate runner and dies saving his old master.

SLAVE'S STORY: RUNNING A THOUSAND MILES TO FREEDOM, A
Series: American Heriitage Film
Producer: Oberon Communications, Inc.
Tech Info: 16 mm/sound/color/1 reel/29 min.
Date/Country: 1972 + USA   Type: Documentary Drama
Distr/Arch: lca
Annotation: The story of the harrowing escape from slavery
of William and Ellen Craft, dramatized and narrated by one
of their descendants. The thousand mile journey is from
Macon, Georgia to Philadelphia, Pa. The ingenious plan:
Ellen (light skinned), dressed as a male planter not well
enough to travel alone, takes her "man" William on the
train - first class - to minister to her needs. This is
one of the most famous slave narratives, recorded by William, 1848.

SLAVE, THE
Nar/Cast: Florence Laurence + James Kirkwood + Harry Salter
+ Mary Pickford + Mack Sennett + Arthur Johnson
Producer: D. W. Griffith + Biograph   Director: D. W. Grif-
fith
Studio/Company: Biograph
Tech Info: 35 mm/silent/bw/998 ft.
Date/Country: 1909 + USA   Type: Feature
Annotation: A Roman costume drama with blacks (whites in
black face) as atmosphere.

SLAVER, THE
Studio/Company: Peter P. Jones Film Company
Date/Country: 1917 + USA
Annotation: A tribal chieftain on the coast of Africa
reverses the slavery pattern: he makes a deal with a white
sea captain to buy a white girl. A black cabin boy saves
her, sacrificing himself in the process.

SLAVERY AND SLAVE RESISTANCE
Nar/Cast: Cleavon Little*
Producer: Arno Press + New York Times
Tech Info: 16 mm/sound/color/24 min./1 reel
Date/Country: 1969 + USA   Type: Documentary
Distr/Arch: corf + iu + adl + nyu + per + vfi
Annotation: Examines the history and long lasting effects of
    slavery and slave resistance in North America from its
    inception during the 17th century up to and through the
    1960's. Shows how some Blacks rioted aboard slave ships,
    sabotaged work orders, and sometimes murdered to gain
    freedom. Narrated by Cleavon Little.

SLAVERY, THE BLACK MAN AND THE MAN
Nar/Cast: Damon Braswell*
Producer: Silvermine   Director: John Chandler
Tech Info: 16 mm/sound/color/22 min.
Date/Country: 1972 + USA   Type: Documentary
Distr/Arch: mac
Annotation: Uses contemporary scenes of poverty/drugs in the
    ghetto, juxtaposed to graphics, picturing slavery to show
    the dramatic relationship between two periods of bondage.
    Damion Braswell* of the Negro Ensemble Company narrates.
    Music by Frank Leadley Moore*.

SLAVERY
Series: History of the Negro People
Producer: NET
Tech Info: 16 mm/sound/bw/1 reel/30 min.
Date/Country: 1953 + USA   Type: Documentary
Distr/Arch: iu
Annotation: Based on actual testimony of former slaves,
    tells of the tragic and sometimes humorous experiences of
    life in the old South. Tells of small incidents in the
    lives of many slaves and depicts the liberation of slaves
    by the Yankee troops. Uses Negro spirituals to help tell
    the story of slavery.

SLAVES AND STATESMEN
Producer: Shanks + Comco Productions
Studio/Company: PBS
Tech Info: 16 mm/sound/color/30 min./1 reel
Date/Country: 1976   Type: TV Docuumentary
Annotation: Film about the life of Booker T. Washington at
    Tuskegee Institute narrated by Hugh Downs.

SLAVES
Nar/Cast: Barbara Ann Teer* + Robert Kya-Hill* + Ossie
    Davis* + Stephen Boyd + Julius Harris* + Eva Jessye* +
    Dionne Warwick* + Aldine King* + James Heath* + Gwendolyn
    Bell*
Screenplay: Herbert Biberman + John O. Killens*
Producer: Philip Langner   Director: Herbert Biberman
Tech Info: 16 mm/sound/color/102 min.
Date/Country: 1969 + USA   Type: Feature
Distr/Arch: wrs
Annotation: In an update of Uncle Tom's Cabin, Boyd is McK-
    ay, the Le Gree character, with Warwick as his mistress

Cassy; Davis as the strong slave Luke who is flogged to
death because he refuses to tell Cassy's whereabouts.
United by his death, the slaves set fire to the cotton
sheds diverting McKay so that Cassy and some of the others
can escape to freedom.

SLENDER THREAD, THE
Nar/Cast: Sidney Poitier* + Anne Bancroft + Telly Savalas
Screenplay: Sterling Silliphant
Producer: Stephen Alexander   Director: Sydney Pollack
Studio/Company: Paramount
Tech Info: 16 mm/sound/bw/3 reels/100 min.
Date/Country: 1966 + USA   Type: Feature
Distr/Arch: fnc
Annotation: Poitier, a psychology student and volunteer
    worker at a crisis clinic in Seattle, receives a phone
    call from a woman (Bancroft) who has taken an overdose of
    barbiturates. Through his patience and actions by a
    police emergency unit, they save her life. Music by
    Quincy Jones*.

SLOW POKE
Nar/Cast: Stepin Fetchit* + Bunny and the Cotton Girls*
Screenplay: Sid Herzig   Director: Sid Herzig
Studio/Company: Educational Pictures + Fox Pictures Release
Tech Info: 16 mm/bw/sound/1 reel/10 min.
Date/Country: 1932 + USA   Type: Musical Short
Distr/Arch: kpf
Annotation: A "lazy" Fetchit performance with music.

SMALL TALK
Series: Our Gang
Nar/Cast: Our Gang + Allen Hoskins* + Edith Fortier*
Screenplay: Robert F. McGowan
Producer: Robert F. McGowan + Hal Roach   Director: Robert
    F. McGowan
Studio/Company: MGM + Roach
Tech Info: super 8 mm/16 mm/sound/1 reel/20 min.
Date/Country: 1929 + USA   Type: Comedy Short
Distr/Arch: bla + roa
Annotation: The gang gets involved in Wheezer's and Mary
    Ann's family problems. Allen Hoskins is Farina.

SMALL TOWN GIRL
Nar/Cast: Nat King Cole* + Jane Powell + Farley Granger +
    Ann Miller
Screenplay: Dorothy Cooper + Dorothy Kingsley
Producer: Joe Pasternak   Director: Leslie Kardos
Studio/Company: MGM
Tech Info: 16 mm/sound/bw/93 min.
Date/Country: 1953 + USA   Type: Feature
Distr/Arch: fnc
Annotation: Farley Granger plays a spoiled young millionare
    who gets jailed for speeding through a small town, and
    stays long enough to fall in love with the local beauty.
    Nat (King) Cole plays himself, and in one appearance per-
    forms "Flaming Heart."

SMART MONEY
Nar/Cast: Edward G. Robinson + James Cagney + Boris Karloff
    Story: Kubec Glasman + John Bright   Director: Alfred E.
    Green
Studio/Company: Warners
Tech Info: 16 mm/sound/bw/83 min.
Date/Country: 1931 + USA   Type: Feature
Distr/Arch: uas
Annotation: Robinson is a gambling barber who carries a rab-
    bit's foot and occasionally rubs the head of Negro for
    good luck. His reputation for winning is so illustrious
    that when he goes to the city to try big time gambling,
    everyone wants to invest in him, including the shoe shine
    boy (black actor uncredited): "Don't Forget Me, Boss."

SMASH YOUR BAGGAGE
Nar/Cast: Roy Eldridge* + Dickie Wells* + Small's Paradise
    Entertainers*   Director: Roy Mack + Joseph Henabery
Studio/Company: Vitaphone
Tech Info: 16 mm/sound/1 reel
Date/Country: 1932 + USA   Type: Musical Short
Distr/Arch: uas
Annotation: The plot devolves on the treasurers of the rail-
    road brotherhood losing funds shooting craps. The locale
    is Grand Central Station where the redcaps work and the
    high point is a benefit revue with a half dozen musi-
    cal/dance numbers.

SMILE ORANGE
Date/Country: 1975 + Jamaica   Type: Feature

SMILE WINS, THE
Series: Our Gang
Nar/Cast: Our Gang + Allen Hoskins* + Jannie Hoskins*
Screenplay: Hal Roach + Robert F. McGowan
Producer: Hal Roach   Director: Robert F. McGowan
Studio/Company: Pathe
Tech Info: bw/silent/2 reels
Date/Country: 1928 + USA   Type: Comedy Short
Annotation: With the help of the gang and a neighbor's
    punctured pipeline, Farina (Allen Hoskins) is able to out-
    wit the landlord, help his invalid mother and to fade out,
    dressed in high hat, swallow-tailed coat, directing his
    chauffeur to drive him to the new mansion.

SMILING GHOST, THE
Nar/Cast: Wayne Morris + Alexis Smith + Willie Best* + Alan
    Hale
Screenplay: Ken Gamet + Stuart Palmer   Story: Stuart Palmer
    Director: Lewis Seiler
Studio/Company: Warner Brothers
Tech Info: 16 mm/sound/bw/71 min.
Date/Country: 1941 + USA   Type: Feature
Distr/Arch: uas
Annotation: Murder mystery, complete with haunted house,
    femme fatal, and Willie Best to be afraid of everything.

SMILING HATE

Studio/Company: Superior Film Company
Date/Country: 1924 + USA   Type: Feature
Annotation: Melodrama about goldmining, thievery, assault,
    and romance, which works itself out properly in the end.
    "Smiling Hate" is the disguise of the owner of Piker's
    Hold gold mine.

SMOOTH_AS_SILK
Nar/Cast: Kent Taylor + Virginia Grey + Jane Adams + Milburn
    Stone + John Litel + Charles Trowbridge + Teresa Harris*
    Director: Charles Barton
Studio/Company: Universal
Date/Country: 1946 + USA   Type: Feature
Annotation: Teresa Harris tries to infuse life into her role
    of maid in this film.

SNIPER'S_RIDGE
Nar/Cast: Al Freeman, Jr.* + Jack Ging
Screenplay: Tom Murizzi
Producer: John Bushelman   Director: John Bushelman
Studio/Company: Fox
Tech Info: 16 mm/sound/bw/61 min.
Date/Country: 1961 + USA   Type: Feature
Distr/Arch: wcf
Annotation: Freeman is Gwathney, one of the battle weary
    soldiers subjected to the command of a tough but cowardly
    superior at the front during the Korean War.

SNOW_WHITE
Nar/Cast: Cab Calloway* and his Orchestra
Producer: Max Fleischer   Director: Dave Fleischer
Studio/Company: Warner Brothers
Tech Info: 16 mm/sound/1 reel/8 min.
Date/Country: 1934 + USA   Type: Animated Short
Distr/Arch: emg + kpf
Annotation: Betty Boop cartoon, with Cab Calloway singing
    the songs on the track.

SNOWS_OF_KILIMANJARO,_THE
Nar/Cast: Gregory Peck + Susan Hayward + Paul Thompson* +
    Everett Smith* + Benny Carter*
Screenplay: Casey Robinson   Story: Ernest Hemingway
Producer: Darryl F. Zanuck   Director: Henry King
Studio/Company: 20th Century Fox
Date/Country: 1952 + USA   Type: Feature
Annotation: loosely based on Hemingway's short story, the
    film tells of writer/hunter's life through flashbacks as
    he lies dying on Safari. Benny Carter* and rhythm section
    in a jazz sequence.

SO_RED_THE_ROSE
Nar/Cast: Margaret Sullavan + Janet Beecher + Walter Connal-
    ly + Randolph Scott + Robert Cummings + Dickie Moore +
    Clarence Muse* + Daniel Haynes* + George Reed*
Screenplay: Maxwell Anderson   Director: King Vidor
Studio/Company: Paramount
Tech Info: 16 mm/sound/bw/2 reels/83 min.
Date/Country: 1935 + USA   Type: Feature

Distr/Arch: uni
Annotation: A movie of the Old South as it goes off to war.
  Daniel Haynes and Clarence Muse portray the two extremes
  of the black response to slavery.

SOLEI-O
Nar/Cast: Robert liensol*   Director: Mal Hondo*
Tech Info: 16 mm/sound/bw/3 reels/106 min./in French with
  English subtitles
Date/Country: 1972 + France + Mauritania   Type: Feature
Annotation: This first feature by a young Mauritanian
  theater director, explores the plight of a black African
  in Paris who seeks work and dignity , but is denied both.

SOLID SENIERS
Nar/Cast: Edna Mae Harris* + "Rubberneck" Holmes*
Date/Country: 194- + USA

SOLO
Nar/Cast: Louis Armstrong* and His Band   Director: Jorn
  Winther
Date/Country: 1965
Annotation: Louis Armstrong and his All Stars Band perform
  "I've Got a Lot of Livin' to Do," "My Man," "Mack the
  Knife" and others.

SOME ARE MORE EQUAL THAN OTHERS
Producer: CBS
Tech Info: 16 mm/sound/bw/40 min.
Date/Country: 1971 + USA   Type: TV Documentary
Distr/Arch: imp
Annotation: Inequities in the bail system, jury selection
  and civil actions are shown through the legal treatment of
  various ethnic minorities.

SOME BABY
Nar/Cast: Ebony Players*
Studio/Company: Ebony Film Corporation
Date/Country: 1918 + USA

SOME OF MY BEST FRIENDS ARE WHITE
Producer: Michael Lathem
Studio/Company: Robeck + BBC-TV Production
Date/Country: 1967   Type: TV Documentary
Distr/Arch: tl
Annotation: An examination of America's racial problem as
  discussed from the point of view of the black middle-
  class. Includes an interview with Gordon Parks*.

SOME TALK ABOUT POOL ROOMS AND GIN MILLS
Producer: Paulist Productions
Tech Info: 16 mm/sound/bw/28 min.
Date/Country: 1967 + USA   Type: Documentary
Distr/Arch: aim + ifp
Annotation: A Black family is forced to shelter a white gun-
  man. Their attitudes toward life are revealed while in
  this situation of tension.

SOME WHITE HOPE
Nar/Cast: Donald McBride
Studio/Company: Vitagraph
Date/Country: 1915 + USA   Type: Comedy Short
Annotation: Story of Hiram Limburger (McBride), a braggart
    who dreams he is being beaten in a boxing match with black
    champion "Lam Bangford," is saved by his wife who wakens
    him with a bucket of water.

SOMETHING OF VALUE
Nar/Cast: Sidney Poitier* + Rock Hudson + William Marshall +
    Ivan Dixon* + Junno Hernandez* + Frederick O'Neil* + Ken
    Renard* + Somadu Jackson*
Screenplay: Richard Brooks   Story: Robert Ruark   Director:
    Richard Brooks
Studio/Company: MGM
Tech Info: 16mm/ sound/ bw/ 113 min.
Date/Country: 1957 + USA   Type: Feature
Distr/Arch: fnc
Annotation: A dramatization of the Mau Mau uprising in Kenya
    which pits native African against British planter and sets
    Kimani (Poitier) against Peter McKenzie (Hudson), his
    erstwhile childhood friend. The film stops short of Keny-
    an independence but William Marshall plays a Kikuyu leader
    who bears some resemblance to Jomo Kenyatta.

SOMETHING TO SHOUT ABOUT
Nar/Cast: Don Ameche + Janet Blair + Jack Oakie + William
    Gaxton + Cobina Wright, Jr. + Veda Ann Borg + Hazel Scott*
    + Teddy Wilson and his band*
Screenplay: Lou Breslow + Ed Ellscu
Producer: Gregory Ratoff   Director: Gregory Ratoff
Studio/Company: Columbia
Date/Country: 1943 + USA   Type: Feature
Annotation: This musical comedy marked Hazel Scott's film
    debut.

SON HOUSE
Producer: Seattle Folklore Society
Tech Info: 25 min.
Date/Country: 1969 + USA
Annotation: Performances on film by the Mississippi Delta
    bluesman Son House*.

SON OF INGAGI
Nar/Cast: Zack Williams* + Four Toppers* + Laura Bowman* +
    Spencer Williams* + Alfred Grant* + Daisy Buford* + Earl
    J. Morris* + Arthur Ray*
Screenplay: Spencer Williams*   Director: Richard C. Kohn
Studio/Company: Harly Wood Productions + Sack Amusement En-
    terprises
Date/Country: 1940 + USA   Type: Feature
Distr/Arch: lc
Annotation: Williams plays a detective in this "African"
    style melodrama about hidden gold, murder and theft, with
    a happy ending.

SON OF KONG

Nar/Cast: Robert Armstrong + Helen Mack + Noble Johnson*
Screenplay: Ruth Rose   Director: Ernest B. Schoedsack
Studio/Company: RKO
Date/Country: 1933 + USA
Annotation: Kong's progeny loses much of his sire's viril-
    ity, in this sequel to <u>King Kong</u>, helping out a motley
    group of whites after a treasure. He also saves Robert
    Armstrong during the big climactic earthquake.' Noble
    Johnson's role is unremarkable.

SON OF SATAN
Nar/Cast: Lawrence Chenault* + Shingzie Howard* + Andrew S.
    Bishop* + Ida Anderson* + Edna Morton*
Studio/Company: Micheaux Film Corporation
Date/Country: 1922 + USA   Type: Feature
Annotation: The plot of this film revolves around the ex-
    perience of a man spending a night in a haunted house in
    order to win a bet.

SONG AFTER SORROW
Series: National Archives Gift Collection
Tech Info: 16 mm/silent/3 reels/bw
Annotation: At the Bibanga Leper Camp patients learn to be
    self-supporting during treatment. (Part of Record Group
    200 HF series, Harmon Foundation Collection).

SONG OF FREEDOM
Nar/Cast: Paul Robeson* + Elizabeth Welch* + Robert Adams* +
    Orlando Martins* + James Solomon + Toto Ware*   Director:
    J. Elder Wills
Studio/Company: British Lion-Hammer
Tech Info: 16 mm/sound/bw/2 reels/70 min.
Date/Country: 1937 + Britain   Type: Feature
Distr/Arch: bud + kpf + mog + cie + rad + emg
Annotation: Paul Robeson plays a London stevedore, a
    descendant of slaves, who longs to return to his homeland
    in Africa to help his oppressed people. To this end, he
    becomes an opera singer which gives him the opportunity to
    raise money and to sing for the film audience.

SONG OF THE SOUTH
Nar/Cast: Ruth Warrick + James Baskett* + Lucille Watson +
    Hattie McDaniel* + Luana Patten + Bobby Driscoll   Story:
    Joel Chandler Harris
Producer: Walt Disney
Studio/Company: RKO Radio + Disney
Date/Country: 1947 + USA   Type: Feature
Annotation: Disney studios combined live and animated action
    in this movie based on Uncle Remus stories with James
    Baskett as the story telling "Uncle." NAACP and IFRG tried
    to stop the filming because of the stereotyped character
    of Uncle Remus.

SONNY FORD, DELTA ARTIST
Producer: William Ferris + Josette Ferris
Tech Info: 16 mm/bw/sound/1 reel/45 min.
Date/Country: 1969 + USA   Type: Documentary
Distr/Arch: iu + pen

Annotation: Documents the life and family of Mississippi
   blues singer James 'Sonny Ford' Thomas, presenting an in
   depth view of the social context from which the blues
   emerged as a musical form. Shows 'Sonny' performing in
   the homes of friends and in local 'juke joints' and
   reveals the involvement and self expression this music
   elicits from the people.

SONNY JIM AT THE MARDI GRAS
Series: Sonny Jim
Producer: Tefft Johnson   Type: Comedy Short
Annotation: A black girl is punished by her mother for al-
   lowing jim to lead her by the hand through the luna park
   steeplechase to the beach.

SOUL CITY
Producer: NET
Tech Info: 16 mm/sound/bw/1 reel/13 min.
Date/Country: 1971 + USA   Type: Documentary
Distr/Arch: iu
Annotation: Focuses on Soul City, a black-controlled commun-
   ity in Warren County, North Carolina, being developed by
   Floyd McKissick*. Observes that this experiment is taking
   place because blacks found that moving into large cities
   in an attempt to escape the conditions of the South did
   not allow them to control their own lives.

SOUL OF NIGGER CHARLEY, THE
Nar/Cast: Fred Williamson* + D'Urville Martin* + Denise
   Nichols* + Pedro Armendariz
Screenplay: Harold Stone   Story: Harold Stone
Producer: Larry G. Spangler   Director: Larry G. Spangler
Studio/Company: Paramount
Tech Info: 16 mm/sound/color/3 reels/109 min.
Date/Country: 1973 + USA   Type: Feature
Distr/Arch: fnc
Annotation: Sequel to Legend of Nigger Charley, a post-Civil
   war slave community in Mexico is saved by Charley and
   Mexican bandito cohorts.

SOUL SOLDIER
Alt Title(s): See The Red White and Black
Nar/Cast: Isabell Sanford* + Rafer Johnson* + Robert DoQui*
   + Lincoln Kilpatrick* + Cesar Romero + Janee Michelle* +
   Isaac Fields* + Otis Taylor* + Bill Collins* + John Fox* +
   Byrd Holland* + Bobby Clark*
Screenplay: Marlene Weld
Producer: Stuart Hirschman + James Northern   Director: John
   Cardos
Studio/Company: Hirschman-Northern Productions
Tech Info: 16mm/ sound/ color/ 84-103 min.
Date/Country: 1970 + USA   Type: Feature
Distr/Arch: mac + sel + wfc + wil
Annotation: Western drama about an all black regiment of the
   U.S. 10th Cavalry stationed at Fort Davis, Texas, 1871,
   under the command of white officers and ironically
   fighting against and defeating red men. The love triangle
   consists of DoQui/ Michelle/ Kilpatrick. Johnson plays

Private Armstrong, a special friend to the Indians.

SOUL TO SOUL
Nar/Cast: Wilson Pickett* + Ike Turner* + Tina Turner* +
   Santana* + Roberta Flack* + Les McCann* + Eddie Harris* +
   Voices of East Harlem*   Director: Denis Saunders
Studio/Company: Cinerama
Tech Info: 16 mm/sound/color/96 min.
Date/Country: 1971 + USA   Type: Entertainment Feature
Distr/Arch: swa
Annotation: Filmed during the week-long celebration of the
   14th anniversary of Ghana's independence in Accra's Black
   Star Square. Additional footage includes urban scenes and
   Roberta Flack's trip to a slave fort in Elmina.

SOULS OF SIN
Nar/Cast: Savannah Churchill* + William Greaves* + Jimmy
   Wright* + Billie Allen* + Emery Richardson* + Louise Jack-
   son* + Powell Lindsay* + Charlie Mae Rae* + Bill Chase* +
   Jessie Walter* + Harris* and Scott*
Screenplay: Powell Lindsay
Producer: William Alexander*   Director: Powell Lindsay
Studio/Company: Alexander Productions
Tech Info: sound/bw
Date/Country: 1949 + USA

SOUND AND THE FURY, THE
Nar/Cast: Ethel Waters* + Margaret Leighton + Joanne
   Woodward + Yul Brynner
Screenplay: Irving Raveth + Harriet Frank, Jr.   Story:
   William Faulkner
Producer: Jerry Wald   Director: Martin Ritt
Studio/Company: Fox
Tech Info: 16 mm/sound/color/115 min.
Date/Country: 1959   Type: Feature
Distr/Arch: fnc
Annotation: Film version of Faulkner's novel about the de-
   cline of a Southern family. Ethel Waters is Dilsey, the
   family cook.

SOUND OF JAZZ, THE
Nar/Cast: Henry "Red" Allen and the All Stars + Billie
   Holiday* + Mal Waldron All Stars + Count Basie's All
   Stars* + Jimmy Rushing* + Jimmy Giuffre* Trio + Thelonius
   Monk*
Producer: Nat Hentoff + Whitney Balliett   Director: Jack
   Smight
Tech Info: 60 min.
Date/Country: 1957 + USA
Annotation: Musical extravaganza including the above listed
   artists performing numbers such as "Wild Man Blues," "Fine
   and Mellow," and "I Left My Baby."

SOUNDER
Nar/Cast: Paul Winfield* + Cicely Tyson* + Kevin Hooks* +
   Taj Majal*
Screenplay: Lonne Elder, III*
Producer: Robert Radnitz   Director: Martin Ritt

Studio/Company: 20th Century Fox
Tech Info: 16 mm/color/sound/3 reels/106 min.
Date/Country: 1972 + USA   Type: Feature
Distr/Arch: fnc
Annotation: Desperate because his family is hungry, a poor
   black sharecropper during the Depression in Louisiana,
   steals meat from a white man's smokehouse and is sentenced
   to a chain gang. In his absence his wife molds a strong
   family unit which survives poverty, loneliness, back-
   breaking farming chores and despair.

SOUNDS OF THE SEVENTIES
Nar/Cast: Taj Mahal*
Producer: Richard W. Jackman
Tech Info: 42 min.
Date/Country: 1971 + Britain
Annotation: Film record of four popular American groups at a
   concert in The Royal Albert Hall in London.

SOUTH AFRICAN ESSAY: FRUIT AND FEAR
Producer: NET
Tech Info: 16 mm/sound/bw/2 reels/59 min.
Date/Country: 1965 + USA   Type: Documentary
Distr/Arch: iu
Annotation: Documents and contrasts the two societies ex-
   isting in South Africa today--the black majority and the
   ruling white minority.   Interviews leaders of both factions to present their views of the apartheid doctrine
   which the whites enforce. Contrasts social and economic
   privileges of the two groups.

SOUTH AFRICAN ESSAY: ONE NATION--TWO NATIONALISMS
Producer: NET
Tech Info: 16 mm/sound/bw/2 reels/59 min.
Date/Country: 1965 + USA   Type: Documentary
Distr/Arch: iu
Annotation: Uses documentary film footage to examine the
   country's Nationalist Party and the policy of strict
   separation of people according to racial and tribal
   origins.   Features interviews with leaders from the
   several groups concerned.

SOUTH OF DIXIE
Nar/Cast: Mantan Moreland*
Date/Country: 1944 + USA   Type: Feature

SOUTH: HEALTH AND HUNGER, THE
Producer: NET
Tech Info: 16 mm/sound/bw/1 reel/23 min.
Date/Country: 1969 + USA   Type: Documentary
Distr/Arch: iu
Annotation: Surveys the inadequate nutrition, the lack of
   water, and too few medical facilities which face many
   black southern residents. Shows how these problems affect
   both the physical and mental development of the people.
   Utilizes the talents of black filmmakers to acquaint pe-
   ople with black America.

SOUTH, THE: ROOTS OF THE URBAN CRISIS
Producer: Encyclopedia Britannica Ed. Corp.
Tech Info: 16 mm/sound/bw/1 reel/26 min.
Date/Country: 1969 + USA   Type: Documentary
Distr/Arch: iu + ebec
Annotation: Illustrates how the cyclical pattern which links
    poverty to violence has many of its roots in the South.
    Describes how increased industrialization has resulted in
    fewer agricultural jobs and a continuing deprivation in
    housing and education.

SOUTHERN CONSUMERS' COOPERATIVE
Producer: NET
Tech Info: 16 mm/bw/sound/1 reel/9 min.
Date/Country: 1968 + USA   Type: Documentary
Distr/Arch: iu
Annotation: Looks at a cooperative in Louisiana started by a
    black priest as a farming enterprise and run entirely by
    Blacks. Shows the cooperative's shrimp boat, loan com-
    pany, gas station, and how it produces candy for large
    chains.

SOUTHERN GIRL'S HEROISM
Date/Country: 1911 + USA   Type: Feature
Annotation: A Civil War melodrama in which a union officer
    kisses "Topsie," the slave of the southern girl with whom
    he is in love, and marches off with both of them in the
    closing sequence.

SOUTHERNER, THE
Nar/Cast: Stepin Fetchit* + Gertrude Howard* + Laurence Tib-
    bett + Esther Ralston
Screenplay: Bess Meredyth + Wells Roof   Director: Harry
    Pollard
Studio/Company: MGM
Date/Country: USA   Type: Feature
Annotation: Tibbett as Jeffrey, the lovably irresponsible
    son of a wealthy Southern family, wanders about for five
    years but returns to beautiful Antonia (Esther ralston).
    Gertrude Howard is Naomi; Stepin Fetchit as Hokey provides
    the humor along with Roland Young and Cliff Edwards as
    Snipe.

SPANKING AGE, THE
Series: Our Gang
Nar/Cast: Our Gang + Allen Hoskins*
Screenplay: Robert F. McGowan
Producer: Hal Roach   Director: Robert F. McGowan
Studio/Company: MGM
Tech Info: bw/silent with synchronized music track and sound
    effects, on disc/2 reels
Date/Country: 1928 + USA   Type: Comedy Short
Annotation: The gang attends a party given by Mary Ann and
    Wheezer; Mary Ann decides to prepare the food herself.
    Allen Hoskins stars as Farina.

SPANKY
Series: Our Gang

War/Cast: Our Gang + Matthew Beard*
Screenplay: Hal E. Roach + H.M. Walker
Producer: Robert F. McGowan + Hal Roach   Director: Robert
    F. McGowan
Studio/Company: MGM
Tech Info: super 8 mm/16 mm/bw/sound/1 reel/20 min.
Date/Country: 1932 + USA   Type: Comedy Short
Distr/Arch: bla
Annotation: Breezy must keep, an eye on baby brother Spanky
    between scenes of the gang's production of "Uncle Tom's
    Cabin." The "Uncle Tom" segments, reworked from "Uncle
    Tom's Uncle" have various gang members in blackface and
    Stymie must handle both Uncle Tom and Topsy.

SPARKLE: FROM GHETTO TO SUPERSTAR
War/Cast: Philip M. Thomas* + Irene Cara* + Lonette McKee* +
    Dorian Harewood* + Tony King* + Dwan Smith* + DeWayne Jes-
    se* + Beatrice Winde* + Mary Alice*
Screenplay: Joel Schumacher
Studio/Company: Warner Brothers
Tech Info: 16 mm/sound/color/93 min.
Date/Country: 1977 + USA   Type: Feature
Distr/Arch: swa
Annotation: Drama of three girl singers who rise from the
    Harlem ghetto to stardom.   Music by Curtis Mayfield*,
    music by Lester Wilson*.

SPARTACUS
Nar/Cast: Kirk Douglas + Jean Simmons + Woody Strode*
Screenplay: Dalton Trumbo   Story: Howard Fast
Producer: Edward Lewis   Director: Stanley Kubrick
Studio/Company: Universal-International
Tech Info: 16 mm/sound/color/184 min.
Date/Country: 1960 + USA   Type: Feature
Distr/Arch: twy + uni
Annotation: Kirk Douglas stars as Spartacus in this film
    about the great slave rebellion in Rome during 1st
    century, B.C. Strode is one of the slaves.

SPEAKER, THE
Producer: American Library Association
Tech Info: 16mm/ sound/ color/ 42 min.
Date/Country: 1977 + USA   Type: Dramatized Documentary
Distr/Arch: oif + ala
Annotation: First Amendment controversy develops when a high
    school student committee invites a scientist to speak on
    his theory that Blacks are genetically inferior to whites.
    The school board bans "the speaker" who is never seen on
    camera.

SPECIAL MESSENGER, A
Studio/Company: Kalem
Tech Info: silent/bw
Date/Country: 1911 + USA
Annotation: A girl spies for the Confederacy while her black
    butler takes care of her ailing lover wounded in the war.

SPENCER'S MOUNTAIN

Nar/Cast: Barbara McNair* + Henry Fonda + Maureen O'Hara
Screenplay: Delmer Daves
Producer: Delmer Daves   Director: Delmer Daves
Studio/Company: Warners
Tech Info: 16 mm/sound/color/119 min.
Date/Country: 1963 + USA   Type: Feature
Distr/Arch: arg + bud + ccc + cha + ics + mac + mod + mot +
    nat + rca + sel + tfc + tmc + twy + unf + wcf + wel +   wil
Annotation: Barbara McNair is the graduation singer at Clay-
    boy Spencer's graduation in this rural comedy-drama about
    the fourth generation of a Wyoming settler family.

SPIDER'S WEB, THE
Alt Title(s): see The Girl From Chicago
Nar/Cast: Evelyn Preer* + Billy Gulfport* + Marshall Rogers*
    + Edward Thompson* + Lorenzo McLane* + Henrietta Loveless*
    + Grace Smith*
Screenplay: Oscar Micheaux*
Producer: Oscar Micheaux*   Director: Oscar Micheaux*
Studio/Company: Micheaux Film Corporation
Tech Info: 35 mm/silent/bw/7 reels/6,913 ft.
Date/Country: 1926 + USA   Type: Feature
Annotation: Using a different cast, Micheaux produced a
    sound version of this picture in 1932 under the title The
    Girl From Chicago. In this version Norma's aunt, not her
    friend, gets involved in playing the numbers in Harlem and
    is accused of murdering the numbers banker. She is saved
    by an investigator for the Justice Department, the young
    man who wins Norma's heart.   Justice Department, the young
    man who wins Norma's heart.

SPIDERS, THE
Nar/Cast: Richard Conte + Faye Marlowe + Mantan Moreland*
Screenplay: Jo Eisinger + W. Scott Darling
Producer: Ben Silvey   Director: Robert Webb
Studio/Company: Fox
Tech Info: 16mm/ sound/ bw/ 62 min.
Date/Country: 1946 + USA   Type: Feature
Distr/Arch: fnc
Annotation: Mantan Moreland plays Henry in this melodrama
    about a private eye (Conte) who has th usual problems with
    a mysterious murderer.

SPIRIT OF YOUTH
Nar/Cast: Joe Louis* + Clarence Muse* + Mantan Moreland* +
    Edna Mae Harris* + Cleo Desmond* + Mae Turner* + Clarence
    Brooks* + Anthony Scott* + Janette O'Dell*
Screenplay: Arthur Hoerle
Producer: Lew Golder   Director: Harry Fraser
Studio/Company: Grand National Films
Tech Info: 16 mm/bw/sound/2 reels/70 min.
Date/Country: 1937 + USA   Type: Feature
Distr/Arch: kpf + thu
Annotation: Poor black fighter climbs to the top of the
    boxing world. Joe Louis plays Joe Thomas.

SPITFIRE
Nar/Cast: Edna Morton* + Edward Brown* + Lawrence Chenault*

Studio/Company: Reol
Tech Info: 16 mm/sound/bw
Date/Country: 1922 + USA
Annotation: Edna Morton is the spitfire of the title and the
    farmer's daughter who brings reality, and love, to the
    experience of the young black novelist.

SPLIT, THE
Nar/Cast: Jim Brown* + Diahann Carroll* + Julie Harris +
    Ernest Borgnine + Gene Hackman + Donald Sutherland
    Director: Gordon Fleming
Studio/Company: MGM
Tech Info: 16 mm/sound/color/3 reels/90 min.
Date/Country: 1968 + USA   Type: Feature
Distr/Arch: fnc
Annotation: Brown is a highly competent thief who decides on
    one   last caper before retiring - robbing the L.A.
    Coliseum. Music score by Quincy Jones*.

SPOOK SPOOFING
Series: Our Gang
Nar/Cast: Our Gang + Allen Hoskins*
Screenplay: Robert F. McGowan
Producer: Robert F. McGowan + Hal Roach   Director: Robert
    F. McGowan
Studio/Company: MGM + Roach
Tech Info: super 8 mm/16 mm/bw/silent/1 reel/22 min.
Date/Country: 1928 + USA   Type: Comedy Shor
Distr/Arch: bla
Annotation: Joe and the gang perpetrate an assortment of
    cruel ghostly jests on superstitious Farina. Finally a
    convenient eclipse of the sun and stormy high winds help
    turn the tables in Farina's favor. Allen Hoskins stars as
    Farina.

SPOOK WHO SAT BY THE DOOR, THE
Nar/Cast: Laurence Cook* + Paula Kelly* + James League*
Screenplay: Melvin Clay   Story: Sam Greenlee*
Producer: Ivan Dixon* + Sam Greenlee*   Director: Ivan
    Dixon*
Studio/Company: United Artist
Tech Info: 16 mm/color/sound/3 reels/102 min.
Date/Country: 1973 + USA   Type: Feature
Annotation: Film adaptation of Greenlee's novel about a
    black man's experience in government secret service and
    what he does with that experience when he is "separated"
    from the C.I.A.

SPOOKS RUN WILD
Nar/Cast: Frederick Ernest Morrison* + The Bowery Boys
    Director: Phil Rosen
Studio/Company: Monogram
Tech Info: 16 mm/sound/bw/60 min.
Date/Country: 1941 + USA   Type: Feature
Distr/Arch: bud + ivy + new + cie
Annotation: "Sunshine" Sammy, the first black to appear in
    Our Gang silents, joins the Bowery Boys in a full length
    feature.

SPOOKS
Nar/Cast: Ebony Players*
Studio/Company: Ebony Film Corporation
Date/Country: 1918 + USA

SPOOKY_HOOKY
Series: Our Gang
Nar/Cast: Our Gang + Billie Thomas*
Screenplay: Hal E. Roach
Producer: Hal Roach   Director: Gordon Douglas
Studio/Company: MGM + Roach
Tech Info: super 8 mm/16 mm/bw/sound/1 reel/10 min.
Date/Country: 1936 + USA   Type: Comedy Short
Distr/Arch: bla + roa
Annotation: The gang is done out of a trip to the circus
  because in trying to retrieve a phoney note on a scary
  night, they catch cold and are forced to stay at home.
  Billie Thomas is Buckwheat.

SPORT_OF_THE_GODS,_THE
Nar/Cast: Elizabeth Boyer* + Edward Zbrams* + Edward G.
  Brown* + Leon Williams* + Lucille Brown* + Lindsay Hall* +
  Stanley Walpole* + Walter Thomas* + Lawrence Chenault* +
  Ruby Mason*   Story: P.L. Dunbar*
Producer: Robert Levy
Studio/Company: Reol
Date/Country: 1923 + USA   Type: Feature
Annotation: Adapted from Dunbar's novel, the story deals
  with a man, Berry Hamilton, whose decency and loyalty are
  repaid by his being jailed for a crime he did not commit.
  His family moves to the North, to avoid humiliation, but
  the city has a deleterious effect on all of them.   When
  Hamilton is finally released from jail, after the real
  criminal confesses, he goes North to find his family and
  finds numerous complications to be resolved.

SPORTING_BLOOD
Alt Title(s): Horseflesh (story)
Nar/Cast: George Reed* + Clark Gable + Ernest Torrence + Ben
  Carter*   Story: Frederick Brennan   Director: Charles
  Brabin
Studio/Company: MGM
Tech Info: 16 mm/sound/bw/82 min.
Date/Country: 1931 + USA   Type: Feature
Distr/Arch: fnc
Annotation: Carter and Reed have bit roles in the the sta-
  bles in this Gable film about gambling and the training
  and racing of thoroughbreds.

SPORTS_CAVALCADE
Nar/Cast: Fay Young*
Studio/Company: All American News
Tech Info: 35 mm/bw/sound/2 reels
Date/Country: 1944 + USA
Annotation: Introductions by Young, "Dean of American Negro
  Sportswriters."

SPRING MADNESS
Nar/Cast: Maureen O'Sullivan + Lew Ayres + Burgess Meredith
   + Willie Best*
Screenplay: Edward Chodorov
Producer: Edward Chodorov   Director: S. Sylvan Simon
Studio/Company: MGM
Date/Country: 1938 + USA   Type: Feature
Annotation: Willie Best plays a small part in this romantic
   comedy about the perennial rites of spring, love and
   matrimony.

SPRUCIN' UP
Series: Our Gang
Nar/Cast: Our Gang + Billie Thomas*
Producer: Hal Roach   Director: Gus Meins
Studio/Company: MGM + Roach
Tech Info: super 8 mm/16 mm/bw/sound/1 reel/17 min.
Date/Country: 1935 + USA   Type: Comedy Short
Distr/Arch: bla + roa
Annotation: The gang changes its opinion about being neat
   when they try to win the attention of the daughter of the
   new truant officer. Finally it's a contest between Spanky
   and Alfalfa - but they get so caught up besting each
   other, that the girl is whisked away by her old boyfriend.
   Billie Thomas stars as Buckwheat.

SPY 13
Alt Title(s): see Operator 13

SPYING THE SPY
Studio/Company: Ebony Films
Tech Info: 16 mm/bw/silent/1 reel/10 min.
Date/Country: 1917 + USA   Type: Dramatic Short
Distr/Arch: kpf + lc
Annotation: The misadventures of Sambo Sam, a black (World
   War I) spy hunter, probably played by Sam Robinson*, who
   captures the wrong German (Schwartz who turns out to be
   black) and ends up in the Coffin club where he becomes an
   unwilling initiate into a secret society. He does however
   end up capturing a spy.

SQUARE JOE
Nar/Cast: Joe Jeanette* + John Lester Johnson* + Bob Slater*
   + Marian Moore*
Studio/Company: E.S.   L. Colored Feature Productions
Tech Info: 35 mm/silent/bw
Date/Country: 1921 + USA   Type: Feature
Annotation: Jeanette and Johnson are boxers in this story of
   black life

SST DEATH FLIGHT
Alt Title(s): SST Disaster in the Sky
Nar/Cast: Brock Peters* + Lorne Greene + Burgess Meredith
Screenplay: Robert Joseph + Myron Bolinsky   Story: Gordon
   Trueblood
Producer: Ron Roth   Director: David Lowell Rich
Studio/Company: ABC
Tech Info: color/90 min.

Date/Country: 1977 + USA   Type: TV Feature
Annotation: Epidemiologist of World Health Organization, Dr.
    Thurman (Peters) comes aboard the maiden flight of the
    first U.S. commercial SST. Flown in by a black helicopter
    pilot, he has deadly Sengalese viral culture put on board
    by a black mechanic. The strong box containing the
    culture is broken open when the plane is sabotaged and
    after a crash landing in Dakar, Dr. Thurman and other
    survivors demonstrate their courage by ministering to the
    injured and infected, along with humane Sengalese
    volunteers.

SST_DIASTER_IN_THE_SKY
Alt Title(s): see SST Death Flight

ST._LOUIS_BLUES,_THE
Nar/Cast: Bessie Smith* + Isabel Washington + Jimmy Morde-
    cai*   Director: Dudley Murphy
Studio/Company: RKO
Tech Info: 16 mm/bw/sound/1 reel/17 min.
Date/Country: 1929 + USA   Type: Dramatic Short
Distr/Arch: kpf + mac + emg
Annotation: Only extant film of Bessie Smith, who falls in
    love with an unfaithful man and sings the blues. Musical
    arrangements by W.C. Handy* and J. Rosamond Johnson*.

ST._LOUIS_BLUES
Nar/Cast: Nat Cole* + Eartha Kitt* + Pearl Bailey* + Cab
    Calloway* + Ella Fitzgerald* + Mahalia Jackson* + Juano
    Hernandez* + Billy Preston*
Producer: Robert Smith   Director: Allen Reisner
Studio/Company: Paramount
Tech Info: 16 mm/bw/sound/3 reels/93 min.
Date/Country: 1958 + USA   Type: Feature
Distr/Arch: fnc
Annotation: Nat King Cole stars in this fictionalized bio-
    graphy of W.C. Handy's (the "father of the Blues") life.
    His film has an all black cast from the various entertain-
    ment fields.

ST._LOUIS_BLUES
Nar/Cast: Dorothy Lamour + Lloyd Nolan + Jessie Ralph +
    Jerome Cowan + Maxine Sullivan*
Screenplay: John C. Moffitt + Malcom Boylan
Producer: Jeff Lazarus   Director: Raoul Walsh
Studio/Company: Paramount
Date/Country: 1939 + USA   Type: Feature
Annotation: Musical set on a showboat on the Mississippi,
    featuring Maxine Sullivan.

ST._LOUIS_GAL
Nar/Cast: Nina Mae McKinney* + Jack Carter*
Studio/Company: Creative Cinema Corporation
Date/Country: 1938 + USA

ST._VALENTINE'S_DAY_MASSACRE
Nar/Cast: Frank Silvera* + Jason Robards + George Segal
Screenplay: Howard Browne

Producer: Roger Corman   Director: Roger Corman
Studio/Company: Fox
Tech Info: 16 mm/sound/color/100 min.
Date/Country: 1967 + USA   Type: Feature
Distr/Arch: fnc
Annotation: Frank Silvera plays Sorello, one of the gang
   members, in this crime melodrama about the Valentine's Day
   (1929) attack by Al Capone's men on Bugs Moran's gang in
   Chicago.

STAGE DOOR CANTEEN
Nar/Cast: Cheryl Walker + William Terry + Count Basie* +
   Ethel Waters*
Screenplay: Delmer Daves
Producer: Sol Lesser   Director: Frank Borzage
Studio/Company: United Artists
Tech Info: sound/150 min.
Date/Country: 1943 + USA   Type: Feature
Annotation: Featuring a tremendous cast, the film is another
   collection of skits and songs with some of the screen's
   top stars entertaining World War II servicemen.

STAGE ENTRANCE
Nar/Cast: Charlie Parker* + Dizzy Gillespie* + Dick Hyman
Producer: Dumont Production   Director: Bill Seasman
Tech Info: 7 min.
Date/Country: 1951 + USA   Type: TV Short
Annotation: Downbeat Awards for 1951 are presented in this
   film short.

STAGE FRIGHT
Series: Our Gang
Nar/Cast: Our Gang + Ernie Morrison* + Allen Hoskins*
Screenplay: Hal Roach
Producer: Hal Roach   Director: Robert McGowan
Studio/Company: Pathe
Tech Info: silent/bw/2 reels
Date/Country: 1923 + USA   Type: Comedy Short
Annotation: A fake prince comes to town to raise money for
   starving 'Trombonians'. To raise the needed funds, a play
   is staged with the gang members as the cast. All goes
   downhill fast, especially after firecrackers disrupt the
   show. Allen Hoskins stars as Farina.

STAGGERLEE: INTERVIEW WITH BOBBY SEALE
Studio/Company: KQED TV--San Francisco
Tech Info: 60 min./bw
Date/Country: 1970 + USA   Type: Documentary
Distr/Arch: adf
Annotation: An interview with Bobby Seale* while in-
   carcerated in a San Francisco jail, where he talks of Huey
   Newton, his son Staggerlee, and his hopes for black
   families.

STALKING MOON, THE
Nar/Cast: Frank Silvera* + Gregory Peck + Eva Marie Saint
Screenplay: Alvin Sargent
Producer: Alan Pakula   Director: Robert Mulligan

Studio/Company: National General
Tech Info: sound/color/109 min.
Date/Country: 1969 + USA   Type: Feature
Annotation: Frank Silvera is Major in this western melodrama
    about Arizona in the 1880's, a veteran scout and a woman
    captive of the Apaches.

STAND UP AND CHEER
Nar/Cast: Shirley Temple + Stepin Fetchit* + Aunt Jemima*
Screenplay: Lew Green   Story: Will Rogers + Phillip Klein
    Director: Hamilton McFadden
Studio/Company: Warner Brothers
Tech Info: 16 mm/bw/sound/80 min.
Date/Country: 1934 + USA   Type: Feature
Distr/Arch: fnc
Annotation: An early Shirley Temple film in which she plays
    a child entertainer trying to convince the new Secretary
    of Amusement that she can contribute to helping the
    country laugh again. Fetchit as George Bernard Shaw does
    his routines with the "hillybilly" and the penguin and
    leads the janitors in the finale. Lois Gardella as "Aunt
    Jemima" sings "I'm Happy."

STAND UP AND FIGHT
Nar/Cast: Robert Taylor + Wallace Beery + Florence Rice +
    Clinton Rosemond*
Screenplay: James Cain + Janee Martin + Harvey Ferguson
    Director: W.S. Van Dyke, III
Studio/Company: MGM
Tech Info: 16 mm/sound
Date/Country: 1939 + USA   Type: Feature
Annotation: Robert Taylor plays a pampered aristocrat who is
    helping build the B and O. Railroad across the the Al-
    leghenies, having to battle Wallace Beery, manager of
    stage coach line along the same route and also a slave
    runner. Clinton Rosemond plays Enoch, one of that number.

STAR FOR A NIGHT
Nar/Cast: Claire Trevor + Jane Darwell + Dean Jagger + Hat-
    tie McDaniel*   Story: Karin Michaelis   Director: Lewis
    Seiler
Studio/Company: 20th Century Fox
Date/Country: 1936 + USA   Type: Feature
Annotation: Three immigrants from Austria write home to
    their blind mother of their supposed success, only to be
    shocked when she arrives for a visit. How they resolve
    this mix up is the plot of the film.   Hattie McDaniel
    plays "Hattie."

STAR IS BORN, A
Nar/Cast: Maidie Norman* + Fredric March + Janet Gaynor
    Director: William Wellman
Tech Info: 16 mm/sound/color/111 min.
Date/Country: 1937 + USA   Type: Feature
Distr/Arch: bud + mog + cie
Annotation: Maidie Norman plays a small role in this
    original version about a woman who becomes a more popular
    film star than the man who "discovered" and married her.

STAR-SPANGLED RHYTHM
Nar/Cast: Victor Moore + Betty Hutton + Katherine Dunham* +
    Eddie Anderson*
Screenplay: Harry Tugend   Director: George Marshall
Studio/Company: Paramount
Tech Info: 16 mm/sound/bw/93 min.
Date/Country: 1942 + USA   Type: Feature
Distr/Arch: uni
Annotation: Another in a series of Paramount's annual all-
    star variety shows, this time with Betty Hutton and Eddie
    Bracken, around whom a story is loosely fashioned. Dunham
    and Anderson do a musical bit together.

STARS IN MY CROWN
Nar/Cast: Juano Hernandez* + Joel McCrea + Ellen Drew + Dean
    Stockwell
Screenplay: Margret Fitts   Story: Joe D. Brown
Producer: William H. Wright   Director: Jacques Tourneur
Studio/Company: MGM
Tech Info: 16 mm/sound/bw/89 min.
Date/Country: 1950 + USA   Type: Feature
Distr/Arch: fnc
Annotation: A homey story of a parson in a small southern
    town shortly after the Civil War. Hernandez plays Uncle
    Famous Prill, an aged Negro.

STARS ON PARADE
Nar/Cast: Bob Howard* + Unamae Carlisle* + King Cole Trio* +
    Benny Carter Choir*
Tech Info: 50 min.
Date/Country: 1944 + USA   Type: Feature
Annotation: Musical film featuring the above in instrumental
    and vocal numbers.

STARTING FROM SCRATCH
Producer: NHK Japan Broadcasting Corp. + UNICEF
Tech Info: 16 mm/sound/color/1 reel/27 min.
Date/Country: n.d.   Type: Documentary
Distr/Arch: iu + un
Annotation: Discusses the self-help projects of the Republic
    of Tanzania which are part of its total program of tribal
    socialism. Shows the role that UNICEF is playing in this
    program by helping to improve health education and nutri-
    tion services. Emphasizes the improving roles of women in
    Tanzanian society.

STEAMBOAT 'ROUND THE BEND
Nar/Cast: Will Rogers + Stepin Fetchit* + Irvin SCobb
Screenplay: Dudley Nichols + Lamar Troth
Producer: Sol Wurtzel   Director: John Ford
Studio/Company: 20th Century Fox
Tech Info: 16 mm/bw/sound/2 reels/80 min.
Date/Country: 1935 + USA   Type: Feature
Distr/Arch: fnc
Annotation: Mississippi river provides the backdrop for
    comedy in this vehicle for Stepin Fetchit as Jonah and
    other character types made popular in Judge Priest.

Several comic sequences parody the old South and poke fun at "numbskull hillbillies."

STEEL HELMET, THE
Nar/Cast: James Edwards* + Gene Evans + William Chun + Robert Hutton + Richard Loo
Screenplay: Samuel Fuller
Producer: Samuel Fuller   Director: Samuel Fuller
Studio/Company: Lippert Pictures
Tech Info: 16 mm/sound/bw/84 min.
Date/Country: 1950 + USA   Type: Feature
Distr/Arch: bud + ics + mac + sel + wcf + wil
Annotation: The strains of combat are shown in this movie about a patrol accidentally thrown together to hold a position until help arrives. Edwards plays a medic with the patrol.

STEPIN HIGH
Nar/Cast: William Lee*
Studio/Company: Superior Art Motion Pictures
Date/Country: 1924 + USA

STIGMA
Nar/Cast: Phillip Thomas* + Cary Harlan Poe + Josie Johnson + Peter H. Clune
Producer: Charles B. Moss, Jr.   Director: David E. Durston
Studio/Company: Cinerama
Tech Info: 16 mm/sound/color/93 min.
Date/Country: 1973 + USA   Type: Feature
Distr/Arch: swa
Annotation: A black doctor, summoned to a white community, investigates a syphilis outbreak the source of which is prominent community members.

STILETTO
Nar/Cast: Alex Cord + Patrick O'Neal + Barbara McNair* + Britt Ekland + Lincoln Kilpatrick*
Screenplay: A.J. Russell
Producer: Norman Rosemant   Director: Bernard Kowalski
Studio/Company: Avco Embassy
Tech Info: 16 mm/sound/color/98 min.
Date/Country: 1969 + USA   Type: Feature
Distr/Arch: mac
Annotation: Story of a Mafia hit man (a "stiletto man") who wants out of the business, so he runs not only from the police but also from the Mafia. McNair is Ahn Dessje, one of the hit man's girlfriends who hides him in her Harlem apartment and becomes a victim of a Mafia attack on him. Kilpatrick is Hannibal Smith.

STILL A BROTHER: INSIDE THE NEGRO MIDDLE CLASS
Nar/Cast: St. Clair Drake* + Dr. Percy Julian* + Nathan Wright* + Julian Bond* + Ossie Davis*
Producer: William Branch* and William Greaves*
Director: William Greaves* Type: Documentary
Tech Info: 16mm/bw/sound/3 reels/90 min. 1968/USA
Distr/Arch: con + cal + mhf
Annotation: A TV documentary dealing with the conflicts of

the black middle class. The major one is whether or not
they should align themselves with members of their race
regardless of their class status or whether they should
emulate white standards in order to rise in the limited
areas provided by the society. Narrated by Ossie Davis.

STORMY WEATHER
Nar/Cast: Lena Horne* + Bill Robinson* + Cab Calloway* +
    Katherine Dunham* + Harold Nicholas + Fayard Nicholas +
    Ada Brown* + Dooley Wilson* + Babe Wallace* + Ernest Whit-
    man* + Zuttie Singleton* + F. E. Miller* + Nicodemus
    Stewart* + Fats Waller*
Screenplay: Jerry Horwin + Seymour Robinson
Producer: William Le Baron   Director: Andrew Stone
Studio/Company: Twentieth Century-Fox
Tech Info: 16 mm/bw/sound/2 reels/77 min.
Date/Country: 1943 + USA   Type: Feature
Distr/Arch: fnc
Annotation: A semi-biography of Bill Robinson, the film is
    the story of a black dancer (played by Robinson) who woos
    a beautiful woman, Selina, played by Lena Horne, and wins
    her after the usual complications. Most of the time is
    spent with the musical/dance performances of the entire
    cast.

STORY OF A THREE DAY PASS, THE
Alt Title(s): La Permission
Nar/Cast: Harry Baird* + Nicole Berger
Screenplay: Melvin Van Peebles*   Story: Melvin Van Peebles*
Producer: Guy Belfond   Director: Melvin Van Peebles*
Studio/Company: O.P.E.R.A. + Sigma III
Tech Info: 16 mm/sound/bw/3 reels/87 min./French with En-
    glish subtitles
Date/Country: 1968 + France   Type: Feature
Distr/Arch: mac
Annotation: Turner (Harry Baird), a G.I. stationed in
    France, gets a three day pass because his captain thinks
    he's a "good Negro." In Paris he meets a white shopgirl
    with whom he has an idyllic week-end love affair which
    they plan to continue, but when he returns to the base,
    his Captain--informed of the affair--demotes and restricts
    him to the base. Music by Van Peebles* and Mickey Baker*.

STORY OF BAMBA, THE
Series: National Archives Gift Collection
Tech Info: 16 mm/silent/3 reels/bw
Annotation: Dramatic story of young Africans breaking away
    from witch doctor practices in their interest in modern
    medicine. (Part of Record Group 200 HF series, Harmon
    Foundation Collection).

STORY OF DR. CARVER
Series: Pete Smith Specialities
Producer: MGM
Tech Info: 16 mm/bw/sound/1 reel/10 min.
Date/Country: 1939 + USA   Type: Dramatized Documentary
Distr/Arch: iu
Annotation: A slave boy with a keen interest in studying is

educated by his master, Carver. The young scientist, George Washington Carver, then devotes his life to the
development of uses of the peanut and other agricultural
products of the South. Shows some of his experimental
work and his achievements at Tuskegee Institute.

STORY OF TEMPLE DRAKE, THE
Nar/Cast: Hattie McDaniel* + Miriam Hopkins + Jack La Rue +
William Gargan
Screenplay: Oliver H.P. Garrett   Story: William Faulkner
Director: Stevan Roberts
Studio/Company: Paramount
Date/Country: 1933 + USA   Type: Feature
Annotation: Based on Faulkner's Sanctuary, the story is of a
reckless young woman forced to go with a mobster after
he's killed her boyfriend. Hattie McDaniel plays in one
of her early Mammy roles (uncredited).

STRAIGHT TO HEAVEN
Nar/Cast: Nina Mae McKinney* + Lionel Monogas* + Jackie Ward
+ James Baskett* + Percy Verwagen*
Studio/Company: Million Dollar Pictures
Date/Country: 1939 + USA   Type: Feature
Annotation: Nina Mae McKinney plays the wife of Joe William
who helps clear her husband (Lionel Monogas) of murder
charges cooked up by Lucky John (Verwagen) the syndicate
head. Baskett plays the detective.

STRANGE CASE OF DR. RX, THE
Nar/Cast: Mantan Moreland* + Lionel Atwell + Patric Knowles
Screenplay: Clarence Upson Young   Director: William Nigh
Studio/Company: Universal
Tech Info: 16 mm/sound/bw/66 min.
Date/Country: 1942 + USA   Type: Feature
Distr/Arch: uni
Annotation: Mantan Moreland is Horatio in this "horror"
melodrama in which the mad doctor/scientist who has the
reputation of terrifying people to such a degree that
their hair turns white. That happens to Horatio, the in-
efficient houseboy.

STRANGE INCIDENT
Alt Title(s): see Ox-Bow Incident

STRANGE ONE, THE
Nar/Cast: Ben Gazzara + James Olson + George Peppard
Screenplay: Calder Willingham
Producer: Stan Spiegal   Director: Jack Garfein
Studio/Company: Columbia
Date/Country: 1957 + USA   Type: Feature
Annotation: Blacks are background figures in this melodrama
about excesses (in brutality/coruption) in a southern
military school. Most ironic moment is the ending in
which the worst trouble maker (Gazzara as Jocko de Paris)
is exposed, ejected and unceremoniously thrown blindfolded
into the Jim Crow car of a train on its way out of town.

STRANGER FROM WAY OUT YONDER, THE

Studio/Company: Lone Star Motion Picture Company
Date/Country: 1922 + USA

STRANGERS_IN_THEIR_OWN_LAND:_THE_BLACKS
Series: Human Relations Film
Producer: ABC
Tech Info: 16 mm/color/12 min.
Date/Country: 1971 + USA   Type: Documentary
Distr/Arch: xex
Annotation: A theater/dance/painting/literature collage
  showing aftistic creativity in the urban black ghettos of
  America. Provided by Center for Southern Folklore.

STREETS_OF_GREENWOOD,_THE
Producer: Jack Willis + John Reavis, Jr. + Fred Wardenburg
  Director: Jack Willis + John Reavis, Jr. + Fred Wardenburg
Tech Info: 16mm/ bw/ 20 min.
Date/Country: 1964 + USA   Type: Documentary
Distr/Arch: mac
Annotation: Records the voter registration drive in Green-
  wood Mississippi, in the summer 1964; shows the bravery
  and determination of the members of SNCC.

STRICTLY_DYNAMITE
Nar/Cast: Mills Brothers* + Jimmy Durante + Lupe Velez
  Story: Robert Colwell + Robert Simon   Director: Elliott
  Nugent
Studio/Company: RKO
Tech Info: 74 min.
Date/Country: 1934 + USA   Type: Feature
Annotation: The Mills Brothers perform in this Durante
  comedy about a radio comic who is having trouble with his
  gags.

STRIKE,_THE
Producer: Jim Simon*   Director: Jim Simon*
Tech Info: animated
Annotation: Animated film produced for Black Psychiatrists
  of America. USA Film Festival Award.

STRIP,_THE
Nar/Cast: Mickey Rooney + Sally Forrest + Louis Armstrong*
  Director: Leslie Kardos
Studio/Company: MGM
Tech Info: 16 mm/sound/bw/85 min.
Date/Country: 1951 + USA   Type: Feature
Distr/Arch: fnc
Annotation: Louis Armstrong supplies the music for this
  film.

STRUGGLE_CONTINUES,_THE
Alt Title(s): see A_LUTA_CONTINUA

STRUGGLE_FOR_LOS_TRABAJOS
Screenplay: William Greaves*
Producer: William Greaves*   Director: William Greaves*
Tech Info: 16 mm/color/35 mm/sound   Type: Documentary
Distr/Arch: wgp

Annotation: What actually happens when a complaint of job
    discrimination is lodged by an individual with the Equal
    Employment Opportunity Commission.

STUDY IN COLOR
Series: Study in Color
Tech Info: 16 mm/sound/28 min./bw
Date/Country: USA   Type: Documentary
Distr/Arch: adl
Annotation: Two players discuss "color" in separate
    monologues, one is white wearing a black mask, the other
    is black wearing a white mask. The theatrical device al-
    lows the audience to see itself in opposite roles.

STUDY OF NEGRO ARTISTS, A
Series: National Archives Gift Collection
Tech Info: 16 mm/silent/4 reels/bw
Annotation: Methods of work and productions of several
    artists. Indicates range of bread-winning activities
    which keep art work going. (Part of Record Group 200 HF
    series, Harmon Foundation Collection).

SUBMARINE EYE, THE
Studio/Company: Williamson Brothers
Date/Country: 1917 + USA   Type: Feature
Annotation: A black helper rescues a young white inventor,
    trapped beneath the sea in a tangled net, by diving in and
    cutting him free.

SUGAR HILL BABY
Studio/Company: Creative Cinema Corporation
Date/Country: 194- + USA

SUGAR HILL
Nar/Cast: Marki Bey*
Screenplay: Tim Kelly
Producer: Elliot Schick   Director: Paul Muslansky
Studio/Company: American International
Tech Info: 16 mm/sound/color/91 min.
Date/Country: 1974 + USA   Type: Feature
Distr/Arch: swa

SULLIVAN'S EMPIRE
Nar/Cast: Bernie Hamilton* + Martin Milner
Screenplay: Frank Chase
Producer: Frank Price   Director: Harvey Hart + Thomas Carr
Studio/Company: Universal
Tech Info: 16 mm/sound/color/85 min.
Date/Country: 1967 + USA   Type: Feature
Distr/Arch: ccc + tmc + uni
Annotation: Bernie Hamilton is Ambudo in this adventure-
    drama about a wealthy American who is kidnapped and held
    for ransom by a revolutionary guerilla leader in South
    America, after making a crash landing near his ranch in
    the Amazon River territory.

SULLIVAN'S TRAVELS
Nar/Cast: Joel McCrea + Veronika Lake + Jesse Lee Brooks* +

Sam McDaniel*
Screenplay: Paul Sturges
Producer: Paul Jones   Director: Preston Sturges
Studio/Company: Paramount
Tech Info: 16 mm/sound/bw/90 min.
Date/Country: 1941 + USA   Type: Feature
Distr/Arch: uni
Annotation: Sullivan's Travels is a satiric comment on
   "socially significant" films and Hollywood publicity ex-
   cesses.   Joel McCrea as film director John L. Sullivan
   finds himself sentenced to hard labor on the chain gang.
   One striking scene in a black church shows the deacon, a
   genuine humanitarian, welcoming the prisoners, mainly
   white, into his church. He also sings the spiritual "Let
   My People Go," an ironic touch, as the men enter.   (No
   credits for black actors listed.)

SUN DOWN LIMITED, THE
Series: Our Gang
Nar/Cast: Our Gang + Allen Hoskins*
Screenplay: Hal Roach
Producer: Hal Roach   Director: Robert McGowan
Studio/Company: Pathe
Tech Info: silent/bw/2 reels
Date/Country: 1924 + USA   Type: Comedy Short
Annotation: After setting off a runaway train, the gang
   members are no longer welcome at the train yard, so they
   build their own train line. All goes well until it gets
   sidetracked and runs amok thru town. Allen Hoskins stars
   as Farina.

SUN SHINES BRIGHT, THE
Nar/Cast: Charles Winninger + Arleen Wheelan + Stepin
   Fetchit*
Screenplay: Laurence Stallings
Producer: Merian Cooper   Director: John Ford
Studio/Company: Argosy Pictures
Date/Country: 1954 + USA   Type: Feature
Annotation: Charles Winninger recreates the role of Judge
   Priest in this John Ford version about a southern judge
   and the particular justice and humor he dispenses. Stepin
   Fetchit is still Jeff, still attending the judge. The
   film also includes a near-lynching scene.

SUN TAN RANCH
Nar/Cast: Byron* and Bean* + Eunice Wilson* + Mildred Boyd*
   + Joel Fluellen* + Austin McCoy* + Bill Walker*
Studio/Company: Norwanda Pictures
Date/Country: 1948 + USA

SUN VALLEY SERENADE
Nar/Cast: Sonja Henie + John Payne + Dorothy Dandridge* +
   Nicholas Brothers*
Screenplay: Robert Ellis + Helen Logan
Producer: Milton Sperling   Director: H. Bruce Humberstone
Studio/Company: 20th Century Fox
Date/Country: 1941 + USA   Type: Feature
Annotation: Musical comedy set in Sun Valley, that has John

Payne chasing Sonja Henie through the snow. Dorothy
Dandridge and the Nicholas Brothers add to the entertainment with specialty numbers.

SUN'S GONNA SHINE, THE
Nar/Cast: Lightnin' Hopkins*
Producer: Les Blanc
Tech Info: 16 mm/sound/1 reel/10 min./color
Date/Country: 1968 + USA   Type: Documentary
Annotation: Companion film to The Blues Accordin' To Light-
  nin' Hopkins. Recreates Hopkins' decision to move from
  cotton chopping to blues singing.

SUNDAY CALM
Series: Our Gang
Nar/Cast: Our Gang + Ernie Morrison* + Allen Hoskins*
Screenplay: Hal Roach
Producer: Hal Roach   Director: Robert McGowan
Studio/Company: Pathe
Tech Info: silent/bw/2 reels
Date/Country: 1923 + USA   Type: Comedy Short
Annotation: The gang members run amok on the way to a family
  picnic. Allen Hoskins stars as Farina.

SUNDAY ON THE RIVER
Nar/Cast: Gordon Hitchens + Ken Resnick
Tech Info: 16 mm/sound/bw/30 min.
Date/Country: 1961 + USA   Type: Documentary
Distr/Arch: rad
Annotation: This film about Harlem Blacks on a Hudson river
  boat trip won a Venice Film Festival award. Folk songs
  and spirituals furnish background music.

SUNDAY SINNERS
Nar/Cast: Mamie Smith* + Alec Lovejoy* + Norman Astwood* +
  Edna Mae Harris* + Cristola Williams* + Sidney Easton* +
  Earl Sydnor* + Gus Smith* + Alberta Perkins* + Dene Larry*
    Story: Frank Wilson*   Director: Arthur Dreifuss
Studio/Company: Goldberg Production
Tech Info: 16 mm/sound/bw/2 reels/65 min.
Date/Country: 1941 + USA   Type: Feature
Distr/Arch: bud + kpf + emg
Annotation: Lyrics and music for this musical feature by
  Donald Heywood*, writer and composer, prominently associ-
  ated with independent black films from 1932.

SUNDOWN TRAIL
Nar/Cast: Louise Beavers*
Date/Country: 1931 + USA   Type: Feature
Annotation: An early Louise Beavers appearance.

SUPER COPS, THE
Nar/Cast: Ron Leibman + David Selby + Pat Hingle + Sheila
  Frazier* + Ralph Wilcox
Producer: William Belasco   Director: Gordon Parks*
Studio/Company: MGM
Tech Info: 94 min./color/16 mm/sound
Date/Country: 1973 + USA   Type: Feature

Distr/Arch: fnc
Annotation: Story of two flamboyant, ingenious policemen
  nicknamed Batman and Robin known for busting dope pushers
  in Bedford- Stuyvesant of Brooklyn.

SUPER FLY T.N.T.
Nar/Cast: Ron O'Neal* + Roscoe Lee Brown* + Sheila Frazier*
  + Robert Guillaume* + Jacques Sernas + William Berger
Screenplay: Alex Haley*   Story: Ron O'Neal* + Sig Shore
Producer: Sig Shore   Director: Ron O'Neal*
Studio/Company: Paramount
Tech Info: 16 mm/color/sound/3 reel/87 min.
Date/Country: 1973 + USA   Type: Feature
Distr/Arch: fnc
Annotation: Sequel to Super Fly with Priest and his lady
  Georgia in Europe where he is convinced to use his hust-
  ling expertise to aid an African nation's fight for
  liberation.

SUPER FLY
Nar/Cast: Ron O'Neal* + Carl Lee* + Julius Harris + Sheila
  Frazier* + Charles McGregor + Curtis Mayfield*
Screenplay: Phillip Fenty   Story: Robert Brady
Producer: Sig Shore   Director: Gordon Parks, Jr.*
Studio/Company: Warner Brothers
Tech Info: 16 mm/sound/color/3 reels/93 min.
Date/Country: 1972 + USA   Type: Feature
Distr/Arch: wsa + swa
Annotation: Ron Neil is the pimp-pusher Priest, who in spite
  of all, manages to defeat the system and his white oppres-
  sors, and walk away with the money and his woman (Sheila
  Frazier). Some sequences reveal the corruption and
  despair of the ghetto drug scene behing the veneer of suc-
  cess. Music by Curtis Mayfield*.

SUPER SLEUTH
Nar/Cast: Jackie Oakie + Ann Southern + Willie Best*
Screenplay: Gertrude Purcell + Ernest Pagano
Producer: Edward Small   Director: Ben Stoloff
Studio/Company: RKO Radio
Date/Country: 1937 + USA   Type: Feature
Annotation: Mystery-comedy as Jack Oakie plays a dim-witted
  movie detective out to solve a real-life mystery, with the
  help of Willie Best.

SUPER SLEUTHS
Studio/Company: Toddy Pictures
Date/Country: 194- + USA

SUPER SPEED
Nar/Cast: Martin Turner* + Reed Howes + Mildred Harris
  Story: J.W. Grey + Henry R. Symonds   Director: Albert
  Rogell
Studio/Company: Harry J.Brown Productions
Tech Info: 35 mm/silent/bw/5 reels/5,227 ft.
Date/Country: 1925 + USA   Type: Feature
Annotation: Martin Turner plays Pat's Valet in this "comedy
  -melodrama about racing, thievery, kidnapping and

romance."

SUPERDOME
Nar/Cast: David Janssen + Donna Mills + Edie Adams + Clifton
  Davis* + Vonetta McGee*
Screenplay: Barry Oringer   Story: Barry Oringer + Bill
  Svanoe
Producer: William Frye   Director: Jerry Jameson
Studio/Company: ABC Circle Films
Date/Country: 1977 + USA   Type: TV Feature
Annotation: The future of many people depends on the Super
  Bowl's outcome which is threatened by a killer.

SUPPOSE THEY GAVE A WAR AND NOBODY CAME
Nar/Cast: Tony Curtis + Brian Keith + Ivan Dixon* + Suzanne
  Pleshette
Screenplay: Don McGuire + Hal Captail
Producer: Fred Engel   Director: Hy Averback
Studio/Company: Cinerama + ABC
Tech Info: 16 mm/sound/color/113 min.
Date/Country: 1970 + USA   Type: Feature
Distr/Arch: fnc
Annotation: The war is the undeclared one between an army
  post and the surrounding civilian community. This comedy
  pokes fun at the foibles of both sides.   Ivan Dixon is
  Sgt. Jones, one of the four members of the Colonel's Com-
  munity Relations Committee.

SUR UN AIR DE CHARLESTON
Alt Title(s): Charleston
Nar/Cast: Catherine Hessling + Johnny Higgins* + Pierre
  Braunberger + Pierre Lestrinquez
Screenplay: Pierre Lestrinquez   Director: Jean Renoir
Studio/Company: Epinay Studios
Tech Info: 35 mm/silent/bw/22 min.
Date/Country: 1927 + France   Type: Dramatic Short
Distr/Arch: bfi + eas
Annotation: Set in the year 2028, a black explorer flies
  from Central Africa (the seat of civilization) to visit
  Europe which he thought was not inhabited. He discovers
  in Paris a "primitive" girl dancing the charleston.   En-
  tranced, he gets back into his space craft with her and
  goes back to Africa.

SURINAM, A SONG OF DEMOCRACY
Producer: Educational Film
Tech Info: 16 mm/sound/color/28 min.
Date/Country: South America   Type: Documentary
Distr/Arch: efd
Annotation: Documentary of the many different nationality
  groups of the Dutch Commonwealth of Surinam (Dutch
  Guinea). Among them: Africans, Chinese, American Indian,
  Europeans, etc.

SURPRISED PARTIES
Series: Our Gang
Nar/Cast: Our Gang + Billie Thomas*
Screenplay: Hal Law + Robert A. McGowan

Producer: MGM   Director: Edward Cahn
Studio/Company: MGM
Tech Info: bw/sound/1 reel
Date/Country: 1942 + USA   Type: Comedy Short
Annotation: Froggy is angry at the gang when they kick him
   out of the club before a big party. He booby traps the
   clubhouse and comes to the party dressed as a girl. Only
   then does he find out the party is for him. Billie Thomas
   stars as Buckwheat.

SWAMI_SAM
Studio/Company: Vitagraph
Date/Country: 1915 + USA   Type: Comedy Short
Annotation: Sam is a black con man successful at his con and
   successful at avoiding the police until a black laundress
   comes to collect his overdue bill and ends up dragging him
   off to the station.

SWANEE_RIVER
Nar/Cast: Don Ameche + Andrea Leeds + Al Jolson + Hall John-
   son Choir* + George Reed*   Director: Sydney Lanfield
Studio/Company: Twentieth Century-Fox
Tech Info: 16 mm/sound/bw/84 min.
Date/Country: 1940 + USA   Type: Feature
Distr/Arch: fnc
Annotation: Al Jolson appears as E.P. Christy, the man who
   founded one of the first Negro minstrel troupes. Black-
   face numbers included.

SWANEE_SHOWBOAT
Nar/Cast: Nina Mae McKinney* + Dewey "Pigmeat" Markham* +
   Mabel Lee* + Helen Barys* + The Eight Black Streaks* + The
   Lindy Hoppers* + Scott* and Whaley* + Swanee Swingsters*
Date/Country: 194- + USA   Type: Feature

SWEET_BIRD_OF_YOUTH
Nar/Cast: Roy Glenn* + Davis Roberts* + Paul Newman +
   Geraldine Page
Screenplay: Richard Brooks
Producer: Pandro Berman   Director: Richard Brooks
Studio/Company: MGM
Tech Info: 16 mm/sound/color/125 min.
Date/Country: 1962 + USA   Type: Feature
Distr/Arch: fnc
Annotation: Roy Glenn is Charles in this adaptation of the
   Tennessee Williams play about an aging Hollywood actress
   and one of her young lovers.

SWEET_CHARITY
Nar/Cast: Sammy Davis, Jr.* + Shirley MacLaine + Ricardo
   Montalban
Screenplay: Peter Stone
Producer: Robert Arthur   Director: Bob Fosse
Studio/Company: Universal
Tech Info: 16 mm/color/sound/157 min.
Date/Country: 1969 + USA   Type: Feature
Distr/Arch: cwf + swa + twy + uni
Annotation: Davis plays Big Daddy in this screen adaptation

of the Broadway musical about a good hearted New York
dancer who always gives her heart to the wrong man.

SWEET_JESUS_PREACHER_MAN
Nar/Cast: Roger E. Mosley* + William Smith + Michael Pataki
  + Sam Laws*
Screenplay: John Cerullo + M. Stuart Madden + Abbey Leitch
  Director: Ronald Goldman + Daniel B. Cady
Studio/Company: MGM
Tech Info: 16 mm/color/sound/3 reels/103 min.
Date/Country: 1973 + USA   Type: Feature
Distr/Arch: fnc
Annotation: Roger Mosley stars as a crook hired by the mob
  to pose as a minister in the community and track down
  other, outside mobsters.

SWEET_LOVE,_BITTER
Alt Title(s): It Won't Rub Off, Baby
Nar/Cast: Dick Gregory* + Robert Hooks* + Don Murray + Diane
  Varsi
Screenplay: Herb Danska* + Lewis Jacobs   Story: John Willi-
  ams* (novel, Nigh Song)
Producer: Lewis Jacobs   Director: Herb Danska*
Studio/Company: Film 2 Associates
Tech Info: 16 mm/bw/sound/3 reels/92 min.
Date/Country: 1967 + USA   Type: Feature
Distr/Arch: mac
Annotation: The film's protagonists are "Eagle" Stokes
  (Gregory), a fading jazz musician with an acid sense of
  humor; David Hilary (Murray), a former college professor
  turned alcoholic; Keel Robinson (Hooks), a black cafe ow-
  ner, embittered toward all whites; and Della (Varsi),
  Keel's white mistress. Danska portrays the friendships
  that develop among these four people and the emotional
  conflicts that eventually tear them apart.

SWEET_RIDE,_THE
Nar/Cast: Tony Franciosa + Michael Sarrazin + Percy
  Rodrigues* + Jacqueline Bisset
Screenplay: Tom Mankiewicz
Producer: Joe Pasternak   Director: Harvey Hart
Studio/Company: Fox
Tech Info: 16 mm/sound/color/110 min.
Date/Country: 1968 + USA   Type: Feature
Distr/Arch: fnc
Annotation: Rodrigues is Lieutenant Atkins in this Malibu
  melodrama about a young woman who is assaulted, beaten and
  dumped out on the highway. Atkins conducts the investiga-
  tion to find the perpetrator.

SWEET_SHOE
Nar/Cast: Rita Rio* and Her All-Girl Band* + Anita Colby* +
  The Four Horsemen Male Quartet*
Date/Country: 194- + USA

SWEET_SWEETBACK'S_BAADASSSSSS_SONG
Nar/Cast: Simon Chuckster* + Hubert Scales + John Dullaghan
  + West Gale + Niva Rochelle + Rhetta Hughes* + Nick Fer-

rari + Ed Rue + Johnny Amos* + Lavelle Roby* + Ted Hayden*
+ Melvin Van Peebles* + Mario Peebles* + Sonja Dunson* +
Michael Augustus + Peter Russell + Norman Fields + Ron
Prince + Steve Cole + Megan Peebles* + Joe Tornatore +
Mike Angel + The Copeland Family* + Jeff Goodman + Curt
Matson + Marria Evonee*
Screenplay: Melvin Van Peebles*
Producer: Yeah, Inc. + Melvin Van Peebles* + Jerry Gross
   Director: Melvin Van Peebles*
Studio/Company: Cinemation Industries
Tech Info: 16 mm/sound/color/3 reels/97 min.
Date/Country: 1971 + USA   Type: Feature
Distr/Arch: wsa
Annotation: A young starving ghetto child is taken in by
   women in a bordello and grows up to be a "Sweetback,"
   whose sexual performances in a number of different set-
   tings are astounding. His experiences with and reaction
   to the racist brutality of the police (especially their
   beating of a young militant) turn him into a fugitive
   whose black consciousness grows and develops as he runs.
   Much of the film is concerned with the communal effort to
   protect him and with his flight--real and symbolic--to the
   border. Orchestration Earth, Wind and Fire*.

SWEETHEARTS_OF_RHYTHM
Nar/Cast: Sweethearts of Rhythm All Girl Band*
Studio/Company: Associated Producers of Negro Motion
   Pictures
Date/Country: 1947 + USA

SWIMMER, THE
Nar/Cast: Burt Lancaster + Janet Landgard + Bernie Hamilton*
Screenplay: Eleanor Perry   Story: John Cheever
Producer: Roger Lewis + Frank Perry   Director: Frank Perry
Studio/Company: Columbia Pictures
Tech Info: 16 mm/sound/color/94 min.
Date/Country: 1968 + USA   Type: Feature
Distr/Arch: bud + ccc + ics + mac + mod + mot + roa + sel +
   unf + wcf + wel + who + wil
Annotation: A middle-aged suburbanite (Burt Lancaster)
   decides to swim home through various people's swimming
   pools - and with every pool, another slice of life is
   revealed. Bernie Hamilton is the chauffeur.

SWING_FEVER
Nar/Cast: Kay Kyser + Marilyn Maxwell + Lena Horne*
Screenplay: Nort Perrin + Warner Wilson
Producer: Irving Stair   Director: Tim Whelan
Studio/Company: MGM
Date/Country: 1943 + USA   Type: Feature
Annotation: Musical comedy which has Kay Kyser playing a
   mousy musician in love with singer Marilyn Maxwell.   Lena
   Horne sings one number, "Indifferent."

SWING_IT_HARLEM
Nar/Cast: Ralph Brown* + Ella Mae Walters*
Date/Country: 1941 + USA

SWING PARADE OF 1946
Nar/Cast: Louis Jordan* + Connie Boswell
Studio/Company: Monogram Pictures
Date/Country: 1946 + USA
Annotation: Musical comedy about a female singer on her way
   up.

SWING TEASE
Alt Title(s): see Sing As You Swing

SWING
Nar/Cast: Cora Green* + Hazel Diaz* + Carmen Newsome* +
   Dorothy Van Engle* + Alec Lovejoy* + Amanda Randolph* +
   The Tyler Twins*   Director: Oscar Micheaux*
Studio/Company: Micheaux Film Corporation
Date/Country: 1938 + USA   Type: Feature
Annotation: Much of the drama in this musical is built
   around the music which is performed from Alabama to New
   York (Harlem). The Tyler Twins perform the dance numbers.

SWINGIN' ALONG
Alt Title(s): Double Trouble
Nar/Cast: Ray Charles* + Peter Marshall + Barbara Eden
Screenplay: Jameson Brewer
Producer: Jack Leewood   Director: Charles Barton
Studio/Company: Fox
Tech Info: 16 mm/sound/color/74 min.
Date/Country: 1960 + USA   Type: Feature
Annotation: Ray Charles is featured as himself in this
   comedy about a congenital bungler who winds up winning a
   song-writing contest.

SWORDS AND HEARTS   Director: D.W. Griffith
Studio/Company: Biograph
Tech Info: 35 mm/silent/bw/1 reel/1030 ft./10-15 min.
Date/Country: 1911 + USA   Type: Dramatic Short
Distr/Arch: moma
Annotation: Civil War drama in which a faithful slave (Old
   Ben) hides the family treasure chest from the Yankee
   soldiers. He reveals the chest later and is rewarded by
   his master with a hoe.

SYMBOL OF THE UNCONQUERED
Nar/Cast: Lawrence Chenault* + Walker Thompson* + Iris Hall*
   + E.G. Tatum* + Jim Burris* + Mattie Wilkes* + Leigh Whip-
   per*
Screenplay: Oscar Micheaux*
Producer: Oscar Micheaux*   Director: Oscar Micheaux*
Studio/Company: Micheaux Film Corporation
Date/Country: 1921 + USA   Type: Feature
Annotation: Beautiful (quadroon) girl goes west to claim her
   dead grandfather's mine and meets with trouble. She also
   falls in love. There is some mistaken identity involved
   in the love affair but the film does not opt for "pas-
   sing."

SYMPATHY FOR THE DEVIL
Alt Title(s): 1 * 1

Nar/Cast: The Rolling Stones + Frankie Dymon, Jr.* + Anne
   Wiozensky
Screenplay: Jean-Luc Godard
Producer: Michael Pearson   Director: Jean-Luc Godard
Studio/Company: New Line Cinema
Tech Info: 16 mm/sound/color/104 min.
Date/Country: 1969 + Britain   Type: Feature
Distr/Arch: nlc
Annotation: While the Rolling Stones work out their song
   "Sympathy for the Devil" in a studio session various se-
   quences are on screen. One has a group of black power
   advocates reading passages from Eldridge Cleaver's and
   Imamu Baraka's (Le Roi Jones) writings and preparing for
   the revolution.

SYMPHONY IN BLACK
Nar/Cast: Duke Ellington* + Billie Holiday* + Earl "Snake
   hips" Tucker*
Producer: Fred Waller
Tech Info: 16 mm/sound/bw/1 reel/9 min.
Date/Country: 1935 + USA   Type: Musical Short
Distr/Arch: emg
Annotation: An elaborate composition, built around 4 phases
   of black life, with the real Lady Day, Billie Holiday.

SYMPHONY IN SWING
Nar/Cast: Duke Ellington and His Orchestra* + Delta Rhythm
   Boys*   Director: Will Cowan
Studio/Company: Universal-International
Tech Info: 15 min.
Date/Country: 1949 + USA   Type: Musical Short
Annotation: A bandstand setting features the above listed
   artists performing "Take the A Train," "Knock Me a Kiss,"
   "Frankie and Johnny" and others.

SYNANON
Nar/Cast: Eartha Kitt* + Bernie Hamilton* + Chuck Connors +
   Stella Stevens
Screenplay: Ian Bernard + S. Lee Pogostin
Producer: Richard Quine   Director: Richard Quine
Studio/Company: Columbia
Tech Info: sound/bw/107 min.
Date/Country: 1965 + USA   Type: Feature
Annotation: The rehabilitation of drug addicts through the
   now famous "synanon" method. Hamilton plays Pete, one of
   the addicts, who is caught getting high on cough syrup but
   later gets back on the withdrawal regimen. Eartha Kitt
   appears as Betty Coleman; a prostitute during her period
   of addiction, she becomes an assistant to the founder of
   Synanon House.

SYNCOPATION
Nar/Cast: Adolphe Menjou + Jackie Cooper + Bonita Granville
   + Todd Duncan* + Frank Jenks
Screenplay: Phillip Yordan + Frank Cowett   Story: Valentine
   Davies   Director: William Dieterle
Studio/Company: RKO Radio
Tech Info: 16 mm/sound/bw/88 min.

Date/Country: 1942 + USA   Type: Feature
Distr/Arch: mog
Annotation: Todd Duncan is featured as Rex Tearbone, a New
  Orleans trumpet player who teaches jazz to Bonita Granvil-
  le, in this film about a New Orleans girl and a Chicago
  boy (Cooper) who are devoted to music (jazz), poetry (Walt
  Whitman) and each other.

SYSTEM TO DESTROY, A
Series: The Black Experience
Producer: University of Michigan Television Center
Tech Info: 16 mm/sound/bw/29 min. (also on videotape)
Date/Country: 1970 + USA
Distr/Arch: umic
Annotation: Black participation in the Civil War and Recon-
  struction. Provided by Center for Southern Folklore.

T.A.M.I. SHOW, THE
Nar/Cast: Chuck Berry* + James Brown* and the Flames + The
  Rolling Stones + The Supremes* + Smokey Robinson and the
  Miracles* + The Barbarians + Marvin Gaye* + Gerry and the
  Pacemakers + Lesley Gore + Jan and Dean
Producer: Lee Savin   Director: Steve Binder
Studio/Company: American International
Tech Info: 16 mm/sound/bw/100 min.
Date/Country: 1964 + USA
Distr/Arch: bud + kpf + nlc + sel + wcf + wil
Annotation: Rock 'n roll spectacular filmed at the Santa
  Monica Civic Auditoriium.

TAFFY AND THE JUNGLE HUNTER
Nar/Cast: Hari Rhodes* + Robert DoQui* + Jacques Bergera
Screenplay: Arthur Hoerl
Producer: William Faris   Director: Terry O. Morse
Studio/Company: Allied Artists
Tech Info: sound/color/87 min.
Date/Country: 1965 + USA   Type: Feature
Annotation: Hari Rhodes as Khali, a friendly African chief,
  warns a jungle hunter (Bergera) of imminent tribal warfare
  in Kenya. Later he helps helps the hunter find his 8 year
  old son who has run away with Taffy a baby elephant the
  hunter has captured.

TAKE A GIANT STEP
Producer: Roundtable
Tech Info: 16 mm/sound/bw/25 min.
Date/Country: 1967   Type: Documentary
Distr/Arch: uca
Annotation: Employing the 'unemployable' of the ghetto in
  the Watts Manufacturing Company.

TAKE A GIANT STEP
Nar/Cast: Ruby Dee* + Johnny Nash* + Frederick O'Neal* +
  Beah Richards* + Estelle Hemsley* + Ellen Holly* + Pauline
  Meyers*
Screenplay: Louis Peterson* + Julius Epstein   Story: Louis
  Peterson*
Producer: Julius J. Epstein   Director: Philip Leacock

Studio/Company: United Artists
Tech Info: sound/bw/100 min.
Date/Country: 1960 + USA   Type: Feature
Annotation: Concerns a black teenager (played by Johnny
    Nash) and his growing awareness of what it is like to be
    black in a white dominated society.

TAKE A HARD RIDE
Nar/Cast: Jim Brown* + Fred Williamson* + Lee Van Cleef +
    Catherine Speak + Jim Kelly*   Director: Anthony Dawson
Studio/Company: 20th Century Fox
Tech Info: 16 mm/sound/color/103 min
Date/Country: 1975 + USA   Type: Feature
Distr/Arch: fnc
Annotation: Entrusted by his dying white boss to return
    $86,000 to his widow, a black wrangler faces many misad-
    ventures as various people try to relieve him of his
    burden. Through these trials, he is aided by a light-
    hearted, light-fingered gambler and a former resident of a
    bordello.

TAKE A LETTER DARLING
Nar/Cast: Dooley Wilson* + Rosalind Russell + Fred McMurray
Screenplay: Claude Binyon   Director: Mitchell Leisen
Studio/Company: Paramount
Tech Info: 16 mm/sound/bw/94 min.
Date/Country: 1942 + USA   Type: Feature
Distr/Arch: uni
Annotation: Dooley Wilson adds his music to the typical
    Rosalind Russell romantic comedy with McMurray as the
    romantic interest.

TAKE MY LIFE
Alt Title(s): Murder Trap
Nar/Cast: Freddie Baker* + Eugene Jackson* + Paul White* +
    Eddie Lynn* + DeForrest Covan* + Monte Hawley* + Jeni
    LeGon* + Lovey Lane* + Robert Webb* + Jack Carter* + Harry
    Levette* + Guernsey Morrow* + Herbert Skinner* + Arthur
    Ray*
Studio/Company: Goldseal
Date/Country: 1941 + USA
Annotation: After a close brush with death, the Harlem Dead
    End Kids (Baker, Jackson, White, Lynn, Covan) abandon
    their life of petty crime and join the Army. (May also
    have been released as Murder Rap.)

TAKE THIS HAMMER
Producer: NET
Tech Info: 16 mm/sound/bw/1 reel/45 min.   Type: Docu-
    mentary
Distr/Arch: iu
Annotation: Presents the defiant bitterness of James
    Baldwin* as he tours Negro areas of San Francisco. Views
    a redevelopment area, where Baldwin describes the building
    of new apartments as a 'Negro removal' project.

TAKE, THE
Nar/Cast: Billy Dee Williams* + Eddie Albert + Frankie

Avalon + Albert Salmi + Vic Morrow + Tracy Reed*
Studio/Company: Columbia + World Film Services
Tech Info: 16 mm/sound/color/3 reel/91 min.
Date/Country: 1974 + USA   Type: Feature
Distr/Arch: swa
Annotation: Billy Dee Williams manages to play the police
   and the thieves against each other, all to his advantage
   and profit.

TAKING CARE OF BUSINESS   Director: Robert Kaylor
Studio/Company: Robert Kaylor
Tech Info: 16 mm/color/sound/1 reel/50 min.
Date/Country: 1973 + USA   Type: Documentary
Annotation: A penetrating look at ex-con, ex-heroin addict
   Charlie McGregor who spent 25 of his 40 years in jail.
   The group encounter session not only shows insights into
   group sessions, but is also a classic example of cinema
   verite.

TAKING CARE OF MOTHER BALDWIN
Producer: Victor Nunez
Tech Info: 16 mm/sound/bw/1 reel/20 min.
Date/Country: 1969 + USA   Type: Dramatic Short
Distr/Arch: iu + persp + vfi
Annotation: Tells the story of a young boy who helps an old
   woman with her chores. Expresses the closeness of the two
   people through visuals, using intermittent clapping and
   singing as sound track. Features a choir singing gospels.

TAKING OF PELHAM ONE TWO THREE, THE
Nar/Cast: Julius Harris* + Walter Matthau + Robert Shaw +
   Martin Balsam + Hector Elizondo + Earl Hindman
Screenplay: Peter Stone   Story: John Godey
Producer: Edgar J. Scherick + Gabriel Katzka   Director:
   Joseph Sargent
Studio/Company: United Artists
Tech Info: sound/color/102 min.   Type: Feature
Annotation: Four people hijack a subway car in New York and
   the action switches from inside the car to the Transit
   Authority's and Police Department's efforts to rescue the
   victims. Julius Harris is a police officer trying to
   track the hijackers and save the passengers.

TAKING OFF
Nar/Cast: Lynn Carlin + Buck Henry + Linnea Heacock + Ike
   and Tina Revue*   Director: Milos Forman
Studio/Company: Universal
Tech Info: 16 mm/sound/color/93 min./3 reels
Date/Country: 1971 + USA   Type: Feature
Distr/Arch: uni + cwf + swa + twy + uni
Annotation: Generation gap comedy tells of a 15 year old
   girl who drops out to the East Village in New York. The
   Ike and Tina Turner Revue performs.

TALE OF A DOG
Series: Our Gang
Nar/Cast: Our Gang + Billie Thomas* + Cordell Hickman*
Screenplay: Hal Law + Robert A. McGowan

Producer: MGM   Director: Cyril Endfield
Studio/Company: MGM
Tech Info: bw/sound/1 reel
Date/Country: 1944 + USA   Type: Comedy Short
Annotation: The gang overhears Buckwheat (Billie Thomas) and
    Big Shot talking about giving 'small pox' to the gang.
    Not realizing 'smallpox' is a dog, they alert the neigh-
    borhood and health authorities and start a panic of out-
    landish rumours in the city.

TALE OF TWO LADIES, A
Series: Epitaph for Jim Crow
Nar/Cast: Dr. Thomas Pettigrew
Producer: NET Network
Tech Info: 16 mm/30 min./bw/sound
Date/Country: 1961 + USA   Type: Feature
Distr/Arch: adl
Annotation: A review of the history of protest against raci-
    al discrimination in the U.S.A.

TALES OF MANHATTAN
Nar/Cast: Charles Boyer + Rita Hayworth + Edward G. Robinson
    + Paul Robeson* + Ethel Waters* + Eddie Anderson* +
    Clarence Muse* + George Reed* + Cordell Hickman* + Hall
    Johnson Chorus*
Screenplay: Ben Hecht
Producer: Boris Moros   Director: Julien Duvivier
Studio/Company: 20th Century Fox
Tech Info: 16 mm/sound/bw/118 min.
Date/Country: 1943 + USA   Type: Feature
Distr/Arch: wrs
Annotation: A string of stories linked together by a coat
    stuffed with money and its effect on the lives of those
    who come into its possession. The coat finally falls into
    the hands of Southern black farm folk (Robeson and Waters)
    who have to decide what to do with the money. Eddie An-
    derson is the preacher who has his own ideas.

TALES: TALL AND OTHERWISE
Producer: Univ. of Michigan Television Center
Tech Info: 16 mm/sound/bw/29 min.
Date/Country: 1967 + USA   Type: Documentary
Distr/Arch: umic
Annotation: Discusses tales like Paul Bunyon and Brer Rab-
    bit, their long life and popularity. Provided by Center
    for Southern Folklore.

TALK OF THE TOWN, THE
Nar/Cast: Jean Arthur + Ronald Colman + Cary Grant + Rex
    Ingram*
Screenplay: Irwin Shaw + Sidney Buchman
Producer: George Stevens   Director: George Stevens
Studio/Company: Columbia
Tech Info: 16 mm/sound/bw/118 min.
Date/Country: 1942 + USA   Type: Feature
Distr/Arch: mac + wel
Annotation: Rex Ingram has a character role (Tilney) in this
    mystery comedy with Cary Grant as a convicted murderer who

escapes from prison and enlists the aid of Jean Arthur and Ronald Colman to prove his innocence.

TALKING DRUMS OF NIGERIA, THE
Screenplay: Peter Seeger + Toshi Seeger
Producer: Folklore Research Film
Tech Info: 16 mm/bw/sound/17 min.
Date/Country: 1964 + Nigeria   Type: Documentary
Distr/Arch: rad
Annotation: A demonstration of the "language" of drums in which the people demonstrate to Pete Seeger the way they communicate with their drums by imitating the sounds of the Yoruba language.

TALL TARGET, THE
Nar/Cast: Dick Powell + Paula Raymond + Ruby Dee* + Will Geer
Screenplay: George W. Yates + Art Cohn   Story: George W. Yates + Geoffery Iomes
Producer: Richard Goldstone   Director: Anthony Mann
Studio/Company: MGM
Tech Info: 16 mm/sound/bw/78 min.
Date/Country: 1951 + USA
Distr/Arch: fnc
Annotation: Dick Powell plays a New York detective who uncovers an assassination plot against Abraham Lincoln on the eve of Lincoln's first inaugural and races against time to foil it. Ruby Dee plays Rachel (Ginny Beaufort's maid), one of the numerous suspects although she does clear herself somewhere near the middle of the film.

TALL, TAN AND TERRIFIC
Nar/Cast: Francine Everett* + Monte Hawley* + Milton Woods* + Mantan Moreland* + Dotts Johnson* + Perry "Butterbeans" Bradford* + Rody Toombs* + Lou Swarz* + Johnny and George* + Edna Mae Harris* + Myra Johnson*
Screenplay: John S. Gordon
Producer: R.M. Savini   Director: Bud Pollard
Studio/Company: Astor Picture Corp.
Tech Info: sound/bw/60 min.
Date/Country: 1946 + USA   Type: Feature
Annotation: Handsome Harry (Hawley), owner of the Golden Slipper nightclub, is in love with Miss Tall, Tan...(Everett) who works there. Harry fights with one of the gamblers at his club and when the gambler later dies, the murder weapon is traced to Harry who is jailed and faces the electric chair. Detective work on the part of Moreland clears Harry who is reunited with Miss Tall, Tan and T...who'd left town to avoid testifying against Harry. Music by Golden Slipper All Girl Band*.

TAMANGO
Nar/Cast: Dorothy Dandridge* + Curt Jurgens + Jean Servais + Alex Cressan
Screenplay: Lee Gold + Tamara Hovey + John Berry   Director: John Berry
Studio/Company: Les Films du Cyclope + Hal Roach Release
Date/Country: 1959 + France   Type: Feature

Annotation: This adaptation of Prosper Merimee's Tamango is
    concerned with the happenings aboard a slave ship plying
    the waters from Africa to Cuba. Dorothy Dandridge is
    Aiche, the island beauty who is torn between loyalty to
    her people in the hold and the passionate sea captain
    (Jurgens).

TANGANYIKA
Nar/Cast: Van Heflin + Ruth Roman + Joe Comadore* + Howard
    Duff + Jeff Morrow
Screenplay: William Sackheim + R. Alan Simmons
Producer: Albert J. Cohen   Director: Andre de Toth
Studio/Company: Universal-International
Tech Info: 16 mm/sound/color/81 min.
Date/Country: 1954 + USA   Type: Feature
Distr/Arch: uni
Annotation: After his partner is killed by a maniacal
    renegade played by Jeff Morrow, Van Heflin seeks the vil-
    lain out to get revenge.   Along the way he meets Ruth
    Roman and Howard Duff in this studio- style safari film
    replete with natives, including one on the credits: An-
    dolo, played by Joe Comadore.

TANZANIA--THE QUIET REVOLUTION
Producer: NET
Tech Info: 16 mm/sound/bw/1 reel/60 min.
Date/Country: 1965   Type: Documentary
Distr/Arch: iu
Annotation: A portrait of the country and peoples of Tan-
    zania and their struggle with the problems of extreme
    poverty, illiteracy, and racism. President Julius K. Ny-
    erere* explains his policy of nonalignment as the only
    practical means of obtaining the needed manpower and money
    to solve these problems.

TARZAN AND HIS MATE
Nar/Cast: Johnny Weissmuller + Maureen O'Sullivan + Neil
    Hamilton + Nathan Curry*   Director: Cedric Gibbons
Studio/Company: MGM
Tech Info: 16 mm/sound/bw/3 reels/105 min.
Date/Country: 1934 + USA   Type: Feature
Distr/Arch: fnc
Annotation: After a short time of marriage-jungle bliss,
    Tarzan and Jane are confronted with Jane's old fiance. he
    has brought along an ivory-collecting friend who tries to
    grab ivcry and Jane for for his own without Tarzan's know-
    ledge. Tarzan fights back with his strength and command
    of the jungle animals, routing the hunter and his savages.
    Curry is one of the natives.

TARZAN AND THE AMAZONS
Nar/Cast: Jchnny Weissmuller + Brenda Joyce   Director: Kurt
    Neumann
Studio/Company: RKO
Tech Info: 16 mm/sound/bw/76 min.
Date/Country: 1945 + USA   Type: Feature
Distr/Arch: cha
Annotation: Safari to find gold in the Amazons "land of the

forgotten time" through the wilds of Africa is led by Boy, against Tarzan's wishes. The Amazons are all white females armed with bows and arrows; Blacks are native bearers who last only until the going gets rough. Tarzan of course has to save Boy's life.

TARZAN AND THE GREAT RIVER
Nar/Cast: Mike Henry + Diane Millay + Rafer Johnson*
Screenplay: Bob Barbash
Producer: Sy Weintraub   Director: Robert Day
Studio/Company: Paramount
Tech Info: 16 mm/color/sound/2 reels/88 min.
Date/Country: 1967 + USA   Type: Feature
Distr/Arch: fnc
Annotation: A modern, educated Tarzan, having turned his pet lion and monkey into a local zoo, learns that a leopard tribe revived by Barcuna (Rafer Johnson) is creating havoc in the area. Exchanging suit for loin cloth, he swings into action to restore peace.

TARZAN AND THE JUNGLE BOY
Nar/Cast: Mike Henry + Rafer Johnson* + Alizia Gur + Steve Bond + Edward Johnson*
Screenplay: Steven Lord
Producer: Robert Day   Director: Robert Gordon
Studio/Company: Paramount
Tech Info: 16 mm/color/sound/3 reels/90 min.
Date/Country: 1968 + USA
Distr/Arch: fnc
Annotation: Tarzan helps a woman photographer find a lost white boy believed living in the jungle for six years. Their travels take them through Zagunda territory where they become involved in the contest between two brothers Nagambi (Rafer Johnson) and Bhara (Edward Johnson) for control of the tribe when the Chief, their father, dies.

TARZAN AND THE LOST SAFARI
Nar/Cast: Gordon Scott + Robert Beatty + Betta St. John + Orlando Martins*   Story: Edgar Rice Burroughs
Producer: John Croydon   Director: Bruce Humberstone
Studio/Company: MGM
Tech Info: 16 mm/color/sound/2 reels/84 min.
Date/Country: 1957 + USA   Type: Feature
Distr/Arch: fnc
Annotation: A luxury airliner crashes in the Arican jungle, landing on the edge of a precipice into which it is about to fall and thereby doom its five passengers. Tarzan rescues them not only from the brink of doom but also from the numerous perils of the jungle. Orlando Martins plays Chief Ogonooro.

TARZAN ESCAPES
Nar/Cast: Johnny Weissmuller + Maureen O'Sullivan + Benita Hume   Director: Richard Thorpe
Studio/Company: MGM
Tech Info: 16 mm/sound/bw/3 reels/89 min.
Date/Country: 1936 + USA   Type: Feature
Distr/Arch: fnc

Annotation: Africans, native to the terrain now presided
over by Tarzan and his happy mate, make things difficult
(with their ju ju and ingrigues) for the blissful pair, so
do some of Jane's relatives and a villainous English explorer who wants ivory and Jane, and Tarzan out of the
way.

TARZAN OF THE APES
Nar/Cast: Elmo Lincoln + Enid Markey + Rex Ingram*   Story:
   Edgar Rice Burroughs   Director: Scott Sidney
Studio/Company: First National
Tech Info: 16 mm/bw/silent/2 reel/60 min.
Date/Country: 1918 + USA   Type: Feature
Distr/Arch: bud + emg + fce + kpf + bla + cie + mog
Annotation: The child of Lord/Lady Greystokes is brought up
   in the wilds of Africa by an ape mother, Kala, after the
   demise of his parents. Kala is killed by a native whom
   Tarzan then kills and is propetiated by the natives like a
   god. When Jane arrives with safari, Tarzan has to save
   her from any number of perils--African and animal - before
   they can swing happily through the trees together. Ingram
   and other Blacks play natives who range from happy to
   superstitious to cowardly; all easily outwitted by Tarzan.
   The most frightened Black is Jane's imported maid,
   Esmeraldy.

TARZAN'S FIGHT FOR LIFE
Nar/Cast: Gordon Scott + Eva Brent   Story: Edgar Rice Bur-
   roughs   Director: Bruce Humberstone
Studio/Company: MGM
Tech Info: 16 mm/color/sound/2 reels/86 min.
Date/Country: 1958 + USA   Type: Feature
Distr/Arch: fnc
Annotation: After rushing his mate to a research scientist
   for an emergency operation, Tarzan helps the medical man
   fight tc keep his jungle hospital open in the face of op-
   position from the local witch doctor.

TARZAN'S PERIL
Nar/Cast: Dorothy Dandriege* + Lex Barker
Date/Country: 1951 + USA   Type: Feature
Annotation: A Tarzan adventure with Dandridge in the lead as
   an African princess, who is kidnapped by a bellicose
   tribal leader but rescued by Tarzan.

TARZAN'S THREE CHALLENGES
Nar/Cast: Jock Mahoney + Woody Strode* + Earl Cameron*
Screenplay: Bernie Giler + Robert Day
Producer: Sy Weintraub   Director: Robert Day
Studio/Company: MGM
Tech Info: 16 mm/color/sound/92 min.
Date/Country: 1963 + USA   Type: Feature
Distr/Arch: fnc
Annotation: Tarzan is asked to go to a Tibetan-like Asian
   country to guard a child on a trip from a monastery to the
   city where he will become the new spiritual leader. His
   Uncle Knan/Tarim (Strode) covets the position for his own
   son and challenges his selection under the ancient law.

Cameron plays Mang.

TARZAN, THE APE MAN
Nar/Cast: Johnny Weissmuller + Maureen O'Sullivan + Neil
   Hamilton + C. Aubrey Smith   Story: Edgar Rice Burroughs
   Director: W.S. Van Dyke
Studio/Company: MGM
Tech Info: 16 mm/color/3 reels/100 min.
Date/Country: 1932 + USA   Type: Feature
Annotation: In this first of the Weissmuller/Tarzan series,
   Tarzan saves Jane, her father and her fiance from hostile
   natives as the trio look for elephant's graveyard.

TARZAN, THE APE MAN
Nar/Cast: Denny Miller + Cesare Danova + Joanna Barnes
   Director: Joseph M. Newman
Studio/Company: MGM
Tech Info: 16 mm/sound/color/82 min.
Date/Country: 1959 + USA   Type: Feature
Distr/Arch: fnc
Annotation: Two men (one has a daughter Jane) decide to make
   fortunes uncovering the legendary elephants' graveyard and
   its ivory. Their trek is interrupted by natives but
   Tarzan rescues Jane and takes her to his tree house.
   Remake of the original 1932 version.

TARZANS DEADLY SILENCE
Nar/Cast: Ron Ely + Robert DoQui* + Kenny Washington* +
   Woody Strode*
Screenplay: Lee Erevin + Jack Robinson + John Considine
   Story: Tim Considine
Producer: Leon Benson   Director: Robert L. Friend
Studio/Company: National General
Tech Info: 16 mm/sound/color/89 min.
Date/Country: 1970 + USA   Type: Feature
Distr/Arch: swa
Annotation: Tarzan is temporarily deafened in this struggle
   to keep a former British Colonel with a love for power
   from assuming control over all African tribes. Marstak
   (Strode) is on the side of the Colonel, against Metusa (Do
   Qui), the son of the tribal chief taken hostage by the
   villains - the "good guys" in the formula.

TASTE OF HONEY, A
Nar/Cast: Paul Danquah* + Rita Tushingham + Murray Melvin
   Director: Tony Richardson
Studio/Company: Continental Pictures
Tech Info: 16 mm/bw/sound/3 reels/100 min.
Date/Country: 1962 + Britain   Type: Feature
Distr/Arch: twy + wrs + kpf
Annotation: Danquah is the black sailor (Jimmy) who gets
   involved with a young white girl, played by Rita
   Tushingham. The film delineates her problems after she
   gives birth to their baby.

TAW
Alt Title(s): Tauw
Nar/Cast: Amadou Dieng* + Mamadou M'Bow* + Fatim Diagne* +

Coumba Mane + Habib Diop*
Screenplay: Ousmane Sembene*
Producer: Ousane Sembene* + Herbert F. Lowe + George
   Carestan   Director: Ousmane Sembene
Tech Info: 16 mm/color/sound/1 reel/27 min./Walof with En-
   glish subtitles
Date/Country: 1970 + Senegal   Type: Dramatic Short
Distr/Arch: tri + nyf + avsl + cph + umch + aph + avei + mar
   + uccav
Annotation: Taw is a 20 year old unemployed youth in
   Senegal's capital, Dakar. The film focuses on the despair
   caused by Senegal's high rate of unemployment and the
   serious differences between generations.

TEACHER'S BEAU
Series: Our Gang
Nar/Cast: Our Gang + Matthew Beard* + Billie Thomas* + The
   Five Cabin Kids*
Producer: Hal Roach   Director: Gus Meins
Studio/Company: MGM + Roach
Tech Info: super 8 mm/16 mm/bw/sound/1 reel/19 min.
Date/Country: 1935 + USA   Type: Comedy Short
Distr/Arch: bla + roa
Annotation: The gang tries various schemes to prevent Miss
   Jones, about to be married, from being replaced by Mrs.
   Wilson - who they are made to believe is an old hag. One
   of their pranks gets back to them when they discover Miss
   Jones' fiance is named Wilson. Matthew Beard stars as
   Stymie and Billie Thomas stars as Buckwheat.

TEACHERS PET
Series: Our Gang
Nar/Cast: Our Gang + Matthew Beard* + Allen Hoskins*
Screenplay: Robert F. McGowan
Producer: Hal Roach   Director: Robert F. McGowan
Studio/Company: MGM + Roach
Tech Info: super 8 mm/16 mm/bw/sound/1 reel/21 min.
Date/Country: 1930 + USA   Type: Comedy Short
Distr/Arch: bla + roa
Annotation: Jackie inadvertently reveals all the gang's
   nasty plans for the new teacher to the pretty lady who's
   given him a lift. He is amazed and humiliated when the
   pretty lady turns out to be the new teacher. Allen
   Hoskins* is Farina.

TEENAGE REBEL
Nar/Cast: Ginger Rogers + Michael Rennie + Mildred Natwick +
   Louise Beavers*
Screenplay: Walter Reisch + Charles Brackett   Story: Edith
   Sommer
Producer: Charles Brackett   Director: Edmund Goulding
Studio/Company: 20th Century Fox
Tech Info: 16 mm/sound/bw/94 min.
Date/Country: 1956 + USA   Type: Feature
Distr/Arch: fnc
Annotation: Tensions arise when a young girl goes to spend
   some time with her mother, who has divorced and remarried.
   Louise Beavers is Willamay.

TELETHON
Nar/Cast: Polly Bergen + Lloyd Bridges + Red Buttons + Jimmy
    Walker* + Sugar Ray Robinson*
Screenplay: William Roberts
Producer: Robert Lovenheim   Director: David Lowell Rich
Studio/Company: ABC Circle Films
Date/Country: 1977 + USA   Type: TV Feature
Annotation: Drama of personal crises with a Las Vegas
    Telethon as its backdrop. Jimmie Walker and Sugar Ray
    Robinson appear as themselves.

TELL ME THAT YOU LOVE ME, JUNIE MOON
Nar/Cast: Liza Minnelli + Emily Yancy* + Fred Williamson*
Screenplay: Marjorie Kellogg   Story: Marjorie Kellogg
Producer: Otto Preminger   Director: Otto Preminger
Studio/Company: Paramount
Tech Info: 16 mm/sound/color/112 min.
Date/Country: 1970 + USA   Type: Feature
Distr/Arch: rbc
Annotation: Story of how some of society's outcasts band
    together for mutual enlightenment and growth.   Williamson
    plays a beach boy, Yancy plays Solana.

TELL NO TALES
Nar/Cast: Melvyn Douglas + Louise Platt + Gary Lockhart +
    Teresa Harris* + Clinton Rosemond*
Screenplay: Lionel Houser   Story: Pauline London
Producer: Edmund Chodorov   Director: Leslie Fenton
Studio/Company: MGM
Date/Country: 1939 + USA   Type: Feature
Annotation: Melvyn Douglas plays a hard working editor out
    to save his paper and find some kidnappers, both before
    it's too late.   Teresa Harris (Ruby) and Clinton Rosemond
    figure in the Negro death wake the editor happens into in
    his search for evidence in the kidnapping case.

TELLING WHOPPERS
Series: Our Gang
Nar/Cast: Our Gang + Allen Hoskins*
Screenplay: Hal Roach
Producer: Hal Roach   Director: Robert McGowan
Studio/Company: Pathe
Tech Info: silent/bw/2 reels
Date/Country: 1926 + USA   Type: Comedy Short
Annotation: Joe and Farina (Allen Hoskins) lose in a lottery
    drawing and Dicky wins the privilege of confronting the
    bully who is terrorizing the gang.   Thinking the bully has
    left town, they return 'telling whoppers' of their con-
    quests, only to be saved by the bully's mother who deals
    with him handily.

TEMPTATION
Nar/Cast: A.S. Bishop* + Lorenzo Tucker* + Hilda Rogers* +
    Alfred "Slick" Chester*   Director: Oscar Micheaux*
Studio/Company: Micheaux Film
Date/Country: 1936 + USA   Type: Feature
Annotation: Lorenzo Tucker, billed by Micheaux as the "black

Valentino" plays in this "adult" drama.

TEN COMMANDMENTS, THE
Nar/Cast: Theodore Roberts + Noble Johnson* + Richad Dix +
   Rex Ingram*
Screenplay: Jeanie MacPherson
Producer: Adolph Zukov   Director: Cecil B. DeMille
Studio/Company: Paramount
Tech Info: silent/bw
Date/Country: 1923 + USA   Type: Feature
Annotation: The prologue depicts biblical stories from Ex-
   odus. The main story is about 2 brothers in love with the
   same girl. Noble Johnson plays the bronze man.

TEN COMMANDMENTS, THE
Nar/Cast: Charlton Heston + Anne Baxter + Yul Brynner +
   Woody Strode*
Screenplay: Aeneas MacKenzie
Producer: Cecil B. DeMille   Director: Cecil B. DeMille
Studio/Company: Paramount
Tech Info: 16 mm/sound/color/219 min.
Date/Country: 1956 + USA   Type: Feature
Distr/Arch: fnc
Annotation: The story of Moses from bulrushes to Mount
   Sinai. Woody Strode in a small part.

TEN MINUTES TO KILL   Director: Oscar Micheaux*
Studio/Company: Micheaux Film Corporation
Date/Country: 1933 + USA   Type: Feature

TEN MINUTES TO LIVE
Nar/Cast: Lawrence Chenault* + Willor Lee Guilford* + Willi-
   am A. Clayton* + A.B. Comathiere* + Laura Bowman* + Tres-
   sie Mitchell* + Mabel Garrett* + Carl Mahon* + Lorenzo
   Tucker*   Director: Oscar Micheaux*
Studio/Company: Micheaux Film Corporation
Tech Info: 16 mm/bw/sound/2 reels/65 min.
Date/Country: 1932 + USA   Type: Feature
Distr/Arch: kpf + lc
Annotation: A mystery-musical built around a threatening
   note which gives the heroine only "ten minutes to live."
   Much nightclub business as the mystery unravels with song
   and dance numbers and a stand up comedy routine.   Billie
   Heywood* is the nightclub M.C.

TEN NIGHTS IN A BARROOM
Nar/Cast: Charles Gilpin* + Lawrence Chenault* + Myra Bur-
   well* + William Clayton* + Harry Henderson* + Ethel Smith*
   + Arline Mickey* + Edward Moore* + William Johnson
Studio/Company: Colored Players of Philadelphia
Tech Info: 35 mm/silent/bw/5 reels/60 min.
Date/Country: 1926 + USA   Type: Feature
Distr/Arch: imp
Annotation: Black version of William Pratt's temperance
   novel. Gilpin plays the father who is overcome by the
   demon drink until his entire family is affected.

TEN PICKANINNIES

Date/Country: 1904 + USA
Annotation: Another forerunner of the Our Gang series.

TEN YEARS OLD
Series: Our Gang
Nar/Cast: Our Gang + Allen Hoskins* + Jannie Hoskins*
Screenplay: Hal Roach
Producer: Hal Roach   Director: Anthony Mack
Studio/Company: Pathe
Tech Info: silent/bw/2 reels
Date/Country: 1927 + USA   Type: Comedy Short
Annotation: Mischief begins when Joe combines his birthday
   party with rich kid Jackie's, the topper comes when Farina
   shows up with a kitten which turns out to be a skunk.

TENDER GAME, THE
Nar/Cast: Ella Fitzgerald* + Oscar Peterson Trio*
Producer: John Hubley
Tech Info: 16 mm/sound/color/1 reel/6 min.
Date/Country: 1958 + USA   Type: Animated Short
Distr/Arch: iu + stu
Annotation: Presents an interpretation using semi-abstract
   animation of the song 'Tenderly,' as performed by Ella
   Fitzgerald and the Oscar Peterson Trio. The story tells
   of a boy and girl falling in love.

TENDERFEET
Nar/Cast: Spencer Williams* + Mildred Washington* + Flora
   Washington* + Spencer Bell* + James Robinson*   Director:
   Spencer Williams*
Studio/Company: Midnight Productions
Tech Info: 35 mm/silent/bw
Date/Country: 1928 + USA   Type: Feature

TENEMENT
Studio/Company: CBS
Tech Info: 16 mm/sound/bw/40 min.   Type: TV Documentary
Distr/Arch: adl
Annotation: Nine families in a ghetto on the South side of
   Chicago talk of their dreams of a better life, of their
   struggle for pride, and their failures, conveying the
   hopelessness and despair of poverty and its special impact
   on the Black American.

TENNESSEE JOHNSON
Alt Title(s): The Man on America's Conscience
Nar/Cast: Van Heflin + Lionel Barrymore + Ruth Hussey + Mar-
   jorie Main + Edward F. Bromberg + Grant Withers + Dane
   Clark + Noah Beery, Sr.   Story: Milton Ginsberg + Alvin
   Meyers   Director: William Dieterle
Studio/Company: MGM
Tech Info: 16 mm/souund/bw/103 min.
Date/Country: 1944 + USA   Type: Feature
Distr/Arch: fnc
Annotation: Released in America under the titleTennessee
   Johnson, the film makes a hero of Andrew Jackson (Heflin),
   a defender of old Southern traditions, in spite of the
   war, emancipation, et cetera, and a villain of Thaddeus

Stevens (Barrymore) who believed in giving the ex-slaves their rights.

TERM OF TRIAL
Nar/Cast: Earl Cameron* + Sir Laurence Olivier + Sarah Miles
Screenplay: Peter Glenville
Producer: James Woolf   Director: Peter Glenville
Studio/Company: Warners
Tech Info: 16 mm/sound/bw/113 min.
Date/Country: 1963 + Britain   Type: Feature
Distr/Arch: wsa
Annotation: Earl Cameron is Chard in this drama of a dedicated London school teacher (Olivier) and his troubled marriage.

TERRA STRANIERA
Nar/Cast: John Kitzmiller*
Date/Country: 1953 + Italy   Type: Feature

TERROR IN THE CITY
Nar/Cast: Lee Grant + Ruth Attaway* + Robert Earl Jones* + Roscoe Lee Browne* + Sylvia Miles
Screenplay: Allen Baron
Producer: Allen Baron + Merrill Brody + Dorothy E. Reed
    Director: Allen Baron
Studio/Company: Allied Artist
Tech Info: sound/color/90 min.
Date/Country: 1966 + USA   Type: Feature
Annotation: Story of a little runaway farm boy and his experiences in New York as he's befriended by a prostitute and a young Puerto Rican who takes the boy under his wing. Browne is a preacher; Jones a farmer, Attaway his wife.

TERRY WHITMORE FOR EXAMPLE
Nar/Cast: Terry Whitmore*
Screenplay: Hasse Seiden
Producer: Hasse Seiden   Director: Bill Brodie
Studio/Company: Grove Press
Date/Country: 1969 + Sweden   Type: Documentary
Annotation: Whitmore who, after having won a medal for heroism, as a marine in Vietnam, defects to Sweden. He tells his own story in this documentary. Whitmore also plays the role of defector in Maya Angelou's Georgia, Georgia.

THANK YOU, JEEVES
Nar/Cast: Arthur Treacher + David Niven + Virginia Field + Willie Best*
Screenplay: Joseph Hoffman   Story: P.G.Wodehouse
Producer: Sol Wurtzel   Director: Arthur Collins
Studio/Company: 20th Century Fox
Date/Country: 1936 + USA   Type: Feature
Annotation: Another film in the Jeeves series has David Niven and Arthur Treacher trying to help a young woman avoid some gunmen. Willie Best plays (and looks) "Drowsy."

THANK YOUR LUCKY STARS

Nar/Cast: Eddie Cantor + Joan Leslie + Hattie McDaniel +
   Willie Best
Screenplay: Norman Panama
Producer: Mark Hellinger   Director: David Butler
Studio/Company: Warner Brothers
Tech Info: 16mm/sound/bw/127 min.
Date/Country: 1943 + USA   Type: Feature
Distr/Arch: uas
Annotation: All-star variety show with the various contract
   stars at Warner Brothers. McDaniel and Best do a Harlem
   production number entitled "Ice-Cold Katie."

THAT_CERTAIN_FEELING
Nar/Cast: Pearl Bailey* + Bob Hope + Eva Marie Saint + Ge-
   orge Sanders   Story: Jean Kerr (play)
Producer: Norman Panama + Melvin Frank + I.A.L. Diamond +
   William Altman   Director: Norman Panama + Melvin Frank +
   I.A.L. Diamond + William Altman
Studio/Company: Paramount
Tech Info: 16 mm/sound/color/102 min.
Date/Country: 1956   Type: Feature
Distr/Arch: fnc
Annotation: Bob Hope as a "ghost" cartoonist in this comedy
   farce that has Eva Marie Saint playing his ex-wife trying
   to instill self-confidence in him. Bailey is a lyrical
   wisecracking maid (she sings two numbers).

THAT_MAN_BOLT
Nar/Cast: Fred Williamson* + Byron Webster + Mike Mayama +
   Teresa Graves*
Screenplay: Quentin Wertz + Charles Johnson   Story: Charles
   Johnson
Producer: Bernard Schwartz   Director: Harry Levin + David
   Lowell Rich
Studio/Company: Universal
Tech Info: 16 mm/sound/color/103 min.
Date/Country: 1973 + USA   Type: Feature
Distr/Arch: cwf + twy + uni
Annotation: Jefferson Lincoln Bolt (Fred Williamson) courier
   by trade and skilled in the martial arts, must deliver one
   million dollars from a bank in Hong Kong to Mexico City.
   Teresa Graves is the woman with whom he becomes involved.

THAT_MAN_OF_MINE
Nar/Cast: Ruby Dee* + Powell Lindsay* + Hazel Tillman* +
   Rhina Harris* + Flow Hawkins* + Betty Haynes* + Toni
   Moore* + Henri Woods* and his Six Hepcats*   Director:
   William Alexander
Studio/Company: Associated   Producers   of Negro Motion
   Pictures
Date/Country: 1947 + USA

THAT'S_ENTERTAINMENT
Nar/Cast: MGM stars + Lena Horne*
Producer: MGM   Director: Jack Haley, Jr.
Tech Info: 16 mm/sound/137 min.
Date/Country: 1974 + USA   Type: TV Feature
Annotation: Highlights from MGM musicals, includes almost

all that studio's stars. Lena Horne sings "Honeysucuckle Rose" from <u>Thousands Cheer</u>. Ethel Waters is credited but doesn't appear.

THAT'S THE SPIRIT
Nar/Cast: Noble Sissle and his band* + Cora La Redd* + The Washboard Serenaders* + Flournoy Miller* + Mantan Moreland*
Studio/Company: Vitaphone
Tech Info: 16 mm/sound/1 reel/9 min.
Date/Country: 1932 + USA   Type: Musical Short
Distr/Arch: unf
Annotation: Moreland and Miller are nightwatchmen easily terrorized by "ghostly" happenings (Moreland's terror even lifts him out of his shoes). La Redd and the Washband Serenaders provide the song and dance numbers. Sissle and his band play "Tiger Rug" and "St. Louis Blues."

THE COLOUR OF LOVE
Alt Title(s): see Les Laches Vivant d'Espoir

THERE WAS A CROOKED MAN...
Nar/Cast: Kirk Douglas + Henry Fonda + Claudia McNeil* + Lee Grant + Alan Hale
Screenplay: David Newman + Robert Benton
Producer: Joseph L. Mankiewicz   Director: Joseph L. Mankiewicz
Studio/Company: Warner Brothers
Tech Info: 16 mm/sound/color/125 min.
Date/Country: 1970 + USA   Type: Feature
Distr/Arch: ker
Annotation: A comic look at some of the myths of the old West in this movie set in a prison in the Arizona territory. McNeil is "Madam."

THEY BEAT THE ODDS
Producer: Dixie-Dash
Tech Info: 16 mm/sound/color/22 min.
Date/Country: 1965 + USA   Type: Documentary
Distr/Arch: dibd
Annotation: Illustrates success of Blacks in many fields; yet, shows how limited opportunities may on the other hand affect a black youth contemplting dropping out of school.

THEY CALL ME MISTER TIBBS
Nar/Cast: Sidney Poitier* + Barbara McNair* + Wanda Spell* + George Spell* + Beverly Todd* + Juano Hernandez* + Martin Landau   Director: Gordon Douglas
Studio/Company: Columbia
Tech Info: 16 mm/color/sound/3 reels/108 min.
Date/Country: 1970 + USA   Type: Feature
Distr/Arch: uas
Annotation: This film, set in San Francisco, has Poitier as a detective looking for the murderer of a call girl. The prime suspect seems to be a Protestant minister who happens to be Poitier's best friend. Barbara McNair plays his wife; Hernandez is Mealie the garbage man. Music score by Quincy Jones*.

THEY_DIED_WITH_THEIR_BOOTS_ON
Nar/Cast: Errol Flynn + Olivia de Havilland + Arthur Kennedy
  + Anthony Quinn + Sydney Greenstreet + Hattie McDaniel*
Screenplay: Wallace Kline + Aeneas MacKenzie   Director:
  Raoul Walsh
Studio/Company: Warners
Tech Info: 16 mm/sound/bw/138 min.
Date/Country: 1942 + USA   Type: Feature
Distr/Arch: uas
Annotation: Romanticized   version   of George Armstrong
  Custer's life. Hattie McDaniel plays her usual role.

THEY_GET_RICH_FROM_THE_POOR
Producer: NBC
Tech Info: 16 mm/sound/color/1 reel/24 min.
Date/Country: 1970 + USA   Type: Documentary
Distr/Arch: iu + fnc
Annotation: Describes crime in New York City, concentrating
  upon dope peddling, gambling, racketeering, and their ef-
  fects upon the community. Notes that a great deal of money
  can be made by exploiting the hopes and dreams of people
  in poor neighborhoods.

THEY_WON'T_FORGET
Alt Title(s): Death in the Deep South (book)
Nar/Cast: Claude Rains + Allyn Joslyn + Edward Norris +
  Gloria Dickson + Otto Kruger + Lana Turner + Elisha Cook,
  Jr. + Clinton Rosemond* + Trevor Bardette + Elliot Sul-
  livan + Frank Faylen
Screenplay: Ward Greene   Story: Ward Greene
Producer: Mervyn LeRoy   Director: Mervyn LeRoy
Studio/Company: Warners
Date/Country: 1937 + USA   Type: Feature
Annotation: In this film, Trump Redwind (Clinton Rosemond),
  a black janitor, discovers the body of a murdered white
  girl.   The police put him through a brutal interrogation
  in an attempt to wring a confession from him. A reworking
  of the Leo Frank case, the film focuses on a Northern
  white school teacher who is accused of killing the girl,
  one of his pupils, and is lynched by a mob.

THEY'RE_OFF
Nar/Cast: Martin Turner* + Peggy O'Day + Francis Ford
Screenplay: Francis Ford   Director: Francis Ford
Studio/Company: New Era Productions
Tech Info: 35 mm/silent/bw/5 reels/4,381 ft.
Date/Country: 1923 + USA   Type: Feature
Annotation: Martin Turner plays "Cellar," the Colonel's
  servant in this melodrama about twin sisters, horse
  racing, mountain life and Southern gentility.

THIEF_OF_BAGDAD,_THE
Nar/Cast: Conrad Veidt + Sabu + June Duprez + John Justin +
  Rex Ingram* + Adelaide Hall*
Screenplay: Miles Mallerson
Producer: Alexander Korda   Director: Michael Powell +
  Ludwig Berger

Studio/Company: London
Tech Info: 16 mm/sound/bw/109 min.
Date/Country: 1940 + Britain   Type: Feature
Distr/Arch: ivy
Annotation: Fantasy woven from the tales of the Arabian
    Nights complete with flying horses, usurped prince.   Rex
    Ingram is the "Genie of the Lamp," Djinni; Adelaide Hall,
    sings "The Princess' Song."

THIEF OF BAGDAD, THE
Nar/Cast: Douglas Fairbanks + Noble Johnson* + Anna May Wong
    + Sam Baker*
Screenplay: Elton Thomas   Director: Raoul Walsh
Studio/Company: United Artists
Tech Info: 16 mm/silent/bw/138 min.
Date/Country: 1924 + USA   Type: Feature
Distr/Arch: emg + kpf + mac + sel + twy + unf + wcf + wil +
    bla + cie + gme + ncs
Annotation: Fairbanks as the Thief of Bagdad falls for the
    princess of the city, poses as a prince to win her love --
    something he eventually does. Noble Johnson, in bearded
    splendor, is the Indian prince in this Arabian Nights
    satire.

THING WITH TWO HEADS, THE
Nar/Cast: Ray Milland + Roosevelt Grier*
Studio/Company: American International
Tech Info: 16 mm/sound/color/93 min.
Date/Country: 1972 + USA   Type: Feature
Distr/Arch: unf

THINKING BOOK, THE
Nar/Cast: Sidney Poitier*
Producer: Bank Street College of Educational Film Produc-
    tions
Tech Info: 16 mm/sound/color/1 reel/10 min.
Date/Country: 1968 + USA   Type: Dramatic Short
Distr/Arch: iu + mghf
Annotation: Presents Sidney Poitier reading the book of the
    same title by Sandal Stoddard. Relates the story of a
    child who prefers to think about important things like
    dust, colors, fruit, and what he loves, instead of the
    mundane tasks of getting up, washing, and dressing. Re-
    commended for young children.

THINKING OUT LOUD
Producer: C.D. Film
Tech Info: 16 mm/sound/bw/22 min.
Date/Country: 1972 + USA   Type: Documentary
Distr/Arch: efs
Annotation: The blues by black artists still living and per-
    forming in their home states: Robert Pete Williams, Scott
    Dunbar and Liza, Furry Lewis, Col. Bill Williams, Sleepy
    John Estes. Provided by Center for Southern Folklore.

THINKING SEVENTEEN
Producer: Richard Zarlow
Tech Info: 16 mm/sound/bw/16 min.

Date/Country: 1969 + USA   Type: Documentary
Distr/Arch: uca
Annotation: A black teen-ager in Oakland, California,
   describes his goals and inner conflicts.

THIRTEEN CLUB, THE
Studio/Company: Biograph
Date/Country: 1905 + USA
Annotation: A black waiter at the Thirteen Club is
   frightened into shakes and bugeyes as he suddenly sees a
   death head centerpiece while setting the table.

THIRTY YEARS LATER
Nar/Cast: William Edmondson* + A.B. Comathiere* + Mabel Kel-
   ly* + Ardella Dabney* + Gertrude Snelson*   Director:
   Oscar Micheaux*
Studio/Company: Micheaux Film Corporation
Tech Info: bw/sound
Date/Country: 1938 + USA   Type: Feature
Annotation: Melodrama about the hidden racial identity of a
   young man who believes he is white (Edmondson). He falls
   in love with a young black woman (Mabel Kelly) who refuses
   to marry him until she later discovers his Negro racial
   heritage, as he does with great pride.

THIS FAR BY FAITH
Nar/Cast: Brock Peters* + Roscoe Lee Brown* + Beah Richards*
   + Glynn Turman* + Edwin Hawkins Singers* + James Baldwin*
   + Geoffrey Holder*   Story: Byron Lewis
Producer: Brock Peters* + Alan Belkin
Studio/Company: Public Broadcasting Service
Tech Info: 16 mm/sound/color/60 min.
Date/Country: 1977 + USA   Type: TV Documentary
Annotation: This film traces the evolution of the American
   black church from its roots on the African continent,
   through the slavery era, Reconstruction and into the 20th
   Century.

THIS IS THE HOME OF MRS. LEVANT GRAHAM
Producer: Eliot Noyes, Jr. + Claudia Weill + New Thing Flick
   Co.
Tech Info: 16 mm/1 reel/15 min./bw
Date/Country: 1971 + USA   Type: Dramatized Documentary
Distr/Arch: pyr + nth
Annotation: This portrait of a black mother and her family
   living in a crowded slum apartment was produced by a black
   culture center in Washington.

THIS TRAIN
Producer: Frank Paine
Tech Info: 16 mm/sound/color/1 reel/4 min.
Date/Country: 1965 + USA   Type: Documentary
Distr/Arch: iu + per + nyu + vfi
Annotation: Depicts a night train speeding across the
   countryside using the folksong 'This Train' sung by Big
   Bill Broonzy* as accompaniment. Shows people embarking as
   the train rests in the depot.

THIS UNION CAUSE
Producer: AFL-CIO Unions
Tech Info: 16 mm/sound/color/23 min.
Date/Country: 1962 + USA   Type: Documentary
Distr/Arch: afl-cio
Annotation: The long struggle to rebuild the labor movement
  in Colonial America, beginning with the use of slaves and
  indentured servants in Colonial America. Provided by
  Center for Southern Folklore.

THOMAS CROWN AFFAIR, THE
Nar/Cast: Judy Pace* + Yaphet Kotto* + Charles Lampkin* +
  Steve McQueen + Faye Dunaway
Screenplay: Alan Trustman
Producer: Norman Jewison   Director: Norman Jewison
Studio/Company: United Artists
Tech Info: 16 mm/sound/color/102 min.
Date/Country: 1968 + USA   Type: Feature
Distr/Arch: uas
Annotation: Kotto is Carl and Pace "a pretty girl" in this
  crime melodrama about a self-made millionaire (McQueen)
  who decides to take the establishment, of which he is a
  part. He does so successfully, outwitting a chic in-
  surance investigator (Dunaway) along the way.

THOMASINE AND BUSHROD
Nar/Cast: Max Julien* + Vonetta McGee* + George Murdock
Screenplay: Max Julien*
Producer: Harvey Bernard + Max Julien*   Director: Gordon
  Parks, Jr.*
Studio/Company: Columbia
Tech Info: 16 mm/sound/color/3 reels/95 min.
Date/Country: 1975 + USA   Type: Feature
Distr/Arch: swa
Annotation: A different style western set in the Southwest
  circa 1912. A young black couple go on a crime spree and
  are aided by poor Blacks, Indians, and whites of the area.

THOUSANDS CHEER
Nar/Cast: Lena Horne* + Hazel Scott* + Kathryn Grayson +
  Gene Kelly
Screenplay: Paul Janrico + Richard Collins
Producer: Joe Pasternak   Director: George Sidney
Studio/Company: MGM
Tech Info: 16 mm/sound/color/126 min.
Date/Country: 1943 + USA   Type: Feature
Distr/Arch: fnc
Annotation: MGM's version of a star-studded variety show
  featuring the biggest stars in their studio. Lena Horne
  sings "Honeysuckle Rose" by Fats Waller* and Andy Razaf is
  backed by Benny Carter* and his band.

THREE IN THE ATTIC
Nar/Cast: Judy Pace* + Christopher Jones + Yvette Mimieux
Producer: Richard Wilson   Director: Richard Wilson
Studio/Company: American International Pictures
Tech Info: 16 mm/color/sound/90 min.
Date/Country: 1968 + USA   Type: Feature

Distr/Arch: mod + mot + unf
Annotation: Tale of unique revenge when 3 women find out
    they've been sleeping with the same man. Pace is Eulice,
    one of the three.

THREE IN THE CELLAR
Alt Title(s): Up in the Cellar
Nar/Cast: Judy Pace* + Joan Collins + Larry Hagman
    Director: Theodore Flicker
Studio/Company: American International
Tech Info: 16 mm/sound/color/92 min.
Date/Country: 1970 + USA   Type: Feature
Distr/Arch: mod + unf
Annotation: Judy Pace is Harlene Jones, secretary-sweetheart
    to Maurice Camber (Hagman), a politically ambitious, mar-
    ried college president. How they finally consummate their
    relationship is part of the comedy which includes the
    bizarre antics of a frustrated college student- poet.

THREE LITTLE GIRLS IN BLUE
Nar/Cast: June Haver + Vivian Blaine + Vera Ellen + "Smokey"
    Whitfield* + George Montgomery
Screenplay: Valentine Davis
Producer: Mack Gordon   Director: Bruce Humberstone
Studio/Company: 20th Century Fox
Tech Info: 16mm/ sound/ bw/ 90 min.
Date/Country: 1946 + USA   Type: Feature
Distr/Arch: fnc
Annotation: Musical set in 1902, about three sisters who go
    to Atlantic City to find husbands.

THREE MEN IN A TUB
Series: Our Gang
Nar/Cast: Our Gang + Billie Thomas*
Producer: Hal Roach   Director: Nate Watt
Studio/Company: MGM
Tech Info: super 8 mm/16 mm/bw/sound/1 reel/10 min.
Date/Country: 1938 + USA   Type: Comedy Short
Distr/Arch: bla
Annotation: Rivalry for Darla's affections involves Alfalfa
    in a boat race with Waldo. The gang's makeshift, duck and
    umbrella powered boat wins when Waldo's powerboat springs
    a leak.   Porky and Buckwheat are seen holding the cork.
    Billie Thomas stars as Buckwheat.

THREE MEN ON A HORSE
Nar/Cast: Frank McHugh + Joan Blondell + Eddie Anderson*
Screenplay: Laird Doyle   Story: J.C. Holm + George Abbott
    Director: Mervyn LeRoy
Studio/Company: Warner Brothers
Tech Info: 16 mm/sound/bw/85 min.
Date/Country: 1936 + USA   Type: Feature
Distr/Arch: uas
Annotation: Three down and out horse players run into a
    drunken poet who is infallable when it comes to picking
    the ponies. Eddie Anderson as Mose adds to the comedy

THREE MUST GET THEIRS, THE

Nar/Cast: Max Linder + Bill Montana + Frank Cooke +
    Catherine Ranhin + Jobyna Ralston + Jack Richardson + Jaz-
    bo
Screenplay: Max Linder   Director: Max Linder
Studio/Company: United Artists
Tech Info: 35 mm/silent/bw/5 reels
Date/Country: 1922 + USA
Annotation: Parody of the Three Musketeers with a black man
    surprisingly appearing in one of the bedroom scenes as the
    musketeers romp through a 16th century French town.

THREE PALS
Nar/Cast: Martin Turner*
Screenplay: L.V. Jefferson   Director: Wilbur McGaugh
Studio/Company: Davis Distributing Division
Tech Info: 35 mm/silent/bw/5 reels/4,987 ft.
Date/Country: 1926 + USA   Type: Feature
Annotation: Martin Turner is Uncle Lude in this "romantic
    melodrama" about old Southern gentlemen, horseracing,
    murder, and blackmail.

THREE PENNY OPERA
Nar/Cast: Sammy Davis, Jr.* + Curt Jurgens + Gert Frobe
Screenplay: Wolfgang Standte + Gunter Weisenhorn
Producer: Kurt Ulrich   Director: Wolfgang Staudte
Tech Info: sound/color/83 min.
Date/Country: 1964 + France + West Germany
Annotation: Davis is the ballad singer in this European
    version of the Weill-Brecht-Blitzstein musical.

THREE SMART BOYS
Series: Our Gang
Nar/Cast: Our Gang + Billie Thomas*
Producer: Hal Roach   Director: Gordon Douglas
Studio/Company: MGM
Tech Info: super 8 mm/16 mm/sound/1 reel/10 min.
Date/Country: 1937 + USA   Type: Comedy Short
Distr/Arch: bla
Annotation: The gang, with painted spots (Buckwheat's (Bil-
    lie Thomas) of course, are white) plan to get the local
    doctor to close the school. Unfortunately, he is a vet
    performing experiments with a monkey. When Buckwheat
    fails to emerge from the doctor's office, the gang
    believes he's been turned into a monkey.

THREE SMART GUYS
Series: Our Gang
Nar/Cast: Our Gang + Billie Thomas*
Screenplay: Hal Law + Robert A. McGowan
Producer: MGM   Director: Edward Cahn
Studio/Company: MGM
Tech Info: bw/sound/1 reel
Date/Country: 1943 + USA   Type: Comedy Short
Annotation: Mickey, Froggy and Buckwheat play hooky at the
    old fishing hole but return to school when a wise old
    fisherman tells them they'll catch the biggest fish by
    studying. Billie Thomas stars as Buckwheat.

THREE SONGS BY LEADBELLY
Nar/Cast: Huddie Ledbetter*
Producer: Folklore Research Films
Tech Info: 16 mm/8 min./color/sound
Date/Country: 1945 + USA   Type: Documentary
Distr/Arch: rad
Annotation: In the only film made of him, Huddie "Leadbelly"
    Ledbetter is seen at his prime (in 1945) singing three
    well known folk songs: "Pick a Bale of Cotton", "Grey
    Goose", "Take This Hammer."

THREE THE HARD WAY
Nar/Cast: Jim Brown* + Fred Williamson* + Jim Kelly* +
    Sheila Frazier*
Screenplay: Eric Bercovici + Jerry Ludwig
Producer: Harry Bernsen   Director: Gordon Parks, Jr.*
Studio/Company: Allied Artists
Tech Info: 16 mm/sound/color/92 min.
Date/Country: 1973 + USA   Type: Feature
Distr/Arch: cin
Annotation: Brown, Williamson, and Kelly defeat
    fascist/racist whites planning genocide against black pe-
    ople in three of the largest cities in the U.S.

THREE TOUGH GUYS
Nar/Cast: Isaac Hayes* + Fred Williamson* + Paula Kelly*
    Director: Duccio Tessari
Studio/Company: Paramount
Tech Info: 16 mm/sound/color/92 min./3 reels
Date/Country: 1974 + USA   Type: Feature
Distr/Arch: fnc
Annotation: A hard hitting priest (an ex-con) and a down at
    the heels black (an ex-cop) join forces to solve a Chicago
    bank robbery that has cost one a parishoner and the other
    his job.

THUNDERBALL
Nar/Cast: Earl Cameron* + Sean Connery
Screenplay: Richard Maibaum + John Hopkins
Producer: Kevin McClony   Director: Terence Young
Studio/Company: Eon Productions + United Artists, Dist.
Tech Info: 16 mm/sound/color/132 min.
Date/Country: 1965 + Britain   Type: Feature
Annotation: Earl Cameron is Pinder in this James Bond action
    melodrama about atomic bombs, hijacking and blackmail by
    an international crime syndicate.

THUNDERBOLT
Nar/Cast: Teresa Harris* + Richard Arlen + George Bancroft +
    Madame Sul-te-Wan* + Oscar Smith* + Nathan Curry* + Mos-
    by's Blue Blowers* + S.S. Stewart*
Screenplay: Jules Furthmann   Director: Joseph Von Sternberg
Studio/Company: Paramount + Famous Lasky Corp.
Tech Info: 16 mm/sound/bw/94 min.
Date/Country: 1929 + USA   Type: Feature
Distr/Arch: mma + uni
Annotation: Teresa Harris is a singer in a Harlem saloon in
    this crime melodrama about Thunderbolt Jim Lang (Bancroft)

Series: Merrie Melodies Cartoon
Nar/Cast: Fats Waller*
Studio/Company: Warner Brothers
Tech Info: 16 mm/sound/20 min.
Date/Country: 1943 + USA   Type: Animated Short
Distr/Arch: uas
Annotation: Cartoon figure of Fats Waller as the hip cat
    with the conflict between the secular and the religious --
    Kit Kat Klub and Uncle Tom's Mission -- worked out musi-
    cally.

TINY TROUBLES
Series: Our Gang
Nar/Cast: Our Gang + Billie Thomas*
Screenplay: Hal Law + Robert A McGowan
Producer: Jack Chertok   Director: George Sidney
Studio/Company: MGM
Tech Info: bw/sound/1 reel
Date/Country: 1939 + USA   Type: Comedy Short
Annotation: Alfalfa trades his baby brother for another in-
    fant who turns out to be a midget-pick pocket fleeing the
    cops. Billie Thomas stars as Buckwheat.

TIRE TROUBLE
Series: Our Gang
Nar/Cast: Our Gang + Ernie Morrison* + Allen Hoskins*
Screenplay: Hal Roach
Producer: Hal Roach   Director: Robert McGowan
Studio/Company: Pathe
Tech Info: silent/bw/2 reels
Date/Country: 1924 + USA   Type: Comedy Short
Annotation: The gang's antics in this short include an
    automobile of their own making and a romp in an amusement
    park. Allen Hoskins stars as Farina.

TIRED BUSINESS MEN
Series: Our Gang
Nar/Cast: Our Gang + Allen Hoskins* + Jannie Hoskins*
Screenplay: Hal Roach
Producer: Hal Roach   Director: Anthony Mack + Charles Oelze
Studio/Company: Pathe
Tech Info: silent/bw/2 reels
Date/Country: 1927 + USA   Type: Comedy Short
Annotation: Joe, the new kid, has to go through initiation
    rites to become a gang member and is admitted only ater
    the gang learns his father is a policeman. Later they
    help the police capture a bank robber. Farina (Allen
    Hoskins) and Mango (Jannie Hoskins) appear.

TNT JACKSON
Producer: Cirio H. Santiago   Director: Cirio H.Santiago
Studio/Company: New World Pictures
Tech Info: 75 min./color/16 mm/sound
Date/Country: 1975 + USA   Type: Feature
Distr/Arch: fnc
Annotation: A beautiful woman, TNT Jackson (Jeanne Bell), is
    also highly skilled in the martial ats and uses her
    talents to wage a one woman war on crime.

TO ALL MY FRIEND'S ON SHORE
Nar/Cast: Bill Cosby* + Gloria Foster* + Dennis Hines*
Screenplay: Allan Sloane
Producer: Gilbert Cates   Director: Gilbert Cates
Studio/Company: Jemmin
Tech Info: sound/color
Date/Country: 1971 + USA   Type: TV Feature
Annotation: A black father, who skycaps at L.A. air
   terminal, copes with his son's fatal disease while
   desperately trying to get his family out of the rat-
   infested ghetto.

TO BE BLACK
Producer: ABC News
Studio/Company: ABC
Tech Info: 16 mm/sound/color/2 reels/54 min.
Date/Country: USA   Type: TV Documentary
Distr/Arch: con
Annotation: This News Documentary reveals the resentments
   and frustrations of black Americans. Its purpose is to
   depict the plight of the black man in America and to hear
   the concerns of black people so that perhaps some solu-
   tions can be found.

TO BE YOUNG, GIFTED AND BLACK
Nar/Cast: Ruby Dee* + Al Freeman, Jr.* + Claudia McNeil* +
   Barbara Barrie + Lauren Jones + Roy Scheider
Producer: NET
Tech Info: 16 mm/color/sound/3 reels/90 min.
Date/Country: 1972 + USA   Type: Drama
Distr/Arch: iu
Annotation: Depicts in play form the life and works of the
   late black playwright Lorraine Hansberry, author of A
   Raisin in the Sun. Portrays her struggles from her first
   visit to the South, to her life on the streets of Harlem.

TO FIND A HOME
Producer: University of Wisconsin
Tech Info: 16 mm/sound/bw/1 reel/27 min.
Date/Country: 1963   Type: Dramatized Documentary
Distr/Arch: iu
Annotation: Presents the story of Paul Reed, a black
   television repairman who lives in a middle-sized northern
   city. With a good income Paul and his wife decide they
   would like a larger house in a more modern neighborhood.
   The discrimination he encounters in searching for a home
   is depicted.

TO HEAR YOUR BANJO PLAY
Producer: Creative Age Films
Tech Info: 16 mm/sound/bw/1 reel/17 min.
Date/Country: 1947 + USA   Type: Documentary
Distr/Arch: iu + mac
Annotation: Pictures American folk singers in various parts
   of the country and discusses briefly the development of
   folk music. Pete Seeger and other singers, including
   mountaineers, sharecroppers, migrant workers, Blacks, and

railroad men are shown.

TO KILL A MOCKINGBIRD
Nar/Cast: Brock Peters* + Estelle Evans + Gregory Peck
Screenplay: Hoorton Foote   Story: Harper Lee
Producer: Alan J. Pakula   Director: Robert Mulligan
Studio/Company: Universal
Tech Info: 16 mm/sound/bw/129 min.
Date/Country: 1962 + USA   Type: Feature
Distr/Arch: cwf + swa + twy + uni
Annotation: Story concerns the defense of a black man on
   trial for allegedly raping a white girl in a small Alabama
   town. Peters is Tom Robinson, the accused.

TO LIVE AND MOVE ACCORDING TO YOUR NATURE IS CALLED LOVE
Series: To Save Tomorrow
Producer: NET
Tech Info: 16 mm/sound/bw/1 reel/29 min.
Date/Country: 1971 + USA   Type: Documentary
Distr/Arch: iu
Annotation: Presents Reverend James Bevel* of the Southern
   Christian Leadership Conference and Almanina Barbour,
   black attorney and director of an experimental project in
   Philadelphia, as they attempt to organize residents to
   cope with community problems.

TO LIVE IN PEACE
Alt Title(s): see Vivere in Pace

TO LIVE WITH HERDS
Screenplay: David MacDougall
Producer: David MacDougall   Director: David MacDougall
Tech Info: 16 mm/sound/bw/68 min./English subtitles
Date/Country: 1973 + Uganda   Type: Documentary
Distr/Arch: rad
Annotation: Study of the tribal life of the Jie, a pastoral
   people of Northeastern Uganda. Following a period of
   relative isolation under the British, the Jie are under
   increasing pressure to change their traditional culture
   and participate in a modern nation state. The film ex-
   amines their predicament in the light of Jie values.

TO SIR, WITH LOVE
Nar/Cast: Sidney Poitier* + Judy Geeson + Lulu + Christian
   Roberts + Suzy Kendall
Screenplay: James Clavell   Story: E.R. Braithwaite*
Producer: James Clavell   Director: James Clavell
Studio/Company: Columbia
Tech Info: 16 mm/color/sound/3 reels/105 min.
Date/Country: 1967 + Britain   Type: Feature
Distr/Arch: arg + bud + ccc + cha + con + cwf + ics + ker +
   mac + mod + mot + roa + sel + swa + tfc + twy + unf + wcf
   + wel + who + wil
Annotation: Poitier plays a young Guyanian engineer who
   takes a job teaching in a rough London school. Gradually,
   as he learns to relate to his students, he earns their
   respect, as they learn to repect themselves.

TO TRAP A SPY
Nar/Cast: William Marshall* + Robert Vaughn + David McCallum
   + Ivan Dixon* + Rupert Crosse* + Fritz Weaver
Screenplay: Sam Rolfe
Producer: Sam Rolfe   Director: Don Medford
Studio/Company: MGM
Tech Info: 16 mm/sound/color/92 min.
Date/Country: 1966 + USA   Type: Feature
Distr/Arch: fnc
Annotation: Marshall is Ashumen who along with Vulcan
   (Weaver) are the villains of this UNCLE spy/action drama,
   as the heads of an international crime syndicate prepare
   to take over a newly independent African nation.   Dixon
   plays Soumarin; Crosse is Nobuk.

TOGETHER BROTHERS
Nar/Cast: Ahmad Nurradin + Anthony Wilson* + Nelson Sims +
   Kenneth Bell + Owen Pace
Producer: Robert L.Rosen   Director: William A. William
Studio/Company: 20th Century Fox
Tech Info: 16 mm/color/sound/3 reels/94 min.
Date/Country: 1974 + USA   Type: Feature
Distr/Arch: fnc
Annotation: Two rival gangs (one black, one Chicano) join
   forces when the only policemen who treated them fairly is
   gunned down by a demented killer. Meanwhile the killer
   stalks a little boy, the only witness to the killing.

TOMBOLO
Nar/Cast: Aldo Fabrizi + Adriana Bennetti + John Kitzmiller*
Screenplay: Indro Montalenli + Glauco Pelligrine + Rodolfo
   Sonego + Giorgio Ferroni   Director: Signor Ferroni
Studio/Company: Grandi Films
Date/Country: 1939 + Italy   Type: Feature
Annotation: Kitzmiller plays Jack, leader of a grop of uni-
   formed American (black) profiteers in this melodrama about
   post World War II Italy.

TOMORROW'S CHILDREN
Nar/Cast: Don Douglas + John Preston + Diane Sinclair +
   Sterling Halloway
Screenplay: Wallace Thurman*   Story: Wallace Thurman* +
   Crane Wilbur   Director: Crane Wilbur
Studio/Company: Bryan Foy Productions
Tech Info: sound/bw/70 min.
Date/Country: 1934 + USA
Annotation: The pros and cons of sterilization dramatized in
   a story which poses the complexities of eugenics.

TONI
Nar/Cast: Charles Blaveete   Director: Jean Renoir
Tech Info: 16 mm/sound/bw/90 min./with English subtitles
Date/Country: 1935 + French   Type: Feature
Distr/Arch: con
Annotation: A film about quarry workers on the Riviera with
   a black character named Dick, who is one of the workers in
   the South of France. No reference to race is made.

TONY'S SHIRT
Studio/Company: Dunbar Film Corporation
Date/Country: 1923 + USA

TOO BUSY TO WORK
Nar/Cast: Will Rogers + Marian Nixon + Louise Beavers* +
   Dick Powell   Story: Ben A. Williams   Director: John
   Blystone
Studio/Company: Fox Film Corp.
Tech Info: sound/bw
Date/Country: 1932 + USA   Type: Feature
Annotation: Will Rogers plays a tramp, who before having
   taken up that line of non-work, had fought in France.
   Returning home, he finds that his now deceased wife had
   remarried and that his daughter thinks him a dead hero.
   Louise Beavers plays a "Mammy" and is listed that way in
   the credits.

TOO LATE BLUES
Nar/Cast: Bobby Darin + Stella Stevens + Rupert Crosse*
Screenplay: Rich Carr + John Cassavetes
Producer: John Cassavetes   Director: John Cassavetes
Studio/Company: Paramount
Tech Info: 16 mm/sound/bw/103 min.
Date/Country: 1961 + USA   Type: Feature
Distr/Arch: rbc
Annotation: Rupert Crosse is Baby Jackson in this drama
   about a dedicated combo of jazz musicians and their strug-
   gle to retain the integrity of their music.

TOOT THAT TRUMPET
Nar/Cast: Louis Jordan* and his Band*
Date/Country: 1946

TOP MAN
Nar/Cast: Louise Beavers* + Donaldo'Connor + Susanna Foster
   + Lillian Gish + Count Basie and his orchestra
Screenplay: Zachary Gold
Producer: Milton Schwartzwald   Director: Charles Lamont
Studio/Company: Universal
Date/Country: 1943 + USA   Type: Feature
Annotation: An Andy Hardy-like film (World War II vintage)
   with O'Connor playing the humorous boy wonder role. Count
   Basie and his orchestra perform in the Big Morale Show.

TOP OF THE HEAP
Nar/Cast: Christopher St. John* + Paula Kelly*
Screenplay: Christopher St. John*
Producer: Christopher St. John*   Director: Christopher St.
   John*
Studio/Company: Fanfare
Tech Info: 16 mm/sound/color/90 min.
Date/Country: 1972 + USA   Type: Feature
Distr/Arch: pru
Annotation: Problems of a black Washington, DC. policeman
   are explored. Music score by J.J. Johnson*.

TOPAZ

Nar/Cast: Roscoe Lee Browne* + Federick Stafford + Dany
   Robin + Karin Dor
Screenplay: Samuel Taylor   Story: Leon Uris
Producer: Alfred Hitchcock   Director: Alfred Hitchcock
Studio/Company: Universal
Tech Info: 16 mm/sound/color/125 min.
Date/Country: 1969 + USA   Type: Feature
Distr/Arch: cwf + swa + twy + uni + wcf
Annotation: Alfred Hitchcock based this spy thriller on a
   spy scandel that rocked NATO in 1962. Browne is Philippe
   Dubois, a florist and secret agent who obtains important
   documents by infiltrating a group of Cuban revolutionaries
   in Harlem.

TOPPER RETURNS
Nar/Cast: Eddie Anderson* + Joan Blondell + Roland Young +
   Carole Landis
Screenplay: Jonathan Latimor + Gordon Douglas
Producer: Hal Roach   Director: Roy Del Ruth
Studio/Company: United Artists
Tech Info: 16 mm/sound/bw/90 min.
Date/Country: 1941 + USA   Type: Feature
Distr/Arch: bud + ccc + ics + roa + sel + wil + cie + thu
Annotation: Another in the Topper series, that has Eddie
   Anderson as a bug-eyed chauffer.

TOPPERS TAKE A BOW
Nar/Cast: Four Toppers* + Spencer Williams* Director:
   Richard C. Kahn
Studio/Company: Hollywood Productions
Date/Country: 1941 + USA   Type: Musical Short
Annotation: A radio station, announced and operated by Wil-
   liams, is having tryouts for a radio spot and a quartet,
   "The Toppers," tries out.

TOPSY AND EVA
Nar/Cast: Rosetta Duncan + Vivian Duncan + Noble Johnson*
Screenplay: Catherine C. Cushing
Producer: Feature Productions   Director: Del Lard
Studio/Company: United Artists Distributed
Tech Info: 35 mm/silent/bw/8 reels/7,456 ft.
Date/Country: 1927 + USA   Type: Feature
Annotation: Loosely based on Uncle Tom's Cabin, the film
   focuses on the friendship between Topsy (played by Rosetta
   Duncan in black face) and Eva. Griffith acted as super-
   viser and "re-made" the film (not given official credit)
   after Lois Weber, the original director, walked off the
   film protesting its racist overtones. Noble Johnson is
   Uncle Tom, Myrtle Ferguson is Aunt Ophelia.

TOUCHING GROUND   Director: Douglas Collins
Studio/Company: New Line Cinema
Tech Info: 16 mm/color/sound/1 reel/18 min.   Type: Documentary
Annotation: Touching Ground presents episodes in the life of
   a black jazz musician, Jim, who is under pressure from
   friends to become more of a militant and political
   activist. But to Jim, life has more to do with music than

with confrontation and conflict.

TOUGH WINTER, A
Series: Our Gang
Nar/Cast: Our Gang + Allen Hoskins* + Stepin Fetchit*
Screenplay: Robert F. McGowan
Producer: Robert F. McGowan + Hal Roach   Director: Robert
   F. McGowan
Studio/Company: MGM + Roach
Tech Info: super 8 mm/16 mm/bw/sound/1 reel/21 min.
Date/Country: 1930 + USA   Type: Comedy Short
Distr/Arch: bla + roa
Annotation: The gang helps Stepin Fetchit read a love let-
   ter; then he tries to help them in cleaning up the candy
   mess they've made. The film is mostly a vehicle for
   Stepin Fetchit. Allen Hoskins stars as Farina.

TOUGH!
Nar/Cast: Dion Gossett* + Christopher Towns* + Renny Roker*
   + Rich Holms* + Sandy Reed* + Philip Hadler* + David Sha-
   fer* + Detra Piernas*
Screenplay: Horace Jackson*
Producer: Horace Jackson* + Thurston Frazier   Director:
   Horace Jackson*
Studio/Company: Dimension Pictures
Tech Info: 16 mm/color/sound

TOWARDS TRUE DEMOCRACY
Producer: Colonial Film Unit for Central Office of Informa-
   tion
Tech Info: 35 mm/bw/sound/20 min.
Date/Country: 1947 + Britain   Type: Documentary
Distr/Arch: iwm
Annotation: Film about the opening of the Nigerian legislat-
   vie council.

TOXI
Date/Country: 195- + Germany   Type: Feature

TOY WIFE, THE
Nar/Cast: Luise Rainer + Melvyn Douglas + Clarence Muse* +
   Robert Young
Screenplay: Zoe Akins
Producer: George Cukor   Director: Merian C. Cooper
Studio/Company: MGM
Tech Info: 16 mm/sound/bw/90 min.
Date/Country: 1938 + USA   Type: Feature
Distr/Arch: fnc
Annotation: An antebellum period piece set in New Orleans
   about a Parisienne lady and how she affects the lives of
   several men in the city. Clarence Muse plays Brutus,
   along with other black actors in livery.

TOYS IN THE ATTIC
Nar/Cast: Dean Martin + Geraldine Page + Charles Lampkin* +
   Frank Silvera* + Wendy Hiller + Yvette Mimieux
Screenplay: James Poe   Story: Lillian Hellman
Producer: Walter Mirisch   Director: George Roy Hill

Studio/Company: United Artists
Tech Info: 16 mm/sound/color/90 min.
Date/Country: 1963 + USA   Type: Feature
Distr/Arch: cha + uas
Annotation: Based on the play by Lillian Hellman which won
    the 1960 Drama Critic's Award, it's the story of two spin-
    ster sisters and their odd devotion to their brother, set
    in a musty old house in New Orleans.   Silvera is Henry;
    Lampkin is Gus.

TRADER_HORN
Nar/Cast: Harry Carey + Edwina Booth + Mutia Onooloo*
Screenplay: Richard Schayer   Story: Ethelreda Lewis
    Director: W.S. Van Dyke
Studio/Company: MGM
Tech Info: 16 mm/sound/bw/102 min.
Date/Country: 1931 + USA   Type: Feature
Distr/Arch: fnc
Annotation: Filmed in East Africa, the Sudan and the Congo,
    this film about Horn (Carey), a hunter and trader who
    loves Africa, and his loyal gun bearer (Onooloo) depicts
    one experience in which he helps educate the son of a
    friend to the ways of Africa, and finds and rescues the
    daughter of a Missionary who was abducted years earlier by
    a mysterious and especially fierce tribe.

TRADER_HORN
Nar/Cast: Rod Taylor + Anne Heywood + Jean Sorel   Director:
    Reza S. Badiyi
Studio/Company: MGM
Tech Info: 16 mm/sound/color/105 min.   Type: Feature
Distr/Arch: fnc
Annotation: Remake of the 1931 Trader Horn with Africans
    appearing of necessity.

TRAP, THE
Series: Charlie Chan
Nar/Cast: Roland Winters + Sidney Toler + Mantan Moreland*
Screenplay: Miriam Kissinger
Producer: James S. Burkett   Director: Howard Bretherton
Studio/Company: Monogram
Tech Info: 16 mm/sound/bw/2 reels/68 min.
Date/Country: 1946 + USA   Type: Feature
Distr/Arch: cin + mog
Annotation: Another Charlie Chan mystery   with   Mantan
    Moreland as Birmingham.

TRAVELS_WITH_MY_AUNT
Nar/Cast: Lou Gossett* + Maggie Smith + Alec McCowen
Screenplay: Joe Presson Allen + Hugh Wheller   Story: Graham
    Greene
Producer: Robert Fryer + James Cresson   Director: George
    Cukor
Studio/Company: MGM
Tech Info: 16 mm/sound/color/109 min.
Date/Country: 1972 + USA   Type: Feature
Annotation: An elderly aunt tries to inspire her nephew with
    the same lust for life she has by staging the kidnapping

of her former lover Zachary Wordsworth, played by Lou Gossett, and engaging her nephew in the rescue.

TREAT 'EM ROUGH
Nar/Cast: Mantan Moreland* + Eddie Albert + William Frawley
Screenplay: Roy Chanslor + Bob Williams
Producer: Marshall Grant   Director: Roy Taylor
Studio/Company: Universal
Date/Country: 1942 + USA   Type: Feature
Annotation: Mantan   plays   "Smoke-Eyes" in this comedy-
    melodrama about a middle weight champion who turns detec-
    tive to help save his father from being disgraced in an
    oil scandal.

TRIAL
Nar/Cast: Juano Hernandez* + Glen Ford + Dorothy McGuire
    Story: Don Mankiewicz
Producer: Charles Schnee   Director: Mark Robson
Studio/Company: MGM
Tech Info: 16 mm/sound/bw/105 min.
Date/Country: 1955 + USA   Type: Feature
Distr/Arch: fnc
Annotation: A Chicano boy is accused of having murdered a
    white girl and various forces use his trial for their own
    purposes. Juano Hernandez plays the judge.

TRIAL: THE FIRST DAY
Series: Trial: The City and County of Denver versus Lauren R
    Watson
Producer: NET
Tech Info: 16 mm/sound/bw/3 reels/90 min.
Date/Country: 1970 + USA   Type: Documentary
Distr/Arch: iu
Annotation: Presents the first day in the trial of black
    defendant Lauren R. Watson, member of the Black Panther
    Party, charged with interfering with a police officer and
    resisting arrest.   Tells how his request for a jury of
    peers was denied.   James Vorenburg, law professor at
    Harvard, explains a jury of peers. Provides personal in-
    terviews with all those associated with the case.

TRIAL: THE FOURTH AND FINAL DAY
Series: Trial: The City and County of Denver versus Lauren
    R. Watson
Producer: NET
Tech Info: 16 mm/sound/bw/3 reels/90 min.
Date/Country: 1970 + USA   Type: Documentary
Distr/Arch: iu
Annotation: Presents the fourth and final day in the trial
    of black defendant Lauren R. Watson. Both sides rest their
    cases after closing arguments. Includes inverviews with
    the judge, the arresting officers, both attorneys, and the
    defendant. Presents some of the jury members' reasons for
    voting as they did following the presentation of the
    verdict.

TRIAL: THE SECOND DAY
Series: Trial: The City and County of Denver versus Lauren

r. Watson
Producer: NET
Tech Info: 16 mm/sound/bw/3 reels/90 min.
Date/Country: 1970 + USA   Type: Documentary
Distr/Arch: iu
Annotation: Presents the second day in the trial of black
    defendant Lauren R. Watson. Establishes the prosecution's
    case and counters with defense attorney Leonard Davies.
    Includes a summation of the day's proceedings.

TRIAL: THE THIRD DAY
Series: Trial: The City and County of Denver versus Lauren R
    Watson
Producer: NET
Tech Info: 16 mm/sound/bw/3 reels/90 min.
Date/Country: 1970 + USA   Type: Documentary
Distr/Arch: iu
Annotation: Presents the third day in the trial of black
    defendant Lauren R. Watson. Depicts the prosecution
    resting its case; and the defense, after making a motion
    for acquittal, presenting its witnesses, whose position is
    that Watson did not resist arrest, but was harassed by the
    officers.

TRIBUTE TO MALCOLM X, A
Producer: NET
Tech Info: 16 mm/sound/bw/1 reel/15 min.
Date/Country: 1969 + USA   Type: Documentary
Distr/Arch: iu
Annotation: Reports the influence of Malcolm X* upon the
    present black liberation movement. Reviews his life
    through an interview with his widow, Betty Shabazz*.
    Shows how Malcom X became a black Moslem minister and a
    leader of the black struggle until his assassination.

TRICK BABY
Nar/Cast: Mel Stewart* + Kiel Martin + Dallas E. Hayes +
    Beverly Ballad + Vernee Watson*
Screenplay: T. Raewyn   Story: Iceberg Slim*
Producer: Marshal Bucklar   Director: Larry Yust
Studio/Company: Universal
Tech Info: 16 mm/sound/color/3 reels/89 min.
Date/Country: 1973 + USA   Type: Feature
Distr/Arch: uni
Annotation: Trick Baby tells of two con artists "Blue"
    Howard, who maintains that "in this world there are only
    two kinds of dudes--hustlers and suckers," and "White
    Folks" who is light enough to pass for white. Together
    they rip off a series of "marks"; then complications arise
    and they find themselves on the run from the mob and a
    crooked black policeman.

TROOPER OF COMPANY K
Alt Title(s): see Trooper of Troop K

TROOPER OF TROOP K
Alt Title(s): Trooper of Company K
Nar/Cast: Noble Johnson* + Beulah Hall*

Studio/Company: Lincoln Motion Picture Company
Date/Country: 1916 + USA
Annotation: Noble Johnson plays "Shiftless Joe" who redeems
    himself in the battle of Carrizal as a member of the
    heroic Afro-American cavalary which fought valiantly
    against the Mexican Carranzista June 1916, during the
    SpanishAmerican war.

TROPICAL AFRICA
Producer: Julien Bryon + Twentieth Century Fund
Tech Info: 16 mm/sound/color/1 reel/20 min.
Date/Country: 1961   Type: Documentary
Distr/Arch: iu + iff
Annotation: Surveys the history of Africa, its current con-
    ditions and problems, and its outlook for the future.
    Highlights, using animation, the history of Africa over
    3,000 years.   Shows how the new Africa is a continent in
    political revolution and undergoing social change.

TROPICI
Alt Title(s): Tropics
Nar/Cast: Joel Baralos + Jamira Santiago
Screenplay: Gianni Amico + Francesco Tullio
Producer: Gianni Barcelloni   Director: Gianni Amico
Studio/Company: Corte-B.B.G. Cinematografia + R.A.I.
Tech Info: 16 mm/sound/bw/3 reels/87 min./English subtitles
Date/Country: 1969 + Italy   Type: Dramatized Documentary
Distr/Arch: nyf
Annotation: In the first part of Tropici, a poor family
    moves from northeastern Brazil to Sao Paulo in hopes of
    finding a better life in the city. The second portion of
    the film is documentary footage about the desperate
    economic condition of the poor in Brazil.

TROPICS
Alt Title(s): see Tropici

TROUBLE MAN
Nar/Cast: Robert Hooks* + Paul Winfield* + Paula Kelly* +
    Ralph Waite + Julius Harris*
Screenplay: John D.F. Black
Producer: Joe D. Freeman   Director: Ivan Dixon*
Studio/Company: 20th Century Fox
Tech Info: 16 mm/color/sound/3 reels/101 min.
Date/Country: 1972 + USA   Type: Feature
Distr/Arch: fnc
Annotation: Robert Hooks plays a Robin Hood/James Bond style
    private detective who gets caught in the middle when rival
    gangs (one black, one white) fight to control the Los An-
    geles crime network.

TROUBLED CITIES, THE
Producer: NET
Tech Info: 16 mm/sound/bw/2 reels/60 min.
Date/Country: 1966 + USA   Type: Documentary
Distr/Arch: iu
Annotation: Probes the attempts which are being made to
    solve the problems brought about by the urban population

explosion. Cites slum areas, racial imbalance in the
schools, and the needs of rural immigrants as some of the
elements involved.   Points out projects in urban renewal
and urban rehabilitation, and anti-poverty programs as
attempted solutions.

TROUBLEMAKER, THE
Nar/Cast: Thomas Aldredge + Joan Darling + Godfrey Cam-
    bridge* + Al Freeman, Jr.*
Screenplay: Buck Henry + Theodore Flicker
Producer: Robert Gaffney   Director: Theodore Flicker
Studio/Company: Janus Films
Tech Info: 16 mm/sound/bw/82 min.
Date/Country: 1964 + USA   Type: Feature
Distr/Arch: mac
Annotation: Story of a naive country boy, who comes to the
    Big Apple to open a coffee house which takes broad,
    satirical strokes at modern city life. Cambridge is a
    fire inspector, Freeman an intern.

TROUBLEMAKERS
Producer: Norman Fruchter + Robert Machover   Director:
    Norman Fruchter + Robert Machover
Studio/Company: Film Makers Cooperative
Tech Info: 16 mm/sound/bw/54 min.
Date/Country: 1966 + USA   Type: Documentary
Distr/Arch: gro + cal + fmc + mmm
Annotation: Filmed in 1966, this documentary focuses on the
    work done by Tom Hayden and other SDS members along with
    members of the Newark Community Union Project to get a
    stop light installed on a busy intersection and make a
    slum lord repair a substandard building. These frustra-
    tions may have in part led to the Newark riots 10 months
    later.

TRUCK TURNER
Nar/Cast: Isaac Hayes* + Yaphet Kotto*
Screenplay: Oscar Williams + Michael Allin
Producer: Fred Weintraub + Paul Heller   Director: Jonathan
    Kaplan
Studio/Company: American International
Tech Info: 16 mm/sound/color/91 min.
Date/Country: 1974 + USA   Type: Feature
Distr/Arch: swa
Annotation: A melodrama set in Los Angeles in which Hayes
    plays a skip tracer (a person who hunts down bail jum-
    pers).

TRUE CONFESSION
Nar/Cast: Carole Lombard + Fred McMurray + John Barrymore +
    Porter Hall + Hattie McDaniel*
Screenplay: Claude Binyon   Story: Louis Verneuil + Georges
    Berr
Producer: Albert Lewin   Director: Wesley Ruggles
Studio/Company: Paramount
Tech Info: 16 mm/sound/bw/84 min.
Date/Country: 1937 + USA   Type: Feature
Distr/Arch: uni

Annotation: Comedy about a young wife who tells so many "little white-lies" that when she is accused of murder, no one believes that she is innocent. Hattie McDaniel is Ella who, along with Barrymore, Hall and especially Lombard as the young wife, infuses the film with merriment.

TRUE GRIT
Nar/Cast: James McEachin* + John Wayne
Screenplay: Marguerite Roberts
Producer: Hal Wallis   Director: Henry Hathaway
Studio/Company: Paramount
Tech Info: 16 mm/sound/color/128 min.
Date/Country: 1969 + USA   Type: Feature
Distr/Arch: rbc
Annotation: McEachin has a bit role in this John Wayne western melodrama.

TRUMPET FOR THE COMBO, A
Producer: National Film Board of Canada
Tech Info: 16 mm/sound/bw/8 min.
Date/Country: 1966 + Canada   Type: Documentary
Distr/Arch: sef
Annotation: Two students, one black and one white, try out for a single spot in the school combo. Discussion of the consequences of the teacher's attempts to influence the outcome.

TUAREGS IN THEIR COUNTRY
Studio/Company: Pathe
Date/Country: 1909 + USA   Type: Documentary
Annotation: Early documentary which attempted to show the beauty of Africa.

TUNNEL, THE
Alt Title(s): see Proud Valley

TURNING WIND, THE
Alt Title(s): see Barravento

TUSKEGEE FINDS A WAY OUT
Studio/Company: Crusader
Date/Country: 1922 + USA   Type: Documentary
Annotation: A rare documentary for the period, about Booker T. Washington's institution in Alabama.

TUSKEGEE SUBJECT 626   Director: Leroy McDonald*
Date/Country: 1975 + USA   Type: Documentary
Annotation: Docu-drama depicting the experience of a black patient with syphilis who was one of the "control group."

TUSKEGEE TRAINS NEW PILOTS
Series: National Archives Gift Collection
Tech Info: 16 mm/2 reels/silent/partly edited
Annotation: Part of Record Group 200 HF series, Harmon Foundation Collection.

TWO BLACK CHURCHES

Producer: Bill Ferris + Yale University Media Design Studio
   + Center for Southern Folklore
Tech Info: 16 mm/sound/color/20 min.
Date/Country: 1975 + USA   Type: Documentary
Distr/Arch: csf
Annotation: The religious services of two churches one in
   rural Mississippi, the other in New Haven, Connecticut,
   are presented. Provided by Center for Southern Folklore.

TWO_BLACK_CROWS_IN_AFRICA
Nar/Cast: George Moran + Charles Mack
Studio/Company: Educational Films
Tech Info: sound/bw/2 reels
Date/Country: USA   Type: Comedy Short
Annotation: One of a number of two-reel comedy shorts made
   by the blackface comedy team, the "Two Black Crows."

TWO_GENTLEMEN_SHARING
Nar/Cast: Robin Phillips + Hal Frederick* + Judy Geeson +
   Esther Anderson* + Earl Cameron* + Carl Adam* + Ram John
   Holder*
Producer: J. Barry Kulick   Director: Ted Kotcheff
Studio/Company: American International Pictures
Tech Info: 16 mm/sound/color/106 min.
Date/Country: 1969 + Britain   Type: Feature
Distr/Arch: unf
Annotation: Film about a young white man (Phillips) - an
   advertising executive - who shares a flat with an equally
   young Jamaican lawyer (Frederick) in London.   An assort-
   ment of problems follows, including the racism of their
   landlady which drives Andrew, the lawyer, and   his
   girlfriend (Esther Anderson) back to the ghetto and to a
   decision to return to Jamaica.

TWO_GIRLS_AND_A_SAILOR
Nar/Cast: Van Johnson + June Allyson + Lena Horne*
Screenplay: Richard Connell + Gladys Lehman
Producer: Joe Pasternak   Director: Richard Thorpe
Studio/Company: MGM
Tech Info: 16 mm/sound/bw/126 min.
Date/Country: 1944 + USA   Type: Feature
Distr/Arch: fnc
Annotation: Another patriotic variety show made during the
   World War II years.   This featuring Van Johnson being
   chased by sisters. "A Tisket a Tasket" by Ella Fitz-
   gerald* and Al Feldman. Lena Horne performs.

TWO_GUN_MAN_FROM_HARLEM
Studio/Company: Merit Pictures
Date/Country: 1938 + USA   Type: Feature
Annotation: Musical western in which a phony deacon becomes
   a two-gun-totin' man. Faithful Mary, a former Father
   Divine "angel" appears.

TWO_IN_REVOLT
Nar/Cast: John Arledge + Louise Latimer + Willie Best*
Screenplay: Frank H. Clark   Story: Earl Johson + Thomas
   Stovey

Producer: Robert Sisk   Director: Glenn Tyron
Date/Country: 1936 + USA   Type: Feature
Annotation: Comedy in which the two main stars are a horse
    and a dog, set in Montana. Among the humans who assist is
    Willie Best as Eph.

TWO LOVES
War/Cast: Juano Hernandez* + Shirley MacLaine + Laurence
    Harvey
Screenplay: Ben Maddow
Producer: Julian Blaustein   Director: Charles Walters
Studio/Company: MGM
Tech Info: 16 mm/sound/color/100 min.
Date/Country: 1961 + USA   Type: Feature
Distr/Arch: fnc
Annotation: Hernandez is Rauhuia in this drama about an
    American born spinster teaching in a remote area of New
    Zealand.

TWO RODE TOGETHER
War/Cast: James Stewart + Richard Widmark + Woody Strode*
Screenplay: Fran Nugent   Story: Will Cook
Producer: Stan Sheptner   Director: John Ford
Studio/Company: Columbia
Tech Info: 16 mm/sound/color/109 min.
Date/Country: 1961 + USA   Type: Feature
Distr/Arch: arg + bud + ccc + cha + con + ics + ker + mac +
    mod + mot + wcf + wel
Annotation: Stewart plays McCabe, a hard drinking sheriff,
    charged with the task of ransoming captives from Indians.
    Strode plays Stone Calf, a Comanche warrior who tries to
    reclaim his squaw and is killed by McCabe.

TWO SMART PEOPLE
War/Cast: Lucille Ball + John Hodiak + Lloyd Nolan +
    Clarence Muse*
Screenplay: Ethel Hill + Leslie Charteris
Producer: Ralph Wheelwright   Director: Jules Dassin
Studio/Company: MGM
Tech Info: 16 mm/sound/bw/93 min.
Date/Country: 1946 + USA   Type: Feature
Distr/Arch: fnc
Annotation: Lucille Ball is a confidence woman out to fleece
    John Hodiak, until she falls in love with him. Then they
    both have to avoid a hit man who is on a train with them.
    Clarence Muse is a porter on the train.

TWO TOO YOUNG
Series: Our Gang
War/Cast: Our Gang + Billie Thomas*
Producer: Hal Roach   Director: Gordon Douglas
Studio/Company: MGM + Roach
Tech Info: super 8 mm/16 mm/bw/sound/1 reel/10 min.
Date/Country: 1936 + USA   Type: Comedy Short
Distr/Arch: bla + roa
Annotation: Recess bell interrupts Alfalfa as he is about to
    set off some firecrackers he and Spanky have conned from
    Buckwheat (Billie Thomas) and Porky. However, Buckwheat

and Porky have the last laugh when the firecrackers go off
in Alfalfa's back pocket.

U.F.O. INCIDENT, THE
Nar/Cast: James Earl Jones* + Estelle Parsons + Bernard
   Hughes
Screenplay: Anderson and Justiz
Producer: Joel L. Cramer   Director: Richard A. Colla
Date/Country: 1975 + USA   Type: TV Feature
Annotation: Based on an incident of a black man (Barney Hill
   Postman) and his white wife who claim they were taken
   aboard a space ship and examined medically.   Racial
   memories for the husband, played by James Earl Jones, con-
   tribute to his heightened fear. Locale, New Hampshire.

ULTIMO PERDONO
Nar/Cast: John Kitzmiller*
Date/Country: 1952 + Italy   Type: Feature

UMOJA: TIGER AND THE BIG WIND
Producer: Carol Monday Lawrence
Tech Info: 16 mm/sound/color/8 min.   Type: Animated Short
Distr/Arch: afr
Annotation: An African folk story is told by an 80-year-old
   black American. Umoja means unity in Swahili.

UN REVE DE DRANEM
Nar/Cast: Dranem
Studio/Company: Pathe Freres
Tech Info: 35 mm/22 m./bw/silent
Date/Country: 1905 + France   Type: Comedy Short
Distr/Arch: saf
Annotation: Dranem is in bed with a white prostitute; but
   twice she is replaced by a black woman with an "Afro."

UNASHAMED
Nar/Cast: Helen Twelvetrees + Robert Young + Louise Beavers*
   + Lewis Stone
Screenplay: Bayard Veiller   Director: Harry Beaumont
Studio/Company: MGM
Tech Info: sound/bw
Date/Country: 1932 + USA   Type: Feature
Annotation: Story of a young brother who kills the fortune
   hunter who has wronged his sister and now stands trial for
   his life. The only person who can save him is his sister
   who won't. Louise Beavers is Armanda in this domestic
   drama in which all is finally resolved - happily.

UNCLE JASPER'S WILL
Alt Title(s): see Jasper Landry's Will

UNCLE PETE'S RUSE
Annotation: Black Pete saves a Confederate soldier from
   capture by having the whole family appear contagious with
   "painted-on" smallpox.

UNCLE REMUS' FIRST VISIT TO NEW YORK
Studio/Company: The Colored and Indian Film Company

Date/Country: 1917 + USA

UNCLE TOM AND LITTLE EVA
Alt Title(s): Pickaninny Blues
Tech Info: 16 mm/bw/sound/1 reel/10 min.
Date/Country: 1932 + USA   Type: Animated Short
Distr/Arch: kpf
Annotation: Another variation on Uncle Tom's Cabin, cartoon
   style.

UNCLE TOM WINS
Studio/Company: Edison
Date/Country: 1909 + USA

UNCLE TOM'S CABANA
Producer: Fred Quimby
Studio/Company: MGM
Date/Country: 1947 + USA   Type: Animated Short
Annotation: A cartoon version of Uncle Tom's Cabin.

UNCLE TOM'S CABIN
Nar/Cast: James B. Lowe* + Margarita Fischer + George Seig-
   mann + Arthur Edmund Carew + Madame Sul-te-Wan   Director:
   Harry Pollard
Studio/Company: Universal
Tech Info: 16 mm/bw/silent/93 min. (also available in 8 mm)
Date/Country: 1927   Type: Feature
Distr/Arch: kpf + min + mog + csv + ivy + csv + nil
Annotation: James B. Lowe plays Uncle Tom in this second
   version of Mrs. Stowe's novel which Harry Pollard made,
   the first with a black actor in the role. The film con-
   tains a baptismal scene not heretofore seen and was later
   reissued (1958) with a prologue by Raymond Massey.

UNCLE TOM'S CABIN
Producer: Edwin S. Porter
Studio/Company: Thomas Edison Company
Tech Info: 16 mm/bw/silent/2 reels/15 min.
Date/Country: 1902 + USA + 18 + Dramatic Short + 19 + moma
Annotation: A string of animated tableaux with painted back-
   drops, cakewalk, and various theatrical illusions; the
   film preserves the style of early popular American
   theater. Porter plays Uncle Tom in blackface.

UNCLE TOM'S CABIN
Studio/Company: Thanhouser
Tech Info: silent/bw
Date/Country: 1909
Annotation: A remake of Uncle Tom's Cabin.

UNCLE TOM'S CABIN
Nar/Cast: Sam Lucas* + Irving Cummings + Marie Eline
Screenplay: Harriet B. Stowe   Story: Harriet B. Stowe
   (novel)
Producer: Carl Laemmle   Director: William R. Daly
Studio/Company: World
Tech Info: bw/silent/75 min.
Date/Country: 1914 + USA   Type: Feature

Annotation: This version stars Sam Lucas (said to be "the
    first black man to have a leading role in films") as Tom
    and has some black stage actors in the cast.

UNCLE TOM'S CABIN
Nar/Cast: Marguerite Clark   Director: J. Searle Dawley
Studio/Company: Paramount
Date/Country: 1918 + USA
Annotation: This version was shot in Mississippi, Marguerite
    Clark plays both Topsy (in black face) and little Eva.

UNCLE TOM'S CABIN
Alt Title(s): see Onkel Tom's Hutte

UNCLE TOM'S GAL
Nar/Cast: Edna Marion
Studio/Company: Universal
Tech Info: bw/silent/2 reels
Date/Country: 1925 + USA   Type: Dramatic Short
Annotation: Edna Marion plays Topsy, Eva and Eliza in this
    version in which a second-rate film company is filming
    Uncle Tom's Cabin.

UNCLE TOM'S UNCLE
Series: Our Gang
Nar/Cast: Our Gang + Allen Hoskins* + Jannie Hoskins*
Screenplay: Hal E. Roach
Producer: Hal Roach   Director: Robert F. McGowan
Studio/Company: Pathe
Tech Info: super 8 mm/16 mm/bw/silent/1 reel
Date/Country: 1926 + USA   Type: Comedy Short
Distr/Arch: bla
Annotation: The gang reenacts Uncle Tom's Cabin. Joe is
    Uncle Tom in black face; Farina is Topsy. Allen Hoskins
    stars as Farina and Jannie Hoskins stars as Mango.

UNCOMMON IMAGES: THE HARLEM OF JAMES VAN DERZEE   Type:
    Documentary

UNDEFEATED, THE
Nar/Cast: James McEachin* + John Wayne
Screenplay: James Lee Barrett
Producer: Robert Jacks   Director: Andrew V. McLaglen
Studio/Company: Fox
Tech Info: 16 mm/sound/color/118 min.
Date/Country: 1969 + USA   Type: Feature
Distr/Arch: fnc
Annotation: McEachin is Jimmy Collins in this 19th century
    western drama about a confederate colonel who wants to
    re-establish the confederacy in Mexico.

UNDERWORLD
Nar/Cast: Alfred "Slick" Chester* + Oscar Polk* + Bill
    Freeman* + Sol Johnson* + Ethel Moses* + Larry Seymour*
Studio/Company: Micheaux Film Corporation
Date/Country: 1937 + USA   Type: Feature
Annotation: Story of a young man, graduate of a Southern
    black college, who becomes a part of the Chicago under-

world.

UNDISPUTED EVIDENCE
Studio/Company: Cotton Blossom Film Company
Date/Country: 1924 + USA

UNE NATION EST NEE
Alt Title(s): A Nation is Born   Director: Paulin Soumanou
    Vieyra*
Tech Info: sound/color/22 min.*french
Date/Country: 1962 + Senegal   Type: Dramatized Documentary
Annotation: This film started as a celebration of the first
    anniversary of the independence of Senegal but developed
    into a five-part background and coverage for several
    celebrations.

UNEXPECTED RICHES
Series: Our Gang
Nar/Cast: Our Gang + Billie Thomas* + Pearl Curtis* +
    Ernestine Wade*
Screenplay: Hal Law + Robert A. McGowan
Producer: MGM   Director: Herbert Glazer
Studio/Company: MGM
Tech Info: bw/sound/1 reel
Date/Country: 1942 + USA   Type: Comedy Short
Annotation: The gang is tricked into digging for 'buried
    teasure' and each dreams about what he'll do with the
    riches. Buckwheat (Billie Thomas) imagines himself riding
    through the black section of town in a chaffeur-drven
    limousine, dispensing watermelon and fried-chicken.

UNION OF SOUTH AFRICA
Series: National Archives Gift Collection
Tech Info: 16 mm/1 reel
Annotation: Part of Record Group 200 HF series, Harmon
    Foundation Collection.

UNKNOWN SOLDIER SPEAKS, THE
Producer: Robert Rossen + Jack Goldberg
Studio/Company: Goldberg Brothers
Date/Country: 1919 + USA   Type: Documentary
Annotation: Documents the contributions of black soldiers in
    American wars.

UP IN THE AIR
Nar/Cast: Frankie Darro + Mantan Moreland*   Director:
    Howard Bretherton
Date/Country: 1941 + USA   Type: Feature
Annotation: See annotation for Chasing Trouble.

UP IN THE CELLAR
Alt Title(s): see Three in the Cellar

UP JUMPED THE DEVIL
Nar/Cast: Mantan Moreland* + Shelton Brooks* + Maceo Shef-
    field* + Clarence Brooks* + Florence O'Brien* + Lawrence
    Criner*
Studio/Company: Toddy Films + Dixie National Pictures, Inc.

Tech Info: 62 min.
Date/Country: 1941 + USA   Type: Feature
Annotation: Two parolees (Moreland and Brooks) are out to
    find their fortune; by posing as a butler and maid they
    catch a jewel thief they framed and become heroes.

UP POPS THE DEVIL
Nar/Cast: Willie Best* + Richard Gallagher + Carole Lombard
    + Stuart Erwin   Story: Albert Hackett + Frances Goodrich
Producer: A. Edward Sutherland
Studio/Company: Paramount
Date/Country: 1931 + USA   Type: Feature
Annotation: The problems a young couple face when the
    writer-husband stays at home to write while the wife goes
    out to earn the family living. Willie Best is introduced
    in this film, billed as "Sleep'n' Eat," the two things the
    role called for him to do.

UP THE DOWN STAIRCASE
Nar/Cast: Jose Rodriquez* + Sandy Dennis + John Fantauzzi* +
    Patrick Bedford + Eileen Heckart + Vinette Carroll*
Screenplay: Tad Mosel   Story: Bel Kaufman
Producer: Alan J. Pakula   Director: Robert Mulligan
Studio/Company: Warner Brothers-Seven Arts
Tech Info: 16 mm/sound/color/123 min.
Date/Country: 1967 + USA   Type: Feature
Distr/Arch: arg + bud + ccc + cwf + ics + ker + kpf + mac +
    mod + mct + roa + swa + twy + unf + wel + who
Annotation: An adaptation of the best-selling novel about a
    young idealistic schoolteacher in a New York City slum
    whose teenage students suffer from a variety of social
    ills including poverty and racism. Eddie Williams
    (Fantauzzi) and Jose Rodriquez are two of those students.

UP THE RIVER
Nar/Cast: Bill Robinson* + Preston Foster + Tony Martin +
    Arthur Treacher
Screenplay: Lou Breslow   Story: Maurine Watkins
Producer: SolMurtzel   Director: Alfred Werker
Studio/Company: 20th Century Fox
Date/Country: 1938 + USA   Type: Feature
Annotation: Comedy about a prison football team whose star
    backfield (Foster and Treacher) goes over the wall on the
    eve of the big game. Bill Robinson is Memphis Jones, one
    of the inmates.

UP TIGHT
Nar/Cast: Raymond St. Jacques* + Julian Mayfield* + Ruby
    Dee* + Frank Silvera* + Roscoe Lee Browne* + Janet Ma-
    cLachlan* + Max Julien* + Juanita Moore* + Alice
    Childress* + James McEachin* + Richard Williams* + Leon
    Bibb*
Screenplay: Jules Dassin + Ruby Dee* + Julian Mayfield*
    Story: Liam O'Flaherty
Producer: Jules Dassin   Director: Jules Dassin
Studio/Company: Jules Dassin Production + Paramount
Tech Info: 16 mm/color/sound/3 reels/94 min.
Date/Country: 1968 + USA   Type: Feature

Distr/Arch: rbc
Annotation: Based loosely on Liam O'Flaherty's novel, The
    Informer, Uptight examines one aspect of the black power
    movement immediately after the King assassination. Film
    set in the Hough area of Cleveland; Julian Mayfield
    (writer) plays the informer.

UPBEAT_IN_MUSIC
Series: The March of Time
Alt Title(s): Music in America
Nar/Cast: Duke Ellington* + Marian Anderson* + Art Tatum* +
    George Gershwin
Producer: March of Time
Tech Info: 16 mm/sound
Date/Country: 1943   Type: Documentary
Distr/Arch: moma

UPTOWN_SATURDAY_NIGHT
Nar/Cast: Harry Belafonte* + Sidney Poitier* + Bill Cosby* +
    Lincoln Kilpatrick* + Roscoe Lee Browne* + John Sekka +
    Ketty Lester* + Rosalind Cash* + Lee Chamberlin* + Richard
    Pryor* + Flip Wilson* + Calvin Lockhart* + Paula Kelly*
Screenplay: Richard Wesley
Producer: Melville Tucker   Director: Sidney Poitier*
Studio/Company: Warner Brothers
Tech Info: 16 mm/color/sound/3 reels/104 min.
Date/Country: 1974 + USA   Type: Feature
Distr/Arch: wsa
Annotation: Sidney Poitier and Bill Cosby are robbed of a
    lottery ticket worth $50,000. To regain the ticket they
    end up in partnership with Harry Belafonte as a black
    version of the Godfather.

UPWARD_PATH
Studio/Company: Democracy Film Corporation
Date/Country: 1919 + USA

VALENTINO
Nar/Cast: Eleanor Parker + Richard Carlson + Anthony Dexter
    + Marietta Canty*
Screenplay: George Bruce
Producer: Edward Small   Director: Lewis Allen
Studio/Company: Columbia
Date/Country: 1951 + USA   Type: Feature
Annotation: A romantized version of Valentino's life.
    Marietta Canty is Tillie.

VALET'S_WIFE,_THE   Director: D.W. Griffith
Studio/Company: American Mutoscope + Biograph
Tech Info: silent/bw/508 ft.
Date/Country: 1908 + USA   Type: Comedy Short
Annotation: Bachelor Reggie Van Twiller lives the high life
    in New York off his rich uncle's beneficence until the old
    man decides to pay him a visit. Reggie must quickly ac-
    quire a wife and child to satisfy the story he has told
    his uncle. His valet obliges with his wife but when Reg-
    gie sends out to the orphanage for an infant on loan, he
    gets a black baby.

VALIANT_IS_THE_WORD_FOR_CARRIE
Nar/Cast: Gladys George + John Howard + Hattie McDaniel
Screenplay: Claude Binyon   Story: Barry Benefield
    Director: Wesley Rugghes
Studio/Company: Paramount
Date/Country: 1936 + USA   Type: Feature
Annotation: The problems faced by a woman with a questiona-
    ble past who tries to raise a couple of children.   Hattie
    McDaniel is the maid.

VANISHING_POINT
Nar/Cast: Barry Newman + Cleavon Little* + Dean Jagger +
    Victoria Medlin
Producer: Michael Pearson   Director: Robert Sarafian
Studio/Company: 20th Century Fox
Tech Info: 16 mm/color/sound/3 reels/107 min.
Date/Country: 1972 + USA   Type: Feature
Distr/Arch: fnc
Annotation: Korean War vet, ex-cop and race car driver
    Kowalski who delivers cars, makes a bet to finish a Den-
    ver-to-San Francisco run in 15 hours thereby becoming the
    object of a three-state police chase to stop him. His
    obsessive flight is radioed by Super Soul (Little) a
    jive-talking, blind, black disc jockey who monitors police
    calls and champions Kowalski's ride as a blow for freedom.

VANISHING_VIRGINIAN,_THE
Nar/Cast: Frank Morgan + Kathryn Grayson + Spring Byington +
    Leigh Whipper* + Louise Beavers*
Screenplay: Jan Fortune   Story: Rebecca Y. Williams
Producer: Edwin Knopf   Director: Frank Borzage
Studio/Company: MGM
Date/Country: 1941 + USA   Type: Feature
Annotation: Louise Beavers plays Aunt Emmeline and Leigh
    Whipper Uncle Josh in this film about southern gentlefolk
    and their doings about the time of the First World War.

VANITY
Nar/Cast: Leatrice Joy + Charles Ray + Noble Johnson* + Alan
    Hale   Director: Donald Crisp
Studio/Company: DeMille Pictures
Date/Country: 1927 + USA   Type: Feature
Annotation: A young socialite dallies with the captain of a
    tramp steamer on the eve of her wedding and gets caught up
    in more than she bargained for. Noble Johnson is Bimbo,
    the ship's cook, who gets into a struggle with Morgan
    (Hale) and is shot by Barbara (Joy).

VARIETY_GIRL
Nar/Cast: Mary Hatcher + Olga San Juan + Pearl Bailey*
Screenplay: Edmund Hartmann
Producer: Daniel Dare   Director: George Marshall
Studio/Company: Paramount
Tech Info: 16 mm/sound/bw/93 min.
Date/Country: 1947 + USA   Type: Feature
Distr/Arch: uni
Annotation: A big Paramount production variety show

featuring their top stars, including Pearl Bailey, held
together by a thread of a plot.

VARIETY LIGHTS
Alt Title(s): see Luci del Varieta

VARSITY SHOW, THE
Nar/Cast: Ford Lee Washington* + John Sublette*
Studio/Company: Warner Brothers
Date/Country: 1937 + USA   Type: Feature
Annotation: Buck and Bubbles (Washington and Sublette) tutor
    the white dancers in this Warner Brothers musical.

VEILED ARISTOCRATS
Nar/Cast: Lawrence Chenault* + Walter Fleming* + Lorenzo
    Tucker*   Director: Oscar Micheaux*
Studio/Company: Micheaux Films
Date/Country: 1932 + USA   Type: Feature

VENUS IN FURS
Nar/Cast: James Darren + Barbara McNair*
Screenplay: Jess Franco
Producer: Harry Alan Towers   Director: Jess Franco
Studio/Company: American International
Tech Info: 16 mm/sound/color/86 min.
Date/Country: 1970 + Britain + Italy + West Germany   Type:
    Feature
Distr/Arch: ivy + unf
Annotation: Barbara McNair (Rita) loses her lover to a
    ghost, the Venus of the title, who has come back to get
    revenge on 3 other people who murdered her during an orgy.

VERONICA
Producer: Jason
Tech Info: 16 mm/sound/color/27 min.
Date/Country: 1969 + USA   Type: Documentary
Distr/Arch: jas
Annotation: A middle-class black girl comments on her ideas
    about the future while attending a predominantly white
    school in Connecticut.

VEUVES (LES) DE QUINZE ANS   Director: Jean Rouch
Date/Country: 1966 + France
Distr/Arch: saf
Annotation: Archived only.

VICIOUS CIRCLE, THE
Studio/Company: Cramerly Picture Corp.
Date/Country: 1937 + USA

VIEW FROM POMPEY'S HEAD, THE
Alt Title(s): Secret Interlude
Nar/Cast: Benny Carter* + Richard Egen + Dana Wynter
Screenplay: Philip Dunne   Director: Philip Dunne
Studio/Company: Fox
Tech Info: 97 min.
Date/Country: 1955 + USA   Type: Feature
Annotation: Benny Carter participates in this adaptation of

Hamilton Basso's novel about a New York lawyer's (Egen)
return to the South and scenes of his past. Two black
butlers appear as background in one scene, no lines or
identification.

VIEWING THE SUPERNATURAL
Series: People Are Taught To Be Different
Producer: NET
Tech Info: 16 mm/sound/bw/1 reel/30 min.
Date/Country: 1956   Type: Documentary
Distr/Arch: iu
Annotation: Uses dance routines and originally scored music
    to portray cultural differences in solving problems
    through religion. Compares experiences of the southern
    Black, the voodoo cult of the Haitian black peasant, and
    the polytheism of the Muria of India.

VIRGIN ISLAND
Nar/Cast: John Cassavetes + Sidney Poitier* + Ruby Dee*
    Story: Robb White
Producer: Leon Clore + Grahame Tharp   Director: Patrick
    Jackson
Studio/Company: Films Around the World
Tech Info: 16 mm/sound/color/94 min.
Date/Country: 1960 + USA   Type: Feature
Distr/Arch: unf
Annotation: Poitier is a friendly islander who helps a young
    American (Cassavetes) and his wife (who have settled into
    housekeeping on an island key) when she is in labor. Ruby
    Dee is Poitier's friend.

VIRGIN OF THE SEMINOLE, THE
Nar/Cast: William Fountaine* + Shingzie Howard*   Director:
    Oscar Micheaux*
Studio/Company: Micheaux Film Corporation
Tech Info: bw/silent
Date/Country: 1922 + USA   Type: Feature
Annotation: An adventure story of the great Northwest and a
    young man who becomes a member of the Canadian Mounties
    and through his heroic actions finds love and happiness.

VIRGINIA JUDGE
Nar/Cast: Stepin Fetchit* + Walter C. Kelly   Director:
    Edward Sedgwick
Studio/Company: Paramount
Tech Info: 16 mm/sound/bw/61 min.
Date/Country: 1935 + USA   Type: Feature
Distr/Arch: uni

VIRGINIA
Nar/Cast: Madeleine Carroll + Fred MacMurray + Sterling
    Hayden + Leigh Whipper* + Louise Beavers* + Darby Jones
    Story: Edward H. Griffith + Virginia Van Upp Director:
    Edward H. Griffith
Studio/Company: Paramount
Tech Info: 16 mm/bw/sound/3 reels/109 min.
Date/Country: 1941 + USA   Type: Feature
Distr/Arch: uni

Annotation: Story of beautiful expatriate Virginian who
   returns to her old family home, complete with dutiful
   slaves (Whipper, Beavers) who present her with their
   savings in worthless confederate money. She battles
   scoundrel carpetbaggers and falls in love with a fellow
   Virginian.

VITE PERDUTE
Nar/Cast: John Kitzmiller*
Date/Country: 1959 + Italy   Type: Feature

VIVA FRELIMO
Producer: Dutch Kenmark T.V.
Tech Info: 16mm/ sound/ 30 min./ color/ Portuguese dialog
   with English subtitles and narration.
Date/Country: 1969 + Mozambique   Type: T.V. Documentary
Distr/Arch: tri + onn + twn
Annotation: A study of the Mozambique Liberation Front, its
   political organization and program of national reconstruc-
   tion inside liberated Mozambique.

VIVA ZAPATA
Nar/Cast: Marlon Brando + Anthony Quinn + Frank Silvera*
Screenplay: John Steinbeck
Producer: Darryl Zanuck   Director: Elia Kazan
Studio/Company: Twentieth Century Fox
Date/Country: 1952 + USA   Type: Feature
Annotation: Frank Silvera plays Huerta in this drama about
   the Mexican rebel leader played by Marlon Brando.

VIVACIOUS LADY
Nar/Cast: Ginger Rogers + James Stewart + Willie Best*
Screenplay: P.J. Wolfson
Producer: Pandro S. Berman   Director: George Stevens
Studio/Company: RKO Radio
Tech Info: 16 mm/sound/bw/90 min.
Date/Country: 1938 + USA   Type: Feature
Distr/Arch: fnc
Annotation: After a whirlwind romance, college professor
   Jimmy Stewart brings wife Ginger Rogers to a staid college
   community, with predictable results. Willie Best plays a
   porter.

VIVERE IN PACE
Alt Title(s): To Live in Peace
Nar/Cast: Gar Moore + John Kitzmiller* + Aldo Fabrizi
Producer: Carlo Ponti   Director: Luigi Zampa
Studio/Company: Lux Films
Tech Info: 16 mm/sound/bw/2 reels/90 min./English subtitles
Date/Country: 1946 + Italy   Type: Feature
Distr/Arch: mac
Annotation: Two American soldiers, one black, one white, are
   hidden by an Italian family in an occupied Italian village
   toward the end of WW II (1945). John Kitzmiller plays the
   black soldier whose wound complicates their escape.

VIXEN
Nar/Cast: Harrison Page* + Erica Gavin

Screenplay: Robert Rudelson
Producer: Russ Meyer   Director: Russ Meyer
Studio/Company: EVE Productions
Tech Info: 16 mm/sound/color/71 min.
Date/Country: 1968 + USA   Type: Feature
Distr/Arch: bac
Annotation: Harrison Page is Niles, a draft dodger from the
    states, at a fishing lodge in British Columbia with a
    friend whose married sister is a nymphomaniac. He gets
    involved with her and a plane high jacker and finally
    decides to stay in the states as the "lesser of two
    evils."

VOICE OF BRITAIN, THE
Nar/Cast: Nina Mae McKinney* + Henry Hall + BBC Dance
    Orchestra   Director: Stuart Legg
Studio/Company: GPO Film Unit Production
Tech Info: 56 min.
Date/Country: 1935 + Britain   Type: Documentary
Annotation: McKinney sings "Dinah" in this production which
    examines the entertainment and cultural contributions of
    BBC Radio.

VOICE OF CONSCIENCE, THE
Annotation: A black woman saves the hero (white) from a
    murder charge by using voodoo to force a confession from a
    black man who is not very sound of mind.

VOICE OF LA RAYA
Nar/Cast: Anthony Quinn
Screenplay: William Greaves*
Producer: William Greaves*   Director: William Greaves*
Tech Info: 16 mm/color/53 min./sound
Date/Country: 1971 + USA   Type: Documentary
Distr/Arch: gre
Annotation: Deals with discrimination against Spanish-
    speaking Americans.

VOICE OF THE DRUM, THE
Producer: Francisoire Films
Tech Info: 16 mm/sound/color/45 min.
Date/Country: 1967 + Ivory Coast + Bauli   Type: Documentary
Distr/Arch: uill
Annotation: The spiritual and symbolic meaning of Baule
    dances.

VOLCANO
Nar/Cast: Clarence Muse* + Babe Daniels + Ricardo Cortez +
    Wallace Beery
Producer: Adolph Zukor   Director: William K. Howard
Studio/Company: Paramount
Date/Country: 1926 + USA   Type: Feature
Annotation: Returning from a convent in Brussels, to her
    home in Martinique, a young girl (Daniels) finds that not
    only has her father died, but that she may be of mixed
    parentage. The movie moves to clear her of this un-
    pardonable sin and unite her with her lover (Cortez).
    Wallace Beery is the quadroon villain; Clarence Muse has a

bit role.

VOODOO DEVIL DRUMS
Studio/Company: Toddy Pictures
Tech Info: 44 min.
Annotation: Voodoo rites, zombies, witchcraft, and magic are
   included in this film.

VOODOO DRUMS
Alt Title(s): see Drums O'Voodoo

VOODOO ISLAND
Series: Central and South American
Nar/Cast: Lowell Thomas
Studio/Company: BBC + Odyssey
Tech Info: color/25 min.
Date/Country: 1967   Type: Documentary
Distr/Arch: tl
Annotation: An   authentic Haitian voodoo ceremony is shown.

VOODOO VENGEANCE
Date/Country: 1913
Annotation: The "black savage" is a stock menacing character
   in this film in which the British successfully put down a
   burgeoning Mau Mau conspiracy.

VOYAGE AU CONGO
Alt Title(s): The Courting of Djinta
Producer: Marc Allegret + Andre Gide
Studio/Company: Gide-Allegret
Date/Country: 1927 + France
Annotation: Tells of the courtship between an African native
   woman and the farmer who comes to live in the village in
   semi-documentary style.

W. C. HANDY
Producer: Vignette Films
Tech Info: 16 mm/sound/color/14 min.
Date/Country: 1967 + USA   Type: Documentary
Distr/Arch: bfa
Annotation: The life and career of the 'Father of the
   Blues', William Christopher Handy.

W.C. HANDY
Producer: Vignette Films
Tech Info: 16 mm/sound/color/14 min.
Date/Country: 1967 + USA   Type: Documentary
Distr/Arch: usc + bfa
Annotation: Traces the contributions of William Christopher
   Handy*, the "Father of the Blues," to American culture.
   Gives background, influences on his career.

W.W. AND THE DIXIE DANCEKINGS
Nar/Cast: Burt Reynolds + Furry Lewis* + Stanley Greene* +
   Art Carney   Director: John V. Avildsen
Studio/Company: Fox
Tech Info: 16 mm/sound/color/94 min.
Date/Country: 1974 + USA   Type: Feature

Distr/Arch: fnc
Annotation: Reynolds as W.W., con artist who tries to help
    Dixie and her Dancekings get their big chance. Uncle Fur-
    ry (Lewis) hides them from Rev. Goce (Carney) after their
    robbery attempt. He also sings "Dirty Car Blues." Greene
    plays a chauffeur.

WABASH AVE
War/Cast: Betty Grable + Victor Mature + Phil Harris +   Col-
    lette Lyons*
Screenplay: Harry Tugend
Producer: William Perlberg   Director: Henry Koster
Studio/Company: 20th Century Fox
Tech Info: 16 mm/sound/bw/92 min.
Date/Country: 1950 + USA   Type: Feature
Distr/Arch: fnc
Annotation: Life in a gas-lit, gay 90's Chicago saloon is
    depicted in this musical comedy.   Collette Lyons plays
    Beulah.

WAGES OF SIN, THE
War/Cast: Lorenzo Tucker* + Katherine Noisette* + Gertrude
    Snelson* + Bessie Gibbens* + Ethel Smith* + Alice Russell*
Studio/Company: Micheaux Film Corporation
Date/Country: 1929 + USA   Type: Feature
Annotation: The problems of two brothers and the strain of
    urban life on their familial relationship - with one
    brother involved in maintaining a motion picture company,
    the other in theft and wild parties.

WALDO'S LAST STAND
Series: Our Gang
War/Cast: Our Gang + Billie Thomas*
Screenplay: Hal Law + Robert A. McGowan
Producer: Jack Chertok + Richard Goldstone   Director:
    Edward Cahn + Steven Granger
Studio/Company: MGM
Tech Info: bw/sound/1 reel
Date/Country: 1940 + USA   Type: Comedy Short
Annotation: A floorshow put on to help business at Waldo's
    lemonade stand fails to convince the sole customer to buy
    lemonade and ties up the rest of the potential customers
    who all work in the show. Billie Thomas stars as Buck-
    wheat.

WALK ON THE WILD SIDE
War/Cast: Laurence Harvey + Capucine + Jane Fonda + Juanita
    Moore*
Screenplay: John Fante + Edmund Morris   Story: Nelson Al-
    gren
Producer: Charles K. Feldman   Director: Edward Dmytryk
Studio/Company: Columbia
Tech Info: 16 mm/sound/bw/114 min.
Date/Country: 1962 + USA   Type: feature
Distr/Arch: bud + cha + con + cwf + ics + ker + mac + mod
Annotation: Drama about a Texas vagabound (Harvey) who goes
    looking for his lost love in New Orleans and finds her
    working in a bordello. Juanita Moore is "Mama."

WALK THE WALK
Nar/Cast: Bernie Hamilton* + Honor Laurence
Screenplay: Joe Zacha
Producer: Joe Zacha   Director: Joe Zacha
Studio/Company: HQZ Productions + Hallmark of Hollywood
Tech Info: sound/color/95 min.
Date/Country: 1970 + USA   Type: Feature
Annotation: Drama about a black theological student, (Bernie
    Hamilton) addicted to heroin, who struggles valiantly and
    finally wins out against the habit only to be re-addicted
    when a doctor gives him drugs to ease his pain after an
    injury.

WALK, DON'T RUN
Nar/Cast: Cary Grant + Jim Hutton
Screenplay: Frank Ross
Producer: Sol C. Siegel   Director: Charles Walters
Studio/Company: Columbia
Date/Country: 1966 + USA   Type: Feature
Distr/Arch: arg + buc + ccc + cha + cwf + ics + mac + mod +
    mot + rca + swa + tfc + wcf + wel + who
Annotation: Music score by Quincy Jones* for this comedy
    about the Olympic games in Tokyo, replete with Russians,
    athletes, spies, and mistaken identity.

WALKING HILLS, THE
Nar/Cast: Randolph Scott + Josh White*
Studio/Company: Columbia
Tech Info: sound/78 min.
Date/Country: 1949 + USA   Type: Feature

WALKING TALL PART 2
Nar/Cast: Bo Svenson + Robert DoQui* + Richard Jaeckel
Screenplay: Howard Kreitsek
Producer: Charles Pratt + BCP Production   Director: Earl
    Bellamy
Studio/Company: Cinerama
Tech Info: 16 mm/sound/color/109 min.
Date/Country: 1975 + USA   Type: Feature
Distr/Arch: swa
Annotation: Robert DoQui is Obra Eaker in this continuation
    of the story of Buford Pusser (Svenson), honest, courage-
    ous, Tennessee sheriff. Here he is searching for the men
    who killed his wife and maimed him.

WALKING TALL
Nar/Cast: Joe Don Baker + Elizabeth Hartman
Producer: BCP Production   Director: Phil Karlson
Studio/Company: Cinerama
Tech Info: 16 mm/sound/color/125 min.
Date/Country: 1973 + USA   Type: Feature
Distr/Arch: swa
Annotation: Melodrama based on the real life story of Buford
    Pusser (Baker), sheriff of a Tennessee county full of
    crime which it seems only he has the conscience, will or
    strength to undo. Blacks are an integral part of the
    story.

WALL OF NOISE
Nar/Cast: Suzanne Pleshette + Ty Hardin + Bill Walker* +
   Napolean Whiting*
Screenplay: Joseph Landon   Story: J. Michael Stein
Producer: Joseph Landon   Director: Richard Wilson
Studio/Company: Warner Brothers
Tech Info: color/sound/112 min.
Date/Country: 1963 + USA   Type: Feature
Annotation: Story of a young, on-the-make trainer, who is
   having a tough time deciding between a new horse or his
   former employer's wife.   Bill Walker plays the role of
   "Money"; Whiting is the preacher.

WALTER ALLEN, AMOS TUTUOLA*, ULLI BEIER
Series: African Writers of Today
Producer: NET
Tech Info: 16 mm/sound/bw/1 reel/29 min.   Type: Documentary
Distr/Arch: iu
Annotation: Introduces series host, Lewis Nkosi*, who begins
   a survey of Africa's writers by conversing with English
   literary critic Walter Allen.   Shifts to Nigeria and a
   visit with Amos Tutuola*, author of The Palm-Wine Drinkard, who talks of the past and his people's story-telling
   ways. Ends with Ulii Beier, German-born editor of the
   African literary magazine Black Orpheus.

WAR CAME TO KENYA
Nar/Cast: Ian Wetherall   Director: Guy Johnson
Date/Country: 1941 + Britain   Type: Documentary
Distr/Arch: iwm
Annotation: Kenya's contribution to the war effort including
   the liberation of Abyssinia. Ian Wetherall narrates.

WAR FEATHERS
Series: Our Gang
Nar/Cast: Our Gang + Allen Hoskins* + Jannie Hoskins*
Screenplay: Hal Roach
Producer: Hal Roach   Director: Robert McGowan
Studio/Company: Pathe
Tech Info: silent/bw/2 reels
Date/Country: 1926 + USA   Type: Comedy Short
Annotation: After disrupting a train on a cross-country
   ride, the gang sneaks off and onto a covered wagon. The
   new vehicle ride leads to various misadventures with
   bandits, Indians and ending in the gang getting a reward
   for helping capture the bandits. Allen Hoskins stars as
   Farina and Jannie Hoskins stars as Mango.

WARM DECEMBER, A
Nar/Cast: Sidney Poitier* + Esther Anderson* + Yvette
   Curtis*
Screenplay: Lawrence Roman
Producer: Melville Tucker   Director: Sidney Poitier*
Studio/Company: First Artists Presentation + National
   General Pictures Release
Tech Info: 16 mm/color/sound/3 reels/100 min.

Date/Country: 1973 + USA   Type: Feature
Distr/Arch: swa
Annotation: Story of an ill-fated romance between a black
   American widower (Poitier) on a visit to London with his
   pre-teenage daughter (Yvette Curtis) and a female diplomat
   (Esther Anderson), a member of an emerging African state's
   embassy. The film provides some insight into African
   culture.

WASHEE_IRONEE
Series: Our Gang
Nar/Cast: Our Gang + Matthew Beard* + Willie May Taylor*
Producer: Hal Roach   Director: James Panott
Studio/Company: MGM + Roach
Tech Info: super 8 mm/16 mm/bw/sound/1 reel/16 min.
Date/Country: 1934 + USA   Type: Comedy Short
Distr/Arch: bla + roa
Annotation: Waldo gets his clothes muddy playing football
   just before he's to play the violin for a ladies' group.
   The gang tries to wash them, but Waldo ends up with hope-
   lessly shrunken clothes. Waldo appears with a lampshade
   shirt, Mom faints, the gang appears and a melee ensues.
   Matthew Beard stars as Stymie.

WASHINGTON_MERRY-GO-ROUND
Nar/Cast: Lee Tracy + Constance Cummings + Walter Connally +
   Clarence Muse*   Story: Maxwell Anderson   Director: James
   Cruze
Studio/Company: Columbia
Date/Country: 1933 + USA   Type: Feature
Annotation: Political intrigues and misdeeds are the central
   theme in this movie about a rookie Congressman (Tracy) and
   his unwillingness to bend to graft. Clarence Muse is
   Clarence, Tracy's valet, who furnishes the comedy.

WASHINGTON: THE MAYOR AND THE CITY
Producer: Jesse Sandler
Tech Info: 16 mm/sound/color/15 min.   Type: Documentary
Distr/Arch: aff
Annotation: Adresses Mayor Walter Washington's attempts to
   rebuild community spirit after the riots in Washington,
   D.C.

WASP_NEST, THE
Series: !Kung and !Gwi Bushmen
Producer: John Marshall
Tech Info: 16 mm/sound/color/1 reel/20 min.
Date/Country: Botswana   Type: Documentary
Distr/Arch: psu + der
Annotation: Film shows the role of !Kung women, gathering
   wild food. Men distribute game and maintain a system of
   favors, while women provide only for immediate families.

WATCH ON THE RHINE
Nar/Cast: Bette Davis + Paul Lukas + Geraldine Fitzgerald +
   Frank Wilson
Screenplay: Dashiell Hammett   Story: Lillian Hellman
Producer: Hal B. Wallis   Director: Herman Shumlin

Studio/Company: Warner Brothers
Tech Info: 16mm/ sound/ bw/ 114 min.
Date/Country: USA   Type: Feature
Annotation: In 1940, an anti-Nazi German patriot, tired of
    fighting underground against the rise of Hitler, brings
    his family to America to live. He soon finds, however,
    that Hitler's tentacles reach across the Atlantic. Frank
    Wilson is Joseph.

WATERMELON MAN
Nar/Cast: Mantan Moreland* + Godfrey Cambridge* + Estelle
    Parsons + D'urville Martin* + Charles Lampkin*
Screenplay: Herman Rancher
Producer: John B. Bennett   Director: Melvin Van Peebles*
Studio/Company: Columbia Pictures
Tech Info: 16 mm/sound/color/3 reels/100 min.
Date/Country: 1970 + USA   Type: Feature
Distr/Arch: swa
Annotation: Van Peebles' American film (directorial) debut
    in this story about a bigot who turns black overnight.
    What happens when that transformation becomes known to his
    associates and friends and the effect on his family are
    the central issues raised by the film.

WATTS FESTIVAL - 69
Producer: Watts Training Center for Film, Television, Radio
Tech Info: 16 mm/sound/bw/20 min.
Date/Country: 1969 + USA   Type: Documentary
Distr/Arch: dbm
Annotation: Documents the Watts festival in 1969 in Los An-
    geles: crafts, booths, people. Provided by Center for
    Southern Folklore.

WATTS TOWERS THEATRE WORKSHOP
Producer: Educational Television Service
Tech Info: 16 mm/color/sound/1 reel/27 min
Date/Country: 1969 + USA   Type: Documentary
Distr/Arch: iu
Annotation: Introduces the Watts Towers Theatre Workshop
    consisting of black teenagers from the Los Angeles Watts
    ghetto. The group, founded in 1963 by Stephen Kyle Kent
    as a Join the Arts project, utilizes everyday events to
    create a situation of active involvement and immediate
    importance for personal and social change. Presents those
    ideas by means of improvisational techniques.

WATTSTAX
Nar/Cast: Isaac Hayes* + Staple Singers* + Jimmy Jones* +
    Little Milton* + Richard Pryor* + The Emotions* + Albert
    King* + Luther Ingram* + Johnnie Taylor* + Rufus Thomas* +
    Carla Thomas*
Producer: Larry Shaw + Mel Stuart   Director: Mel Stuart
Studio/Company: Columbia
Tech Info: 16 m/sound/color/3 reels/100 min.
Date/Country: 1973 + USA   Type: Documentary
Distr/Arch: swa
Annotation: Filmed at the Watts Summer Festival, August,
    1972, the film interweaves the various stars with street

life in Watts.   Richard Pryor does the comedy bits that
have since brought him national prominence.

WATTS! RIOT OR REVOLT?
Studio/Company: CBS-TV
Tech Info: 16 mm/bw/45 min.
Date/Country: 1966 + USA   Type: Documentary
Distr/Arch: adl
Annotation: Film examines the riot of Watts, Los Angeles, in
    1965 in the context of the civil rights struggle. Con-
    tains newsreel footage and interviews with community
    leaders.

WATUSI
Nar/Cast: George Montgomery + Taina Elg + David Farrar + Rex
    Ingram*
Screenplay: James Clavell   Story: H. Rider Haggard
Producer: Al Zimbalist   Director: Kurt Newmann
Studio/Company: MGM
Tech Info: 16 mm/sound/color/85 min.
Date/Country: 1959 + USA   Type: Feature
Distr/Arch: fnc
Annotation: Son of a famous white hunter retraces his
    father's steps seeking African diamond mines of King
    Solomon. Rex Ingram plays Umbopa (the Robeson role) in
    this remake of King Solomon's Mines.

WAY DOWN SOUTH
Nar/Cast: Bobby Breen + Clarence Muse* + Allan Mowbray +
    Ralph Morgan + Steffi Duna* + Sally Blane* + Lillian Yar-
    bo* + Matthew Beard* + Jack Carr* + Marguerite Whitten* +
    Hall Johnson Choir*
Screenplay: Clarence Muse* + Langston Hughes*   Story: Lang-
    ston Hughes*
Producer: Sol Lessor   Director: Bernard Vorhaus
Studio/Company: RKO Radio
Date/Country: 1939 + USA   Type: Feature
Annotation: When the master of the plantation is killed and
    before the heir becomes of age, a mean, Simon LeGreeish
    adminstrator is appointed. How the heir and slaves join
    forces to oust the adminstrator is the movie plot.
    Clarence Muse aided in the direction.

WAY IT IS, THE
Producer: NET
Tech Info: 16 mm/sound/bw/1 reel/60 min
Date/Country: 1967 + USA   Type: Documentary
Distr/Arch: iu
Annotation: Documents the chaos of a ghetto school and what
    is being done in one particular school to remedy this
    situation. Focuses on Junior High School No. 5, Bedford-
    Stuyvesant section of Brooklyn, where the workers with a
    New York University special learning project are shown in
    classrooms, teachers' meeting, and visits with parents.

WAY TO HAPPINESS, THE
Date/Country: 194- + USA

WAY WEST, THE
Nar/Cast: Roy Glenn* + Kirk Douglas + Robert Mitchum
Screenplay: Ben Maddow
Producer: Harold Hecht   Director: Andrew V. McLaglen
Studio/Company: United Artists
Tech Info: 16 mm/sound/color/122 min.
Date/Country: 1967 + USA
Distr/Arch: uas
Annotation: Roy Glenn is Saunders in this western drama
    about a wagon train led by Sen. William Tadlock (Douglas).
    In one scene Saunders, distressed by his emotional respon-
    se to his son's death, orders his slave to whip him.

WE GOT TO LIVE HERE
Producer: Robert Machover + Norm Fruchter
Tech Info: 16 mm/sound/bw/20 min.
Date/Country: 1966 + USA   Type: Documentary
Distr/Arch: uca
Annotation: The history of the development of a slum in
    Newark, New Jersey and its toll in human despair.

WE SHALL OVERCOME
Producer: Jack Summerfield
Tech Info: 16 mm/sound/color/10 min.
Date/Country: 1965 + USA   Type: Documentary
Distr/Arch: mac
Annotation: A civil rights movement documentary with inter-
    views and rallies unified by the song for which the film
    is titled.

WE WORK AGAIN
Studio/Company: WPA Film
Date/Country: 1936 + USA   Type: Newsreel
Annotation: Newsreel showing scenes of Blacks participating
    in various WPA work projects in the U.S.

WE'LL NEVER TURN BACK
Producer: Harvey Richards + Student Non-Violent Coordinating
    Committee
Tech Info: 16 mm/sound/bw/30 min.
Date/Country: 1963 + USA   Type: Documentary
Distr/Arch: mac + uca
Annotation: A black voter registration campaign in Missis-
    sippi.

WE'VE COME A LONG, LONG WAY
Nar/Cast: Elder Michaux*
Producer: Jack Goldberg   Director: Jack Goldberg
Studio/Company: Goldberg Production
Date/Country: 1945 + USA   Type: Documentary
Annotation: A documentary cavalcade of the Negro race, with
    narration by Elder Michaux.

WE'VE GOT THE DEVIL ON THE RUN
Nar/Cast: Elder Micheaux*
Producer: Elder Solomon Lightfoot Micheaux*
Date/Country: 1934 + USA

WEAPONS OF GORDEN PARKS
Studio/Company: Contemporary + McGraw Hill
Tech Info: 16 mm/color/sound/1 reel/28 min.
Date/Country: 1967 + USA   Type: Documentary
Distr/Arch: con
Annotation: The story of the internationally known black
    photographer seen at work, in his home, with his family,
    and on the streets of Harlem, as part of his past life is
    recreated.

WEDDING WORRIES
Series: Our Gang
Nar/Cast: Our Gang + Billie Thomas*
Screenplay: Hal Law + Robert A. McGowan
Producer: MGM   Director: Edward Cahn
Studio/Company: MGM
Tech Info: bw/sound/1 reel
Date/Country: 1941 + USA   Type: Comedy Short
Annotation: Darla's father is going to remarry, but Froggy's
    horror story about stepmothers sets the gang in action to
    sabotage the wedding. Billie Thomas stars as Buckwheat.

WELCOME TO L.A.
Nar/Cast: Keith Carradine + Sally Kellerman + Geraldine
    Chaplin + Harvey Keitel + Sissy Spacek + John Considine +
    Viveca Lindfors + Richard Baskin + Denver Pyle + Diahann
    Abbott*
Screenplay: Alan Rudolph
Producer: Robert Altman   Director: Alan Rudolph
Studio/Company: United Artists
Tech Info: 16 mm/color/sound
Date/Country: 1977 + USA   Type: Feature
Distr/Arch: uas
Annotation: Welcome to L.A. centers around a songwriter
    (Keith Carradine), heir to his father's million dollar
    yoghurt business, and his interactions with the other L.A.
    characters in the film. Diahann Abbott is Denver Pyle's
    receptionist.

WELL SPENT LIFE, A
Producer: Les Blank   Director: Les Blank
Studio/Company: Flower Films
Tech Info: 16 mm/44 min./color/sound/1 reel
Date/Country: 1971 + USA   Type: Documentary
Distr/Arch: gro + ff
Annotation: Film portrait of Mance Liscomb, Texas blues
    singer, as he talks of love, music, marriage, religion,
    youth and importance of an education. The film includes
    footage of town, neighbors and farms.

WELL, THE
Alt Title(s): Deep Is the Well
Nar/Cast: Maidie Norman* + Ernest Anderson* + Christine
    Larsen + Bill Walker* + Alfred Grant* + Benjamin Hamilton
    + Gwendolyn Laster* + George Hamilton
Screenplay: Russell Rouse + Clarence Green
Producer: Leo C. Popkin + Clarence Green   Director: Russell
    Rouse + Leo C. Popkin

Studio/Company: United Artists
Tech Info: 16 mm/bw/sound/3 reels/89 min.
Date/Country: 1951 + USA   Type: Feature
Distr/Arch: bud + unf + kpf + mac
Annotation: Racial tensions mount when a missing black girl
    is last seen talking to a white stranger. The town is on
    the verge of open riot, but when the girl is discovered
    down an abandoned well, all sides join in to save her.

WEST AFRICA (NIGERIA)
Series: Africa in Change
Producer: Encyclopedia Britannica Films, Inc.
Tech Info: 16 mm/sound/color and bw/1 reel/23 min.
Date/Country: 1963   Type: Documentary
Distr/Arch: iu + ebec
Annotation: Points out the three geographically and
    culturally different regions of Nigeria. Emphasizes the
    role of education in uniting the varied peoples of this
    African country.

WEST AFRICA: ANOTHER VIET NAM?
Producer: Granada International
Tech Info: 16 mm/sound/bw/40 min.
Date/Country: 1968 + Guinea + Bissau   Type: Documetary
Distr/Arch: impact + grove
Annotation: Documents the struggle of one guerilla unit in
    Guinea-Bissau.

WEST INDIES CALLING
Screenplay: John Page
Producer: Donald Alexander   Director: John Page
Studio/Company: Paul Rotha Productions for Ministry of In-
    formatin
Tech Info: 35 mm/bw/1300 ft./15 min.
Date/Country: 1943 + Britain   Type: Documentary
Distr/Arch: iwm
Annotation: Illustration of a BBC radio broadcast by West
    Indians in Britain explaining to the British people the
    contribution made by West Indians to the war effort.

WEST INDIES, THE
Studio/Company: Encyclopaedia Britannica Educational Corp.
Tech Info: color/22 min.
Date/Country: 1965   Type: Documentary
Distr/Arch: ebec + uwy
Annotation: Substandard living conditions of West Indians
    are contrasted with the scenic beauty of the islands.

WEST OF THE PECOS
Nar/Cast: Willie Best* + Richard Dix + Martha Sleeper +
    Louise Beavers*
Screenplay: Milton Krims + John Twist   Story: Zane Grey
    Director: Paul Roser
Studio/Company: RKO Radio
Date/Country: 1934 + USA   Type: Feature
Annotation: Typical western in which the hero first feuds
    with then falls in love with the heroine, while fighting
    offIndians and clearing himself of a rustling charge.

Willie Best is billed as "Sleep-'n-Eat" which he does in this film. Louise Beavers is Mauree.

WEST OF ZANZIBAR
Nar/Cast: Anthony Steel + Sheila Sim + Edric Connor* + Orlando Martins* + Peter Illing* + Juma*
Screenplay: Max Catto + Jack Whittingham
Producer: Leslie Norman   Director: Harry Watt
Studio/Company: J. Arthur Rank Production
Tech Info: sound/color
Date/Country: 1955 + Britain   Type: Feature
Distr/Arch: fnc
Annotation: In this sequel to Ivory Hunter, Anthony Steel goes after ivory poachers on the preserve he helped establish. Blacks provide the atmosphere (Martins as M'Kwongwi, Connor as Ushingo, Illing as Khingoni, Juma as Juma) in this adventure filmed in Mombasa and Zanzibar.

WESTERN VENGEANCE
Nar/Cast: Martin Turner* + Franklyn Farnum + Doreen Turner
    Director: J.P. McDowan
Studio/Company: Independent Pictures
Tech Info: 35 mm/silent/bw/5 reels
Date/Country: 1924 + USA   Type: Feature
Annotation: Martin Turner plays Luke Mosby in this melodrama about outlaws and gold mines.

WHAT A GUY
Nar/Cast: Ruby Dee* + Mantan Moreland* + Anna Lucasta*
Producer: Ted Toddy
Studio/Company: Toddy Pictures + Lucky Star Productions
Date/Country: 1947 + USA

WHAT A MISSIONARY DOES IN AFRICA
Series: National Archives Gift Collection
Tech Info: 16 mm/silent/3 reels/bw
Annotation: The life, problems and work of the average missionary, with a survey of the church's program in Africa. (Part of Record Group 200 HF series, Harmon Foundation Collection).

WHAT ABOUT PREJUDICE?
Studio/Company: McGraw Hill Films
Tech Info: 16 mm/bw/sound/1 reel/10 min.
Date/Country: 1959 + USA   Type: Dramatic Short
Distr/Arch: kpf
Annotation: A film designed to promote discussion among high school students. A ficticious tale about an unmentioned minority member, Bruce Jones.

WHAT AFRICA IS
Series: National Archives Gift Collection
Tech Info: 16 mm/silent/1 reel/bw
Annotation: The country, its people, religious beliefs and tribal organizations. (Part of Record Group 200 HF series, Harmon Foundation Collection).

WHAT COLOR ARE YOU?

Producer: Encyclopædia Britannica Educational Corp.
Tech Info: 16 mm/sound/color/1 reel/15 min.
Date/Country: 1967 + USA   Type: Dramatized Documentary
Distr/Arch: iu + ebec
Annotation: Answers the questions of three boys, each representing a different race, about the color of skin and
  discusses the biological role of genes and chromosomes in
  pigmentation. Uses animation to provide chronological
  sequence and historical context to support arguments.

WHAT_DO_YOU_PEOPLE_WANT
Producer: John Evans
Tech Info: 16 mm/sound/color/30 min.
Date/Country: 1968 + USA   Type: Documentary
Distr/Arch: imp
Annotation: Filmed are meetings of the Black Panther Party
  and a California rally. Appearances by: Stokely Car-
  michael*, Rap Brown*, Catherine/Eldrige Cleaver*, James
  Forman* Bobby Seale*.

WHAT_EVER_HAPPEND_TO_BABY_JANE
Nar/Cast: Bette Davis + Joan Crawford + Maidie Norman*
Screenplay: Lukus Heller   Story: Henry Farrell
Producer: Robert Aldrich   Director: Robert Aldrich
Studio/Company: Warner Brothers
Tech Info: 16 mm/sound/bw/132 min.
Date/Country: 1962 + USA   Type: Feature
Distr/Arch: arg + bud + ccc + cha + ker + mac + mod + mot +
  nat + roa + sel + swa + tfc + tmc + unf + wcf + who + wil
Annotation: Horror film about two aging sisters who prey on
  each other in a decaying home. Maidie Norman plays the
  concerned maid.

WHAT_GOES_UP
Nar/Cast: Eddie Green*
Studio/Company: Sepia Art Picture Company
Date/Country: 1939 + USA

WHAT_HARVEST_FOR_THE_REAPER
Producer: NET
Tech Info: 16 mm/sound/bw/59 min.
Date/Country: 1968 + USA   Type: TV Documentary
Distr/Arch: imp
Annotation: How the migrant labor system affects black pe-
  ople economically.

WHAT_PRICE_HOLLYWOOD
Nar/Cast: Louise Beavers* + Eddie Anderson* + Constance Ben-
  nett + Lowell Sherman   Story: Adela Rogers St. John
  Director: George Cukor
Studio/Company: RKO Radio
Tech Info: 16 mm/sound/bw/88 min.
Date/Country: 1932 + USA   Type: Feature
Distr/Arch: fnc
Annotation: The story of a waitress-turned actress on her
  way up, the director who helps her ascent, and the polo
  player who marries her, briefly. Anderson is James and
  Beavers is Cassie, domestics in this tale which emphasizes

the transitory nature of movie fame.

WHAT'S BUZZIN' COUSIN
Nar/Cast: Ann Miller + Eddie Anderson* + John Hubbard
Screenplay: Harry Scruber   Story: Aben Korndel   Director:
    Charles Barton
Studio/Company: Columbia
Date/Country: 1943 + USA   Type: Feature
Annotation: Ann Miller inherits a hotel in a ghost town and
    enlists Eddie Anderson to make it into a nightspot.

WHAT'S THE USE?
Studio/Company: Trowship Film Company
Date/Country: 191- + USA

WHEN A MAN LOVES
Nar/Cast: Noble Johnson* + John Barrymore + Dolores Costello
    + Warner Oland   Director: Alan Crosland
Studio/Company: Warner Brothers Pictures
Tech Info: silent/bw/35 min./10 reels
Date/Country: 1927 + USA   Type: Feature
Annotation: Noble Johnson plays an Indian during Louis XV's
    reign who makes advances to a woman loved by a man about
    to take his vows as a priest.

WHEN BOYS ENCOUNTER PUBERTY
Series: People Are Taught To Be Different
Producer: NET
Tech Info: 16 mm/sound/bw/1 reel/30 min.   Type: Docu-
    mentary
Distr/Arch: iu
Annotation: Uses dance routines and originally scored music
    to portray male adolescent rituals as a means of passing
    boys to manhood. Compares Americans, the Pokot of Kenya,
    and the Nupe of northern Nigeria.

WHEN CUPID WENT WILD
Nar/Cast: Ebony Players*
Studio/Company: Ebony Film Corporation
Date/Country: 1918 + USA

WHEN DO WE EAT?
Studio/Company: Artcraft
Date/Country: 1918 + USA
Annotation: An Uncle Tom-type character portrayed in a
    show-within-the-film by stock company actors.

WHEN GIANTS FOUGHT
Tech Info: silent/bw
Date/Country: 1926 + Britain   Type: Feature
Annotation: Story of Tom Molyneux, pioneer black boxer.

WHEN MEN BETRAY   Director: Oscar Micheaux*
Studio/Company: Micheaux Film Company
Date/Country: 1928 + USA   Type: Feature

WHEN THE BOYS MEET THE GIRLS
Nar/Cast: Connie Francis + Harve Presnell + Louis Armstrong*

Screenplay: Robert Kent
Producer: Sam Katzman   Director: Alvin Ganzer
Studio/Company: MGM
Tech Info: 16 mm/sound/color/97 min.
Date/Country: 1965 + USA   Type: Feature
Distr/Arch: fnc
Annotation: An updated version of <u>Girl</u> <u>Crazy</u> (1943)
   featuring Louis Armstrong as himself and with his
   songs/music.

WHEN_THE_WIND_BLOWS
Series: Our Gang
Nar/Cast: Our Gang + Allen Hoskins*
Screenplay: Robert F. McGowan
Producer: Robert F. McGowan + Hal Roach   Director: James W.
   Horne
Studio/Company: MGM
Tech Info: super 8 mm/16 mm/sound/bw/1 reel/20 min.
Date/Country: 1930 + USA   Type: Comedy Short
Distr/Arch: bla
Annotation: While Jackie and officer Kennedy chase real and
   phantom burglars, Farina appears in the ramshackle barn he
   calls home, tending baby brother with a contraption that
   rocks the cradle and spins a laundry line at the same
   time.   Farina is frightened by the wind and noise outside
   and at one point kid brother is doused with flour and
   frightens Farina even more as a 'ghost.'

WHEN_YOU_HIT,_HIT_HARD
Nar/Cast: Ebony Players*
Studio/Company: Ebony Film Corporation
Date/Country: 1918 + USA

WHERE_IS_JIM_CROW?
Producer: KQED
Tech Info: 16 mm/sound/bw/30 min.
Date/Country: 1964 + USA   Type: TV Documentary
Distr/Arch: uca
Annotation: A series of 5 "conversations", 30 minutes each,
   with: Brock Peters*, Godfrey Cambridge*, Lena Horne*,
   Nancy Wilson*, Stokely Carmichael* covering such subjects
   as: the problems of the black entertainer, the role of
   black women in film and television, the civil rights move-
   ment, class implications of violence. Available
   separately.

WHERE_IS_MY_MAN_TONIGHT?
Date/Country: 194- + USA

WHERE_IS_PREJUDICE?
Producer: NET
Tech Info: 16 mm/bw/sound/2 reels/60 min.
Date/Country: 1967 + USA   Type: Documentary
Distr/Arch: iu
Annotation: Shows twelve college students of different races
   and faiths participating in a week-long workshop to test
   their common denial of prejudice. Reveals latent
   prejudices by candid discussion and questioning. Relates

how the participants are unable to cope with this revela-
tion.

WHERE'S POPPA?
Nar/Cast: George Segal + Ruth Gordon + Garrett Morris* + Ron
  Leibman + Paul Sorvino + Joe Keyes, Jr.*
Screenplay: Robert Klane
Producer: Jerry Tokofsky + Marvin Worth   Director: Carl
  Reiner
Studio/Company: United Artists
Tech Info: 16 mm/sound/color/87 min.
Date/Country: 1970 + USA   Type: Feature
Distr/Arch: uas
Annotation: George Segal is a small time New York lawyer who
  has a mother he wants to put in an old folk's home but
  can't. He tries to scare her to death, but she won't
  scare. Garrett Morris is Garrett.

WHICH WAY IS UP?
Nar/Cast: Richard Pryor* + Lonette McKee* + Margaret Avery*
  + Marilyn Coleman* + Danny Valdez*
Screenplay: Carl Gottlieb + Cecil Brown*   Director: Michael
  Schultz*
Studio/Company: Universal
Tech Info: 16 mm/sound/color/94 min.
Date/Country: 1977 + USA   Type: Feature
Distr/Arch: swa
Annotation: A remake of Lena Wertmuller's comedy, The Seduc-
  tion of Mimi. Pryor plays an orange picker Leroy Jones,
  his father, and a preacher. He has both a wife and a
  mistress and there are numerous opportunities for him to
  perform, playing three roles: Leroy Jones, Rufus Jones,
  and Rev. Lenox Thomas.

WHILE THOUSANDS CHEER
Alt Title(s): Crooked Money
Nar/Cast: Kenny Washington* + Gladys Snyder* + Jeni LeGon* +
  Florence O'Brien* + Ida Belle* + Mantan Moreland* +
  Reginald Fenderson* + Lawrence Criner* + Monte Hawley* +
  Edward Thompson* + Lena Torrance* + Joel Fluellen* + Harry
  Lavette*
Studio/Company: Million Dollar Productions
Date/Country: 1940 + USA   Type: Feature
Annotation: Kenny Washington, former football all-American
  stars in this film about attempted corruption of the sport
  and the players. This may also have been released under
  Gridiron Graft.

WHISPERING GHOSTS
Nar/Cast: Milton Berle + Brenda Joyce + Willie Best*
Screenplay: Lou Breslow   Story: Phillip McDonald
Producer: Sol M. Wurtzel   Director: Alfred Werker
Studio/Company: 20th Century Fox
Tech Info: 16 mm/sound/bw/75 min.
Date/Country: 1942 + USA   Type: Feature
Distr/Arch: fnc
Annotation: An assortment of wierd characters, including
  Milton Berle, board the wrecked hulk of a ship looking for

a lost treasure. Willie Best, Berle's valet Euclid White,
is among them.

WHITE CARGO
Nar/Cast: Hedy Lamarr + Walter Pidgeon + Frank Morgan +
    Oscar Polk* + Leigh Whipper* + Darby Jones*
Screenplay: Leon Gordon   Story: Ida Vera Simonton (novel)
Producer: Victor Saville   Director: Richard Thorpe
Studio/Company: MGM
Tech Info: 16 mm/bw/sound/90 min.
Date/Country: 1942 + USA   Type: Feature
Distr/Arch: fnc
Annotation: Hedy Lamarr plays the dark-skinned Tondeleyo who
    drives white men wild in Africa, if "dry-rot" doesn't get
    them first.   Leigh Whipper plays Jim Fish; Oscar Polk,
    Umeela. Darby Jones is the Doctor's (Frank Morgan's)
    houseboy.   Gypsy Rhouma played Tondeleyo in the 1930
    version.

WHITE DAWN
Nar/Cast: Lou Gossett* + Warren Oates + Timothy Bottoms +
    Simonie Kopapik   Director: Philip Kaufman
Studio/Company: Paramount
Tech Info: 16 mm/sound/color/110 min./3 reels
Date/Country: 1974 + USA   Type: Feature
Distr/Arch: fnc
Annotation: A true adventure of 80 years ago relates the
    ultimately tragic adoption by native Eskimos of three
    marooned whalers, one of whom is played by Lou Gossett.
    Feelings of mutual curiosity and fear slowly turn to trust
    and   warmth then degenerate to mistrust and finally
    vengeance as the two alien cultures threaten each other.

WHITE HUNTER
Nar/Cast: Warner Baxter + June Lang + Wilfrid Lawson + Gail
    Patrick + Alison Skipworth + Ernest Whitman* + Ralph
    Cooper*
Screenplay: Sam Duncan + Kenneth Earl   Director: Irving
    Cummings
Studio/Company: 20th Century Fox
Date/Country: 1936 + USA   Type: Feature
Annotation: Shot on location in California, this "African"
    film has the white hunter (Baxter) leading a safari which
    includes the man who hounded him out of England (Lawson)
    and his former love (Lawson's wife) and the young woman
    with whom he falls in love (Lawson's daughter).   Ernest
    Whitman plays Ahdi and Ralph Cooper is Ali in this
    "jungle" melodrama.

WHITE MAN'S COWBOY
Series: Kenya Trilogy
Producer: Anthony-David Productions
Tech Info: 16 mm/sound/color/1 reel/28 min.
Date/Country: 1973 + Kenya   Type: Documentary
Distr/Arch: fnc
Annotation: Depicts through interviews colonial attitudes
    during the British East Africa period with African respon-
    se/reactions.

WHITE_ROSE,_THE
Nar/Cast: Lucille La Verne + Mae Marsh + Porter Strong
Screenplay: Irene Sinclair (pseudonym for D.W. Griffith)
Producer: D.W. Griffith   Director: D.W. Griffith
Studio/Company: United Artists
Tech Info: 16 mm/silent/bw/120 min.
Date/Country: 1922 + USA   Type: Feature
Distr/Arch: moma
Annotation: Blacks (real and simulated) have an important
    role in this film about a young woman who has an il-
    legitimate child by a pastor whose Christian spirit seems
    missing. "Auntie" Easter and Apollo, (Lucille LaVerne and
    Porter Strong in black face) care for Bessie Williams (Mae
    Marsh).   In fact they are the real Christians who, along
    with a gospel choir, help her back to health.

WHITE_WITCH_DOCTOR
War/Cast: Susan Hayward + Robert Mitchum + Mashood Ajala* +
    Joseph C. Narcisse* + Elzie Emanuel* + Everett Brown* +
    Otis Greene*
Screenplay: Ivan Goff + Ben Roberts
Producer: Otto Lang   Director: Henry Hathaway
Studio/Company: 20th Century Fox
Tech Info: sound/color
Date/Country: 1953 + USA   Type: Feature
Annotation: Filmed in the Congo, White_Witch_Doctor is the
    story of a wife of a missionary doctor who wants to stay
    in Africa to continue the work of her dead husband and a
    white hunter who wants to find a way out of Africa.
    Everett Brown is the Bakuba king; Otis Greene, Bakuba boy;
    Mashood Ajala, Jacques the gunbearer.

WHITE_ZOMBIE
War/Cast: Bela Lugosi + Madge Bellamy + John Harron + Joseph
    Cawthorn + Robert Frazer + Clarence Muse*
Screenplay: Garnett Weston   Story: Garnett Weston
    Director: Victor Halperin
Studio/Company: United Artists
Tech Info: 8 mm/16 mm/sound/2 reels/68 min.
Date/Country: 1932 + USA   Type: Feature
Distr/Arch: bud + emg + fnc + kpf + mac + swa + tmc + unf +
    wcf + who + csv + man + ncs + nil
Annotation: The story deals with the occult practices in a
    remote section of Haiti, where the dead are dug up from
    their graves and by a process of sorcery, reanimated and
    put to work in the fields and sugar mills as slaves.

WHO_DO_YOU_KILL?
Producer: CBS
Tech Info: 16 mm/sound/bw/2 reels/50 min.
Date/Country: USA   Type: Dramatized Documentary
Distr/Arch: iu + carouf
Annotation: Dramatizes events resulting from a Negro child
    being bitten by a rat in a slum neighborhood. Depicts the
    filth in which the tenement dwellers of Harlem live.
    Shows the difficulties experienced by blacks seeking em-
    ployment.

WHO KILLED AUNT MAGGIE?
Nar/Cast: Willie Best* + Edgar Kennedy   Director: Arthur
    Lubin
Studio/Company: Republic
Tech Info: 16 mm/sound/bw/54 min.
Date/Country: 1940 + USA   Type: Feature
Distr/Arch: ivy
Annotation: Best has some comedy lines in this George
    Kennedy mystery comedy.

WHO KILLED COCK ROBIN?   Director: Walt Disney
Tech Info: sound/color
Date/Country: 1935 + USA   Type: Animated Short
Annotation: This Disney cartoon was on the National Board of
    Review's list of ten best films. It satirized many of the
    famous, including Stepin Fetchit who is roughed up by two
    scarecrow cops because he is suspected of murder
    (Robin's).

WHO'S WHO IN COLORED AMERICA
Studio/Company: Toddy Pictures
Date/Country: 194-   Type: Documentary

WHOOPEE
Nar/Cast: Eddie Cantor   Story: Florenz Ziegfeld   Director:
    Thornton Freeland
Studio/Company: MGM
Date/Country: 1930 + USA   Type: Feature
Annotation: Eddie Cantor as the "nervous wreck" emerges from
    his momentary oven hiding place blackfaced a la minstrel
    routine in this filmed version of a Flo Ziegfeld produc-
    tion.

WHOOPIN' THE BLUES, SONNY TERRY
Producer: Jack Agins   Director: Jack Agins + Rick Paup
Tech Info: 16 mm/sound/color/14 min.
Date/Country: 1969 + USA   Type: Documentary
Distr/Arch: ppl
Annotation: Sonny Terry* sings, tells stories about his
    life, plays some of his own compositions for blues
    harmonica in Oakland, California.

WHY BRING THAT UP?
Nar/Cast: George Moran + Charles Mack + Evelyn Brent
    Story: Octavus Roy Cohen   Director: George Abbott
Studio/Company: Paramount
Tech Info: 35 mm/sound/bw
Date/Country: 1929 + USA   Type: Feature
Annotation: The recording stars and ex-minstrel team, Moran
    and Mack (known as the two "Black Crows"), bring their
    burnt cork routine to film for the first time in this
    musical comedy-drama titled for one one of their catch
    lines.

WHY WORRY?
Nar/Cast: Byron Smith* + Mae Morris* + Frank Brown*
Studio/Company: Lone Star Motion Picture Company

Tech Info: bw/silent
Date/Country: 1923 + USA   Type: Comedy Short
Annotation: An ingenious brother and sister come to the city
   for the first time. Their naivete gets them into comic
   but also romantic situations.

WIDOW'S_BITE,_THE
Series: Christie Comedy
Nar/Cast: Spencer Williams* + Evelyn Preer* + Edward Thompson*
Screenplay: Octavus Roy Cohen + Spencer Williams*
Producer: Al Christie
Studio/Company: Paramount
Tech Info: 35 mm/bw/sound/2 reels
Date/Country: 1929 + USA   Type: Comedy Short
Annotation: One of the Christie series done in "Negro dialect."

WIFE_HUNTERS,_THE
Nar/Cast: Bob White* + Jessie Purty* + Edward Townsend* + V.
   Stevens* + P. Massey* + H.C. Grant* + J.T. Walton* + J.G.
   Selby*
Studio/Company: Lone Star Motion Picture Company
Tech Info: 35 mm/silent/bw
Date/Country: 1922 + USA   Type: Feature
Annotation: This story of black life was filmed on location
   in Vicksburg, Mississippi.

WIGGLE_YOUR_EARS
Series: Our Gang
Nar/Cast: Our Gang + Allen Hoskins*
Screenplay: Robert F. McGowan
Producer: Robert F. McGowan + Hal Roach   Director: Robert
   McGowan
Studio/Company: MGM + Roach
Tech Info: super 8 mm/16 mm/bw/silent/1 reel
Date/Country: 1929 + USA   Type: Comedy Short
Distr/Arch: bla
Annotation: Joe would like to get the same attention Mary
   lavishes on Harry because he can wiggle his ears. After
   Harry leaves Mary for Jean, Joe gets his chance and with
   some mechanical assistance wiggles his way into Mary's
   heart. Allen Hoskins stars as Farina.

WILBY_CONSPIRACY,_THE
Nar/Cast: Sidney Poitier* + Michael Caine + Nicol Williamson
   + Prunella Gee* + Saaed Joffrey* + Persis Khambatta*
Screenplay: Rod Amateau + Harold Nebenzal
Producer: Martin Baum   Director: Ralph Nelson
Studio/Company: United Artists
Tech Info: 16 mm/sound/color/3 reels/105 min.
Date/Country: 1975 + USA
Distr/Arch: uas
Annotation: Set in South Arica this melodrama revolves
   around the conflict between those who uphold apartheid and
   others who aid fugitives to fight it. Caine accidentally
   becomes involved in assisting Poitier, one of the fugitives.

WILD IN THE COUNTRY
Nar/Cast: Rafer Johnson* + Elvis Presley + Hope Lang
Screenplay: Clifford Odets   Story: J.R.Salamanea
Producer: Jerry Wald   Director: Philip Dunne
Studio/Company: Fox
Tech Info: 16 mm/sound/color/114 min.
Date/Country: 1962 + USA   Type: Feature
Distr/Arch: mac + mod + sel + wil
Annotation: Elvis Presley is a young man with problems who
   goes from jail to parole to romance and college, the lat-
   ter two under the tutelage of Hope Lange. Rafer Johnson
   in a small role plays Davis.

WILD IN THE STREETS
Nar/Cast: Richard Pryor* + Shelley Winters + Christopher
   Jones + Diane Varsi
Screenplay: Robert Thorn   Story: Robert Thorn
Producer: Samuel Z. Arkoff   Director: Barry Shear
Studio/Company: American International Pictures
Tech Info: 16 mm/sound/color/96 min.
Date/Country: 1968 + USA   Type: Feature
Distr/Arch: arg + bud + ccc + cha + cwf + mac + mod + mot +
   sel + tfc + unf + wcf + wel + who + wil
Annotation: Drama about the explosive movement of the young
   to win the vote at age 15 and take over the U.S. govern-
   ment, with the "older generation" forcibly retired at age
   35. Richard Pryor is "Stanley X."

WILD POSES
Series: Our Gang
Nar/Cast: Our Gang + Matthew Beard*
Producer: Robert F. McGowan + Hal Roach   Director: Robert
   F. mcGowan
Studio/Company: MGM + Roach
Tech Info: super 8 mm/16 mm/bw/sound/1 reel/20 min.
Date/Country: 1933 + USA   Type: Comedy Short
Distr/Arch: bla + roa
Annotation: Spanky foils a photographer's attempt to take
   his picture (helped by the gang), responding to the phot-
   ographer's pleas for cooperation with a punch in the nose.
   Matthew Beard stars as Stymie.

WILD RIVER
Nar/Cast: Montgomery Clift + Lee Remick + Robert Earl Jones*
   + Jo Van Fleet
Screenplay: Paul Osborn
Producer: Elia Kazan   Director: Elia Kazan
Studio/Company: 20th Century Fox
Tech Info: 16 mm/color/sound/115 min.
Date/Country: 1960 + USA   Type: Feature
Distr/Arch: fnc
Annotation: In this, movie about the South and how it was
   affected by the coming of the TVA in the early thirties,
   Kazan focuses on the economic and social upheaval it
   caused using as a specific example, Ella Garth (Van
   Fleet), an octogenarian who refuses to move even though
   she will be flooded out. Robert Earl Jones plays Ben, a

dignified farmhand, who insists on staying by her side.

WILLIAM ABRAHAM*
Series: African Writers of Today
Producer: NET
Tech Info: 16 /sound/bw/1 reel/29 min.   Type: Documentary
Distr/Arch: iu
Annotation: Presents Nkosi* and Soyinka* in Accra inter-
    viewing Professor Abraham, philosopher and author of The
    Mind of Africa. Focuses in detail on the function of the
    writer in Africa.

WILLIAM: FROM GEORGIA TO HARLEM
Series: The Many Americans
Producer: Universal Creative Personal and Arts Guild
Tech Info: 16 mm/sound/color/15 min.
Date/Country: 1969 + USA   Type: Documentary
Distr/Arch: lec
Annotation: The adjustment of a black youth as a result of
    migration to the North.

WILLIE CATCHES ON
Studio/Company: McGraw Hill
Tech Info: 16 mm/sound/color/15 min.   Type: Documentary
Distr/Arch: roa
Annotation: The story of how a sense of discrimination is
    developed early in life, and how to adjust to a society
    with a double standard, one for Whites the other for
    Blacks.

WILLIE DYNAMITE
Nar/Cast: Roscoe Oiman* + Diana Sands* + Thalmus Rasulala* +
    Joyce Walker*
Screenplay: Ron Cutler
Producer: Richad Zanuck + David Brown   Director: Gilbert
    Moses*
Studio/Company: Universal + 16 + 16 mm/sound/color/4
    reels/102 min. + 17 + 1974 + USA   Type: Feature
Distr/Arch: uni + cwf + twy + wow
Annotation: The movie, in which the title character is a
    pimp in New York City, makes a serious effort to under-
    stand the code of the streets and the day-to-day struggle
    of the people who live there. This was Diana Sands' last
    movie. Music score by J.J. Johnson*.

WILMA
Nar/Cast: Shirley Jo Finney*
Screenplay: Bud Greenspan   Story: Bud Greenspan (book,
    Wilma)
Producer: Bud Greenspan + NBC-TV   Director: Bud Greenspan
Studio/Company: NBC-TV
Tech Info: sound/color
Date/Country: 1977 + USA   Type: Feature
Annotation: Film biography of Wilma Rudolph who conquered a
    childhood polio affliction to win three gold medals as a
    runner in the 1960 Olympics.

WILMINGTON

Producer: San Francisco Newsreel
Tech Info: 16 mm/sound/bw/15 min.
Date/Country: 1968 + USA   Type: Documentary
Distr/Arch: twn
Annotation: Unrest in the state of Delaware after the death
   of Martin Luther King.

WINGS FOR THIS MAN
Studio/Company: Army Air Force Productions
Date/Country: 1944 + USA
Annotation: Filmed at Tuskegee Army Air Field, Alabama,
   Blacks in the Army Air Force.

WINGS OVER HONOLULU
Nar/Cast: Wendy Barrie + Ray Milland + Louise Beavers*
Screenplay: Isabel Dawn + Boyce de Gau   Story: Mildred Cram
Producer: E.M. Asher   Director: H.C. Potter
Studio/Company: Universal
Date/Country: 1937 + USA   Type: Feature
Annotation: The tedium and boredom of being a Navy wife is
   depicted in this film, as a young newlywed must cope with
   loneliness while her husband is out flying in war games.
   Louise Beavers gets screen credit as "Mammy."

WINNER TAKE ALL
Nar/Cast: Clarence Muse* + James Cagney + Marian Nixon
   Story: Gerald Beaumont   Director: Roy Del Ruth
Studio/Company: Warners
Tech Info: 16 mm/sound/bw/66 min.
Date/Country: 1933 + USA   Type: Feature
Distr/Arch: uas
Annotation: Cagney plays a boxer through various ups and
   downs with Clarence Muse as his trainer.

WITH JUST A LITTLE TRUST
Studio/Company: Teleketus
Tech Info: 16 mm/sound/color/15 min.   Type: Documentary
Distr/Arch: roa
Annotation: The relationship between a mother and her grown
   daughter under the stresses and strains of harsh, ghetto
   life is depicted.

WITHIN OUR GATES
Nar/Cast: Evelyn Preer* + Lawrence Chenault* + William
   Starks* + Mattie Edwards* + E.G. Tatum* + Grant Edwards* +
   Charles Lucan*   Director: Oscar Micheaux*
Studio/Company: Micheaux Film Corporation
Date/Country: 1920 + USA   Type: Feature
Annotation: The film has as its plot the murder of Philip
   Girdlestone, presumably by Jasper Landry, a share cropper,
   or so one of the characters attests. Micheaux included a
   vivid lynching scene, which caused some controversy.

WITHOUT LOVE
Nar/Cast: Spencer Tracy + Katherine Hepburn + Nina Mae McK-
   inney*
Screenplay: Donald Ogden Stewart
Producer: Lawrence A. Weingarten   Director: Harold S. Buc-

quet
Studio/Company: MGM
Tech Info: 111 min.
Date/Country: 1945 + USA   Type: Feature
Annotation: a Tracy-Hepburn comedy based on the Philip Barry
   play, with an appearance by Nina Mae McKinney.

WITHOUT_PITY
Alt Title(s): see Senza Pieta

WITNESS:_A_TESTAMENT_OF_APARTHEID_IN_SOUTH_AFRICA
Producer: Knight Films
Tech Info: 16 mm/sound/color/30 min.*english narration
Date/Country: 1971 + South Africa + England   Type: Docu-
   mentary
Distr/Arch: tri
Annotation: This film introduces the effects of the racist
   policy of apartheid for the dispossessed majority of
   Blacks and other colored citizens and also includes a re-
   enactment, intercut with photos of the actual event, of
   the 1960 Sharpeville massacre.

WOMAN_FROM_MONTE_CARLO,_THE
Nar/Cast: Lil Dagover + Clarence Muse* + Walter Huston +
   Warren William + Dewey Robinson Story: Georges Nepoty +
   Claude Farrere   Director: Michael Curtiz
Studio/Company: First National
Date/Country: 1931 + USA   Type: Feature
Annotation: Lil Dagover plays the wife of a naval captain
   accidentally caught on board ship when it is attacked -
   her testimony of the occurence which caused the loss of
   lives and the ship exonerates her husband, but scuttles
   her marriage. Dewey Robinson plays the cook.

WOMAN_GOD_CHANGED,_THE
Nar/Cast: Seena Owen + E.K. Lincoln + Henry Sedley + Lillian
   Walker* + H. Cooper Cliffe   Director: Robert G. Vignola
Studio/Company: Cosmopolitan Prod.
Tech Info: 35 mm/silent/bw/7 reels
Date/Country: 1921 + USA   Type: Feature
Annotation: Melodrama told in flashbacks by a black maid.
   The story line involves a dancer who shoots her common-law
   husband for his dalliance with a chorus girl.

WOMAN'S_A_FOOL
Nar/Cast: Jean LaRue* + Alabama Blossom* + Birdina Hackett*
   + Billy Fuller* + Hollywood Jitterbugs* + Red Calhoun* and
   his Band* + Ida Cox*
Studio/Company: Astor Pictures
Date/Country: 194- + USA

WOMAN'S_PRISONER
Nar/Cast: Ida Lupino + Jan Sterling + Juanita Moore* + Cleo
   Moore
Screenplay: Crane Wilbur + Jack DeWitt
Producer: Bryan Foy   Director: Lewis Seiler
Studio/Company: Columbia
Date/Country: 1955 + USA   Type: Feature

Annotation: Tensions at a woman's prison erupt in predictable violence. Juanita Moore plays "Polyclinic" Jones and
Ida Lupino is the callous superintendent.

WOMAN'S_WORST_ENEMY,_A
Studio/Company: Foster Photoplay Company
Date/Country: 191- + USA

WOMEN_AT_THE_TOP
Producer: Canadian Broadcasting Corp. + UNESCO + Leo Rampen
Tech Info: 16 mm/sound/color/1 reel/26 min.
Date/Country: 1967 + Cameroun + Nigeria   Type: Documentary
Distr/Arch: usunesco + mghf
Annotation: Three "well-educated" women in West Africa dis-
cuss their lives.

WOMEN_OF_THE_TOUBOU
Producer: Anne Balfour-Fraser
Tech Info: 16 mm/sound/color/1 reel/25 min.
Date/Country: 1974 + Chad   Type: Documentary
Annotation: Filmed for the first time, the women of the
nomadic Toubou are shown as respected and admired equals
within their tribal community.

WOMEN,_THE
Nar/Cast: Norma Shearer + Joan Crawford + Butterfly McQueen*
+ Rosalind Russell
Screenplay: Anita Loos + Jane Murfin
Producer: Hunt Stromberg   Director: George Cukor
Studio/Company: MGM
Tech Info: 16 mm/sound/bw/134 min.
Date/Country: 1939 + USA   Type: Feature
Distr/Arch: fnc
Annotation: Butterfly McQueen is scarcely noticed among this
Park Avenue collection of females at each other's throats
in this adaptation of Clare Booth's highly successful
Broadway comedy.

WONDER_BAR
Nar/Cast: Al Jolson + Kay Francis   Story: Geza Herczeg
Director: Lloyd Bacon
Studio/Company: 1st National
Tech Info: 16 mm/sound/bw/84 min.
Date/Country: 1934 + USA   Type: Feature
Distr/Arch: uas
Annotation: Musical that has Jolson in blackface going to
black heaven, complete with black St. Peter, angels and
black Gabriel.

WOODCUTTERS_OF_THE_DEEP_SOUTH
Producer: Lionel Rogosin
Tech Info: 16 mm/sound/color/90 min.
Date/Country: 1973 + USA   Type: Documentary
Distr/Arch: imp
Annotation: The paper and pulpwood workers unite to overcome
racism in the company headquartered in Mississippi and
Alabama.

WOODEN GIRAFFE, THE
Producer: Kerwin Duffy Productions
Tech Info: 16 mm/sound/color/1 reel/26 min.
Date/Country: 1967   Type: Documentary
Distr/Arch: iu
Annotation: Presents the story of African woodcarving art in
    Zambia, featuring carvings done by the natives of Barot-
    seland. Highlights other aspects of African culture.

WOODPILE, THE
Producer: Paulist Productions
Tech Info: 16 mm/sound/bw/29 min.
Date/Country: 1965 + USA   Type: Documentary
Distr/Arch: aim
Annotation: The decision to hire the company's first black
    executive is the problem confronted in this film.

WOOING AND WEDDING OF A COON, THE
Date/Country: 1905 + USA   Type: Comedy Short
Annotation: Two actors in blackface in an early derisive
    depiction of a newlywed Negro couple.

WORDS AND MUSIC
Nar/Cast: Mickey Rooney + Tom Drake + Lena Horne* + Judy
    Garland
Screenplay: Fred Finklehoff   Story: Guy Bolton
Producer: Arthur Freed   Director: Norman Tunrog
Studio/Company: MGM
Tech Info: 16 mm/sound/color/100 min.
Date/Country: 1948 + USA   Type: Feature
Distr/Arch: fnc
Annotation: Musical biography of the song writers Rodgers
    and Hart featuring many top MGM stars, including Lena
    Horne.

WORLD MOVES ON, THE
Nar/Cast: Stepin Fetchit* + Madeline Carroll + Franchot Tone
    + Louise Dresser + Dudley Diggs   Story: Reginald Berkeley
        Director: John Ford
Studio/Company: Fox
Tech Info: 16 mm/sound/bw/90 min.
Date/Country: 1934 + USA   Type: Feature
Distr/Arch: fnc
Annotation: An anti-war epic that spans a century (1825-
    1925), World begins and ends in New Orleans. In one scene
    Fetchit is drafted into the French army because of a mis-
    understanding.

WORLD OF JULIAN BOND, THE
Producer: NET
Tech Info: 16 mm/bw/sound/1 reel/11 min.
Date/Country: 1968   Type: Documentary
Distr/Arch: iu
Annotation: Reviews the career of Julien Bond*, of the Ge-
    orgia legislature. Discusses Bond's protest candidacy at
    the Democratic National Convention in 1968 as he became
    the first black man nominated for the vice presidency.

WORLD, THE FLESH, AND THE DEVIL, THE
Nar/Cast: Harry Belafonte* + Inger Stevens + Mel Ferrer
  Director: RandallMcDougall
Studio/Company: MGM
Tech Info: 16 mm/sound/bw/3 reels/95 min.
Date/Country: 1959 + USA   Type: Feature
Distr/Arch: fnc
Annotation: After a nuclear war, only 3 people are left, a
  black man, a white woman, a white man. The struggle for
  the girl is set against a bleak, deserted New York City.

WRONG ALL AROUND
Nar/Cast: Ebony Players*
Studio/Company: Ebony Film Corporation
Date/Country: 1917 + USA

WRONG MR. JOHNSON
Studio/Company: Lone Star Motion Picture Company
Date/Country: 1922 + USA

WRONG MR. RIGHT, THE
Nar/Cast: Dewey "Pigmeat" Markham* + John Murray
Date/Country: 194- + USA

WUSA
Nar/Cast: Paul Newman + Moses Gunn* + Joanne Woodward +
  Anthony Perkins
Screenplay: Robert Stone
Producer: Paul Newman + John Foreman   Director: Stuart
  Rosenberg
Studio/Company: Paramount
Tech Info: 16 mm/sound/color/115 min.
Date/Country: 1970 + USA   Type: Feature
Distr/Arch: fnc
Annotation: Newman as an itinerant radio announcer who gets
  a job on a super patriotic southern radio station. Moses
  Gunn plays a hood. Apperance by Preservation Hall Jazz
  Band*.

XALA
Nar/Cast: Thierno Leye* + Seum Samb*
Screenplay: Ousman Sembena*   Story: Ousmane Sembene* +
  Youngousse* + Seye* + Diaynaba Dieng* + Makhouredia
  Grieye* + Miriam Niang*
Producer: Societe Nationale Cinematographie   Director:
  Ousmane Sembene*
Tech Info: 16 mm/sound/color/4 reels/123 min./Wolof and
  French with English subtitles
Date/Country: 1975 + Senegal   Type: Feature
Distr/Arch: nyf
Annotation: The Africa depicted in Xala is rendered im-
  potent-- cursed by the residue of Colonialism as is El
  Hadji Abdoukader Beye, the middle-aged protagonist who
  cannot consummate his third marriage. This satire of
  neo-colonialism in post-independence Africa is Sembene's
  fourth feature film.

XAVIER UNIVERSITY, AMERICA'S ONLY CATHOLIC COLLEGE FOR NEGRO

YOUTH
Series: National Archives Gift Collection
Tech Info: 16 mm/silent/1 reel/bw
Annotation: Surveys the range of facilities at Xavier, type
    of student and social life in informal, journalistic style
    without attempting a specific theme. (Part of Record
    Group 200 HF series, Harmon Foundation Collection).

YALE VS. HARVARD
Series: Our Gang
Nar/Cast: Our Gang + Allen Hoskins* + Jannie Hoskins*
Producer: Hal Roach   Director: Robert F. McGowan
Studio/Company: MGM
Tech Info: bw/silent/2 reels
Date/Country: 1927 + USA   Type: Comedy Short
Annotation: The gang faces tough football competition again-
    st the gas house team. Allen Hoskins stars as Farina and
    Jannie Hoskins stars as Mango.

YAMACRAW
Nar/Cast: James P. Johnson* + Jimmy Mordecai*   Director:
    Murray Roth
Studio/Company: Vitaphone
Date/Country: 1930 + USA   Type: Musical Short
Annotation: A vignette of black life--the dilemma sur-
    rounding the move from country to city, leaving the secur-
    ity of the known for the uncertain promise of opportunity
    ahead. Music by James P. Johnson.

YAMBA
Alt Title(s): see Baks

YANKEE CLIPPER, THE
Nar/Cast: William Boyd + Elinor Fair + Walter Long + Zack
    Williams*   Director: Rupert Julian
Date/Country: 1927 + USA   Type: Feature
Annotation: Zack Williams has a small part as a cook aboard
    The Yankee Clipper which, under the command of William
    Boyd, bests the British vessel in a race from China to
    Boston.

YE OLDE MINSTRELS
Series: Our Gang
Nar/Cast: Our Gang + Billie Thomas*
Screenplay: Sam Baerwitz
Producer: MGM   Director: Edward Cahn + Bud Murray
Studio/Company: MGM
Tech Info: bw/sound/1 reel
Date/Country: 1941 + USA   Type: Comedy Short
Annotation: The gang puts on a minstrel show to raise money
    for the Red Cross. Billie Thomas stars as Buckwheat.

YEARS OF RECONSTRUCTION, 1865-1877, THE
Series: American History
Producer: McGraw Hill
Tech Info: 16 mm/sound/color/1 reel/25 min.
Date/Country: 1968 + USA   Type: Documentary
Distr/Arch: iu + mghf

Annotation: Shows the economic, social, and political problems which faced the South after the Civil War. Concludes with the compromise election of 1876 where Hayes
   was elected president with the understanding that federal
   troops would be withdrawn from the South

YES SIR, MR. BONES
Nar/Cast: Monette Moore*   Director: Ron Ormond
Tech Info: 54 min.
Date/Country: 1951 + USA
Annotation: Concerns showboat minstrels and features the
   vocalist Monette Moore.

YONDER COME DAY
Producer: Milton Fruchtman
Tech Info: 16 mm/sound/color/51 min.
Date/Country: 1974   Type: Documentary
Distr/Arch: capc
Annotation: Bessie Jones* shares slave songs and games with
   Yale University students: they in turn share with students
   in the New Haven schools.

YOU CAN'T CATCH IT
Producer: Education Development Center
Tech Info: 16 mm/sound/color/40 min.
Date/Country: 1973 + USA   Type: Documentary
Distr/Arch: afr
Annotation: Informational film about sickle cell anemia.

YOU CAN'T CHEAT AN HONEST MAN
Nar/Cast: W.C. Fields + Eddie Anderson* + Edgar Bergen +
   Constance Moore   Story: Charles Bogle + W.C. Fields
Producer: Lester Cowen   Director: George Marshall
Studio/Company: Universal
Tech Info: 16 mm/sound/bw/74 min.
Date/Country: 1939 + USA   Type: Feature
Distr/Arch: cwf + swa + twy + uni
Annotation: Anderson plays "Cheerful," a minor circus pro-
   prietor, in this comedy in which Fields plays Whipsnade,
   the circus performer. His troupe also includes McCarthy
   and Bergen who are a continuous trial to him. Whipsnade
   is a blusterer who listens to no one, and Cheerful is able
   to watch the police close in on the boss after he has
   refused to listen to Cheerful's warning.

YOU CAN'T KEEP A GOOD MAN DOWN
Studio/Company: Lone Star Motion Picture Company
Date/Country: 1922 + USA

YOU CAN'T RUN AWAY FROM IT
Nar/Cast: Louise Beavers*   Director: Dick Powell
Date/Country: 1956 + USA   Type: Feature

YOU CAN'T TAKE IT WITH YOU
Nar/Cast: Jean Arthur + Lionel Barrymore + James Stewart +
   Edward Arnold + Mischa Auer + Ann Miller + Spring Byington
   + Donald Meek + Lillian Yarbo* + Eddie Anderson* + Robert
   "Smokey" Whitfield*

Screenplay: Robert Riskin   Story: George S. Kaufmann + Moss
    Hart
Producer: Frank Capra   Director: Frank Capra
Studio/Company: Columbia
Tech Info: 16 mm/sound/bw/127 min.
Date/Country: 1938 + USA   Type: Feature
Distr/Arch: mac
Annotation: Movie based on a Moss Hart - George Kaufmann
    play about what happens when two eccentric families meet
    to celebrate an engagement. Lillian Yarbo plays Rheba;
    Eddie Anderson plays Donald.

YOU DIG IT
Screenplay: Leon Williams*
Producer: Mobilization for Youth   Director: Richard Mason*
Tech Info: 16 mm/bw/sound/1 reel/28 min.
Date/Country: 1969 + USA   Type: Dramatic Short
Distr/Arch: kpf
Annotation: An all-Black production, including direction,
    photography and sound by students of the Cultural Arts and
    Education Program (under the direction of Woodie King*)
    shows New York's Lower East Side from the inside.

YOU HIDE ME   Director: Kwate Nee-Owoo*
Tech Info: 16 mm/sound/20 min./bw/English narration
Date/Country: 1972 + Britain   Type: Feature
Distr/Arch: tri
Annotation: The first film on African art to be produced by
    an African film-maker, You Hide Me deals with the cultural
    agression waged by European colonial regimes in Africa.

YOU MUST BE JOKING!
War/Cast: Tracy Reed* + Terry Thomas + Lionel Jeffries
Screenplay: Alan Hackney
Producer: Charles Schneer   Director: Michael Winner
Studio/Company: Columbia
Tech Info: 16 mm/sound/bw/100 min.
Date/Country: 1965 + Britain   Type: Feature
Distr/Arch: roa + twy
Annotation: Tracy Reed is Poppy Pennington in this farce
    about "initiation" rites for service men in the British
    Army Medical Corps.

YOU'RE OUT OF LUCK
War/Cast: Frankie Darro + Mantan Moreland*   Director:
    Howard Bretherton
Date/Country: 1941 + USA   Type: Feature
Annotation: See annotation for Chasing Trouble.

YOUNG AMERICA
War/Cast: Spencer Tracy + Doris Kenyon + Louise Beavers* +
    Tommy Coulon
Screenplay: John F. Ballard   Director: Frank Borzage
Studio/Company: Fox Film Corporation
Tech Info: sound/bw
Date/Country: 1932 + USA   Type: Feature
Annotation: Spencer Tracy and his wife take in a young boy
    who has a few brushes with the law and help straighten him

out.   Louise Beavers plays the maid.

YOUNG MAN WITH A HORN
Nar/Cast: Kirk Douglas + Sammy Davis* + Lauren bacall +
   Juano Hernandez* + Louis Armstrong*
Screenplay: Carl Foreman + Ed Worth   Story: Dorothy Baker
Producer: Jerry Wald   Director: Michael Curtiz
Studio/Company: Warners
Tech Info: 16 mm/sound/bw/3 reels/111 min.
Date/Country: 1950 + USA   Type: Feature
Distr/Arch: arg + mac + who
Annotation: The world of the jazz musician is brought to the
   screen in the story of Rick Martin, Jazz trumpeter.   Kirk
   Douglas stars   as a Bix Beiderbecke- like character who un-
   compromisingly works to develop his artistry and technique
   in the up-hill climb to success and stardom, only to skid
   back down to the bottom following an unhappy marriage.
   Hernandez and Davis are featured as jazz musicians who
   influence Martin musically and are sympathetic to him.

YOUNG MR. LINCOLN
Nar/Cast: Henry Fonda + Alice Brady + Marjorie Weaver +
   Arleen Whelan   Director: John Ford
Studio/Company: Twentieth Century Fox
Tech Info: 16 mm/sound/bw/100 min.
Date/Country: 1939 + USA   Type: Feature
Distr/Arch: fnc
Annotation: Deals peripherally with the race problem as a
   part of the period.

YOUNG ONE, THE
Nar/Cast: Bernie Hamilton* + Zachary Scott + Leon Bibb* +
   Key Meersman
Screenplay: Luis Bunuel + H.B. Addis
Producer: George P. Werker   Director: Luis Bunuel
Studio/Company: Valiant Films
Date/Country: 1961 + Mexico   Type: Feature
Distr/Arch: mac
Annotation: Hamilton plays a jazz musician who escapes from
   a Southern town to a nearby island to avoid being lynched
   on a rape charge. There a young girl is attentive to him
   causing her guardian (Scott) to get jealous. Tensions
   mount when the guardian learns that Hamilton is a wanted
   man.

YOUNG PUSHKIN
Nar/Cast: V. Litovsky + L. Paramof + A. Aharazin   Director:
   Arady Narodistky
Studio/Company: Len Film
Date/Country: 1935 + Russian   Type: Feature
Annotation: Russian film with English subtitles, about Push-
   kin's life roughly covering the years, 1811-1817.

YOUNG RUNAWAYS, THE
Nar/Cast: James Edwards* + Isabell Sanford* + Kevin Coughlin
   + Patty McCormack
Screenplay: Orville Hampton
Producer: Sam Katzman   Director: Arthur Dreifuss

Studio/Company: MGM
Tech Info: 16 mm/sound/color/91 min.
Date/Country: 1968 + USA
Distr/Arch: fnc
Annotation: Edwards is Sgt. Joe Collyer and Sanford is Sarah
  in this melodrama about three teenagers who run away from
  home to Chicago's "hippie" district.

YOUNG SAVAGER, THE
Nar/Cast: Joel Fluellen* + Burt Lancaster + Shelley Winters
Screenplay: Edward Anholt
Producer: Pat Duggan   Director: John Frankenheimer
Studio/Company: United Artists
Tech Info: 16 mm/sound/bw/100 min.
Date/Country: 1961 + USA   Type: Feature
Distr/Arch: uas
Annotation: Fluellen is clerk of the court in this drama
  about a politically ambitious D.A. and his prosecutor who
  are forced to make serious ethical and moral decisions in
  the prosecution of three teenage Italian gang members ac-
  cused of stabbing to death a Puerto Rican boy.

YOUNG SHERLOCKS
Series: Our Gang
Nar/Cast: Our Gang + Ernie Morrison* + Allen Hoskins*
Screenplay: H. M. Walker
Producer: Hal Roach   Director: Robert McGowan
Studio/Company: Pathe
Tech Info: silent/bw/2 reels
Date/Country: 1922 + USA   Type: Comedy Short
Annotation: Ernie spins a tall tale of how he and Jackie
  solve a kidnapping and use the reward to set up
  'Freetown', a community just for kids.   Ernie Morrison
  stars as Sunshine Sammy and Allen Hoskins stars as Farina.

YOUNG WOMAN, THE
Alt Title(s): See Diankha-Bi

YOUNGBLOOD   Story: John O. Killens*
Annotation: This film deals with initiation, responsibility
  and the problem of identity within current black urban
  life.   It shows that Blacks in the urban ghetto have always been forced to view life on an adult level.

YOUR CHEATIN' hEART
Nar/Cast: Rex Ingram* + George Hamilton + Susan Oliver
Screenplay: Stanford Whitmore
Producer: Sam Katzman   Director: Gene Nelson
Studio/Company: MGM
Tech Info: 16mm/ sound/ bw/ 99 min.
Date/Country: 1964 + USA   Type: Feature
Distr/Arch: fnc
Annotation: Biographical drama about country and western
  singer Hank Williams, telling his rags to riches story and
  his problems with alcohol. Ingram appears in the prologue
  as Teetcs, an old man who befriends the orphaned Hank and
  teaches him the basics of music, singing, and guitar play-
  ing.

YOUR OWN BACK YARD
Series: Our Gang
Nar/Cast: Our Gang + Allen Hoskins*
Screenplay: Hal Roach
Producer: Hal Roach   Director: Robert McGowan
Studio/Company: Pathe
Tech Info: silent/bw/2 reels
Date/Country: 1925 + USA   Type: Comedy Short
Annotation: Farina (Allen Hoskins) stars as a lonely, 'dusky
    juevnile' whose attempts to play with his white
    counterparts are continually rebuffed. Pranks are played
    on him, like having him chased by toothpaste-mouthed dogs
    who look mad, but when finally he falls asleep, in a beg-
    gar's chair, he wakes with enough money to buy new
    clothes.

YOUTH TAKES A FLING
Nar/Cast: Joel McCrea + Andrea Leeds + Willie Best*
Screenplay: Myles Connolly
Producer: Joe Pasternak   Director: Archie Mayo
Studio/Company: Universal
Tech Info: sound/bw
Date/Country: 1938 + USA   Type: Feature
Annotation: Comedy about a woman (Andrea Leeds) who sets out
    to and gets her man, (Joel McCrea), a midwestern innocent.
    Willie Best has a bit role as George.

YWCA, HARLEM, NEW YORK
Series: National Archives Gift Collection
Tech Info: 16 mm/silent/1 reel/bw
Annotation: Part of Record Group 200 HF series, Harmon
    Foundation Collection.

ZACHARIAH
Nar/Cast: Don Johnson + John Rubenstein + Pat Quinn +
    Country Joe and the Fish + Elvin Jones*
Screenplay: Joe Massot + Phillip Austin + Peter Bergman +
    David Ossman + Philip Proctor
Producer: George Englund   Director: George Englund
Studio/Company: ABC Picture Corporation
Tech Info: 16 mm/sound/color/3 reels/92 min.
Date/Country: 1971 + USA   Type: Feature
Distr/Arch: fnc
Annotation: Parody of the Western genre includes homosexual
    overtures on the part of a gay old man who tries to dis-
    suade young Zachariah from being a gunfighter. Elvin
    Jones plays Job Cain, the bad guy everyone is gunning for.

ZAMBA
Nar/Cast: June Vincent + Beau Bridges + Darby Jones* +
    Theron Jackson*
Screenplay: Barbara Worth
Producer: Maurice H. Conn   Director: William Berke
Studio/Company: Eagle-Lion
Tech Info: 16 mm/sound/bw/75 min.
Date/Country: 1949 + USA   Type: Feature
Distr/Arch: ivy + mog

Annotation: A young boy who had to parachute from a burning plane is separated from his mother in the African jungle and is adopted by a gorilla named Zamba. How he grows up and his eventual rescue is the story line. Darby Jones and Thereon Jackson are natives - Keega and Bayla.

ZANZIBAR
Nar/Cast: Clarence Muse* + Lola Lane + James Craig + Eduardo Ciannelli
Screenplay: Maurice Tombruel   Director: Harold Schuster
Studio/Company: Universal
Date/Country: 1940 + USA   Type: Feature
Annotation: Lola Lane leads an expedition into the bush to gain control of the skull of a revered tribal sultan, because with it the British will be able to control the natives. Muse plays a native "Bino."

ZENOBIA
Nar/Cast: Oliver Hardy + Harry Langdon + Billie Burke + Jean Parker + Stepin Fetchit* + Hattie McDaniel* + Hall Johnson Choir*
Producer: A. Edward Sutherland for Hal Roach   Director: Gordon Douglas
Studio/Company: Universal
Date/Country: 1939 + USA   Type: Feature
Annotation: Slapstick comedy of antebellum South with the Declaration of Independence recited by "one of Mr. Roach's comic pickaninnies." Stepin Fetchit is "Zero", Hattie McDaniel is "Dahlia".

ZIEGFELD FOLLIES
Nar/Cast: William Powell + Lucille Ball + Esther Williams + Fred Astaire + Lena Horne* + Red Skelton + Judy Garland + Gene Kelly + Kathryn Grayson + Cyd Charisse + Avon Long*
Producer: Arthur Freed   Director: Vincente Minnelli
Studio/Company: MGM
Tech Info: 16 mm/sound/color/110 min.
Date/Country: 1946 + USA   Type: Feature
Distr/Arch: fnc
Annotation: Avon Long and Lena Horne have a spot in this musical tribute to Ziegfeld and his follies.

ZIGZAG
Nar/Cast: William Marshall* + Anne Jackson + George Kennedy
Screenplay: John Kelley
Producer: Robert Enders   Director: Richard Colla
Studio/Company: MGM
Tech Info: 16 mm/sound/color/104 min.
Date/Country: 1970 + USA   Type: Feature
Distr/Arch: fnc
Annotation: Marshall is Morrie Bronson in this melodrama about an insurance investigator (Kennedy) who, having been diagnosed as suffering from a fatal brain tumor, figures out an ingenious plan to provide financially for his family. When he recovers his problems begin.

ZOU ZOU
Nar/Cast: Josephine Baker* + Jean Gabin

Producer: Marc Allgret   Director: Marc Allgret
Tech Info: 90 min.
Date/Country: 1935 + France

ZULU KING, THE
Tech Info: bw/silent
Date/Country: 1913 + USA   Type: Comedy Short
Annotation: Black natives choose a hen-pecked white man, who
  is fleeing from his wife, to become king of the Zulus.

ZULU'S HEART, THE
Producer: D.W. Griffith   Director: D.W. Griffith
Studio/Company: Biograph
Tech Info: 35 mm/silent/bw/776 ft.
Date/Country: 1908 + USA   Type: Dramatic Short
Annotation: A Zulu chief whose four year old daughter dies
  of fever displays sensitivity and compassion for the wife
  and child of a Boer, risking his life to save mother and
  child from his own South African tribesmen.   Whites in
  black face play the African roles in this film, touted:
  The Zulu's Heart, "the savage beast becomes compassionate
  through grief" in the Biograph bulletin.

ZULU
Nar/Cast: Stanley Baker + Michael Caine + Jack Hawkins
Screenplay: John Prebble + Cy Endfield
Producer: Stanley Baker + Cy Endfield   Director: Cy End-
  field
Studio/Company: Embassy Pictures
Tech Info: 16 mm/color/sound/130 min./4 reels
Date/Country: 1964 + Britain   Type: Feature
Distr/Arch: roa + unf + mab + aim + aca + as + bud + ccc +
  cwf + mac + mot + swa + twy + wcf + who
Annotation: A handful of British soldiers withstand the as-
  sault of 4,200 Zulu warriors for   24   hours   at Rorke's
  drift, an outpost in South Africa. Foreword by Richard
  Burton.

1-2-3 GO
Series: Our Gang
Nar/Cast: Our Gang + Billie Thomas*
Screenplay: Hal Law + Robert A. McGowan
Producer: MGM   Director: Edward Cahn
Studio/Company: MGM
Tech Info: bw/sound/1 reel
Date/Country: 1941 + USA   Type: Comedy Short
Annotation: After Mickey is hit by a car, the gang works up
  a safety society which gets city-wide recognition. Billie
  Thomas stars as Buckwheat.

100 RIFLES
Nar/Cast: James Brown* + Raquel Welch + Burt Reynolds +
  Fernando Lamas
Screenplay: Clair Huffaker + Tom Gries
Producer: Tom Gries   Director: Marvin Schwartz
Studio/Company: Twentieth Century Fox
Tech Info: 16 mm/color/sound/3 reels/100 min.
Date/Country: 1969 + USA   Type: Feature

Distr/Arch: fnc
Annotation: U.S. Deputy Brown chases bank robber Reynolds
   into Mexico, where they get involved helping Yanqui Indians against an oppressive Mexican general. Brown falls in
   love with the Yanqui leader Welch, but to no avail. She
   is killed in the final shootout.

13 FRIGHTENED GIRLS
Nar/Cast: Judy Pace* + Joyce Taylor + Murray Hamilton
Screenplay: Robert Dillon
Producer: William Castle   Director: William Castle
Studio/Company: Columbia
Tech Info: 16 mm/sound/color/89 min.
Date/Country: 1963 + USA   Type: Feature
Distr/Arch: cwf + mod + mot + nat + new + roa + swa + wcf
Annotation: An action melodrama about a teen-aged girl who
   takes up spying and gets into trouble.

13 WEST STREET
Nar/Cast: Bernie Hamilton* + Alan Ladd + Rod Steiger
Screenplay: Bernard Schoenfeld
Producer: William Bloom   Director: Philip Leacock
Studio/Company: Columbia
Tech Info: 16 mm/sound/bw/80 min.
Date/Country: 1962 + USA   Type: Feature
Distr/Arch: mod + roa + tfc
Annotation: Hamilton has a small role in this melodrama
   about a space scientist's compulsion for revenge against a
   brutal gang of teenagers who attack and beat him.

14TH GENERATION AMERICANS
Series: Epitaph for Jim Crow
Nar/Cast: Dr. Thomas Pettigrew
Producer: NET + Harvard University
Tech Info: 16 mm/bw/sound/1 reel/30 min.
Date/Country: 1961 + USA   Type: Documentary
Distr/Arch: adl
Annotation: The history of the black American and contribu-
   tions by black people to all aspects of American life are
   emphasized. Thomas Pettigrew narrates.

1861-1877: CIVIL WAR AND RECONSTRUCTION
Series: History of the Negro in America
Tech Info: 16 mm/sound/bw/1 reel/20 min.   Type: Documentary
Distr/Arch: con
Annotation: A study of the role of slavery in the Civil War
   and the Reconstruction era. Examines the political conflicts over the issue of slavery which led to the War and
   illustrates how the Emancipation Proclamation and the
   Thirteenth, Fourteenth and Fifteenth Amendments sought to
   protect and preserve the newly won freedom of black people.

1877-TODAY: FREEDOM MOVEMENT
Series: History of the Negro in America
Tech Info: 16 mm/sound/bw/1 reel/20 min.
Distr/Arch: con

Annotation: A history of the century-long struggle of Black
    Americans for the rights and freedom which were promised
    them at the end of the Civil War. Follows the Afro-
    American from his tenant-farmer existence in the post-war
    South to black ghettoes of the cities; from the cultural
    renaissance of the New Negro of the 1920's through the
    Depression and into the 1950's and the flowering of the
    civil rights movement.

2ND BEST SECRET AGENT IN THE WHOLE WIDE WORLD, THE
Nar/Cast: Sammy Davis, Jr.* + Tom Adams + Peter Buel
    Director: Lindsay Shonteff
Studio/Company: Embassy
Tech Info: 16 mm/sound/color/96 min.
Date/Country: 1965 + Britain   Type: Feature
Distr/Arch: mac + mod
Annotation: Sammy Davis sings in this action comedy-drama
    about secret agents, Russians and a Swedish scientist.

20 MILLION SWEETHEARTS
Nar/Cast: Pat O'Brian + Dick Powell + Ginger Rogers + The
    Mills Brothers*   Story: Paul Moss + Jerry Wald
    Director: Ray Enright
Studio/Company: First National
Tech Info: 89 min.
Date/Country: 1934 + USA   Type: Feature
Annotation: The Mills Brothers are featured in this musical
    with a radio station setting.   O'Brian is a talent
    procurer, Powell a crooner and Rogers his sweetheart.

20TH CENTURY
Nar/Cast: John Barrymore + Carole Lombard + Fred "Snowflake"
    Toones*
Screenplay: Ben Hecht + Charles McArthur   Story: Ben Hecht
    + Charles McArthur   Director: Howard Hawkes
Studio/Company: Columbia
Date/Country: 1934 + USA   Type: Feature
Annotation: Comedy about a producer who makes an unknown a
    star only to lose her and then meet her on a train on her
    way to get married.   Fred Toones (Snowflake as he is
    credited) plays a porter.

220 BLUES
Producer: King Screen Prod.
Tech Info: 16 mm/color/sound/1 reel/17 min.
Date/Country: 1970 + USA   Type: Dramatized Documentary
Distr/Arch: iu + bfa
Annotation: Dramatizes the problem of racial identification
    faced by a black high school star who must decide whether
    or not to run in a championship meet with the possibility
    of receiving a college scholarship. Contrasts the concept
    of separatism, and loyalty to Blacks only as one's source
    of pride and dignity, with that of cooperation and working
    within the white system.

3 FOR A BEDROOM C
Nar/Cast: Gloria Swanson + James Warren + Fred Clark +
    Ernest Anderson*

Screenplay: Milton Bren   Story: Goddard Lieberson
Producer: Edward L. Alperson   Director: Milton Bren
Studio/Company: Warner Brothers
Date/Country: 1952 + USA   Type: Feature
Annotation: Story of a glamorous movie star and a conserva-
    tive college professor and their romance on a cross-
    country train trip with various supporting cast members
    supplying humor, including Ernest Anderson as Fred.

36 HOURS TO KILL
Nar/Cast: Brian Donlevy + Gloria Stuart + Stepin Fetchit*
Screenplay: Lou Breslow + John Patrick   Story: W.R. Burnett
    Director: Eugene Forde
Studio/Company: 20th Century Fox
Date/Country: 1936   Type: Feature
Annotation: Gangster movie with unusual twist, right after
    gangster Douglas Fowley gets promoted to Public Enemy /1,
    he wins a sweepstake and tries to get the money without
    getting the attention. Stepin Fetchit has a bit part.

45 FATHERS
Nar/Cast: Jane Withers + Thomas Beck + Louise Henry + The
    Hartmans + Richard Carle + Nella Walker + Sammy Cohen +
    Hattie McDaniel*
Screenplay: Frances Hyland + Albert Ray   Story: Mary Bickel
Producer: John Stone   Director: James Tinling
Studio/Company: Twentieth Century Fox
Date/Country: 1937 + USA   Type: Feature
Annotation: Judith Frazier (Jane Withers) becomes the ward
    of a gun club. Hattie McDaniel plays Beulah.

5 CARD STUD
Nar/Cast: Dean Martin + Robert Mitchum + Yaphet Kotto*
Screenplay: Marguerite Roberts
Producer: Hal Wallis   Director: Henry Hathaway
Studio/Company: Paramount
Tech Info: 16 mm/sound/color/103 min.
Date/Country: 1968 + USA   Type: Feature
Distr/Arch: fnc
Annotation: Yaphet Kotto (Little George) is one of a group
    of stud poker players in a game which ends with the
    violent death of a supposedly cheating player. Each of
    the group mysteriously meets his death (including Little
    George) in this western melodrama of the 1880's, except
    Van (Dean Martin), before the identity of the killer is
    discovered.

1 * 1
Alt Title(s): see Sympathy for the Devil

Appendix

abc
ABC-TV News
7 West 66th St.
New York, N.Y. 10019

aca
Academy Films
748 N. Seward St.
Hollywood, California 90038

aci
ACI Films Inc.
11th Flr.
35 W. 45th St.
New York, NY 10036

acusa
Angola Committee, USA
Box 27101
Detroit, MI 48227
(313) 836-2210

adf
American Documentary Films
336 West 84th Street
New York, NY 10024

adl
Anti-Defamation League of
B'Nai B'rith
315 Lexington Avenue
New York, NY 10016

aef
American Education Films
132 Lasky Dr.
Beverly Hills, CA 90212

af
African Filmstrips
51 E. 42nd Street
New York, NY 10017

aff
Alfred Ehrhardt Film
Loppenstr. 38
D2 Hamburg 61
West Germany

afgr
Afrographis
P.O. Box 8361
Los Angeles, CA 90008

afl-cio
Education Department
815 16th St. NW

Washington, D.C. 20006

afr
Afram Associates, Inc.
68-72 East 131st St.
New York, NY 10037

aft
American   Film   Theatre/
 Cinebill
1350 Avenue of the Americas
New York, NY 10019

aim
Association Instructional
 Materials
866 Third Avenue
New York, NY 10022

aims
AIM   Instructionsl   Media
 Services, Inc.
626 Justin Avenue
Glendale, CA 91201

ait
Agency for Instructional
 Television
Box A
Bloomington, IN 47401

ala/oif
Office   for   Intellectual
 Freedom
American Literary Assoc.
50 E. Hurcn St.
Chicago, IL 60611

alb
Alba House
7050 Pinehurst
P.O. Box 35
Dearborn, MI 48126

amc
American Metal Climax, Inc.
1270 Avenue of the Americas
New York, NY 10020

aof
Andy Olenyik Films
10927 Carroll Wood Way
St. Louis, MO 63128

aph
Augsburg Publishing House
426 South Fifth St.
Minneapolis, Mn 55415

arg
Argosy Film Service
1939 Central St.
Evanston, IL 60201

asf/as
Association-Sterling Films
600 Grant Avenue
Ridgefield, N.J. 07657

ast
Astral Films, Ltd.
224 Davenport Road
Toronto, Ontario M5R 1J7
Canada

atl
See atlap

atlap/atl
Atlantis Productions, Inc.
850 Thousand Oaks Blvd.
Thousand Oaks, CA 91360

aufs/ff
Fieldstaff Films
American Universities Field
  Staff
535 Fifth Avenue
New York, NY 10017

aved
AV-ED Films
7934 Santa Monica Blvd.
Hollywood, CA 90046

avei
Audio-Visuals
Box 370
Elkhart, IN 46514

avsl
Audio-Visual Services Library
Christian Church Disciples
  of Christ
222 South Downey Avenue
Indianapolis, IN 46219

bac
Bread and Circus
630 Ninth Avenue
New York, NY 10036
(212) 541-9664

bafc
Broadcasting and Film Commission
Natl. Council of Churches
  of Christ
475 Riverside Drive
New York, NY 10027
(212) 870-2200

bbc
The   British Broadcasting
  Corp.
P.O. Box 500
Toronto, Ontario M5W 1E6,
  Canada

bfa
BFA Educational Media
2211 Michigan Avenue
P.O. Box 1795
Santa Monica, CA 90406
(213) 829-2901

bfc
Baptist Film Centers
2930 Flowers Road
Chamblee, GA 30341

bfi
The National Film Archive
British Film Institute
81 Dean Street
London W1V 6AA
Great Britain

bla
Blackhawk Films
Eastin-Phelan Corporation
1235 West 5th Street
Davenport, Iowa 52808
(319) 323-9736

bris
British Information Service

bu
Krasker Memorial Film Library
Boston Univ./School of Edu.
765 Commonwealth Avenue
Boston, Mass. 02215
(617) 353-3272

buc
Buchan Pictures
122 W. Chippewa St.
Buffalo, NY 14202
(716) 853-1805

bud

Budget Films
4590 Santa Monica Blvd.
Los Angeles, CA 90029
(213)660-0187

byu
Brigham Young Univ.
Educational Media Svs.
290 Herald R. Clark Bldg.
Provo, Utah 84602

cafm
Cathedral Films
2921 W. Alameda Ave.
P.O. Box 1608
Burbank,   CA   91507
   (213)848-6637

cal
See ucemc

can
Canyon Cinema
Industrial Center Building
Room 220
Sausalito, CA 94965
(415)332-1514

canbc
Canadian Broadcasting Corp.
P.O. Box 500, Terminal A
Toronto, Ontario
Canada

car
See carouf

carouf/car/carsl
Carousel Films
1501 Broadway
New York, NY 10036
(212)345-0315

carsl
See carouf

cbfms
Conservative   Baptist
 Foreign Mission Society
P.O. Box 5
Wheaton, IL 60187
(312)665-1200

cbs
See cbsf

cbsf/cbs
CBS Films, Inc.

51 West 52nd St.
New York, NY 10019
(212)765-4321

cc
Cecilia Conway
1720 Allard Road
Chapel Hill, NC 27514

ccc
Cine-Craft Co.
1720 W. Marshall
Portland, OR 97209
(503)228-7484

ccmfi
CCM Films, Inc.
866 Third Ave.
New York, NY 10022

ccunesco
UNESCO Canadian Commission
222 Queen Street
Ottawa, Canada

cdc
Cinerama   Distributing
  Corporation
141 South Robertson Blvd.
Los Angeles, CA 90052
(213)278-5271

cemc
Center for Mass Communica-
      tions   of   Columbia
      University Pres
136 South Broadway
Irvington, NY 10533

cf
Churchill Films
662 North Robertson Blvd.
Los Angeles, CA 90069
(213)657-5110

cfi
Canadian Film Institute
1762 Carling Ave.
Ottawa 13, Ontario
Canada

cfi
Consolidated Film   In-
      dustries
959 Seward Street
Hollywood, CA 90028
(213)462-3161

cfm_
Classic Film Museum
4 Union Square
Dover-Foxcroft, ME 04426
(207) 564-8371

cha/char_
Charard Motion Pictures
2110 E. 24th St.
Brooklyn, NY 11229
(212) 891-4339

char_
See cha

cie_
Cinema Eight/Cinema   Concepts
91 Main St.
Chester, Conn 06412
(203) 526-9513

cin_
Cintec Productions
611 W. Pacific Coast Hwy.
Long Beach, CA 90806

cinemv_
See civ

civ/cinemv_
Cinema 5
595 Madison Ave.
New York, NY 10022
(212) 421-5555

cmi_
Calmalma Media Institute,
Inc.

coksby_
Cokesbury
Service Dept.
100 Maryland Ave. NE
Washington, D.C. 20002

col_
See colsc

colsc/col_
Colorado State College
Instructional   Materials
Center
Attn: Booking Agent
Greeley, Colorado

colu_
Columbia Cinematique

711 Fifth Avenue
New York, NY 10022

cor_
See corf

corf/cor_
Coronet Instructional Media
65 E. South Water St.
Chicago, IL 60601

cou_
Cousino Visual Ed. Serv.
1945 Franklin Ave.
Toledo, OH 43624
(419) 246-3691

cox_
Paul Cox
Classroom Film Dist. Inc.
5610 Hollywood, CA 90028
Hollywood, CA 90028
(213) 466-1651

cph_
Concordia Publishing House
3558 Jefferson Ave.
St. Louis, MO 63118
(314) 664-7000

crnf_
Corinth Films
410 East 62nd Street
New York, NY 10021
(212) 421-4770

csf_
Center   for   Southern
Folklore
1216 Peabcdy Avenue
P.O. Box 4081
Memphis, TN 38104
(901) 726-4205

csv_
Cine Service Vintage Films
85 Exeter St.
Bridgeport, CT 06606
(203) 372-7785

cup_
Center for Mass Communications   of   Columbia
University Press
562 West 113th St.
New York, NY 10025
(212) 678-6751

cwf
Clem Williams Films
2240 Noblestown Rd.
Pittsburgh, PA 15205
(512) 921-5810

db/m
DB/M Productions
8738 Holloway Drive
West Hollywood, CA 90069

dc/dic
Doubleday Multimedia
P.O. Box 11607
Santa Ana CA 92705

der
Documentary Edu. Resources
Center for Documentary
  Anthropology
24 Dane St.
Somerville, Mass. 02143
(617) 666-1750

dfp
Department of Film Produc-
tion
University of Mississippi
Division of Special
  Activities
University, MS 38677
(601) 232-7211

dibd
Dibie-Dash Productions
4949 Hollywood Blvd. Suite
  217
Los Angeles, CA 90027

dic
See dc

dir
Directions One
328 E. 48th St.
New York, NY 10017

dis
Walt Disney Prod.
800 Sonora Ave.
Glendale, CA 91201
(213) 845-3141

dync
Dynamic Films, Inc.

eas
See imp

eba/ebec
Encyclopaedia   Britannica
  Ed. Corp.
425 N. Michigan Ave.
Chicago, IL 60611
(312) 321-6800

ebec
See eba

edc
EDC Distribution Center
39 Chapel St.
Newton, MA 02160

efd
Educational Film   Distrib-
  utors Ltd.
285 Lesmill Rd.
Don Mills
Ontario McB 2V1, Canada

efe
Educational Film   Enterprises, Inc.
6770 Hollywood Blvd.
Hollywood, CA 90028

efs
Educational Film Services
28 Fisher Avenue
Boston, MA 02120
(617) 440-7603

emg
Em Gee Film Library
16024 Ventura Blvd.
Encino, CA 91316
(213) 981-5506

fa
Friends of Angola
1648 Roxana Rd. NW
Washington, D.C. 20012
(202) 293-7193

fac
FACSEA
972 Fifth Ave.
New York, NY 10021
(212) 737-9700

fce
Film Classic Exchange
1914 S. Vermont Ave.
Los Angeles, CA 90007
(213) 731-3854

ff_
See aufs

fft/ffth_
Films for the Humanities
Harold Mantell Inc.
P.O. Box 378
Princeton, NJ 08540
(609) 921-2803

ffth_
See fft

fi_
See fnc

fif_
Faces Internationsl Films
8444 Wilshire Blvd.
Beverly Hills, CA 90211
(213) 653-8260

flf_
Flower Films
John   T.   Harms,   General
  Manager
11305 Q-Ranch Rd.
Austin, TX 78757
(512) 258-1776

fmc_
Film-Makers Cooperative
175 Lexington Ave.
New York, NY 10016
(212) 889-3820

fnc/fi_
Films Incorporated
1144 Wilmette Ave.
Wilmette, IL 60091
(312) 256-6600

fon_
Films of the Nations
7820 20th Ave
Brooklyn, NY 11214

fsu_
Florida State University
Instructional Media Center
Tallahassee, Fla. 32306
(904) 644-2820

gis_
Ghana Information Service
c/o Ghana Mission to the
  U.N.

964 Third Avenue
New York, NY 10017

gms_
Griggs-Moviedrome
263 Harrison St.
Nutley, NJ 07110

gre_
See wgp

gro_
See grove

grove/gro_
Grove Press Film Division
53 East 11 Street
New York, NY 10003
(212) 677-2400

hfsc_
Harvard Film Study Center

hraw_
Hold, Rinehart and Winston
383 Madison Avenue
New York, NY 10017

ics_
Institutional   Cinema
  Service
915 Broadway
New York, NY 10010
(212) 673-3990

ieucla_
Institute of   Ethnomusi-
  cology
Univ. of California
Los Angeles, CA 90024
(213) 825-4761

ifb_
International Bureau Inc.
332 South Michigan Ave.
Chicago, IL 60604
(312) 427-4545

iff_
International Film Foundation, Inc.
475 Fifth Ave. Suite 916
New York, NY 10017
(212) 685-4998

ifp_
Independent   Film Producers
  Co.

P.O. Box 501
Pasadena, CA 91102

ill_
See uill

ima_
Images   Motion   Picture
  Rental Library
2 Purdy Ave
Rye, NY 10580
(914) 967-1102

ime_
Imperial Entertainment
15 Park Row
New York, NY 10038
(212) 267-5315

imp/eas_
International   Museum   of
  Photography[3]
George Eastman House
900 East Avenue
Rochester, NY 14603

imp/impact_
Impact Films
144 Beecher St.
New York, NY 10012
(212) 674-3315

impact_
See imp

imr_
Image Resources
267 W. 25th St.
New York, NY 10001

ind_
See iu

iowa_
Iowa Films,   Audio-Visual
  Center
Univ. of Iowa
Iowa City, Iowa 52242
(319) 353-5885

iqf_
I.Q. Films
P.O. Box 326
Wappingers   Falls, NY 12590
(914) 297-0070

isr_
Films of Israel

c/o Alden Films
7820 20th Ave
Brooklyn, NY 11214
(212) 331-1045

isr_
Indiana University   In-
  stitute for Sex Research[2]
Morrison ≤416
Indiana University
Bloomington, IN 47403

iu/ind_
Audio-Visual Center
Indiana University
Bloomington, IN 47402
(812) 337-2103

iuasp_
Indiana University   African
  Studies Program
223 Woodburn Hall
Indiana University
Blooomington, IN 47402
(812) 337-6734
(Research   Collection--Not
  for distribution)

ivy_
Ivy Films/16
165 W. 46th St.
New York, NY 10036
(212) 765-3940

iwm_
Imperial War Museum[4]
Lambeth Road
London SE1 6HZ
Great Britain

iws_
Iowa State University
Media Resources Center
121 Pearson Hall
Ames IA 50010
(515) 294-4111

jan_
Janus Films
745 Fifth Avenue
New York, NY 10022
(212) 753-7100

jas_
Jason Films
2621 Palisade Ave.
Riverdale, NY 10463

jhb
Baker, John H.[1]
3456 South High Street
Columbus, OH 43207

jou
Journal Films, Inc.
930 Pitner Ave.
Chicago, IL 60202
(312) 328-6700

ka
Kaiser Aluminum Room 864
3001 Lakeside Dr.
Oakland, CA

kb
Knowledge Builders
Lowell Ave and Cherry   Lane
Floral Park, NY 11001

kent
Audio Visual Services
Kent State Univ.
Education Bldg. 215
Kent, OH 44242
(216) 672-2454

ker
Kerr Film Exchange
3034 Canon St.
San Diego, CA 92106
(714) 224-2406

kil
The Killiam Collection
Rental Division
6 E. 39th St.
New York, NY 10016
(212) 684-3920

kje
Kelly Jordan Enterprises
342 Madison Avenue
New York, NY
(212) 687-1720

kpf/par
KitParker Films
Box 227
Carmel Valley, CA 93924
(408) 659-4131

lc
Library of Congress[5]
Motion Picture Section
1st and B Streets N.E.
Washington, D.C. 20540

lca/lec/lcoa
Learning Corp. of America
1350 Ave. of the Americas
New York, NY 10019
(212) 397-9330

lcoa
See lca

lec
See lca

lew
Lewis Film Serv.
1425 E. Central
Wichita, KS 67214
(316) 263-6991

lfa
Lutheran Film Associates
360 Park Avenue S.
New York, NY 10010
(212) 532-6350

luc
Lucerne Films
P.O. Box 625
N. Bergen, NJ 07047
(212) 424-5571

luther
Lutheran Film Associates
315 Park Ave. South
New York, NY 10010
(212) 677-3950

mab/mac
Macmillan/Audio-Brandon
  Films, Inc.
34 MacQuesten Parkway South
Mt. Vernon, NY 10550
(914) 664-5051

mac
See mab

man
Manbeck Pictures
3621 Wakonda Dr.
Des Moines, IA 50321

mar
Marquis Film Distributors
416 W. 45th St.
New York, NY 10036

mar

Maryknoll Publications
Department 2T
Maryknoll, NY 10545

mar_
Marlin Motion Pictures Ltd.
47 Lakeshore Rd., East
Port Credit, Ontario L5G
   1C9
Canada

mghf/mhf_
McGraw Hill Films
330 West 42nd Street
New York, NY 10036

mhf_
See mghf

min_
Minot Films
Minot Bldg.
Milbridge, ME 04568

mla_
Modern Learning Aids Div of
   Ward's Natural Science
P.O. Box 302
Rochester, NY 14603

mma_
See moma

mmm_
Mass Media Ministries
2116 N. Charles St.
Baltimore, MD 21218
(301) 727-3270

mod_
Modern Sound Pictures, Inc.
1402 Howard Street
Omaha, Nebraska 68102
(402) 341-8476

mog_
Mogull's
235 W. 46th St.
New York, NY 10036
(212) 757-1414

mom_
Modern Mass Media
315 Springfield Ave.
Summit, NJ 07901

moma/mma_
The Museum of Modern Art

Dept. of Film[6]
11 West 53rd Street
New York, NY 10019
(212) 245-8900

mot_
Mottas Films
1318 Ohio Ave. NE
Canton, OH 44705
(216) 494-6058

mp_
Mountain Plains

msu_
Michigan State University
Instructinal Media Center
East Lansing, MI 48824

mtp_
Modern   Talking   Picture
   Service
2323 New Hyde Park Road
New Hyde Park, NY 11040
(516) 437-6300

nac_
National   Audio-Visual
   Center
Washington, D.C. 20409

nacc_
National   Council   of
   Churches
Broadcasting and Film Com-
   mission
456 Riveside Drive
New York, NY 10027

nars_
Audiovisual   Archives
   Division[7]
National Archives and Re-
   cords Service
Washington, D.C. 20408
(202) 936-6725

nat_
Adrian O. Natalini
321 Custer
Evanston, IL 60202

nbcee_
NBC Education Enterprises
30 Rockefeller Plaza
New York, NY 10020

ncs_

National Cinema Service
333 W. 57th St.
New York, NY 10019
(212) 247-4343

nef
National Educational Film
  Center
Finksburg, MD 21048
(301) 795-3000

new
Newman Film Library
400 32nd St. SE
Grand Rapids, MI 49508
(616) 243-3300

nfb
See nfbc

nfbc/nfb
Natl. Film Board of Canada
1251 Avenue of the Americas
New York, NY 10020
(212) 586-2400

nfbc/nfb
Natl. Film Board of Canada
P.O. Box 6100 Station A
Montreal, Quebec HRC 3H5
Canada

nge/ngs
Natl. Geographic   Educa-
  tional Serv.
P.O. Box 1640
Washington, DC 20013

ngs
See nge

nil
Niles Film Products, inc.
1141 Mishawaka Avenue
South Bend, IN 46615
Order toll free   (800) 348-
  2462

nlc
New Line Cinema
853 Broadway, 16th Floor
New York, NY 10003
(212) 674-7460

nth
New Thing
1811 Columbia Road, N.W.
Washington, D.C. 20001

nyf
New Yorker Films
43 West 61st Street
New York, NY 10023
(212) 247-6110

nyu
New York University
Fil Library
26 Washington Pl.
New York, NY 10003
(212) 777-2000

obe
Vaughn Obern
704 Santa Monica Blvd.
Santa Monica, CA 90403

ode/odeo
Odeon Films, Inc.
1619 Broadway
New York, NY 10019
(212) 541-5677

odeo
See ode

oeca
OECA
Canada Sq.
2180 Yonge St.
Toronto, Ontario
Canada M45 2C1

off
Official Films, Inc.
Linden and Grand Aves.
Ridgefield, NJ 07657

ohn
Ohio Newsreel
P.O. Box 19241
Cincinnati, OH 45219
(513) 561-6900

oif
See ala

oks
See osu

ore
Orion Enterprises, Inc.
614 Davis Street
Evanston, IL 60201

orr

Orrin Enterprises
175 Beach 27 St.
Far Rocaway, NY 11691
(212)327-7149

osu/oks_
Oklahoma State University
Audio-Visual Center
Stillwater, OK 74074
(405)325-4011

oxf_
See oxford

oxford/oxf_
Oxford Films
1136 N. Las Palmas Ave.
Los Angeles, CA 90038
(213)461-9231

panwa_
Pan   American World Airways
200 Park Avenue
New York, NY 10017

par_
See kpf

pard_
Paradigm Film Productions
6305 Yucca St.
Los Angeles, CA 90028

pcn_
Psychological   Cinema
  Register
Audio-Visual Svs.
The Penn. St. University
University Park, PA 16802

pen_
Pennebaker, Inc.
56 W. 45th Street
New York, NY 10036
(212)986-7020

per_
Perennial   Education,   Inc.
P.O. Box 236
1825 Willow Road
Northfield, IL 60093

persp_
Perspective Films
360 W. Erie Street
Chicago, IL 60610
(312)332-7676

pho_
Phoenix Films
470 Park Ave. S
New York, NY 10016
(212)684-5910

pic_
Pictura Films Distribution
  Corp.
43 West 16th St.
New York, NY 10011
(212)691-2930

ppl_
Pleasant Pastures Ltd.
57 Greek Street
London WIV6DB
England

pru_
Productions Unlimited
1301 Ave. of the Americas
New York, NY 10019
(212)541-6670

psfc_
Pacific St. Film Collective
280 Clinton St.
Brooklyn, NY 11201

psu_
The   Pennsylvania   State
  University
Audio-Visual   Services,   6
  Willard Bldg.
University Park, PA 16802
(814)865-6315

pyr_
Pyramid Films
P.O. Box 1048
Santa Monica, CA 90406
(213)828-7577

rad/radim_
Film Images/Radim Films
17 West 60th Street
New York, NY 10023
(212)279-6653

radim_
See rad

rbc_
rbc Films
933 N. LaBrea Ave.
Los Angeles, CA 90038
(213)874-7330

red
Rediscovery Productions
2 Halfmile Common
Westport, CN 06880
(203)226-4489

refl
Religious and Educational
  Film library
17 Park Place
New York, NY 10001

rk
Robert Koestler*
4243 North Lincoln
Chicago, IL 60618

roa/roaf
ROA Films
1696 North Astor Street
Milwaukee, WS 53202
(414)271-0861

roaf
See roa

saf
Service des Archives du
  Film⁹
78390 Bois D'Archy
France

sef
See ste

sel
Select Film Library
115 W. 31st St.
New York, NY 10010
(212)594-4500

serb
Seious Business Co.
1609 Jaynes St.
Berkeley, CA 94703

sfi
Sportlite Films
20 N. Wacker Dr.
Chicago, IL 60606

sm
Sterling Movies U.S.A.
866 Third Avenue
New York, NY 10022
(212)586-1717

soh
Soho Cinema
225 Lafayette St.
New York, NY 10012
(212)966-1416

sta
Standard Film Service
14710 West Warren Avenue
Dearborn, MI 48126
(313)581-2250

ste/sef
Sterling Educational Films
241 E. 34th St.
New York, NY 10016
(212)683-6300

stu
Stanford University

suf
Film Rental Center of
  Syracuse Univ.
1455 E. Colvin St.
Syracuse, NY 13210
(315)479-6631

swa
Swank Motion Pictures
201 South Jefferson Ave.
St. Louis, MO 63166
(314)534-6300

tch
Office of Instructional
  Support Services
439 Thorndike Hall
Teachers College Library
525 West 120th St.
New York, NY
(212)678-3822

tex/texflm
Texture Films
1600 Broadway
New York, NY 10019
(212)586-6960

texflm
See tex

tfc
Trend Films Corp.
P.O. Box 69680
Los Angeles, CA 90069

tfc

Teaching Film Custodians
25 W. 43rd St.
New York, NY 10036

tfcr
"The" Film Center
908 12th St., NW
Washington, D.C. 20005
(202) 393-1205

thu
Thunderbird Films
3501 Eagle Rock Blvd.
Los Angeles, CA 90054
(213) 256-1034

tim
See timlif

timlif/tim/tl
Time-Life Multimedia
Time and Life Building
New York, NY 10020
(212) 586-1212

tl
See timlif

tmc
The Movie Center
57 Baldwin St.
Chalestown, MA 02129
(617) 242-3456

tnf
Trans-National Films
48 W. 69th St.
New York, NY 10023
(212) 873-2190

transw/twf
Transworld Films, Inc.
332 S. Michigan
Chicago, IL
(312) 922-1530

tri
Tricontinental Film Center
333 Sixth Avenue
New York, NY 10014
(212) 989-3330

tribu
Tribune Films
38 West 32nd St.
New York, NY 10001
(212) 594-5287

twcf
Twentieth Century Fox Film
   Corp.
10201 W. Pico Blvd.
Los Angeles, CA 90064

twf
See transw

twn
Third World Newsreel
26 W. 20th St.
New York, NY 10011
(212) 243-2310

twy
Twyman Films, Inc.
329 Salem Avenue
Dayton, OH 45401
(800) 543-9594

uas
United Artists
729 Seventh Avenue
New York, NY 10019
(212) 575-4715

uca
See ucemc

uccav
Office for Audio-Visuals
United Church of Christ
1505 Race St.
Philadelphia, PA 19102

ucemc
University of California
Extension Media Center
Berkeley, CA 94720
(415) 642-0460

ucemc/cal/uca
Univ. of California
Extension Media Center
2223 Fulton Street
Berkeley, CA 94720
(414) 845-6000

uco
Educational Media Center
University of Colorado
Bureau of Audio-Visual In-
   struction
Stadium Bldg.
Boulder, CO 80309
(303) 443-2211

ueuwis_
Univ. of Wisconsin Ext.
Bureau of Audio-Visual In-
   st.
1327 Univ. Ave. P.O. Box
   2093
Madison, WS 53701
(608) 262-1644

ueva_
Universal   Education   and
   Visual Arts
1501 Broadway
New York, NY 10036

uil_
See uill

uill/ill/uil_
Univ. of Illinois
Visual Aids Service
Div. of Univ. Extension
1325 S. Oak St.
Champaign, IL 61820
(217) 333-1360

umavec/umic_
The Univ. of Michigan
Audio-Visual Edu. Center
416 Fourth St.
Ann Arbor, MI 48103

umch_
United Methodist Church
Board of Global Ministeries
   Service Div.
7820 Reading Rd.
Cincinnati, OH 45237
(513) 761-2100

umic_
See umavec

umn_
See umnav

umnav/umn_
Univ. of Minnesota
Audio-Visual   Library
   Service
3300   University   Avenue,
   S.E.
Minneapolis, MN 55414
(612) 373-3810

un_
United Nations Office of
   Public Information

United Nations Plaza
New York, NY 10017

une_
See uon

unebr_
Univ. of Nebraska-Lincoln
Instructional Media Center
Univ. of Nebraska
Lincoln, Nebraska 68508
(402) 472-2171

unf_
United Films
1425 South Main
Tulsa, OK 74119
(918) 583-2681

uni_
Universal 16
425 North Michigan Avenue
Chicago, IL 60611
(312) 822-051

untv_
Mr. Tom Shull, Chairman
US Broadcasters' Committee
   for the United Nations
P.O. Box 20
Grand Central Sta., NY

uon/une_
University of Nevada
Audio-Visual Center
Education Bldg.
Reno, NV 89507
(702) 784-6671

usc_
University   of   Southern
   California
Div. of Cinema
Film Dist. Section
University Park
Los Angeles, CA 90007

usf_
U.S. Film Office
230 Park Ave.
New York, NY 10017
(212) 689-5859

usunesco_
United States Natl. Commission for United Nations
   Educational, Scientific,
   and Cultural Organization

Washington, D.C. 20520

uut_
University of Utah
Educational Media Center
Milton Bennion Hall 207
Salt Lake City, UT 84110
(801) 322-6112

uwap_
University of Washington
    Press
1416 NE 41st St.
Seattle, WA 98105

vfi_
Viewfinders, Inc.
P.O. Box 1665
Evanston, IL 60204
(312) 869-8602

vtn_
Video Tape Network
115 3. 62nd Street
New York, NY 10021
(212) 759-8735

wasu_
Audio-Visual Center
A Division of the Library
Washington State Univ.
Pullman, WA 99163
(509) 335-4535

wcf_
Westcoast Films
25 Luke St.
San Francisco, CA 94107
(415) 362-4700

webc_
Group W Productions, Inc.
Westinghouse Broadcasting
    Co.
240 W. 44th St.
New York, NY 10036
(212) 736-6300

wel_
Weling Motion Pictures
454 Meacham Ave.
Elmont, NY 11003
(516) 354-1066/6/8

weta_
WETA-TV
3620 27th Street, S.
Attention: David Deutsch

Arlington, VA 22206
(804) 820-4500

wgp/gre_
William Greaves Prod.
1776 Broadway (Suite 902)
New York, NY 10019
(212) 586-7710 or   (516) 775-
    1285

who_
Wholesome Film Center
20 Melrose St.
Boston, MA 02116
(617) 426-0155

who_
World Health Organization
Film Catalogue
Avenue Appia
1211 Geneva 27
Switzerland

wil_
Willoughby-Peerless
110 W. 32nd St.
New York, NY 10001
(212) 564-1660

wil_
Willoughby-Peerless
415 Lexington Ave
New York, NY 10017
(212) 687-1000

wrs_
Walter Reade 16
241 E. 34th St.
New York, NY 10016
(212) 683-6300

wsa_
Warner Bros.
Non-theatrical Div.
4000 Warner Blvd.
Burbank, CA 91505
(213) 843-6000

wsu_
Wayne State Univ.
Audio-Visual   Productions
    Center
680 Putnam
Detroit, MI 48202

xer_
See xex

xex/xer
Xerox Film
245 Long Hill Rd.
245 Long Hill Rd.
Middletown, CT 06457

yal
Yale   University   Media
  Design Studio
305 Crown Street
New Haven, CT 06520
(203) 436-4771

zip
See zph

zph/zip
Zipporah Films
54 Lewis Wharf
Boston, Mass 02110
(617) 742-6680

[1] Private collector of Jazz Films. Some available for rental.

[2] The film collection of the Institute for Sex Research is open only to qualified scholars and scientists who have demonstrable need for access. Arrangements must be made well in advance of any visit. Due to legal and other con- straints, no films may be loaned or copied. Inquiries should be sent to Joan Scherer Brewer, Information Service Officer, 416 Morrison Hall, Bloomington, Indiana 47402.

[3] The International Museum of Photography is located in the former residence of George Eastman; the primary concern of the film museum is the preservation of rare films. Screenings of both 35mm and 16mm films are possible. Scholars/researchers should make reservations in advance. Screening fees are charged. For further information write or call Marshall Deutelbaum, International Museum of Photography, complete address above.

[4] All films listed in the archive of the Imperial War Museum are British official films (except END OF THE DIALOGUE, made by Blacks), are Crown Copyright, not available for rental. However, copies may be purchased or viewed at the museum in London.

[5] All Library of Congress Films listed in the filmography are housed in the Motion Picture Section, which maintains the film collections for scholarly study and research. Public projection, preview, and loan services are not available. The section staff answers written and telephone inquiries about the holdings and makes appointments for the use of the reference facilities by individual scholars. The viewing facilities, which consist of several 16mm and 35mm viewing machines, may be used free of charge by serious researchers only; viewing times must be scheduled in ad- vance. Inquiries should be addressed to: Motion Picture Section, Library of Congress, Washington, D.C. 20540.

Films not restricted by copyright or donor agreement may be duplicated. In some cases a copyright search must be made and donor permission acquired. The cost is calculated on a price per foot basis and depends on the type of material held and type of copy desired. The Library requires payment in advance and whole roll printing only. For further information contact: Patrick Sheehan or Barbara Humphrys, Motion Picture Section, Library of Congress, Washington, D.C. 20540.

[6]Primarily an Archive, the Museum does have some films which circulate. See the MMA catalog.

[7]Inquiries by mail or phone regarding viewing. Individual researchers may study films in the motion picture research room, and groups may view them in the National Archives Theater, provided reference prints are available. In either case, reservations are generally needed. There is no charge for screening films at the National Archives. Reproduction services are available for filmmakers and other users; however, some films may be encumbered by copyright and/or other restrictions imposed by Government agencies or other sources. Inquiries concerning films or film services should be addressed to the Director, Audiovisual Archives Division, National Archives and Records Service, Washington, D.C. 20408. (Motion picture research room telephone number: (202) 963-6725.)

[8]Private collector of films mainly on Jazz and Blues (1929-1970's). Catalog of holdings available soon. Occasional screenings on the premises. Write for information.

[9]General Conditions Regarding Consultation of the Materials Preserved at the "Services Des Archives du Film": The consultation of cinematographic films at the Archives is possible for the benefit of professionals with proper credentials and under certain precise conditions. These conditions take into account particularly the rules of the collection as defined by the Rules Governing Use of the Services Des Archives du Film, which those making inquiries are requested to consult.

The request for consultation, obligatorily made by letter, must contain a precise goal of research, study, or analysis. The Service reserves the right to refuse requests for consultation which are incompatible with its archival obligation or which do not demonstrate a clearly expressed professional or research nature.

Bibliography

Black Film Reference

Bogle, Donald. Toms, Coons, Mulattoes, Mammies, and Bucks. New York: Viking Press, 1973.

Cripps, Thomas. Slow Fade to Black: The Negro in American Film, 1900-1942. New York: Oxford University Press, 1976.

Landay, Eileen. Black Film Stars. New York: Drake Publishers, 1973.

Leab, Daniel. From Sambo to Superspade: The Black Experience in Motion Pictures. Boston: Houghton Mifflin, 1976.

Mapp, Edward. Blacks in American Films: Today and Yesterday. Metuchen, New Jersey: The Scarecrow Press, 1972.

Maynard, Richard, ed. The Black on Film: Racial Stereotyping. New Jersey: Hayden Book Co., Inc., 1974.

Murray, James. To Find an Image: Black Films From Uncle Tom to Superfly. New York: Bobbs - Merrill, 1973.

Noble, Peter. The Negro in Films. London: Skelton Robinson, 1948; reprinted New York: Arno Press, 1970.

Null, Gary. Black Hollywood: The Negro in Motion Pictures. Secaucus, New Jersey: The Citadel Press, 1974.

Patterson, Lindsay, ed. Black Films and Filmmakers. New York: Dodd Mead, 1975.

Pines, Jim. Blacks in Cinema: The Changing Image.   London:
    Cassell and Collier Macmillan, 1974.

Powers,   Anne.   Blacks   in   American   Movies: A   Selected
    Bibliography.   Metuchen,   New   Jersey: The   Scarecrow
    Press, 1974.

                         Filmographies

Cyr, Helen W.   A Filmography   of   the Third World: An An-
    notated List of 16mm Films.   Metuchen, New Jersey: The
    Scarecrow Press, 1976.

Ferris,   Bill and Judy Peiser, eds.   American Folklore Films
    and Videotapes: An Index.   Center   for   Southern
    Folklore, Memphis, 1976.

Meeker, David.   Jazz in the Movies: A Guide to Jazz Musici-
    ans 1917-1977. New Rochelle: Arlington House Publica-
    tions. (First published in London, 1977.)

Ohrn, Steven and Rebecca Riley, compilers.   Africa from Reel
    to Reel.   African Studies Association, Waltham,   Mass.,
    1976.

Sampson, Henry T. Blacks in Black and White: A Source Book
    on Black Films, (1904-1950).   Metuchen, New Jersey:
    Scarecrow Press, 1977.   New Jersey: Scarecrow Press,
    1977.

Index of Black Performers

Man // You Can't Take It With You

Anderson, Ernest // In This Our Life // Peanut Man // Tick-
...Tick...Tick // Till the End of Time // Well, The // 3
for Bedroom C

Anderson, Esther // Two Gentlemen Sharing // Warm December,
A

Anderson, Ida // Son of Satan

Anderson, Ivie // Bundle of Blues, A // Day at the Races, A

Anderson, Myrtle // Green Pastures

Anderson, Robert // Crowning Experience, The

Anderson, Theresa // Jezebel

Andrade, Elisa // Sambizanga

Andrews, Billy // Crimson Fog, The

Angelou, Maya // Roots

Ansah, Tommy // Bushbaby, The

Arblanche, Kitty // Crimson Fog, The

Archer, Osceolo // Affair of the Skin, An

Armstrong, Henry // Keep Punching // Pittsburgh Kid, The

Armstrong, Louis // Artists and Models // Atlantic City //
Auf Wiedersehn // Beat Generation, The // Cabin in the Sky
// Doctor Rhythm // Every Day's a Holiday // Ex-Flame //
Five Pennies, The // Glenn Miller Story, The // Glory Al-
ley // Going Places // Hello, Dolly // Here Comes the
Groom // High Society // I'll Be Glad When You're Dead You
Rascal You // Jam Session // Jazz on a Summer's Day // La
Paloma // La Route du Bonheur // Louis Armstrong // Louis
Armstrong // Louis Armstrong and the All Stars // Man
Called Adam, A // Negro in Entertainment, The // New
Orleans // Paris Blues // Pennies from Heaven // Rhapsody
in Black and Blue // Satchmo the Great // Solo // Strip,
The // When the Boys Meet the Girls // Young Man With a
Horn

Arrindell, Helene // Nothing But a Man

Ashby, Irving // "King" Cole and His Trio

Ashford, Emmett // Bingo Long Traveling All-Stars and Motor
Kings, The

Aspinal, Nguba // Countdown at Kusini

Astwood, Norman // Murder on Lenox Avenue // Sunday Sinners

Family // Dixie Jamboree // DuBarry Was a Lady // Election
Lay // Expert, The // Facts of Life, The // Follow the
Ecys // General Spanky // Girl Missing // Girls About Town
// Glad Rag Doll // Goddess, The // Holiday Inn // I Dream
of Jeannie // I Want a Divorce // I'm No Angel // Imita-
tion of Life // In the Money // Jack London // Jackie
Robinson Story, The // Ladies of the Big House // Lady's
From Kentucky, The // Last Gangster, The // Life Goes On
// Love in a Eungalow // Made for Each Other // Make Way
for Tomorrow // Mr. Blandings Builds His Dreamhouse // My
Elue Heaven // No Time for Comedy // Peck's Bad Boy with
the Circus // Rainbow on the River // Reap the Wild Wind
// Reckless Living // Scandal Street // Seven Sweethearts
// Shadow of the Thin Man // She Done Him Wrong // Sundown
Trail // Teenage Rebel // Too Eusy to Work // Top Man //
Unashamed // Vanishing Virginian, The // Virginia // West
of the Pecos // What Price Hollywood // Wings over
Honolulu // You Can't Run Away From It // Young America

Bechet, Marieluise // Moon Over Harlem

Bechet, Sidney // L'Inspecteur Connait la Musique // La
   Route du Eonheur // Mcon Over Harlem // Serie Noire

Belafonte, Harry // Angel Levine, The // Bright Road // Buck
   and the Preacher // Carmen Jones // Island in the Sun //
   Odds Against Tomorrow // Uptown Saturday Night // World,
   the Flesh, and the Devil, The

Belafonte, Marguerite // Night of The Quarter Moon, The

Bell, Gene // Minstrel Man

Bell, Gwendolyn // Slaves

Eell, Spencer // Tenderfeet

Eelle de Knight, Fannie // Hallelujah

Eelle, Ida // While Thousands Cheer

Eengeloun, Alice // Moe

Benglia, Habib // Roots of Heaven, The

Eennett, Hope // Life Goes On

Eennett, Marilyn // Rockin' the Blues

Berry Erothers // Panama Hattie

Berry, Chuck // Jazz on a Summer's Day // T.A.M.I. Show, The

Best, Dearnie // Shanghai Chest, The

Eest, Willie // Arizonian, The // Blondie // Body Disappears, The // Breezing Home // Cabin in the Sky // General
   Spanky // Ghost Breakers, The // Gold Is Where You Find It

// Hidden Hand, The // Hold That Blonde // Home in Indiana // I Take This Woman // Kentucky Kernals // Little Miss Marker // Littlest Rebel, The // Make Way For a Lady // Merrily We Live // Monster Walks, The // Murder on a Bridle Path // Murder on a Honeymoon // Nancy Drew, Trouble Shooter // Nothing But the Truth // Pillow to Post // Racing Lady // Red Dragon, The // Red Stallion // Smiling Ghost, The // Spring Madness // Super Sleuth // Thank You, Jeeves // Thank Your Lucky Stars // Two in Revolt // Up Pops the Devil // Vivacious Lady // West of the Pecos // Whispering Ghosts // Who Killed Aunt Maggie? // Youth Takes a Fling

Bethea, David // Green Pastures

Bey, Marki // Landlord, The // Sugar Hill

Bibb, Leon // For Love of Ivy // Lost Man, The // Up Tight // Young One, The

Biron, Lillian // Dark and Cloudy

Bishop, Andrew // Brand of Cain, The // Ghost of Tolston's Manor // House Behind the Cedars, The // Son of Satan // Temptation

Black Diamond Dollies // Midnight Menace

Black, Valerie // Beware

Blake, Eubie // Eubie Blake Plays // Harlem is Heaven // Noble Sissle and Eubie Blake // Pie, Pie Blackbird // Scott Joplin // Sissle and Blake

Blake, Ruby // Sepia Cinderella

Blake, Sam // Man of Two Worlds

Blakely, Don // Short Eyes

Blakey, Rubel // Harlem Follies

Blane, Sally // Way Down South

Bledsoe, Jules // Drums of the Congo // Show Boat

Blossom, Alabama // Woman's a Fool

Blue, Vida // Black Gunn

Boles, Lottie // Realization of a Negro's Ambition, The

Bond, Judie // Guns of the Trees

Bond, Julian // Greased Lightning // It's Nation Time

Bonny, Fred // Drums O'Voodoo

Lilith // Lost Continent, The // Riot // Shadows

Carter, Ben // Bowery to Broadway // Crash Dive // Dark Alibi, The // Dixie Jamboree // Gone With the Wind // Harvey Girls, The // Maryland // Night Without Sleep // Safari // Scarlet Clue, The // Sporting Blood

Carter, Benny // "King" Cole and His Tric // Clash by Night // Snows of Kilimanjaro, The // Stars on Parade // View from Pompey's Head, The

Carter, Douglas // Love is an Awful Thing

Carter, Frank // Foolish Lives

Carter, Freddie // Jivin in Be Bop

Carter, Jack // Devil's Daughter, The // Miracle in Harlem // St. Louis Gal // Take My Life

Carter, Laveda // Harlem Follies

Carter, Terry // Abby // Black on White // Foxy Brown

Casey, Bernie // Big Mo // Black Chariot // Black Gunn // Brothers // Cleopatra Jones // Cornbread, Earl and Me // Guns of the Magnificent Seven // Hit Man // It Happened at Lakewood Manor // Panic on the 5:22 // Tick...Tick...Tick

Cash, Rosalind // Amazing Grace // Cornbread, Earl and Me // Hickey and Boggs // Melinda // New Centurians, The // Omega Man, The // Uptown Saturday Night

Catlett, Sidney // Harlem Follies // Jammin' the Blues

Cato, Minta // Girl From Chicago, The

Caviness, Cathryn // Blood of Jesus

Chamberlin, Lee // Uptown Saturday Night

Charles, Ray // Blues for Lovers // Swingin' Along

Chase, Anazette // Greatest, The

Chase, Bill // Souls of Sin

Chatman, Frank // Foolish Lives

Cheev, Lawyer // Music Hath Charms

Chenault, Lawrence // Birthright, ≤1 // Brute, The // Burden of Race, The // Call of His People, The // Children of Fate // Crimson Fog, The // Crimson Skull, The // Devil's Disciple, The // Ghost of Tolston's Manor // Gunsaulus Mystery // Homesteader, The // House Behind the Cedars, The // Prince of His Race, A // Scar of Shame // Schemers, The // Son of Satan // Spitfire // Sport of the Gods, The

The

Connor, Edric // Cry, The Beloved Country // Roots of Heaven, The // West of Zanzibar

Cook, Earle Browne // Dungeon, The

Cock, Laurence // Spock Who Sat By the Door, The

Cock, Louise // Exile, The

Cooke, Marie // Boarding House Blues

Cooley, Isabelle // Anna Lucasta

Cooper, Ralph // Am I Guilty? // Bargain with Bullets // Blonde Venus // Dark Manhattan // Luke Is Tops, The // Gang War // White Hunter

Copeland Family // Sweet Sweetback's Baadassssss Song

Core Harris // Harlem Hotshots

Corman, Lawrence // Black Gold

Cormick, Walter // Midnight Ace, The

Cornell, Anna // Harlem Follies

Cosby, Bill // Bill Cosby on Prejudice // Hickey and Boggs // Let's Do It Again // Man and Boy // Mother, Jugs and Speed // Piece of the Action, A // To All My Friend's on Shore // Uptown Saturday Night

Costanzo, Jack // "King" Cole and His Trio

Costell, Frank // Lying Lips

Couch, Robert // Hallelujah

Coulibalz, Moussa // Les Princes Noirs de Saint-Germain des Pres

Coutinho, Jorge // Ganga Zumba

Cowan, DeForrest // No Time for Romance // Take My Life

Cowan, Verlie // Betrayal, The // Betrayal, The

Cox, Ida // Woman's a Fool

Cox, Jewell // Foolish Lives

Cox, Jimmie // Disappearance of Mary Jane, The

Cramer, Harold // Boarding House Blues

Crawford, Aurelia // Les Princes Noirs de Saint-Germain des

Pres

Criner, John // Gang Smashers

Criner, Lawrence // Am I Guilty? // Eargain with Bullets // Duke Is Tcps, The // Flying Ace, The // Gang Smashers // Gang War // Life Gces On // Millionaire, The // Miracle in Harlem // Mr. Smith Goes Ghost // One Cark Night // Up Jumped the Cevil // While Thousands Cheer

Crockett, J. // $10,COC Trail, The

Cronk, Eilly // Lcuis Armstrong and the All Stars

Crosse, Rupert // Reivers, The // Shadows // To Trap a Spy // Too Late Elues

Crothers, Scatman // "King" Cole and His Trio // Coonskin // Great White Hope, The // Lady Sings the Blues // Lady in a Cage // Silver Streak // Sins cf Rachel Cade, The

Crcwell, William // Eirthright, ≤1 // Dungecn, The // House Behind the Cedars, The

Cruter, Gil // Cclored Champions of Sport

Cuban Dancers // Rockin' the Elues

Cumbuka, Ji-Tu // Lost In the Stars // Roots

Cumby, William // Green Pastures

Curley, Ian // Jivin in Be Bop

Curry, Nathan // Congo Maisie // Tarzan and His Mate // Thundericlt

Curtis, Willa Pearl // Native Son // Queen Bee // Unexpected Riches

Curtis, Yvette // Warm Cecember, A

Latney, Ardelle // Eroken Violin, The // Thirty Years Later

Dandridge, Dcrcthy // Eahama Passage // Bright Road // Carmen Jcnes // Lecks Ran Red, The // Drums of the Congo // Flamingc // Four Shall Lie // Harlem Globetrotters, The // Hit Parade of 1943, The // Island in the Sun // Jungle Queen // Lady frcm Iouisiana // Malaga // Mcment of Danger // Moo Cow Boogie // Pcrgy and Bess // Remains to be Seen // Sun Valley Serenade // Tamango // Tarzan's Peril

Dandridge, Putney // Harlem is Heaven

Dandridge, Ruby // Cabin in the Sky // Midnight Shadow

Daniels, Eilly // Eeat Generation, The // Night of The Quarter Moon, The // Sepia Cinderella

ly's Blues // Ride 'em Cowboy // St. Louis Blues // Tender
Game, The

Five Cabin Kids, The // Beginner's Luck // Gifts in Rhythm
// Teacher's Beau

Five Racketeers // All-Colcred Vaudeville Show

Flack, Rcberta // Erothers and Sisters in Concert // Legend
of John Henry, The // Scul to Soul

Fleming, Walter // Veiled Aristccrats

Fletcher, Lusty // Boarding Hcuse Blues // Killer Diller //
King fcr a Day

Florent, Napolean // Man cf Two Wcrlds

Flowers, Nathlyn // Ccuntdcwn at Kusini

Fluellen, Joel // Burning Crcss, The // Chase, The // Decks
Ran Red, The // Duffy of San Quentin // Friendly Per-
suasicn // Great White Hope, The // He Rides Tall // Jackie Rotinscn Story, The // Learning Tree, The // No Time
fcr Rcmance // Porgy and Bess // Raisin in the Sun, A //
Roustatcut // Sheriff, The // Sitting Bull // Sun Tan
Ranch // While Thousands Cheer // Young Savages, The

Fcrtier, Edith // Small Talk

Fcster, Daisy // Eroken Violin, The

Foster, Frances // Legacy cf Blccd

Foster, Cloria // Angel Levine, The // Ccmedians, The //
Cccl Wcrld, The // Man and Boy // Ncthing But a Man // To
All My Friend's on Shore

Fcuntaine, William // Deceit // Dungeon, The // Hallelujah
// Jasper Landry's Will // Virgin of the Seminole, The

Four Congaroos, The // Killer Diller

Four Hamptons // Lionel Hampton and Herb Jeffries

Fcur Horsemen Male Quartet // Sweet Shoe

Four Master Keys // Rcmance on the Beat

Four Tones // Harlem Rides the Range // One Dark Night

Fcur Tcrrers // Mystery in Swing // Son of Ingagi // Tcppers
Take a Bow

Fox, John // Soul Soldier

Fcxx, Redd // Cotton Comes to Harlem // Norman...Is That
You?

Jones // What Goes Up

Green, Joe // Black Six, The // Nobody's Children

Green, Kenneth // Hero Aint Nothin But a Sandwich, A

Greene, Laura // Putney Swope

Greene, Loretta // Black Girl

Greene, Otis // White Witch Doctor

Greene, Reuben // Boys in the Band, The

Greene, Sparky // American Shoeshine

Greene, Stanley // Nothing But a Man // W.W. and the Dixie Dancekings

Gregg, Richard // Dixie Love

Gregory, Dick // Sweet Love, Bitter

Grier, Pam // Arena, The // Beyond the Valley of the Dolls // Big Bird Cage, The // Black Mama, White Mama // Bucktown // Coffy // Foxy Brown // Friday Foster // Greased Lightning // Hit Man // Scream Blacula Scream

Grier, Roosevelt // Skyjacked // Thing with Two Heads, The

Griffin, Alex // Nobody's Children

Griffin, Douglas // House Behind the Cedars, The

Griggers, Roscoe // Music Hath Charms

Gross, Leon // Harlem Hotshots

Gude, Seydou // Moi un Noir

Gueye, Awa // Diankha-Bi

Gueye, Ita // Liberte Un

Gueye, Makhouredia // Lambaaye

Gueye, Mody // Lambaaye // Njangaan

Gueye, N'dack // Reou Takh

Guilford, Willor Lee // Daughter of the Congo // Easy Street // Ten Minutes to Live

Guillaume, Robert // Super Fly T.N.T.

Gulfport, Billy // Spiders Web, The

Gunn, Bill // Ganja and Hess

No Tales // Thunderbolt

Harrison, Richard B. // Easy Street

Hart, Fred // His Great Chance

Hartman, Ena // Girl Nobody Knows, The // New Interns, The // Our Man Flint

Hartman, Ras Daniel // Harder They Come, The

Haven, Shirley // No Time for Romance

Havens, Richie // Catch My Soul

Hawkins, Alfred // Dirty Gerty from Harlem, USA

Hawkins, Charles // Double Deal // Gang Smashers

Hawkins, Erskine // Deviled Hams

Hawkins, Flow // That Man of Mine

Hawley, Monte // Am I Guilty? // Double Deal // Duke Is Tops, The // Gang Smashers // Gang War // Ghost of Tolston's Manor // Life Goes On // Lock Out, Sister // Mantan Messes Up // Merrie Howe Carfe // Mr. Smith Goes Ghost // Mystery in Swing // One Dark Night // Take My Life // Tall, Tan, and Terrific // While Thousands Cheer

Hayden, Ted // Sweet Sweetback's Baadassssss Song

Hayes, Isaac // Brothers and Sisters in Concert // Three Tough Guys // Truck Turner

Haynes, Betty // That Man of Mine

Haynes, Daniel // Escape From Devil's Island // Hallelujah // Last Mile, The // So Red the Rose

Haynes, Hilda // Diary of a Mad Housewife // Gone Are the Days

Haynes, Lloyd // Good Guys Wear Black, The // Greatest, The

Haywood, Donald // Exile, The

Heard, Nathan C. // Gordon's War

Heath, Gordon // Les Laches Vivant d'Espoir // Sapphire

Heath, James // Slaves

Heath, Mark // Call Me Bwana

Heathman, Josephine // Hello Bill

Heavenly Choir // Blood of Jesus

Krakatoa, East of Java // Live and Let Die // Shango

Holder, Ram John // Leo the Last // Two Gentlemen Sharing

Holeby, Walter // Giant of His Race, A // Shot in the Night, A

Holiday, Billie // "Sugar Chile" Robinson - Billie Holiday - Count Basie and His Sextet // New Orleans // Sound of Jazz, The // Symphony in Black

Holland, Byrd // Soul Soldier

Holly, Ellen // Take a Giant Step

Hollywood Jitterbugs // Woman's a Fool

Holmes, "Rubberneck" // Solid Senders

Holms, Rich // Tough!

Homes, Mabel // Giant of His Race, A

Hondo, Med // Moe

Honi Coles and Choley Atkins // Rock 'N' Roll Revue

Hooks, Kevin // Aaron Loves Angela // Hero Aint Nothin But a Sandwich, A // Sounder

Hooks, Robert // Frederick Douglass // Hurry Sundown // Last of the Mobile Hot Shots // Sweet Love, Bitter // Trouble Man

Hope, "Boots" // Broken Violin, The

Hopkins, Jack // For His Mother's Sake

Hopkins, Linda // Rockin' the Blues

Horne, Lena // Bip Bam Boogie // Blonde Venus // Boogie Woogie Dream // Broadway Rhythm // Cabin in the Sky // Death of a Gunfighter // Duchess of Idaho // Duke Is Tops, The // Harlem Hotshots // Harlem on Parade // Hi-de-ho Holiday // I Dood It // Mantan Messes Up // Meet Me in Las Vegas // Panama Hattie // Stormy Weather // Swing Fever // That's Entertainment // Thousands Cheer // Till the Clouds Roll By // Two Girls and a Sailor // Words and Music // Ziegfeld Follies

Hoskins, Allen // Ask Grandma // Baby Brother // Baby Clothes // Back Stage // Bargain Day // Barnum and Ringling, Inc. // Bear Shooters // Better Movies // Big Business // Big Show, The // Big Town, The // Bouncing Babies // Boxing Gloves // Boys Will be Joys // Boys to Board // Bring Home the Turkey // Buccaneers, The // Buried Treasure // Cat, Dog and Co. // Champeen, The // Chicken Feed // Circus Fever // Cobbler, The // Commence-

ment Day // Cradle Robbers // Crazy House // Derby Day //
Dog Days // Dog Heaven // Dogs of War // Edison, Marconi
and Co. // Election Day // Every Man for Himself // Fair
and Muddy // Fast Company // Fast Freight // Fire Fighters
// First Seven Years, The // Fish Hooky // Fly My Kite //
Fourth Alarm, The // Giants vs. Yanks // Glorious Fourth,
The // Good Cheer // Heebee Jeebees // Helping Grandma //
High Society // Holy Terror, The // It's a Bear // Jubilo
Jr. // July Days // Lazy Days // Little Daddy // Little
Mother // Lodge Night // Love Bug, The // Love Business //
Love My Dog // Mary, Queen of Tots // Mayor of Hell, The
// Moan and Groan, Inc. // Monkey Business // Mysterious
Mystery, The // No Noise // Noisy Noises // Official Of-
ficers // Old Wallop, The // Olympic Games // One Terrible
Day // One Wild Ride // Playin' Hookey // Pleasant
Journey, A // Pups is Pups // Railroadin' // Rainy Days //
Reckless // Saturday Morning // Saturday's Lesson //
School Begins // School's Out // Seein' Things // Seeing
the World // Shivering Shakespeare // Shivering Spooks //
Shootin' Injuns // Small Talk // Smile Wins, The // Spank-
ing Age, The // Spook Spoofing // Stage Fright // Sun Down
Limited, The // Sunday Calm // Teacher's Pet // Telling
Whoppers // Ten Years Old // Thundering Fleas // Tire
Trouble // Tired Business Men // Tough Winter, A // Uncle
Tom's Uncle // War Feathers // When the Wind Blows // Wig-
gle Your Ears // Yale vs. Harvard // Young Sherlocks //
Your Own Back Yard

Hoskins, Jannie // Baby Brother // Big Business // Bring
Home the Turkey // Chicken Feed // Commencement Day //
Fourth Alarm, The // Glorious Fourth, The // Good Cheer //
Monkey Business // Olympic Games // Playin' Hookey //
Smile Wins, The // Ten Years Old // Thundering Fleas //
Tired Business Men // Uncle Tom's Uncle // War Feathers //
Yale vs. Harvard

Houston, Eddye L. // Go Down Death

Howard, Bob // Howard's House Party // Junction 88 // Murder
With Music // Stars on Parade

Howard, Gertrude // Hearts in Dixie // I'm No Angel // Show
Boat // Southerner, The

Howard, Shingzie // Children of Fate // Dungeon, The //
House Behind the Cedars, The // Jasper Landry's Will //
Prince of His Race, A // Son of Satan // Virgin of the
Seminole, The

Hubba Hubba Girls // Oop Boop Sh'bam

Huey, Richard // Caldonia

Hughes, Rhetta // Sweet Sweetback's Baadassssss Song

Humes, Helen // Be Bata Leba // Jivin in Be Bop

Hunter, Floyd // Hello Bill

Hurd, Hugh // For Love of Ivy // Shadows

Hurlic, Lucky // Helldorado

Hurlic, Philip // Penrod and Sam

Hurricanes, The // Rockin' the Blues

Hussein, M. // Angelo

Hyson, Roberta // Framing of the Shrew, The // Georgia Rose // Melancholy Dame

Illing, Peter // West of Zanzibar

Inglehart, Jim // Beyond the Valley of the Dolls

Ingram, Clifford // Hearts in Dixie

Ingram, Rex // A Thousand and One Nights // Anna Lucasta // Big Parade, The // Cabin in the Sky // Captain Blood // Congo Crossing // Dark Waters // Elmer Gantry // Emperor Jones, The // Fired Wife // God's Little Acre // Green Pastures // Huckleberry Finn, The Adventures of // Hurry Sundown // Journey to Shiloh // King Kong // King of Kings, The // Moonrise // Sahara // Sign of the Cross, The // Talk of the Town, The // Tarzan of the Apes // Ten Commandments, The // Thief of Bagdad, The // Watusi // Your Cheatin' Heart

Ink Spots, The // Great American Broadcast, The // Ink Spots, The

Isham Jones and His Orchestra // Meet the Maestros

Jacks, S.T. // Millionaire, The

Jackson Five // Brothers and Sisters in Concert // Rhythm Rodeo

Jackson, Al // Boy! What a Girl! // Children of Fate

Jackson, Aunty // Saturday Morning

Jackson, Ian // Roots of Heaven, The

Jackson, Ernestine // Aaron Loves Angela

Jackson, Eugene // Circus Fever // Hearts in Dixie // Love Bug, The // Mysterious Mystery, The // Shootin' Injuns // Take My Life

Jackson, Freddie // Double Deal // Merrie Howe Carfe

Jackson, Horace // Living Between Two Worlds

Jackson, Jesse // It's Nation Time

Jones, Quincy // Harlem Jazz Festival

Jones, Robert Earl // Lying Lips // Notorious Elinor Lee, The // One Potato, Two Potato // Terror in the City // Wild River

Jones, Thaddeus // Maryland

Jordan, Louis // Beware // Beware // Caldonia // Follow the Boys // Look Out, Sister // Reet, Petite and Gone // Swing Parade of 1946 // Toot That Trumpet

Jordan, Sam // Flying Ace, The

Jordan, Taft // Duke Ellington and His Orchestra

Joyce, Adrian // For His Mother's Sake

Joynes, Roxie // Caldonia

Juanita Hall Choir // Miracle in Harlem

Julien, Max // Mack, The // Psych-Out // Savage Seven, The // Thomasine and Bushrod // Up Tight

Juma // Safari // West of Zanzibar

Kain, Gylan // Right On

Kalana, Thais Nehli // Loyal Hearts

Kane, Sally // Diankha-Bi

Keith, Rosaline // Bad Boy

Kelly, Jim // Black Belt Jones // Enter the Dragon // Melinda // Take a Hard Ride // Three the Hard Way

Kelly, Matel // Midnight Ace, The // Thirty Years Later

Kelly, Paula // Andromeda Strain, The // Lost In the Stars // Spook Who Sat By the Door, The // Three Tough Guys // Top of the Heap // Trouble Man // Uptown Saturday Night

Kelson, Anna // Flames of Wrath, The

Kemp, Mae // Call of His People, The

Kennedy, Ann // Scar of Shame

Kerr, J. Herbert, Jr. // Place Called Today, A

Keyes, Joe, Jr. // Where's Poppa?

Khambatta, Persis // Wilby Conspiracy, The

Kiallo, Madeline // Kodou

// Nothing But a Man

Lincoln, Rosalie (Rosa Lee) // Absent // Rhythm Rodeo

Lindsay, Powell // Love in Syncopation // Souls of Sin //
That Man of Mine

Lindy Hoppers // Swanee Showboat

Liney, Jack // Dark Manhattan

Lipscomb, Mance // Le Blues Entre les Dents

Liston, Sonny // Moonfire

Little Richard // Girl Can't Help It, The

Little, Cleavon // Blazing Saddles // Day the Earth Moved,
The // Greased Lightning // Vanishing Point

Lockhart, Calvin // Beast Must Die, The // Cotton Comes to
Harlem // Dandy in Aspic, A // Dark of the Sun // Halls of
Anger // High Commissioner // Honey Baby, Honey Baby //
Joanna // Leo the Last // Melinda // Myra Breckinridge //
Only When I Larf // Salt and Pepper // Uptown Saturday
Night

Logan, Ruby // One Dark Night

Long, Avon // Centennial Summer // Finian's Rainbow //
Romance on the High Seas // Ziegfeld Follies

Long, Walter // His Great Chance // Shot in the Night, A

Louis, Joe // Fight Never Ends, The // Spirit of Youth

Love, Garfield // Rhythm in a Riff

Lovejoy, Alec // Birthright, ≤2 // Black and Tan // Brand of
Cain, The // Moon Over Harlem // Murder on Lenox Avenue //
Sunday Sinners // Swing

Lovejoy, Alice // God's Stepchildren

Loveless, Henrietta // Brand of Cain, The // Spiders Web,
The

Lowe, James // Blue Streak Series // Uncle Tom's Cabin

Lucas, Charles // Homesteader, The // Within Our Gates

Lucas, George // Deceit

Lucas, Sam // Uncle Tom's Cabin

Luciano, Felipe // Right On

Lunceford, Jimmy // Blues in the Night

McCann, Les // Soul to Soul

McClain, Billy // Bargain with Bullets // Nagana

McClennan, Frank H. // Blood of Jesus

McCoo, Arthur // Betrayal, The

McCoy, Austin // No Time for Romance // No Time for Romance // Sun Tan Ranch

McCurdy, Anna Marie // Crowning Experience, The

McCurdy, George // Crowning Experience, The

McCurry, John // Bingo Long Traveling All-Stars and Motor Kings, The

McDaniel, Etta // Lawless Nineties, The // Pittsburgh Kid, The

McDaniel, Hattie // Affectionately Yours // Alice Adams // Aniversary Trouble // Arbor Day // Battle of Broadway // Blonde Venus // Bride Walks Out, The // Can This be Dixie // China Seas // Family Honeymoon // First Baby, The // Gentle Julia // George Washington Slept Here // Gold West, The // Gone With the Wind // Great Lie, The // Hearts Divided // High Tension // Hypnotized // In This Our Life // Janie // Johnny Vagabond // Judge Priest // Little Colonel, The // Little Men // Lost in the Stratosphere // Mad Miss Manton, The // Male Animal, The // Margie // Maryland // Music is Magic // Nothing Sacred // Operator 13 // Postal Inspector // Prisoner of Shark Island, The // Reunion // Saratoga // Shopworn Angel, The // Show Boat // Since You Went Away // Song of the South // Star for a Night // Story of Temple Drake, The // Thank Your Lucky Stars // They Died With Their Boots On // True Confession // Zenobia // 45 Fathers

McDaniel, Sam "Deacon" // All Through the Night // Am I Guilty? // Bad Men of Missouri // Bargain with Bullets // Dark Manhattan // Flamingo Road // Foxes of Harrow, The // Great Lie, The // Louisiana Purchase // Pride of the Blue Grass // Sullivan's Travels

McEachin, James // Buck and the Preacher // Fuzz // Hello, Dolly // If He Hollers, Let Him Go // Lawyer, The // Play Misty for Me // True Grit // Undefeated, The // Up Tight

McElrath, Joyce // Beale Street Mama

McGarrity, Everett // Hallelujah

McGee, Vonetta // Blacula // Brothers // Detroit 9000 // Hammer // Lost Man, The // Melinda // Shaft in Africa // Superdome // Thomasine and Bushrod

McGinty, Artilbelle // Chicago After Dark

McGuire, Lawrence // Hearts of the Woods

McKee, Lonette // Sparkle: From Ghetto to Superstars // Which Way Is Up?

McKinney, Chick // Drums O'Voodoo

McKinney, Nina Mae // Black Network // Dark Waters // Devil's Daughter, The // Gang Smashers // Hallelujah // In Old Kentucky // Life is Real // Night Train to Memphis // On Velvet // Pie, Pie Blackbird // Pinky // Reckless // Safe in Hell // Sanders of the River // St. Louis Gal // Straight to Heaven // Swanee Showboat // Without Love

McLane, Lorenzo // Spiders Web, The

McMillen, Allen // Chicago After Dark

McMillion, Walter // Go Down Death

McMowan, Edward // For His Mother's Sake

McNair, Barbara // Change of Habit // If He Hollers, Let Him Go // Mother Goose a Go-Go // Organization, The // Spencer's Mountain // Stiletto // They Call Me Mister Tibbs // Venus in Furs

McNeely, Howard Louis // Jackie Robinson Story, The

McNeil, Claudia // Black Girl // Last Angry Man, The // Raisin in the Sun, A // There Was a Crooked Man... // To Be Young, Gifted and Black

McQueen, Butterfly // Affectionately Yours // Amazing Grace // Cabin in the Sky // Duel in the Sun // Gone With the Wind // I Dood It // Killer Diller // Mildred Pierce // Phynx, The // Women, The

McRae, Carmen // Hotel

McShee, Brownie // Le Blues Entre les Dents

Melo, Breno // Black Orpheus

Meyers, Pauline // Take a Giant Step

Michaels, Dan // Black King, The

Micheaux, Elder // We've Got the Devil on the Run

Michelle, Janee // Soul Soldier

Mickey, Arline // Children of Fate // Ten Nights in a Bar-room

Milburn, Amos // Basin Street Revue // Rhythm and Blues Revue

Miller Brothers and Lois // Hi-de-ho

Miller Sisters // Rockin' the Blues

Miller, F.E. // Double Deal // Lucky Ghost // Mystery in Swing // Rockin' the Blues // Stormy Weather

Miller, Fay // Hell's Alley

Miller, Flournoy E. // Bronze Buckeroo // Harlem Rides the Range // Harlem on the Prairie // Jimtown Speakeasy // Mantan Runs for Mayor // Mayor of Jimtown // Midnight Lodge // Mr. Creeps // Mr. Washington Goes to Town // Professor Creeps // Return of Mandy's Husband // She's Too Mean to Me // That's the Spirit

Millinder, Lucky // Paradise in Harlem // Rhythm on the Run

Mills Brothers // Big Broadcast, The // Chatterbox // Cowboy Canteen // Fight Never Ends, The // He's My Guy // Operator 13 // Reveille With Beverly // Rhythm Parade // Sing as You Swing // Strictly Dynamite // 20 Million Sweethearts

Mills, Jerry // Railroad Porter, The

Mines, Callie // Birthright, ≤1

Mingus, Charles // All Night Long

Mitchell, Abbie // Eyes of Youth // Scapegoat, The

Mitchell, Billy // Professor Creeps

Mitchell, Don // Scream Blacula Scream

Mitchell, Gwen // Shaft

Mitchell, Knolly // Black King, The

Mitchell, Tressie // Ten Minutes to Live

Mkopi, Johan // Bushbaby, The

Modisane, Bloke // Dark of the Sun

Monagas, Lionel // Brand of Cain, The // Drums O'Voodoo // Keep Punching // Millionaire, The // Romance on the Beat // Straight to Heaven

Monk, Thelonius // Jazz on a Summer's Day // Sound of Jazz, The

Monroe, Millie // Mr. Smith Goes Ghost

Moody, Lynn // Roots

Moore, Archie // Carpetbaggers, The // Fortune Cookie, The // Huckleberry Finn, The Adventures of

Moore, Charles // Exile, The // Homesteader, The

Moore, Edward // Ten Nights in a Barroom

Moore, Gertrude // His Great Chance

Moore, Juanita // Girl Can't Help It, The // Imitation of Life // Lydia Bailey // Mack, The // Rosie // Singing Nun, The // Up Tight // Walk on the Wild Side // Woman's Prison

Moore, Katherine // Dirty Gerty from Harlem, USA

Moore, Lisa // Hit Man

Moore, Marian // Square Joe

Moore, Matt // Bad Boy

Moore, Melba // Lost In the Stars

Moore, Monette // Yes Sir, Mr. Bones

Moore, Ray // Rhythm in a Riff

Moore, Tim // Boy! What a Girl! // His Great Chance

Moore, Tommivetta // Broken Strings

Moore, Tommy // Mystery in Swing

Moore, Toni // That Man of Mine

Mordecai, Jimmy // Yamacraw

Moreland, Mantan // Amateur Detective // Basin Street Revue // Bowery to Broadway // Cabin in the Sky // Charlie Chan in the Secret Service // Chasing Trouble // Chinese Cat, The // Chinese Ring, The // Come on Cowboy // Comic, The // Crime Smasher // Dark Alibi, The // Docks of New Orleans, The // Dreamer, The // Ellery Queen's Penthouse Mystery // Eyes in the Night // Farewell to Fame // Feathered Serpent, The // Footlight Serenade // Four Shall Die // Frontier Scout // Gang Smashers // Golden Eye, The // Harlem on the Prairie // In the Night // Irish Luck // Jade Mask, The // Jazz Festival // Juke Joint // King of the Zombies // Laughing at Danger // Law of the Jungle // Lucky Ghost // Mantan Messes Up // Mantan Runs for Mayor // Melody Parade // Mexican Spitfire Sees a Ghost // Millionaire Playboy // Mr. Creeps // Mr. Washington Goes to Town // Next Time I Marry // Night Club Girl // One Dark Night // Phantom Killer, The // Professor Creeps // Return of Mandy's Husband // Revenge of the Zombies // Rhythm and Blues Revue // Rock 'N' Roll Revue // Rockin' the Blues // Sarong Girl // Scarlet Clue, The // Shadow Over Chinatown // Shanghai Chest, The // She's Too Mean to Me // Sky

Dragon, The // South of Dixie // Spiders, The // Spirit of Youth // Strange Case of Dr. Rx // Tall, Tan, and Terrific // That's the Spirit // Trap, The // Treat 'Em Rough // Up Jumped the Devil // Up in the Air // Watermelon Man // What a Guy // While Thousands Cheer // You're Out of Luck

Moreland, Marcella // Am I Guilty?

Morris, Earl J. // Broken Strings // Bronze Buckeroo // Son of Ingagi

Morris, Garrett // Car Wash // Cooley High // Where's Poppa?

Morris, Greg // Countdown at Kusini // New Interns, The // COM-TAC 303

Morris, Mae // Why Worry?

Morris, Mercury // Black Six, The

Morrison, Ernie // Fire Fighters

Morrison, Ernie // Back Stage // Big Business // Big Show, The // Boys to Board // Buccaneers, The // Champeen, The // Cobbler, The // Commencement Day // Cradle Robbers // Derby Day // Dogs of War // Fast Company // Flying Wild // Giants vs. Yanks // It's a Bear // July Days // Lodge Night // Mr. Wise Guy // No Noise // One Terrible Day // Our Gang // Penrod // Pleasant Journey, A // Quiet Street, A // Saturday Morning // Seein' Things // Stage Fright // Sunday Calm // Tire Trouble // Young Sherlocks

Morrison, Ernie, Sr. // Circus Fever // Fire Fighters // Lodge Night // Love Bug, The // Pleasant Journey, A // Quiet Street, A // Saturday Morning

Morrison, Florence // Penrod

Morrow, Guernsey // Am I Guilty? // Take My Life

Morton, Edgar Lewis // Chicago After Dark

Morton, Edna // Burden of Race, The // Call of His People, The // Ghost of Tolston's Manor // Schemers, The // Simp, The // Son of Satan // Spitfire

Mosby's Blue Blowers // Thunderbolt

Moseley, Thomas // Crimson Fog, The // Hell's Alley

Moses, Ethel // Birthright, ≤2 // God's Stepchildren // Gone Harlem // Harlemania // Underworld

Moses, Lucia Lynn // Scar of Shame

Mosley, Roger E. // Darktown Strutters // Leadbelly // Sweet Jesus Preacher Man

Moten, Etta // Flying Down to Rio // Gold Diggers of 1933

Mukwanazi, David // Magic Garden, The

Murray, Art // Bargain with Bullets

Murray, John "Rastus" // Fight that Ghost // House Rent Party

Muse, Clarence // Act of Murder, An // Alias Mary Dow // Attorney For the Defense // Black Moon // Broadway Bill // Broken Earth // Broken Strings // Buck and the Preacher // Cabin in the Cotton, The // Car Wash // Count of Monte Cristo, The // Dirigible // Flying Down to Rio // Follow Your Heart // From Hell to Heaven // Fury of the Jungle // Gentleman From Dixie // Harmony Lane // Hearts in Dixie // Heaven Can Wait // Hell's Highway // Huckleberry Finn // Invisible Ghost, The // Is My Face Red // Jam Session // Joe Palooka in the Knockout // Last Parade // Laughing Irish Eyes // Laughter in Hell // Maryland // Massacre // Mind Reader, The // Muss 'Em Up // Night and Day // O'Shaughnessy's Boy // Peanut Man // Porgy and Bess // Prestige // Rain or Shine // Rainbow on the River // Riding High // Road to Mandalay // Royal Romance, A // Safe in Hell // Secret Witness // Secrets of a Nurse // Shadow of a Doubt // Show Boat // So Red the Rose // Spirit of Youth // Tales of Manhattan // Toy Wife, The // Two Smart People // Volcano // Washington Merry-Go-Round // Way Down South // White Zombie // Winner Take All // Woman from Monte Carlo, The // Zanzibar

Nance, Ray // Duke Ellington and His Orchestra

Nar Sene, Momar // La Noire de...

Narcisse, Joseph C. // White Witch Doctor

Nash, Johnny // Key Witness // Take a Giant Step

Nder, Sala // Samba Tali

Ndiaye, Tabara // Ceddo

Nelson, David // Right On

Nelson, Howard // Nobody's Children

Newell, Inez // Dirty Gerty from Harlem, USA

Newsome, Carmen // Birthright, ≤2 // God's Stepchildren // Lying Lips // Notorious Elinor Lee, The // Swing

Newsome, Don // If He Hollers, Let Him Go

Newton, Jack // For His Mother's Sake

Ngakane, Lionel // Cry, The Beloved Country // Safari

Niang, Isseu // Lambaaye // Mandabi // Samba Tali

Niang, Mareme // Baks

Nicholas Brothers // All-Colored Vaudeville Show // Barbershop Blues // Black Network // Dixieland Jamboree // Down Argentine Way // Great American Broadcast, The // Orchestra Wives // Pie, Pie Blackbird // Pirate, The // Sun Valley Serenade // Zee also Nicholas, Fayard and Nicholas, Harold

Nicholas, Denise // Blacula

Nicholas, Fayard // Big Broadcast of 1936 // Liberation of L.B. Jones, The // Zee also Nicholas Brothers

Nicholas, Harold // Big Broadcast of 1936 // Carolina Blues // Zee also Nicholas Brothers

Nichols, Denise // Let's Do It Again // Soul of Nigger Charley, The

Nicholson, Calvin // Flaming Crisis, The

Nix, Victor // Greatest Sin

Noel, Hattie // King for a Day

Noisette, Katherine // Daughter of the Congo // Exile, The // Wages of Sin, The

Nollan, K.D. // Come Back

Norcom, Alfred // Regeneration

Norman, Maidie // About Mrs. Leslie // Big Mo // Bright Road // Burning Cross, The // Final Comedown, The // Peanut Man // Say Goodbye, Maggie Cole // Star is Born, A // Well, The // What Ever Happened to Baby Jane

Norton, Ken // Mandingo

Obileye, Yomi // Countdown at Kusini

Odetta // Autobiography of Miss Jane Pittman, The // Sanctuary

Oduor, Paul // Lion, The

Offley, Hilda // Miracle in Harlem

Ogunnaike, Kola // Countdown at Kusini

Oiman, Roscoe // Willie Dynamite

Okorodudu, Helen // Countdown at Kusini

Oliver, George // Murder With Music

Oliver, Thelma // Pawnbroker, The

Oliviera, Domingas // Sambizanga

Olusola, Elsie // Countdown at Kusini

Onikoyi, Rasheed // Countdown at Kusini

Oncoloo, Mutia // Trader Horn

Original Dixieland Jazz Band // March of Time // March of Time

Ovey, George // Dark and Cloudy

Owens, Virgil // Absent

Pace, Judy // Brian's Song // Cool Breeze // Cotton Comes to Harlem // Fortune Cookie, The // Slams, The // Thomas Crown Affair, The // Three in the Attic // Three in the Cellar // 13 Frightened Girls

Page, Harrison // Beyond the Valley of the Dolls // Vixen

Pancho and Dolores // Jivin in Be Bop

Pagiun, Robert // Lying Lips

Parker, Charlie // Stage Entrance

Parker, Dolores // "King" Cole and His Trio

Parker, Leonard // Nothing But a Man

Parks, Trina // Darktown Strutters

Patrick, F. // $10,000 Trail, The

Patterson and Jackson // Killer Diller

Patterson, J. Patrick // Joint is Jumping, The

Patterson, Marguerite // Foolish Lives

Patterson, Warren // Boy! What a Girl!

Patton, Jonella // Foolish Lives

Paul, Ike // Broken Violin, The

Pawley, William, Jr. // Crowning Experience, The

Payne, Freda // Book of Numbers, The

Payton, Lew // Jezebel // Lady for a Night // Lady's From Kentucky, The

Pointer Sisters, The // Car Wash

Poitier, Sidney // All the Young Men // Band of Angels //
Bedford, Incident, The // Blackboard Jungle, The //
Brother John // Buck and the Preacher // Cry, The Beloved
Country // Defiant Ones, The // Duel at Diablo // Edge of
the City // For Love of Ivy // Go, Man, Go // Goodbye, My
Lady // Greatest Story Ever Told, The // Guess Who's
Coming to Dinner // In the Heat of the Night // Let's Do
It Again // Lillies of the Field // Long Ships, The //
Lost Man, The // Mark of the Hawk, The // No Way Out //
Organization, The // Paris Blues // Patch of Blue, A //
Piece of the Action, A // Porgy and Bess // Pressure Point
// Raisin in the Sun, A // Red Ball Express // Slender
Thread, The // Something of Value // They Call Me Mister
Tibbs // Thinking Book, The // To Sir, With Love // Uptown
Saturday Night // Virgin Island // Warm December, A //
Wilby Conspiracy, The

Poke, Leon // Midnight Menace

Polk, Oscar // Cabin in the Sky // Gone With the Wind //
Green Pastures // Underworld // White Cargo

Pope, Leo // Eleven P.M.

Popwell, Johnny // Heart is a Lonely Hunter, The

Poree, Anita // Living Between Two Worlds

Porter, Uriel // Man of Two Worlds

Preer, Evelyn // Birthright, ≤1 // Blonde Venus // Brown
Gravy // Brute, The // Conjure Woman, The // Deceit //
Devil's Disciple, The // Dungeon, The // Framing of the
Shrew, The // Georgia Rose // Gunsaulus Mystery //
Homesteader, The // Hypocrite, The // Lady Fare, The //
Melancholy Dame // Music Hath Charms // Oft in the Silly
Night // Spiders Web, The // Widow's Bite, The // Within
Our Gates

Premice, Josephine // Autobiography of Miss Jane Pittman,
The

Prescod, Pearl // Beware of Children

Press, Gloria // God's Stepchildren

Preston, Billy // St. Louis Blues

Price, Victor // Come Back

Priest, Martin // Nothing But a Man

Pringle, Joan // J.D.'s Revenge

Pryor, Richard // Bingo Long Traveling All-Stars and Motor

Kings, The // Busy Body, The // Car Wash // Greased Light-
ning // Hit // Lady Sings the Blues // Mack, The // Phynx,
The // Silver Streak // Uptown Saturday Night // Which Way
Is Up? // Wild in the Streets

Purty, Jessie // Wife Hunters, The

Quarles, Vivian // Modern Cain, A

Qubeka, Harriet // Magic Garden, The

Rae, Charlie Mae // Souls of Sin

Rahn, Muriel // King for a Day

Rainey, Pat // Dreamer, The

Ralph, Sheryl Lee // Piece of the Action, A

Rama-Take // Cain

Ramokgopa, Tommy // Magic Garden, The

Randall, Lord // Romance on the Beat

Randol, George // Exile, The // Harlem on the Prairie

Randolph, Amanda // Black Network // Comes Midnight // Lying
Lips // Notorious Elinor Lee, The // She's Working Her Way
Through College // Swing

Randolph, Forbes // Cotton-Pickin' Days

Randolph, Lillian // Am I Guilty? // Life Goes On // Mr.
Smith Goes Ghost

Rasulala, Thalmus // Autobiography of Miss Jane Pittman, The
// Bait, The // Blacula // Cool Breeze // Roots // Willie
Dynamite

Rathebe, Dolly // Magic Garden, The

Ray, Arthur // Am I Guilty? // Burden of Race, The // Gang
Smashers // One Dark Night // Professor Creeps // Son of
Ingagi // Take My Life // Ties of Blood

Ray, Ellen // Come Back

Red Lilly Chorus // Harlem Hotshots

Redd, Frances // Midnight Shadow

Redman, Don // I Heard

Reed, Clarence // Daughter of the Congo

Reed, George // Absent // Birth of a Nation, The // Green
Pastures // Hold Your Man // Home in Indiana // Huckleber-

ry Finn // Kentucky // Maryland // Red Lights // Show Boat // So Red the Rose // Sporting Blood // Swanee River // Tales of Manhattan

Reed, Sandy // Tough!

Reed, Terry // Hammerhead

Reed, Tracy // Car Wash // Casino Royale // Devils of Darkness // Dr. Strangelove or: How I Learned to Stop Worrying and Love the Bomb // Main Chance, The // Maroc 7 // Shot in the Dark, A // Take, The // You Must Be Joking!

Renard, Ken // Lydia Bailey // Murder With Music // Something of Value

Reynolds, George // Lying Lips

Reynolds, Steve // Bull Doggers, The // Crimson Skull, The // Flying Ace, The // Regeneration

Rhodes, Dotty // It Happened in Harlem // Romance on the Beat

Rhodes, Hari // Blindfold // Detroit 9000 // Drums of Africa // Fiercest Heart, The // Matt Helm // Mirage // Nun and the Sergeant, The // Return to Peyton Place // Roots // Satan Bug, The // Shock Corridor // Taffy and the Jungle Hunter

Rhythm Rascals Orchestra // Girl From Chicago, The

Rich, Ron // Fortune Cookie, The

Richards, Beah // Gone Are the Days // Great White Hope, The // Guess Who's Coming to Dinner // Hurry Sundown // In the Heat of the Night // Miracle Worker, The // Outrage // Take a Giant Step

Richardson, Daisy // Jivin in Be Bop

Richardson, Emery // Beware // Boarding House Blues // Souls of Sin

Richmond, June // Dreamer, The // Murder in Swingtime // Reet, Petite and Gone

Riley, Juanita // Blood of Jesus

Rio, Rita // Sweet Shoe

Robbins, James // Bad Boy

Roberts, Davis // Chase, The // Halls of Anger // Hotel // Killers, The // Quick, Before It Melts // Sweet Bird of Youth

Roberts, Elyce // Rockin' the Blues

Tondaleyo // Sepia Cinderella

Toombs, Rody // Tall, Tan, and Terrific

Toones, Fred "Snowflake" // Biscuit Eater, The // Cabin in
the Cotton, The // Go Into Your Dance // Lady By Choice //
Lawless Nineties, The // 20th Century

Tops and Wilda // Chicago After Dark // Love in Syncopation

Torrance, Lena // While Thousands Cheer

Toto, Ecco Homo // King Solomon's Mines

Toure, Aida // Diankha-Bi

Toure, Petit // Moi un Noir

Towns, Christopher // Tough!

Townsend, Edward // Wife Hunters, The

Treadville, Bettie // One Dark Night

Tube, Sandy // Boesman and Lena

Tucker, Earl "Snake Hips" // Symphony in Black

Tucker, Lorenzo // Black King, The // Daughter of the Congo
// Easy Street // Harlem Big Shot // One Round Jones //
Reet, Petite and Gone // Temptation // Ten Minutes to Live
// Veiled Aristocrats // Wages of Sin, The

Turman, Glynn // Cooley High // Five on the Black Hand Side
// Hero Aint Nothin But a Sandwich, A // J.D.'s Revenge //
Minstrel Man // River Niger, The

Turner, Ike // Big T-N-T Show, The // Soul to Soul // Taking
Off

Turner, Joe // Rhythm and Blues Revue

Turner, Mae // Am I Guilty? // Life Goes On // Spirit of
Youth

Turner, Martin // A Ropin' Ridin' Fool // Cruise of the Hel-
lion, The // Family Secret, The // Ghost Rider, The //
Knockout Kid, The // Lost Express, The // Midnight Faces
// On the Stroke of Twelve // Rainbow Rangers // Royal
American, The // Sell 'Em Cowboy // Silent Sheldon //
Super Speed // They're Off // Three Pals // Western
Vengeance

Turner, Raymond // Love Mart, The

Turner, Tina // Big T-N-T Show, The // Soul to Soul //
Taking Off

Turnham, Francis // Bargain with Bullets

Tutt, J. Homer // Birthright, ≤1 // Broken Violin, The

Tyler Twins // Swing

Tynes, Gwendolyn // Fight Never Ends, The

Tyson, Cicely // Autobiography of Miss Jane Pittman, The //
Comedians, The // Heart is a Lonely Hunter, The // Hero
Aint Nothin But a Sandwich, A // Last Angry Man, The //
Man Called Adam, A // River Niger, The // Roots // Sounder

Uggams, Leslie // Black Girl // Roots // Skyjacked

Valade, Herman Dela // In the Depths of our Hearts

Valdez, Danny // Which Way Is Up?

Van Engle, Dorothy // Brand of Cain, The // Swing

Van Peebles, Melvin // Sweet Sweetback's Baadassssss Song

Varieties Dance Girls // Killer Diller

Vaughan, Sarah // Basin Street Revue // Harlem Jazz Festival
// Jazz Festival // Rhythm and Blues Revue

Vereen, Ben // Louis Armstrong: Chicago Style // Roots

Vernon, Lou // Betrayal, The // Exile, The

Verwayen, Percy // Burden of Race, The // Call of His People, The // Conjure Woman, The // Daughter of the Congo
// Hello Bill // Simp, The // Straight to Heaven

Vieyra, Paulin Soumanou // Afrique Sur Seine

Voices of East Harlem // Soul to Soul

Wade, Ernestine // Unexpected Riches

Wagner, Leon // Bingo Long Traveling All-Stars and Motor
Kings, The

Waker, Joyce // Willie Dynamite

Walker, Bill // Big Mo // Harlem Globetrotters, The // Kil-
lers, The // Kisses For My President // Night Without
Sleep // No Time for Romance // Queen Bee // Sun Tan Ranch
// Wall of Noise // Well, The

Walker, Hughie // Romance on the Beat

Walker, Jimmy // Let's Do It Again // Midnight Menace //
Telethon

Walker, Joyce // Education of Sonny Carson, The

Wells, Dickie // Smash Your Baggage

West, Hank // For His Mother's Sake

Whipper, Leigh // Bahama Passage // Due Process of Law Denied // King of the Zombies // Mission to Moscow // Of Mice and Men // Ox-Bow Incident // Symbol of the Unconquered // Vanishing Virginian, The // Virginia // White Cargo

White, Arthur // Jittering Jitter-Bugs

White, Betty // Coonskin

White, Beverly // Killer Diller

White, Bob // Wife Hunters, The

White, Josh // Walking Hills, The

White, Lolsy // Lionel Hampton and Herb Jeffries

White, Paul // Take My Life

White, Slappy // Amazing Grace // Man From O.R.G.Y., The

White, Talford // Flaming Crisis, The

White, Tony Joe // Catch My Soul

Whitfield, Robert "Smokey" // Another Part of the Forest // Jungle Gents // Right Cross // Second Woman, The // Three Little Girls in Blue // You Can't Take It With You

Whiting, Napoleon // Black Samson // Living Between Two Worlds // Wall of Noise

Whitman, Ernest // Cabin in the Sky // Congo Maisie // Daughter of Shanghai // Drums of the Congo // Green Pastures // Jesse James // Maryland // My Brother Talks to Horses // Pittsburgh Kid, The // Prisoner of Shark Island, The // Return of Frank James // Stormy Weather // White Hunter

Whitmore, Terry // Georgia, Georgia

Whitney, Salem Tutt // Birthright, ≤1 // Daughter of the Congo

Whitten, Marguerite // Mystery in Swing // Professor Creeps // Way Down South

Wilcois, Izinetta // Moon Over Harlem

Wilcox, Ralph // Claudine // Gordon's War // River Niger, The

Wild West Rodeo // Saddle Daze

Tenderfeet // Toppers Take a Bow // Widow's Bite, The

Williams, Theodore // Modern Cain, A

Williams, Tunji // Man of Two Worlds

Williams, Virgil // In the Depths of Our Hearts

Williams, Zack // Four Feathers, The // Hearts in Dixie //
Maryland // Merry Widow, The // Professor Creeps // Son of
Ingagi // Yankee Clipper, The

Williamson, Fred // Black Caesar // Black Eye // Bucktown //
Hammer // Hell Up in Harlem // Legend of Nigger Charley,
The // M*A*S*H* // Soul of Nigger Charley, The // Take a
Hard Ride // Tell Me That you Love Me, Junie Moon // That
Man Bolt // Three Tough Guys // Three the Hard Way

Wills, Harry // Harry Wills in Training

Wilson, Anthony // Together Brothers

Wilson, Don // Dirty Gerty from Harlem, USA

Wilson, Dooley // Cairo // Casablanca // Keep Punching //
Stormy Weather // Take a Letter Darling

Wilson, Eunice // All-Colored Vaudeville Show // Brand of
Cain, The // Dixieland Jamboree // No Time for Romance //
Sun Tan Ranch

Wilson, Flip // Uptown Saturday Night

Wilson, Frank // All-American Sweetheart // Beware // Bub-
bling Over // Devil Is Driving, The // Emperor Jones, The
// Girl From Chicago, The // Green Pastures // Melody
Makers Series // Murder on Lenox Avenue // Paradise in
Harlem

Wilson, Irene // Georgia Rose

Wilson, Marcellus // Boarding House Blues

Wilson, Nancy // Brothers and Sisters in Concert

Wilson, Teddy // Benny Goodman Story, The // Boogie Woogie
Dream // Harlem Hotshots // Hollywood Hotel // Something
to Shout About

Wiltshire, George // It Happened in Harlem // Killer Diller
// Midnight Menace

Winde, Beatrice // Sparkle: From Ghetto to Superstars

Winfield, Paul // Conrack // Gordon's War // Greatest, The
// Green Eyes // Hero Aint Nothin But a Sandwich, A //
Huckleberry Finn // Hustle // It's Good to be Alive //
Lost Man, The // Sounder // Trouble Man // RPM

Index of Black Authors

Index of Black Screenplay Writers

Goodwin, Robert L. // Black Chariot

Greaves, William // Fighters, The // In the Company of Men // On Merit // Power Versus the People // Struggle For Los Trabajos // Voice of La Raya // EEOC Story

Gunn, William // Angel Levine, The // Ganja and Hess // Landlord, The

Haley, Alex // Super Fly T.N.T.

Hansberry, Lorraine // Raisin in the Sun, A

Hatcher, Margerine // In the Rapture

Hughes, Langston // Rhythm of Africa // Way Down South

Jackson, Horace // Bus Is Coming, The // Tough!

Johnson, George P. // By Right of Birth

Jones, Evan // Fight Against Slavery, The

Julien, Max // Cleopatra Jones // Thomasine and Bushrod

Killens, John O. // Odds Against Tomorrow // Slaves

King, Mel // All Night Long

Lee, Carl // Cool World, The

Lee, Leslie // Almos' a Man

Lyles, Aubrey // Mayor of Jimtown

Mahomo, Nana // Last Grave at Dimbaza

Maldoror, Sarah // Sambizanga

Markham, Dewey "Pigmeat" // One Big Mistake

Maurice, Richard // Eleven P.M.

Mayfield, Julian // Up Tight

Micheaux, Oscar // Betrayal, The // Broken Violin, The // God's Stepchildren // Spiders Web, The // Symbol of the Unconquered

Miller, Flournoy E. // Harlem Rides the Range // Mayor of Jimtown // Double Deal

Mills, Jerry // Grafter and the Maid, The

Modisane, Blake // Come Back, Africa

Moss, Carlton // Negro Soldier, The // Paul Laurence Dunbar:

America's First Black Poet

Muse, Clarence // Broken Strings // Way Down South

Parks, Gordon // Diary of a Harlem Family // Flanio

Peebles, Melvin // Sweet Sweetback's Baadasssss Song

Peterson, Louis // Take a Giant Step

Randol, George // Rhythm Rodeo

Rhone, Trevor D. // Harder They Come, The

Robinson, Matt // Amazing Grace // Detroit 9000

Russell, Charlie L. // Five on the Black Hand Side

Samb-Makharam, Ababaear // Et La Neige N'Etait Plus

Sarr, Mamamou // Afrique Sur Seine

Seck, Fraore // Njangaan

Seck, Sherif Adrame // Njangaan

Sembene, Cusmane // Borom Sarret // Ceddo // La Noire de...
  // Mandabi // Taw // Xala

Senghor, Blaise // Grand Magal a Touba

St. John, Christopher // Top of the Heap

Teague, bcb // Hey, Cab!

Thiam, Mcmar // Baks

Thurman, Wallace // Tomorrow's Children

Traore, Mahama // Diankha-Bi // Garga M'Bosse // Lambaaye

Van Lierop, Robert // A Luta Continua // O Povo Organizado

Van Peebles, Melvin // Greased Lightning // Story of a Three
  Day Pass, The

Watkins, Battie // Hell's Alley

Webb, Jean // Hell's Alley

Williams, Leon // You Dig It

Williams, Oscar // Black Belt Jones // Final Comedown, The

Williams, Spencer // Blood of Jesus // Framing of the Shrew,
  The // Harlem Rides the Range // Lady Fare, The // Music
  Hath Charms // Oft in the Silly Night // Son of Ingagi //
  Widow's Bite, The

Index of Black Producers

Alexander, William // Fight Never Ends, The // Klansman, The
// Souls of Sin

Allassane, Moustapha // An Adventurer Returns

Benbow, Lillian // Countdown at Kusini

Bourne, St. Clair // Let the Church Say Amen

Dixon, Ivan // Spook Who Sat By the Door, The

Dones, Sidney P. // '10,000 Trail, The

Dudley, Sherman H., Jr. // Reckless Money // Scar of Shame

Fabio, Cheryl // Rainbow Black: Poet Sarah W. Fabio

Faye, Safi // Kaddu Beykat

Foster, Bill // "Buck and Bubbles" Series // Birth Mark //
Brother // Butler, The // Fall Guy, The // Florida Crackers // Grafter and the Maid, The // Railroad Porter, The

Goodwin, Robert L. // Black Chariot

Greaves, William // Fighters, The // First World Festival of
Negro Arts, The // In the Company of Men // On Merit //
Power Versus the People // Struggle For Los Trabajos //
Voice of La Raya // EEOC Story

Greenlee, Sam // Spook Who Sat By the Door, The

Hatcher, William C. // In the Rapture

Index of Black Directors

Anderson, Madeline // I am Somebody

Bennerson, Sam // Cotton Comes to Harlem

Beye, Ben Diogaye // Les Princes Noirs de Saint-Germain des Pres // Samba Tali

Crain, William // Blacula

Danska, Herb // Right On // Sweet Love, Bitter

Davis, Ossie // Black Girl // Cotton Comes to Harlem // Countdown at Kusini // Gordon's War // Kongi's Harvest

Diop-Mambety, Djitril // Badou Boy

Dixon, Ivan // Spook Who Sat By the Door, The // Trouble Man

Fabio, Cheryl // Rainbow Black: Poet Sarah W. Fabio

Faye, Safi // Kaddu Beykat

Franklin, Wendell James // Bus Is Coming, The

Gerima, Haile // Harvest A: 3000 Years

Goodwin, Robert L. // Black Chariot

Gordy, Berry // Mahoghany

Greaves, William // Fighters, The // In the Company of Men // On Merit // Power Versus the People // Still a Brother: Inside the Negro Middle Class // Struggle For Los Trabajos // Voice of La Raya // EEOC Story

Green, Eddie // Mr. Adam's Bomb

Poitier, Sidney // Buck and the Preacher // Let's Do It
    Again // Piece of the Action, A // Uptown Saturday Night
    // Warm December, A

Randol, George // Darktown Strutters Ball // Midnight Shadow
    // Rhythm Rodeo

Robertson, Hugh A. // Black Music in America: From Then
    Till Now

Samb-Makharam, Ababacar // Et La Neige N'Etait Plus // Kodou

Sarr, Mamamou // Afrique Sur Seine

Schultz, Michael // Car Wash // Cooley High // Greased
    Lightning // Which Way Is Up?

Sembene, Ousmane // Borom Sarret // Ceddo // La Noire de...
    // Mandabi // Xala

Senghor, Blaise // Grand Magal a Touba

Shah, Krishna // River Niger, The

Simon, Jim // Strike, The

St. Jacques, Raymond // Book of Numbers, The

St. John, Christopher // Top of the Heap

Thiam, Momar // Baks // Karim // Sarzan

Traore, Mahama // Diankha-Bi // Garga M'Bosse // Lambaaye //
    Njangaan // Reou Takh

Van Lierop, Robert // A Luta Continua // O Povo Organizado

Van Peebles, Melvin // Don't Play Us Cheap // Night the Sun
    Came Out, The // Story of a Three Day Pass, The // Sweet
    Sweetback's Baadassssss Song // Watermelon Man

Vieyra, Paulin Soumanou // Afrique Sur Seine // Lamb // Moe
    // Une Nation est Nee

Warren, Mark // Come Back, Charleston Blue

Wiggins, William H., Jr. // In the Rapture

Williams, Oscar // An Afro-American Thing // Final Comedown,
    The // Five on the Black Hand Side

Williams, Spencer // Beale Street Mama // Blood of Jesus //
    Dirty Gerty from Harlem, USA // Girl in Room 20, The // Go
    Down Death // Jivin in Be Bop // Juke Joint // Marching On
    // Melancholy Dame // Of One Blood // Tenderfeet

Zebba, Sam // Pincho